C000270491

PATRICK HILLERY

PATRICK HILLERY
The Official Biography

by

John Walsh

NEW
ISLAND

PATRICK HILLERY – THE OFFICIAL BIOGRAPHY
First published 2008
by New Island
2 Brookside
Dundrum Road
Dublin 14

www.newisland.ie

ISBN 978-1-84840-009-2

British Library Cataloguing Data. A CIP catalogue record for this book is available from the
British Library.

Book design and Origination by TypeIT, Dublin.

Printed in the UK by CPI Mackays, Chatham ME5 8TD

10 9 8 7 6 5 4 3 2

Contents

Acknowledgments

This book would not have possible without the help and support that I received from a wide range of people and institutions. Dr Tom Mitchell and Prof Eunan O'Halpin first raised the idea of the project in December 2005 and were supportive throughout the occasionally tortuous process of research and writing. My colleagues in the School of Education, Dr David Limond and Dr Damian Murchan, also offered advice and practical help.

I owe a debt of gratitude to my publisher, New Island Books, and especially to Edwin Higel, who was enthusiastic about the project from the outset. Mariel Deegan, Inka Hagen and Deirdre Nolan all made an essential contribution in preparing the work for publication; Gráinne Killeen gave invaluable advice on publicising the book. John P. Ryan prepared the index to his usual high professional standard. Deirdre O'Neill offered constant encouragement and expertise; she deserves thanks in particular for doing so much to bring the book to fruition in reasonable time, despite the reluctance of the author to relinquish it.

The late Dr Patrick Hillery gave me fourteen interviews over the course of a two-year period; he was consistently open and often fascinating, showing a remarkable facility to recall events from several decades earlier. Dr John Hillery provided invaluable assistance and responded patiently to a multitude of last-minute queries. Dr Maeve Hillery offered her unique insights about her husband's life and career; she also guided me through her vast collection of photographs. I spent two enjoyable and informative days with Michael Hillery in Miltown Malbay; he contributed his own special memories of his uncle. I am also indebted to David and Caitriona Hillery; Professor Brian Hillery; Paddy Casey in Spanish Point; PJ Donnellan; and Seamus Talty, who shared his extensive knowledge of the history of west Clare. Teresa Queally, archivist in the parish office in Miltown Malbay, proved adept at unearthing family records going back to the early nineteenth century.

Archivists and librarians at various institutions did a great deal to facilitate the research for the book. Seamus Hefferty and all the staff of UCD Archives, the custodians of the Hillery Papers, were consistently helpful and efficient in responding to apparently endless requests for documentation. I also wish to thank Catriona Crowe and the production staff in the National Archives, Fr Peter Queally in Rockwell College, the staff of the National Library, the National Photographic Archive, Blanchardstown Library, the Library of Trinity College Dublin and the Dr Patrick J. Hillery Library in Miltown Malbay.

Many prominent participants in the events of Hillery's career gave generously of their time and recollections, including Tony Brown, John Cooney, Evelyn Conlon, Seán Donlon, James Dukes, Edwin FitzGibbon, John Horgan, Professor John Kelly, Dennis Kennedy, Neville Keery, John McColgan, Joe O'Keeffe and Peig O'Malley. Peter Feeney readily discussed his own documentary about Hillery's life and provided interesting background about various aspects of the former president's career. Former political colleagues and opponents of Paddy Hillery also contributed their recollections, including Dr Garret FitzGerald and Gerard Collins.

The Centre for Contemporary Irish History in Trinity College, Dublin, provided essential support for the project over the last three years. The Centre received valuable research funding from CRH during this period. I also wish to acknowledge generous support from the Trinity

College Dublin Association and Trust and the Provost's Academic Development Fund.

Other researchers were generous in giving me the benefit of their expertise: in particular Tom Rigney and Alan Power provided invaluable information drawn from their own research. I greatly appreciated the support and advice of friends and colleagues throughout the process. Without taking pages to describe what each of them did, I want to thank Ciara Breathnach, Simon Boucher, Aoife Bhreathnach, Noel Coghlan, Shane Martin, Aoife Nolan, Kate O'Malley, Peter Rigney and Eavan O'Brien.

The support of my family was indispensable to the successful completion of the book. Thanks are due to Siobhan and Kevin, not least for their tolerance of constant queries and skilled technical assistance during various minor crises. Finally I can only express profound gratitude to my parents, John and Maura, for their constant support and encouragement, especially during the final stages of the project, when looming deadlines ensured that the boundary between dedication and obsession was not always clear.

John Walsh

Introduction

Paddy Hillery was born less than a year after the foundation of the Irish Free State; he died as the era of the Celtic Tiger was drawing to a close. His life spanned the first three generations of independent Ireland. He was a pivotal figure in Irish public life for almost four decades. He held the unique distinction of serving as a cabinet minister, European Commissioner and President of Ireland, a troika of offices held by no other Irish politician. He made an extraordinary contribution, in a characteristically understated fashion, to the peaceful, democratic and prosperous Irish state of the twenty-first century. Yet, so far, remarkably little has been written about Hillery's life and career. He himself did not write memoirs and no biography of Paddy Hillery has previously been published.

This is a political biography, which is designed to provide a balanced assessment of Paddy Hillery's public life and career. His personal life and family are part of the book, as they are central to an understanding of the man. I have also sought to convey an image of the authentic Paddy Hillery, which was often concealed behind a veil of public reticence, particularly during his term as President. He was not only a leading political figure; he was also a man of great personal charm, kindness and generosity. This work seeks to explore the political fortunes and the personal qualities of Paddy Hillery.

The book is an official biography in the sense that it was written with the full approval and collaboration of Dr Hillery. But it is not authorised in any conventional sense of the word. The only condition that Paddy Hillery imposed when I first started the work was that any of the material he made available would be published only in the book itself and would not appear in any other form before publication. This is a condition that I was happy to fulfil. Neither Dr Hillery nor his family sought any control or influence over the content of the work. For various reasons Paddy Hillery did not wish to see any of the draft chapters; at my request he checked the transcripts of his own interviews to confirm his original recollections. The general effect of this process was to make his recollections more rather than less interesting. The interpretations and conclusions in the work are entirely my own; so too are any errors or omissions.

This book is based principally on archival material, which was not previously available or was not fully exploited with regard to Hillery's career. I was fortunate to gain access to the Hillery Papers in the UCD Archives, which are not generally available to researchers. I also made extensive use of two other private collections held by the Hillery family. Paddy Hillery made available a private collection of papers, composed mainly of notes that he made in his retirement on the events of his career. These notes were originally intended to serve as the basis for his memoirs; they were interesting particularly for the unvarnished comments on other public figures and institutions in which he served. I also received original transcripts from tapes recorded by Hillery between 1969 and 1982. This material took the form of a diary, although it does not form a continuous narrative; the records begin following the outbreak of the Troubles in Northern Ireland and essentially conclude before the end of his second term as President, with a couple of brief entries subsequently. Despite the gaps, this contemporaneous material was extremely valuable, especially for the events of 1970 and his term as a European Commissioner.

I benefited greatly from a series of in-depth interviews with the late

Dr Hillery. I found very little of his fabled reticence, but a great deal of generosity with his time and memories. These interviews were invaluable in providing Paddy Hillery's unique perspective on historical events in which he was deeply involved; the process also opened up new lines of enquiry for the research. His recollections have been used in conjunction with the archival record and I found remarkably few differences between the two, despite the considerable lapse between the time of the interviews and many of the events described in the book. I also conducted several interviews with former officials who worked closely with Dr Hillery and journalists who covered the major events of his career, as well as former political colleagues and opponents.

The book also draws upon a wide range of other archival sources. The McQuaid Papers in the Dublin Diocesan Archives provide a rich source of material on Dr Hillery's term as Minister for Education. The records of the Department of the Taoiseach in the National Archives yielded valuable material on Hillery's interaction with Seán Lemass and Jack Lynch. The files of the Department of Foreign Affairs gave much essential information on the Irish government's response to the outbreak of conflict in Northern Ireland, particularly Hillery's appeal to the United Nations in 1969. The back issues of national and local newspapers in the National Library were useful in identifying public and media reaction to initiatives pursued by Hillery and in charting attitudes within the print media to his role as President. No book on Paddy Hillery would be complete without reference to Clare and particularly his beloved Spanish Point. The parish records in Miltown Malbay were invaluable for background information on the Hillery family.

Hillery was an Irish nationalist throughout his career, but his nationalism was combined with a profound commitment to democracy and a passionate egalitarianism. He gradually developed a broad international outlook, which was best expressed in his support for Irish engagement in the process of European integration. He was driven by compelling personal convictions rather than conventional political ambition; it is the apparent contradiction between distaste for self-promotion and the considerable achievements of his political career that makes him a fascinating subject for a biographer. The subtlety and complexity of his political views also provide fertile ground for exploration.

Patrick Hillery was a nationalist who was vehemently opposed to armed struggle; an Irish patriot who advocated sharing sovereignty with European institutions; and a pragmatic politician who introduced radical social reforms. His essential decency and integrity were universally acknowledged by contemporaries, but his force of character and political abilities were all too often underestimated. He was a reluctant public figure initially, but became a skilled practitioner of the art of politics and a tenacious exponent of policies in which he believed. While his early ambivalence about a public career gradually faded, he always retained personal characteristics that made him an unusual and indeed exceptional participant in front-line politics. Hillery was a shy man who became a formidable politician, a successful public figure who was wary of the limelight.

1.

Miltown Malbay

Spanish Point, the original home of Paddy Hillery, was officially known as Breaffa but gained its modern name when ships from the Spanish Armada were wrecked off its coastline in 1588.[1] The townland of Breaffa, which formed part of the ancient parish of Kilfarboy in west Clare, came under the control of the Moroney family during the eighteenth century. Spanish Point was first developed in the early 1800s by Thomas Moroney, who turned it into a popular summer holiday destination for the Protestant gentry.[2] Moroney was the leading member of a company that built the Atlantic Hotel in 1810 and he established permanent lodges to accommodate the regular visitors. Spanish Point became a well-known seaside resort on the shores of the Atlantic Ocean, frequented by members of the social and political elite throughout the nineteenth century. Miltown Malbay too owed its early development largely to the expansionist activity of the Moroney family. The Moroneys built Miltown House in Spanish Point as their residence and this did much to stimulate the development of the neighbouring village.[3] Miltown Malbay emerged around the beginning of the nineteenth century; it was a village with 110 houses and 600 people by 1821.[4] The village developed rapidly in the following two decades, emerging as a recognisable town with a population of 1,295 on the eve of the famine in 1841. The impact of the famine and the subsequent wave of emigration curtailed its expansion, but did not lead to a dramatic decline in the population of the town itself. It had a population of 1,330 in 1861 and it remained a prosperous small town for the rest of that century.[5]

Yet if the expansionism of the Moroneys contributed to the development of the town, their financial exactions and oppressive tactics alienated them from the local tenant farmers and the traders of Miltown Malbay. They gained an unenviable reputation for rack-renting and ruthless use of force against disaffected tenants in the late nineteenth century, particularly when the estate came under the direction of Mrs Lucinda Moroney in the 1880s. The landlords in west Clare were by no means universally unpopular, but the Moroneys provoked widespread and frequently violent discontent through their refusal to reduce rents and their determination to evict tenants who fell into arrears. The movement to establish tenant rights led to bitter clashes between the landlord family and the local tenants.

The Hillery family were tenant farmers for most of the nineteenth century, living in the rural hinterland of Miltown Malbay. They farmed a smallholding at Poulawillin, a couple of miles outside the town, renting land owned by the Moroneys. Pat Hillery, the grandfather and namesake of Paddy Hillery, was the first member of the family to settle in the town itself. It was not a voluntary move on his part but an enforced departure from the land. A branch of the Land League was established in Miltown Malbay in 1879, demanding fair rent and security of tenure; when the Moroneys resisted these demands a campaign for the non-payment of rents began.[6] Pat Hillery actively supported the Land League and refused to pay rent to the Moroneys. He was evicted from Poulawillin in September 1881, but this was only the beginning of his involvement in the land agitation. Pat Hillery was arrested by the Royal Irish Constabulary (RIC) early in 1882; he was accused of involvement in the murder of Mrs Moroney's herdsman. He was sent to jail in Clonmel but was not convicted of the charge and was released from custody later in the same year.[7] Hillery was a colourful and impetuous character, known as 'Rory of the Hill'; this was not a personal nickname but a general designation for those involved in violent agitation against the authorities. While the nature of his activity is not fully documented, it is probable that Pat Hillery went considerably beyond the peaceful methods of the Land League in opposing the authorities who had evicted him from his home.

Pat Hillery married Margaret Vaughan in July 1888; the couple had five children over the following decade. Michael, the eldest of the family, was born on 30 March 1889.[8] He had two younger brothers who survived into adulthood: Tom (born 1890) and PJ (born 1893).[9] Margaret and Pat Hillery also had two other children: Mary Ellen and John, who died in childhood. Pat Hillery established a pub and grocery business in Miltown Malbay in 1891, using money provided by Margaret who had recently returned from North America. But he did not long enjoy his new profession as a publican. He was arrested once again, apparently on charges related to agrarian crime, and jailed in Enniskillen. He contracted TB around this time and was released from prison in 1899 when it became clear that he was dying. His ten-year-old son, Michael, left a poignant entry in the family records for that year: 'My da died Oct 1899. May he RIP. The Lord have mercy on his soul and relieve him from whatever trouble he is in. Amen.'[10] Pat Hillery died in Miltown Malbay at the early age of 46; his premature death left his widow to raise a young family on her own.

Fortunately Margaret Hillery was a woman of formidable will and considerable ingenuity. She took over the pub and turned it into a prosperous business venture. Margaret successfully expanded the family business; recognising a valuable opportunity, she set up the first petrol pump in Miltown Malbay just outside the door of the pub. This venture later developed into a garage run by the Hillery family. Margaret also established the first hackney service in Miltown Malbay, which she ran in collaboration with her younger son PJ.[11] Two of Margaret's sons worked in different branches of the family business. PJ Hillery eventually took over the pub, while Tom developed and managed the garage. Margaret was the driving force behind the considerable achievements enjoyed by the Hillery family in the first two decades of the twentieth century.

Michael Hillery took a very different path to his younger brothers. He completed secondary education at Rockwell College in Cashel and secured a scholarship to the Royal College of Surgeons to study medicine in 1906. This was an unusual accomplishment at the beginning of the twentieth century, but it was only the beginning of an extraordinary sequence of academic achievements. He was a brilliant student, winning a series of awards and medals in each year of his course.[12] In 1911 alone he secured medals for first place in the practice of medicine, surgery and midwifery.[13] He qualified as a doctor in 1912 and almost immediately was appointed to a post in the Meath Hospital in Dublin. He also served as a lecturer in the College of Surgeons not long after his graduation.[14] Yet his greatest ambition was to establish his own practice in Clare and he soon returned to Miltown Malbay to work as a GP. Michael first established his surgery in an upstairs room over the family pub in the main street of the town.[15] It was the beginning of a family practice in west Clare that lasted for most of the twentieth century.

Michael Hillery married his second cousin Ellen MacMahon, known locally as Nellie, on 3 July 1919.[16] Following their marriage Michael moved his practice across the street to his wife's house, where he established a surgery and nursing home.[17] Nellie's family were affluent traders in Miltown Malbay; her father, James McMahon, owned a flourishing business, including a bakery and a pub.[18] The McMahons were prominent and wealthy members of the middle class in Miltown Malbay. The Hillery family had secured respectability in the town much more recently; they owed their prosperity largely to the efforts of Margaret Hillery. Yet Michael enjoyed considerable status as a doctor and he was wealthy enough to buy property in the neighbourhood. Several Protestant families owned houses in Spanish Point, including Captain Ernest Ellis, whose house was known as Wellington. Michael Hillery bought the house in the 1920s from Captain Ellis, who left with his family for Northern Ireland following the war of independence.

Michael and Nellie Hillery were deeply involved in the nationalist struggle for independence between 1919 and 1921, along with many of their contemporaries in Miltown Malbay. Éamon de Valera, who was then best known as the sole surviving commandant of the 1916 Rising, was elected as MP for East Clare in 1917 at a fateful by-election which signalled that the separatist Sinn Féin movement was emerging as the dominant voice of nationalist Ireland. De Valera would represent Clare for over forty years, first as the president of Sinn Féin, then as the leader of Fianna Fáil after 1926 and finally as Taoiseach of the independent Irish state. But in the short-term it was the military wing of the separatist movement that had the most marked impact in Clare. The Irish Volunteers established a strong presence in the county during the war of independence and took the offensive against the RIC, which was increasingly unable to maintain its control over the area. British military forces were stationed in west Clare to support the police and the Volunteers, who increasingly became known as the Irish Republican Army (IRA), conducted guerrilla warfare against the Crown forces on a similar pattern to many other areas of the country. The war in west Clare was dominated by IRA ambushes of police patrols and attacks on army barracks in outlying areas. The crown forces relied heavily on the Black and Tans, a force of ex-soldiers who became notorious for their brutality.

Michael Hillery served as the medical officer of the Mid-Clare Brigade of the IRA, while Nellie often acted as a nurse for wounded Volunteers, who were sheltered in her home in Miltown Malbay.[19] The most celebrated incident involved Ignatius O'Neill, a prominent figure in the local IRA. O'Neill was a childhood friend of Nellie Hillery, whose family lived only a couple of doors from the O'Neills on the main street of Miltown Malbay. O'Neill had served in the British army and was in receipt of a British military pension while he was fighting the Crown forces throughout the war of independence.[20] He narrowly escaped death following an ambush that went wrong. A small force of Volunteers, led by Martin Devitt, attacked an RIC patrol at Crowe's Bridge near the village of Inagh on 20 February 1920. But the police repelled the attack and Devitt was killed.[21] The engagement was the most severe setback suffered by the local IRA during the conflict. O'Neill was seriously wounded but managed to escape from the scene of the ambush; he was sheltered by a local family sympathetic to the Volunteers. Michael Hillery was called out to treat his injuries and immediately determined that the wounded man needed medical care in a nursing home. As it was impossible to bring a wounded IRA officer to a hospital, the doctor found a different solution. O'Neill was instead taken to Hillery's own home on the main street of Miltown Malbay.[22] The Hillery family hid him in an upstairs room, where the doctor treated his wounds. O'Neill's injuries required surgery but he could not be moved immediately, so he was kept in the house on the same street as the police barracks. It was a hair-raising experience for Nellie Hillery, who constantly feared that the house would be raided and O'Neill arrested. Eventually Michael Hillery smuggled him out under the cover of darkness and he was taken to Dublin for surgery.[23] The treatment was successful and O'Neill soon resumed his involvement in the local IRA, taking over as commander of the Fourth battalion of the Mid-Clare Brigade later in 1920.

The treatment of Ignatius O'Neill was not an isolated incident. Michael Hillery was a constant presence attending wounded or dying IRA men following ambushes or other clashes with the British forces. He treated several men who were injured in an attempt to burn down the military barracks in Lahinch; one Volunteer, Pat Murtagh, was badly burned, and Hillery drove him to Dublin for treatment.[24] The most significant military clash where Michael Hillery provided medical support to the local Volunteers was the Rineen ambush. An IRA force, led by Ignatius O'Neill, ambushed a police lorry in the Rineen area between Miltown Malbay and Ennistymon on 22 September 1920; all six of the RIC men perished.[25] A stronger force of soldiers arrived shortly after the ambush, exchanging fire with the Volunteers and pursuing them across the hills, but the IRA raiding party managed to escape.[26] They did suffer some casualties of their own; O'Neill himself was wounded, so too was another Volunteer, Michael Curtin. It was Michael Hillery who treated the IRA casualties of the ambush. O'Neill was taken to a remote farmhouse owned by the Moloney family in the townland of Illaunbawn, on the side of a hilltop which gave a wide view of the surrounding countryside. Michael Hillery made an arduous and dangerous trek through the countryside by night to reach O'Neill at Illaunbawn. On this occasion the IRA officer was not moved into Miltown Malbay, probably because the danger of discovery was too great. O'Neill appears to have led a charmed life. He again recovered from his wounds and was leading an attack on a police barracks within a month. He was a revered figure in Miltown Malbay during and immediately after the war of independence.

Michael Hillery was fortunate to escape the reprisals that followed the Rineen ambush. The Black and Tans took their revenge on the local population; groups of drunken soldiers descended on Miltown Malbay, Lahinch and Ennistymon, looting and burning property as they went. Several houses in Miltown Malbay were burned to the ground and most of the others were damaged; the Black and Tans raided the Hillery pub and fired shots through the windows of the house, although the family's property escaped the worst excesses of the attack.[27] Michael Hillery was treating the wounded Volunteers when the attack occurred, but his car was burned out, apparently as a warning to break his links with the IRA. Similar scenes of destruction occurred in Lahinch and the town hall was burned down in Ennistymon; six people were killed in the reprisals.[28]

Nellie Hillery feared that her husband would suffer the same fate. Michael's part in supporting the IRA was well known in the neighbourhood and he was constantly under suspicion by Crown forces. Paddy Hillery remembered that 'My mother often spoke of the strain when the police called on my father to halt on his return from a sick call and he had to put his medical bag on the ground. She feared they would shoot as he was obviously under suspicion'.[29] Her fears were perfectly understandable considering some of the risks that Michael Hillery was willing to take in treating and sheltering local Volunteers.

But whatever about his apparent disregard for his own safety, Michael Hillery was not indifferent to the risks to his wife and family. Their eldest child, Eleanor, was born in April 1920, in the midst of the struggle in which her parents were embroiled; they had a son, Des, in May of the following year.[30] The situation in Miltown Malbay was so dangerous that their first two children were sent away from home shortly after their birth. Michael Hillery was arrested and jailed in Limerick for a short time, but was soon released. He escaped largely unscathed from the bitter conflict between the IRA and the British forces in Clare. He won in the process a lasting reputation as a dedicated medical practitioner and a fearless supporter of the nationalist movement.

The Truce in July 1921, which suspended the military conflict between the British forces and the IRA, also signalled the end of Michael Hillery's participation in the national revolution. He was not a political activist, but a doctor giving support to a movement whose objectives he shared. He took no part in the bitter split within the Sinn Féin movement following the signature of the Anglo-Irish Treaty in December 1921; he stayed resolutely aloof from the civil war that followed between the supporters of the Irish Free State and its republican opponents. He had friends and patients on both sides of the civil war divide. Ignatius O'Neill became an officer in the Free State army, but most of his former comrades supported the anti-Treaty side.[31] Michael Hillery avoided involvement in the party politics of the new Irish state, dedicating himself entirely to his medical practice and his family.

Patrick John Hillery was born on 2 May 1923 in Miltown Malbay, less than a year after the foundation of the new state. He was the third in a family of four; his younger sister, Bernadette, who was known as Berry, was born two years later in April 1925.[32] The young Paddy enjoyed a secure and prosperous family background. Michael Hillery had developed a flourishing medical practice by this time, which ranged over a wide area of west Clare. He was a greatly respected figure in the local community. His standing was due in part to his distinguished record as a doctor and his involvement in the war of independence; but it also had much to do with his concern for the poor in his native town. He did not charge fees for many patients, knowing that they could not afford to pay even modest medical bills. A large proportion of his patients gave him gifts instead; chickens and geese appeared in Spanish Point on a regular basis and food was always plentiful in the Hillery household.[33] Michael Hillery's generosity was renowned in Miltown Malbay. He frequently covered his patients' bills at the local pharmacy, charging their prescriptions to his own account. His generosity caused some concern to his wife, who was anxious about his precarious position as a general practitioner. While he was a very successful GP, his income at first depended on the private practice and it was his sole means of supporting a young family. The young Paddy recalled his mother's worries, which did not greatly disturb him at the time:

> I remember as a child my mother saying, 'Michael, would you ever take the money they offer you'. But it was only as I grew older that I realised her anxiety must have been great; there was no pension if he died and he was doing everything possible to kill himself from work. She must have been very anxious for her future and the future of the children if anything happened.[34]

Nellie Hillery's anxiety was understandable; her husband's practice and their family's survival depended entirely on his continuing good health. But Michael Hillery's dedication to his medical practice made him one of the most popular and successful GPs in the county; he drew patients from well beyond Miltown Malbay and not all of them were poor. His success in his chosen profession ensured that he was able to provide a comfortable upbringing for his children; his son commented many years later that 'he had an enormous practice, we were never short'.[35]

Despite Michael Hillery's experience and his academic accomplishments, he experienced considerable difficulty in acquiring a dispensary post funded by the state, which provided a guaranteed minimum income. Ironically it was the Irish language policy of the new Irish state, created by the nationalist struggle in which he was a prominent local participant, which presented the greatest obstacle to his appointment. The Irish Free State introduced a series of initiatives to promote the Irish language, including a requirement that applicants for certain public offices appointed by the state had to possess a working knowledge of Irish. Michael Hillery had little or no Irish; when he first applied for a dispensary post, he lost out to a new graduate who lacked his experience or qualifications but had the all-important asset of a superior grasp of the national language.[36] Yet this proved a temporary setback. He learned Irish with the assistance of John 'Bob' Fitzpatrick, a teacher in the local national school, who had taught himself the language to ensure that he could meet the demands of the revised curriculum.[37] Bob Fitzpatrick was a central figure in the life of the town; he was involved in the local GAA, the golf club and debating society. He was a highly intelligent, assertive and affable man, who was widely viewed as a personality of importance in the village, on the same level as the parish priest and the doctor. It is not known whether it was Fitzpatrick's instruction that made the difference, but Michael Hillery certainly acquired a sufficient knowledge of Irish to hold state medical appointments. He secured the post of medical officer for Miltown Malbay, holding the position until his retirement in 1957; he also became Coroner for west Clare.[38]

The young Paddy Hillery attended the local national school in Miltown Malbay. It was in fact three two-teacher schools on the same site; boys and girls first entered the infants' school, which had mixed classes. Then, after the first two grades, the pupils were promoted to separate senior schools for boys and girls.[39] In the boys' national school, the teachers were Pat O'Brien and Dr Hillery's friend, Bob Fitzpatrick. The school buildings were in a dilapidated condition, with rat holes in the floors; it was particularly cold in winter and the children were asked to bring in sods of turf to feed the fire. They were also required to keep the school clean by sweeping the floor. Despite the conditions it was usually a relaxed environment, except when the school received a visit from the inspector. The new Department of Education maintained many features of the stringent regime of school inspection practiced by the commissioners of national education under British rule. The inspectors gave a rigorous assessment of the work of teachers, awarding a merit mark in each subject, which could range from 'very satisfactory' to 'not satisfactory'; an unsatisfactory report from the inspector could threaten a teacher's job. As a student the young Paddy Hillery was surprised by the impact on apparently self-assured adults of a visitation by the dreaded inspector: 'In general teachers were terrified by inspectors who usually arrived without warning. Once when the inspector made a visit, I was in Mr O'Brien's class; I answered every question and the Misses O'Brien [sisters of Pat O'Brien] who had a shop in the main street purred over me as I passed home from school.'[40] The parish priest, Fr Denis Murphy, who doubled as the school manager, also made regular visits to the school, although usually without inspiring the same terror as the inspector.

The national school was the beginning and end of formal education for the majority of the children in Miltown Malbay. Paddy Hillery was one of the few in his class who went on to secondary school; many of his classmates left school at thirteen or fourteen to work on the land or in shops in the town, while others attended local secondary schools. His life began to diverge from the experience of his local contemporaries in 1935, when his parents sent him to Rockwell College, a secondary boarding school for boys in Cashel, County Tipperary. Michael Hillery had preceded him as a student at Rockwell and had a high regard for the Holy Ghost Order which managed the college. It was a difficult transition for a twelve-year-old boy, who was separated from his family and friends for the first time. Yet what Hillery missed most was Spanish Point itself and its closeness to the sea: 'If you're reared near the sea and you're sent off inland, you feel it, I didn't realise it at the time, but other times when I was away from the sea I was uncomfortable'.[41] His abiding memories of the first days at Rockwell were of 'big rooms, the enormous corridors, huge dormitories and refectories and a young child's loss of the beloved seaside of Miltown Malbay.'[42] It was a vivid illustration of the central importance of Spanish Point in his life. He formed an enduring attachment to Spanish Point which remained with him throughout his adult life.

Yet his initial loneliness passed quickly as he settled into the rhythm of life at the boarding school. The Holy Ghost priests ran the college, with assistance from prefects who were training for the priesthood; the prefects took day-to-day responsibility for discipline in the dormitories and common areas of the school such as the refectory. The college also employed a considerable number of lay teachers. Hillery did well in his first-year exams, securing first place in his class in three subjects and second place in three more.[43] This marked the high point of his academic career at Rockwell. He himself admitted: 'That was the last of my interest in study at school: I did not exhibit any interest in books again until I was in medical school learning my profession'.[44] He did not take academic work too seriously, becoming immersed in various sports and enjoying the camaraderie of the boarding school environment. He played hurling and Gaelic football, but was particularly absorbed with rugby. His interests provided a good fit with Rockwell's traditions; while the school had an impressive academic reputation, the Holy Ghost fathers placed a high value on participation in competitive sports and particularly cherished the college's strong record of achievement on the rugby field. Fortunately, Hillery excelled in rugby and played for the school's Junior Cup team alongside Bertie O'Hanlon, who later became an Irish rugby international. Hillery became captain of the Junior Cup team in 1938 and was selected as a member of the Senior Cup team in the same year, a notable achievement for a boy of fifteen.[45] His sporting endeavours were not crowned with success on this occasion. His team were narrowly defeated by Crescent College in the first match of the Junior Cup, while the senior side was edged out by Presentation, Cork.[46] But despite the lack of success he greatly enjoyed the team spirit fostered by competitive sport and relished as well the atmosphere of the Cup matches.[47] Hillery's involvement in rugby was the driving passion of his time at Rockwell.

Despite his participation in the school's main sport, Hillery was not by any means a model student. His academic record was mediocre after the first year and he had his fair share of clashes with authority. He rebelled against some of the strict rules maintained by the school management. The boys were divided into senior and junior groups; the two groups were kept apart not only in their dormitories, but also in the school refectory and during their leisure time. Hillery broke this rule in his final year at Rockwell by speaking to the vice-captain of his Junior Cup team in the refectory. He fell foul of the dean of discipline, Fr Barrett, for this infraction and Hillery's status as captain of the rugby team did not save him from a severe caning on his hands.[48] The harsh punishment for such a minor breach of the rules did not greatly bother him; like most boys of his generation he accepted physical punishment as a normal part of the educational experience. Moreover, by the standards of the time, Rockwell was mild in administering physical punishment to its pupils, especially in comparison with schools run by other religious orders in the same period. Hillery's occasional clashes with authority did not affect his generally positive experience of the school. He greatly enjoyed his time at Rockwell and valued the strong sense of community that he found in the school.[49] He appreciated too the opportunity to develop at his own pace, without undue academic pressure. Hillery remembered Rockwell with great affection and paid a handsome tribute to the school in an interview many years later: 'They were good, they didn't push you. At that time it was a bit like the old university, you know, you just mixed with the others, you were there for the experience. I felt that Rockwell was my university'.[50]

2.

Dr Hillery

Hillery's time at Rockwell drew to a close in the summer of 1939. He undertook the matriculation exam for the NUI and qualified for entry to University College Dublin. He could have remained in secondary school for another year and was urged to do so by the priests at Rockwell. Whatever their concerns about his application to academic work, they were keen to retain his talents as a rugby player, offering him the opportunity to be captain of the Senior Cup team if he stayed on.[1] But by this time Hillery wanted to move on from secondary education. He was determined to qualify as a doctor and to work in the family practice in Miltown Malbay. Paddy's decision to choose a career in medicine reflected the profound influence of Michael Hillery on his son. The elder Hillery passed on his passion for medical practice to three of his four children. Eleanor was the first to qualify as a doctor, while Berry also followed her father into the medical profession.

Hillery went to Dublin to enrol for medicine in UCD at the early age of 16. But an unexpected problem arose to delay his progress. He enrolled with the medical faculty for the autumn term without difficulty, but after

two months in Earlsfort Terrace he was informed that he was too young
to pursue the course. The faculty required students to attain the age of 18
during their first year; there was a minimum age limit for entry to various
medical laboratories, notably the anatomy lab. This was dictated mainly by
concern to protect the tender virtue of young students from early
exposure to the organs of the human body.[2] Nellie Hillery travelled to
Dublin to negotiate on his behalf with the UCD authorities, but to no
avail and he was obliged to return home. He remained in Clare until the
following summer, enjoying the mid-century equivalent of a gap year. He
spent much of the year working with his elder brother. Des, the only one
of Michael Hillery's children who did not enter the medical profession,
took up farming in Spanish Point. Paddy helped out on the farm, went
swimming in the Atlantic Ocean and learned to play the piano.[3] He might
have reflected that there were worse ways to spend a year. He certainly
enjoyed his respite and returned to Earlsfort Terrace to start the medical
course in the autumn of 1940.

He soon displayed an impressive commitment to his chosen profession.
His studies in UCD brought out a drive for academic achievement that
had not been evident in his time at Rockwell. He gained honours in his
medical exams throughout the six-year course. He also developed a wider
interest in science, in addition to his core preoccupation with medicine.
He interrupted his medical studies in 1942 to undertake a one-year
science course leading to a separate qualification; he was awarded a B.Sc.
with honours in 1943. He took particular satisfaction in the science
degree, as it involved a greater emphasis on original thinking than his
medical studies.[4] But nevertheless medicine remained his first love and
he was determined to master the discipline as thoroughly as possible. He
succeeded as a medical student primarily by hard work and the ability to
memorise large tracts of material. Hillery secured the final medical
qualification in 1947, graduating from UCD with first-class honours.

Hillery's dedication to learning his profession left him with little time
for other interests and he was particularly detached from politics as a
student. None of his classmates in Earlsfort Terrace would have identified
him as a future politician; he was entirely apolitical throughout his medical

training. He was a student in UCD for most of the Second World War, but was hardly affected by the conflict. He remembered the war as a distant reality but not an immediate threat: 'I don't think it affected UCD much; we were a bit isolated. We had a great time compared to what they had in England'.[5] Hillery's perception reflected his own disinterest in politics perhaps more than the prevailing feeling in UCD in the early 1940s. Ireland's neutrality certainly meant a degree of self-imposed isolation during the war, but this did not prevent students in UCD from holding passionate opinions in favour of the western Allies or Germany. There was a vocal pro-German element in the college, which had occasional clashes with pro-British students from Trinity College. Hillery was aware of these rivalries but entirely detached from them. Medicine, not politics, was the dominant passion of his life in college and as a young doctor.

Following his graduation from UCD, Hillery was accepted as a resident doctor at the Mater Hospital in Dublin. There was no formal requirement to undertake an internship before qualifying as a doctor in the 1940s and only a small proportion of the medical graduates secured jobs in the major hospitals. Hillery was one of the few who did, largely due to his impressive examination results; he secured a place as a house surgeon in the Mater, working under the direction of a distinguished surgeon, John Corcoran.[6] Yet it was essentially a residential internship rather than a proper medical post. Hillery was paid 30 shillings a week as a junior doctor in residence at the hospital, but was required to contribute 25 shillings for his keep.[7] The young doctor soon gained considerable expertise in routine surgical procedures and impressed his superiors at the Mater. He received a highly favourable reference from Corcoran, who became his friend as well as his supervisor:

> I must say I have not known a better man; able and energetic, courteous and punctual, he has never failed to carry out his duties with the utmost efficiency giving at all times entire satisfaction to patients and colleagues alike…His diagnosis and treatment of the cases which came under his care left nothing to be desired.[8]

The post in the Mater was, however, a temporary position and Hillery secured a further residency in the National Maternity Hospital in Holles Street. He did not stay there very long, taking advantage of an unexpected opportunity to complete his training in North America. The Master of the Hospital, Dr Alec Spain, who had recently returned from Canada, informed the junior doctors that resident positions were available at the Hotel Dieu, a hospital in Kingston, Ontario.[9] Hillery decided to apply almost immediately. Many of his contemporaries were seeking to complete their training or to get jobs in Britain, where the National Health Service had recently come into being. This option did not appeal to Hillery: 'I didn't want to go to England; it was in a bad way just after the war anyway. I had an attitude that I didn't want to go there.'[10] It was not simply the difficult post-war conditions in Britain that deterred Hillery; as the product of a staunchly nationalist upbringing in west Clare, he had no great liking for the British state and no desire to work in England. Canada offered an attractive alternative, which had the lure of being relatively unknown.

It was not primarily hope of financial reward that led Hillery to cross the Atlantic in 1948. He did not emigrate in search of work; his ultimate ambition was to practise as a country doctor in Clare. Instead he was seeking further opportunities to complete his training and widen his knowledge of the discipline. He was not alone in taking up the offer; two of his colleagues, Paddy Maloney and Michael Raftery, joined him at the Hotel Dieu.[11] Several other doctors from the National Maternity Hospital also travelled to Canada, securing posts in a hospital in Ottawa. Hillery remained in Canada for about one year, working first in the hospital at Ontario and later taking up a post at a hospital in Regina, the provincial capital of Saskatchewan. He also worked for several months in the Saskatchewan Hospital, a psychiatric institution in the town of North Battleford. His experience of the Canadian health system was mixed. The provincial government in Saskatchewan invested generously in health care and provided a wide range of public medical services. Hillery was impressed by several large-scale publicity campaigns promoted by the authorities, which were designed to raise public awareness about serious illnesses; an official campaign about cancer sought to ensure early treatment of the disease. The authorities of Saskatchewan also highlighted the dangers of venereal disease, using advertising on envelopes to underline their message about the perils of syphilis. This form of advertising had some unexpected consequences for the young Clare man:

> They had a big campaign against syphilis. This made a big problem for me; when they franked the letters they had 'Stamp out syphilis in Saskatchewan' and these letters were going home to my mother! They had a number of different campaigns but that one was a bit embarrassing back in Miltown Malbay.[12]

This occasional embarrassment did not undermine his general appreciation for the commitment of the local authorities to public health. But he had a much more serious concern about the medical practices in his own workplace. Hillery was deeply dissatisfied with the dominant philosophy within the Saskatchewan Hospital concerning the management of mentally ill patients. The institution focused on the containment rather than the rehabilitation of inmates; he was disturbed at the harsh and repressive treatment of the patients.[13] The experience reinforced his strong distaste for the coercive management of mentally ill patients and left him with a lifelong aversion to snow, as it was winter for most of his time in Saskatchewan. There were other, more personal reasons for his growing disenchantment with Saskatchewan. He was lonely, having been separated from his family and friends for a prolonged period and once again found that he missed the familiar seaside environment at Spanish Point. The immediate trigger for his decision to leave Canada was not homesickness, but a message from Miltown Malbay that his father was ill. While the elder Hillery's bout of illness did not turn out to be serious, Paddy decided to return to Clare; even without the news from home, he would not have stayed much longer in Canada.

Hillery returned to Miltown Malbay initially to help out in the family practice during his father's illness. He also took up a temporary appointment as a locum in a dispensary in the nearby village of Craggaknock.[14] It was his first experience of medical practice in rural Clare and reinforced his long-standing ambition to work as a family doctor. Hillery returned to Ireland at a time of considerable political change and far-reaching developments in the Irish health service. De Valera's dominance of Irish politics had been temporarily interrupted, when Fianna Fáil lost office in 1948 after sixteen years in power. The new inter-party government, headed by John A. Costello, was an eclectic combination of parties and individuals, united mainly by their common hostility to de Valera.[15] Noel Browne, a young doctor who had lost most of his family to tuberculosis, became Minister for Health on his first day in the Dáil.[16] Browne took the lead in a nationwide campaign against tuberculosis, which reached frighteningly high mortality rates by the 1940s. Browne achieved outstanding success in the campaign against the disease, assisted by the appearance of the BCG vaccine and extensive funding from the Hospital Sweepstakes.[17] Paddy Hillery was largely indifferent to the political changes of the late 1940s, but was greatly interested in the campaign against TB. He saw the treatment of tuberculosis as a rapidly growing area, where he could make a valuable contribution; he also believed that expertise in the area was essential for an aspiring young doctor. He decided that 'I would have to get into the treatment of tuberculosis – that was the big thing in Ireland at the time and you would have to know it anyway if you wanted to get a job anywhere'.[18] So he secured a post in 1950 as an assistant medical officer at Peamount Hospital near Newcastle, in south county Dublin.

Peamount was founded in 1912 by the National Women's Health Association as a TB hospital. It continued to operate primarily as a sanatorium for the treatment of patients with tuberculosis until the early 1960s.[19] The one-year post at Peamount was Hillery's first real job in an Irish hospital. Although he took the position mainly to secure expertise in the treatment of TB, he was paid a salary as a resident doctor. Peamount was undergoing a rapid expansion at the time; three new wards were opened in 1949, adding an additional 120 beds to the hospital.[20] The appointment at Peamount was undoubtedly a good career opportunity for Hillery. He was starting work in a sanatorium at the dawn of a new era in the treatment of tuberculosis.[21] The only drawback was his cool relationship with Dr Joseph Logan, the Resident Medical Superintendent. Logan, who had taken over as medical director at Peamount two years earlier, was a central figure in the development of the hospital over the following generation.[22] He seemed to regard Hillery with some suspicion; the younger man in turn found Logan overbearing and excessively concerned with administrative detail.[23] But fortunately these differences did not extend to the rest of Hillery's colleagues. He got on very well with Jack Sherry, the Deputy Medical Superintendent, who was Logan's chief assistant. Sherry, who was from Foxford in Mayo, became a close friend of Hillery and was the best man at his wedding five years later. The two men remained friendly until Sherry died prematurely of leukaemia in 1965.

Hillery's term at Peamount brought some unexpected benefits, especially the opportunity to participate in an international study, which was funded by the United Nations Children's Fund (UNICEF). The study entailed a tour of European cities to investigate tuberculosis in children. Logan discovered that the Department of Health had received an invitation for an Irish doctor to join the group; the medical director told Hillery of the opening, asking the junior doctor if he had any French. Hillery had studied French at Rockwell and eagerly accepted the opportunity. Logan's action suggested that the differences between the two men were peripheral or at any rate did not affect their professional relationship. Hillery applied to join the study group, without expecting anything to come of it quickly:

> I entered for the *bourse* and went to Clare to take my week off. When I arrived in Spanish Point, Mrs Shannon at the Post Office had a message for me to go at once to 2 rue de Parc de Passey in Paris to join the other doctors from other countries who were already there.[24]

Des Hillery immediately drove his brother to Dublin airport and he arrived in Paris for the first time later on the same day. He was the sole

Irish member of the group, which included doctors from Britain,
continental Europe and South America.[25] The study involved a serious
investigation of the treatment of tuberculosis in several European
countries; it was essentially an exercise in postgraduate work for the
doctors. But in an era when travel was considerably more difficult and
expensive than it became in the late twentieth century, it was also an
unparalleled opportunity; Hillery was able to tour a series of major
European cities and experienced the rich cultural heritage of continental
Europe. The tour began in Paris, where the doctors witnessed the latest
French medical studies in the Pasteur Institute. Hillery loved his first
impressions of Paris and found time to go sightseeing. He also managed
a convivial evening in a suburban bar with a doctor from Guatemala and
had no idea how he found his way back to his residence.[26] The group
then inspected sanatoria in the mountains of southern France, Switzerland
and Italy; along the way they visited Lyon and the Swiss city of Lausanne.
The tour concluded in Rome, where the doctors had an audience with
Pope Pius XII.[27] It was the first time Hillery had met the reigning pontiff;
it would not be the last. He was blissfully unaware that he would later be
received by four popes, as a cabinet minister and President.

It was during his time as a junior doctor that Hillery took up golf,
which was to become the most valued and lasting pastime of his life. He
began to play the game when he was a resident intern in the Mater
Hospital.[28] Shortly afterwards he was involved in revitalising the golf club
in Spanish Point and he became its captain in 1952. He played golf there
regularly with his lifelong friend and neighbour, Paddy Casey, whom he
had known since they went to national school together. Both men took
their golf seriously, as Paddy Casey recalled: 'It was a nine-hole course
and it was pretty rough at the time, there wouldn't be any markings or
anything…and the stake was a half-crown and we fought for that half-
crown the same as if it was the claret jug.'[29] Hillery always retained a strong
attachment to his local golf course, but also became a member of Lahinch
golf club and played the South of Ireland championship at Lahinch several
times.[30] He was an outstanding amateur golfer, who played off a handicap
as low as seven at one stage. He found golf an essential source of relaxation

throughout his political career. While he was Minister for Education, he sometimes played golf tournaments under the alias of 'PJ Spain', to avoid being interrupted by urgent messages from his department: 'The secretary at Lahinch gave me the name. It was because people used to come looking for me, when they would want something they would come up the course after me.'[31] The heavy commitments imposed by his public career later curtailed Hillery's golfing, but never led him to abandon it; golf remained one of the enduring passions of his life.

Hillery was still working at Peamount when the inter-party government collapsed. Noel Browne's attempt to introduce the Mother and Child scheme, proposing free ante- and post-natal care for mothers and free medical care for children under the age of sixteen, was strongly opposed by the Irish Medical Association and the Catholic hierarchy. The Cabinet disowned the minister and Browne was forced to resign in April 1951.[32] The government fell within a month on an unrelated issue, although it was certainly damaged by the debacle over the Mother and Child scheme. Hillery was sympathetic towards Browne rather than the doctors who opposed him.[33] But the young Clare man took no part in the public controversy over the scheme. He remained entirely apolitical, showing no interest in politics at any level.

Hillery was following in the footsteps of his father, from Rockwell to medical training in Dublin and back to Clare as a doctor. His willingness to go to Canada for postgraduate work and his concern to secure the best possible training reflected the central importance of medicine in his life. Hillery showed a relentless drive to enhance his medical expertise and widen his experience throughout his early career as a doctor. His sole ambition was to go into general practice in his native town. He later ruefully described his aspiration to be a country doctor as 'a modest ambition, one never to be achieved.'[34]

3.

Candidate

'But I remember when I went home and I was sitting down in the front of the house at home in Spanish Point and I was kicking stones and gravel. My mother was looking at me and she said, "what are you worried about? You mightn't get elected at all." She had read my mind.'[1] Hillery's memory of his first reunion with his family following his selection as a candidate speaks volumes about his attitude towards politics in May 1951. Candidates rarely welcome reassurance from a close family member that they may not be elected, but that was evidently Nellie Hillery's intention in this instance. Paddy Hillery was already regretting his impulsive decision to allow a Fianna Fáil convention to nominate him and wondering what he had got himself into. This was not a case of pre-election nerves or the false reluctance sometimes adopted by practiced politicians. Hillery's reservations were very real and flowed from his own personality and life experience. Hillery did not expect any involvement in politics and never contemplated the prospect at all until the eve of the general election in 1951. It was not simply that he did not seek a party nomination; he was taken aback to be approached and shocked to find himself a candidate. While local political activists in Clare recognised his potential, his candidacy was most unexpected to Hillery himself.

Following the collapse of the first inter-party government, an election was called for 30 May. It was only at this late stage that Hillery emerged as a possible candidate. The main instigator of Hillery's political career was Patrick J. Hogan, an old IRA man who had served in the war of independence and was the chair of the Fianna Fáil cumann (branch) in Miltown Malbay. Hogan, who worked as a draper in the town, was a former neighbour of Hillery's mother.[2] Hillery later recalled that Hogan 'told me afterwards that there was an election called and he had no work done for the organisation and then "I got a brainwave", he said. I was the brainwave!'[3] Hillery had no previous involvement in politics of any kind and neither he nor his family were associated with Fianna Fáil. But the long-time Fianna Fáil activist saw Hillery's undoubted potential as a candidate. His father was a highly respected figure with an extensive medical practice throughout west Clare. Paddy himself was a native of Miltown Malbay and was also known in his own right from his time as a locum in a local dispensary; he could appeal effectively to local loyalties. Moreover he was a highly qualified doctor at a time when considerable social prestige still attached to the medical profession. His status as a complete political novice counted for little set against these substantial assets. Time would prove that Hogan was a shrewd judge of Clare politics.

When the election was called Hillery was still working in Dublin, serving out his term at Peamount. Hogan phoned the hospital at Peamount on Saturday 5 May to persuade Hillery to go forward; the young doctor was not there but Hogan told the other staff that he wanted Hillery to run for the Dáil and he needed to know his answer urgently. The selection convention was to be held on the next day, Sunday 6 May, at 3pm. Hillery was enjoying a relaxed evening with one of his colleagues but this was about to be rudely interrupted:

> I was out with Jack Sherry, and he asked if I wanted to go
> to Tom Murphy's farewell party in Naas but I said, no, drop
> me off at Peamount. I went in and had all these people

shouting at me. The people in the residence there said people were on from Clare several times, they want you to go for the Dáil – and I laughed. I knew nothing about it.[4]

Hillery's initial reaction was revealing. He had difficulty taking the idea seriously, not least because he had never expressed any interest in politics. But Hogan was deadly serious; in several phone calls that night, he strongly urged Hillery to go forward, telling him that his parents were in favour of the idea and that the younger man would not have to do anything himself to get selected. This assurance caused a comical misunderstanding, which reflected Hillery's complete inexperience in politics at the time: 'They said "you don't have to do anything, you can stay where you are". I understood that to mean that if I was selected I could stay where I was! But they were talking about getting through a convention.'[5] Hillery's colleagues in Peamount were also enthusiastic about the prospect of a TD in their ranks; the strongest voice in favour was Mark Clinton, then the farm manager for the sanatorium, who was later to be a Fine Gael TD and minister. Although he was already a Fine Gael activist, Clinton urged his colleague to seize the opportunity: 'If you can accept the policy at all, take it'.[6] Despite Hogan's assurances and the eager advice of his colleagues, Hillery was deeply uncertain about getting involved in politics, but he eventually agreed that the Miltown Malbay activists could put his name before a selection convention: 'It was not a decision, it was an "ok, so". How are important decisions made by individuals? There was no thought given to it by me – no worry like "what will I do if I win?" '[7] He understandably assumed that he was unlikely to be selected, as the convention would be held on the following day: 'I thought there was no way you could be selected in that time. It would usually be weeks going around getting different votes from different cumainn, you know.'[8] But Hogan was as good as his word. Paddy Hillery was one of the four candidates selected by the Fianna Fáil convention.[9] He found himself on the ticket with Éamon de Valera, the founding father and leader of the party, now in his seventies but still the most dominant and controversial figure in Irish politics. The other Fianna

Fáil candidates were Seán O'Grady, a TD since 1932 and former member of the Mid-Clare Brigade of the IRA, and Michael Considine, an affable county councillor and licensed trader in Ennis.[10] Hillery attributed his selection with characteristic modesty to his father's outstanding reputation in the county and to a desire within the party for new, young candidates. There was no doubt some truth in both of those explanations. But the younger Hillery was also well known in Miltown Malbay and the local organisation believed correctly that he would make a popular candidate.

The decision of the convention confronted Hillery with an unexpected dilemma. He had agreed impulsively to let his name go forward and was not at all sure that he wanted to be a candidate: 'But I woke up in the morning in a terrible state. I remember sitting on the steps—there is an old house in Peamount where Lady Aberdeen lived—and I said this was a dreadful mistake as far as I was concerned. But sometimes it's in my nature to do things like that'.[11] After some soul-searching Hillery did not decline the nomination; instead he agreed to contest the election, but was determined to maintain his medical career whatever the result. He had worked assiduously to earn his medical qualifications; medicine was his chosen career and he had no intention of abandoning it for politics. He would have been horrified in May 1951 had he realised that he was about to embark on a political career spanning almost forty years.

The beginning of Hillery's political career had some comical interludes, not least his first encounter with the party's headquarters. Shortly after his selection he received another call at Peamount, this time from a considerably more eminent political figure than Patrick Hogan. De Valera telephoned the sanatorium to give instructions to his newest running mate. Once again Hillery was absent but he found the fact of de Valera's call distinctly unnerving. When he actually spoke to de Valera, Hillery initially thought that his new party leader was warning him to give up the drink:

> I was to go to FF headquarters and sign the pledge. This did
> not appeal to me at all, but it had nothing to do with Fr

Mathew [Theobald]. It was a pledge to 'sit, act and vote with the party'. That did not cheer me up either. A call from Dev was unexpected. It also brought home to me that there was more involved than Paddy Hogan and Miltown Malbay.[12]

Hillery's conversation with de Valera underlined the reality of his new status as a party candidate. He dutifully followed de Valera's instructions and went into Fianna Fáil's headquarters in Mount Street to meet the party's long-serving general secretary, Tommy Mullins. Hillery confided to Mullins his anxiety about his political inexperience. The genial official sought to reassure him but succeeded only in highlighting Hillery's status as de Valera's youngest running mate. 'I said "I know absolutely nothing about politics, I shouldn't be here". His reply was "at the end of one campaign with this man you will know all you need to know"'.[13]

At the outset of the campaign, Hillery's election seemed an unlikely prospect to seasoned political observers. Fianna Fáil hoped to take three seats out of four in Clare, but its prospects of doing so were remote in an election that brought no great upsurge in support for de Valera's party. The other incumbent deputies were Paddy Hogan of the Labour Party and Tom Burke, a popular independent who was elected largely on the basis of his reputation as a skilled bonesetter. Fianna Fáil was not likely to unseat either of them. While Clare was not traditionally fertile ground for the Labour Party, Hogan (a namesake of Patrick Hogan of Miltown Malbay) operated to a large extent as a rural independent and benefited from his involvement in the war of independence, when he had been jailed for a time along with Michael Hillery.[14] Tom Burke based his appeal to the voters entirely on his service to the community as a bonesetter; he was also a native of Miltown Malbay, but received support throughout the constituency.[15] Fianna Fáil may have hoped that Hillery would take a seat at Burke's expense, but 'the Bonesetter' was a popular figure in the county, not least with Fianna Fáil supporters whose transfers had helped to elect him in 1948.[16] Fine Gael had failed to take a seat in the 1948 election but was mounting a strong campaign in Clare three years later, running two new candidates, Bill Murphy, a farmer from Ennistymon, and Vincent McHugh from Ennis.[17] The election would see a resurgence for Fine Gael following its participation in government for the first time in sixteen years.

A local Fianna Fáil councillor told Michael Hillery that his son would probably get in if Fianna Fáil secured a third seat. The old doctor was annoyed at this, believing that his son could be elected regardless of Fianna Fáil's ability to win an extra seat.[18] But the re-election of the two sitting Fianna Fáil TDs was conventional political wisdom on the eve of the election. De Valera had been returned at every election since the East Clare by-election in 1917 and he was certain to top the poll. Hillery recalled that de Valera 'was there only for one weekend and he got all the votes.'[19] While O'Grady lacked his leader's extraordinary popularity, he was a central figure in local Fianna Fáil politics. O'Grady enjoyed considerable prestige due to his status as a veteran of the old IRA. He was also an experienced politician, who had served as a Parliamentary Secretary, chair of Clare County Council and a TD for nineteen years.[20] Hillery was a political neophyte contesting his first election and he was not expected to win it. De Valera's political adviser, Pádraig Ó hAnnracháin, who accompanied the Chief on his election tour of Clare, encouraged Hillery to run again, urging him not to be discouraged by failing at his first attempt.[21] Similarly an encounter with one of the party's most prominent local figures left Hillery in no doubt that his prospects were generally regarded as bleak. Shortly after his selection he went to Ennis to meet Seán Ó Ceallaigh, a teacher in Ennis technical school who was the secretary of the Fianna Fáil organisation in the county.[22] Ó Ceallaigh was a leading organiser for the party in Clare; he later became Hillery's running mate and was himself elected as a TD. At his first meeting with the young candidate, however, Ó Ceallaigh did not seem impressed. He was pessimistic about Hillery's chances and sceptical at his decision to run for election at all:

> When I met him he did not show any great enthusiasm
> for my candidacy and as he walked looking straight ahead

he said, 'you have no sense, young man, getting involved in politics'. Since I thoroughly agreed with him it made me feel that I had made a serious mistake.[23]

The encounter with Ó Ceallaigh underlined that Hillery remained profoundly ambivalent concerning his involvement in politics. The pessimistic views of leading party members in Clare and nationally were shared to a considerable extent by Hillery himself. He did not think he was likely to be elected and had mixed feelings about the possibility of defeat. His own reservations about running for office had not abated. He had no ambition to be a TD and intended to work full-time as a doctor. But equally he did not want to lose the election once he had committed to running; 'You see, once you are going you don't want to be beaten'.[24] Moreover, he was concerned not to let down his family and supporters in Miltown Malbay, who very much wanted him to win the election.[25] This ambiguity about politics lay at the heart of his first campaign and indeed of his early years in the Dáil.

The campaign itself was uncharted territory for Hillery. It took some time for him to adapt to the demands of political campaigning. He struggled particularly with public speaking, even to friendly audiences: 'I stood up in a couple of places and I couldn't get anything out at all, I'd say I'll be back and I'll talk to you, this was even in a quiet meeting with Fianna Fáil members.'[26] Hillery's reticence was explained in part by his natural shyness, but he was also keenly aware that he knew very little about politics or local political issues. He set out diligently to remedy this problem, studying the leaflets and briefing material prepared by Fianna Fáil nationally. When Michael Hillery was temporarily laid low by illness at the beginning of the campaign, Paddy was covering his father's practice as well as running for the Dáil. Despite the considerable workload this was undoubtedly an advantage, as it brought him into contact with patients throughout west Clare. He later recalled waiting to deliver a baby for one of his father's patients in Quilty and reading the party's election leaflets by the fireside, 'because I didn't know anything about politics'.[27] This ignorance did not last long; he was soon able to deliver a stump speech that extolled Fianna Fáil's record in government up to 1948 and urged the people of Clare to play their part in giving a majority to de Valera again.[28] Yet Hillery remained extremely nervous before speaking in public throughout the campaign. He was unable to eat before speaking and marvelled at de Valera's ability to consume a hearty meal before addressing a meeting: 'I was amazed at how he ate. I was all the more impressed at his appetite as my taste for food disappeared with public appearance'.[29]

The young candidate was even more impressed by de Valera's hold on the local electorate. The Fianna Fáil leader spent only four days in Clare as part of his national tour. He did public meetings in different towns over a long weekend, including Kilrush, Kilkee, Ennistymon, Kilmihil, Killaloe and Ennis. All the meetings attracted large crowds and Hillery recalled the enthusiasm of the local people for de Valera:

> His speeches were lectures, more seeking accuracy than stimulation, but small changes of tone or emphasis brought cheers as evidence of their desire to encourage him. In Ennistymon the streetlights went out at their usual hour while Dev was still explaining. He said 'táimid ins an dorchadas' ['we are in the darkness'] and quickly a shout from the crowd came back 'we were there before!' and brought a big cheer. They felt as old companions of his.[30]

De Valera was certainly enormously popular in Clare, but he had his opponents even in the Banner County. Local politics in Clare was a colourful, exciting and raucous business in the 1950s. Fine Gael organised a public meeting in Ennis, which was addressed by Dr J.H Counihan, a leading local opponent of de Valera; in the course of a highly charged speech, Counihan declared that 'de Valera would return like a dog to his vomit'.[31] This provoked a memorable riposte two days later from Seán MacNamara, a long-time Fianna Fáil activist from north Clare, who claimed that Counihan had given aid and comfort to the British forces during the war of independence, in stark contrast to Hillery's father:

> I was at a meeting and Seán McNamara, an old IRA man
> … came out with the most extraordinary statement about
> Dr Counihan. He said that while Dr Hillery's father was
> attending to the IRA in Rineen, Dr Counihan was picking
> shot out of the arses of British soldiers and getting paid for
> it by John Bull.[32]

Whatever Counihan was actually doing during the war of independence, the row underlined that the movement for national independence and the civil war still formed the backdrop for party politics a generation later. As his family had remained aloof from nationalist politics after the war of independence, Hillery had little direct experience of the intensity of the divisions provoked by the split over the Treaty and inflamed by the civil war. The campaign left Hillery with no illusions about the fierce animosity between leading supporters of Fianna Fáil and Fine Gael, which still persisted in the 1950s. But he never shared this ingrained hostility; indeed his close friend Paddy Casey was an active supporter of Fine Gael. Hillery's distaste for civil war rhetoric became a consistent feature of his political career.

The Fianna Fáil campaign was organised around a series of public meetings, which were usually held wherever large numbers of people gathered – notably cattle fairs in the main towns and especially at church gates after Mass every Sunday. As the population was overwhelmingly Catholic and the vast majority attended Mass, Sunday was the most important day for public meetings. The candidates sought to address all the congregations as they exited the churches after Mass; this often became a race between candidates to arrive first at the church gates, which would establish the right to speak first and catch the full congregation before they left for home. Hillery recalled that 'there were disputes about who was first; longwinded ones saw the crowd disperse before other speakers got a chance. Since I had little to say I was not worried about getting in first'.[33] Hillery's speeches were generally brief and avoided any attacks on political opponents. His broadly positive approach to the campaign was evident at Fianna Fáil's final major rally in Ennis, which was addressed by de Valera. Hillery praised de Valera as 'the leader of the Irish people' and appealed to young people to vote for Fianna Fáil. He drew attention to the party's success in bringing Ireland safely through the Second World War and also emphasised Fianna Fáil's record in delivering social reforms.[34] Any reference to the civil war or the past sins of the party's opponents was notably absent. His previous detachment from politics meant that he had no history of bad blood with the party's opponents. But Hillery's political instincts were also beginning to appear: 'I saw too that long-windedness lost the audience, as did offensive statements about public men'.[35] In this case Hillery's initial reticence served him well.

Despite his political inexperience Hillery enjoyed some important advantages. He commanded the enthusiastic support of a large extended family, who threw themselves eagerly into the campaign. Hillery was joined in canvassing west Clare by his brother Des and brother-in-law Bill Ryan; from an older generation his uncle PJ Hillery also helped out in the campaign.[36] Most significantly, Michael Hillery openly participated in a political contest for the first time since the Treaty, drawing upon his wide network of connections throughout the county to promote his son. Michael Hillery's reputation as a much admired country doctor and medical officer to the local IRA in the war of independence was an invaluable asset to his son's campaign. The Fianna Fáil organisers were delighted by Michael Hillery's association with the party and the leaflet issued for all four party candidates referred to 'Dr M.J. Hillery, Spanish Point, who was prominently identified with the I.R.A in Black and Tan days and is now extending his whole-hearted support to the Fianna Fáil candidates'.[37] Like most good political propaganda, this was not precisely true: the elder Hillery was determined to secure Paddy's election and was not greatly concerned by the rest of the Fianna Fáil ticket. The younger man drew considerable support from his native town, where he was able to rely on the votes of former patients from his own year in the dispensary as well as those who knew and respected his family.[38] Local loyalty to a successful son of Miltown Malbay was another element in the groundswell of support for Hillery. These were all significant assets for a first-time candidate, which guaranteed that Hillery would challenge strongly for a seat.

It is impossible to know if local and family connections alone would have secured Hillery's election. But he was not entirely dependent on such inherited advantages; he benefited too from his own positive approach to the campaign. Hillery's quiet manner and low-key rhetoric on the hustings marked out a personal and generational distinction with his older counterparts in Fianna Fáil, O'Grady and Considine. O'Grady was deeply immersed in the tradition of Civil War politics and delighted in attacking the party's opponents, especially the old enemy of Fine Gael. At the same rally in Ennis where Hillery spoke, O'Grady called on the people of Clare 'to strike another blow for Ireland' by returning three Fianna Fáil candidates; his speech combined nationalist rhetoric with an extended onslaught on the failures of the inter-party government.[39] Considine explicitly invoked the memory of the civil war, telling the audience in Ennis 'that was what they fought and suffered for in 1922 – to maintain the Republic they had now'. Moreover he appealed for support on the basis of Fianna Fáil's 'proper national outlook' and the party's determination to prevent 'persons with imperialistic tendencies' from retaining power.[40] The confrontational style of the older Fianna Fáil candidates contrasted sharply with Hillery's low-key, conciliatory approach, but there was also a clear divergence in the substance of their appeals for support. Hillery's more positive, pragmatic appeal to the people of Clare was very different from the nationalist rhetoric employed heavily by O'Grady and Considine.

O'Grady's confrontational style, which had probably served him well in the past, proved counterproductive in 1951. He singled out James Dillon, Minister for Agriculture in the outgoing government, for special attention at various public meetings. O'Grady denounced Dillon's policies on agriculture, claiming that Dillon had made Ireland the only country in Western Europe where bread and flour were still rationed.[41] The merits of his criticisms were lost on the voters, however, when the veteran TD also made contemptuous references at various times to 'James Mary Dillon'.[42] It was hardly the sole occasion in the campaign where Dillon was denounced from a Fianna Fáil platform, but the veteran TD's choice of language was spectacularly ill advised in a rural constituency where traditional Catholicism was the norm and the name of Mary was widely regarded with veneration. Hillery recalled that O'Grady's comments at one public meeting brought 'shouted outrage from a lady in the gallery' and provoked anger among those who felt that he was insulting the name of Mary.[43] The younger man realised that O'Grady was losing ground: 'Seán O'Grady, he was drumming it away and it suddenly dawned on me, he's losing votes. At one meeting down in Kilrush they walked away, he kept insulting the opposition. While he probably felt fully satisfied that he had a good song to sing, they didn't like it'.[44] O'Grady's attacks did no damage at all to Dillon but rebounded on himself. The main beneficiary was O'Grady's junior colleague and rival. O'Grady may well have sensed the threat from Hillery to his seat and hoped to solidify his position by marking himself out as the most vocal and effective critic of Fianna Fáil's traditional opponents. This was a standard political tactic in the 1950s and provided a convenient way of reminding supporters of O'Grady's long-standing connections with the party. But if this was O'Grady's intention the move backfired disastrously.

The election on 30 May brought defeat for two incumbents and success for the young pretender. When the votes were counted on the following day it was immediately evident that de Valera would top the poll once again; he was elected on the first count with 13,850 first preferences in a very high poll of over 41,000.[45] Bill Murphy was also elected for Fine Gael, easily seeing off the challenge of his party rival from Ennis. The party leader's substantial surplus guaranteed the election of a second Fianna Fáil candidate – the only issue to be decided was which one. Hillery secured an impressive lead over his party rivals, winning 4,063 votes and taking fourth place on the first count, behind de Valera, Murphy and Hogan. The younger man enjoyed a lead of more than 1,500 votes over Considine and an even larger margin over O'Grady.[46] Hillery was in a commanding position from the start, although he had to endure a long, nerve-wracking wait until the count was concluded. The distribution of de Valera's surplus marginally favoured O'Grady, but Hillery secured enough votes to remain well ahead of the incumbent deputy. The elimination of Considine, whose transfers favoured Hillery by more than two to one, gave Hillery a decisive advantage over O'Grady.[47] The young doctor won the third seat, ousting the veteran politician and revolutionary. The struggle for the last seat saw a close battle between two sitting deputies; Paddy Hogan narrowly defeated Tom Burke on the final count.[48]

Hillery's election was a significant accomplishment for a first-time candidate with no political experience. He certainly owed much of his support to his extensive family and local connections in west Clare; in particular Michael Hillery's generation of service as a highly regarded rural doctor did a great deal to ensure his son's election. But this was not the whole story. Paddy Hillery developed his own mild-mannered and conciliatory political style, which presented a favourable contrast with many older politicians of both main parties. Hillery's lack of any personal or family background in politics meant that he had no inclination to attack Fianna Fáil's opponents or to rake up the embers of the civil war. His low-key style and lack of any previous political record did him no harm at all in appealing to a local electorate, which greatly admired de Valera but was disillusioned with the more virulent strains of civil war politics. Hillery had not plotted and planned his elevation to the Dáil; it had happened to a large extent by accident or by the designs of others. He had, however, shown many of the attributes of a successful politician in his first campaign – hard work, tenacity, an affable personal manner and a sensible political caution. Hillery's first campaign showed that he had the ability to become a popular candidate in his own right.

Yet Hillery's ambivalence about involvement in politics did not end with his victory. He remarked in retirement that losing the election was 'my last hope' of avoiding further entanglement in politics.[49] This comment was an exaggeration of his feelings at the time; he had wanted to win the election and had worked hard to do so. He was far from exultant, however, at becoming a member of the Dáil. He still felt that his future lay in medicine, as a country doctor, who might in time take over his father's practice. The idea of becoming a professional politician held no appeal for him and he aimed instead to combine his new political role with his primary focus on medical practice. If he thought about it at all he assumed that politics was simply a temporary deviation in his chosen career path, which he would leave behind in due course. The lingering ambiguity that lay at the core of his approach towards politics would define Hillery's first eight years as a TD.

4.

In the Shadow of the Chief

Clare returned two new TDs to the 14ᵗʰ Dáil, Paddy Hillery and Bill Murphy. Both men began as political outsiders who were elected at the expense of more prominent party candidates and they became friendly as new members of the Dáil. But Hillery's path to office was more unconventional. Murphy had previous political experience as a county councillor and Fine Gael activist. Hillery's involvement in the political arena was still very recent and some echoes of his previous detachment from party politics lingered during his early years as a TD, occasionally with comical results. The newly elected deputy had difficulty in finding Leinster House on the day that he arrived to take his seat: 'I went to Dublin holding a letter from the returning officer saying that I had been returned for the constituency of Clare. Then I had to look for Leinster House and got a strange look from a garda of whom I asked where it was'.[1] The irony of this episode was that Hillery was emphatically not a country boy on his first day in the city. He was no stranger to Dublin, having studied and worked there for several years. Moreover he had already travelled widely in Europe and North America. But he was nevertheless unaware of the precise location of the national parliament; it would be hard to find a more striking illustration of his detachment from political life before 1951. It would be some time before Hillery's reluctance to engage fully in party politics was overcome and while he later became a highly skilled practitioner of the art, some aspects of his original detachment from politics left their imprint on his political style.

The first duty of the new Dáil was to choose between the rival claims of de Valera and the outgoing Taoiseach, John A. Costello, to form a government. As neither Fianna Fáil nor the inter-party government had come close to an overall majority, fourteen Independent deputies held the balance of power. Tensions mounted in the corridors of Leinster House, as both sides sought to win over the Independents while politicians and journalists tried to work out the permutations that could either re-elect Costello or return de Valera to office. Hillery found that backbench deputies were given no information about what their leaders were doing and had as little knowledge about what would actually happen as average members of the public. He was pursued by journalists, who assumed that as de Valera's junior colleague in Clare he had privileged access to information. Malachy Hynes, a journalist who was also a native of Miltown Malbay, was particularly persistent in demanding information and was not convinced by Hillery's assurances that he had no idea what was going on: 'Malachy Hynes came after me and could not believe that I was not in on the negotiations of senior members of the party and was very annoyed that I would not disclose the information for which they all hungered.'[2] De Valera manoeuvred with his customary skill to cobble together a majority. Frank Fahy, the Ceann Comhairle, who was a member of Fianna Fáil, fortuitously announced that he was unable to stand again for the office due to ill health; his return to the Fianna Fáil benches gave de Valera an additional vote.[3] Then Paddy Hogan, the Labour TD for Clare, was elected unanimously as Ceann Comhairle; this move neutralised another vote for the outgoing government. But the decision ultimately rested with the Independents and the outcome was unclear right up until the hour of the vote on 13 June 1951. De Valera's victory was assured when he secured the backing of five Independents, including Noel Browne.[4] The outcome was still extremely close; Costello's nomination for Taoiseach was defeated by only two votes, while de Valera was elected by 74 votes to 69.[5] The Fianna Fáil leader led a minority government and his ability to govern effectively was constrained by his reliance on the support of the Independents and his own increasing ill health.

De Valera's return to power did not greatly affect the status of his junior colleague, although it certainly did impinge upon the younger man's workload. Hillery was a newly elected government backbencher; like most of his colleagues in rural constituencies, he immediately found that the role was dominated by a heavy burden of constituency work, combined with virtually no influence in the party or the Dáil. He wryly recalled that 'my mother said that it was superior to be a backbencher of the government than the opposition. I found that the public seeking help also believed that and I had an enormous postage to deal with, as well as notes made from callers and notes at meetings'.[6] Hillery's workload was dramatically increased due to his position as the Taoiseach's junior colleague. As de Valera lived and worked in Dublin, Hillery was the only government TD who was easily accessible to party supporters and other constituents seeking assistance; he therefore faced an even larger volume of constituency queries. Moreover de Valera did not do constituency work, instead referring all constituency queries to his running mate. The Taoiseach's private secretary, Kathleen O'Connell, passed on to Hillery any correspondence from people seeking favours or assistance with local issues in Clare.[7] Hillery believed that de Valera was acting in a scrupulous fashion to avoid any personal representations to one of his ministers: 'If he got a request from somebody for a favour he passed it on to me. I understood he felt (correctly) that he could not take the usual course of asking the appropriate minister to do something as a minister could hardly refuse the Taoiseach'.[8] This sense of propriety was undoubtedly part of de Valera's rationale, although it was hardly the sole explanation for the wholesale delegation of constituency duties to his junior colleague. It was also convenient for the ageing Taoiseach, preoccupied with governmental and party affairs, to farm out the extensive volume of constituency business to a young and energetic newcomer. The increasing problems with de Valera's health also made extensive delegation of local business to Hillery essential; the Taoiseach was absent for over four months in the Netherlands for eye treatment in 1951 and 1952. But whatever de Valera's reasons, the consequences for Hillery were the same: 'I was swamped with constituency work'.[9]

The Dáil in the 1950s was closer to a nineteenth-century parliament than to the highly developed structures for political information, campaigning and constituent service that characterised Leinster House at the end of the twentieth century. The nature of the Dáil in 1951 ensured that constituency service genuinely meant personal service by TDs. There were no secretarial or research allowances for deputies when Hillery was first elected; neither staff nor typing services were generally available to TDs at the time. The absence of staff or significant resources meant that members of the Dáil replied to letters from constituents personally. Hillery himself wrote responses to constituency queries in his own hand during his first term as a TD.[10] He also took up individual cases with ministers or senior officials, often calling personally to departments or state offices on behalf of constituents. Not all TDs took constituency work so seriously; Hillery recalled that 'Some people got elected without working, but others had to work like mad'.[11] The workload was undoubtedly heavier for rural deputies, who tended to face a much higher demand for constituency service. One of Hillery's colleagues found the burden so onerous that he appealed in vain to the people of his constituency to stop tormenting him: 'Paddy Maguire, a doctor, he was from Monaghan and he put a notice in the paper that he couldn't handle all the letters he was getting and asking them to stop. Then it doubled immediately!'[12]

The national parliament was also a traditional institution in its membership and political ideology. The Dáil was still dominated by the leading members of the revolutionary generation, who had participated in the movement for national independence and the subsequent bitter conflict over the Treaty. The veterans of the nationalist movement were strongly represented within the two major parties. A majority of deputies were old enough to have personal experience of the civil war; some had actively participated in the conflict, while others had lost relatives or close friends. The events of a generation before still aroused fierce animosity and had the power to generate bitter clashes in the Dáil. Hillery felt shock and revulsion at the ferocity of the civil war rhetoric and the intensity of the loathing between some members on different sides of the House: 'I hated it when they started shouting at one another. I couldn't understand the hatred. It's hard to bring it all back now. People were there who had brothers and sisters killed; there was real bitterness there'.[13] His strong aversion to civil war rhetoric became an enduring theme of Hillery's political career. At least in part because he was repelled by the continuing verbal hostilities over the civil war, Hillery did not like or enjoy the political theatre of the Dáil in his time as a backbench TD. He did not become a frequent contributor to parliamentary debates until his appointment as a minister. This was not simply a matter of distaste for civil war polemics, but also reflected the reality that his priorities lay elsewhere. Hillery was preoccupied not only with the large-scale demand for constituency service, which was central to the work of any rural TD, but also with his blossoming career as a doctor.

Hillery's term at Peamount ended shortly after his election and he returned to Miltown Malbay to work in his father's practice. He seemed on the verge of fulfilling his cherished ambition to become a country doctor, taking on greater responsibilities within the family practice.[14] The Hillery practice was widely accessible to people of all social classes because the fees were low and indeed were waived completely for some patients.[15] Hillery travelled extensively throughout west Clare on maternity work, assisting with the delivery of babies. This involved a considerable amount of night work in addition to his daytime commitments in the practice. He soon acquired a well-deserved reputation as a capable and conscientious family doctor, following the example set by his father. His favourable reputation in west Clare was enhanced by a rumour, which was not entirely unfounded, that he was giving money to patients. This arose when Hillery delivered a baby for a Traveller family at a campsite and noticed that an adult Traveller within the same community was suffering from tuberculosis: 'I felt sorry for him as I told him he would have to go to hospital. I gave him some money. The following day I had a queue outside my surgery as the word went out that I was giving out money'.[16] Fortunately for Hillery, this episode proved the exception rather than the rule. He greatly enjoyed the work and wrote later that he was more contented as a country doctor than at any time in his political career: 'I loved the time I spent in country practice.'[17] Certainly his commitment to pursuing a career in general practice remained steadfast.

Even in his chosen profession, however, the younger Hillery could not escape from politics. Local people seeking a clinic of a more political kind were soon knocking on the door of the family surgery: 'My father had this experience as a doctor and helped to meet the new arrivals brought in by my election with a patience which was a lesson to me'.[18] Hillery found himself dealing with a wide variety of constituency queries in the course of his medical work. Perhaps the most persistent cases concerned claims for pensions, particularly invalidity pensions and old IRA pensions for those who had served in the war of independence. His dual functions as a country doctor and politician involved him in unusual and occasionally hilarious episodes on his medical house calls, especially where the claims for pensions were at issue:

> Once at dusk I called for directions at a house where I knew I had to cross fields. The man offered to accompany me. We crossed over a wall (made of stones enclosed in sods as was usually the case). We walked quite a bit until my eyes, accommodating [to the dark], showed we were repeatedly passing recognisable landmarks. We were circling. I spoke and he got us on track with some fuss about his sight. Then he said 'I was thinking of applying for the blind pension: Could you do anything for me?' He gave me the scenic route to convince me that he needed the blind pension!'[19]

Hillery was highly entertained by the devices adopted by local people to secure what they regarded as their entitlements from a distant and penny-pinching administration in Dublin. He enjoyed living and working in Clare far too much to be disturbed by the considerable demands of his constituents. Moreover in taking up claims for pensions and social welfare on an official basis, he was continuing a family tradition. Michael Hillery had acted as an informal adviser to local people on similar issues for many years. Unlike his father, however, Paddy Hillery maintained a dual career as politician and doctor for most of the 1950s. He was both a busy local GP and a hardworking constituency representative, sometimes discharging both functions at the same time.

Hillery's balancing act between politics and medicine was by no means easy. It was a particularly difficult balance to maintain when the Dáil was in session; he often had commitments to parliamentary duties in Dublin and general practice in Clare on the same day. It was not unusual for Hillery to see patients in Miltown Malbay during the day and then drive to Dublin in time for votes in the Dáil around 10.30pm. He then drove back to Clare on the same evening, doing a round trip of about 320 miles each day.[20] This pattern occurred with increasing frequency throughout the 1950s, as Hillery took on an expanded range of medical responsibilities. Michael Hillery was seriously ill for the final three years of his life and Paddy gradually took over the family practice. After his father's retirement in February 1957, Paddy Hillery was appointed to succeed him as medical officer of Miltown Malbay; he became Coroner for West Clare in the following year.[21] Michael Hillery died in October 1957 at the age of 68. The Clare Champion provided a respectful and affectionate obituary for the old doctor, noting with complete accuracy that 'his devoted attention to his patients, day and night, was undoubtedly responsible for shortening his life.'[22] Paddy Hillery appeared to be following in his father's footsteps in more ways than one, maintaining an immensely demanding medical practice, in tandem with the additional burden of a political career. The combined workload was gruelling and unsustainable in the long term. It was evident that a choice would have to be made between politics and medical practice sooner or later.

Yet Hillery's dual career certainly did not disturb the people of Clare; his work as a family doctor enhanced his stature and brought him into contact with a wide range of local people from diverse backgrounds. His dual status led to another incident that became legendary in the Hillery family. His nephew Michael recalled the story of how politics and medicine became intertwined in the mind of an anxious father-to-be:

> Dr Paddy had just done a house call and he was about to go to bed when there was a knock on the door. He opened the window and popped his head out; the man said 'Dr Paddy, my wife is about to have a child'. My uncle thought he might get a few hours' sleep, he asked 'Is she in labour?' The man said 'Oh no, Doctor, we were always Fianna Fáil to the bone.'[23]

The young doctor was concerned about the possibility of a false alarm on the part of his patient, but had reckoned without the patient's desire to highlight his political insurance policy. The distinction between the two roles became blurred in the eyes of some constituents, who might seek assistance in securing a pension at their doctor's surgery or ask for help with a social welfare claim while their local GP was completing his house calls. There is little doubt that Hillery's genuine commitment to family practice did much to sustain his political career, at a time when he was deeply ambivalent about his future participation in politics. It was ironic that his work as a doctor contributed to developing an unforeseen future in politics – one that would take him away from his cherished medical practice. Hillery's diligence in pursuing both strands of his career served to consolidate his position as a TD. It was no accident that he was easily re-elected to the Dáil throughout the 1950s.

De Valera's minority government did not complete its full term; the Dáil was dissolved after less than three years as the Taoiseach chose to go to the country in May 1954. The contest that followed underlined Hillery's growing popularity in Clare. The circumstances were very different from his first campaign; he was now an incumbent TD who was widely favoured to hold his seat. De Valera opened his own campaign in late April in Miltown Malbay, sharing the platform with Hillery, the leading political figure in the town. The Taoiseach told an enthusiastic crowd of supporters that 'his party colleagues' had suggested the meeting, which was probably true but also ensured that Hillery got the credit for securing the party leader's appearance in the town so early in the campaign.[24] De Valera's appearance was an obvious gesture of support for his young running mate and testified to Hillery's increasing stature within local politics. The internal competition between the Fianna Fáil candidates was much less pronounced on this occasion, as the party was concerned primarily with holding its own; taking a third seat was not practical politics, as Paddy Hogan, the Ceann Comhairle, was returned automatically to the Dáil and Clare was effectively a three-seat constituency for electoral purposes. Hillery's erstwhile rival, Seán O'Grady, who was now a Senator, did not stand again and Thomas O'Meara, the third Fianna Fáil candidate, had virtually no chance of securing a seat. O'Meara openly admitted that he did not expect to be elected, telling the party's final rally in Ennis with commendable honesty that 'he was a poor platform speaker and it was never his intention to be a deputy, but he was selected by the party'.[25] Hillery was de Valera's leading running mate and had little to fear from internal party competition.

Hillery himself was more confident and fluent in his public appearances, showing no signs of the stage fright that had afflicted him in 1951. Moreover he found his own voice as a politician, emphasising in his speeches the need for social and economic progress. When he addressed the Fianna Fáil rally in Ennis alongside de Valera, he claimed with some justification that Fine Gael had no policy but 'put out the government' and was seeking support from those 'discontented with everything Fianna Fáil had done'.[26] Significantly, he did not reproach Fine Gael for its alleged failings on the national question, but attacked the main opposition party for proposing to cut taxes rather than investing in social services. While he made the obligatory references to Fianna Fáil's nationalist traditions and the central part played by de Valera in establishing full Irish sovereignty in the 1930s, Hillery also warned that past glories were not enough for the Irish people. He set out his own view of the challenge facing Fianna Fáil in a striking passage that escaped much notice at the time:

> It was not enough to drive the enemy from the country. They had to prove the capability of the Irish people to work for Ireland and to give the people a better standard of living than the English gave them and to prove that they can maintain their freedom and not neglect their people as the British and Cumann na nGaedhael neglected them.[27]

Hillery's criticism of the evils of British rule and the failures of Cumann na nGaedhael, the party which preceded Fine Gael, were standard themes of Fianna Fáil rhetoric. But his implicit message was that the achievement of economic and social development was the challenge facing his generation. Hillery's statement reflected his own convictions and not the standard party line. The passage had little in common with the high-flown nationalist rhetoric employed by de Valera and bore a much greater resemblance to the pragmatic approach developed not long afterwards by his chief lieutenant and eventual successor, Seán Lemass. Moreover while Hillery's speech was based on the argument that only Fianna Fáil could deliver economic and social progress, his statement also contained a strong hint of impatience that successive governments of all parties had failed to give the Irish people 'a better standard of living'. The speech did not disturb Hillery's party leader, who was standing beside him on the platform, but it underlined in unmistakable terms that Hillery was developing his own independent political convictions.

The election on 18 May brought a change of government at national level, but merely confirmed the stability of political alignments in Clare. All four TDs were returned to the 15th Dáil, with de Valera topping the poll once more and Murphy taking the second seat.[28] Hillery's first preference vote increased dramatically by over 2,000 and his election was assured from the outset. He was elected on the seventh count, defeating his nearest rival, the Labour Party candidate, Gerard Griffin, by a margin of two to one.[29] Hillery's performance was impressive, not least in the context of the overall results, which brought defeat for Fianna Fail. The party lost four seats, while Fine Gael gained ten seats and returned to power. Costello took office at the head of a second inter-party government, composed of Fine Gael, Labour and Clann na Talmhan, while de Valera was again consigned to the opposition benches. Hillery was not greatly disturbed by Fianna Fáil's removal from office. As a backbench TD his life did not change very much, although he enjoyed a considerable reduction in his workload; an opposition TD at the time received fewer demands for assistance than his counterparts on the government benches. The difference was graphically illustrated by the experience of Hillery's fellow deputy for Clare. He met Bill Murphy shortly after the change of government: 'I said "How do you like it, Bill, you're in government" and he groaned, "I got a shoebox of letters this morning"'.[30] As it turned out, de Valera's setback and Hillery's respite both proved temporary.

The second inter-party government was more stable than the first but it did not prove more durable. Costello sought a dissolution of the Dáil in February 1957, after two and a half years in office, as the government could no longer command a parliamentary majority. The third general election of the decade, which was held on 5 March 1957, was the first to produce a definitive verdict. Fianna Fáil won over half the seats in the Dáil and secured an overall majority for the first time since 1944.[31] The seventy-five-year-old de Valera formed his final government, in which Lemass soon emerged as the dominant figure. The campaign in Clare was described by *The Clare Champion* as the 'quietist election on record'; only Fianna Fáil and Fine Gael contested the poll in Clare and the election produced no changes at all.[32] If the ballot underlined the local dominance of the two main parties, it also served to confirm Hillery's success in carving out a secure political base. Seán O'Grady, whom Hillery had displaced in 1951, attempted to make a political comeback and contested the election on the same ticket as Hillery and de Valera. The result was a personal triumph for de Valera, who was elected on the first count with a huge vote of over 16,000. This overshadowed Hillery's less spectacular but equally decisive victory; he was elected on the second count, outpolling O'Grady by over 4,000 votes. O'Grady came in at the bottom of the poll and barely saved his deposit.[33] The outcome reflected Hillery's standing as a highly respected local figure and popular representative. Despite his initial reluctance he had shown an unexpected aptitude for politics.

Yet it was also true that Hillery had no wider political ambitions at this stage. He rebuffed more than one overture from de Valera, who sounded out his junior colleague about becoming a Parliamentary Secretary. When de Valera returned to power in 1957, he offered Hillery a junior post in the government, but the younger man firmly declined the offer. This was not de Valera's only attempt to persuade his junior colleague to accept ministerial office. The Taoiseach acted with the political subtlety that was his trademark, seeking to encourage Hillery to express an interest in joining the government without approaching him directly:

> He did some tricks after that, he used to call me in and ask me how I was doing. And once there was a vacancy in the government, people were waiting for an announcement and he asked me in, we had a long chat; he didn't say anything about the vacancy. But I think he was letting me ask.[34]

De Valera undoubtedly faced some local pressure from his supporters in Clare to appoint Hillery as a Parliamentary Secretary. The Taoiseach may also have hoped to promote a young colleague whom he respected. He had already appointed Jack Lynch, who was a contemporary of Hillery, to the Cabinet as Minister for Education in 1957. But Hillery did not regard his involvement in politics as a long-term career and told de Valera of his feelings:

> Dev had tried me out a couple of times and once I made it clear to him that my interest was medical practice. I asked him if in the event of taking part in the government I

could apply for a dispensary; he groaned. But I never regarded politics as anything but a temporary derailment — an aberration from which I would one day escape.[35]

De Valera did not press the matter any further and Hillery held no government office until his senior colleague's retirement as Taoiseach in June 1959.

After eight years as a TD, Hillery still believed that his future lay in medicine rather than politics. Indeed he seriously considered standing down as a TD to devote himself fully to medical practice towards the end of de Valera's final term as Taoiseach: 'I remember I was treating Canon O'Reilly and I said "Canon, I'm giving up politics, I can't take it all." The following day it was announced that Dev was running for the Park. There were only the two of us there so if both of us disappeared the constituency would be in an awful state. That kind of tied me in'.[36] The official announcement that de Valera would be the Fianna Fáil candidate for President in 1959 put Hillery's hopes for political retirement on hold. As it was widely (and correctly) assumed that de Valera would win the election, Hillery was about to become the only sitting Fianna Fáil TD in Clare. He was undoubtedly concerned that his departure would leave his constituents and the local organisation in the lurch. But Hillery's plans for withdrawing from politics were tentative and might not have come to fruition in any event. The election of Seán Lemass as de Valera's successor ensured that they never would. Hillery was still uncertain about the future place of politics in his life and was not at all sure that he belonged in the political arena.[37] Lemass's accession would dispel those reservations and resolve the ambiguity at the heart of Hillery's working life for the most of the previous decade.

5.

Marriage and Family

Hillery's life changed dramatically in the summer of 1955. He set out to secure a postgraduate qualification in paediatrics. He hoped to obtain a dispensary post in Clare and required a hospital residency in paediatrics to ensure that he was qualified for a dispensary. He contacted his friend and former mentor, John Corcoran, who arranged for Hillery to spend two months in the Children's Hospital in Harcourt Street before sitting the examination for the Diploma in Child Health.[1] He undertook the hospital work during the summer holidays while the Dáil was in recess. Hillery's drive to succeed in his profession was the central motivation of his life at the time; politics was still firmly behind medicine in his order of priorities. But he never completed the diploma, not least because he got married in the autumn of 1955.

Mary Beatrice Finnegan was the daughter of Irish emigrants in England. Her father, John Finnegan, who was from Dunmore in east Galway, went to England at the age of 16 to find work. He became the manager of a building firm in Sheffield and later set up his own company. He was a successful building contractor, who provided employment for many of the Irish emigrants in the city. John Finnegan married Winifred Donnellan, the daughter of a prominent Irish employer in Sheffield who had established his fortunes in the local construction industry. Their daughter Mary Beatrice – known universally as Maeve – was born in Sheffield on 3 September 1924. Winifred died when Maeve was only four years old, and her father later remarried. John Finnegan retained strong connections with his native county and Maeve returned to her father's family in Dunmore for the summer holidays each year. She was in Galway when the Second World War broke out; Britain declared war on Germany on 3 September 1939, which happened to be her fifteenth birthday.[2] As Sheffield was a major centre of manufacturing industry, it was an obvious target for German bombing raids. John Finnegan decided that his daughter should not return to wartime England and so Maeve remained with her grandmother in Ireland for most of the war, making intermittent visits to Sheffield to see her father. She completed her final year of secondary education at Taylor's Hill school in Galway, where she sat the matriculation examination in 1940.

Maeve, like her future husband, went to college at 16, entering the Pre-Med course at University College, Galway in October 1940; she was also too young to be registered as a medical student and had to wait an additional year to enrol for medicine. Despite this initial obstacle, she treasured the closeness and carefree atmosphere of college life in Galway in the early 1940s: 'Some of the happiest days of my life were spent there. It was a small university, there were only about 700 students at that time, so everybody knew everybody else.'[3] But Galway lacked sufficient hospital capacity in the early 1940s to provide adequate facilities for clinical training and medical students in UCG were obliged to spend several months in Dublin hospitals to complete their studies. Maeve transferred to UCD for the final three years of the medical course. She was in the same final year class as Paddy Hillery, although they did not meet until several years later.

Following her graduation from UCD in 1947, Maeve was appointed as a house doctor in Jervis Street Hospital; in the following year she became the resident anaesthetist in Jervis Street, at a time when she was the only female doctor resident in the hospital. Maeve held the same position in St James' Hospital for two years, where she was one of only two specialists in anaesthetics; the area was headed by a consultant who was, however, an intermittent presence in the wards and Maeve served as the sole anaesthetist on a day-to-day basis. This was a highly demanding and responsible post for a young doctor, which was made all the more challenging by the shortage of advanced medical equipment.[4] Maeve returned to her father's home in England in the early 1950s, securing a job at the Royal Hospital in Sheffield that entailed a considerable volume of maternity work. The role was equally arduous and the conditions for the junior medical staff were considerably worse than in Dublin:

> We used to think it was bad in Dublin. I had to arrange my duties so that I wouldn't be on duty the same night as one of the male anaesthetists, because we shared a room on a return of a fire escape. That was the accommodation we had at night… But of course it was postwar and people had had terrible hardships and you were just glad to be leading a normal type of life again, so people didn't really demand too much.[5]

Maeve also worked in Bolton Royal Infirmary following her time in Sheffield. As a young doctor she accumulated an impressive range of experience in the medical establishments of Ireland and England. Yet when she returned to Dublin in 1955 it proved impossible to get a job in an Irish hospital; this was due at least in part to a marked tendency among senior doctors to give preference to male candidates. Maeve was in many respects a pioneer as a female anaesthetist in Ireland, working in a male-dominated environment in Jervis Street and effectively running the anaesthetics section in St James' Hospital. But following her service in the British National Health Service, she found no job opportunities in Dublin despite her considerable experience and accomplishments. She decided to emigrate to Canada and applied successfully for a post as an anaesthetist in a hospital at Montreal. Maeve was on the verge of leaving Ireland, perhaps for good, in the summer of 1955.

Maeve met Paddy Hillery entirely by chance. He recalled it as a series of happy coincidences:

> I needed to do two months to be allowed to sit an exam, to work with children. Then one of the girls working in Harcourt Street went off to do Lough Derg or something like that and asked Maeve to do duty for her. It was only for two days.[6]

Paddy and Maeve started to go out together almost immediately. She abandoned her plans to work in Canada. They were engaged within months of their first meeting.[7] They intended to get married in the cathedral in Ennis, but their plans were upset by the death of the longest serving member of the Irish hierarchy. Dr Michael Fogarty, the bishop of Killaloe, died on the eve of their wedding in October 1955; the deceased prelate lay in state for three days in the cathedral prior to his funeral.[8] So Paddy and Maeve were married instead in the chapel of St Flannan's College, Ennis on 27 October 1955.[9] Monsignor Michael Mooney, who was a cousin of Maeve, officiated at the ceremony. Mooney, who became principal of St Jarlath's College in Tuam, acted as a quiet adviser to his brother-in-law during Hillery's term as Minister for Education.

The new couple were united by their intelligence, force of character and a shared passion for medicine. Perhaps most of all, both were deeply concerned for the welfare of their children and were determined that politics would not distort their upbringing. Their first child, John, was born on 18 June 1957. John was barely two years old when his father became Minister for Education in June 1959. This meant that Hillery could no longer commute from Spanish Point to Dublin on a daily basis. He and Maeve moved to Dublin permanently, first living in Clontarf for a short time; they later bought a house in Shankill where they lived for ten years.[10] Then in 1969 the Hillery family moved to a more spacious house in Sutton. The new house looked out on Dublin Bay, an important consideration for Paddy, who was always happiest living by the sea.

Paddy Hillery retained strong links with his native town, not least through his remaining family and friends in Miltown Malbay. He also kept the family home in Spanish Point. His strong connections with his relatives were reinforced by a family tragedy shortly after his appointment as a minister. Des Hillery died suddenly in August 1959, following treatment for a brain tumour; he was just 38 years old. Des' tragically premature death was a devastating shock to his younger brother. It was even more traumatic for his widow, Bridget, and their young family. Des and Bridget had six children: the eldest, Michael, was 11 while the youngest, also named Des, was born six months after his father's death. Paddy was deeply involved in the upbringing of his brother's family, staying in regular contact with Bridget and providing a reassuring presence for their children. Michael remembered being brought with his younger siblings in the state car to see Santa Claus: 'He kept up the little things that my father was doing, which was very important to us at the time.'[11] Michael retained a vivid memory of Paddy's concern to help his brother's children. When Michael attended St Flannan's College between 1962 and 1967, Paddy called into the school to see his nephew on a regular basis. His first visit caused much excitement among the students and gave Michael's standing among his peers an invaluable boost:

> When I went to Flannan's in my first year, he called in after about a month of my being there and he was Minister for Education at the time, so we all got a half-day from his visit. The other students used to ask when he was calling again, hoping we would get a half-day every time he called.[12]

Michael's enhanced stature among his classmates proved temporary, however, as the half-day was a once-off affair. The school authorities could hardly have done anything else, considering the frequency of Hillery's visits to St Flannan's during his nephew's time there. Michael later secured a degree in agricultural science in UCD, staying with his uncle's family in Dublin for four years while he was completing the course.

Both Paddy and Maeve sought to ensure that their children were not adversely affected by the demands on his time or caught in the harsh spotlight of publicity. John was accustomed from the outset to the benefits and drawbacks of being the child of a government minister. He was used to his father constantly being in the public eye:

> What people took as extraordinary I took as ordinary, because that's how I grew up. Among my earliest memories about public life, the first one would be of him opening the Rhinoceros House in the Zoo. I was about six or seven at the time. He opened it and stood aside to let the president of the Zoo in and I ran in first. Apparently I was on the news that evening.[13]

Paddy was often away at weekends, attending to constituency business in Clare; sometimes Maeve or John would go with him, although his weekends were usually dominated by local politics. But he made sure that he saw John regularly during the week, regardless of what else was going on at the time. John attended Willow Park primary school and Blackrock College, a selection reflecting Paddy's high opinion of the Holy Ghost Order that managed both schools. John vividly remembered his father's concern to balance his political commitments with family life:

> Anywhere I went with my father, the memory I have is of people considering him their property. But he always made efforts that we would meet, once a week at least for lunch, if not twice. Those were the days of the long school lunch break and I would come in and meet him in town for lunch and then go back to school.[14]

This pattern began when Paddy was Minister for Education and continued until he left for Brussels as a European Commissioner in 1973.

Paddy took up painting shortly after his elevation to the Cabinet; it remained a frequent pastime and an essential source of relaxation throughout his political career. John shared his father's interest in painting and they went together to a painting school at Keel on Achill island in the late 1960s. The school was always held in August and unhappily coincided with the final peak of the loyalist marching season in Northern Ireland, notably the parade of the Apprentice Boys in Derry. This meant that Paddy's time in Keel was usually cut short; it was from Achill that he was called back in August 1969 to an emergency meeting of the government, when the crisis in the North erupted. Nevertheless he insulated his children to a large extent from the pressures that affected him on a daily basis. John realised later the extent to which he was sheltered from the more difficult aspects of his father's public career:

> I remember being in the house in Dublin and my father being very anxious, listening to the radio, and I know now it was a general election and I don't know why he was back in Dublin rather than in Clare, he had to come back for something, but he was listening to the results come in and I had no idea of its import, that he could be out of a job.[15]

John, however, soon developed a keen interest in politics. He went canvassing with his father in June 1969 during Paddy's final election in Clare. His father later made a characteristic wry comment that 'John is much more interested in politics than I would ever be.'[16]

Paddy and Maeve adopted their second child, Vivienne, who was born on 11 April 1969; she was adopted almost immediately after her birth. John, who had been an only child until he was twelve, was delighted to have a baby sister: 'That was great, to have a sibling at last.'[17] Vivienne's adoption coincided with the most demanding and difficult phase of her father's career. As Foreign Minister he was out of the country a great deal, while the outbreak of the Troubles in Northern Ireland inevitably had implications for his family. Their move to Sutton happened within a couple of days of Paddy Hillery's address to the UN Security Council in August 1969.[18] He was preoccupied with the crisis in Northern Ireland and could not give much attention to the mundane business of moving house. Maeve managed the process, viewing the new house and

arranging the sale of their home in Shankill. Paddy's enforced
detachment from the process had some entertaining results. It transpired
that they were due to move out on the day that he returned from New
York, as Maeve later recalled:

> He had been to the UN. He came back about three
> o'clock in the morning and went to bed and CIÉ were
> coming the next morning to move us out of the house.
> The house was empty at that stage apart from the bed and
> a few other things. I still remember some of the men…they
> were creeping around the house and whispering to one
> another, because they knew what he had been doing. One
> of them came up to me and he whispered 'Do you think
> we'll be able to take the bed soon, Ma'am?' So I said, well,
> I suppose you'll have to.[19]

The move to Sutton went ahead despite this minor hitch. Paddy and his
family lived in Sutton only on an intermittent basis over the next two
decades, as his career took him first to Brussels and then back to Áras an
Uachtaráin as President. But he greatly valued his home in Sutton,
retaining the house for the rest of his life and returning to live there once
more following his retirement.

Hillery was considered a target for both republican and loyalist
paramilitary groups: as a result security around his family was increased
and the Special Branch established a permanent presence at his home.
This was not all bad, at least as far as John was concerned:

> There was a Special Branch man and a uniformed guard in
> a security hut on the lawn of our house in Sutton. The
> advantage of that was that my cousin Michael…and I
> always had two people to play football with; so we used to
> have games of two–a–side football in the garden.[20]

Yet there was a darker side associated with the security presence. There were genuine fears that Hillery's family might be in danger and the increased security measures remained an integral feature of their lives throughout the early 1970s. The family's private visits to Maeve's relatives in Sheffield often brought a security operation by British police, who feared an attack against the Irish Foreign Minister on their territory.

Paddy Hillery's appointment to the European Commission in 1973 affected his family in a different way. It meant that some degree of separation became inevitable, as John was still completing secondary education at Blackrock; he continued to live in Sutton, while the rest of the family relocated to Brussels. Maeve found a house on the Avenue Parmentier, close to the city centre, where they settled for the following four years.[21] Paddy sought to minimise the impact of the separation by returning home from Brussels on Thursday evenings for most of his time as a Commissioner. He used to schedule meetings in Dublin on Fridays and spend much of the weekend with his son. This practice continued when John began to study medicine at the Royal College of Surgeons in 1975.

It was Hillery's elevation to the presidency in 1976 that brought the family back under the same roof, the old Viceregal lodge in the Phoenix Park, which had become Áras an Uachtaráin. John lived at the Áras until 1982, while he was completing his medical studies. Vivienne was enrolled in primary school at Mount Sackville in west Dublin, within easy commuting distance of the Áras. Neither Paddy nor Maeve regarded the sprawling house in the middle of the Phoenix Park as an ideal place to raise a family. There was initially no private residence for the family within the house and the limitations of the Áras were exacerbated by the lack of adequate funding for the establishment. Maeve set out to preserve her children's privacy in an environment where maintaining a normal lifestyle was extremely difficult. She was equally concerned to ensure that they would not acquire any sense of entitlement from living in a state house with domestic staff. John recalled that 'When he became President she took steps to ensure that firstly we weren't in the public eye but secondly that we didn't feel that we were little princes and princesses... She made sure there was a private house and we weren't being served on.'[22] Maeve ensured that a separate kitchen was installed for the family and turned the west wing of the Áras into a private family space.

John followed his father into medicine, specialising in psychiatry. He worked especially in the area of disability, treating children with mental disabilities. John moved out of the President's house following his wedding. He married Carolyn Curtin in London on 22 January 1983.[23] Paddy decided not to go to London for the wedding, although he wanted to attend the service. He believed that it would be impossible to maintain a private ceremony if he went to London. The presence of the Irish head of state in the British capital at the height of the Troubles and following tension between the two governments over the Falklands War would certainly have triggered significant interest by the British media and probably a major security operation as well.

Hillery's second term as President was marked by profound personal tragedy. Vivienne was diagnosed with non–Hodgkin's lymphoma in 1985. Hillery had just returned from the National Ploughing Championships when his daughter complained that she was feeling unwell:

> Vivienne said there was something wrong. So I got a doctor in and he asked Eoin O'Malley to look at it. I remember it well, I brought her to the Mater in the morning. Then I was opening some function…I was so worried about Vivienne in the hospital. He was doing a biopsy.[24]

Eoin O'Malley, who was Professor of Surgery at UCD, was an old friend of Paddy Hillery. It soon became apparent that Vivienne was seriously ill. The prognosis for patients with non–Hodgkin's lymphoma was poor in the 1980s. Yet Vivienne received excellent specialist care in the Mater Hospital and her condition was responding to treatment. She maintained a resolutely positive approach, bearing the illness with considerable fortitude. Her brother recalled that 'she did the treatment, then went home and got on with her life.'[25] It appeared at one stage that she was on the verge of a full recovery. Then Paddy received news from the hospital that the treatment had failed: 'It was a prolonged illness, and then when they thought they had cured it, I got a phone call.'[26] John remembered that 'she was doing well and then suddenly it all went wrong.'[27] The treatment, which was not nearly as sophisticated as it later became, was unable to overcome the disease. Vivienne died at the Mater Private nursing home on 26 March 1987, aged only 17.

Vivienne's death was a devastating blow to her parents. Paddy and Maeve dealt with their loss privately and with considerable dignity. No formal announcement was made from Áras an Uachtaráin and the funeral service was a private ceremony, which was attended only by Vivienne's family and close friends.[28] Vivienne's illness and death was the most difficult and traumatic period of Paddy Hillery's life. Any disappointments or setbacks in his public life paled into insignificance beside the tragedy of losing his daughter. Peig O'Malley, his private secretary, saw his shock and grief at first-hand; she worried that he might not recover from it.[29] But his private secretary was amazed at his resilience. Hillery continued his public engagements with only a short interruption and went ahead with his visit to the institutions of the European Community later in the same year. He was badly shaken by Vivienne's death, but his private grief was largely hidden from public view. Yet his family were well aware of his grief. John and Carolyn moved into Áras an Uachtaráin when Vivienne became ill; they remained after her death to support her parents.[30]

Retirement in 1990 was a liberation for Paddy Hillery in many respects. He greatly valued the opportunity to spend more time with his family. Almost immediately after his retirement, the whole family went on holiday to Florida; he and Maeve accompanied John, Carolyn and their children to Disneyland. Then when the rest of his family returned to Ireland, Paddy and Maeve took a house in Singer Island, on the Atlantic coast north of Miami, for an extended holiday. Their stay in Florida became an annual feature of his retirement. He and Maeve went to Florida for about three months every year from 1991 until 2007, usually from January to April. Paddy had always devoted as much time as he could to his family when John and Vivienne were children; now he greatly enjoyed the opportunity to spend more time with his grandchildren. Paddy Hillery was a devoted husband and father. He and Maeve did a great deal to ensure that their children enjoyed a happy if unusual upbringing, in circumstances where a conventional private life was almost impossible.

6.

Reluctant Minister

For most politicians, appointment to a Cabinet post is a celebrated landmark, marking the achievement of a coveted office and frequently the culmination of years of work and planning. It was a milestone too for Hillery – a profoundly unwelcome one. His appointment as Minister for Education in June 1959 came at a time when he was reconsidering his future in politics. He had, however, reckoned without Seán Lemass. Hillery would never have been a minister but for Lemass's intervention. It is entirely possible that the Clare man would have retired from politics completely before he had served a full decade in the Dáil.

Lemass's election as Taoiseach on 23 June 1959 opened a new era, which would bring about far-reaching changes in Irish society and Ireland's place within Europe. The advent of Lemass was regarded as a watershed in Irish public life at the time, not least because he succeeded the dominant figure in Irish politics for over a generation, Éamon de Valera. If anything, Lemass's election appears even more significant in retrospect. The new Taoiseach's time in power was relatively short, compared to his legendary predecessor – a total of seven-and-a-half years.

But Lemass's term of office initiated a lasting transformation of independent Ireland, marked especially by the gradual transition from a protectionist regime to free trade; the development of coherent economic planning; the far-reaching expansion of the educational sector; and the beginnings of liberalisation in social values and legislation. Lemass's accession also had momentous consequences for Hillery.

The new Taoiseach initially made only modest changes to the government which he inherited from de Valera, appointing only two new ministers – one was the Meath TD Michael Hilliard as Minister for Posts and Telegraphs; the other was Hillery himself, who received his first government post as Minister for Education.[1] Hillery had anticipated Lemass's unopposed succession but not his own elevation to the Cabinet. Lemass was determined to appoint Hillery and was not deterred by the younger man's reluctance. Political geography influenced Hillery's appointment, as he shared a constituency with the former Taoiseach and Clare had never lacked representation within a Fianna Fáil government.[2] Yet Lemass's resolve to bring Hillery into the Cabinet also reflected a wider concern to promote capable younger members of the party and to initiate a gradual modernisation of the government. Over 45 years later, Hillery retained a vivid memory of the no-nonsense way in which he was appointed.

> I went into the Dáil and Lemass was duly elected by the party. I was going out and Mick Hilliard said 'I want you, come with me'. So I went with him and was wondering what he was at. The next thing he landed me in an office in front of Seán Lemass and Lemass said 'I want you in the Cabinet. I am not letting you off as Dev did'. I said 'I can't do a thing like that, I have people booked in for babies!' He said 'you can finish all the work you are doing but I want you in the Cabinet.' He wasn't taking no for an answer.[3]

Hillery's choice between politics and medicine was resolved, though not in the way he had originally anticipated: 'It was a conclusion. It wasn't the one I wanted, but I had to get rid of half my work. I would have got rid of the politics.'[4] Lemass's forceful style certainly played its part in getting Hillery to accept ministerial office for the first time. But that was not the whole story – even Lemass's powers of persuasion might have failed if Hillery did not already hold a high opinion of the new Taoiseach. Hillery not only respected Lemass's impressive record as a minister, but was attracted by his political approach. The younger man recognised that Lemass aimed to sideline the traditional Civil War divisions which had defined the previous generation and to place economic development at the heart of his agenda: 'It was exciting with Lemass. He was through all the politics of Fianna Fáil, his brother was murdered, but he was stepping away from the bitterness, you know; he never went in for shouting or downing the other people [the opposition]. He had a kind of politics that I could go along with'.[5] Hillery's respect for Lemass's forward-looking and innovative political approach was the most important factor in overcoming the younger man's genuine reluctance to pursue a career in politics.

Hillery's appointment as Minister for Education was a decisive turning point in his life. He could no longer combine politics with medical practice. His new position did not prevent him from fulfilling the commitments he had already made to patients: indeed he delivered the baby of a national schoolteacher in west Clare soon after his appointment – undoubtedly a first for any Minister for Education.[6] But his elevation to the Cabinet marked the end of his promising career as a country GP. The family's medical practice in Clare passed instead to his sister Eleanor. Hillery was still in Clare most weekends for constituency work and he maintained close contact with his family in Miltown Malbay, but he would not live in the county again on a permanent basis. He regretted leaving medicine behind and it took some time for him to acclimatise to the dramatic change in his personal circumstances:

> Now there was no contact with the patients. No way to
> practice all the skills and knowledge I had worked to learn
> either. I think in retrospect that I missed the human contact

and that was the worst loss. Once when my P. S. [Private
Secretary] Jimmy Dukes said, 'I think you need to see a
doctor', I replied 'I need to see a patient!'[7]

Hillery also had to adapt to the political requirements of the position,
especially in responding to the critical interrogation of opposition
deputies at Ministerial Questions in the Dáil. Few ministers claim to enjoy
parliamentary questions, but Hillery also disliked much of the partisan
bickering in the Dáil. He felt keenly the contrast between his parliamentary duties and the medical career that he had given up; 'all the theatre
of the Dáil was irritating in view of what I was leaving behind'.[8] So
despite his acceptance of the position, Hillery's reaction to his
appointment was a long way removed from the response of a more
conventional politician. He was aware, however, that in some ways his
elevation to the Cabinet was obviously beneficial, not least because it
simplified his work commitments. His initial workload as Minister for
Education was considerably less than his double burden as a rural TD and
country doctor for the previous eight years. This testified to the enormous
workload that he had taken on previously, but it was also a sign of the
times: the role of the minister in managing and directing educational
policy was still in its infancy.

    Hillery was a new minister who lacked any experience of the
educational system beyond his own participation in it. He was concerned
to gain a full understanding of the major issues facing his department and
to develop his own ideas for resolving long-standing educational
problems. He had a very capable private secretary in James Dukes, who
was succeeded in 1960 by the equally diligent Tom Leahy. The secretary
of the department, Dr Tarlach Ó Raifeartaigh, was an intellectual and
classical scholar whom Hillery came to like and respect.[9] The new
minister relied particularly on the senior assistant secretary, Seán
MacGearailt, who emerged as a key figure in driving forward reforming
policies in the 1960s. Hillery was not, however, an amiable front man for
influential officials, as some ministers undoubtedly were; he set out to
learn his brief and to put his own stamp on educational policy.[10]

When Hillery became Minister for Education in June 1959, his new department was a political backwater. James Dukes believed that the senior officials regarded Education as a junior department, understaffed, under-resourced and unable to take on any additional responsibilities: 'they were up to their ears with work and it was very tight where money was concerned.'[11] The financial constraints imposed by the Department of Finance, which had secured cuts in education spending in the 1950s, reinforced the prevailing official reluctance to take a proactive approach. Dukes recalled: 'We were completely under the thumb of Finance'.[12] The Cinderella status of the Department of Education was well established. The department faced continual criticism from educational interest groups either frustrated with the slow pace of change or outraged that change was happening at all. Hillery managed small-scale crises on a routine basis, facing almost daily demands from officials for his intervention to deal with dissatisfied school managers or religious superiors unhappy at the department's approach:

> You were always hit, every day you got up you were going to be hit by someone. A former secretary once said that 'the only relief was a change of assailant' as one was beaten about the head daily on matters educational.'[13]

Moreover, successive ministers had pursued a limited and minimalist approach in education, accepting the predominant role of private interests, notably the churches. The Catholic and Protestant churches played a crucial part in providing both primary and secondary education. The Catholic Church was the most powerful stakeholder in the Irish educational system: the vast majority of schools were owned and managed by Catholic religious authorities. Education was a sensitive area in Church–State relations, which was perceived to require cautious and careful management by politicians who wished to avoid a belt of the crozier. Hillery's senior colleague Jim Ryan, the Minister for Finance, accurately expressed the traditional view of the Department of Education:

> Jim Ryan said to me, 'What job have you?' I said,
> 'Education,' and he said, 'You can take care of the bishops
> for us.' The Church ruled, the nuns and priests, and the
> officials were full of stories about what this priest said and
> that priest said. The civil servants saw that the Church was
> in charge.[14]

Leading politicians, officials and clergy shared a conservative consensus that the state's role in education should be strictly limited to aiding established private interests. Hillery's term would mark a decisive break with this comfortable consensus. The Department of Education badly needed effective leadership from its political head and had generally not received it for most of the previous generation. Hillery believed that the department in the late 1950s was 'essentially inert. I was trying to get the department moving.'[15] While Hillery was initially a reluctant minister, he soon came to realise the scale of the challenges that he faced in education and also saw opportunities for far-reaching changes, which had not even been contemplated in the previous generation.

Embracing gradualism

The state's policy towards education was ill-defined to the point of incoherence when Hillery took office in 1959. While his predecessor Jack Lynch had initiated some incremental reforms in primary education, the government essentially had no policy for the expansion of second-level education and there was no official commitment to support the future development of the educational sector as a whole. Hillery began to chart a new course for government policy on education in October 1959. Noel Browne and Jack McQuillan, the left-wing Independents who had recently formed the small National Progressive Democrat party (NPD), put down a motion in the Dáil calling for the extension of the statutory school-leaving age to at least 15 years. Hillery respected the two radical mavericks, privately describing them as 'the only real opposition', and had no illusions about their ability to embarrass unwary government ministers.[16] On this occasion Browne and McQuillan's manoeuvre provided the opportunity for a low-key but significant advance in the government's position. The new minister defended the educational system against criticisms by Browne, but also indicated that it was his 'earnest wish' to enable all children to continue in post-primary education at least up to the age of 15, arguing that the most effective way to achieve this objective was to provide the necessary facilities.[17] Hillery also promised to extend the scholarship scheme to create wider opportunities of second-level and university education for talented pupils. He had given the first definite indication of a new government policy for the gradual expansion of the educational sector.

The new policy was given the full support of the government through a statement made by the Taoiseach. Lemass intervened personally on 28 October 1959 in the debate on the motion by Browne and McQuillan.[18] Lemass made a commitment that 'The aim of government policy is to bring about a situation in which all children will continue their schooling until they are at least 15 years of age.'[19] Lemass pledged to achieve this objective as soon as possible, without immediately extending the age of compulsory attendance on a statutory basis.[20] The Taoiseach assured the Dáil that the government fully agreed with the aim of the motion, but disagreed with the method proposed by the Opposition TDs, namely the immediate raising of the legal school-leaving age.[21] Lemass and Hillery instead outlined a policy based on a measured expansion of post-primary facilities and scholarships. It was not at all the radical approach sought by Browne, which involved the introduction of free and compulsory education up to the age of 15; but Lemass's policy statement established a definite gradualist approach towards the expansion of post-primary education.[22] The Taoiseach's intervention in the debate, only four months after his election, underlined the increasing priority that would be accorded to education under his leadership. Hillery appreciated Lemass's commitment to educational reform and welcomed the Taoiseach's occasional public interventions to highlight the importance of education.[23] Lemass and Hillery established in October 1959 a cautious but definite policy approach by the state, which was designed to achieve a gradual expansion of the educational system, while avoiding any short-term commitment to the extension of the statutory school-leaving age.

This gradualist approach to educational expansion provided for useful practical improvements in the primary school system. Hillery authorised a range of reforming measures to deal with the most obvious flaws in the system. He maintained and extended the incremental reforming approach in the primary sector, which had been initiated by Jack Lynch. The programme for the building of primary schools was accelerated due to substantially increased state investment by 1961–2. The allocation for the primary school building programme almost doubled in this period.[24] Hillery introduced new state grants for primary schools, including a new scheme providing funding for the painting and decoration of national schools.[25] The scheme made grants available from April 1962 towards the cost of painting national schools externally every four years and for internal decoration every eight years.[26] While the maintenance of the schools remained a local responsibility, the department usually provided a grant of two-thirds of the expenditure incurred on painting the building. This hardly seems like a radical advance by more recent standards, but it represented a genuine improvement from the tight-fisted and minimalist approach of the 1950s. Hillery and Ó Raifeartaigh believed that regular painting of the buildings would reduce the number of national schools that required replacement: the secretary urged school managers to co-operate with the scheme to avoid the 'premature reconstruction' of national schools.[27] The scheme was a modest improvement based partly on pragmatic official calculations designed to save money in the long term; but it was also the first state programme that directly funded the upkeep of national schools.

Hillery also acted to reduce the pupil–teacher ratio and to improve staffing levels in national schools, particularly by creating new posts for lay national teachers.[28] He sought to increase the supply of trained teachers to the national schools, authorising a major programme of rebuilding and reconstruction for St Patrick's Training College, Drumcondra, to deliver more places for teacher training.[29] The department secured a bank loan of £750,000 for the college to finance the building work and provided the remainder of the necessary funding in direct grants.[30] Hillery promoted piecemeal reforms in the course of his first term, which were designed to alleviate obvious shortcomings in the educational system, especially its limited physical capacity, the appalling condition of many national schools and the inadequate numbers of teachers.

Few shortcomings in the Irish educational system were more evident than the inadequacy of the local authorities' scholarships scheme. While the Department of Education provided scholarship schemes for pupils from the Gaeltacht and third-level students who were willing to pursue their university courses through Irish, the local authorities provided the only general scheme of scholarships. Local authorities throughout the state awarded only 619 scholarships for post-primary schools in 1960.[31] The level of support for university scholarships was even worse: local authorities awarded only 155 university scholarships nationally in 1961.[32] The overall funding for the scheme on a national basis was extremely limited, not least because there was no contribution at all from the Exchequer; the scheme was funded entirely from the local rates.

Hillery regarded the existing scheme as farcical due to its limited scope and the failure of many councils to provide adequate support for maintenance as well as fees. He lobbied Lemass successfully for state investment to provide an adequate scholarships scheme: 'I started off by persuading Lemass that we had to get better scholarships. The scholarships at that time were only useful to people with money. It was no good to the people that needed it, they had to pay the full fee of staying in digs and so on.'[33] Hillery secured the support of the government for a greatly expanded scholarships scheme, which would be funded in part by the Exchequer. He outlined the terms of the Local Authorities Scholarships (Amendment) Bill to the Dáil on 25 July, describing the lack of adequate support for scholarships as 'a serious defect' in the educational system.[34] The new measure was intended not to provide direct state scholarships on a general basis but to increase and supplement the funding provided by the local authorities. The Bill provided additional funding of approximately £300,000 from the national government for the local authority scholarships over four years. The new legislation was also designed to encourage local councils to increase their contribution to the scholarships scheme by raising additional funding on the rates.[35] The Exchequer contribution was designed to increase steadily in proportion to the funding raised by the local authority to achieve a ratio of five to four between state and local contributions after four years. It was envisaged that four years after the establishment of the new scheme the total allocation for scholarships would be roughly quadrupled, rising from £150,000 provided by the local authorities alone in 1960–61 to £540,000 under the new scheme by 1965–6.[36] The scholarships would be allocated on the basis of a competitive examination at national level set by the department: up to one quarter of the scholarships would be awarded on merit alone without any means test.

The most significant innovation of the Scholarships Bill was the introduction of direct payments by the national government towards the cost of local authority scholarships. While the department already provided limited scholarship programmes, mainly for the promotion of the Irish language, the legislation signalled a new approach by the state, which provided funding for a general scheme of scholarships for the first time. The legislation also enabled the minister to sanction the terms of the local authority schemes, giving the department significant influence over the terms and value of the scholarships.[37] The Bill established a new framework for the award of scholarships by the local authorities and transformed the financial provision for post-primary and university scholarships.

The obvious advantages of the legislation guaranteed it an easy passage through the Dáil, despite some criticism of its terms by opposition TDs. Noel Browne attacked the Bill as a pre-election manoeuvre by the government.[38] The Bill was, however, approved without a division at any stage on 2 August 1961, within a month of its introduction.[39] As the Dáil was dissolved on 1 September for a general election, Browne's suspicions about the timing of the Bill were well founded, but the importance of the new legislation transcended pre-election politics. The legislation marked the first real attempt by the state to widen educational opportunity, especially in second-level education. The new Scholarships Act contributed immediately to a major increase in the number of scholarship candidates. In 1962, 5,622 candidates took the post-primary scholarship examinations, compared to only 3,122 in 1961. The Department of Education was providing £60,000 annually towards the cost of local authority scholarships by 1963–4.[40] The number of scholarships for post-primary schools more than doubled between 1961 and 1962, rising from 831 to 1,927. The university scholarships saw a more modest increase from 155 to 254 over the same period.[41] The direct support for scholarships from the national government promoted a rapid expansion in the scholarship scheme, especially at post-primary level.

The new legislation was shaped by the idea of greater educational opportunity for the talented child. Hillery argued on 25 July that the individual talent of the Irish people was an invaluable resource and that the aim of the Bill was 'to bring forward for the benefit of the nation as a whole, the country's best talent, wherever it is to be found.'[42] He summarised his objective in the Dáil on 1 August: 'The principle is that if there are brains in the country, we should get them through the full course of education as far as we can afford to do so and that they should earn their way on merit.'[43] Hillery emphasised the necessity to enable talented children from all social classes to progress up the educational ladder, presenting the extension of scholarships as a social and educational necessity. The initiative was essentially a pragmatic attempt to help talented children. Hillery understandably took pride in the scholarships legislation; but he would soon move well beyond the incremental approach embodied in the Act to more radical measures designed to achieve equality of educational opportunity.

Diluting the language revival

The new minister also made his influence felt on the department's policy towards the Irish language. The first major reform introduced during Hillery's term was the oral test in Irish at Leaving Certificate level. The oral test had been initiated by Lynch and was implemented for the first time as part of the Leaving Certificate examination in 1960.[44] While this initiative was inherited from Lynch, Hillery did not hesitate to introduce far-reaching policy changes in the department's traditional approach to the revival of the Irish language. He approved Circular 11/60 on the teaching of Irish, which was issued to the primary school authorities in January 1960.[45] The circular announced that inspectors would in future give greater importance to oral than to written Irish in assessing the work of teachers. In addition, teachers of junior classes, where the department had required teaching through the medium of Irish since the 1920s, were allowed to change 'the emphasis from teaching through Irish to the teaching of Irish Conversation', if they considered that greater progress would be made in oral Irish.[46] While the circular appeared only to give greater freedom to teachers to determine their teaching methods on the basis that the standard of oral Irish would improve, the department had effectively abandoned the traditional policy of teaching through Irish in national schools.[47] Circular 11/60 marked a subtle but vital policy shift by the Minister for Education; it formed part of a more general reassessment of the Irish language policy by the department under Hillery.

The official reappraisal was reflected in the reform of national teacher-training announced by Hillery in 1960. The system of training for national schoolteachers was built to a large extent around the Preparatory Colleges during the first generation of the independent Irish state. The Colleges were state secondary schools that provided education through Irish for candidates who gave a commitment to enter the teaching profession.[48] There were five Preparatory Collages, five Catholic and one Protestant (Coláiste Moibhí in Shankill, Co. Dublin). The students from the Preparatory Colleges received access to the training colleges for national schoolteachers on a preferential basis, as 25 per cent of all places were reserved for them, and they entered the training colleges without further competition on fulfilling the minimum Leaving Certificate requirements for entry. The system was intended to promote the revival of the Irish language in the national schools at a time when the state faced difficulties in obtaining candidates for the teaching profession with the required knowledge of Irish.[49] The senior officials of the department itself increasingly regarded the system as a liability: it was costly to run six secondary schools, and the academic contribution of the colleges was difficult to defend, as the standard of the Preparatory College students at the Leaving Certificate was lower than the standard reached by successful candidates in the open competition for the training colleges.[50] Hillery put a proposal to the Cabinet on 9 November 1959 for the closure of the five Preparatory Colleges serving Catholic pupils and the establishment of an extended scholarship scheme for Gaeltacht students.[51] The Cabinet approved Hillery's initiative by 15 December 1959.[52] He announced on 24 May 1960 the abolition of the Preparatory College system as a means of recruitment for Catholic teachers.[53] Although Coláiste Móibhí continued to operate, the other five colleges were closed in July 1961.[54]

The department announced a revised scheme of scholarships for Gaeltacht pupils to replace the Preparatory Colleges in accordance with Hillery's proposal.[55] The extended scholarships' scheme provided for an increase in the number of secondary school scholarships awarded annually to Gaeltacht pupils by the department from eighteen to eighty. Similarly, the number of university scholarships for Gaeltacht students increased from five to fifteen.[56] As an average of fifty Gaeltacht students had secured places in the Preparatory Colleges between 1957 and 1959, the extended scheme of scholarships marked a moderate improvement in the educational opportunities offered by the state to native speakers of Irish.[57] The introduction of a wider scholarships' scheme as an alternative to the Preparatory Colleges reflected Hillery's emphasis on the extension of scholarships as an essential element in expanding educational opportunity.

The initiative also marked a significant revision of the government's policy for the revival of the Irish language. Hillery's announcement had removed an important element of the Irish language policy in the national schools. The traditional language revival methods employed in the schools required a regular supply of teachers using Irish as their vernacular: the abolition of the Preparatory Colleges terminated the sole official process for supplying such teachers.[58] It was a policy change of considerable importance, achieved with almost no opposition or even public attention.

Seán O'Connor, a leading official of the department who disagreed with
the abolition of the Preparatory Colleges, believed that 'by the issuing of
the January Circular on the teaching of Irish and the closing of the
Preparatory Colleges, Dr Hillery ensured the disestablishment of the Irish
language.'[59] O'Connor's sweeping assertion exaggerated the impact of the
changes. The requirements for Irish to be taken as a compulsory subject
for the award of the Intermediate and Leaving Certificate examinations
remained in place. O'Connor himself also acknowledged that there was
no deliberate attempt by the minister to dismantle the Irish language
revival in the schools.[60] But the minister and senior officials of the
department believed with considerable justice that the teaching methods
employed to achieve the revival of Irish in the schools had proved
ineffective. The reappraisal also reflected a more significant change for the
Department of Education; Hillery himself remarked that 'it was important
that the revival of the Irish language was not the purpose of the
Department of Education primarily'.[61] James Dukes commented simply
that 'He tried to bring a bit of sense into it.'[62] While the established policy
objective of language revival was maintained, Hillery heavily diluted the
traditional policy of reviving Irish through the schools.

The move to Belfield

If the government was beginning to implement a workable policy for the
expansion of the educational sector as whole during Hillery's first two
years in office, the department's approach for the development of higher
education remained ill defined. The timing of Hillery's appointment did,
however, plunge him into the midst of a long-running and heated debate
about the future of University College Dublin. The department under
Hillery gave an official seal of approval to the move of UCD to Belfield.
The new minister inherited the report of the Commission on
Accommodation Needs for the colleges of the NUI.[63] The decision on
the move to Belfield was, to all intents and purposes, already taken by the
time Hillery took office. De Valera's final government accepted the
Commission's recommendation for the transfer of UCD from Earlsfort
Terrace to the new site at Belfield shortly before Hillery's appointment.

An inter-departmental committee, headed by Máirtín Ó Flathartaigh of the Department of Education, endorsed the immediate development of accommodation for the college's Faculty of Science on the new site in November 1959.[64] This verdict was not entirely unanimous; the Department of Finance's representative on the committee expressed serious reservations about the development of the site at Belfield.[65] Hillery did not share such reservations and it would have almost impossible to unpick the Cabinet decision even if he had. He presented a proposal to the government on 22 February 1960, advocating the immediate development of a new science building at Belfield; the Cabinet agreed to provide state funding for the project.[66]

Hillery then proposed a supplementary estimate in the Dáil on 23 March 1960 providing for a token allocation of £10 to the Belfield development.[67] This was not a cunning attempt to sabotage the project by the Department of Finance; the token Vote was designed to secure the approval in principle of the Dáil for the transfer of the college to Belfield. While the full allocation for the development of the new site would not be authorised in the short term, Hillery announced the government's decision to provide immediately for a new science building on the Belfield site, at a total cost of £250,000. As the college authorities were able to raise £100,000 for the new building, the state would provide the remainder of the funding. The minister commented that the transfer of the college as a whole could well require up to 20 years.[68] While only the funding for the new science building was provided initially, the government had made a long-term commitment to the establishment of a new campus at Belfield.

Hillery's opening speech to the debate made the case for the transfer of UCD, relying heavily on the conclusions of the Commission on Accommodation Needs. The option of redeveloping Earlsfort Terrace through extensive use of compulsory acquisition was rejected both by the Commission and by the minister, who argued that the property rights of householders and institutions in the area deserved respect.[69] The other main alternative to the development of the site at Belfield, namely the amalgamation of UCD with Trinity College Dublin, had been strongly advocated by Aodhogán O'Rahilly in a Reservation to the report of the Commission.[70] But, with the exception of the dissenting voice of O'Rahilly, the Commission had not given any consideration to the possibility of merger, as their terms of reference excluded Trinity College. Furthermore, merger did not appear a practical proposition to the Commission due to the ban on the attendance of Catholics at Trinity College maintained by the hierarchy. Hillery too rejected the possibility of amalgamation on 23 March, largely on the basis that such a solution would undermine the fundamental right of parents to guarantee the denominational education of their children.[71] He noted that Article 42 of the Constitution required the state to respect the lawful preference of parents not to send their children to any educational institution designated by the state in violation of their conscience. Hillery argued that he was obliged to respect the consciences of all Irish citizens, Catholic or Protestant, in considering the question of university amalgamation. He asserted that the basic principle of 'the non-forcing of conscience' would be the decisive factor in considering any redistribution or amalgamation of faculties at university level.[72]

Hillery's statement was drafted by Ó Raifeartaigh, who was his most influential adviser on higher education.[73] Significantly John Charles McQuaid, the long-serving Catholic Archbishop of Dublin, wrote to both the minister and the secretary of the department on 24 March 1960, to offer his congratulations on Hillery's statement in the Dáil. The archbishop, who vehemently opposed any suggestion of merger between Trinity College and UCD, thanked Hillery for his courage in guaranteeing Catholics the right to their own university education.[74] McQuaid also warmly praised Ó Raifeartaigh for the excellence of the minister's speech and commented, 'for your share in securing our right to Catholic education, I am very grateful'.[75] Hillery's statement underlined not only the influence of Ó Raifeartaigh, but also the government's determination to avoid any conflict with the Catholic bishops. Yet McQuaid's influence was not decisive in this instance, no matter how much he welcomed the decision. The project for a new campus had acquired virtually unstoppable momentum by the late 1950s, not least due to the determination of the UCD authorities to bring about the transfer and their successful lobbying of de Valera's government in 1959. Hillery himself was supportive of the move to Belfield, but he had little freedom of action on the matter even if he had wished to pursue a different course. The development of the Belfield site represented a satisfactory solution for a government that had no desire for conflict with the educational or ecclesiastical authorities.

The debate on Hillery's token Estimate underlined that Fine Gael's parliamentary party was also solidly supportive of the proposal. James Dillon, the leader of Fine Gael and former Finance Minister Patrick McGilligan both warmly endorsed Hillery's approach.[76] Browne and McQuillan emerged as the most vociferous opponents of the move to Belfield. Browne attacked the transfer as 'the decision of old men' who lacked appreciation of the needs of the modern world and he called for some form of amalgamation between the two universities in Dublin.[77] But Hillery won the day without much difficulty. There was no vote at all, although Browne recorded his dissent from the transfer of UCD to Belfield: the Dáil passed the estimate without a division on 31 March.[78] The relative ease with which Hillery secured the agreement of the Dáil to the development of the new campus at Belfield illustrated the pragmatic case for the government's decision. Certainly any attempt to promote university amalgamation would have encountered much fiercer resistance.

The controversy on the transfer of UCD to Belfield allowed Hillery to open up a broader debate on the development of higher education. He saw the need to plan effectively for the future expansion of higher education and accepted Ó Raifeartaigh's advice that 'the universities would not tolerate interference from a politician and the only way I could deal with them would be through a commission'.[79] Hillery announced his intention on 23 March 1960 to establish a new Commission of Inquiry on Higher Education.[80] The new Commission would evaluate a wide variety of issues related to the long-term development of higher education. The minister provided wide-ranging terms of reference for the Commission, which was formally established on 4 October 1960. Hillery requested that the Commission make recommendations in relation to university, professional, technological and higher education generally.[81] The Commission was instructed to give special attention to the general organisation of higher education and the procedures for making academic and administrative appointments in the universities; the new group would also examine the possibility of providing courses of higher education through Irish.[82] The only restriction imposed on the new group by Hillery was that the transfer of UCD to Belfield did not come within its terms of reference, as the government and the Dáil had already approved the transfer of the college to the new site.[83]

Hillery hoped to set up a small expert group that would examine the issues in a sharply focused way and report quickly; this would allow him to make the necessary decisions to support the expansion of higher education in the short term.[84] But the Commission that actually emerged following detailed consultation within the government and higher levels of the civil service was very different from Hillery's original idea: 'the meeting of the government and the consultation with the departments caused me to come out with a commission of 26 people.'[85] He had reckoned without the Cabinet's concern to cover its flanks by providing representation for all relevant interests. The government set out to ensure that no influential interest group would be offended by exclusion from the Commission. Other ministers and senior officials sought with some success to ensure that their nominees secured places on the Commission. Seán MacEntee, the long-serving Minister for Health and Social Welfare, was particularly interested in higher education and insistent on influencing the composition of the Commission. MacEntee bombarded Hillery with letters outlining his views about the membership of the Commission and the general deficiencies of higher education in Ireland.[86] Hillery successfully resisted MacEntee's proposal that his wife Margaret be a member of the Commission. Although Margaret MacEntee, a lecturer in UCD, was undoubtedly qualified for membership of a review group on higher education, Hillery was concerned to avoid any hint of impropriety. He feared that appointing the wife of a Cabinet Minister would create the perception that the Commission was a puppet of the government.[87] The disagreement involved Hillery in a clash with MacEntee at a Cabinet meeting on 13 September 1960 and also provoked a rift between Hillery and another senior minister, Paddy Smith:

> Before the meeting, I told Lemass of my stand and he nodded. In the meeting room before the meeting started Paddy Smith came to my place at the table to ask me to put MacEntee's wife on the Commission. I refused. Smith did not speak to me for some years after that except to mouth insults at the restaurant table. In the meeting MacEntee proposed his wife [for the Commission]. I was supported in my position by Oscar Traynor for whom I felt deep gratitude as he was a man respected by the others and he made it clear that he thought MacEntee's proposal was not acceptable.[88]

MacEntee was gravely offended by Hillery's action and the incident led to a temporary rift between the two men. The coolness did not last, however, as MacEntee let the matter drop after a short time. He soon resumed his previous practice of firing letters at Hillery on various issues and later became an admirer of Hillery's educational policies.[89] Hillery won his point on that occasion, but he could do little to limit the overall size of the Commission, which was approved by the government in September 1960. At twenty-six members, the new group was simply too large to function effectively or report in a timely fashion; the Commission included eminent academics from the universities, representatives of business interests, trade unions and semi-state bodies, as well as Catholic and Protestant bishops.[90] The government appointed Justice Cearbhall Ó Dálaigh, then a member of the Supreme Court, as chairman of the Commission. Hillery was disappointed by the eventual make-up of the Commission and rightly anticipated a much longer timeframe for its work than he had originally hoped.[91] Their deliberations were certainly prolonged, and the group's report was not submitted until 1967, more than two years after the end of Hillery's term as Minister for Education.

The delay severely limited the influence of the Commission itself and meant that no long-term policy for the development of higher education would be implemented during Hillery's time as minister, thanks to the government's decision to sacrifice efficiency to political expediency.

Early years

Hillery's elevation to the Cabinet helped to maintain Fianna Fáil's dominance of Clare politics. The general election on 4 October 1961 was the first poll in Clare for half a century without de Valera's name on the ballot. The new minister consolidated his hold on the local electorate. He topped the poll for the first time, securing just over 1.5 quotas.[92] Hillery's surplus ensured the election of his running mate, none other than Seán Ó Ceallaigh, the veteran organiser who had serious reservations about Hillery's candidacy ten years before. The younger man harboured no resentment about Ó Ceallaigh's qualms in 1951, not least because they were shared even more strongly by Hillery himself. Few doubted his aptitude for politics a decade later; the election confirmed Hillery's status as the leading Fianna Fáil politician in the county.

Hillery's first two years as Minister for Education brought few major changes and little indication of the radical policy initiatives which would define his second term in Education. But while most of the reforms promoted by Hillery up to 1961 were small-scale and incremental, such changes were still significant as the first indicators of new policy thinking. Hillery pursued a cautious but definite policy for educational expansion, which had been given the full support of the government by Lemass. The most significant legacy of Hillery's first term as Minister for Education was not any particular initiative, but the cautious beginning of sustained activism by the state in education. As a new minister he was seeking to learn his brief and was still formulating his own ideas about educational reform. But his early experiences as a minister had an important effect on Hillery himself; he gained first-hand knowledge of the severe inequalities and shortcomings in the Irish educational system and became convinced that far-reaching changes were needed. He later attributed his motivation to:

... the social interest which insisted on the injustice in a large section of children having no prospect of going ahead to post-primary education and beyond because they had not got the money. I improved the scholarships scheme but this was only a stopgap until a comprehensive plan was introduced.[93]

Hillery now faced the challenge of developing such a 'comprehensive plan' and converting reforming intentions into educational reality.

7.

Quiet Reformer

' To do what is possible is my job and not to have the whole matter upset because of some supposed principle or ideal.'[1]

Hillery's pragmatic defence of his policy approach on 11 June 1963 appeared to identify him as a cautious piecemeal reformer who was wary of radical innovation. This impression was profoundly misleading. Certainly Hillery steadfastly refused to endorse the ideal of free post-primary education and rarely enunciated an overall vision for the future of Irish education. But Hillery's second term as minister between 1961 and 1965 brought a series of far-reaching reforms in Irish education. More significantly, useful piecemeal reforms were no longer the summit of the department's ambitions. Hillery's term of office launched a process of radical reform which would continue for the following decade and laid the foundations for a lasting transformation of the Irish educational sector.

The OECD pilot study

The most influential initiative of Hillery's tenure as Minister for Education was taken almost as soon as he returned to the Department of Education after the general election in October 1961. Hillery played a crucial part in opening up the Irish educational system to international influences, disseminated especially by the Organisation for Economic Co-operation and Development (OECD). The international organisation, which began its official existence as the Organisation for European Economic Co-operation in 1948, expanded its membership to include the United States of America and Canada in September 1961, when it was restructured as the OECD.[2] The newly-reconstituted OECD vigorously promoted the idea that education should be regarded as a key factor in economic development. OECD officials were greatly influenced by human capital theory, which held that investment in people produced a greater return of investment than investment in physical capital. The OECD's first major event was a policy conference on 'Economic Growth and Investment in Education', which was held in Washington between 16 and 20 October 1961.[3]

Hillery was initially uncertain of the benefits of participating in the OECD conference. He believed that 'I knew what I wanted before the OECD study'.[4] It was Seán MacGearailt who persuaded Hillery to accept the OECD invitation:

> Seán came in one day and he said there was an OECD conference. I said 'but Seán, I know what I want'; but he said 'This is the way to get it – they could do what you wanted.' He was right, [it was the way] to get a structure and support for it.'[5]

Hillery accepted MacGearailt's argument that the imprimatur of an independent international body was necessary to validate the case for reform in Irish education.[6] The minister agreed to Irish representation at the conference in the full knowledge that OECD involvement in the evaluation of the Irish educational system was the likely outcome.

Two Irish representatives attended the Washington Conference, MacGearailt himself and John F. McInerney, deputy assistant secretary to the Department of Finance.[7] The OECD's Directorate of Scientific Affairs issued a proposal just before the conference for the establishment of pilot studies on long-term educational needs in developed countries.[8] The Directorate identified an increased supply of skilled technical workers as an essential requirement for economic growth in most member states; their proposal emphasised too that the achievement of 'social aims' demanded the expansion of educational facilities. The OECD proposal was based on the assumption that investment in education was one of the key instruments in the achievement of social and economic progress.[9] The OECD officials aimed to achieve a critical survey of the entire educational system of one or more member states; this would offer valuable guidance for policymaking in the member state concerned and would provide a model for future studies in other developed countries.[10]

The Washington Conference agreed an international initiative, the *Education Investment and Planning Programme* (EIPP), based on the Directorate's proposal.[11] Keill Eide, a senior OECD official, approached the Irish representatives, suggesting that they should advise the Irish government to undertake the proposed pilot study.[12] The Irish officials immediately agreed to recommend co-operation with the pilot study to their ministers. Only the delegations of Ireland and Austria volunteered to co-operate with the project initially; the representatives of most other states showed little enthusiasm for exposing their educational problems to international evaluation, although some would join the EIPP at a later stage.[13]

Hillery was well aware of the wide-ranging implications of the project. He had been in office long enough to recognise the marked inequalities and deficiencies that characterised the Irish educational system; he knew that the survey would illuminate these shortcomings and hold them up to international scrutiny.[14] O'Connor correctly drew attention to the considerable political risk involved for the incumbent minister: 'The OECD would publish details of these inadequacies for the world to see. If blame was to be assigned – and he never doubted that the picture

painted by the report, when it appeared, would be grossly unfavourable –
then his government would be the target. He could easily refuse, as many
other countries did, and nobody might ever know.'[15] Hillery himself
recorded in a private note that the initiative 'meant opening cupboards
and all the dark holes and highlighting everything that was lacking and
planning for ten years ahead.'[16] He was not indifferent to the political
implications, but he was willing to take the risk to achieve his policy
objectives; he realised that the pilot study would pave the way for far-
reaching changes in the Irish educational sector and lay the basis for
coherent planning of educational needs.[17] Hillery fully supported the
initiative from the outset; he recommended to the government the
appointment of an Irish survey team to conduct the pilot study along the
lines proposed by the OECD. He announced on 22 June 1962 that the
project would be implemented by a national survey team under the
auspices of the OECD and the Department of Education.[18] O'Connor
regarded this move as 'one of the most important policy decisions and, in
my opinion, one of the most courageous ever made about Irish
education.'[19]

It was certainly the most significant policy decision taken by Hillery
in the course of his six-year term in Education. Hillery showed political
courage in authorising a comprehensive evaluation of the Irish
educational system by an independent survey team, but arguably it was
a calculated gamble on his part rather than a leap into the unknown. A
critical analysis of the Irish educational system would prove a potent asset
for a reforming minister, who sought a coherent rationale for the policy
changes that he believed to be necessary. The report of the survey team,
Investment in Education, profoundly influenced important reforms that
were implemented by Hillery's successor, George Colley. Hillery could
not have anticipated the full extent of the influence achieved by
Investment, but he could confidently expect that the report would offer
a blueprint for reform and would provide a powerful source of legitimacy
for greater activism by the state in Irish education. Hillery saw the project
not as a potential threat, but as an opportunity; time would prove that his

assessment was right – it was not the government, but traditional stakeholders within the educational system, especially the Catholic Church, who had most to fear from *Investment in Education*.

Hillery's support for the OECD project was essential in securing its rapid adoption by the government. The pilot study would not have proceeded so rapidly, or perhaps even at all, without his endorsement of Irish participation in the Washington Conference and his active support for the project within the government. He was not a lone voice arguing for the initiative; the political context was very favourable for the adoption of the pilot study. The proposal was swept through the bureaucratic thickets of the Irish political system with remarkable speed. The government was beginning the preparation of the *Second Programme for Economic Expansion*, and Lemass endorsed the survey of long-term educational needs as an essential element in a process of national economic planning.[20] Leading officials in the departments of Education and Finance also favoured the OECD initiative: T.K. Whitaker, the influential secretary of the Department of Finance, firmly backed the project and secured general agreement for the initiative from other government departments by December 1961.[21] Hillery himself obtained the government's approval for the establishment of the survey team in June 1962 and he announced its membership on 29 July.[22] Patrick Lynch, Professor of Economics at UCD and a former adviser to Taoiseach John A. Costello, became head of the survey team. Hillery greatly respected Lynch and was keen to secure his participation in the project. The national team also included William J. Hyland, a statistician originally from Cork who was then working with the UN Statistics Office, Pádraig Ó Nualláin, a senior inspector within the department, and Martin O'Donoghue, a lecturer in Economics at Trinity College Dublin.[23] The work of the survey team was overseen by a National Steering Committee; Hillery selected Seán MacGearailt as chair of the committee. [25] The rapid official decision in favour of the study meant that Ireland became the first OECD member state to volunteer for participation in the project.[26] The survey team began its work in

October 1962, barely a year after the idea was first floated at the
Washington Conference.

Perhaps as important as the establishment of the pilot study itself was
the mission assigned to the survey team. Hillery announced the terms of
reference for the project in the Dáil on 3 July 1962. The team was asked
to undertake a comprehensive survey of the state's long-term needs for
educational resources. The terms of reference for the study were definite
and specific, requiring the team to evaluate the educational system in the
context of existing policies and to undertake a detailed assessment of the
workings of the system on the basis of relevant statistical data.[27] While
specific policy recommendations were not envisaged by the terms of
reference, the survey team was asked to undertake a full evaluation of
long-term educational needs and an assessment of future essential demand
for facilities at different levels. The study was designed to develop
educational targets, which would be closely related to future needs for
skilled manpower, for the following 10-15 years.[28] The team was also
required to consider the implications of future levels of enrolment for the
expansion of educational resources and the level of state spending in
education.

The department drew the terms of reference almost entirely from the
proposal for the pilot studies in developed countries issued by the
Directorate of Scientific Affairs on 12 October 1961.[29] The sole element
not derived from the OECD proposal was the proposed evaluation of the
implications of providing educational aid to developing countries. The
inclusion of aid to developing countries in the survey team's terms of
reference reflected the Irish tradition of missionary and educational work
in Africa, especially by the religious orders.[30] Although the OECD
emphasised that the responsibility for the pilot survey rested with teams
appointed by the national authorities, the international organisation
undoubtedly exerted a pervasive influence over the scope and objectives
of the new study. Hillery and his senior officials were content to adopt the
OECD blueprint for the pilot study almost without amendment.

When Hillery addressed the inaugural meeting of the Steering

Committee in October 1962, he portrayed educational expansion as a key factor in delivering economic prosperity. He adopted the ideas and rhetoric of the OECD to make a compelling case for investment in education by the Irish state. The minister argued that the role of education in promoting economic development had been given inadequate attention in the past but investment in education was now widely recognised as a major factor in economic development.[31] Hillery was concerned to assure his audience that the needs of the economy did not provide the sole imperative for the study, asserting that the survey team would take account of the wider aims of education. He showed considerable skill in attempting to place the pilot study, with its strong economic orientation, in a wider social and educational context. He sought to demonstrate that the new ideas of the OECD initiative could be consistent with traditional educational and spiritual values. Hillery argued that economic expansion and the full development of the potential of individual citizens both depended on the delivery of the necessary educational resources. The new study was designed to evaluate the educational needs of an expanding economy, but also the economic implications of the increasing demand for education.[32] Hillery was not speaking simply for himself; he was expressing the newly adopted educational policy of the government. Hillery's speech represented an emerging consensus among politicians and senior officials in favour of investment in education as a key element in national economic development.

The launch of the pilot study in June 1962 reflected a definite policy commitment by the Irish government to coherent planning of educational needs, in the wider context of economic and social development. Hillery referred frequently to the work of the survey team as a means of achieving proper planning of future developments in education. He declared in the Dáil on 27 May 1964 that future spending on education would be based upon the assessments of the survey team, especially their estimates of manpower needs. Hillery believed correctly that the analysis of the educational problems to be provided by the survey team would demand vastly increased expenditure, but emphasised that 'it will be expenditure on a studied plan and not just the lashing out of money in a haphazard fashion.'[33] The report was completed shortly before the end of Hillery's term in Education and it was to be his successor, George Colley, who had the opportunity to implement many of the policy changes which flowed from the critical analysis provided by the survey team. But this should not obscure the importance of the decision to establish the pilot study in the first instance. While other influential figures also supported the original OECD initiative, Hillery played a crucial part in securing the rapid approval of the project by the government and in establishing the survey team itself. The establishment of the *Investment in Education* study marked the first explicit acknowledgement by any Irish government of the need for a comprehensive reappraisal of the educational system, which would go far beyond the incremental reforms already started by the Department of Education. The work of the survey team paved the way for coherent educational planning based upon accurate statistical information. The adoption of the pilot study in 1962 was a key policy decision which shaped the reform and expansion of the Irish educational sector over the following decade.

A new era – Special education

The department under Hillery also took an innovative approach to the development of special education. Although primary schools for blind and deaf pupils had existed since the nineteenth century, the department gave formal recognition to special education as a distinctive sector for the first time in the early 1960s. Special training for teachers of pupils with disabilities was provided for the first time in 1961, when a training course for such teachers was established in St Patrick's Training College.[34] Schools for blind or partially-sighted children became special schools in a real sense in 1962, when the department authorised a special teacher–pupil ratio of one to fifteen and provided a grant for specialised equipment for such schools.[35] This initiative was a watershed in the development of special education and it was soon followed by the introduction of special staffing measures for schools serving pupils with impaired hearing. The department had already recognised the first schools for mentally handicapped pupils in 1955. Special education in this area began to expand significantly in the early 1960s, as official recognition was given to special schools for students suffering from moderate mental disabilities and behavioural problems.[36] Hillery's term saw the first meaningful attempt by the Irish government to develop an area which had previously been neglected by the state.[37] Hillery understandably took pride in the decisions taken on his watch to recognise special education and particularly the early initiatives to provide schools for students with mental disabilities.[38] The department's initiatives certainly represented only a modest beginning in the area of special education. Nevertheless the initiatives taken by Hillery reflected his proactive, reforming approach in dealing with various educational problems by the early 1960s.

Incremental advances

The launch of the pilot study was an initiative that was rich in potential, but it did not preclude immediate short-term measures to alleviate pressing educational problems, even if such measures provided only imperfect and temporary solutions. Hillery sought to improve the pupil–teacher ratio at primary level, but soon found that the traditional distribution of teachers between large and small schools presented a particularly intractable problem. The historical development of the Irish educational system had led to a proliferation of small national schools (76 per cent of all national schools taught fewer than 100 pupils in the early 1960s).[39] The small schools were heavy users of teaching resources, containing over half of all national schoolteachers, but only 38 per cent of all pupils.[40] This imbalance in the distribution of teachers helped to create a situation in which 84 per cent of the pupils in large schools were to be found in classes of 40 or more.[41] Most primary schools in urban areas had very large classes; this trend was particularly marked in Dublin, where 737 primary school classes in 1964 contained 50 or more pupils.[42]

The only long-term solution to this haphazard use of teaching resources was a radical restructuring of the primary system involving the amalgamation of small schools; this did not become practical politically until the publication of *Investment in Education*, which starkly illustrated how traditional practices led to gross inefficiency and waste of teaching resources. As the work of the survey team was still ongoing for most of his term, Hillery resorted to short-term remedies intended to tackle the worst effects of the school accommodation crisis.

A survey of national schools in the Dublin area was undertaken by the department in 1964 with the objective of reducing large classes to a more manageable size. The department sought to reduce class sizes firstly by the reorganisation of existing classes; where this proved impractical, Hillery authorised the provision of prefabricated classrooms. The use of prefabricated structures became an important element of the department's strategy to reduce the pupil–teacher ratio. Official approval was given for the supply of 112 prefabricated classrooms and the appointment of 104 additional teachers in the Dublin area between June and September 1964.[43] These measures reflected the scale of the overcrowding problem in urban primary schools and the recognition by the department that effective short-term remedies were urgently required. Hillery reinforced the practical measures to reduce class sizes by requiring all national schools in Dublin to establish a maximum class size of 50 pupils in infants' classes from 1 July 1964. Circular 16/64 required national school managers to limit the admission of new infant pupils to a maximum of 50 per class.[44] These incremental measures undoubtedly had some effect, but at the cost of making prefabricated classrooms a semi-permanent feature for many schools.

The minister's efforts to enhance the resources available to the national schools were not restricted to the increased supply of accommodation and teachers. Hillery announced a scheme to establish libraries in national schools for the first time; the scheme provided grants from November 1963 for the establishment of school libraries in five counties initially, namely Laois, Leitrim, Monaghan and the rural areas of Limerick and Waterford.[45] The department arranged to supply reference works to all national schools in these areas, at a cost of £20,000, between January and March 1964.[46] The scheme was introduced on a phased basis and was intended to lead to the establishment of reference libraries in all national schools; the initiative was gradually extended to the entire country between 1964 and 1968.[47] The new scheme was the first public initiative to provide for permanent reference libraries in primary schools, and marked a significant advance in the academic support provided by the state for the national school system.

Despite these incremental advances, Hillery was criticised by the Opposition for failing to offer a coherent programme of reform. On 23 May 1962, the leader of Fine Gael, James Dillon, attacked Hillery's failure to offer 'a comprehensive review' of the system and a plan for the future.[48] In the same Dáil debate Noel Browne criticised the minister for failing to deliver fundamental reform of an unequal and inefficient system. Browne ridiculed Hillery as 'a sort of political castrate in charge of this tremendously important department'.[49] Hillery's response highlighted his own unhappiness with the condition of the educational system, as well as his feeling that he was being unfairly targeted for problems which had accumulated for over a generation. He reminded the Dáil on 6 June 1962 of the underdeveloped and underfunded system that he had inherited: 'we had a 50-year backlog of bad schools', and pointed with some justification to the 'silent progress' of the previous five years.[50] But while Hillery defended the gradualist policy of the government, his dissatisfaction with the existing system of post-primary education was obvious. He told TDs that 'the main flaw in our post-primary education … was that it was not open to all and there were no signs of it becoming open to all'.[51] He recognised that a substantial proportion of children did not receive any post-primary education and pledged to bring forward plans for the expansion of second-level education 'in the near future'. Hillery's commitment to a significant initiative at post-primary level foreshadowed the launch of the groundbreaking proposal for comprehensive schools in 1963.

'A revolutionary step': comprehensive schools

The development of the minister's initiative was encouraged by public criticism of the existing educational system, which was most forcefully expressed by Tuairim, a political research society founded in 1954 to provide a platform for members of the post-Treaty generation.[52] The government also faced increasing pressure for educational reform from its political opponents. The Labour Party issued a policy document in March 1963 entitled *Challenge and Change in Education*. The Labour policy, composed mainly by Barry Desmond and Catherine McGuinness, was a manifesto for a radical reform of the educational system. Labour endorsed the raising of the school-leaving age, initially to 15 but later to 16, and sought the establishment of a National Planning Branch within the department to implement rational planning of educational needs.[53] The document sought the introduction of free post-primary education for all children as 'a social and economic necessity of the first importance'.[54] The Labour Party's reforming approach mirrored many of the sentiments expressed by Hillery and Lemass, although Labour advocated more rapid and ambitious changes than the government was willing to endorse in 1963. The launch of Labour's education policy intensified the political pressure on Hillery to bring forward his own initiative. Ó Raifeartaigh privately informed the Catholic bishops in February 1963 that the minister wished to make a public statement on his plans for education in the short-term, as the Labour Party was about to publish its policy document and 'he wants to forestall them.'[55] Hillery already intended to launch a new initiative for post-primary education before the publication of the Labour policy, but he was undoubtedly concerned to limit the political impact of *Challenge and Change*. The launch of Labour's policy influenced the timing of Hillery's initiative in May 1963, providing an additional incentive for an early announcement of his plans.

Hillery made an initial proposal for a new type of post-primary school in a memorandum to the Department of the Taoiseach on 7 July 1962, following the report of the Inter-Departmental Committee on western small farms.[56] The memo highlighted that post-primary education was often not available at all in the western small farm areas, and, where schools were available, the facilities were completely inadequate. Hillery proposed the establishment of several new post-primary schools, offering a comprehensive course of three years for pupils aged from twelve to fifteen; the curriculum of these schools should be broad-based but maintain 'a very definite practical bias'.[57] This concept envisaged central schools serving a wide area which would require transport services to bring in all pupils outside a three-mile radius of the school.[58] Hillery sought to secure the agreement of the Cabinet Committee dealing with the report on small farm areas that the state would provide a new type of second-level school. If this principle was accepted, then the Department of Education could prepare plans to implement a pilot scheme in the areas with the most pressing educational needs.[59]

The Taoiseach intervened to support Hillery's initiative. Lemass asked the ministers on the Committee to indicate whether they would agree to a new educational initiative, to be announced firstly in a public statement by the Taoiseach.[60] Hillery's initiative received support from several ministers, including his predecessor, Jack Lynch, as Minister for Industry and Commerce.[61] The initiative was, however, strongly opposed by the Department of Finance. Whitaker criticised the proposal in a lengthy reply to Nicholas Nolan, the secretary to the government, on 18 July, drawing attention to the extensive costs involved and seeking a thorough review of its financial implications.[62] He argued that full consultation with educational interests, including the churches, school managers and teaching unions, would be necessary before any commitment was made by the government. Whitaker also issued a clear warning 'that any announcement made at this stage in connection with these proposals should be limited to a general statement to the effect that special attention is being given to the question of improving post-primary educational facilities in the western rural areas.'[63] Whitaker categorically rejected Hillery's attempt to secure agreement in principle for the proposal from relevant ministers. The Department of Finance was entirely opposed to any endorsement of the proposal in the short term; Whitaker had grave reservations about the initiative on financial and educational grounds.

Hillery, however, was not deterred by the Department of Finance's negative response. He issued an uncompromising defence of the original proposal on 26 July, rejecting the criticisms made by the Department of Finance. The minister dismissed Whitaker's concern about the need for wider consultation, with a pointed reminder that such consultation was appropriately left to the Department of Education. Hillery argued that a vague reference to a potential extension of existing facilities in the Taoiseach's statement would 'in many ways be worse than making no reference at all to education in any statement that may be issued.'[64] Private interests had already failed to provide secondary education in the western small farm areas and were most unlikely to do so in the future; the areas concerned were too thinly populated to make the running of a secondary school a viable proposition. Hillery believed that any reference to education in Lemass's statement should not only acknowledge the exceptional problems in providing second-level education for the western small farm areas but should also contain 'a firm statement of intention to take special measures in order to cater for them.'[65]

Lemass resolved the dispute in Hillery's favour by including a short but positive reference to the proposal in a public statement for Muintir na Tíre Rural Week. The speech was delivered on Lemass's behalf by Charles Haughey, the Minister for Justice, on 14 August 1962.[66] The Taoiseach's statement acknowledged that special problems existed with regard to post-primary education in the western small farm areas and indicated that Hillery was preparing proposals to remedy these deficiencies.[67] Lemass's statement cautiously floated the idea of a new type of post-primary school, provided by the state, as a solution to the underdevelopment of second-level education in sparsely-populated rural areas.[68] The section of

Lemass's statement on education attracted little public attention at the time, but the Taoiseach had signalled a new departure in educational policy.

The next move lay with Hillery, and he sought to develop a compelling case for reform in second-level education. He asked Ó Raifeartaigh to set up an advisory group within the department, which would produce detailed proposals for change. Hillery said:

> I needed people who were equipped with educational expertise and who were open to the idea of change. Dr Terry Ó Raifeartaigh was able to name those likely to answer this description and was most helpful. It was clear to me from an earlier encounter with the more senior inspectors that the older ones would not want change.[69]

Ó Raifeartaigh set up the internal committee in June 1962 to advise Hillery on future educational needs in post-primary education. The committee, which was chaired by Dr Maurice Duggan, also included Dr Finbar O'Callaghan, Tomás Ó Floinn, Liam Ó Maolchatha and Mícheál Ó Súilleabháin.[70] While Duggan himself was a senior inspector, it was significant that most members of the group were middle-ranking inspectors or officials who were impatient with the timidity and inertia of the department in the previous generation. The establishment of the internal committee was a means to an end. Hillery was concerned to overcome the traditional attitude, shared by many senior officials and inspectors, that reshaping the educational system was beyond the capacity of the department:

> This was the way to overcome the first obstruction – the attitude in the department that the situation was unchangeable – that the system was working – that the Department of Finance would not tolerate the idea of the spending necessary – that the Church would obstruct it

and would not like to see the State coming into the field
of Education.[71]

Changing traditional attitudes within the department itself was an essential
first step in developing reforming policies and transforming the restricted
role of the state in education.

The advisory group certainly fulfilled Hillery's expectations. He
himself prepared a brief outline for their attention and the group drafted
a detailed proposal for the reform of second-level education.[72] The
officials produced an interim report on 8 December 1962, which argued
that a minimum period of post-primary education was a national
necessity. The committee recommended free and compulsory second-
level education for all children up to the age of 15.[73] They rejected the
idea of large comprehensive schools modelled on the English system as
impractical. The report proposed instead a common post-primary course
for junior cycle pupils in secondary and vocational schools.[74] Hillery did
not, however, endorse all the recommendations of the internal report.
The department's initiative, entitled *Proposal for Comprehensive Post-Primary
Education: Pilot Scheme Related to Small Farm Areas,* used certain elements
of the report by Duggan's committee, such as its arguments for a common
post-primary course for all pupils aged 12 to 15.[75] But the official proposal
also included a definite recommendation for several comprehensive
schools of between 150 and 400 pupils; the final version also quietly left
out the committee's suggestion of free post-primary education for all
children up to the age of 15.[76] Hillery was convinced that he could not
propose free education as part of the new scheme, believing that the
opposition generated by such a proposal would wreck the initiative. 'It
wasn't about free education. The whole thing would have collapsed due
to the opposition.'[77] The report was more important in supporting the
case for major changes in second-level education than as a direct influence
on Hillery's proposals for reform. But the work of the advisory group was
certainly significant as an indication of new thinking about educational
policy among the officials of the department.

The final proposal approved by Hillery in January 1963 identified key problems in post-primary education. The availability of secondary education depended entirely on private initiative, implying that more remote regions were unlikely ever to have a secondary school as no incentive existed for the private sector to provide one for only a few pupils. The most striking defect of the system was summarised bluntly; a large proportion of pupils would never receive post-primary education 'under the present system of private enterprise'.[78] Moreover, the department's paper identified further problems flowing from this 'fundamental structural defect' in the educational system.[79] Many rural secondary schools were too small, employing inadequate numbers of staff and therefore providing only a limited curriculum giving little or no attention to continental languages or science. The proposal also described private schools under one-man management as 'inherently unstable'.[80] This was a revealing comment, which gave a clear indication of dissatisfaction on the part of Hillery and the senior officials with the tight control of schools by individual clergy. The submission also expressed grave concern at the rigid separation between secondary and vocational education, noting that the two strands of the post-primary system operated in 'separate watertight compartments'.[81] The solution was the establishment by the state of comprehensive post-primary schools, which were initially described as 'Junior Secondary Schools'.[82] This proposal formed the basis of the policy announcement made by Hillery in May 1963.

The plan for reform made rapid progress through the administrative and political obstacles that could have blocked its path, due to Hillery's effective lobbying and the support of the Taoiseach. The proposal was submitted to the Department of Finance and was blocked once again.[83] Hillery then appealed directly to the Taoiseach. He made the case for comprehensive schools to Lemass on 9 January 1963, proposing a pilot scheme for comprehensive schools in the western small farm areas.[84] Hillery noted that private interests had failed in the relevant areas to provide for education and so could not credibly object to state action. He hoped that the pilot scheme would provide a model of post-primary education, which could later be extended to the whole country. Hillery acknowledged both the considerable expense of the plan and the possible opposition of private interests, including the Catholic hierarchy, but urged that it was necessary and probably inevitable. He even argued that the comprehensive schools plan might well prove to be the only opportunity to introduce a 'really satisfactory system of post-primary education'.[85]

Hillery suggested that his department's proposal should be forwarded to the Cabinet Committee on Small Farms. The Taoiseach backed Hillery's initiative but found a more effective means of promoting it. Lemass withheld the proposal from the Cabinet Committee, instead arranging a meeting involving only Hillery, the Taoiseach himself and Jim Ryan.[86] The Taoiseach explicitly endorsed the new initiative in his response on 14 January, although he also noted his own lack of knowledge about the cost of the plan and other practical problems.[87] He warned the minister that public confusion about the government's policy would persist until Hillery's plan was announced. Lemass gave Hillery clear directions on the procedure to be followed in the meeting with Ryan, warning him to 'come to this meeting with the nature of the decisions you desire very clear in your mind' – Lemass even sought in advance a draft of the decisions as Hillery wished to have them recorded.[88] The Taoiseach's commitment to Hillery's proposal and his determination to fast-track it through the normal procedures were evident.

Hillery's officials rapidly drafted the summary of the decisions requested by Lemass.[89] The draft laid out a new system of post-primary education based on comprehensive courses and, where necessary, comprehensive schools; as a first step in this direction, a pilot scheme for comprehensive schools would be introduced in more remote rural areas.[90] Hillery sought authorisation to consult with the Catholic bishop in each area to give effect to the proposal, as it was envisaged that the pilot scheme would involve only Catholic schools.[91] Hillery secured agreement from Jim Ryan for the plan by following the procedure recommended by Lemass, despite some delay caused by the Department of Finance. Hillery

was delighted by his success, but was brought down to earth abruptly by
the Taoiseach:

> Jim and Lemass agreed and I was floating out the door, and
> Lemass said 'You'll never get that through the government.'
> I said, 'What will I do then?' 'Announce it,' he said.[92]

Lemass warned Hillery to launch the scheme publicly without bringing
it to the Cabinet for approval. So Hillery launched the initiative for
comprehensive schools at a press conference on 20 May 1963.

Hillery's policy announcement on 20 May drew public attention to
major weaknesses in the existing second-level sector, which provided the
rationale for the comprehensive schools proposal. These flaws included
the failure of the system to provide post-primary education for a
substantial number of children and the complete absence of coordination
between secondary and vocational schools.[93] Hillery pointed out that one
third of Irish children received no post-primary education; opposition
politicians and commentators claimed that the figure was closer to half,
but nobody disputed the reality of deeply entrenched social inequalities
within second-level education. He declared that these children were
'today's Third Estate, whose voice amid the babel of competing claims
from the more privileged, has hitherto scarcely been heard.'[94] Hillery
proclaimed equality of opportunity as a guiding principle of state policy.
He announced that the state would take the initiative by providing a
number of new post-primary schools catering in the first instance for
specific regions. Hillery proposed a comprehensive post-primary day
school, providing a three-year course leading to the Intermediate
Certificate Examination.[95] The new comprehensive school would provide
for at least 150 students and would be open to all within a ten-mile radius
of the school; pupils would enter the comprehensive school after the sixth
standard in primary school.[96] The comprehensive school would offer a
wide range of subjects to pupils, including all those available in the
secondary and vocational schools. Hillery specifically rejected selection

at an early age, ruling out any system similar to the 11-plus examination in Britain; he aimed instead to provide a broad, comprehensive curriculum for children in the 12 to 16 age group.[97] The school buildings would be financed largely by the state, while the running costs would be funded through annual grants from the department and the Vocational Education Committees (VECs). The salaries of the teachers in comprehensive schools would be paid as usual by the department.[98] Hillery's announcement marked a sweeping policy change from the practice of successive governments since the foundation of the Irish state. The national government would intervene directly to provide broadly based second-level education for the first time.

Hillery offered a clear vision of the role of comprehensive schools and their place in the educational system; he envisaged that pupils of the comprehensive schools would move into secondary or technical education at the age of 15 or 16. Hillery hoped that local technical schools would function as a 'senior storey' of the comprehensive school or as a separate institution for comprehensive students.[99] More significantly, he proposed a radical new departure in technical education to accommodate pupils who did not intend to proceed with academic education after the age of 15. Hillery announced his intention to establish Regional Technological Colleges, in conjunction with the VECs; the Regional Colleges would provide courses for a new public examination, the Technical Schools Leaving Certificate.[100] The objective of the new examination was to enable technical students to achieve a standard of education comparable in status with the Leaving Certificate courses provided by the secondary schools; the new qualification was intended to provide a gateway to third-level education or employment training for skilled technical and managerial positions. The regional colleges were designed to accommodate not only pupils from the new comprehensive schools, but any students who displayed 'practical aptitudes'.[101] The existing vocational schools would provide many of the recruits for the new colleges. The regional technological colleges were originally intended as a bridge to third-level education or skilled technical employment for students with technical aptitudes. Hillery's proposal was a serious attempt to widen educational opportunity and to enhance the status of the technical sector.

The wide-ranging initiative also sought to improve coordination between the secondary school system and the vocational schools by introducing a common examination. Hillery announced the extension of the two-year day course in vocational schools to make it a three-year course.[102] This paved the way for vocational students to take the Intermediate Certificate examination in a number of subjects by 1966. The Intermediate Certificate itself would be revised to provide a broadly common examination for students from the secondary and vocational sectors. The measure, which was intended to achieve parity in standards and evaluation between the different systems, was an important educational reform.[103]

Hillery's policy initiative of 20 May 1963 aimed to promote equality of educational opportunity and to improve the coordination between the very different strands of the educational system. The initiative deserves to be considered not only with regard to its specific achievements but also in the context of the underdeveloped Irish educational system in the early 1960s. The comprehensive schools proposal was initially implemented as a pilot project involving only three schools, in Cootehill, County Cavan, Shannon, County Clare and Carraroe, County Galway, which opened in September 1966.[104] But Hillery's announcement marked the first major initiative by the Irish state to provide for second-level education, outside the specific area of technical instruction. The direct intervention of the national government to establish a new form of post-primary school was unprecedented.

Hillery's proposal was significant too because it owed much to economic imperatives as well as social and educational demands. He himself hoped that the reforms would 'give the country a systematic supply of youth with a sufficient technical education'.[105] The proposed regional technological colleges were clearly intended to provide a supply of skilled technical workers to meet the demands of an expanding economy. It was, however, the educational potential of the regional colleges that made this innovation one of the most radical of the reforms announced by Hillery. While the first Regional Technical Colleges were not established until 1969, the RTCs became an integral part of the third-level system in the following decade.[106] Certainly the RTCs performed very different functions from the role initially envisaged by Hillery, not least because the proposal for separate second-level courses leading to a Technical Schools' Leaving Certificate was shelved by his successors. But the foundation of the regional colleges was a significant extension of educational opportunity, even if the implementation of the initiative was a long way off in 1963.

Hillery's initiative also involved a sustained effort to raise the quality and status of technical education, which was reflected not only in the plan for the regional technical colleges but also in the reform of the examination system. Hillery initiated a revision of the Intermediate Certificate examination to provide a common system of assessment for all post-primary schools in the junior cycle. A curriculum committee was established within the department, chaired by Tomás Ó Floinn, which drafted the revised programme for the Intermediate Certificate and drew up the curriculum for the comprehensive schools.[107] The minister's hope that the new common examination would enhance the status of vocational education was, however, certainly too optimistic. It was always unlikely that the deep divisions between vocational and secondary education could be overcome simply by a common examination. But the revised state examination at least provided a greater degree of coordination between two systems, which had previously operated on an entirely separate basis. Certainly the revised examination system marked the first real effort by the state to coordinate the activity of the vocational sector and the private secondary schools. Hillery's policy announcement was an influential reforming initiative, which heralded a radical policy departure in second level education. Hillery himself believed that the initiative marked the most important development in education since the establishment of the vocational system in 1930.[108] This was hardly an exaggeration, considering the minimalist activity of the Department of

Education over the previous generation. The initiative as a whole marked the first real attempt by the Irish state to deliver second-level education for the children of all its citizens.

The proposals unveiled by Hillery secured a positive reception in the media. The *Irish Press* gave a highly favourable response to the announcement, describing the plan on 22 May 1963 as 'revolutionary' and 'a welcome move to streamline the system and bring into line with modern needs.'[109] Such a response was perhaps not surprising, in the context of the newspaper's long-standing connections with Fianna Fáil, but *The Irish Times* was almost equally effusive; an editorial on 21 May welcomed the plan and praised the comprehensive model adopted by the minister.[110] The initiative received a less positive response from the teaching unions, as the union leaders were angered by the lack of any consultation with them before the policy announcement. Charles McCarthy, the general secretary of the Vocational Teachers Association (VTA), expressed great disappointment at the minister's failure to consult vocational teachers, although he also welcomed the extension of the vocational school courses and the announcement of the regional technological colleges.[111] The most influential stakeholder in the educational system, the Catholic hierarchy, made no immediate response to the initiative.

Hillery informally consulted the bishops well before the initiative was announced, raising his ideas privately with Dr William Conway, the newly appointed Archbishop of Armagh. Conway was sceptical about the plan itself and dismissive about Hillery's motivation in bringing it forward:

> I sent for Conway, and I remember it was a long summer's evening. I had him into the department and I told him what I wanted and I talked to him until it got dark; he said something then that disappointed me; 'I see that you are a young man and you want to make a name for yourself.' But the last thing I wanted in the world was to make a name for myself; but it showed the thinking that was there, that

was seen as the only motivation for the changes, you know.[112]

The initial reaction of the bishops to the proposal was hostile. Hillery was undoubtedly correct in commenting that 'The hierarchy were totally against it'[113] The bishops agreed to oppose any attempt to establish state secondary schools at their general meeting on 1 October 1962.[114] The Bishop of Elphin, Dr Vincent Hanly, emerged as a key critic of the plan within the hierarchy. Ó Raifeartaigh attempted to reassure the bishops in February 1963, briefing Hanly and his colleague, James Fergus, Bishop of Achonry, on the key features of the forthcoming policy announcement. But the hierarchy's representatives expressed strong objections to several elements of the initiative, and were particularly opposed to the idea that vocational school students might be allowed to undertake the Intermediate Certificate course.[115] Hanly wrote to Fergus that 'since our meeting with Dr Ó Raifeartaigh on Friday I cannot help feeling that we are on the edge of an educational crisis.'[116] He believed that the comprehensive schools plan would cause the conversion of vocational schools into state secondary schools, which would compete successfully with the voluntary secondary schools. Hanly feared that Hillery's plan would undermine private denominational education, replacing it with a network of non-denominational state schools at post-primary level. This suspicion was certainly unfounded. Hillery had no intention of undermining denominational education; the first four comprehensive schools were intended to be Catholic schools. But the initiative was launched publicly in the absence of any agreement with the Catholic bishops. Hillery aimed to bypass the opposition of the hierarchy by announcing the principle of comprehensive schools first and engaging in negotiation afterwards; he was operating on the basis that 'it is easier to get forgiveness than permission.'[117]

The policy announcement itself did little to reconcile the bishops to the minister's plans. The hierarchy agreed at their general meeting on 25 June 1963 that the initiative was 'a revolutionary step'; the minister would act to establish post-primary schools, while vocational education would be transformed.[118] The bishops were determined that a clerical manager, appointed by the local bishop, should control any new school, with the power to appoint staff and determine the curriculum in accordance with Catholic teaching. They also sought assurances that there would be no co-education and that the new schools would not adversely affect existing secondary schools. Hillery, accompanied by Ó Raifeartaigh and MacGearailt, began the negotiations with the bishops by meeting Hanly and Fergus to discuss the new scheme on 28 June 1963.[119] The bishops argued that the entry of the state into the field of general post-primary education was a revolutionary measure. They were dissatisfied with the proposed reform of vocational schools and the lack of any clarity in Hillery's statement concerning the possibility of co-education. Hillery emphasised that private education had failed to provide for certain regions of the country and so intervention by the state was necessary.[120] The meeting was inconclusive and revealed considerable differences between the department and the hierarchy not only on the management of the new schools, but also on the broader role of the state in second level education.

The negotiations between the officials and the hierarchy on comprehensive schools proved slow and tortuous. Hillery believed that the bishops were seeking to frustrate or at least delay the scheme:

> They dragged their feet. I sent Dr Ó Raifeartaigh and Seán O'Connor around to the bishops and the answer each time was 'that has to wait for the bishops' meeting.' Then the bishops' meeting came and it became 'a problem for the individual bishops'.[121]

The minister's appraisal of the hierarchy's approach was well founded. Dr Fergus, joint secretary of the hierarchy, wrote to Hillery on 29 October 1963 to communicate the bishops' severe reservations about the initiative. He warned Hillery that, due to a principle of Canon Law, individual bishops were precluded from accepting the proposal until the Irish bishops had made a collective decision.[122] Fergus sought clarification on a wide range of issues, including the functions of the board of management and the teaching of religion in the new schools; he also requested definite assurances that the department was not proposing co-educational schools.[123] The hierarchy feared that the reform of the vocational system would threaten the viability of private secondary schools, as they would be obliged to compete with state-funded vocational schools, which might soon offer a similar type of education.[124]

Hillery dealt with the hierarchy's objections in a conciliatory fashion. He clarified that the board of management would operate in a similar way to the national school managers; appointments would be made by the board of management subject to the approval of the minister.[125] He promised the hierarchy that he would gladly facilitate training in the teaching of religion for all teachers. While Hillery agreed that single-sex schools would be preferable, he carefully did not rule out mixed schools in areas with a widely dispersed population; co-education was essential to the success of the new schools in rural areas with a low population. Hillery met another deputation from the hierarchy, led by William Conway, in December 1963. The bishops sought assurances that religion would be taught in all post-primary schools and demanded the establishment of Deeds of Trust for the comprehensive schools, which would guarantee denominational education. Conway also made a strong case for greater financial aid to existing secondary schools.[126] Hillery sought to accommodate the concerns of the bishops on matters of detail, while remaining firm on the basic principle of the comprehensive schools scheme. He confirmed that Christian Doctrine would be taught as part of the syllabus in all post-primary schools. The minister was flexible on the terms for the Deed of Trust, readily accepting input from the bishops; indeed he was willing to allow the local bishop to nominate all three Trustees for the comprehensive schools.[127] Hillery also accepted the case for increased state aid to secondary schools. The Standing Committee of the hierarchy agreed on 7 January 1964 that, in view of the assurances given by the minister and his officials, individual bishops should be authorised to hold discussions with the department for the establishment of comprehensive schools.[128] This marked a breakthrough in the negotiations, but it did not yet guarantee the establishment of the new schools; it remained for the department to secure the consent of individual bishops for comprehensive schools in their dioceses.

Hillery's negotiations with the hierarchy on the comprehensive schools plan injected greater urgency into the department's efforts to facilitate the expansion of secondary education. The cost of building secondary schools fell entirely on the private stakeholders until the 1960s; this was a bone of contention between the department and the secondary school managers. Hillery recommended to Lemass on 4 February 1964 that a scheme of building grants should be established to provide direct state assistance in financing the secondary school building programme.[129] Lemass immediately backed the proposal and the new initiative was announced publicly on 13 February 1964, only nine days after it had first been proposed by Hillery. The Taoiseach himself made the announcement in St Patrick's Training College, Drumcondra, that the government would initiate 'a new departure' for secondary education. Lemass indicated that Hillery would soon introduce a scheme of direct building grants to secondary schools for the first time.[130] The timing of the announcement was dictated by party politics. Lemass's urgency was explained by the imminence of two by-elections, to be held on 19 February in Kildare and Cork, which would be crucial for the stability of his minority government. But the introduction of capital grants was also designed to satisfy the hierarchy and to secure their collaboration with the comprehensive schools initiative. The new scheme, which came into effect from May 1964, provided for grants to the secondary school authorities which would cover up to 60 per cent of the costs incurred in building or extending eligible secondary schools.[131] Despite its highly political timing, Lemass's announcement marked a significant advance from the conservative and minimalist approach followed by successive governments in education.

The considerable attempts by Hillery to satisfy the concerns of the hierarchy did not pave the way for comprehensive schools as smoothly as he had hoped. Conway congratulated Lemass and Hillery on the scheme for building grants, acknowledging that it would help to relieve the financial burdens shouldered by clerical schools and religious congregations.[132] The archbishop was certainly more concerned about securing specific concessions than disputing the principle of the scheme at this stage. But most bishops remained reluctant to collaborate with the foundation of comprehensive schools. While the hierarchy was no longer opposed to the scheme in principle, several bishops continued to raise objections to the establishment of the new schools in their dioceses. Hillery failed in May 1964 to secure the agreement of Joseph Rodgers, Bishop of Killaloe, for a new comprehensive school at Shannon.[133] Michael Browne, Bishop of Galway, was staunchly opposed to the entire initiative. Browne sought Hillery out at the opening of St Munchin's secondary school in Limerick and warned him against going ahead with comprehensive schools at all.[134] The department faced an impasse in its negotiations with the bishops by the summer of 1964.

'They will have a strike in the exams ...'

The prolonged negotiations over the comprehensive schools became intertwined with another sensitive area in the relations between church and state, the conflict between the minister and the lay secondary teachers. The Association of Secondary Teachers, Ireland (ASTI), which represented the interests of lay teachers in the secondary schools, embarked on large-scale industrial action in 1964 to vindicate their claim to maintain a higher salary than primary teachers. The cumbersome industrial relations procedures for considering salary claims from the teaching profession were an invitation to strife. Claims by each group of teachers were assessed by separate conciliation and arbitration panels, opening the way to competing pay claims by primary and secondary teachers that sought to change the relative position of each group. The Irish National Teachers Organisation (INTO) secured a considerable salary increase in 1963, which narrowed the gap in salary between primary and secondary teachers. Their success immediately triggered a pay claim by the ASTI to restore the previous relativity in salaries between the two groups.[135] This claim was rejected by the arbitrator, and the Standing Committee of the ASTI warned Hillery in March 1964 of their 'grave dissatisfaction' with the arbitration findings.[136] Ó Raifeartaigh warned Hillery of what was to come:

> The secretary came in [to my office] in his usual seemingly absentminded way and said 'They will have a strike in the exams sir.'[137]

The secretary's prediction soon proved accurate. The ASTI threatened to impose a ban on co-operation with the Certificate examinations by its members, unless the minister acted to deliver their salary claim. Hillery was confronted with the real prospect that the state exams would not be held at all, as most of the examiners who marked the papers and many of the exam superintendents were secondary teachers.[138] But it was virtually impossible for the minister to meet the ASTI demand; this would have obliged Hillery to overrule the arbitrator and infuriate the INTO by unilaterally widening the salary gap between primary and secondary teachers.[139] Even if Hillery had wished to do so, he could not have secured the support of the government. Lemass was opposed to any move that would undermine the existing industrial relations process, and he refused to meet ASTI representatives in the course of the dispute on the basis that the association was seeking to 'strike at the roots of the Conciliation and Arbitration machinery'.[140] Hillery warned the ASTI leaders in early May that he could not intervene to change the decision of the independent arbitrator, but they felt that applying enough pressure would force him to yield: 'When I told them that they had created an insoluble problem, they replied airily "You'll think of something" and went their way.'[141] The minister, however, refused to back down and the ASTI instructed their members to withhold any co-operation with the

Certificate exams. The stage was set for the most bitter and protracted dispute of Hillery's term as Minister for Education.

Hillery was determined to ensure that the Leaving Certificate exams at least would be held; the challenge of recruiting examiners was sufficiently daunting that he was initially willing to drop the Intermediate Certificate for 1964. But when he brought the issue before the government, he not only secured support for going ahead in the face of the ASTI exam ban, but was also persuaded to hold the junior cycle exam as well.[142] The minister sought to secure the collaboration of the school managers in providing superintendents for the exams, but failed to get it. The managerial authorities elegantly evaded this request by assuring Hillery that they would give the same co-operation as they had given in previous years – and no more.[143] The managerial bodies requested that the ASTI withdraw its threat of industrial action, but they tacitly supported the secondary teachers once the action went ahead. Most managers did nothing to assist the department in holding the exams while some actively supported the ASTI.[144] The ASTI enjoyed close connections with the managerial bodies and especially with the Catholic Church. The association's officers met Archbishop McQuaid privately in May 1964 and he sought unsuccessfully to act as an intermediary between the ASTI and the government.[145] The Catholic managerial bodies were already concerned at the implications of the comprehensive schools scheme for secondary education. Moreover, they were seriously alarmed by the increasing activism of the state in education and by Hillery's willingness to take major initiatives without consulting them.[146] It was a salary dispute that triggered the bitter conflict between the Department of Education and the secondary teachers, but the tacit support of most school managers for the ASTI was influenced by a wider suspicion of Hillery's reforming policies and by resentment, especially among the Catholic managerial bodies, at the growing influence of the state in education.

It was obvious that if Hillery and the officials wished to hold the exams, they would have to do so on their own. The department put advertisements in the national newspapers to recruit examiners and supervisors. Hillery also issued a statement criticising the managerial bodies for their failure to co-operate with the department in holding the exams and appealed for support from the wider community.[147] This appeal for public support was more successful than Hillery had anticipated; on 2 June he was able to tell the Dáil that satisfactory arrangements had been made to hold both state exams, which would commence on the following day.[148] The department succeeded in holding the exams and assessing the results despite the fierce opposition of the ASTI. This was no mean achievement, not least because the exams were conducted in a sulphurous atmosphere, dominated by public recrimination and unprecedented rancour between the department and many secondary teachers. Exam superintendents made numerous complaints that efforts were made to intimidate them by individual teachers. A supervisor from Limerick, Michael O'Connor, stated that ASTI members harassed him and claimed that 'a large car pulled up and photographed me in gangster style as I was leaving the Post Office after posting the exam envelopes.'[149] There was no doubt that at least some of the allegations of intimidation were well founded. The ASTI itself denied that any intimidation had taken place. But the Standing Committee had instructed its members on 12 May to follow a policy of 'complete non-fraternisation with superintendents' at exam centres; they asked every member 'to find out and forward to Head Office the name, address and occupation' of any superintendent appointed by the department in their local area, presumably with a view to exerting pressure on them to withdraw.[150] While the ASTI officers publicly warned against intimidating superintendents, local members either took action on their own account or felt that they were following the openly proclaimed strategy of the association to disrupt the exams.

Hillery also received reports that several school managers had ostracised superintendents and attempted to obstruct the holding of the exams. He complained directly to McQuaid about the behaviour of various school managers in Dublin, who had declined to offer meals to superintendents.[151] Hillery also brought a more serious complaint by supervisors at the Cistercian College, Roscrea, to McQuaid's attention; this time it was alleged that most members of the order had refused to co-operate with the superintendents and teachers had constantly harassed them. The minister told McQuaid bluntly that the reports were 'a terrible indictment of members of a prominent Religious Order' and hoped that no other school authorities had shown such 'utter irresponsibility.'[152] Hillery warned that he might have to make a public statement about the situation in due course, on the basis that the actions of many school managers were already 'a source of public scandal'.[153] Hillery was undoubtedly correct in believing that a high proportion of school managers aided and abetted the ASTI in their efforts to disrupt the exams. It was no accident that the association's Standing Committee formally expressed its thanks to the managerial bodies on 15 June 'for their co-operation and support in the dispute with the Minister for Education'.[154] While not all managers actively set out to assist the ASTI, some certainly did and the managerial bodies as a whole refused to co-operate with the department. Hillery's correspondence with McQuaid highlighted that the department was not simply in dispute with the ASTI, but embroiled in an undeclared conflict with the secondary school managerial authorities.

The dispute over the state exams inflamed the existing tensions between Hillery and the Catholic educational authorities. But even before the bitter dispute with the ASTI, Hillery was already exasperated with the hostility of most Catholic bishops towards the comprehensive schools plan. His concerns were expressed in a draft letter to Conway in May 1964, in which Hillery warned that he was 'seriously disturbed at some recent trends as between Church and State in education'.[155] The minister was critical of the attitude of the school managers towards the exam ban and the opposition of various bishops to comprehensive schools. He complained that he was being 'held back by invisible threads' in his attempt to provide second-level education for the children of poor families.[156] The letter was drafted by officials and it expressed Hillery's concerns in a measured and diplomatic way, but his frustration with the hierarchy's tactics was unmistakable. The letter was not sent at the time, probably because Hillery was preoccupied with the exam dispute. But Hillery's anger with the obstructionist approach of the Catholic bishops was expressed more bluntly in a private note, which he composed around the same time. If Hillery's public initiatives alarmed managers and bishops, his private views on the Catholic Church's dominant role in education were potentially explosive:

> I can go along with organised religion as long as it is used for the good of people or the glory of God, whatever difficulties I may have in forming satisfactory personal images on these points, but it seems to me that the 'authority' of the church is used to *prevent* new developments and so deprive persons of education in case the priests' little castles would fall. And so the Glory – the only Glory they recognise – of the hierarchy and priests would diminish. They can delay if I deal with them in a courteous way.[157]

The final terse comment signalled the depth of Hillery's frustration and his determination to proceed even at the risk of open conflict with the hierarchy. As it turned out a clash between the minister and the bishops was averted, though not by any great outbreak of goodwill on either side. The ASTI dispute provided an unexpected but potent weapon for Hillery. MacGearailt compiled a dossier of complaints from superintendents at exam centres concerning intimidation by some ASTI members at the height of the industrial action. Moreover the assistant secretary also chronicled the actions of those clerical and religious managers, who had assisted efforts to disrupt the exams and ostracised exam superintendents.[158] Hillery initially intended to send a copy of the dossier to all the bishops, combined with a demand that the hierarchy should publicly condemn the actions of the school managers.[159] But this letter was never sent; a draft version still survives in Hillery's personal papers. Instead, Hillery accepted MacGearailt's advice to use the file in a less public but more effective fashion. Hillery asked Hanly and Fergus to meet him privately in the department:

> But I sent for them, and it was the time I was trying to get them to accept what I was doing. I said, 'I have this record of what priests and nuns did during the strike and I don't think the public would like to see this.'[160]

He believed that he had no alternative but to threaten the bishops that the dossier would find its way into the public domain. He was prepared to follow through with a public statement on the dispute and to confront the hierarchy openly if necessary. But the behind-the-scenes intrigue succeeded where more conventional negotiations had fallen short. Hanly and Fergus quietly informed Hillery that the bishops would drop their objections to the first wave of comprehensive schools:

> Soon after there was some function on, I think it was the primary teachers who had a Mass and a cup of tea; but they asked to see me, the two of them and they said 'we were thinking about what you told us and we'll agree to your [plan], whatever you are doing in education'. They said 'we don't want another Dr Browne'. It was a big break-through.[161]

The bishops were undoubtedly concerned to avoid public revelations of the extensive involvement by school managers in the recent dispute, which would have caused a great deal of embarrassment to the Catholic Church. It was significant too that the episcopal representatives mentioned their wish to avoid 'another Dr Browne'. It was only twelve years since Noel Browne had resigned as Minister for Health, following the rejection of the Mother and Child scheme by the inter-party government; the opposition of the hierarchy was widely regarded as a key factor in the defeat of the scheme and Browne's retreat into the political wilderness.

The shadow of the Mother and Child scheme still lay over church-state relations, providing a useful backdrop for Hillery in this instance. The bishops backed away from the dreaded prospect of a confrontation with another reforming minister, who on this occasion commanded the crucial support of the Taoiseach.

The hierarchy was still by no means reconciled to comprehensive schools as a model for future development in second-level education, but they had accepted the foundation of the new institutions on a pilot basis in rural areas, in line with Hillery's original proposal. Although further disputes inevitably arose between the department and the bishops, especially concerning co-education, the hierarchy had reluctantly accepted the principle of comprehensive education. The eventual outcome of the negotiations may appear relatively modest. Only a small number of comprehensive schools were built over the following two decades. But the initiative triggered further radical changes in second level education; community schools incorporating key features of the comprehensive model became an integral part of the educational sector in the 1970s. The bishops also implicitly accepted the direct intervention of the state to provide broadly based post-primary education, which had been denounced as revolutionary in June 1963.

Hillery played his hand with considerable political skill. He was unyielding on the principle of establishing comprehensive schools, but made concessions to the hierarchy on various points of detail within the scheme. He took a broadly conciliatory approach until close to the end of the negotiations, offering assurances to deal with specific concerns raised by the bishops. But in the end it was not primarily the commitments given by Hillery, but his assurance that the department's file on the ASTI dispute would never see the light of day which influenced the bishops. Hillery succeeded, where others had failed, in navigating the complex labyrinth of negotiation with the Catholic hierarchy. Hillery's success in establishing the right of the state to make policy and intervene effectively in second level education was the most significant achievement of his term in Education.

Politics in Clare

His own constituency was not neglected in the general movement towards educational reform. Hillery opened a new national school in Miltown Malbay in 1963, to replace the dilapidated building in which he himself had been educated.[162] He also took the decision to include Shannon in the first wave of comprehensive schools; there was a genuine educational case for a post-primary school to serve the industrial development zone in Shannon, but the decision had an obvious political dimension. Hillery's record as Minister for Education was a significant asset to the government nationally when Lemass called a general election in March 1965. Fianna Fáil allocated one of its television broadcasts to education and Hillery presented the broadcast on 30 March.[163] It is unlikely that his efforts had much impact on the outcome nationally; Fianna Fáil's campaign was fought under the slogan 'Let Lemass Lead On' and was dominated by the party leader.[164] But Hillery's performance received a decisive local endorsement in the general election on 7 April. Hillery secured 14,372 first preferences, over one-third of the total vote in the constituency.[165] It was the most striking electoral triumph of his career: his vote in Clare reached a comparable level to de Valera's in the previous generation. Hillery's popularity delivered a significant increase in Fianna Fáil's local vote and Ó Ceallaigh was also easily re-elected. The party also improved its position at a national level, winning exactly half the seats in the Dáil and Lemass returned to power with a working majority.

The Hillery legacy

Hillery's considerable achievements in education have been overshadowed not only by the genuine accomplishments of his successors, especially Donogh O'Malley, but also by O'Malley's skilful use of the media to promote himself and his initiatives. The announcement of free post-primary education by O'Malley in September 1966 ensured that his name was forever associated with the transformation of the Irish educational system. Yet it was Hillery who took the lead in launching the reforming policies, which began the transformation of the educational sector. He also did a great deal to transform the Cinderella status of the Department of Education. The department under Hillery adopted a proactive function in managing and directing the expansion of the educational system for the first time. The appointment of the survey team in 1962 was one of the most influential policy decisions of the Lemass era. The survey team would influence Irish educational policy long after Hillery ceased to be Minister for Education. Hillery's other great contribution to the expansion of Irish education was the policy announcement on 20 May 1963. His statement launched an open-ended process of educational reform and reflected a new commitment by the Irish state to broadly based second level education. The comprehensive schools pilot project was the first of the major reforming initiatives, which transformed the Irish educational system in the 1960s. The successful launch of reforming policies in education owed a great deal to the constructive interaction between Hillery and Lemass. Hillery benefited greatly from Lemass's policy activism and took full advantage of the Taoiseach's support to pursue a gradualist policy of reform.

Education became a key area of concern for the Irish state from 1959, following a generation in which educational provision was largely delegated to the churches and the department was assigned a distinctly subordinate role. Hillery transformed the department from a political backwater into a major reforming ministry. His term of office brought the development of sustained intervention by the state in the educational system as a whole, as well as the development of key policy themes that would be pursued by his immediate successors. But Hillery did not simply prepare the way for more dramatic and far-reaching initiatives promoted by his successors; his proactive reforming approach marked a decisive break with the conservative consensus of the previous generation and delivered lasting changes in the state's educational policy.

8.

Lemass's Lieutenant
1965–1966

If education moved from being a peripheral concern to a central preoccupation of the political establishment during Hillery's tenure, his next portfolio had been at the heart of political and economic developments in the Irish state for over a generation. Following Fianna Fáil's re-election in April 1965, Lemass appointed Hillery as Minister for Industry and Commerce. His new department was the Taoiseach's old stamping ground; the department under Lemass's direction had been instrumental in constructing the protectionist regime that he was now moving to dismantle. While Lemass as Taoiseach co-operated more closely with T. K. Whitaker in the Department of Finance than with his former officials in Industry and Commerce, the department remained important across a wide range of economic policy issues. Industry and Commerce also took in the increasingly fraught area of labour relations and industrial disputes. Hillery was keenly aware of the department's traditional role in economic development and of its high status as Lemass's former bailiwick.

He was worried at his own lack of expertise in the economic arena and expressed his concerns at a farewell party given by the senior officials in his former department:'I remember I said to Dr O'Raftery,"I'm not a bit sure of myself in this new one". He said "you'll gobble it up, sir".'[1] Hillery drew some reassurance from this, but he might have experienced still more trepidation had he realised that his political life for the next four years would be dominated by industrial relations troubles and the politics of labour.

Lemass's selection of Hillery as Minister for Industry and Commerce was part of a generational change in the government, as the Taoiseach promoted several prominent younger TDs to key positions. Lemass's final government in April 1965 brought the most radical changes in the Cabinet of his time in power.[2] Jack Lynch succeeded Jim Ryan, a founding member of the party, as Minister for Finance; Hillery took over from Lynch at Industry and Commerce. Donogh O'Malley and George Colley entered the Cabinet for the first time. Charles Haughey remained as Minister for Agriculture, while Brian Lenihan had recently made his mark as a reforming Minister for Justice. Only Lemass himself and Frank Aiken, Minister for External Affairs, remained of the generation that had fought in the war of independence and the civil war.[3] Hillery owed his appointment not just to his relative youth (he was 42 in May 1965) but also to his firm support for the Taoiseach's policies. He shared Lemass's vision of a prosperous, outward-looking Ireland, taking its place within an expanding European Economic Community (EEC). Hillery had never displayed much sympathy for the traditional Sinn Féin virtues of protectionism and self-sufficiency even as a candidate in harness with de Valera. As a minister under Lemass, he embraced the new orthodoxy of export-led investment, tariff reduction and preparation for EEC membership. Hillery recognised the scale of the challenge faced by the Irish economy in preparing for eventual accession to the EEC:'Economically we were unfit and needed to boost our economic activity. We had to think as a competitive economy. Most of all our people had to be ready, workers and management in particular'.[4] This was very much in line with Lemass's convictions and reflected the Taoiseach's influence on the younger man at this stage of his career.

The managerial approach within Hillery's new department marked a dramatic change from his previous experience in education. The officials within the Department of Industry and Commerce maintained established working practices, which made for a more settled environment than the frenetic atmosphere in the Department of Education. Lemass had initiated a regular meeting between the minister, the secretary and assistant secretaries, which was held every Monday, to review the developments of the previous week and discuss issues to be decided in the following week. Hillery not only maintained this practice but found it valuable enough that he extended it to other departments where he served as a minister.[5] Industry and Commerce also operated more formal procedures for access to the minister, much to Hillery's relief. Probably due to his inexperience, Hillery had allowed senior officials free access to his office in Education and was frequently interrupted by officials gravely concerned at the latest educational crisis. Industry and Commerce did things very differently. Hillery liked and respected J. C. B. McCarthy, the secretary, not least because of the way in which he managed the department. Hillery left a vivid portrayal of McCarthy's *modus operandi*:

> No one ran into your office, you got a buzzer, and J. C. B. McCarthy was very calm. An official in Education would run in with a terrible problem. JCB would buzz and he would say 'Minister, I have three possible solutions for a problem and I would like to discuss it with you, if I may'. I thought that was beautiful, because the problem didn't come first![6]

McCarthy was a shrewd operator, who had a keen appreciation of how to manage politicians as well as officials. He worked in a very different way from the scholarly and mildly eccentric Ó Raifeartaigh. Yet the differences between the two departments had more to do with institutional development than differing personalities. Industry and Commerce benefited from its long association with Lemass, its place at the heart of protectionist economic policy and its vital role in developing Irish industry. All of these elements established Industry and Commerce unmistakably as a major department of government and contributed to the development of its distinctive working methods; the department's institutional history since 1922 also underpinned the self-assurance of its officials. The Department of Education was only just establishing itself as a major force in its own area by the early 1960s. It was hardly surprising that a more frenetic and volatile atmosphere prevailed in Marlborough Street than in the more secure environment of Industry and Commerce.

The structured management system in his new department provided at least one major advantage for Hillery. It helped to ease the transition from an area with which he was instinctively familiar after almost six years in office, to a new sphere which he knew hardly at all. He had no previous experience of industrial policy or labour relations; nor had he displayed a particular interest in the area as a backbench TD. Yet this background was not unusual for a minister; it was (and still is) common for ministers to head departments for which they have no particular expertise or knowledge, especially in the economic area. Hillery soon overcame his initial apprehension and came to welcome the change to a new ministry following such a long tenure in education. If the department's established procedures undoubtedly helped to cushion the impact of the change, Hillery's impressive work ethic also ensured that he quickly settled in to his new post. He was initially surprised by the extent to which the minister was in demand to speak at functions for industrial and commercial associations and confided to Lemass his alarm at the extent of the after-dinner speeches expected of him:

> I had dinners every night, with different associations. I said to Lemass, 'This speech-making is killing me!' He said, 'Have your own meal at home and then go out and say that dinner table now is my desk; I'm working now.' That saved me a lot.[7]

Hillery also felt uncomfortable relying simply on a civil service draft for after-dinner speeches to industrialists. His solution was to write speeches himself on the different areas of the department's activity and use them as a basis for amending texts given to him by officials. This practice, which he maintained throughout his career, had the added bonus of ensuring that he quickly gained a high level of knowledge about the work of his department.[8]

While Hillery was a highly creative minister in education, his position in Industry and Commerce was both more comfortable and more constrained. Hillery had taken the lead in carving out a new role for the state in directing educational expansion and inaugurated an era of exceptional creativity in policy formulation. But there was little scope for radical innovation in an economic portfolio by the mid-1960s. The government's economic strategy was clearly established in the *Second Programme for Economic Expansion*, published in 1963.[9] Any changes in economic policy were usually driven by the Taoiseach, in conjunction with the Department of Finance; Lemass continued to play a central part in Dáil and public debates on the economy. This made Hillery's job easier in some respects, although it also meant that he enjoyed considerably less freedom of action than in education. The Taoiseach's key role was if anything reinforced by a gradual deterioration in the economy, as the rapid expansion of the early 1960s began to lose momentum. The Labour government under Harold Wilson, which came to power in Britain in October 1964, immediately imposed a 15 per cent surcharge on manufactured imports; this measure severely affected Irish exports to Britain.[10] The progress of the Irish economy was also undermined by domestic factors. The consequences of the ninth-round wage agreement negotiated by Lemass in January 1964, which guaranteed a pay increase of 12 per cent to all industrial workers, were being felt by 1965; incomes rose by 20 per cent in two years, outstripping the level of national production by a factor of three.[11] Other economic indicators were also deteriorating; the expansion in industrial employment showed a marked decline in the first quarter of 1965, while prices and expenditure on imports increased in the first half of the year.[12] The government moved to introduce a raft of anti-inflationary measures in July 1965, including restrictions in bank credit for imports, cutbacks in state expenditure and controls on hire-purchase facilities for consumer goods.[13] The urgency of the situation was highlighted when Lemass himself announced most of these measures in the Dáil on 13 July. The Taoiseach also moved a new Control of Prices (Amendment) Bill, giving the Minister for Industry and Commerce the power to control prices on a general basis; the intention was to block all price increases except those dictated by unavoidable changes in the cost of imported materials.[14] It was striking that Lemass, rather than Hillery, introduced the legislation and outlined a detailed rationale for the measures to restrict imports and domestic consumption.

The Taoiseach's speech on 13 July was bleak and emphasised the extent of the economic difficulties that the measures were intended to contain.[15] Hillery, speaking in the same debate on the following day, adopted a more optimistic tone. He described the reversion to price control as 'not a change but a digression from normal government policy', arguing that external circumstances and internal trends required 'a period of rest and consolidation' in the government's economic programme.[16] Hillery presented the measures as a relatively gentle intervention in the economy, which was designed to protect the country's future economic prospects and even suggested that the government was following the medical principle of 'Primum non nocere – first, do not do harm.'[17] His positive portrayal of the government's actions contrasted sharply with Lemass's grim warning that special measures had to be taken now to avert a possible recession either later in the year or at some future date.[18] It was hardly surprising that opposition TDs highlighted the apparent divergence between Lemass and Hillery; James Tully, the Labour TD for Meath, commented sardonically that 'having listened to the Taoiseach and the minister, one wonders whether or not they were talking about the same situation.'[19]

Yet this was essentially a difference of style rather than substance. Hillery's speech reflected his political style, which was usually constructive and low-key. He was also seeking to counter criticisms of the government's record by Fine Gael, which accused Lemass (with good reason) of a dramatic U-turn in restoring price control and claimed less convincingly that the government's actions foreshadowed a major economic crisis. Hillery dismissed opposition claims that Lemass's statement indicated 'anything like a crisis or an impending crisis'; it was merely a temporary response to unfavourable economic trends.[20] Despite its more optimistic tone, Hillery's speech was broadly consistent with Lemass's statement from the previous day. This was most obvious in his attitude to price control. Hillery regarded 'the normal play of competition as the best regulator'; he commented explicitly that 'interference with economic processes must not be lightly undertaken' and would be minimal if it was found to be necessary.[21] This was essentially the same as Lemass's view on 13 July that an effective system of price control could not be achieved indefinitely in a free society, but was at best a temporary expedient.[22] This view of price control as a necessary evil may have influenced Hillery's decision to permit a significant modification of the Bill as it was rushed through the Dáil. On 21 July he accepted an amendment from the Labour leader, Brendan Corish, which required manufacturers and importers to notify the minister of any proposed price increases in commodities covered by the legislation.[23] The effect of the amendment was to give six months' notice to the firms concerned of any decision to impose orders under the Act.[24] This change allowed the legislation to operate more effectively, and alleviated some of the potential problems involved in regulating a system of price control. As a reluctant exponent of price control, Hillery accepted an amendment that would make the use of his powers under the Act less onerous and less frequent.

While Hillery's involvement in economic policy initiatives was essentially peripheral, industrial relations were a very different matter. Hillery was preoccupied from the outset of his term with sustained problems of industrial strife. He played a central part over the following four years in attempting to manage the volatile relationship between the state and the trade unions and in seeking to integrate organised labour within an industrial relations framework that would facilitate the

achievement of the state's economic objectives. Hillery took over as
Minister for Industry and Commerce just as the industrial relations
climate dramatically deteriorated. The national agreement in 1964 did
not fully contain industrial disputes even in its first year, and fuelled rising
expectations among workers for future wage increases.[25] The level of
industrial conflict escalated rapidly in 1965, with several major strikes in
various sectors of the economy. A relatively small number of prolonged
disputes attracted the most public attention and had the most severe
impact on the economy.[26] A strike in the printing industry in 1965 lasted
for ten weeks, causing most newspapers to cease publication for a time;
an even more protracted dispute closed three paper mills in Dublin and
Waterford for eighteen weeks in 1966. Strikes also affected the banks, the
motor assembly industry and Dublin Port in the first half of 1966.[27] Two
semi-state bodies contributed more than their fair share of industrial
unrest; a major bus strike occurred in CIÉ in 1965, while the ESB was
involved in a series of industrial disputes.[28]

Lemass, seriously alarmed by the wave of strikes, warned Hillery of
the necessity for a new code of conduct governing industrial relations.
The Taoiseach urged Hillery on 17 June 1965 to convene a conference
of workers' and employers' organisations 'to consider in a comprehensive
way the possibilities of introducing a new era in industrial relations that
would operate to reduce the danger of strikes.'[29] Lemass hoped that such
a conference might develop 'a code of good conduct' based on moral
rather than legal force. But Hillery was dubious about the prospects for
the success of such an initiative in the prevailing climate, and proceeded
more cautiously by initiating separate informal discussions with the Irish
Congress of Trade Unions and the Federated Union of Employers
(FUE). The wider initiative suggested by Lemass never materialised. But
the Taoiseach was already contemplating legislative changes to establish
a more orderly system of industrial relations and did not rule out legal
restrictions on industrial action. He told Hillery in June that agreement
with the trade unions on a new framework for industrial relations might
not be possible and 'a Bill for consideration by the Dáil must be ready
for the Autumn, whether agreed or not'.[30] Hillery agreed to bring

forward proposals for change, although he also noted that his discussions with employer and union representatives were being pursued 'with all possible speed' and warned that Congress favoured no changes in existing legislation.[31] While events did not move as quickly as Lemass had hoped, Hillery undertook a major review of industrial relations legislation in the autumn, which produced highly controversial proposals for reform.

The initiative for significant changes in the law on industrial relations came from Lemass, although Hillery's department produced two new Bills that embodied the proposed reforms.[32] The Industrial Relations (Amendment) Bill sought to enhance the authority of the Labour Court by giving it the power to enforce binding arbitration of disputes in certain circumstances and extending its remit to include all industrial workers. The Trade Union Bill sought to withdraw legal protection from picketing in any unofficial action; the legislation set out to impose requirements for a secret ballot and a qualified majority in any vote of union members for strike action. The Bill also sought to encourage the formation of recognised groups of unions in each industry and to promote the voluntary amalgamation of trade unions.[33] The government approved the main elements of both Bills in March 1966.[34] The proposed reforms were designed to increase the efficacy of the Labour Court as a dispute-resolution body, to enhance the authority of trade union leaders over their members and to restrict unofficial action by militant groups.

The legislation was not a charter for strike-breaking, but it went far beyond what union leaders could support and even further from what they could persuade their members to accept. When Hillery circulated the proposals to Congress and the FUE in April 1966, the legislation drew an overwhelmingly hostile response from the trade unions. The leadership of Congress firmly opposed the attempt to transform the Labour Court into an arbitration board with the power to enforce its decisions; they were also hostile to the proposed restrictions on industrial action.[35] Most union leaders were suspicious of the government's intentions and strongly opposed to any change in the voluntary system of wage bargaining. The government proceeded cautiously in the face of vehement trade union opposition. Hillery introduced the two Bills in the Dáil in June 1966, but no attempt was made to drive the legislation through the Oireachtas. Instead, Hillery and leading officials of his department undertook detailed consultations with trade union leaders. The proposed legislation was put on ice for almost three years. It was not until February 1969 that Hillery proposed an amended version of the original plan in the Dáil.[36] It soon became obvious that the reform of the legal framework for industrial relations would be a protracted and tortuous process, which did not guarantee any short-term solution to the high level of disputes.

It was against this background of industrial conflict and deadlock that Hillery proposed a significant innovation in the official institutions that interacted with trade unions. Hillery suggested to Lemass the creation of a new Department of Labour early in June 1966; the Taoiseach rapidly adopted the idea, despite the opposition of Jack Lynch. Hillery was, however, surprised by Lemass's next move, which occurred in the midst of a parliamentary debate on 7 June:

> I was in the Dáil chamber and Lemass came and sat beside me. He said, 'If I set up a Department of Labour will you take it?' Obviously he thought it would not be easy or helpful in terms of ambition. I said yes.[37]

As soon as Hillery agreed to head the new department, Lemass announced the initiative immediately in the Dáil. 'So whatever business I had in the Dáil at the time, he wrote a little speech on a piece of paper and stood up, announcing that we were going to have a Department of Labour.'[38] Lemass was not alone in regarding the new department as a difficult and unrewarding assignment. Brendan O'Regan, the chairman of Bord Fáilte, who was friendly with Hillery, told him that taking the Department of Labour was a bad career move.[39] But Hillery was genuinely interested in developing a new framework for resolving labour disputes and believed that he could contribute to the creation of a better industrial relations climate as Minister for Labour.[40] It was not a highly political decision or one that might benefit Hillery's career – his appointment was not really a promotion at all, but at best a sideways move to a department of comparable importance. Moreover, it was evident in June 1966 that the new department would have to cope with intractable problems associated with high wage demands, increasing trade union militancy in certain sectors of the economy and weak central institutions governing industrial relations both at governmental and interest-group levels. It was equally obvious that the Department of Labour would not provide much political capital for its ministerial occupant. Hillery was well aware of the challenges when he took the new post, although he certainly underestimated the degree of controversy and unpopularity that would surround the Department of Labour in an era of widespread industrial conflict.[41] His decision to accept the ministry underlined one of his most unusual features as a politician, his lack of conventional political ambition. Hillery was certainly driven to achieve major policy goals and he was ambitious to succeed in whatever department he accepted; but his career was not built around a burning desire to reach the top of the greasy pole by leading either his party or the government.

Lemass secured the approval of the government to draft a Bill to establish the new department on 10 June 1966 and the legislation was on the statute book barely a month later.[42] The Department of Labour came into being on 13 July 1966.[43] Lemass conducted a reshuffle of the Cabinet on the same day, and Hillery became the first Minister for Labour since 1922. It was apparent that delivering more effective management of industrial relations lay at the core of the new department's mission, not least because its establishment was publicly announced in the midst of a serious strike in the ESB.[44] While the creation of the new department would not resolve the intractable labour disputes that dominated the industrial relations scene, the initiative recognised the importance of the area in an unmistakable fashion and enhanced the government's ability to engage effectively with the trade unions and employers.

Hillery enjoyed his relatively brief term as Minister for Industry and Commerce and would later look back on it with some nostalgia. It was in some respects the most straightforward and least demanding post of his lengthy ministerial career. But it was evident too that he did not have the

time or opportunity to leave a significant imprint on policy as he had
done in education. The only major innovation for which Hillery was
directly responsible, the creation of the Department of Labour, occurred
right at the end of his tenure. Lemass's dominance across most aspects of
economic policy was a notable feature of Hillery's term. Hillery did not
resent his subordinate role and was comfortable with Lemass's decisive
governing style. Yet the younger man was not simply a loyal assistant of the
Taoiseach; especially on industrial relations, Hillery was developing his
own distinctive ideas, which were very different from the Taoiseach's
interventionist approach. Hillery's firmly held views on the management
of industrial disputes would lead to frequent private disagreement with
Lemass.

9.

The Politics of Labour
1966–1969

The first challenge facing the new Minister for Labour was to establish his own department. The Department of Labour was essentially carved out of Lemass's old empire in Industry and Commerce. The new department was firmly associated with industrial relations from the outset; it was widely believed, not least by Lemass himself, that the primary reason for its existence was to relieve the turmoil caused by industrial conflict. Hillery was concerned, however, that he not be seen simply as the Minister for Strikes. In his first major speech after taking over as Minister for Labour, he publicly emphasised that the new department was not simply designed 'to bring orderliness into the area of industrial relations', but was also responsible for the implementation of the government's manpower policies, and for the protection of the health and safety of workers.[1] Hillery was correct, at least in principle. The functions transferred from Industry and Commerce to Labour included worker protection, health and safety issues and manpower policy, as well as industrial relations. Yet crucially all of the new department's responsibilities involved interaction with the trade union movement, and Hillery's central concern for the following three years would be to manage the turbulent relationship between the Irish state and organised labour.

The practical issues involved in establishing the new department were soon resolved. Lemass's first piece of advice to Hillery after announcing the establishment of the new department was typically pragmatic: 'go off and get a building now'.[2] Hillery, accompanied by Paddy McCarthy, a senior official who headed the Labour Division within Industry and Commerce, inspected Annesley House on Mespil Road. The building had been destined for the IDA but Hillery appropriated it instead for the Department of Labour.[3] Over 500 civil servants were involved in establishment of the new department, with the transfer of the Labour Division from Industry and Commerce and the agency dealing with employment exchanges from Social Welfare. The transfer of the staff was accomplished rapidly, but not without some tension between Hillery and one of his fellow ministers. George Colley, who took over as Minister for Industry and Commerce, was unhappy at the extent of the transfer and made his feelings known to Hillery: 'When I left, George was meant to come over from Education. He called over to see me and asked "are you leaving me any staff, are you taking all the staff?"'[4] Colley got little satisfaction from the exchange, as Hillery did not choose the vast majority of the staff being transferred himself, and the officials who determined the allocation were following Lemass's instructions to establish the new department as quickly as possible. Tadhg Ó Cearbhaill, then assistant secretary to the government, was swiftly appointed as secretary of the Department of Labour; Paddy McCarthy took up the new post of Chief Adviser in the new department.[5] Hillery soon came to appreciate Ó Cearbhaill's ability and unfailing good humour in coping with the severe demands on the fledgling department.[6] McCarthy's detailed knowledge of industrial relations as a former chief conciliation officer of the Labour Court would also prove invaluable to the new Minister for Labour. Hillery was undoubtedly fortunate in having officials of the calibre of Ó Cearbhaill and McCarthy in his new department; he needed all the official ingenuity at his disposal to grapple with the intractable problems of labour relations.

The new Minister for Labour saw the development of initiatives for the retraining and protection of workers, in preparation for the challenges of free trade and accession to the EEC, as a key part of his brief. Hillery acted to introduce redundancy payments for workers who were laid off; it was the first time such a scheme had been established in the Republic. The Redundancy Payments Act, 1967, which came into effect on 1 January 1968, covered about 600,000 workers.[7] The legislation provided for payments to all full-time workers who were insured for benefits under the Social Welfare Act, excluding part-time employees who worked fewer than 21 hours per week.[8] The scheme, which was financed by contributions from workers and employers, involved both a lump-sum payment and modest weekly payments to workers who lost their jobs. The Department of Labour inaugurated a resettlement scheme at the same time, providing allowances for workers who had to move away from their homes to take up new employment, which was financed entirely by the state.[9] The new schemes were designed to cope with the demands of an expanding economy and offer a measure of protection to workers who were laid off due to rationalisation in Irish industry or the introduction of new technologies. Hillery hoped that the legislation would encourage greater flexibility in the labour force and help Irish industries to meet the demands of competition in the European Community.[10] He also sought to promote the retraining of workers to acquire new skills, as an equally important element in preparing Ireland for the challenges of EEC membership. The Industrial Training Authority (AnCo), which was established in 1967, took over responsibility from An Chéard Chomhairle for regulating the system of apprenticeship. Hillery sought to ensure that the new Authority provided training in vocational skills for adult workers, which it did with varying degrees of success.[11] These initiatives were significant reforms which were arguably more important than any measure taken by Hillery to contain industrial disputes, although they did not attract nearly as much attention as the widespread discord in labour relations.

The Department of Labour had barely been established when Hillery faced severe pressure to resolve the wave of strikes. Influential elements within the business community demanded immediate action by the government to control industrial disputes. The Chambers of Commerce of Ireland appealed to Lemass in June 1966 for effective intervention by the government to resolve strikes 'having vicious impact on our economy' and warned of 'irreparable damage' if urgent action was not taken.[12] While Lemass had no intention of imposing the legal controls on union activity sought by employers, he certainly favoured vigorous intervention by ministers to resolve industrial disputes. While Hillery was still Minister for Industry and Commerce, Lemass often expressed concern about the prolonged nature of various disputes and raised the possibility of direct intervention by the minister. In May 1966, the Taoiseach asked Hillery how the long-running strike in the paper mills might be resolved, giving a broad hint that ministerial involvement might be desirable: 'Is this completely deadlocked or is there any chance of a Labour Court or other intervention resulting in an agreement?'[13] Hillery's reply was emphatic and rejected any possibility of ministerial intervention: 'The Labour Court people have been keeping in touch with the situation and I would not favour intervention by anyone else.'[14] The exchange signalled key differences between the two men on the management of industrial relations.

Soon after the creation of the Department of Labour, Hillery faced strong pressure from Lemass to intervene in several ongoing strikes. The Taoiseach frequently phoned Hillery to make a strong case for ministerial action, but Hillery was determined not to intervene in strikes on a regular basis. He had a clear view of what would happen if he did: 'any intervention meant the strikers gained the day. I thought that was where Lemass was wrong and Jack was wrong.'[15] Lemass was sensitive to the demands of the trade union movement, which he had attempted to accommodate in a national understanding; he was also deeply concerned that industrial conflict should be contained due to its damaging economic impact.[16] Hillery was, however, resolutely opposed to ministerial intervention on a general basis, believing that constant involvement by the minister in mediating strikes would decisively undermine the Labour Court and exacerbate industrial militancy over time. The sharp divergence between the two men introduced a new note of tension into their working relationship and at one point Hillery even felt that his time as Minister for Labour might be short-lived:

> Lemass kept asking me to intervene. I refused, and at one time I felt he might be tempted to fire me but he did not. 'People would expect the new minister for Labour to intervene,' he said on the phone. But I did not yield.[17]

In fact, Hillery never came close to being sacked or moved to another department. While Lemass was undoubtedly frustrated at Hillery's stand, he did not seek to overrule the younger man. The Taoiseach was willing to allow a strong-minded minister to develop his own approach to a considerable extent. Hillery believed that Lemass respected his strongly-held views on industrial relations, although 'that was hard for him because he was a better politician than I was'.[18] The new Minister for Labour was well aware that brokering the solution to an industrial dispute ended the immediate disruption and relieved public pressure on the government. But he believed that direct intervention was subject to the law of unintended consequences, generating a series of unanticipated and damaging effects even in the short term. Hillery was convinced that ministerial intervention to concede pay claims marginalised the existing structures for resolving disputes, undermined union leaders if militant strike committees were able to make major gains and generated competition among unions for more favourable pay settlements.[19] Moreover, the cost of increased pay deals, which were the usual result of political intervention, would be passed on to the wider community, as excessive wage inflation would contribute to rising prices and damage economic productivity. This analysis was well founded in many respects and later became widely accepted in the era of social partnership – but it was well before its time in the late 1960s.

Despite their occasional differences, Lemass respected Hillery and generally approved of his performance as a minister. Moreover the older man increasingly saw Hillery as a potential successor. Although he faced no political pressure to do so, Lemass decided to retire in the autumn of 1966. Lemass and Hillery regularly met for lunch in the government dining room and at one of these lunches Lemass raised the issue of the succession. He told the younger man that he was retiring soon and quietly sounded him out about taking over as Taoiseach: 'He said, "You could do it"; and I said I wouldn't. He was the type that would just accept what you said.'[20] Lemass also approached Jack Lynch around the same time as his overture to Hillery; Lynch, too, initially rejected the prospect of becoming Taoiseach.[21] Lemass was seeking a candidate who would unite the party and appeal effectively to the wider electorate; it was significant that he considered Lynch and Hillery the potential successors who would best accomplish these objectives. When Lemass announced his intention to retire in November 1966, Fianna Fáil faced the prospect of a deeply divisive internal contest for the first time since its foundation. The two leading candidates to succeed the Taoiseach, Charles Haughey and George Colley, each commanded fervent loyalty from their own supporters, but neither was broadly acceptable within the party or even the government. Lemass headed off the divisive contest by persuading Lynch to stand.[22] Hillery was one of the ministers who advised the Taoiseach to approach Lynch:

> When I got talking to Lemass and he asked me what I thought; so I said, "You're in a fix now because the party is divided between these two boys and they are not wanted." Jack was ahead of me in the government. He was popular with the party, terribly popular with the country. I said [to Lemass], 'you'll have to ask him'.[23]

Lynch easily won the support of the Fianna Fáil parliamentary party, decisively defeating George Colley after the withdrawal of all the other contenders, and was elected as Taoiseach on 10 November. Hillery was confirmed as Minister for Labour in Lynch's first government. Hillery enjoyed a casually friendly relationship with the new Taoiseach, although they were not close political allies in 1966.

Lemass's retirement removed both the most dominant public figure of the era and the leader who had done most to shape Hillery's political career. Although the Clare doctor began his career as de Valera's junior colleague, Lemass was Hillery's mentor in politics and exerted a lasting influence on the younger man's political outlook. Yet Hillery had already charted his own course as Minister for Labour under Lemass and he would take a still more independent line following Lynch's elevation. Hillery was conscious of the sharp divergence in political style between Lynch and Lemass:

> Jack was more like Dev, I would say. I wasn't in government with Dev, but I remember Kevin Boland saying one day that they [the Cabinet] were 'let talk anyway'. Lemass would cut you off! But Jack would be sitting there and you would wonder was he there at all. He would be chewing a piece of paper and you would wonder was he listening.[24]

Lynch's laid-back and consensual political style gave all of his ministers greater freedom of action than they had enjoyed under Lemass. The new regime enhanced Hillery's ability to blaze a new trail in the Department of Labour.

Hillery's strategy was more idealistic and less overtly political than the former Taoiseach's favoured approach. He believed that in the short-term strikes had to be allowed to take their course without any direct political intervention. This meant that the government had to be willing to accept some disruption to services if necessary and to take the public criticism for not intervening in disputes.[25] In the meantime, the new Department of Labour would seek to develop the existing industrial relations structures and establish a system of negotiation and dispute-resolution that commanded widespread acceptance from the trade unions. This strategy was not hostile to organised labour; Hillery accepted the increasing power of trade unions in the workplace as a reality and sought to bring the

unions within a new labour relations framework that would deliver
industrial stability. He was, however, undoubtedly attempting to change
attitudes within the trade union movement and persuade union members
to reassess their tactics. He hoped that his refusal to intervene in disputes
on a general basis would lead to a reappraisal of the value of militant
action within the trade union movement:

> I believed that the unions had to learn. There had to be a
> balance between protection of the rights of workers and
> the rights of the other people in the community and
> especially those who suffered not having an alternative to
> the service being withdrawn.[26]

Hillery aimed to encourage a more measured approach by unions in
pursuing claims that might affect the interests of society as a whole. His
objectives command respect and he was certainly correct that the
interventionist strategy favoured by Lemass had done little to stop the
escalation of industrial disputes in the mid-1960s. Yet Hillery's strategy
also had its limitations; he overestimated the degree of influence that many
union leaders could exercise over their members, and underestimated the
tenacity that many union members would show in pursuing strike action,
regardless of any expectation of political intervention. Implementing his
approach in the volatile industrial relations climate of the late 1960s also
posed formidable challenges and risked a backlash from the trade union
movement.

The creation of the new department and Hillery's reluctance to resolve
strikes in favour of the unions led to considerable tension between the
new Minister for Labour and some prominent union leaders, which
culminated in a memorable public clash between Hillery and John
Conroy, the general president of the Irish Transport and General Workers'
Union (ITGWU). Conroy served as President of Congress in 1967–8 and
was one of the most influential union leaders of his generation. The
veteran union leader emerged as the most prominent critic of the
Department of Labour. He claimed in an article for *Liberty* magazine in

1966 that the department's declared programme of promoting retraining and redundancy payments meant only that the government had a hidden agenda to undermine job security and intensify unemployment.[27] Conroy also consistently attacked Fianna Fáil's increasing connections with big business, which were underlined in particular by the activity of Taca, a support group of wealthy corporate figures which channelled extensive financial support to Fianna Fáil.[28] There was undoubtedly a wider political context to Conroy's frequent criticisms of the government. The ITGWU under his leadership re-affiliated with the Labour Party from January 1968, resuming an old relationship sundered by the split in the labour movement over the 'red scare' in the 1940s. Shortly after the union's decision to renew its historic links with the party, Conroy denounced government departments on 22 November 1967 as 'among the worst wage-payers and exploiters of manual workers', arguing that ministers would never act voluntarily to ensure that their own workers were paid a 'living wage'.[29] It was against this backdrop that Hillery decided to respond to what he regarded as constant sniping from the union leader.

Hillery made an outspoken public attack on Conroy at a Fianna Fáil function in Bray on Saturday 25 November. He first criticised the ITGWU's decision to affiliate with the Labour Party, arguing that the Transport Union had declared itself to be 'antagonistic' to Fianna Fáil and would have to be treated 'not alone as a trades union but as an active political party'.[30] This was the element of his speech most widely reported – and criticised – in the newspapers the following Monday. But the key theme of Hillery's address was not so much a complaint at the union's political alignments as an extended denunciation of Conroy's rhetoric and tactics. Hillery attacked the union leader's 'recent outpourings' as destructive and demoralising at a time when he might have been expected to take a constructive approach as President of the ICTU. He denounced Conroy's rhetoric as nothing more than 'dishonest grievance peddling'.[31] Hillery's speech caused widespread consternation, not least within the government itself. *The Irish Times* issued a magisterial rebuke on 27 November, wondering 'What got into Dr Paddy Hillery?' The newspaper's editorial commented gravely that 'These are the thoughts that may strike

Dr Hillery in the silent watches of the night; but they need not have been voiced on a public platform'.[32] But the shock at Hillery's outspoken comments was also apparent in official circles, where there was considerable surprise that the usually mild-mannered minister had spoken out at all and even more that he had fired a political broadside against the most powerful union in the country. Jack Lynch hastened to explain away Hillery's comments; a spokesman for Lynch briefed political journalists that Hillery had departed from his script to make off-the-cuff remarks on the political situation.[33] This was a convenient explanation, but unfortunately almost the exact opposite of the truth. Hillery had personally written a script for his speech in Bray, which was considerably more outspoken than the one he actually delivered: 'Tadhg O Cearbhaill persuaded me to cut out a great piece of it. I showed it to Tadhg to avoid surprising him in the newspapers. I met Ken Whitaker [later] and he said, "You shouldn't attack the trade unions." He should have seen the original of the speech!'[34] Hillery's speech in Bray was not a spontaneous outburst at a gathering of the party faithful, but a deliberate and premeditated criticism of the most powerful union leader in the country. It was certainly a striking departure from his usual low-key and cautious political style, but it was a calculated statement and not a political gaffe.

Not everyone was disappointed at his attack on Conroy. The formidable veteran Seán MacEntee, no longer a minister but still a TD, wrote to congratulate Hillery on his comments: 'A few straight punches like yours may, probably would, tumble Conroy from the perch on which Fianna Fáil did a great deal to put him.'[35] Most political observers assumed that Hillery was driven simply by dismay at the restoration of the ITGWU's historic link with the Labour Party. There is little doubt that Hillery was concerned at the Transport Union's decision to return to the Labour Party fold, but this was not the primary motivation for his public attack on Conroy. Hillery was not a conventional party politician. He disliked partisan bickering and rarely got embroiled in personal confrontation with opponents of the party. It was ironic too that Hillery's views on Taca were not greatly different from Conroy's, although he did not share the union leader's fondness for socialist rhetoric. Hillery regarded himself as a 'social republican', who was firmly on the centre-left of the political spectrum. He described Fianna Fáil in July 1966 as the real party of Labour: 'If Ireland had a better Labour Party than Fianna Fáil, I would be in it, but Fianna Fáil rests for its support on the ordinary worker in city and town and country'.[36] This was a sincerely held view that he maintained throughout his political career. But while his analysis of Fianna Fáil was historically valid, the rise of Taca meant that the party's claim to represent the 'men of no property' rang increasingly hollow by the late 1960s. It was probably Hillery's awareness of the essential truth of the case against Taca that made some of Conroy's attacks so unwelcome; the union leader was striking uncomfortably close to the bone. Hillery's speech can certainly be seen as an attempt to reassert Fianna Fáil's credentials as the party of urban workers.

Yet an equally compelling motivation for his outspoken response was widely overlooked. Hillery was consistently protective of the civil servants who worked with him and was genuinely angry at Conroy's attacks on the Department of Labour: 'When the Department of Labour was set up, he attacked and he was making out that this department was a kind of political instrument [for the government]. He made awful speeches'.[37] Hillery was not attempting to split the ITGWU, still less to initiate a modern 'red scare' campaign against left-wing union leaders.[38] He was seeking instead to defend his department and to open up a debate on the role of powerful unions in modern Irish society. He set out to emphasise that union leaders had wider obligations to the nation, which went beyond their commitment to their members or sectional agendas. This message was largely lost in the controversy over Hillery's criticism of the Transport Union's link to the Labour Party and raising that particular issue in such a prominent way was undoubtedly a tactical mistake. But a key theme underlying Hillery's speech, which passed largely unnoticed by the media, was that union leaders should adopt a more constructive and less confrontational strategy in their dealings with the government. Whitaker was entitled to question the wisdom of trying to achieve this objective by staging a fight with one of the most powerful union leaders in the country; but Hillery generally sought to engage with the unions, not to undermine them, even if his frustration with Conroy erupted publicly on this occasion.

Despite his public attack on Conroy, Hillery was concerned to establish a constructive relationship between his department and the trade unions; he succeeded with most leading figures in the Irish labour movement. Hillery established a particularly friendly and constructive relationship with Young Jim Larkin, general secretary of the Workers Union of Ireland (WUI) and son of the legendary Big Jim Larkin, who had led the Dublin workers in the 1913 Lockout. Hillery worked closely with Larkin and Jimmy Dunne, a leading Dublin trade unionist who served as President of Congress in 1968–9, in seeking to resolve several major industrial disputes.[39] Even the minister's relations with the ITGWU were not permanently damaged by his clash with Conroy. Shortly afterwards, the union leader defended publicly the union's decision to affiliate to the Labour Party, but did not attack Hillery personally.[40] Conroy later invited Hillery to speak at the union's annual conference, and the minister accepted; while their world-view remained poles apart, neither could afford to ostracise the other. Hillery's concern to develop a constructive dialogue between the government and the trade unions lay at the heart of his vision for industrial relations and provided much of the rationale for his distinctive approach towards industrial disputes.

Hillery declined to intervene directly in successive strikes by power workers in Bord na Móna, which began in November 1967 and dragged on until March 1968.[41] He also remained aloof from an even more bitter and intractable dispute involving the maintenance craft workers in most areas of Irish industry. The origins of the dispute were to be found in a national agreement made by the FUE with the maintenance workers in 1966, which established a single rate of pay for maintenance craft workers throughout Irish industry. Paddy McCarthy predicted disaster as soon as the agreement expired in 1968, warning Hillery of wide-ranging industrial action: 'In two years' time when this is up we'll have a big strike in all the factories'.[42] This prediction proved entirely accurate. The FUE initiative led to the creation of a single negotiating body for the maintenance workers in different factories – the newly-formed national group of maintenance craft unions. This group, consisting of 18 different unions, lacked internal coherence and agreed on little except the need for a substantial pay increase in 1968. The FUE, having let the genie out of the bottle two years before, resolved to stand firm within the government's pay guidelines, which proposed an increase of around £2 per week. The two sides were firmly entrenched in their attitudes and ready for a trial of strength. The group of unions served strike notice without waiting for a hearing of the Labour Court in January 1969.[43] The employers, meanwhile, warned Hillery to stay out of the dispute: 'There was a strike and the employers sent me word, an unnecessary word, that they were going to face the unions and I was to stay out of it. I had no intention of going into it'.[44]

The strike continued for over five weeks and had a devastating short-term impact across Irish industry and on workers not directly involved in the dispute. While the number of maintenance craft workers in most factories was not very large, they were widely spread throughout the manufacturing sector and trade union solidarity naturally applied wherever pickets were placed by the group of unions. About 31,000 employees were out of work at the height of the strike, including only a small proportion drawn from the unions directly involved in the dispute.[45] Hillery resolutely refused to get involved despite the wide-ranging effects of the strike and the failure of several attempts to mediate between the parties by the Labour Court. He believed that the tactics of the group of unions were 'totally unreasonable', but recognised that the dispute could only be solved by negotiation; he had reservations about the wisdom of the stand taken by the employers and especially about their ability to maintain it.[46]

The outcome vindicated his judgement. The dispute ended with the capitulation of the employers. The FUE appealed privately to Hillery to intervene, hoping to gain political cover to concede the claim from the government, but Hillery refused the poisoned chalice.[47] Then the employers' united front collapsed in spectacular fashion; Arthur Rice, Personnel Director of Jacobs, who was the chair of the FUE negotiating committee, found that his own firm had settled with the unions without telling him.[48] He resigned from the committee and the remaining FUE representatives hastened to concede the claim, giving the maintenance unions a wage settlement of about 20 per cent, which was probably even more than they had been looking for in the first place. The result confirmed Hillery's worst fears about the confrontational dynamic that heavily influenced both unions and employers in Irish industrial relations. He deplored the intransigence and ruthless tactics of the craft unions involved in the dispute, but was equally unhappy about the hard-line stand taken by the employers. The strike reinforced Hillery's convictions about the folly of attempting to settle disputes by confrontation rather than negotiation. He recorded his own views privately shortly after the dispute concluded:

> Employers continue to go up the blind alley of taking a stand. While this is a rational reaction to an unreasonable request, it becomes totally irrational in the knowledge which we now have, that the taking of stands means a temporary taking of stands with a total concession at the end of a strike period. In other words, we have the total concession of the claim, plus the strike of varying length, plus the absence of meaningful negotiation.[49]

Hillery was also exasperated by demands from employers, with E. C. Bewley of Jacobs prominent among them, for action by the government to control trade unions, which would merely have inflamed the dispute further:

> Another blind alley, up which employers go screaming, is that the government should do something about these workers. They have yet to learn that the government does not intend to do anything which the employers should be doing themselves.[50]

The maintenance dispute highlighted the limitations of Hillery's power as Minister for Labour, but it also largely vindicated his strategic approach;

even if he had intervened, he could only have provided a political fig leaf to cover the retreat of the employers.

The strategy adopted by Hillery did not mean a complete rejection of political intervention in strikes. Hillery was pragmatic enough to accept that intervention was inevitable in some cases, whether due to the particularly virulent nature of a dispute, its impact on the economy or simply the force of public pressure for a settlement. He acted quietly but effectively to resolve a long-standing conflict between the US multinational General Electric and the ITGWU over union recognition. The corporation refused to recognise trade unions in its Irish subsidiary, 'Emerald Isle', which had been established in the Shannon industrial development zone. Lemass disliked both the company's name and its attitude towards union recognition, but the issue was still unresolved when he retired in November 1966.[51] The EI company soon became the centre of a bitter dispute between General Electric and the union movement. The ITGWU mounted pickets at the EI plant in Shannon in March 1968; the company organised a fleet of private buses to ferry in workers past the pickets and secured an injunction in an attempt to restrain picketing at their premises.[52] The dispute escalated dramatically, as General Electric sought to keep the unions out at any price and the Transport Union continued its campaign even in the face of legal penalties. As feelings ran high on both sides, there were violent clashes between picketers and EI staff, while a bus that had been used to ferry EI workers was later burned out at a garage in Bunratty.[53] The conflict was deeply embarrassing to the government, which wanted to maintain the flow of American investment but was unhappy about General Electric's hostility to unions. Hillery moved to break the deadlock by appealing directly to the head of the corporation:

> I rang the President of General Electric in New York and said I felt he should intervene in the problem of EI in Shannon; that GE did not have a mission against trade unions in Ireland, were getting a good product and had nothing to gain from the struggle against unionisation.[54]

Hillery's intervention paved the way for negotiations between representatives of General Electric and ITGWU officials in Dublin. While the minister was not directly involved in the discussions, he met privately with senior company executives to facilitate an agreement between the corporation and the Transport Union. The negotiations were successful and the corporation agreed to recognise the ITGWU as the sole union representing its workers in Shannon.[55] Hillery worked constructively with John Conroy in resolving the conflict, despite their earlier clash and their wider political differences.

The other major dispute that demanded Hillery's direct involvement was in the ESB; in this case intervention was unavoidable as the strike led to the worst crisis in the power supply since the foundation of the state. The semi-state company, which held sole responsibility for supplying electricity to industry and domestic users, had a deplorable industrial record in the 1960s. The management of the company was in dispute with almost all grades of their employees at various times and the ESB experienced no fewer than thirty-eight strikes in the seven years from 1961 to 1968.[56] A major strike in June 1966 interrupted the power supply and the government responded by introducing legislation to limit the right to strike by workers in the ESB. The Electricity (Special Provisions) Act, 1966, made it an offence for ESB workers to go on strike in certain circumstances and imposed severe financial penalties for engaging in strike action that threatened the public supply of electricity.[57] This rigorous measure introduced an unprecedented element of legal coercion into Irish industrial relations. But the government undoubtedly hoped that the existence of the legislation would be a sufficient deterrent, and that it would never be used; the provisions of the Act would remain dormant until the government brought it into effect. Hillery piloted the legislation through the Dáil, although the proposal to restrict industrial action by the power workers was instigated originally by Lemass and the Department of Transport and Power. Hillery told the officers of Congress in August 1966 that he wished merely to avoid strikes in the ESB, and established a joint working party of departmental officials and trade unionists to examine the question.[58] The minister hoped to use the possible repeal of the legislation as a bargaining chip to secure more stable industrial relations in the ESB. But the discussions went nowhere, and early in 1968 the ESB faced the worst industrial crisis in its history.

The official union leadership in the ESB wished to reach a comprehensive agreement on pay and avoid a further strike, but they were effectively sidelined by the Day Workers Association, an unofficial group which secured widespread support among over 1,000 unskilled and semi-skilled manual workers in the ESB.[59] The unskilled workers were deeply discontented at the slow progress of pay negotiations and decided on strike action in March 1968. Although the Labour Court had decided to hear the ESB workers' pay claim on 1 April, the unofficial strike committee went ahead with their action and mounted pickets on 27 March. Hillery held last-minute talks with the official union leadership in the ESB in an attempt to persuade the workers to await the Labour Court hearing, but to no avail.[60] Congress criticised the unofficial action and the ESB Group of Unions instructed their members to report for work as normal. But these appeals had virtually no impact; pickets were placed on all generating stations and the vast majority of skilled workers in the ESB refused to pass the pickets.[61] The crisis had an immediate and dramatic impact on the power supply; the ESB asked all employers throughout the country 'not to switch on until further notice', and many firms simply shut down over the following four days.[62] Much of the country was plunged into darkness as the supply of electricity to domestic users was sharply curtailed. Hillery felt he had no alternative but to invoke the powers restricting strike action in the ESB; he immediately secured the government's agreement to bring the legislation into effect. 'I think Jack [Lynch] was away when I brought it in. Kevin Boland objected but I felt logically – I have to go through with this now.'[63] Hillery ruled out more draconian measures, which were suggested by excitable journalists, such as calling in the army to take over the power supply. Instead he publicly defended the order restricting picketing, while conducting private discussions with Congress officers and union leaders to resolve the strike.[64] Hillery was well aware that the Congress leadership was firmly opposed to the unofficial strike, and desperately wanted to have the restrictive legislation repealed; he calculated that their overriding concern to get rid of the legislation could bring a swift resolution of the dispute. Hillery's assessment of the official union position was well-founded, but the long arm of the law, which moved in this case with unexpected speed, upset his calculations.

Within two days of the start of the strike, fifty-three ESB workers were in jail. Several groups of unofficial strikers were brought before the courts on the second day of the dispute. Justice Ó hUadhaigh in Dublin District Court imposed fines on those who had picketed the ESB stations in defiance of the legislation. The strikers refused to pay the fines and the judge immediately sent the men to jail on 28 March, handing down three-month sentences for non-payment.[65] Another group of striking workers in Cork also went to jail on the following day. Hillery was shocked by the action of the judges: 'But the district justice in an awful hurry put them in jail, three months in jail, and the whole thing shut down.'[66] The minister had hoped that the cases would take a few days to go through the courts; in the meantime, senior union leaders had agreed to support his appeal to the strikers to suspend their action pending the Labour Court hearing. The jailing of the unofficial strikers not only destroyed any hopes of an immediate return to work, but also caused widespread outrage within the trade union movement and threatened a dramatic escalation of the dispute. The unofficial strike committee immediately announced that their action would continue and they could now expect overwhelming support from other ESB workers.[67] The leaders of Congress were seriously alarmed, fearing that the jailing of the men could trigger a general strike and a mass movement of workers to challenge the authority of the state.[68] The government's inept attempt to resolve the strike by restrictive legislation had backfired in the most spectacular fashion imaginable.

Hillery recognised the wider implications of the dispute and acted decisively to bring the crisis to an end. He conducted intensive negotiations over a two-day period with Jim Larkin and Jimmy Dunne of Congress, as well as the leaders of the ESB unions; he also agreed to bring representatives of the unofficial strikers into the negotiations. The leadership of Congress played a central part in resolving the crisis, issuing proposals on 29 March that were broadly acceptable both to Hillery and the unofficial strike committee. The ICTU plan recommended that all legal steps against the strikers should be halted straightaway, the jailed workers were to be released and the strike leaders should recommend an immediate return to work.[69] Congress' demand for the release of the workers already imprisoned threatened to scupper the negotiations, as it was painfully obvious from the events of the previous week that the minister could not dictate to the courts. Hillery broke the deadlock by instructing the ESB to pay the fines and ensure the release of the workers.[70] Following eight hours of late-night negotiations on Saturday 30 March, a settlement was reached. The strike committee recommended an immediate return to work by all ESB employees; there would be no victimisation of the unofficial strikers; it was agreed that the Labour Court would consider the workers' pay claim and a public inquiry would be held into industrial relations within the company.[71] In a comical finale to the dispute, the workers were released in the early hours of Sunday morning and taken home in taxis paid for by the ESB. The power supply was fully restored by Monday 1 April, and Hillery acted to revoke the order restricting strike action as soon as the crisis was past. He also moved swiftly to set up the public inquiry, appointing a committee on 11 April headed by Professor Michael Fogarty, Director of the Economic and Social Research Institute (ESRI), to investigate industrial relations and negotiating practices at the ESB; Paddy McCarthy represented the official view on the committee.[72]

The Fogarty inquiry did not end industrial relations strife within the company, but its two reports produced useful recommendations for more effective management of future disputes. The committee recommended the repeal of the Electricity (Special Provisions) Act, 1966; they also argued that strikes had to be accepted occasionally even in the ESB and that attempting to maintain the electricity supply at all costs was not only counterproductive, but usually aggravated industrial disputes.[73] The report underlined a significant change in official thinking away from trade union legislation and ministerial intervention towards a greater preoccupation with voluntary reform of trade union structures and developing new attitudes towards industrial relations.[74] The crisis of March 1968 accelerated a gradual reassessment in official attitudes towards industrial relations. Hillery himself drew some hard lessons from the crisis. He abandoned any attempt to restrict the right to strike, even in extreme circumstances; he secured the repeal of the highly contentious legislation governing the ESB in May 1969.[75] Hillery also tacitly abandoned the previous official endeavour to change trade union tactics by legislation, although he continued to employ the possibility of legal changes as a bargaining counter to influence trade union leaders. Hillery's vision for a stable system of industrial relations, characterised by negotiation rather than confrontation, remained consistent throughout his term. But his tactics evolved over time as he moved steadily away from the traditional path of piecemeal intervention towards a concerted attempt to enhance the authority of the institutions that were designed to mediate disputes. The ESB strike, where he could hardly avoid intervention, and the protracted maintenance workers' dispute in the following year, where he firmly resisted the temptation to get involved, both influenced Hillery's efforts to establish a new framework for the future.

By 1969, Hillery was profoundly sceptical of any attempt to legislate in the field of industrial relations against the opposition of organised labour. He told the Dáil on 6 March 1969 that any attempt to implement reforms unilaterally would be futile if the unions simply refused to co-operate with the revised procedures governing industrial relations. He pledged to avoid 'any radical unacceptable change' in the law on industrial relations.[76] Hillery specifically ruled out a statutory incomes policy, in which wages and incomes would be regulated by a central authority, backed by the force of law. He argued that such a solution would involve an attempt to coerce workers that was both unacceptable and impractical in a democratic state.[77] This did not mean that he was resigned to industrial turmoil; he sought to develop an effective voluntary framework for settling disputes that commanded wide acceptance from both unions and employers. Hillery proposed important reforms of industrial relations law in March 1969 that went some way towards achieving his objective, although the proposed amendments were far less sweeping than the original reforms sought by Lemass in 1966. Hillery abandoned the more radical elements of the earlier plans, notably the proposal to allow the Labour Court to issue legally binding rulings on disputes in certain circumstances.[78] Yet the revised version of the Industrial Relations Bill contained some valuable innovations.

The legislation provided for the appointment of Rights Commissioners, who would investigate disputes stemming from breaches of the rights of workers, as defined in agreements or custom and practice. The Commissioners were intended to give a rapid and authoritative opinion on cases relating to dismissals or disciplinary action against individual workers. The intention behind the move was not only to protect workers' rights but also to provide a more effective mechanism for the resolution of disputes involving individuals and to free the Labour Court to deal with collective disputes, usually involving contentious pay claims.[79] The legislation also proposed changes to make the Labour Court 'a more effective instrument in promoting industrial peace'; the minister was given the power to appoint additional members to the Court and a new rule was introduced that the Court would investigate a dispute only at the request of the parties. Workers employed by the state, who were not already covered by existing conciliation and arbitration schemes, were given access to the Labour Court for the first time.[80] The legislation was designed to enhance the authority and status of the Labour Court and to improve the effectiveness of the institutions dealing with the resolution of industrial disputes. The Industrial Relations Bill was approved by the Dáil without a division on 24 April 1969 and enacted before the end of Hillery's term.[81] While Hillery avoided any fundamental changes in the procedures governing industrial relations, the new legislation delivered some valuable reforms. The appointment of two Rights Commissioners under the Act provided an additional resource for the resolution of disputes at an early stage. The first Commissioners operated entirely within a voluntary system, acting effectively as 'industrial ombudsmen' rather than judges.[82] But the Rights Commissioners would later acquire

a vital statutory role in the protection of workers' rights; the creation of
the service in 1969 was a significant innovation in Irish industrial relations,
even if it attracted relatively little attention at the time. The Act also
reinforced the role of the Labour Court as a key institution in resolving
disputes, although it did not require the parties to accept the Court's
rulings. The legislation reflected the transition in official thinking, in
which Hillery had played an influential part, away from short-term
political intervention in strikes towards the development of effective
public institutions for the resolution of disputes.

The wider reform of trade union law envisaged by Lemass three years
before was quietly dropped. The minister reintroduced the Trade Union
Bill to the Dáil in the midst of the strike by the maintenance workers.
Hillery advocated a major reform of trade union structures in his speech
on 6 March 1969, calling for a reduction in the number of unions and the
introduction of effective procedures to limit the power of small groups of
militant activists.[83] He was critical of the limited authority exerted by
Congress over its member unions, claiming that 'their only capacity is to
carry out a paper war on anybody who tries to make changes from
outside'.[84] But ultimately Hillery did not proceed with the legislation in
the face of strong opposition from Congress; the Trade Union Bill was
quietly allowed to lapse before the dissolution of the Dáil in May 1969.
The government had no stomach for controversial legislation on the eve
of a general election. Hillery, however, used the debate on 6 March to
outline his vision of industrial relations. While he supported the principle
of voluntary wage-bargaining, he emphasised that the freedom given to
employers and trade unions had to be matched by responsibility. Hillery
challenged unions and employers to acknowledge their wider obligations
to society as a whole and accept a moral responsibility to resolve their
disputes through negotiation: 'there ought to be a very strong moral
obligation to use the dispute-settling machinery before thought is given
to ordering strikes, lockouts and pickets'.[85] Hillery's appeal to arguments
based on moral force rather than legal compulsion reflected his
recognition of the realities of Irish industrial relations. He knew that strike
action by workers could not be curtailed by legal penalties, nor could

employers be compelled to maintain government pay guidelines in the face of industrial turmoil. Hillery sought consistently to persuade and cajole unions and employers into developing a new framework for the negotiation and resolution of disputes. This approach certainly had its limitations, but it was arguably the only realistic strategy available in the turbulent conditions of the late 1960s.

Hillery's term as Minister for Labour was certainly less rewarding electorally than his previous assignment in education. The general election in June 1969 presented the most daunting prospect for Hillery since his original victory in 1951. The constituency revision, orchestrated by Kevin Boland as Minister for Local Government to enhance Fianna Fáil's prospects of winning the election, caused major local difficulties for Hillery. The revision put a substantial section of north Clare into a new Clare–South Galway constituency.[86] Boland's sleight of hand transferred areas where Hillery enjoyed considerable support into the new constituency, although it also delivered two seats out of three for Fianna Fáil in Clare–South Galway. Moreover, Hillery faced a formidable challenger within his own party. Sylvester Barrett, an auctioneer and valuer from Clarecastle, emerged as a major rival to Hillery in the late 1960s. Following the death of Hillery's friend and political opponent Bill Murphy, the sole Fine Gael TD for Clare, Barrett secured the Fianna Fáil nomination for the by-election and was elected by a wide margin in March 1968.[87] Barrett's victory ensured that Fianna Fáil briefly held all three seats in Clare, although this would not be maintained in a general election; in any event, the oldest of the incumbent deputies, Seán Ó Ceallaigh, retired in 1969. But the party's local predominance encouraged internal dissension and infighting. Barrett set about building his own base within the constituency and began to gain ground at Hillery's expense. On this occasion being a minister was no great advantage, as it ensured that Hillery could not be in Clare nearly as much as his local challenger. The election in the summer of 1969 was as much a contest between Hillery and Barrett as it was between Fianna Fáil and the fragmented forces of the Opposition.

Hillery suffered from a dangerous liability that has often cost prominent figures their seats in Irish elections; he was perceived to be safe following his extraordinary performance four years before. Barrett made liberal use of this public perception. Michael Hillery recalled Barrett's tactics in 1969: 'He was going around saying that Dr Paddy had buckets of votes.'[88] This was possibly the oldest political ploy on record, but it was also one of the most effective. The party's third candidate, Jack Lynch, was a namesake of the Taoiseach and a farmer from Kilfenora.[89] The majority of Lynch's votes were taken from Hillery, not due to his name but largely because he shared the same base in west Clare. Hillery was anxious about the election result, recognising that his vote was being eroded by several elements largely beyond his control; he canvassed heavily over the three weeks of the campaign. The outcome on 18 June showed that he was right to be concerned. Hillery's vote was more than halved from the previous election. The result was a triumph for Barrett, who topped the poll and was elected on the first count.[90] But the outcome was by no means a disaster for Hillery; he polled only 161 votes less than Barrett and was easily re-elected on the third count. *The Clare Champion* hailed the result as a 'magnificent vote' for Barrett, but Hillery was relieved to have weathered the storm.[91] Despite the dramatic drop in his vote, it was a creditable performance considering the damaging local effect of Boland's gerrymandering and the strength of Barrett's performance. Hillery's popularity in Clare withstood its harshest test since he was first elected.

Hillery's term in the Department of Labour brought him few personal advantages and certainly did little to sustain his position as a rural deputy. The first Minister for Labour in over a generation did not court popularity and nor did he receive it among influential elements of organised labour and private business. Hillery's efforts to promote a reappraisal of trade union tactics proved fruitless, at least in the short term. His hopes of a dramatic change in attitudes among union members were always ambitious, and indeed unrealistic, at a time when the cost of living was rising rapidly and demands from workers for a greater share of the new national prosperity were growing steadily more vocal. Employers, too, were often deeply discontented with the minister's refusal to intervene in disputes or to curtail strikes by legislative action. Yet Hillery was successful in developing a gradual change in the state's approach towards industrial relations. He initiated a difficult transition away from the quick fix of political intervention in disputes, occasionally reinforced by the blunt instrument of legislation to control strikes, towards a greater reliance on effective official institutions for dispute resolution. The attempt to control strike action in the ESB through legal restrictions was undoubtedly a major blunder, but it was very much an exception to the rule during Hillery's eventful term as Minister for Labour. The legislation adopted at Hillery's instigation in 1969 testified to a significant change in official attitudes and the development of a more sophisticated approach towards industrial relations by the state. Despite occasional high-profile clashes with union leaders, Hillery also succeeded in establishing a constructive interaction on industrial disputes between the state and the leadership of the Irish Congress of Trade Unions. While this was not always enough to settle the most intractable disputes during Hillery's term, it was nevertheless an essential advance in stabilising the industrial relations scene. Incremental reform and a consistent emphasis on the need to replace confrontation with negotiation at all levels were the hallmarks of Hillery's term in Annesley House. The minister's attempts to devise a more stable framework for labour relations enjoyed at best partial success, but foreshadowed both the national agreements of the early 1970s and the more enduring system of social partnership which was established in the late 1980s. While he certainly did not achieve all that he set out to do, Hillery began the painful and difficult process of modernising Irish industrial relations.

10.

Foreign Minister
1969

The general election in June 1969 was a personal triumph for Jack Lynch. Fianna Fáil secured an overall majority after 12 years in office and Lynch won a popular mandate in his own right for the first time. Yet the election resolved almost nothing – it failed to secure Lynch's position as party leader, nor did it enhance his standing among prominent members of the Cabinet, who regarded him as a caretaker Taoiseach, to be replaced in due course by a more forceful figure. Several leading Cabinet Ministers operated like feudal barons from an earlier age, acknowledging only the most grudging fealty to a distant and barely tolerated overlord. Neil Blaney, Minister for Agriculture, and Kevin Boland, Minister for Local Government, formed a powerful axis within the Cabinet, whose influence flowed especially from their dominant role in the party organisation and their nationalist credentials. Both men were long-serving ministers and the sons of prominent founder members of Fianna Fáil – unlike Lynch himself, who had no such traditional connections with the party. Blaney and Boland ran the Fianna Fáil organisation, taking responsibility for organising by-election campaigns in most constituencies. The sole constituency where they were not in control of by-election campaigns was Clare, where Hillery deliberately restricted their involvement. Hillery disliked both men and did not want them interfering in his constituency: 'I didn't let them into Clare. I didn't need them, I didn't like them'.[1] Hillery enjoyed much more friendly relations with Charles Haughey, who as Minister of Finance was the most influential member of Lynch's first administration. Haughey was a more pragmatic figure than Blaney and was associated with the new business and political elite of the 1960s rather than traditional nationalism. Yet Haughey was also willing to act independently of the Taoiseach and was positioning himself to succeed Lynch in due course.

Lynch did not attempt to use the election result to stamp his authority on the government, instead continuing to operate as a cautious, consensual leader. Hillery in 1969 was neither as prominent within the party organisation as Blaney, nor as powerful in the Cabinet as Haughey. But Hillery, unlike some of his associates, did not make the mistake of underestimating the Taoiseach. Indeed, he believed that Lynch's approach owed as much to political calculation as to his personal style: 'It's hard to pass judgment on the man. He was so relaxed, you know, he had a great presence. But he was in no hurry to deal with situations'.[2] Whether it was a product of calculation or naivety, Lynch's permissive approach to turbulent ministers would come back to haunt him within a year of his re-election. But the Taoiseach did undertake a limited reshuffle of his Cabinet in July 1969 and made one of the shrewdest – or the most fortunate – decisions of his leadership, promoting Hillery to the crucial and highly sensitive post of External Affairs.

Hillery's promotion to External Affairs came about because Lynch moved to replace Frank Aiken, who had served in every Fianna Fáil government since 1932. Aiken, a long-time lieutenant of de Valera, had been Minister for External Affairs for 12 years; he had been particularly prominent at the United Nations, where he had taken a principled and frequently independent line between the Western powers and the Soviet

Union. Lynch had never been close to Aiken and his departure signalled that the Taoiseach was seeking to complete the generational transition initiated by Lemass. Lynch's Cabinet in 1969 was the first Irish government that contained no veterans of the Irish independence struggle. Yet with this exception, Lynch's new government bore a striking resemblance to the old one; Hillery was the main beneficiary of the limited cabinet changes. Hillery, who was at home in Clare, received a phone call from Lynch a couple of days before the Dáil met to re-elect the Taoiseach. He was about to leave for the ICTU conference in Bundoran in his final engagement as Minister for Labour: 'But I was down in Clare and Jack phoned; he said "I have a problem with some of your colleagues and I want to see you."'[3] Lynch had experienced difficulty in persuading some of his most powerful and assertive ministers, especially Blaney and Boland, to accept the positions he was assigning to them. Hillery pointed out that he had to attend the trade union conference, but promised Lynch not to add to his problems: 'I said, well, look Jack, I'll do any post you ask me.'[4] Lynch did not offer a specific position over the phone, and Hillery went on to Bundoran without knowing what post he would hold in the next government. He returned from the trade union congress late the night before the Dáil reassembled on 2 July; it was only on the morning of the vote that Hillery discovered he was about to become the new Minister for External Affairs.[5] There was no need for Lynch to overcome any lingering reluctance to serve on Hillery's part, as Lemass had done ten years before. Hillery readily accepted the move and looked forward to the challenge of steering Ireland into the European Communities. But it was the gathering storm clouds in Northern Ireland that would dominate his first year as Foreign Minister.

Hillery's principal collaborator for the next three and a half years was Hugh McCann, the experienced secretary of the department. But the official closest to Hillery was John McColgan, a young civil servant from north Dublin who served as private secretary from July 1969 until December 1971. This marked the beginning of one of the most important and valued associations of Hillery's career. The two men became close personal friends and McColgan later joined Hillery in Brussels as a key member of his *cabinet* in the European Commission. McColgan adapted quickly to Hillery's working habits and recognised his desire to create a sense of order in his workplace:

> He hated people creating fuss around him. When I said that somebody wanted to see him, he would ask – 'is there a real problem, John, or are they just trying to transfer their anxiety?'[6]

There was some initial tension between Hillery and McCann. The minister was exasperated by McCann's habit of rushing into his office to impart some news or seek an urgent decision. At one stage the new minister told McColgan that 'your job is to keep that man out of my office'. But this did not signal any personal animosity between Hillery and McCann. Hillery simply hated excitement or commotion in any part of his daily work, and he especially detested it in his private office. This reflected his early experiences in the Department of Education, when he had not controlled access to his office and had been besieged by worried officials. There was no fundamental conflict between the secretary and his political superior. Hillery later developed a high opinion of McCann's judgment and professionalism.[7] He relied heavily on McCann in dealing with Northern Ireland. The secretary established a good personal relationship with successive British ambassadors, particularly Sir John Peck, and maintained regular contacts with the British envoys as the situation deteriorated in Northern Ireland. McCann played an important behind-the-scenes role in communicating Irish concerns to the British during the first years of the Troubles.

External Affairs became Foreign Affairs on Hillery's watch; the government agreed to change the name of the department on his recommendation in 1971.[8] Hillery promoted the change on the basis that Foreign Affairs was the more usual and appropriate term among similar departments internationally. He personally was dissatisfied with the traditional term; he told the Dáil in January 1971 that it was 'of British

Commonwealth origin'.[9] It was a revealing comment that reflected Hillery's concern to distance Irish institutions from past British influences. The move was also influenced by Ireland's impending accession to the European Communities and Hillery's conviction that the new term commanded greater international respect.

The North

The crisis in Northern Ireland erupted within six weeks of Hillery's appointment to External Affairs. Following the partition of the island in 1922, a cold war had prevailed between the Irish state and the unionist government in Belfast, which lasted for over a generation.[10] The political life of Northern Ireland was characterised by the domination of the Unionist Party; its society was marked by discrimination against the Catholic minority in housing, the civil service and local government. The Royal Ulster Constabulary was overwhelmingly a Protestant force, while Stormont also maintained a part-time paramilitary force, the B Specials, which was entirely loyalist and deeply hostile to Catholics.[11] Lemass had broken up some of the ice floes by meeting with Terence O'Neill, the Prime Minister of Northern Ireland, in 1965. The improved relations generated by this initiative proved short-lived. O'Neill, a moderate unionist, sought to conciliate Catholics by proposing incremental reforms; his efforts were inadequate to satisfy most Catholics but outraged a substantial section of his own party. The Northern Ireland Civil Rights Association (NICRA), which was founded in 1967, demanded far-reaching reforms including 'one man, one vote' in local elections, fair distribution of council housing and the disbanding of the B Specials.[12] The drift towards crisis was exacerbated by violent repression of civil rights protests by the RUC in 1968 and a growing loyalist backlash against any real reform. When O'Neill agreed to concede major reforms in local government, his support within the Unionist Party rapidly evaporated. He was forced to resign due to an internal party revolt in April 1969. His successor, Major James Chichester-Clark, sought to pursue a similar course based on incremental reform, but the shelf-life for this policy had already expired. An increasingly vocal and influential element of the minority was no longer willing to accept unionist ascendancy.

The catalyst for the outbreak of violence was the Apprentice Boys' parade in Derry on 12 August, which marked the finale of the loyalist marching season.[13] The march took place at a time of escalating sectarian tension, as the community division in the North was exacerbated by the incompatible demands of strong elements on each side. Hardline loyalist groups sought to use the marching season to underline their dominance, while the unity of the civil rights movement fractured, as socialists and militant republicans moved to exploit the growing wave of protests. Hillery received well-founded reports that rioting would occur if the parade went ahead. He went to London at the beginning of August, accompanied by Hugh McCann, in an attempt to persuade the British government to ban the parade. Hillery met Michael Stewart, the Foreign Secretary, on 1 August, warning him that Derry had become a 'powder keg' and that holding the parade in the present circumstances was 'sheer madness'; it should be banned or at least restricted to Protestant areas of the city.[14] Stewart discounted Hillery's concerns and endorsed the view of the Stormont authorities that banning the parade was unnecessary. Hillery generally took a moderate line, not raising the bogey of partition but focusing on the contentious parade and urging the British side to exert greater pressure on Stormont to implement the reform programme. But Stewart was uncomfortable discussing Northern Ireland with Hillery at all and emphasised that the Irish government had no right to influence British policy on the North: 'I must say to you that there is a limit to the extent to which we can discuss with outsiders – even our nearest neighbours, this internal matter'.[15] The meeting was entirely futile. The British insistence that Northern Ireland was strictly an internal matter and no concern of the Irish government represented a formidable obstacle to Hillery's representations. Moreover, Stewart relied on assurances from the Home Office that the Stormont authorities could control the parade. It did not take long for this approach to lead to disaster.

Hillery's warnings were prescient. The parade went ahead on 12 August and rapidly triggered widespread violence in Derry; there were fierce clashes between nationalist demonstrators mainly from the Bogside and loyalists supporting the Apprentice Boys. The RUC became embroiled in a violent confrontation with nationalists in the Bogside; militant republicans later associated with the Provisional IRA took the lead in organizing resistance to the police and the Bogside became a virtual no-go area for the security forces.[16] The violence spread to Belfast on the following day, as rioting broke out at interfaces between Catholic and Protestant areas and the Stormont government called out the B Specials. The special constables mounted sectarian attacks on nationalist communities in Belfast over the following week, which resulted in widespread destruction and the expulsion of Catholic residents who were burned out of their homes.[17] The unionist government was unable to restore order or to control its own supporters; eight people died in the space of a week as Northern Ireland witnessed the worst sectarian violence since the 1920s.

The government in Dublin was equally unprepared for the widespread outbreak of sectarian conflict. The Cabinet held an emergency meeting on 13 August, receiving reports of rioting and police attacks on nationalists in Derry throughout the day.[18] Hillery was not present at the first meeting of the crisis; he had gone to the painting school at Keel with his son, as he often did in mid-August. His absence, even within the country, underlined that most Irish ministers were taken by surprise by the extent of the crisis in August 1969. Even Hillery, who had predicted that the parade would cause trouble in Derry, was shocked by the scale and sustained intensity of the violence. Hillery rushed back to Dublin as soon as he was informed of the outbreak of conflict; in his absence, the government decided to demand a United Nations peacekeeping force for Northern Ireland, and ordered the Irish army to establish field hospitals along the border to treat Catholics injured in the disturbances.[19] Lynch made a televised address to the nation on the evening of 13 August, in which he warned that 'the Irish government can no longer stand by and see innocent people injured and perhaps worse.'[20] While Lynch had no intention of ordering Irish troops across the border, he felt obliged to take a tough public line in response to the rioting in Derry and severe pressures within his own government. The Taoiseach demanded early negotiations with Britain to review the constitutional position of Northern Ireland and identified 'the reunification of the national territory' as the only permanent solution for the problem.[21] There was no prospect whatsoever of constitutional negotiations between the two governments in the autumn of 1969; Lynch's speech was a skilful exercise in traditional nationalist rhetoric, which sought to reassure nationalist public opinion that the government would act to protect the beleaguered minority, while carefully avoiding any commitment to intervene directly north of the border. The reality was that the Irish government was essentially helpless when the crisis erupted in the North, although it could certainly have made the situation a great deal worse by sending troops across the border. British intervention, long contemplated with grave misgivings in London and Belfast, was now inevitable. Several thousand British troops were deployed on the streets of Belfast and Derry on 14–15 August, ostensibly at the request of the Stormont authorities, but actually in response to appeals from nationalist politicians who feared a full-scale pogrom against unprotected Catholics.[22] The situation remained volatile for several days and it appeared that the violence might spill over the border.

The Irish government was deeply divided in its response to the escalating crisis. Lynch sought to contain the situation and ensure that the Irish state was not drawn into the conflict, while also struggling to keep his government together. But the most powerful members of his Cabinet pursued a very different agenda. Blaney and Boland took the lead in demanding an aggressive response by the Irish state, seeking intervention by the Irish army in Derry. They were not seeking simply to protect beleaguered Catholics; both men saw the outbreak of violence as an opportunity to undermine partition and force Britain to concede a united Ireland.[23] Their hardline stand invoked the traditional certainties of rhetorical nationalism and had a powerful appeal in the volatile conditions of August 1969. Hillery fully shared the genuine outrage within the Cabinet at the loyalist attacks on unprotected Catholic communities. He recognised too the overwhelming pressures on Lynch to act effectively in the defence of Northern nationalists:

> There were pressures to 'do something'; to answer our supporters about our policy of uniting the national territory; to not stand by as those in the North nearest to us in kinship were attacked, humiliated, and sometimes killed; always under threat of death ... There was great and heartfelt emotion.[24]

Hillery himself was a nationalist whose family had been active in the struggle for Irish independence and who represented a county known for its fervent republican tradition. He was sincerely opposed to partition and despised the Unionist regime in Stormont. But he was also an intelligent and pragmatic politician, who was deeply concerned about the vulnerable position of the nationalist community within Northern Ireland. He feared that reckless action by the Irish government could trigger a loyalist backlash and widespread slaughter of unprotected Catholics. His concerns were shared by senior figures within Fianna Fáil, including his former colleague Seán MacEntee, who warned Hillery in stark terms of the dangers facing Northern nationalists: 'I was worried for the Catholics in the Six Counties. MacEntee wrote to me ... in relation to the provocative nature of any activity on our part to become involved: and his message was there was half a million people hostage to our behaviour.'[25]

Hillery was a moderate within the government from the outset of the Northern conflict, even if this was not always obvious only to those who heard his uncompromising public statements about unionist discrimination and British ineptitude. He was appalled by the militant rhetoric of other senior ministers and alarmed by their apparent willingness to contemplate a military solution. 'When it blew up, a meeting was like a ballad session. They were all warriors. I remember government meetings and you would be a traitor, not to be looking for war. They were caught, they were republicans and now was an

opportunity to become active republicans.'[26] Hillery was one of the first
Irish ministers to recognise the dangers in attempting to live up to a
generation of anti-partition rhetoric. He held quiet reservations even
about Lynch's speech on 13 August, recognising the power of rhetoric to
inflame the situation and create unrealistic expectations:

> I missed the government meeting when the first challenge
> came in the Apprentice Boys parade, which found joy in
> going through the Catholic areas of Derry. It was then the
> heroes got Jack Lynch to go on the radio [and TV] saying
> 'We will not stand by'. This became 'stand idly by' and was
> repeatedly thrown at Jack and his supporters in this new
> form as an implication of failure to take a promised
> stand.[27]

Hillery firmly supported Lynch's moderate line within the Cabinet, but
feared that the majority might be swayed by the hardline nationalism of
Blaney and Boland, as Northern Ireland seemed about to slide into civil
war. A viable alternative to military intervention was urgently needed and
it was to be found in frenetic Irish diplomacy, culminating in Hillery's
appeal to the United Nations.

The Cabinet agreed on 14 August that Hillery should go immediately
to London with instructions to demand British agreement for a UN
peacekeeping force.[28] Hillery left for London on the same day. The Irish
Foreign Minister sought a meeting with Stewart or James Callaghan, the
Home Secretary, but was told that neither of the Labour ministers was
available. British ministers were deeply reluctant to discuss the crisis with
the Irish government at all. Hillery secured a meeting the next day with
Lord Chalfont, the Minister of State at the Foreign Office, accompanied
by a junior Home Office minister, Lord Stonham. The meeting on 15
August was tense and even less successful than Hillery's previous
encounter with Stewart. Hillery made the case for a UN peacekeeping
force or alternately a joint British/Irish force to maintain order in the
North; in accordance with the government's instructions he also sought

consultations on the constitutional status of Northern Ireland.[29] Partition did not, however, figure heavily in the discussion, as Hillery emphasised the failure of the Stormont authorities either to deliver far-reaching reforms or to protect the minority; he was well aware that the British ministers could not make any concessions on the constitutional position of the North. But Chalfont was unyielding on all fronts, categorically rejecting the proposal for a UN peacekeeping force; he warned Hillery that Northern Ireland was an integral part of the United Kingdom, and maintaining law and order in the UK was 'primarily our concern'. Hillery refused to accept that maintaining peace in Northern Ireland was solely an internal affair for the British government; he warned bluntly that 'We can blindfold ourselves with technicalities but people are getting killed now'.[30] He demanded the immediate disbandment of the B Specials, whom he described as 'a partisan, armed mob, such as is found only in dictatorships'. But Chalfont even refused to give any assurances about the disarming of the B Specials or the implementation of reforms in Northern Ireland. The British minister was adamant that he could not consult with the representative of 'a foreign government' on developments in Northern Ireland: 'This is a domestic affair.'[31] Chalfont effectively told the Irish government to mind its own business. Hillery knew as he left the meeting that an appeal to the United Nations was inevitable.

When Hillery reported the unfavourable outcome of his meeting with Chalfont, the Cabinet took several key decisions on 16 August. The government agreed that Hillery should proceed immediately to New York and raise the Irish proposal for a peacekeeping force with the Security Council of the United Nations; he was also instructed to have 'the situation in the North of Ireland' placed on the agenda for the UN General Assembly. Equally important was the decision that the Exchequer would provide 'aid for the victims of the current unrest in the Six Counties', by allocating a sum of money, with the amount and the channel of disbursement to be determined by the Minister for Finance.[32] The Government Information Bureau announced on 21 August that the fund would be administered mainly by the Irish Red

Cross Society; the statement indicated that the money would be used to alleviate distress caused by the recent disturbances.[33] A committee of ministers was soon established to oversee the operation of the relief fund, but the committee had only a single meeting and then ceased to function; instead, Haughey maintained control over the administration of the fund.[34] The disbursement of the money became a key issue in the arms crisis during the following year and was the subject of an investigation by the Public Accounts Committee in 1971. This investigation was unable to reach definitive conclusions on how most of the money was spent, but uncovered sufficient evidence to indicate that much of the fund was diverted to other purposes, including the purchase of arms on the continent.[35] This arms deal formed part of a covert operation designed to support militant republicans north of the border, in defiance of the declared policy of the Taoiseach. Hillery, who was out of the country much of the time and preoccupied with international diplomacy, had no inkling of what was going on behind the scenes in Dublin.

The Cabinet's decisions on 16 August preserved the unity of the government in the short term, but a high price would be paid later for papering over the cracks between moderates and hardliners. The attempt to involve the UN was dictated primarily by the divisions within the government and the pressures on Lynch to take action in response to the crisis. This did not mean, however, that it was simply a cynical or meaningless exercise; compared to the likely alternatives, Hillery's appeal to the UN Security Council was a prudent and responsible initiative by the Irish government – or at least by the section of the government that was precariously resisting demands for armed intervention.

Appeal to the Security Council

The Foreign Minister nevertheless had reservations about attempting to raise the situation in Northern Ireland with the UN. Hillery had asked Seán Lemass long before the crisis erupted why the former Taoiseach had never taken the question of partition before the UN: 'Lemass said "Only if you're ready to accept the decision for all time"'.[36] By 1969

Hillery understood Lemass's cryptic warning only too well. Britain held a veto as one of the five permanent members of the Security Council; the Irish could not hope to win a vote on partition. Moreover, Hillery was deeply concerned about the consequences of losing a vote at the Security Council, fearing that partition would be 'copper-fastened for all time in the UN'.[37] The Department of External Affairs under Aiken maintained a policy of not raising partition formally at the United Nations, on the basis that it would be unlikely to achieve anything useful and would destroy any prospect of a lasting settlement between North and South.[38] Hillery fully accepted the necessity to raise the crisis at the UN in the extraordinary circumstances of the time, but he did so in a clear-sighted fashion. He had no illusions that it would be possible to get the UN on the record against partition, or to secure UN agreement for a peacekeeping force. Instead, he set out to have the Irish case formally considered by the Security Council and deliberately avoided placing partition at the core of his appeal.[39] Hillery's department advised the government that the attempt to raise the situation in Northern Ireland at the UN should be based on 'violations of human rights and fundamental freedoms', as an effort to highlight partition in the application to the Security Council would be tactically unwise and counterproductive.[40] Hillery generally followed this tactical approach in his negotiations with other delegations and in his speech to the Security Council itself.

The Foreign Minister left for New York immediately after the Cabinet meeting on Saturday 16 August and gave a press conference on his arrival at Kennedy Airport; later that evening he met Con Cremin, the vastly experienced Irish Permanent Representative to the United Nations, and they discussed how to bring the issue before the Security Council.[41] The first hurdle to be overcome was procedural – getting the issue on the Council agenda so that it could be debated publicly; this would be no mean feat, as nine positive votes out of fifteen were required to adopt the agenda. Hillery and Cremin first approached the President of the Council, Ambassador Jaime de Pinies of Spain. The Spanish ambassador told them that 'as President of the Council he was 100 per cent at our disposal, and as a representative of Spain, 1,000 per cent.'[42] De Pinies' enthusiastic support for the Irish position had much to do with the ongoing controversy between his country and the UK over the British presence in Gibraltar. Cremin submitted a formal application to the President on 17 August, seeking an urgent meeting of the Security Council in connection with 'the situation in the Six Counties of Northern Ireland'.[43] Hillery then began intensive lobbying of the national delegations represented on the Security Council, seeking their support to have the crisis in Northern Ireland inscribed on the Council's agenda. He was initially hopeful that the Irish could gain enough votes to get Northern Ireland on the agenda and guarantee a full debate by the Security Council, although he realised almost immediately that there was no chance of securing a peacekeeping force.[44] Hillery's optimism was sustained by a discussion with U Thant, the Burmese Secretary-General of the United Nations, on Monday 18 August. U Thant was sympathetic and suggested that he might be able to nominate a personal representative as a UN observer in Northern Ireland; the Secretary-General urged Hillery to concentrate on 'the human rights aspect' of the situation.[45] U Thant's message reinforced the tactical approach favoured by Hillery and key officials of his department. Hillery sent a message to Lynch in Dublin on the evening of 18 August warning that 'we will hardly get a peacekeeping force' and suggesting that he might make some progress 'if he had authority to move on to civil rights and seek a UN presence on that basis'.[46] Lynch readily agreed to back Hillery's judgment of the situation; it marked a subtle shift from seeking a peacekeeping force to a more symbolic UN presence, in the form of an observer appointed by the Secretary-General, who would be able to monitor the implementation of civil rights. This would have been a major diplomatic victory for the Irish delegation. But a positive vote in the Security Council was still required to discuss the item at all and as the meeting on 20 August drew closer the prospects for such a vote became steadily less favourable.

The British Foreign Office mounted a diplomatic counter-offensive to ensure that the Irish move was defeated. Lord Caradon, the British

ambassador to the UN, took the lead in lobbying members of the Security
Council; British diplomats also moved to exert pressure on the
governments of member states to vote down the proposal. Hillery
discovered that the British lobbying was highly effective:

> I asked to meet the representatives of the member states
> ... They were all very friendly and many traced Irish
> ancestry; the Permanent Representatives of the nations
> beamed on me when we passed each other. Then as they
> got instructions from their governments they distanced
> themselves a bit. The British diplomatic machine was
> working at full power.[47]

The British side held several key advantages in keeping the Irish initiative
off the agenda. They relied heavily on Article 2.7 of the United Nations
Charter, which prohibited intervention by the UN in matters within the
'domestic jurisdiction' of any state; even governments sympathetic to the
Irish case were reluctant to sanction UN involvement in an area under the
jurisdiction of another sovereign state. The principle of domestic
jurisdiction was a powerful weapon in Britain's armoury at the UN in the
autumn of 1969.

The British delegation pointed to the Downing Street Declaration, an
agreed statement of principles between the British government and the
Stormont administration issued on 19 August 1969. Following the crisis
of the previous week, British ministers acted decisively to compel the
adoption of a sweeping civil rights programme by Stormont. The
Declaration imposed a firm commitment on the unionist authorities to
implement wide-ranging reforms in Northern Ireland, including impartial
allocation of public housing, reform of the local government franchise,
the establishment of a Commission of Complaints and measures to
overcome discrimination in the public administration.[48] An inquiry by
Sir John Hunt into security was established at the same time; the Hunt
report in October led to the disbandment of the B Specials.[49] It was not
coincidental that the Declaration was adopted on the day before Hillery's

address to the Security Council. The joint statement reaffirmed that responsibility for Northern Ireland was 'entirely a matter of domestic jurisdiction'.[50] Lord Caradon quoted the Declaration extensively to illustrate his government's commitment to the full realisation of civil rights in Northern Ireland.[51]

The British representatives also commanded considerable leverage to place pressure on wavering delegations through traditional political and trading alliances.[52] The Irish delegation had expected the support of the African and Asian members of the Council, but found that most developing states were unwilling to commit themselves, influenced by British pressure or by fear of creating a precedent for UN intervention in sovereign states.[53] Pakistan was the only developing country that made a definite commitment to voting for inscription of the Irish initiative. Moreover, no help could be expected from the United States, which was supportive of Britain's position; the US ambassador, Charles Yost, told Cremin that he would abstain in the vote on instructions from the State Department.[54] The Irish delegation reported to McCann in Dublin on 19 August that the outcome was still uncertain, but they were much less hopeful about winning a vote.[55]

The Irish representatives received some help from an unexpected quarter – the Soviet ambassador. Hillery and Cremin met Vladimir Zakharov of the USSR on 18 August and initially received a non-committal reception:

> The Russian alone [of all the envoys] was claiming no Irish grandmother. I met him at his embassy and he listened without committing himself. When we left, Con Cremin said; 'You would not know who was the higher authority here, it could be the chauffeur because of his position in the Communist Party.'[56]

But on receiving instructions from Moscow, the ambassador warmly assured Hillery that he could rely on the full support of the Soviet delegation. The Irish minister also received a favourable mention in

The Royal College of Surgeons, Ireland, *c.*1911:
(l–r) Dr Michael J. Hillery, Dr O'Donoghue (back row)
Dr J.M. Horan, Dr Ashe

Courtesy of Michael Hillery

Eleanor, Des, Paddy and Berry (from bottom).

Courtesy of Michael Hillery

Wedding photograph, Paddy and Maeve Hillery, St Flannan's College, Ennis, October
1955: (l–r) Bill Ryan, Des Hillery, Fr Michael Mooney, Dr Jack Sherry, Paddy Hillery,
Maeve Hllery, Angela Finnegan, Eileen Finnegan and Berry Hillery

Courtesy of Michael Hillery

Paddy and Maeve at Spanish Point.

Courtesy of Dr Maeve Hillery

The Minister for Education practices judo, 1963.

Courtesy of Dr Maeve Hillery

De Valera in Sutton, just after the arms crisis, June 1970: (l–r) Paddy Hillery, Éamon de Valera, Maeve (with Vivienne), John.

Courtesy of John Hillery

Paddy Hillery and Jack Lynch sign the Treaty of Accession to the European Communities, Palais d'Egmont, Brussels, 22 January 1972.

Courtesy of Dr Maeve Hillery

Hillery with Willy Brandt, Chancellor of the Federal Republic of Germany.

Courtesy of the National Library of Ireland

Martyn Turner cartoon on Hillery's first year in Brussels

Courtesy of Martyn Turner

Martyn Turner cartoon on Hillery's appointment as a
European Commissioner, 1973

Pravda, the official journal of the Soviet Communist Party, along with
Bernadette Devlin, the radical left-wing activist who had recently been
elected as an MP. His mission to the UN was featured in the same issue
as a photograph of Devlin breaking a brick to provide her with
ammunition in a street demonstration.[57] Soviet backing was undoubtedly
a double-edged sword, but Hillery at this stage was grateful for whatever
support he could get. He later remarked to John McColgan that his
experience as Minister for Education had served him well in dealing with
the Soviets: 'Once you have dealt with the Irish bishops, the Russians are
a doddle.'[58]

The Irish case gained more from the quiet assistance of the French
ambassador, Armand Bérard. The French government would not support
inclusion of the item on the Council agenda, maintaining that it would
compromise the principle of domestic jurisdiction, but the French
delegation also told their British counterparts that the Irish should at least
be given a hearing.[59] The most influential intervention was made by the
delegation of Finland. The Finnish ambassador, Max Jacobson, told
Cremin that he could not vote for inscription, but was willing to propose
a motion allowing the Irish Foreign Minister to address the Council
before any vote on the adoption of the agenda. Jacobson had 'found a
degree of support for it' among other members, 'although Britain was
very reluctant'.[60] De Pinies, who remained staunchly supportive of the
Irish case, was pessimistic about the outcome of a vote and advised Hillery
that 'the Finnish procedure would be the best possible'.[61] The Finnish
proposal was the one ultimately adopted by the Security Council, and
provided the key to avoiding a damaging defeat for Irish diplomacy at
the United Nations.

After two days of lobbying, Hillery was convinced that the Irish could
not win a majority in the procedural vote. Instead, the Irish
representatives sought to secure a hearing for their case before the
Council, but to avoid a vote on the issue at all costs. Hillery fully shared
his department's opinion that 'the worst possible result would be to
appear to put a UN body on record as endorsing the status quo'.[62] The
Irish lobbying had not secured the necessary votes to put their initiative

on the agenda, but it had generated widespread support among the
Council members for allowing Hillery to present the Irish case. The
proposal circulated by the Finnish ambassador provided an escape route
for the Security Council; most member states wished to avoid either
alienating Britain or giving a straightforward rebuff to Ireland, which
enjoyed a favourable reputation for its commitment to the United
Nations and its participation in UN peacekeeping missions. Hillery and
Lord Caradon met briefly on 18 August to discuss the forthcoming
debate, at the request of the British representative. Caradon, under
pressure from Whitehall to secure the defeat of the Irish initiative,
demanded irritably 'Do you realise what you're doing, young man?'[63]
Hillery knew exactly what he was doing. He sought an international
forum to make the Irish case on the crisis in the North, without
exacerbating the violence; he also had to escape without a decisive public
setback for his long-term objectives.[64] He was fortunate in dealing with
a British minister of Caradon's stature and background. Hugh Foot had
resigned his previous post at the UN in protest at British imperial policies
in Africa; Harold Wilson appointed him as UN ambassador and Minister
of State at the Foreign Office, with the title of Lord Caradon, in 1964.[65]
He enjoyed a deserved reputation for a broad-minded outlook and
distaste for traditional European imperialism, which served him well in
his role at the UN. Caradon showed considerable understanding of the
Irish position and did not attempt to block Hillery's request for a hearing
before the Council. But there was no arrangement between Hillery and
Caradon; the Irish delegation did not know in advance what Caradon
would do.[66] Cremin told Hugh McCann in a phone call to Dublin on
19 August that the British representative might well object to the
minister being heard. The Irish ambassador also thought that the British
were likely to insist on a vote if they were confident of the outcome.[67]
Hillery prepared for the confrontation before the Security Council
without knowing what the British would do and without being certain
even that he would be allowed to speak.

It was one of the most dramatic moments of Hillery's career, preceded
by extraordinary tension and an unprecedented level of media interest in

the activity of an Irish Foreign Minister. He gave TV interviews to two of the major US channels, CBS and ABC news, on 18 August; he also gave a press conference to UN correspondents on the same day, briefed Irish journalists on 19 August and did several other interviews over the course of the week.[68] Hillery's six days at the UN were marked by a frenetic round of diplomatic lobbying, consultations with UN officials, television appearances and interviews; in the midst of the organised chaos, the Irish delegation set to work preparing a speech, on the assumption that Hillery would be allowed to give it. Hillery's speech was a collective effort, drawing on the expertise of several officials in the Irish Mission, but it was finalised by Hillery himself only a few hours before the Council meeting. Paddy McKernan and Declan Connolly of the Department of External Affairs wrote the first draft. Hillery then hammered out a revised version in concert with Con Cremin and Paddy Power, the legal adviser to the Irish Mission, on the evening of 19 August. Hillery himself was reworking the speech for most of the night:

> I took the draft to work on and was still working on it in the heat of my bedroom at 5 o'clock on the morning of the meeting of the Security Council … in the morning the speech was arriving sheet by sheet from the typist and there was a race between the typist and the Council. Luckily the Council was late starting and with the delay we succeeded in having a typewritten script to hand before the meeting began.[69]

The Security Council meeting was fixed for 10.30am on Wednesday 20 August, but the President did not open the session until about 1pm; the delay was caused by intensive consultations between delegations and especially between envoys and their governments.[70] Caradon succeeded in resisting pressure from his superiors in London to force a vote and this removed the final obstacle to Hillery's appearance before the Council. The proceedings of the Council were televised around the world and Hillery was informed as he entered the Council chamber that he would have a worldwide audience of 120 million people.[71] The meeting itself proceeded almost exactly as Hillery and Cremin had hoped. The provisional agenda consisted solely of the Irish application for a peacekeeping force in Northern Ireland. Caradon appealed to the Council not to adopt the agenda, primarily on the basis that it would undermine the principle of domestic jurisdiction even to consider the Irish request. But he raised no objection when Ambassador Jacobson proposed that Hillery should be invited to make a statement to the Council, for the purpose of explaining the Irish position, before any vote was taken on the agenda.[72] Cremin reported to McCann later on the same day that if Caradon had forced a vote at that stage, 'it is very probable that he would have not only succeeded in voting us down but also, of course, prevented the minister from speaking at all'.[73]

Having overcome the initial procedural hurdle, Hillery proceeded to make the most difficult and important address of his career. He began by making the case for the Security Council to consider the situation in Northern Ireland, noting that while the Irish government accepted the practical reality of British control in the North, it did not concede Britain's right to exercise jurisdiction there.[74] While he reiterated the long-standing nationalist position that unity was the only lasting solution, he also declared that the Irish government sought to secure unity by peaceful means and drew attention to Lemass's policy of economic co-operation between North and South. Hillery soon ranged far beyond traditional anti-partition rhetoric, focusing especially on the threat to peace in Northern Ireland and on the denial of civil rights to the Catholic minority. He criticised the Apprentice Boys' parade in Derry on 12 August as sectarian and provocative, attacking 'the tragic folly of the Six-County government in allowing that parade to go on and the profound misjudgement exhibited by the British authorities ...'[75] Hillery emphasised the failure of the Stormont authorities to deliver meaningful reforms and their inability to maintain law and order in an impartial fashion; here at least his arguments were clearly credible and were underlined in striking fashion by the events of the previous fortnight, if not the previous twelve months. He argued that 'the persistent denial of civil rights' was the most immediate cause of the demonstrations and protests of the previous year. The Council would be justified in considering the Irish request solely on the basis of the entrenched discrimination against the minority. Hillery scored a telling point with the developing states by quoting Michael Stewart on the importance of human rights; the Foreign Secretary, in an address to the General Assembly on 14 October 1968, had declared that 'no country can say that the human rights of its citizens are an exclusively domestic matter.'[76]

Hillery concluded on a note of careful moderation, emphasising that the Irish government was anxious to act through the UN to defuse the crisis in the North and to prevent the conflict from 'spreading beyond the area itself and leading to friction between two neighbouring Member States'.[77] His final appeal to the Council was a carefully coded plea to avoid a negative vote:

> We sincerely trust that our hopes will not be disappointed, that the Council will not close the door to our appeal, and that in particular, it will not appear to have pronounced negatively – and perhaps inadvertently so – on the merits of a national issue which has been a source of constant concern and preoccupation to the Irish nation during the last fifty years.[78]

Hillery's speech was notable for its moderate tone and content and for the fact that it was not mainly about the evils of partition, nor did it follow the common nationalist narrative featuring seven centuries of British oppression. His statement was a subtle balancing act, which placed the cause of civil rights and the danger of sectarian conflict at the heart of the Irish appeal to the Security Council, while maintaining the traditional nationalist thesis that partition was the root cause of the conflict. It was carefully crafted so as to promote the Irish case effectively before an international audience, without provoking a vote that Ireland could not win. Hillery's speech was about the most moderate public statement of government policy that could have been made by any Irish minister in the extraordinary circumstances of the time.

The Soviet ambassador was the only representative who spoke in favour of the Irish application. Ambassador Zakharov adopted a harsher tone than Hillery, attacking Britain for encouraging religious divisions in Northern Ireland and failing to overcome inequality and discrimination.[79] Most other representatives did not participate in the debate. Their silence reflected a widely held reluctance by members of the Council to take a stand on the issue and an equally widespread hope that a vote could be avoided. Lord Caradon played a constructive part in the diplomatic dance. He referred to 'the careful and restrained speech' made by Hillery and made a similarly restrained response. He acknowledged the need to establish civil rights in Northern Ireland; he quoted liberally from the Downing Street Declaration, assuring the Security Council that the British government and the Stormont authorities were united in their determination 'to achieve equality'.[80] While this might not have been strictly true of Chichester-Clark's administration, it certainly represented the position of the Labour government. Caradon implicitly conceded Hillery's point that the minority had not enjoyed equal rights for the previous generation.

Yet the British ambassador's urbane tone did not stop him landing a couple of blows of his own; the most telling was his assertion that the Irish state had effectively recognised the fact of partition and accepted its consequences, whatever theoretical position was stated by the Irish Constitution.[81] Caradon's comment on the constitutional issue was uncomfortably close to the bone for the Irish delegation, not least because it contained a strong element of truth. He also pointed out correctly that British troops had been welcomed by Catholics in the North and made the much more contentious claim that the British army was acting as a peacekeeping force. Caradon's statement essentially reaffirmed the British position in moderate language; it gave no ground at all on the key point that Northern Ireland was solely a matter for the British government, in consultation with the Stormont authorities. Yet Caradon sought to contain the diplomatic confrontation wherever he had the freedom to do so. He concluded his address by indicating that he would not object if the Council decided to adjourn without voting on the provisional agenda. The delegate of Zambia then proposed to conclude the meeting and the Spanish President immediately declared that the Security Council would adjourn by unanimous consent of the members.[82]

Hillery was greatly relieved by the outcome. He had succeeded in bringing the Irish case before the Security Council and had avoided a vote that would have been interpreted as a justification of the political and constitutional status quo. He also secured a notable propaganda victory in publicising the Irish case on Northern Ireland in an international forum before a global audience. Cremin reported to McCann later on the same day that 'the outcome was the "least bad" which we could have expected, and the general reaction to the minister's speech was very favourable'.[83] While it was not entirely unprecedented for a member state which was not represented on the Council to be heard before the adoption of the agenda, it was a highly exceptional procedure very rarely seen at the United Nations.[84] Moreover Hillery was very fortunate in avoiding a vote. Cremin estimated that Ireland could rely on only five definite votes and would certainly have failed to secure the necessary majority to get the issue on the agenda. The Irish delegation believed that Lord Caradon had received instructions from the Foreign Office to force a vote, but persuaded his senior colleagues to modify these instructions shortly before the meeting in response to the predominant feeling on the Council.[85] The Irish government did not secure a peacekeeping force, but then neither Hillery nor any other informed observer had expected them to do so.[86] Lynch was satisfied with the outcome, sending a message of congratulations to Hillery and the Irish officials on the afternoon of 20 August.[87] The appeal had served its purpose admirably from the Taoiseach's point of view, relieving pressure on the government and keeping the hawks at bay in Dublin.

Yet the appeal to the UN was not solely about containing political factionalism at home. Hillery secured some valuable gains from his address to the Security Council. The efforts of the Government Information Bureau (GIB) were a very different matter. The GIB launched a large-scale propaganda offensive around the same time to publicise the crisis in the North and win international support for the Irish government's position. The effect of this campaign in generating foreign media coverage or support was limited and it caused tension between the GIB and the Department of External Affairs.[88] Hillery himself was sceptical about the benefits of the propaganda drive and believed that the GIB's efforts, in New York at least, were not merely futile but counterproductive.[89] He was concerned that his initiative at the UN would be presented in the Irish media simply as 'political pyrotechnics', which were of no real value.[90] Dennis Kennedy, the Diplomatic Correspondent of *The Irish Times*, essentially took this view, believing that the initiative was a piece of political theatre with minimal diplomatic effect: 'It might be more accurate to describe it as a propaganda triumph rather than a diplomatic one'.[91] This was not entirely a fair portrayal of Hillery's initiative. There was certainly no diplomatic breakthrough in relations between the Irish government and their British counterparts. Hillery's statement and Caradon's response underlined the gaping fissure that still divided the two governments on Northern Ireland; even with a deliberate attempt on both sides to lower the political temperature, it was obvious that the two governments were poles apart in their view of the crisis. Yet it was striking that despite the persistence of major differences between the two governments, the diplomatic conflict at the UN was successfully contained. There were equally some real diplomatic benefits, which were not obvious at the time. The initiative increased the pressure on British ministers to accelerate the pace of reform in the North. Perhaps more significantly, Hillery's appeal to the UN underlined the Irish view of the severity of the crisis both internationally and to the British government. The crisis had been brought before the most prominent and important body within the international organisation, reflecting the reality that the Irish state had a vital interest in the future of Northern Ireland and would not accept that it was simply an internal affair between Westminster and Stormont.

But no amount of skilful diplomatic manoeuvres could overcome the divisions within the government. Hillery advised the Taoiseach on 26 August that the Irish delegation at the UN should maintain pressure on

Britain to enter talks by seeking to have the situation in Northern Ireland considered by the General Assembly.[92] He also recommended that a focus on human rights in Northern Ireland would command greater support among the UN member states than 'the territorial aspect' of partition. The motivation for Hillery's proposal had more to do with internal Irish politics than with international diplomacy; he felt that having raised the issue before the Security Council, 'we shall be under very great pressure at home, including in the Dáil ... to maintain the momentum and have the question aired in the General Assembly at its forthcoming session'.[93] Lynch supported Hillery's move, which was in line with a previous Cabinet decision, but it was far from sufficient to satisfy the hardliners within the government.

While Hillery was in London on 15 August, Kevin Boland had demanded the mobilisation of the part-time second line reserve and the withdrawal of the Irish military contingent on peacekeeping duties in Cyprus, with the clear intention of enhancing the army's capacity to intervene in the North. When the government declined to take these measures, Boland announced his resignation and stormed out of the meeting.[94] He was persuaded not to stand down by President de Valera on the basis that it would merely allow Fine Gael to form a government.[95] But tensions continued to run high within the Cabinet in early September, when another controversy flared up over the peacekeeping mission in Cyprus. The government had agreed in June to send out a force to extend the Irish involvement in the UN mission, but several ministers objected to going ahead with the deployment due to the situation in the North. While Blaney and Boland took the lead in exerting pressure on the Taoiseach, Haughey was also firmly associated with a hardline stand in the autumn of 1969; so too was Jim Gibbons, the Minister for Defence. Lynch phoned Hillery on 8 September to express his concern about a government meeting that was due to be held on the following day:

> Jack phoned; he was obviously agitated. He said, and he is
> usually right in his information, that tonight would be a

bad night in Belfast and then he said, 'I don't know which
way to turn and what will I do tomorrow?' Tomorrow was
a government meeting in which all the hawks would want
to invade the North with a force that wasn't capable of
doing so, and apart from their incapacity, by their very
action would precipitate an attack on the hostages, the
400,000 Catholics in the North. He was obviously
distressed, his line is the strong one; they will call him
weak.[96]

Lynch and Hillery discussed what to do if there was a further outbreak
of violence; Hillery thought that the Irish application to the Security
Council could be reactivated, although he was doubtful whether this
would achieve anything satisfactory. Lynch's worst fears about street
violence in Belfast were not realised on this occasion and the government
meeting on 9 September was relatively calm. Hillery made the case for
maintaining Irish participation in the Cyprus force and the eventual
decision was a compromise – to prepare the replacement force but not to
send it yet.[97] The government also agreed that Hillery, rather than Lynch,
would represent Ireland at the General Assembly the following week; this
rescinded an earlier decision taken at the height of the crisis in August that
the Taoiseach should go personally to New York.[98] The decision to send
Hillery made sense following his appearance before the Security Council
and also reflected a marginal easing of the tension north of the border. The
deployment of British troops had stabilised the situation in the North
following the disturbances in August, although this interlude of relative
peace was to prove tragically brief.

Final act at the UN

The second Irish initiative of the autumn was played out in the less high-
powered surroundings of the General Committee, which determined the
agenda for the twenty-fourth session of the General Assembly. Hillery
could hardly have been blamed for suffering an oppressive sense of *déjà vu*;
to make any progress, he was faced with the formidable challenge of

persuading the 25 nations represented on the Committee to accept Northern Ireland as part of the UN's agenda for the session.[99] Con Cremin initially reported that the prospects of getting the issue on the agenda were 'fairly encouraging', but noted with masterly understatement that the British 'could make things a little awkward'.[100] Hillery, who arrived in New York on 14 September, was pessimistic about his chances almost immediately. The violence on the streets of Northern Ireland had subsided and the urgency of the crisis no longer justified an appeal to the UN; most member states were wary of involvement in what appeared to be a long-standing territorial dispute. Hillery's frustration was vividly apparent in entries to his diary on 15-16 September: 'I get depressed and agitated every time I think of the task given to me here because I quite realise that the long term goal of reunifying our country will hardly be done through the United Nations.'[101] Hillery was deeply concerned that several members of the government had unrealistic expectations of what might be achieved at the UN: 'The long-term prospect of helping partition through getting support here for resolutions from time to time, year in, year out, does not at all fit with the attitude of many people in the government, certainly, whose desire it was to use the present situation as an excuse to get in and finish the partition question.'[102] He suspected that at least some of his associates in the government preferred to prolong the crisis with the aim of undermining partition:

> Now if I deal with the UN in the only way the UN will let me deal with it, with human rights to be pushed forward and the political question to be raised in the long term, this goes completely against the thinking of these men. Indeed they would prefer, I think, the present agitation to persist as an opportunity for getting in on the political question of reunification and certainly they don't want to look forward to years of negotiation, pushing and pressurising, but rather seem to consider that a quick success would be possible.[103]

Hillery aimed to exert pressure on the British government to secure the rapid implementation of the reforms and to guarantee civil rights for the minority in Northern Ireland; he also hoped to develop international support for Irish unity as a long-term objective. But a powerful group within the government believed that partition could be ended in the short-term and wished to exploit the opportunity offered by the outbreak of violence. This was an irreconcilable difference and Hillery was right to question where it might lead:

> These two things, what we [Hillery and Lynch] are doing and what they are thinking are quite contradictory. It may be that when they realise fully that the action they have asked me to take runs counter to the device ... they are using to get in on the North of Ireland picture, they may do something impatient, or they may just blame me for distracting them from their first intentions.[104]

Hillery's reflections in the autumn of 1969 proved all too accurate. The divisions within the government would explode with devastating effect in May 1970.

Yet in the meantime Hillery pursued the latest Irish initiative in New York despite his reservations about its usefulness and his wider concerns about the stance of powerful ministers at home. The publicity advantages of the initiative were insignificant, while a perceived failure at the UN could be expected to have domestic political repercussions, not least in provoking a hostile reaction to the international organisation from members of the government.[105] The British government was lobbying intensively to keep the item off the agenda, although Cremin was still hopeful of success until a couple of hours before the meeting on 17 September. Then four delegations, which had expressed support for the Irish initiative, withdrew their backing on the eve of the vote.[106] Hillery recorded in his diary that he expected a defeat at the General Committee: 'My final headcount, just before the meeting began, confirmed what I feared in the last few days, that we would be beaten in a vote.'[107] As defeat in any UN forum was the worst possible outcome, he sought once again to sidestep a vote. Hillery's task was greatly helped by the embarrassment of several delegations, including the United States, Denmark and France, which had received instructions to vote down the Irish application but had no desire to get embroiled in the dispute if a vote could be avoided.[108]

The discussion in the General Committee followed a broadly similar pattern to the debate in the Security Council. Hillery was invited to speak on the provisional agenda although Ireland was not a member of the Committee. He took a deliberately low-key approach, focusing mainly on the procedural argument for the General Assembly to consider the issue. His statement was relatively brief and concentrated on civil rights, asserting that 'human rights and fundamental freedoms' had been denied to a large section of the population in the North of Ireland.[109] Lord Caradon replied for the UK, again urging member states not to flout the principle of domestic jurisdiction; more unexpectedly, he appealed to Hillery to withdraw the proposal 'in the genuine interests of the people of Northern Ireland'.[110] This appeal presented Hillery with an awkward dilemma. He could not unilaterally withdraw the item at the request of the British minister without provoking a fierce backlash within the government; yet he faced certain defeat in the vote if he persisted in the face of Caradon's appeal. Hillery initially did not comment on the appeal at all, allowing the debate to continue, until Angie Brooks of Liberia, the chair of the Committee, asked him if he wished to respond to the British request. Hillery did so with considerable skill, walking a tightrope between withdrawing the item or rejecting Caradon's appeal; he told the Committee that the promises of reform followed fifty years of misrule and indicated that he 'would have to reflect' on the consequences for the reforms before he could agree to withdraw the proposal.[111] It was a fine example of deliberate political prevarication; he had no intention of withdrawing the issue from the UN himself but was willing to see it deferred, so that it would be held over the British government as a potential source of political leverage in the future.

Hillery's intervention achieved the desired result. Following a proposal to suspend consideration of the issue by Nigeria and Chile, Brooks announced that the item would be deferred until the next meeting.[112] This caused some palpitations among the Irish delegation, who feared that the vote might come up again on the following day, but the Committee did not consider the issue again.[113] The proposal was simply allowed to fade away, much to the relief of the Irish delegation. The outcome of the meeting testified to the general reluctance of most member states to vote on the issue. The US deputy permanent representative, William Buffum, spoke for many when he commented that the debate confronted his delegation with 'a very unhappy dilemma'.[114] Although the US dilemma at least would have been resolved in Britain's favour, most representatives were concerned to avoid a vote and were greatly relieved at the outcome. Diplomatic pressure from other member states undoubtedly influenced the decision by the British not to force a vote, which they would easily have won. It was the best possible outcome that the Irish delegation could have achieved and was considerably better than Hillery had expected just before the meeting.

Although he had escaped the embarrassment of losing a vote, Hillery had no obvious gains to show for his second appearance at the UN in six weeks. Irish journalists were not slow to point out that he had failed in his stated objective of securing a debate in the General Assembly on Northern Ireland.[115] Yet Hillery's moderate approach and persistent lobbying of UN member states yielded some useful results. Firstly he generated goodwill for the Irish position by avoiding inflammatory nationalist rhetoric and co-operating with efforts by other member states to avoid or at least contain the diplomatic confrontation between Ireland and Britain. This tactical approach encouraged several national representatives to refer favourably to the Irish case in the general debate which occurred at the start of the session. Among the eclectic combination of countries which expressed concern about the crisis in Northern Ireland were Iceland, France, Brazil and the Ivory Coast.[116] Hillery was particularly gratified by the comments of Maurice Schumann, the French Foreign Minister. Schumann promised at a meeting with Hillery on 20 September that he would raise the issue in his speech to the General Assembly. He was as good as his word, commenting that 'even our dear Ireland – to which European civilisation has incurred a debt that is more than one thousand years old – is being threatened by numerous and unjust rendings'.[117] While such support was relatively low key, it served Hillery's purpose of keeping Northern Ireland in the public domain at the UN. He informed Lynch on 23 September that he would have the opportunity to present 'a rational approach' to the problem in his own speech in the general debate. He aimed to underline that Irish attempts to raise the issue could be revived at any time and to generate international pressure on Britain to open talks with the Irish government.[118] Hillery recognised the need to move on from propaganda – a necessary feature of his appearance before the Security Council – to effective diplomacy, which would inevitably be a long-term undertaking and would require sustained engagement with the British government.

A more significant benefit of Hillery's initiatives at the UN, which could not be acknowledged publicly, was the valuable breathing space that his diplomatic efforts gained for Lynch. The Irish appeal to the UN temporarily placated the hawkish members of the Cabinet and gave Lynch time to develop his own response to the Northern crisis. While Hillery was still in New York, the Taoiseach gave the first real indication of new policy thinking on Northern Ireland, in his speech to a Fianna Fáil function in Tralee on 20 September 1969. Lynch looked forward to the ultimate achievement of a united Ireland, but unequivocally rejected the use of force to achieve nationalist objectives, emphasising that his government's policy was 'to seek the reunification of the country by peaceful means'.[119] Moreover, he acknowledged openly that Irish unity was a long-term objective and could only be achieved by winning the agreement of the majority in Northern Ireland. Lynch declared that his policy was based on 'seeking unity through agreement in Ireland between Irishmen'.[120] He held out the prospect of a federal solution in which the Stormont Parliament would retain most of its powers in a united Ireland and pledged that a united Irish state would protect the civil and religious liberties of Ulster Protestants.[121] Not all of what he said was new – a federal solution had been suggested by both de Valera and Lemass; all of his predecessors had also stood firmly against any attempt to coerce the North through physical force. But the Taoiseach's policy statement marked a significant departure from the precepts of traditional nationalism, with its insistence that British interference and unionist intransigence were the central obstacles to restoring the historic unity of the Irish nation. Lynch acknowledged explicitly that the Irish state had to win the consent of the Ulster Protestant community to a united Ireland; he implied no less clearly that the state would have to transform itself to achieve long-term national aspirations. Lynch's speech was the first public expression of the moderate line that he would pursue over the following three years, based on seeking peaceful and democratic change in the status of Northern Ireland.

The Taoiseach's policy statement, combined with Hillery's moderate presentation of Ireland's case at the UN, had a significant impact in laying the groundwork for talks between Irish and British representatives. Hillery hoped that the Secretary-General might intervene to broker discussions between the two governments, either directly or by sending a personal representative to Northern Ireland. Hillery had three meetings with U Thant in August where this option was explored and the Irish Foreign Minister also floated the idea publicly.[122] The British were implacably opposed to any intervention by the UN and Caradon dismissed the idea as an attack on domestic jurisdiction.[123] Yet the first tentative moves towards bilateral Anglo–Irish discussions began in September 1969. Hillery met Caradon several times in New York; their first discussion on 15 September focused on the Irish attempt to have the crisis debated by the General Assembly and consisted mainly of unproductive sparring over the usefulness of the Irish initiative. Hillery was not impressed by Caradon's warnings of dire consequences in the North if the Irish got their way about a debate: 'I listened to him for a long time and I finally told him that it was not my intention or the intention of the government to make matters worse, but that there were 700 years of history in every Irishman and Irishwoman and we couldn't, no government could, pretend that this was a problem to be solved by the British.'[124] But significantly, their discussions continued after the Irish proposal was effectively shelved, with

Caradon particularly concerned to maintain contact with Hillery. The Irish minister suspected that Caradon was simply taking out insurance against a resurrection of the Irish initiative for a debate, but it soon became clear that the British ambassador had wider concerns. On 25 September, as Hillery was preparing his own speech to the General Assembly, Caradon asked to see him; the British minister wished to pass on a message from his government, which had not yet reached the Taoiseach in Dublin. The message was a general assurance that the British government would speak to Irish ministers – but not yet:

> ... that in view of the Taoiseach's statement in Tralee published in Sunday's papers and in view of my statesmanlike handling of the matter in the UN up to now, that they would like me to know that while their main objective was to restore peace to the area, that certainly was not the finish of their thinking, that the British government was planning for the future and obviously from what he said did not exclude us from discussions. He was woolly and at the same time delivered their message that there will be talks but not now.[125]

While Caradon was vague about the nature of the talks offered by his government, the substance of the message was clear enough: it signalled a reassessment of the previous British line that Northern Ireland had nothing to do with the Irish government. Hillery recognised the importance of the message, even if it was disappointingly tentative from his perspective.[126] The possibility of talks with British representatives influenced his approach to the General Assembly speech on the following day, as Caradon no doubt intended. Hillery consulted T.K. Whitaker, who was in New York. Whitaker also believed that there was a genuine prospect of talks between Irish and British representatives; he advised Hillery not to inflame the situation in his address. Hillery then edited the speech to remove some of the more contentious references that might provoke a negative reaction in Westminster.[127] The prospect of Anglo-Irish talks in the short-term was a valuable prize that he was determined not to jeopardise.

Yet Hillery's first address to the General Assembly as Foreign Minister on 26 September was not markedly different in its tone from his previous speeches at the UN, although the focus of the speech was necessarily much broader. He discussed a wide variety of international issues, including Ireland's support for a comprehensive nuclear test ban treaty, the role of the UN in the Middle East and his concern about the conflict between Nigeria and Biafra.[128] But he devoted over half of his speech to the crisis in Northern Ireland, reiterating many of the same themes that he had enunciated before the Security Council, including the familiar demand for civil rights and the necessity for Britain to enforce reforms as a matter of urgency. Hillery appealed for the achievement of Irish unity by agreement, in a deliberate echo of Lynch's speech in Tralee. He emphasised the 'legitimate concern' of the Irish government with the future administration of Northern Ireland and the need for the two governments to 'consult and work together in the spirit of the Charter' to achieve a just and lasting solution.[129] While the British ambassador did not respond directly to this appeal for talks, Hillery's private meetings with Caradon gave the Irish minister a reliable indication of the development of official British thinking. It would be several months before substantive talks occurred at ministerial level, but the first tentative move towards Anglo-Irish discussions on the North occurred in the autumn of 1969.

Hillery's intensive diplomacy during this period amounted to much more than a public relations exercise. While the Irish initiatives at the UN might have appeared a mere publicity stunt to many observers, they had a real diplomatic and political value. Hillery's mission to the UN Security Council was designed to contain political tensions at home and to divert the pressure for military action from a powerful faction within the government; it achieved both objectives in the short term. It was not Hillery's fault that the day of reckoning between moderate and militant nationalists within the Cabinet was postponed, not averted. Hillery's appearance before the Security Council marked the first step in a gradual move by the Irish state to internationalise the conflict in Northern Ireland, which was followed up by Hillery himself and his successors throughout the 1970s. The Irish initiatives did much to highlight the crisis at an international level and generated diplomatic pressure on the British government to recognise that the Irish state had a vital interest in the future governance of Northern Ireland. Hillery's skilful management of the appeal to the UN ensured not only that Anglo-Irish relations survived virtually unscathed, but also that the initiatives helped to promote greater engagement between the two governments.

11.

Arms Crisis

'Further bloodshed among fellow Irishmen would create new and deeper scars in our people'.[1] Hillery's statement on 14 May 1970, in the midst of the marathon Dáil debate following the sacking of Charles Haughey and Neil Blaney, reflected his staunch opposition to the use of force to achieve nationalist objectives. Hillery was to be the first Irish foreign minister to deal with political violence as a regular feature of life in Northern Ireland. Militant republicanism was immeasurably strengthened by the unionist reaction to the civil rights movement and heavy-handed security measures on the part of the police and later the British army. Traditional advocates of physical-force nationalism were quick to take advantage of the volatile situation to launch a renewed campaign of political violence. The crisis was intensified by the emergence of deep divisions within the Irish government over Northern policy, which became interwoven with a fierce internal power struggle in Fianna Fáil. This struggle came to a head in May 1970, when the Taoiseach sacked senior ministers who were accused of involvement in an illegal attempt to import arms. Hillery firmly opposed military intervention or covert support for political violence in Northern Ireland: he sought instead to put diplomacy centre stage in the Irish government's response to the crisis. He argued for a workable and realistic policy towards Northern Ireland, involving reforms within the Northern state and peaceful change in the relationship between North and South.

Lynch consistently emphasised that the government was committed to ending partition by peaceful means. He told the Dáil on 22 October 1969 that 'the use of force would not advance our long-term aim of a united Ireland' and warned that the government would 'not connive at unofficial armed activity here directed at targets across the border'.[2] This position was consistent with the Taoiseach's speech at Tralee in September and Hillery's address to the Security Council. But it soon became apparent that an influential section of the government did not share the views of the Taoiseach or the Foreign Minister on the use of force to resolve the long-standing grievance of partition. The most prominent opponent of Lynch's stand was one of the most powerful figures in Fianna Fáil. Neil Blaney told a Fianna Fáil meeting in Letterkenny on 8 December 1969 that violence flowed from the continuation of partition. He believed that 'the ideal way of ending partition' was by peaceful means: 'But no one has the right to assert that force is irrevocably out. No political party or group at any time is entitled to predetermine the right of the Irish people to decide what course of action on this question may be justified in given circumstances.'[3] Blaney claimed that Fianna Fáil had never ruled out the use of force if the nationalist people of the North came under 'sustained and murderous attack' from the unionist regime. Blaney's speech amounted to open defiance of his party leader. Lynch immediately reiterated that his government rejected the use of force against the unionist majority, although he did not take any action against Blaney.[4]

Blaney and his allies mounted a thinly veiled challenge to Lynch's authority at the Fianna Fáil Ard Fheis in January 1970. Blaney's supporters distributed a leaflet among delegates to the annual conference, entitled 'Back Blaney'. The message given to delegates was stark and left little to the imagination:

If you want a united Ireland in your lifetime support Neil
T. Blaney at this Ard Fheis. Events inside the North prove
that the day is drawing nearer. Irish people are preparing
for the final struggle against British rule in Ireland.[5] The
Seventies are the Decade of Victory in the national struggle.

At the same conference Kevin Boland, one of the two Honorary
Secretaries of Fianna Fáil, made a speech warning that no group or
parliament had the right to divide the country.[6] Boland privately regarded
the crisis as 'the most favourable time in all our history for the
achievement of the national objective.'[7] Lynch saw off the challenge by
making a compelling speech, which combined a fierce attack on partition
with a commitment to achieving unity by peaceful means. He described
partition in colourful terms as 'a deep, throbbing weal across the land,
heart and soul of Ireland', which ate into Irish national consciousness like
a cancer: but he also emphasised that sectarian divisions predated partition
and that peaceful means provided the only path to unity.[8] He told
delegates bluntly that 'the plain truth, the naked reality, is that we do not
possess the capacity to impose a solution by force.'[9] Lynch warned too that
a solution imposed by force could not endure and pledged that his
government would explore every peaceful avenue of 'removing the
injustice of partition'.[10] Despite its anti-partition rhetoric, Lynch's speech
represented a subtle retreat from the rhetorical certainties of traditional
nationalism. The speech fulfilled its immediate purpose – Lynch received
an enthusiastic response from delegates and secured further breathing
space in dealing with his powerful opponents. But Lynch was unable or
unwilling to deal with the glaring contradiction between his stated
position and the militant strategy openly recommended by senior
members of the Cabinet. The government was essentially too divided in
early 1970 to have a coherent policy.

It was against the background of sectarian tension in Northern Ireland
and political turbulence in the South that Hillery sought to develop a
political and diplomatic alternative to physical force nationalism. His
department produced a memorandum on 'Policy in relation to Northern

Ireland', which was submitted to the Cabinet on 28 November 1969. The memo presented an analysis of the Northern state that was largely rooted in traditional nationalism. Northern Ireland was characterised as a political failure and 'an economic absurdity'; the unionist ruling class had maintained control for almost fifty years by exploiting religious fears within the Protestant majority and through discrimination of all kinds against the minority.[11] Yet its policy recommendations were creative, pragmatic and forward-looking. External Affairs urged that the 'reunification of Ireland should be sought by peaceful means through co-operation, agreement and consent between Irishmen'.[12] The department advised that, in the short term, the Irish government should do nothing to impede the implementation of the reforms in the North, applying pressure to the Stormont authorities and the British government to secure the full achievement of the reform programme. The memo recommended more intensive bilateral talks with the British, preferably private discussions without any publicity: 'Maximise discreet contact with Whitehall on the question both at the diplomatic level and at the ministerial level – under cover of other activities if necessary.'[13] The department also advised the early removal of Irish troops from the border, greater co-operation with Northern Ireland and initiatives by the Irish government to reassure Northern Protestants that their civil rights would be protected in a united Ireland; it was noted that changes would be required to ensure that 'a United Ireland would be a pluralistic rather than a confessional society'.[14] Perhaps the most influential recommendation was for the establishment of a section dealing specifically with Northern Ireland in the department itself. Hillery was surprised by the lack of such a dedicated section when he first succeeded Aiken.[15] No official within External Affairs was assigned to report on Northern Ireland; neither Aiken nor his predecessors regarded the North as an appropriate area for professional diplomacy. This deeply flawed method of operation played its part in ensuring that the Irish state was ill-prepared for the outbreak of violence in August 1969.

The memo fully reflected Hillery's views on the appropriate tactics and policies to be pursued by the government and he ensured that it was circulated to the Cabinet for the information of his colleagues. He also acted to improve the supply of information on the crisis available to External Affairs. Hillery operated through informal channels initially, but later set up an official structure within the department to provide political reporting on developments in the North. Eamonn Gallagher, a young diplomat and native of Donegal, was in Letterkenny in the autumn of 1969 and began to make reports to McCann on his own initiative. Hillery soon became aware of Gallagher's activity and encouraged it, allowing him to operate with considerable autonomy. Although Gallagher was still technically attached to the Political Division in Iveagh House, he became the department's point man on Northern Ireland, rapidly establishing a wide range of contacts with various strands of nationalist opinion.[16] He forged links with John Hume and Ivan Cooper, who had been leading figures within the civil rights movement in Derry and were elected to the Stormont Parliament as independent nationalist representatives in 1969. Gallagher maintained particularly close connections with Hume, visiting Derry on a regular basis to discuss the political situation with him and assiduously feeding Hume's views back to the department.[18] Gallagher also established good relations with James Doherty, chairman of the Nationalist Party, and Gerry Fitt, Westminster MP for West Belfast and the leading figure in Republican Labour.[19] Gallagher emerged as the department's unofficial envoy to Northern nationalists. He also developed a wider role as an influential policy adviser, reporting directly to Hillery and Lynch.

Hillery was reticent at first about formalising the department's operation in the North, mainly as a result of the fall-out from the activities of Army Intelligence in Northern Ireland during 1969–70, which became a prominent part of the arms crisis. But he soon concluded that the need for accurate political information was paramount; he expressed frustration that he could get a detailed political report from the embassy in Lagos about the civil war between Nigeria and Biafra, but no comparable flow of information about the conflict in Northern Ireland.[20] Hillery authorised the creation of an Anglo-Irish Political and Information Division within Iveagh House towards the end of 1971; the new section came into being on 1 February 1972. The mission of the new division was to assess the situation in Northern Ireland and advise the government on an appropriate policy response. Hillery told Seán Donlon, who was a prominent member of the division from its inception, that he wanted Irish officials to talk to all political representatives who had no connections with violence. The minister was keenly aware of the political sensitivity of Irish officials operating in the North; he warned Donlon that the division's role within Northern Ireland was related purely to gathering information – 'whatever you say, say nothing.'[21] The section's contacts in the early phase of its activity were predominantly on the nationalist side of the sectarian divide, although this reflected the entrenched nature of the conflict in the early 1970s rather than Hillery's preferences. Hillery, however, broke new ground in applying professional diplomacy to the situation in Northern Ireland for the first time since the foundation of the state.

While Hillery's concerns about the need to observe political discretion were undoubtedly genuine, he permitted official activity in Northern Ireland that went beyond political reporting and information gathering. The department, working mainly through Gallagher, quietly encouraged a new political combination that would embrace the moderate nationalist forces in the North. John Hume took the lead in promoting the formation of a broadly based political movement. The Social Democratic and Labour Party (SDLP) was formed in August 1970, bringing together a wide range of nationalist parties and individuals. Gerry Fitt was the first leader of the new party; its leading representatives included Hume, Cooper and Austin Currie.[22]

Hillery adopted the broad strategy outlined by the departmental memo over the following year, seeking to achieve progress through quiet dialogue with the British at both official and ministerial level. He succeeded in developing contacts with Oliver Wright, the UK government's representative in Belfast; Wright was essentially Whitehall's watchdog over the Stormont authorities. Sir Andrew Gilchrist, the British ambassador to Ireland, arranged a meeting between Hillery and Wright in Dublin on 12 November 1969. The two men had a general discussion, which was largely confined to outlining their respective positions on the North and considering how the major differences between the two governments might be managed. Hillery summed up the meeting soon afterwards in a private note: 'There was no substance really, it was a measurement of how much we understood the total situation and a clearing that we were at least aware of their problems and that they would understand ours.'[23] Yet the meeting also represented a clear signal that the British government was willing to engage with their Irish counterparts on Northern Ireland; the initiative for the meeting came from the British side.[24] The meeting was followed by private talks between Irish diplomats and British officials, including Ronnie Burroughs, Wright's successor as Whitehall's representative in Belfast, in the spring of 1970.[25] Hillery also moved to initiate talks with British ministers on the North under the guise of other issues, as recommended by the departmental memo. He met George Thomson, the Commonwealth Secretary, several times to discuss Anglo-Irish free trade issues and Ireland's negotiations for accession to the EEC; at Hillery's instigation, the talks invariably included Northern Ireland as well. The Labour government was willing to allow such talks but insisted on keeping them secret.[26] Hillery urged Thomson to accelerate the pace of reform within Northern Ireland, seeking the rapid implementation of reforms to eliminate discrimination and gerrymandering, which would give some practical evidence that Lynch's moderate policy was working. The Irish minister also emphasised the need for the British authorities to protect the minority from attack by loyalist extremists.[27] Thomson himself was sympathetic to Irish demands for reform. Although he had little power to affect the situation directly, he was willing to pass on the content of the discussions to Harold Wilson. The talks served a useful purpose in opening up another channel of communication at a time when public discussions between Irish and British ministers on the North were rare and often counterproductive when they did occur.

Hillery's diplomatic activity meant that he was out of the country much of the time. This inevitably meant that he was detached from security and intelligence developments in Dublin. But he was only too well aware of the tensions within the government over the unfolding crisis in Northern Ireland. He was angry at the militant line taken by Lynch's opponents within the Cabinet. Hillery's concerns were vividly expressed in a private note, composed after a government meeting in the autumn of 1969:

> A government meeting is not a ballad singing session. Frankly, the army was not equipped or capable of doing what some people would like it to do. The whole lot smothered in lashings of creamy patriotic ballad singing type of thing ... It would appear that they want to take the right posture but get no scratches. Indeed the subject could be raised whether we are capable of minding the piece we have got [the Republic] or whether any thought whatever has been given to it.[28]

Hillery was staunchly opposed to military intervention by the Irish army, recognising that any resort to force would be futile and disastrous. The Irish army was underfunded and inadequately equipped for sustained military action, which would involve conflict not only with the RUC and the B Specials but probably also the British army. He feared that extreme rhetoric and opportunistic 'ballad singing' by Irish ministers would have disastrous consequences for the whole island. Hillery believed that public militancy by other ministers would decisively undermine his attempts at constructive diplomacy: 'the mouthing of such inanities within the government and maybe without would make it impossible for any serious member to carry out a task on behalf of that government.'[29] He felt too that Blaney and his allies were attempting to manoeuvre the government into a position where intervention in Northern Ireland became inevitable; 'they were trying to create a situation where you couldn't refuse to go in and help.'[30]

Hillery was even more strongly opposed to supplying arms to Northern nationalists. He was influenced by his department's contacts with moderate nationalists in the North, especially John Hume and James

Doherty, who were passionately opposed to any attempt to arm the minority. Doherty gave Eamonn Gallagher a grim warning of the consequences for the Catholic population if guns were sent across the border:

> On the subject of gunrunning Mr Doherty said that hints had been made to him some time ago that guns could be made available to protect the minority. His reply was that 100 coffins should be sent with each gun and he would guarantee to send them back across the border filled with 'our own people'.[31]

Hillery was convinced that giving guns to the minority would merely provoke a ferocious loyalist backlash, with horrifying consequences for vulnerable Catholic communities. Moreover, he recognised that supplying guns to elements in the North outside the effective control of the Irish government was a recipe for catastrophe: 'You could start the war by giving guns to people who recklessly would start without sufficient brains or care for the finish.'[32] Supplying guns would be seen by unionists, not unreasonably, as an act of war and could trigger massive civil strife; then the logical outcome was that the Irish state would be forced to intervene in Northern Ireland and would be drawn into open military conflict with Britain.

He was deeply concerned, however, that British troops might be unable to protect Catholic communities in remote border areas from attack by loyalists. He recognised that Catholics in such communities had legitimate fears if a full-scale civil war erupted in the North – an eventuality that appeared perfectly possible in 1969. But Hillery rejected the idea that the best way to protect vulnerable Catholics was to give them guns. Instead, he adopted a twin-track solution. He constantly warned British ministers of their obligation to protect the Catholic minority and privately favoured a strong British military presence in Northern Ireland as long as the crisis continued. His taped recollections reveal a very different line about the British presence from the one he was obliged to take publicly: 'I came to the conclusion that we should make sure that the British Army had all the authority it wanted to take care of the unionist elements if they attacked the minority.'[33] But Hillery also advised the Cabinet that military planning was needed to safeguard the minority if there was a drastic deterioration in the situation in the North. The army should be prepared to perform two essential functions in a worst-case scenario:

1. Be ready to implement a commando type of exercise to save people in the border areas while the British Army was dealing with the rest.
2. Be in a sufficient state of preparedness to protect our own territory from Ulster type of invasions (UVF) should this arise.[34]

He recommended that preparations be made to protect isolated Catholic communities against a full-scale loyalist pogrom on the basis that British forces might be fully occupied in Belfast and Derry; the army should also be ready to repel incursions into the state by Protestant paramilitary groups, such as the Ulster Volunteer Force (UVF). He favoured the training of small commando units that could intervene rapidly and effectively in a Doomsday scenario. He believed this was the only effective action that the Irish government could take in the circumstances.[35] It is a striking indication of the feverish atmosphere within the government in 1969–70 that Hillery's proposal was denounced by at least one member of the Cabinet as dangerously moderate. In the midst of a semi-hysterical debate when Hillery advanced the idea, Jim Gibbons declared, 'You are accepting the border!'[36] No action was taken on this proposal, probably because Gibbons was opposed to it.

Hillery's proposal for the training of commando units, who would act only in the event of a full-scale civil war in Northern Ireland, was designed to avoid confrontation with British forces and contain the conflict rather than exacerbating it. Hillery rejected the ambivalence about the use of force to achieve political objectives, which was the hallmark of militant nationalists within the government. His own proposal for limited military action in a Doomsday scenario carried its fair share of risks; it could easily have been regarded in Westminster as a preparation for a full-scale Irish invasion of the North. But crucially Hillery was not proposing immediate action, but urging forward planning for a worst-case scenario. He was also seeking to head off more dangerous plans being canvassed around the Cabinet table.

Hillery believed at the outset of the crisis that Haughey and Blaney were simply seeking to displace Lynch by invoking rhetorical nationalism and presenting the Taoiseach as weak and ineffective on the national question, while they hid behind his policy of unity by peaceful means.

> In the early days I felt that the activities of these ministers were calculated to displace Jack Lynch and had motivation far away from the declared patriotic urge. But later I allow that they felt it was an opportunity [to end partition]. It was not.[37]

Hillery did not appreciate initially how far some of his fellow ministers were willing to go to achieve traditional nationalist objectives. He did not know at the time that a powerful section of the government in Dublin was actively involved in supporting militant republicans in Northern Ireland, who were instrumental in forming the Provisional IRA. The Provisional Army Council emerged in December 1969, following the split in the republican movement over the Marxist leadership's political strategy and its rejection of armed struggle.[38] An influential section of the political and security establishment in Dublin regarded the split in the IRA as a positive development, and saw the breakaway movement as a useful ally in the struggle to end partition. The attempt to exploit the crisis by an element within the government provided the context for the abortive attempt to import arms through Dublin in the spring of 1970, which were to be supplied to the Provisional IRA in Northern Ireland.

The key figures directly involved in the attempt to bring in arms were Captain James Kelly, an officer of Irish Military Intelligence, John Kelly of the Belfast Citizens' Defence Committee, and Albert Luykx, a Belgian businessman based in Dublin. Luykx was a Flemish collaborator with the Nazis in his native region, who had fled to Ireland following the Second World Ward. It is obvious that the individuals concerned did not act on their own initiative and that they received high-level support from senior ministers in Dublin. Captain Kelly testified to the Public Accounts Committee that he had acted with the knowledge and approval of Haughey and Blaney as members of the government's Northern Ireland committee.[39] Military Intelligence was deeply involved in clandestine meetings with militant republicans concerning the supply of arms. The importation of arms was to be cleared through customs by the Department of Finance.[40] The investigation by the Public Accounts Committee underlined that a substantial proportion of the relief fund for victims of distress in Northern Ireland was instead used to buy arms. The evidence given before the Committee indicated that approximately £32,000 from the fund was spent on the purchase of arms in West Germany.[41] The Committee reported that approximately £29,000, less than a third of the original allocation for relief, was actually spent on the relief of distress in Northern Ireland, while most of the remaining money was diverted for other purposes, including the arms deal, or possibly spent in Belfast 'on undetermined purposes'.[42] It was not hard to imagine what such purposes were in 1970. Hillery's department received confidential information from Gerry Fitt in December 1970 that the fund had been used to support the Provisional IRA. Fitt informed an Irish official that 'the misuse of the fund was both obvious and tragic in Belfast since about January of this year. Thugs and lay-abouts … were clearly in receipt of Irish money and, in his opinion, were employed to stir up trouble at will.'[43]

Senior ministers were effectively running their own Northern Ireland policy, which was in direct conflict with the policy of the Taoiseach. Hillery concluded later that 'there was a government within the government', suggesting that Lynch was misled by leading members of the Cabinet.[44] Captain Kelly, however, consistently maintained that the operation to import arms received support at the highest level and was sanctioned specifically by Jim Gibbons as Minister for Defence.[45] Gibbons equally trenchantly maintained that it was not; the conflict of evidence was to be a key feature of the arms trial in September–October 1970. Hillery understood how Captain Kelly could have felt that he was acting in line with the government's intentions: 'Oh yes, I would feel the same if ministers came to me, I would feel they were representing the government.'[46] But Hillery was emphatic that Lynch did not know what was going on:

> He ultimately ended up with a situation that quite appalled him. Jack had a kind of innocence about him. I remember one time [long before] there was a creamery problem; the people who tested the milk went on strike and the creameries couldn't take the milk from the farmers and Jack said why don't they just take the milk without testing it. Somebody said they would water it; he couldn't believe it. But I thought that was the utmost innocence. Then I just thought of that when the time came and he was suddenly faced with treachery in the government.[47]

The events of April and May 1970 reinforce Hillery's contention that Lynch did not know of the attempt to import arms for the Provisional IRA. The attempt to bring in arms failed, in part because no attempt was made to secure an end user's certificate, the essential legal requirement for arms importation, which could be issued only by the departments of Defence or Justice. The failure to secure an end user's certificate is difficult to reconcile with the claim by the leading figures involved that the operation was authorised at the highest level. If the ministers involved knew, however, that it was a covert operation, undertaken without the knowledge of the Taoiseach or the collective agreement of the government, the failure to seek an end user's certificate to legalise the importation was entirely understandable. The Belgian authorities stopped the consignment of weapons in Antwerp due to the lack of the necessary authorisation.[48] Captain Kelly and Albert Luykx then sought to arrange the transport of the arms from Vienna to Dublin on a regular Aer Lingus flight; this was also held up by the absence of an end user's certificate. The secretary of the Department of Justice, Peter Berry, was by now fully informed of the plot and he alerted Special Branch, who placed 'a ring of steel around Dublin Airport'.[49] Berry informed Lynch that ministers were involved in an attempt to supply arms to the IRA on 13 April.[50] The secretary then gave Lynch a full Garda report concerning the plot on 20 April and urged him to take action against the ministers implicated in the affair. Lynch did not tell Berry what he intended to do but was extremely angry at any suggestion that the government as a whole might be involved.[51]

There is no doubt that Lynch lost control over leading members of his government and that as a result, the state's policy towards Northern Ireland in 1970 was confused, uncertain and contradictory. The divisions within the government ensured that its initial response to the crisis was incoherent and sometimes actively damaging to the Taoiseach's stated objective of achieving peaceful change. The government was displaying a high level of political schizophrenia on the national question. Lynch and Hillery sought peaceful change by diplomatic means, while Blaney and his allies used belligerent rhetoric and sought actively to destabilise the Northern state. Hillery rightly identified the severe pressure on Lynch within the government:

> Jack complained to me about the pressures put on him at some of these meetings by the gung ho ministers. He occupied the unenviable position of either leading the country into a disaster or stopping the wave for battle and taking the position of not being one of the warriors or even interfering with the warriors as they 'freed' Ireland.[52]

This summed up Lynch's dilemma – how to contain the hawkish ministers without appearing to abandon traditional republican objectives. He could well be overthrown as leader of Fianna Fáil if his opponents managed to portray him as weak on the national question or failing to take any effective action to achieve the party's traditional objective of Irish unity. Moreover the opposition of senior ministers such as Haughey and Blaney presented particularly intractable problems. Blaney in particular commanded considerable support within the organisation, which was heightened by his militant stance on the national question. While Haughey in 1970 did not command the same level of support within the party as Blaney, he was a respected Minister for Finance, the son-in-law of the previous Taoiseach and the director of Fianna Fáil's successful general election campaign in 1969. The two ministers were the most prominent and powerful figures within Fianna Fáil. It was hardly surprising that Lynch was reluctant to take decisive action against them – removing the party's power brokers was not a simple undertaking.

The struggle for power within Fianna Fáil emerged openly in the late spring of 1970. Lynch acted to regain control of his government's policy on Northern Ireland, which had departed radically from the approach of unity by peaceful means laid down by the Taoiseach. Hillery suspected that trouble was brewing, although he had no inkling of what was actually going on. His apprehension was vividly expressed at a meeting with Dennis Kennedy early in 1970, when Hillery suddenly asked the *Irish Times* journalist, 'What's Blaney up to?'[53] Kennedy expressed surprise that Hillery would be asking a journalist such a question; surely he would know more himself about the actions of his Cabinet colleague. Hillery in fact had no idea of what his formidable colleague was doing and hoped that Kennedy might know more than he did. Hillery suspected that Blaney was attempting to undermine Lynch's moderate policy, but knew nothing about the plot to import arms until a week before the crisis broke publicly. Lynch sent for Hillery on Thursday 30 April to tell him about the involvement of senior ministers in attempted gunrunning:

> In the meantime the Taoiseach sent for me. He told me that he had some evidence that ministers were involved in the importation of arms and he was very agitated, not trusting anyone really. In fact he did say 'the only one I can trust is Childers and he is too naïve to be any good to me'. However, he did say he was going to talk to Blaney and

Haughey and I told him I was meeting Blaney at 2pm.
When I got to meet Blaney and before I sat to talk to him
he said 'The top man has sent for me and I can't talk to
you now' and I didn't see him again [that day]. The day
after he phoned to tell me that he had, as he put it, got the
bomb, and that Charlie Haughey had got the bomb as
well.[54]

The Taoiseach was determined to stop any attempt to import arms for the
IRA. He sought to secure the resignations of Haughey and Blaney, but
both men protested their innocence of any involvement in illegal activity
and refused to resign. Their refusal to go and Lynch's unwillingness to
sack them immediately testified to the Taoiseach's precarious position
within his own government. Lynch's next move was to raise the issue of
arms importation with the government collectively for the first time. He
told a meeting of the Cabinet on Friday 1 May that ministers had been
implicated in supplying arms to elements of the Northern IRA. Hillery
believed that Lynch was hoping to reassert his authority over the
government without provoking an open split, despite his obvious anger
at the attempt to import arms illegally:

However, Friday morning came, there was a government
meeting and the Taoiseach outlined what had happened
and went through the procedure anyway of saying that it
mustn't happen again. We went over the Northern policy
… the government meeting ended with everybody
thinking that the case was closed as far as the Blaney–
Haughey episode [was concerned], both were mentioned
at the government meeting and that was that.[55]

Hillery's account makes clear that the government confirmed its support
for the policy of unity by peaceful means; but it was also evident that
Lynch was not yet ready to move against his leading opponents. Lynch
warned ministers to avoid involvement in policy towards Northern

Ireland without his approval and imposed an immediate end to any collaboration with elements in the IRA. But he also indicated that there would be 'no implications' for the two ministers involved in the attempt to import arms.[56] The Taoiseach gave the impression that it was the end of the matter: 'At this first breaking of the news Jack said that he wanted ministers to stay away from this kind of activity. It seemed to be something with which he had dealt and did not want it to happen again'.[57]

The most plausible explanation for Lynch's apparently inconsistent reaction to the plot is that he was deeply uncertain about how to deal with it and not at all sure upon whom he could rely. He might well have preferred to reprimand the two ministers privately and avoid taking any immediate action against them.[58] This was almost certainly never a viable option and soon became politically impossible. The story of the botched attempt to import arms was now leaking out; the information was given to Liam Cosgrave, the leader of Fine Gael, by sources within the Gardaí. The same information was leaked to the *Sunday Independent*, although the editor decided not to publish it. Cosgrave went to Lynch on the evening of 5 May to confront him with details of the abortive plan to import arms.[59] Cosgrave's intervention brought the crisis to a head and provoked a belated but highly effective response from Lynch.

Hillery soon became aware that the crisis was only beginning. He had a lunchtime engagement at the Spring Show in the RDS on 5 May and in a bizarre turn of events travelled there with Neil Blaney, who was also invited as Minister for Agriculture. As the two ministers left Government Buildings, they were greeted by a group of media photographers who were taking photos of Blaney.[60] Although neither man was aware of it, Blaney was then enjoying his last day as a government minister. Lynch told the Dáil on the same day that he had accepted the resignation of Micheál Ó Móráin as Minister for Justice.[61] Lynch had sought Ó Móráin's resignation, replacing him with Desmond O'Malley, the Taoiseach's own Parliamentary Secretary. Ó Móráin's departure was closely linked with the crisis. Lynch later told the Dáil that the minister was asked to resign on grounds of ill health: while Ó Móráin was certainly ill, Lynch replaced him to secure a loyal and politically reliable minister at the Department of Justice.[62] Ó Móráin's removal was a prelude to more radical cabinet surgery within the next 24 hours. There were strong indications that the crisis was about to break, but Hillery, like most other ministers, did not know what was about to happen.[63] The Foreign Minister continued with his own schedule, opening an exhibition of tapestries for the French ambassador in Dublin on 5 May and then departing for London on a late-night flight. He had arranged a meeting with George Thomson, officially to discuss the EEC negotiations, but also for talks about Northern Ireland. Hillery intended to impress on Thomson the need for rapid implementation of the reform programme and effective action by the British government to protect the minority. But the meeting was overtaken by events in Dublin.

Lynch moved decisively to reassert control over the government. A press statement early in the morning of 6 May announced that the Taoiseach had dismissed Haughey and Blaney, while Kevin Boland had resigned as Minister for Local Government.[64] The sacking of Haughey and Blaney marked the culmination of the internal power struggle within Fianna Fáil, which was inextricably linked with the fundamental conflict between the Taoiseach and his most powerful ministers over policy on Northern Ireland. Boland, who had no involvement in the attempt to import arms, resigned in solidarity with his close ally, Blaney. Following a lengthy period of indecision and hesitation, Lynch had nailed his colours to the mast. The Taoiseach's announcement marked a seismic shift within the governing party and triggered the most intensive bout of infighting since Fianna Fáil's foundation. It remained to be seen whether the Taoiseach or even the government itself would survive.

Hillery had hardly arrived in London when the crisis erupted at home. The minister met briefly with Donal O'Sullivan, the Irish ambassador in London, before going to bed: Tom Cummins, the Irish ambassador to the Holy See, was also at the embassy. Hillery himself recalled the events that followed:

> It seemed I was awakened immediately. The two
> Ambassadors O'Sullivan and Cummins (without his

dentures) were in my room. There was a crisis in Dublin. The Taoiseach had fired Haughey and Blaney and Kevin Boland had resigned. I was required back in Dublin.[65]

It was John McColgan who called the Irish embassy in London to give Hillery the news. McColgan himself received word of the sackings, not from the Taoiseach's office, but from a 'very supercilious individual' in the British embassy in Dublin, who woke him up at home early on the morning of 6 May.[66] The private secretary then called the Irish embassy in London and told O'Sullivan to get the minister out of bed. Hillery did not sound surprised when he heard the sensational news. His first reaction was succinct: 'So it's happened then'. He immediately made his decision on what to do, giving McColgan quick instructions to contact the Taoiseach's private secretary: 'Ring Bertie O'Dowd and get him to tell Jack that I'm cancelling my meetings here and I'll be home on the first plane.'[67] Hillery did not know in advance of Lynch's move, but he undoubtedly expected something like it. Whatever he had thought after the government meeting the previous week, which had appeared to paper over the cracks between the Taoiseach and his leading opponents, Hillery's keen political sense told him that the conflict within the government could not be contained indefinitely. It was striking that Hillery was not summoned back to Dublin; McColgan called the minister on his own initiative and Hillery decided unhesitatingly to return to the political fray as soon as he received the news.

While Hillery had not been forewarned of Lynch's intention to sack Haughey and Blaney, there was no doubt where he stood. Hillery had consistently supported the Taoiseach's policy of unity by agreement since the previous autumn and he had done more than any other minister to give some credibility to the policy, especially through his address to the UN Security Council and his efforts at quiet diplomacy with the British government. He decided to return to Dublin immediately to reinforce the Taoiseach's position. His support for Lynch within the government and the parliamentary party would be crucial not only during the next week but over the following two years.

Hillery had to abandon the meeting with Thomson to rush back to Dublin. Instead Donal O'Sullivan met the Labour minister later that day. Not surprisingly, the meeting was overshadowed by events in Dublin – Thomson expressed shock at the dismissals and was particularly disturbed by Haughey's apparent involvement in the affair. The ambassador reported to Hugh McCann that Thomson 'had a particularly high regard for the man in question'.[68] O'Sullivan told Thomson that the situation in Dublin was 'obviously extremely fluid', which if anything was something of an understatement. Hugh McCann's report to Hillery on the meeting indicated that O'Sullivan had emphasised the uncertainty surrounding the survival of Lynch's government and warned that British ministers had to help the Irish administration through the crisis: 'who could tell what would happen in the next week. There could be an entirely different atmosphere in seven days time. Therefore it is very important, and he stressed this, that the British should give all possible moral support in the circumstances.'[69] O'Sullivan was particularly concerned that the British government should increase the pressure on the administration in Northern Ireland to implement reforms of local government, housing and other areas. Thomson agreed fully that it was essential to press ahead with reforms, saying that 'the scandal of Northern Ireland must be rectified' and that they would have to deal once and for all with the result of fifty years of neglect.[70] Thomson was sympathetic to the Irish case and agreed to convey the ambassador's concerns to Harold Wilson. O'Sullivan, however, made sure that the British minister took the point about the unstable situation in Dublin: 'the ambassador stressed that he was talking on behalf of the Administration as it existed in Dublin this morning and left Thompson [sic] with the warning that the elements of sanity in Dublin might not prevail and that he might be speaking on very different instructions next week.'[71] The meeting underlined the genuine sense of uncertainty and anxiety among Irish officials about the political situation at home. It also indicated, however, that the ambassador was willing to use the crisis to place renewed pressure on the British government, by conjuring up images of wild men holding the reins of powers in Dublin.

Hillery himself shared the concern that the 'elements of sanity' might not prevail at home. The sense of drama surrounding the crisis was heightened by a minor accident at the airport, when a supply truck hit the wing of his plane just before it was due to take off.[72] The accident did not prevent his return journey but ensured that Hillery was late in arriving at a crucial Cabinet meeting called by Lynch to discuss the crisis. The Taoiseach publicly announced that a special meeting of the Fianna Fáil parliamentary party would be held at 6 p.m. that evening to consider the situation. Lynch had to ensure that the Cabinet first agreed its strategy to present a united front at the party meeting. This did not prove a simple undertaking. The Cabinet was still meeting when Hillery arrived in the Dáil:

> When I got to Leinster House the members of the government were gathered like the Apostles waiting for the Holy Ghost in the Upper Room and had been there for some time without finding a way to deal with the situation. They did not know what the party would do or how it would react in the face of the patriotic nature of the allegations.[73]

Their uncertainty was entirely understandable. Lynch and his supporters had no way of knowing how the wider party would respond to the unprecedented public conflict within Fianna Fáil and feared that the deposed ministers might well be able to attract support on the basis that their actions were dictated by patriotic motives, particularly the concern to help the Northern nationalists in their hour of need. In these circumstances seeking an immediate vote of confidence in Lynch's leadership was fraught with danger: even if the Taoiseach won the vote, it could provoke a major split and the fall of the government. Hillery, perhaps benefiting from having had more time for reflection than some of his colleagues, proposed that any vote at the party meeting should deal only with the right of the Taoiseach to appoint ministers:

> We were going to the party meeting, and if there was a
> vote of confidence [in Jack Lynch], that's the end of any
> politician; anyone who had a vote of confidence lost the
> next, in a couple of days. So I said, 'Look, propose O'Malley
> for Minister for Justice and if they turn that down you are
> still standing; and you can go to the country if you like.'[74]

Hillery's political logic was impeccable; a vote on O'Malley's nomination
avoided the dangers of a vote of confidence in the Taoiseach. If it went
wrong, the potential minister could be sacrificed without bringing down
the government or the party leader. Lynch adopted a different version of
this tactic and sought the parliamentary party's endorsement only for the
right of the Taoiseach to appoint three new ministers, who were yet to be
nominated: this proposal was accepted without any dissent.[75] Hillery
deliberately sat near Blaney and heard him mutter 'that's all right'.[76] Lynch
also gave the TDs a briefing on the unsuccessful attempt to import arms.
The party leader faced no serious challenge at the meeting, which was
remarkably placid considering the extraordinary political situation. Fianna
Fáil deputies emerged from the crisis meeting after less than an hour,
proclaiming the virtues of party unity. A plausible explanation for the
relatively muted reaction of the TDs was provided by Hillery's
parliamentary colleague and rival in Clare, Sylvester Barrett:

> I met Sylvie Barrett, who knew his politics, on the stairs
> and asked, 'Will we have great trouble with the Party for
> firing them?' He replied that 'the more he fired the better',
> referring to the ever present ambitions for promotion
> among many members of the Dáil.[77]

Personal ambition was an element in the response of some TDs, but more
significant was pragmatic political calculation. It made little sense to
destabilise an already fragile government in the midst of a profound
political crisis in Dublin and escalating sectarian violence in Northern
Ireland. Fianna Fáil TDs were well aware that only the opposition parties

would benefit if Lynch's government collapsed. Moreover the tactical approach proposed by Hillery was a shrewd political move – even Lynch's most fervent critics were reluctant to question the right of the Taoiseach to make ministerial appointments. His leading opponents wanted to overthrow Lynch, not to break Fianna Fáil's hold on power. The government had survived the first hurdle, but the crisis was by no means over.

Hillery emerged as a key supporter of the embattled Taoiseach over the following weeks. He was particularly prominent in supporting Lynch during the week that followed the dismissal of the ministers. It was Hillery who undertook the thankless task of defending the government in an RTÉ interview on the evening of the sackings. He recalled that 'Jack had a habit of getting me to do things. That night he said, "They want someone down in RTÉ, would you go down?" One [interviewer] took the side that the government was wrong because they were into this arms carry on, the other took the side that it was wrong to fire the ministers without trial'.[78] Hillery defended Lynch's action on the basis that political office was not simply a job and ministers had to observe a more rigorous standard of conduct than ordinary employees: 'suspicion is enough to remove a minister from office if not to remove an ordinary man from his job.'[79] Hillery was also consistently supportive of Lynch in the marathon Dáil debate, which followed the sackings. An initial vote approving O'Malley's nomination as Minister for Justice was followed by a 35-hour debate on the nomination of three new ministers, which lasted until 9 May. The proceedings then rolled on into a confidence debate on 13–14 May. The debate proved one of the longest and most acrimonious in the history of the Dáil. Hillery was regularly in attendance throughout the proceedings, but made his most significant contribution in the confidence debate on 14 May.

He staunchly defended Lynch's actions in sacking the ministers on the basis that the Taoiseach had rightly acted to remove any member of the government who failed to accept his public commitment to achieving unity by peaceful means. Hillery carefully avoided any comment on the specific accusations of arms importation against the dissident ministers, focusing instead on their obvious dissent from Lynch's policy as stated in Tralee.[80] He made a diversionary attack on the Opposition, deriding claims that Fianna Fáil was hopelessly divided and drawing attention to divisions between Fine Gael and Labour on their attitude towards accession to the EEC.[81] But Hillery devoted most attention to Northern Ireland and it was here that he made a striking and innovative contribution: he not only denounced the use of force, but called for a new and fundamentally different political approach to Northern Ireland on the part of Irish nationalists. Hillery emphasised that the first step towards a peaceful solution was the implementation of reforms to eliminate the entrenched discrimination in housing, employment and local government against the Catholic minority. Redressing the real grievances of Northern nationalists was a core element of Hillery's approach and a constant feature of his speeches since 1969. But he went much further on this occasion, calling for 'reconciliation among Irish people' as the next essential step towards peace and warning his fellow TDs that reconciliation between the nationalist and unionist traditions would be complex and difficult:[82] 'It is steeped in history, replete with mistakes, errors, and I think that politicians on all sides of this House and in all parts of this country should remind themselves that mistakes can be made on all sides'.[83] This was a thinly veiled warning that politicians in the Dáil should take responsibility for their own behaviour with regard to the North. Hillery proceeded to condemn any attempt by one tradition on the island to dominate the other:

> It is not possible and, as I said earlier, not desirable, that one sole tradition in Irish history should make an attempt to dominate another. We have seen how such an attempt failed utterly in the North. Shall we, for our part here, now attempt to translate that failure to the whole of the country, or shall we take the alternative of trying to understand that the only solution to the Irish question is that which recognises the value of all our Irish traditions? Starting from

such a recognition we could work to bring them together peacefully.[84]

Hillery raised a key question ignored by hardline nationalists, including the dissidents within his own party – would the oppression of nationalists by Stormont not simply be repeated in reverse if unionists were to be coerced into a united Ireland? He argued that the unionist tradition was itself Irish and had to be equally respected by the Irish state. This approach, whatever its limitations, had the great advantage of denying any legitimacy to the use of force against the Protestant community in Northern Ireland.

Hillery asserted the right of the Irish government to act as a peaceful guarantor of the position of the nationalist minority: he believed correctly that such a role for the Irish state would be accepted by the British government, even if British ministers were not yet willing to acknowledge it publicly. He declared that unity would never be achieved by violence, which would only cause further bloodshed and deepen existing divisions: any attempt to arm the minority was dangerous and counter-productive. The supply of guns to paramilitary forces in the North undermined the government's official policy, damaged Ireland's moral authority internationally and threatened 'the life and peace of all our country'.[85] He denounced political violence and sectarian rhetoric in a striking passage, which could have applied equally to hardline unionists and traditional nationalists such as Blaney and Boland:

> We are peacemakers: we do not rant and rave against any part of our own country. We do not rant and rave against any group or section of our people. We do not demand anyone's surrender. It is difficult for us in this part of the country to control our emotions and strength of our feelings but I am certain that the policy of reunification with other Irishmen cannot be achieved by attacking those other Irishmen.[86]

Having categorically rejected the use of force, Hillery emphasised that the Irish government would rely on diplomatic and political initiatives to transform the situation in Northern Ireland and called upon all Irish nationalists to follow its lead:

> At this critical stage in our history we must use other means and keep on using them. Nobody, no matter what position he holds, has a right to act as if these other means will fail ... We must never overlook the reality that, if the unity of our country is to be restored, it must be based on a meeting of minds, a meeting of hearts of all classes and creeds of people in this country.[87]

Hillery here did not simply endorse peaceful means of resolving the national question but also implicitly challenged key elements of traditional nationalist ideology. He rejected a key assumption of traditional nationalist thinking since 1922 – that Britain caused the problem of partition and held the primary responsibility to solve it by delivering territorial unity on the island of Ireland. He certainly did not absolve Britain of responsibility; no Irish minister would be more critical of British policies in Northern Ireland. But Hillery argued that achieving Irish unity was primarily about achieving reconciliation between the divided traditions on the island. It was essentially an Irish problem, which would be resolved only by agreement between unionists and nationalists, North and South. Hillery certainly wished to see the achievement of Irish unity, but recognised that it could not simply be delivered by Britain. This amounted to a quiet rejection of the traditional nationalist view of the North as the fourth green field, tragically separated from the rest of the nation only by the machinations of the devious British.

Hillery's speech concluded with a conventional restatement of his support for the Taoiseach, praising Lynch for taking action to ensure that the government was united behind his policy. But while Lynch's speeches during the Dáil debate focused on defending his own position and explaining the sackings, Hillery outlined several key elements of a new policy by the Irish government, including reform of the Northern state, recognition of the legitimacy of the unionist tradition and an implicit acknowledgement that unity was a long-term objective, to be achieved only by agreement. All of these ideas amounted to a far-reaching departure from traditional nationalism. The significance of Hillery's comments was not fully appreciated in the closing stages of a prolonged and impassioned debate, but they did not pass entirely unnoticed. The next speaker in the debate, Fine Gael TD Richard Barry, immediately endorsed Hillery's comments on Northern Ireland, agreeing that all parties should 'come to a new decision on our approach to Northern affairs'.[88] More prominent representatives of the opposition also welcomed the minister's comments, including Dr Garret FitzGerald for Fine Gael and Barry Desmond of the Labour Party.[89] Hillery's speech foreshadowed the gradual development of a new policy by the Irish state, which would be based explicitly on the idea of unity by agreement.

Lynch won the vote of confidence by 72 to 64, retaining the support of the deposed ministers and their closest allies.[90] The Taoiseach's position was still precarious, depending as it did on the support of politicians who despised him and whose careers he had derailed. But the leading members of the government reconstituted by Lynch had taken a clear stand against political violence and militant nationalism; this position attracted the full endorsement of the opposition parties and commanded overwhelming support within the Dáil. Moreover, the stand taken by Lynch and his allies also received the imprimatur of President de Valera. De Valera acted with characteristic political subtlety to make his views known to Hillery, his former running mate in Clare. Hillery received a message from Áras an Uachtaráin in June 1970 that the President wished to drop by his home in Sutton 'to see the baby' – Paddy and Maeve's infant daughter, Vivienne. The President and Sinéad de Valera duly arrived at Hillery's home to see the baby and de Valera quietly called Hillery aside to deliver his message: 'Dev said re Taoiseach's stand: see it out to the end and the people will see you are right; and give my regards to Muintir an Clár.'[91] De Valera was constrained from speaking out publicly due to his position as President, but his support for Lynch soon became known within Fianna Fáil.

The power struggle within Fianna Fáil then moved to the courts. Haughey and Blaney were arrested and charged with conspiracy to import arms on 28 May; Capt Kelly, Luykx and John Kelly were also charged.[92] The two ex-ministers denied any involvement in the attempt to import arms.[93] While the charges against Blaney were dropped in July, the four other defendants were returned for trial in the Central Criminal Court. The extraordinary story of the arms trial itself, from the collapse of the first trial to the eventual acquittal of all the defendants, has been told many times, most recently by O'Brien in his study of the arms crisis.[94] The verdict of the court on 23 October 1970 ignited a political firestorm. Haughey claimed complete vindication, congratulated his 'fellow patriots' on their acquittal and called for Lynch's resignation.[95] It was a political blunder and a rare departure by Haughey from his calculating position of public support for the official party line. Lynch and Hillery were both out of the country during the arms trial, as they were attending the annual session of the UN General Assembly in New York. But Lynch immediately signalled that he would meet any challenge head on, telling Irish journalists that Haughey had no place in his government and emphasising that 'Republicanism does not mean guns. It does not mean using guns.'[96] When Lynch arrived at Dublin Airport on 26 October, his allies had organised a formidable reception committee. The Taoiseach was greeted by all but two members of the Cabinet, a large majority of Fianna Fáil TDs and President de Valera's private secretary. Hillery commented that 'you create these impressions. So much of politics is perception'.[97] Most opposition to Lynch within the parliamentary party evaporated in the face of this show of strength; Haughey's leadership challenge collapsed almost as soon as it materialised.

In this instance Hillery himself was one of the two ministers not at Dublin Airport. His absence did not reflect any political reluctance – he was in the middle of the Atlantic at the time. He had decided to return from New York on board an ocean liner, the *France*, along with Hugh McCann and John McColgan. Hillery heard the arms trial verdict while he was on the high seas. His isolation from the latest political crisis did not particularly trouble him:

There was a priest from a Dublin order on the ship and he went out to phone Dublin and came back and said, 'Charlie Haughey has been acquitted.' In Dublin, Charlie said something like, 'Jack should consider his position now.' I was in mid-Atlantic and the priest said to me, 'Where would you like to be now?' I said, 'I'd like to be in the middle of the Atlantic on an ocean liner having a drink.'[98]

It was a rare moment of detachment for Hillery from the turmoil within the governing party and the wider crisis in Northern Ireland.

The arms crisis remains profoundly controversial; it has provoked dozens of books and articles, many of them by participants in the crisis seeking to justify themselves and discredit their enemies. Much of the commentary on the arms crisis in the last decade has tended to accept the view, effectively promoted by some of the defendants and their supporters, that Lynch knew all along about the plot to import arms and acted only when it was about to come into the public domain.[99] This version of events owes more to propaganda than it does to reasoned analysis. Hillery, like other ministers loyal to Lynch, was convinced that the Taoiseach did not know about the plot and that he was deeply shocked when the details of involvement by ministers were brought to his attention. Hillery recalled Lynch's comments to him shortly after the crisis broke, which reflected the Taoiseach's shock and anger at the plot:

Jack said to me at one stage, 'What can I do? I can't trust anyone.' I said, 'You're telling me this!' [that he did not trust his ministers] So I said, 'You have to keep going now.' He didn't think there was anyone he could trust.[100]

Even Lynch's most vociferous critics within the party, such as Kevin Boland, did not accuse him of authorising the conspiracy and then backing away from it, but of opportunism and treachery in acting against the real instigators of the plot.[101] It is true that Lynch did not act immediately on information he received from Berry in April 1970, but his hesitation was caused by the political dilemma of how to deal with the leading power brokers within Fianna Fáil, not any involvement in the plot itself. This is not to absolve Lynch of any responsibility for what occurred. As Taoiseach he should have known what his ministers were doing, and acted sooner to stop them undermining his own policy, both openly and covertly. But the primary responsibility for the arms crisis lies with the ministers who opposed and sought to undermine Lynch's moderate policy, not with the Taoiseach or his allies who sought to uphold it.

Hillery was critical of the green-tinted version of history propagated by supporters of the former ministers. His note on the arms crisis in retirement expressed his own frustration at an early and successful example of spin:

> Though they were freed by the courts, in later years a feeling was allowed to emerge and was to some extent nurtured that if they had not been fired they would have brought the freedom of Ireland. The aura of being charged is held onto in spite of being freed and their failure grew into a great imagined interference by Jack Lynch in a potentially successful movement towards a united Ireland.[102]

He was keenly aware that the ex-ministers and their allies sought to turn the arms crisis to their advantage by portraying the government as unpatriotic and opportunistic. Hillery did not question the verdict itself, but he believed that Haughey and Blaney sought to maintain an aura of martyrdom in the national cause, which was enhanced by the collapse of the proceedings against them. Hillery was undoubtedly correct that a nationalist mythology grew up around the events of 1970, which condemned Lynch and his colleagues for 'standing idly by' and abandoning the North to the unionists and the British. This position found an echo among a section of Fianna Fáil's organisation and was given voice by dissident members at the party's Ard Fheis in 1971.[103] Neither the majority of the population nor the political elite never accepted this hard-line nationalist analysis, but it posed great danger to Lynch's position within his own party. Even in retirement, Hillery was concerned to counter the lingering echoes of this analysis, which he regarded as untrue and dangerous.

The overhaul of the government paved the way for a more coherent and effective policy towards Northern Ireland. The crisis clarified where the government stood, even if the debate and the trial itself shed more heat than light on the actual events involved in the attempt to import arms. The policy of the state towards Northern Ireland was already changing even before the events of May 1970. Hillery was certainly aware that militant anti-partitionist rhetoric would do nothing to ease the plight of Northern nationalists, but could do a great deal to exacerbate it and legitimise support for political violence. The arms crisis accelerated the transformation of the government's policy and helped to trigger a careful departure from the ideological purity of traditional nationalism.

A secret memorandum, written by Eamonn Gallagher shortly before the arms crisis erupted, gave a clear insight into the transformation of the state's approach. Gallagher gave a bleak and perceptive analysis of the political situation in Northern Ireland, warning that the society contained a substantial section 'ardently committed to the preservation of their own personality and peculiarities to the point of suicidal resistance if attacked direct'.[104] He pointed particularly to the recent successes achieved by unionists opposed to reform, notably the Revd Ian Paisley's election to the Stormont Parliament, as evidence that intransigent unionist opposition could 'make the state ungovernable'.[105] He also gave a stark warning about the consequences of serious civil strife, noting that he had heard some suggestions that civil war might be in the interests of the minority: 'In my opinion, whatever the gain may be, if any, the price of civil war in terms of eventual reunification does not bear rational examination – this apart altogether from the loss of lives and destruction which would be the result.'[106] Gallagher advised that the first essential step was reform within Northern Ireland, followed by reconciliation between the divided communities and between North and South: 'When this has achieved a certain strength, we can then think of reunification.'[107] It was clearly implied that Irish unity would be dependent on achieving the eventual consent of the Protestant community.

Gallagher's memo did not become the official policy of the government, although Gallagher himself was undoubtedly influential as an adviser to Lynch. Yet events in both North and South drove the Irish government towards a new approach, which displayed many of the features outlined by Gallagher in April 1970. Hillery had already emphasised the importance of guaranteeing civil rights for the nationalist minority in his address to the UN Security Council. Following the arms crisis, the Irish government adopted a coherent policy, seeking reform within Northern Ireland and gradual progress toward political unity. Lynch made a televised address on RTÉ on 11 July 1970, which shared many common features with Hillery's speech two months before. The Taoiseach argued 'all Irish traditions are intertwined: let us cherish them all'.[108] He condemned violence and told his audience that 'This whole unhappy situation is an Irish quarrel', dropping the traditional nationalist position that Britain was essentially to blame for the problem of partition, which had been an essential element of Fianna Fáil rhetoric for a generation. Lynch reiterated that unity was his objective, but made clear that unity would be achieved only by agreement between the divided traditions on the island of Ireland.[109] The unification of Ireland was transformed from an immediate objective – at least in rhetorical terms – to a long-term aspiration; unity would come after the resolution of pressing short-term issues within Northern Ireland and would be achieved by reconciliation between the divided communities. The new policy of unity by agreement appeared to offer some prospect of stabilising the perilous situation in the North, securing equality for the nationalist minority and safeguarding the position of the Irish state itself. The Irish approach still contained significant shortcomings, underestimating the depth of unionist opposition to any move towards a united Ireland, however gradual it might be or regardless of the generosity of the terms that the Irish government was willing to offer. Moreover it was not at all clear that reforms within Northern Ireland would be enough to satisfy the Catholic minority even in the short term. But the Irish government was at least united behind a coherent and relatively moderate approach to the crisis in Northern Ireland.

Hillery would not have admitted that any significant policy change had occurred. He rightly invoked the authority of de Valera and Lemass for the government's opposition to violence. But Hillery and Lynch were attempting to develop a viable policy in response to the outbreak of the Troubles; unity by agreement might not have been acceptable to unionists but it marked a significant departure from traditional nationalist orthodoxy. The revised policy gave Hillery a practical strategy for engaging with British ministers and provided a compelling justification for Irish diplomatic and political intervention in Northern Ireland. The government's stand against violence and in favour of reform also gave important moral and political support to the beleaguered representatives of constitutional nationalism in the North, who sought to survive in the face of unionist intransigence and the hardline militarism of the Provisional IRA.

The explosion of political and sectarian violence in Northern Ireland presented the most formidable challenges for any Irish foreign minister since the Second World War. The crisis in Northern Ireland not only reopened the apparently dormant conflict between nationalists and unionists, but also unleashed forces that were profoundly destabilising in the Republic. Hillery was preoccupied with diplomatic efforts to contain the crisis in Northern Ireland and exert pressure on British ministers to deliver a far-reaching reform of the Northern state. Much of his activity between August 1969 and May 1970 was essentially defensive, geared towards damage limitation in Belfast or containing political tensions in Dublin. The inflammatory rhetoric and covert activity of other senior ministers ran counter to Hillery's diplomacy and actively contributed to the growing instability and violence in Northern Ireland. But the situation could easily have been much worse in 1970. If the militant nationalist strategy favoured by Blaney and his allies had succeeded, then arms

importation would have been a mere overture to massive civil conflict in
the North, opening up the very real prospect of civil war on the island of
Ireland, armed intervention by the Irish state and a military clash with
Britain. Hillery played a crucial part in ensuring that such a nightmare
scenario never became a reality.

12.

A House Divided
1970–1972

Northern Ireland was the key fault-line within Fianna Fáil in the
early 1970s. While Lynch had asserted his authority over the
government in May 1970, the debate within the party had yet to be won.
If the party organisation was won over by the militant nationalist line of
Blaney and Boland, then Lynch's days were numbered and his policy of
unity by agreement would be thrown overboard. The stakes were high in
the internal party struggle. The immediate future of Anglo-Irish relations
would be determined by the outcome, while the danger of a dramatic
escalation in the conflict to the whole island was very real. Hillery was
often viewed by journalists and later by scholars as an effective but low-
key minister, a quiet man who disliked political conflict and was not really
a major figure in Fianna Fáil politics. Even the most cursory assessment
of his role in the political crisis following the arms trial is enough to dispel
this impression. Hillery was a pivotal figure in the Fianna Fáil government
between 1970 and 1972, not simply due to the position he held, but also

because he emerged as a key ally of Lynch in the internal battles with militant nationalists. The internal party struggle ended some political careers, but it enhanced Hillery's standing and kept Lynch's embattled government in office.

'This will have to be beaten'

The sacking of the ministers in May 1970 triggered not only an immediate political crisis but also a more prolonged struggle for dominance within the governing party. Lynch's government survived the short-term crisis in the Dáil and Hillery was able to launch new diplomatic initiatives to engage with the British government. But the party leadership still faced a formidable challenge in persuading the Fianna Fáil organisation that the Taoiseach's actions were justified and in defending the policy of unity by agreement. The deposed ministers, especially Blaney and Boland, had no intention of fading quietly into the background, and hoped to mobilise nationalist feeling within the party against Lynch. The Taoiseach's other leading opponent, Charles Haughey, took a more calculating approach, avoiding any direct clash with the leadership and gradually distancing himself from his former associates. But nevertheless, the opponents of Lynch's policy commanded considerable support within Fianna Fáil and a substantial section of the organisation felt a deep emotional attachment to traditional anti-partitionism: it was by no means clear in June 1970 that the Taoiseach's moderate line on the North would prevail.

The arrest of two of the ex-ministers on suspicion of involvement in the plot to import arms exposed the deep divisions within Fianna Fáil. Following the arrest of Haughey and Blaney on 28 May, a furious Boland accused Lynch of 'felon setting' and 'unparalleled treachery', demanding a special party Ard Fheis to remove him as leader.[1] The former minister lacked the support to sustain a serious challenge against the Taoiseach, and his intemperate attack was a political blunder that probably helped Lynch in the short term. Boland was quickly expelled from the Fianna Fáil parliamentary party; he was also forced to resign as Honorary Secretary of Fianna Fáil on 22 June.[2] Hillery agreed to take his place as a party officer at Lynch's request. The move reflected Hillery's considerable popularity within the party and his absolute reliability in the ongoing political crisis. Hillery recorded his personal feelings about Boland's actions in a brief note written on 10 June: 'Whatever sorrow I felt at the breaking down of the government or whatever sympathy I felt with the albeit totally illogical stand of Kevin Boland, I have now to confess that I was fooled by Kevin's illogicality which is just a cover up for his antagonism for George Colley and Jack Lynch.'[3] Hillery was also concerned by moves against Lynch instigated by members of Taca, which was closely associated with Haughey and Blaney. Hillery became aware of attempts by members of Taca to promote the ex-ministers and undermine Lynch's leadership:

> Taca, in the line of the one-eyed man, bought 80 tickets for
> the Cáirde Fáil dinner to prepare a cheering situation for
> the entry at appropriate moments of Boland and Blaney,
> in an attempt to embarrass and perhaps frighten Jack
> Lynch. This will have to be beaten.[4]

While this was hardly the most serious threat faced by Lynch, Hillery's concern at such a mundane political stunt underlined his anxiety at the internal political situation within Fianna Fáil and his determination to defeat the dissidents.

Hillery recognised from the outset the need to secure the support of the party organisation for the government's line. He quietly took measures to ensure the support of the local organisation in Clare. He briefed his key activists and supporters on the reasons for the government's stand, and sought to head off any possible dissent by other elected representatives. Hillery spoke to Jack Daly, a prominent Fianna Fáil activist in Clare, on 2 June, to sound out opinion among local members. Daly, who was supportive of Hillery and Lynch, wrote to him later on the same day to report that there were a number of 'malcontents', who were trying to stir up opposition to the Taoiseach but that so far they had not succeeded in gaining much support.[5] Daly, however, feared that local activists in Clare, a constituency with a strong republican tradition, could be won over by hardline nationalist rhetoric: 'Generally speaking with regard to Clare's stand in any possible split, I would be extremely worried. Unfortunately there is an element in the Party through the County who could be easily led and swayed with this type of wild talk.'[6] Daly also expressed concern that some local representatives and perhaps even Sylvester Barrett TD might back the agitation against Lynch. While there was some opposition to Lynch's leadership in Clare, Daly's worst fears were not realised. Hillery himself spoke privately to Barrett, and his constituency colleague remained loyal to the leadership. In addition, key activists such as Daly and local district councillor Frank Collins were fully supportive of Hillery's position. Hillery's quiet lobbying and his personal popularity in Clare undoubtedly reduced dissent among local members. But at least as important in calming troubled waters were his public initiatives as Foreign Minister, notably his dramatic visit to the Falls Road in early July 1970.

The enthusiasm of the local party organisation knew no bounds when Hillery visited the Falls Road without giving any warning to the unionist authorities and then took the Irish case to London for talks with the Foreign Secretary (see pp. 258-260). The officers of the Fianna Fáil *Comhairle Dáil Ceanntair* in Clare issued a letter to their members in July 1970, warmly congratulating Hillery for his recent attempts to advance the cause of the Northern nationalists. The local organisation declared that the Foreign Minister's initiatives deserved 'the highest commendation, particularly from his constituents in Clare' and argued that 'his dignified and outspoken statements to British ministers' had given him a favourable image in international politics.[7] The Fianna Fáil members were particularly gratified that Hillery had gone to the Falls Road, noting that he had 'succeeded in visiting Belfast during the recent trouble despite the very tight British security which surrounded the area at the time'.[8] Hillery's decision to visit the Falls Road without telling the British or unionist authorities, which caused outrage in Stormont and Westminster, merely heightened his popularity among the local party activists. There is little doubt that the visit had a similar effect within the wider Fianna Fáil organisation: being attacked by Unionist MPs in the House of Commons did a leading Fianna Fáil politician no harm at all.

The enthusiastic support of the Clare organisation, however, threatened to become problematic for Hillery when the local officers proposed to organise a large-scale reception for him on his return to the county. An open letter, which was signed by the officers and local councillors, as well as Sylvester Barrett, appealed to all supporters to welcome Hillery when he returned to Clare on Saturday 18 July: 'Let this be a Rousing Reception. Let us demonstrate to the people of the North and of the South that the Banner County endorses the recent magnificent actions of Dr Paddy Hillery'.[9] It was proposed to greet Hillery at the county boundary and to escort him with a fleet of cars through Ennis and home to Miltown Malbay. For a rural TD such support was gratifying; for a Foreign Minister it was embarrassing and potentially damaging. Such a large welcoming party was open to criticism as inappropriate and triumphalist; moreover, it would provide unionist politicians in Northern Ireland with a fresh cause for complaint against the Irish government and might even offer a pretext for further violence on the streets of the North. The official reception was cancelled at Hillery's request.[10] But the abortive move by the local officers reflected Hillery's success in maintaining the support of the party organisation in Clare; it underlined, too, his stature as the leading political figure in the county since the retirement of Éamon de Valera from active politics. Despite apparently more urgent concerns, Hillery did not forget the importance of his local base and he was certainly successful in containing the tensions unleashed by the crisis within his local organisation. Resolving the ongoing conflict within the national organisation, however, would require a much more direct and confrontational approach.

'You can have Boland, but you can't have Fianna Fáil'

The internal conflict came to a head at the party's first Ard Fheis after the ministerial sackings, with Hillery playing a central role in upholding the government's line. The divisions within Fianna Fáil over government policy on Northern Ireland were not simply about personality or political ambition, although personal rivalry between the leading figures certainly inflamed and embittered the debate. Lynch and Hillery emphasised that Irish unity could be achieved only through peaceful and diplomatic means; this line received widespread support within the party but was rejected by a vocal minority. While the dissidents within Fianna Fáil did not generally advocate force as a desirable route to Irish unity, they regarded the use of violence against the Northern state as legitimate, and saw political violence as an acceptable response to unionist domination or the British military presence. It is true that Blaney emphatically denied, in his speech to the Ard Fheis in February 1971, that he favoured the use of violence to secure political objectives in Northern Ireland. He added, however, that Northern nationalists were entitled to 'look to the South for help'.[11] The nature of the help to be provided by the Irish state was shrouded in ambiguity; but strikingly, there was no statement that such help would have to be restricted to peaceful and diplomatic means.

Some of the rank-and-file supporters of Blaney's line at the Ard Fheis were considerably more blunt. Tim Buckley, a delegate from the Tullamore Cumann, accused the Taoiseach of hypocrisy and attacked the Fianna Fáil officers for invoking the memory of Wolfe Tone: 'Tone, he said, was a man of violence. He not only imported guns, he imported men to use those guns.'[12] After this statement, the delegate's comment that he did not advocate force appears redundant. The Fianna Fáil opponents of the government's policy were at best ambiguous on the use of force and in some cases, embraced it as a necessary response to the crisis in Northern Ireland. There was no room for compromise between the position of the leadership and the views of the dissidents. The conflict could be resolved only by the removal of the Taoiseach and his key allies (including Hillery), or by the complete rout of the dissident group. The implications of the debate went much further than the fate of individual politicians. The outcome would determine the response of the Irish state to the political and sectarian conflict engulfing Northern Ireland, while it would also solidify or destroy the Republic's cautious engagement with its nearest neighbour. The scene was set for the most turbulent and divisive Ard Fheis in Fianna Fáil's history.

Hillery himself did not anticipate his pivotal role at the party conference. When he accepted the post of joint Honorary Secretary in 1970, he had assumed that it was essentially a formal position and that there would be no need for him to address the Ard Fheis:

> Jack phoned and asked me to take the post of Secretary of the Party. I said yes, but had no idea that addressing the Ard Fheis would be involved. It was usual to have the non-Oireachtas official read the report, so I thought, if I thought of it at all.[13]

Hillery was theoretically correct. The party appointed two Honorary Secretaries, usually a minister and a voluntary party officer. The voluntary secretary, Joe Groome, would normally be expected to present the report to the conference. But the 1971 Ard Fheis was not a normal occasion; it marked the final reckoning between Lynch and the dissidents led by Blaney and Boland.

The rival camps within the party both prepared for a decisive struggle. The leadership circulated a list of reliable candidates for the party officer positions and the influential Committee of Fifteen. Paddy Smith, a long-serving TD and Lynch loyalist, was selected as chair of the Ard Fheis.[14] The faction opposed to the Taoiseach set out to provoke confrontation on the floor of the conference itself with the intention of undermining Lynch's leadership and demonstrating the strength of the dissident group within the party. Despite having planned to organise the Ard Fheis in his favour, Lynch seemed taken by surprise initially when trouble erupted almost as soon as the conference began in the RDS on 22 February 1971.[15] The Taoiseach received a standing ovation when he opened the Ard Fheis that morning, but this was the lull before the storm. The delegates opposed to the leadership were vocal, well-organised and determined to attack the party establishment from the outset. When Smith proposed the standing orders for the Ard Fheis, pandemonium broke out even before a single motion was debated – as The Irish Times reported on the following Monday:

When the chairman, Mr Patrick Smith, proposed standing
orders, a young woman took over the rostrum and shouted
him down. Both of them were supported by sections of
the delegates and the young woman, who was protesting
about the cutting of time for delegates' speeches, said it
'completely took away the democratic rights of the
delegates'. After about 15 minutes, during which time there
was almost continuous shouting in the hall, standing orders
were adopted by a show of hands.[16]

The initial clash over the conference procedures between Paddy Smith
and Joan Buckley, a dissident delegate from Tullamore, indicated that a
long and acrimonious weekend lay ahead. The restriction of the speaking
time for most delegates to three minutes was justified by the party officers
on the basis that close to 5,000 members were attending the Ard Fheis.
The procedures were undoubtedly designed to restrict the scope for
dissident speakers to dominate the conference; but such a restriction on
speaking time was far from unusual at the conference of any major
political party. Moreover, the events that followed provided eloquent
testimony to the fact that the rules did not prevent opponents of the
leadership from making their case. The leadership undoubtedly
commanded the support of the large majority of delegates. The party
officers easily won the procedural vote; later Lynch's supporters triumphed
in all the internal elections and most of his opponents were swept off the
Committee of Fifteen.[17] But the initial row also confirmed that the
fundamental split in Fianna Fáil could no longer be glossed over; a vocal
minority within the party was bitterly opposed to Lynch's leadership.[18]
The conflict had to be settled one way or another.

It soon became apparent that the row over procedures was merely a
preliminary skirmish. The real battle commenced when the secretary's
report was presented to the Ard Fheis. The dissidents took the opportunity
to open a debate on the arms trial. Eamonn Keane, a delegate from
Tallaght, called on the Ard Fheis to reject the report because it failed to
refer to the removal of four senior ministers and leading party officers in

1970. Paul Butler of the Robert Emmet Cumann attacked the attempt to prosecute the defendants in the arms trial and accused prominent members of the party of perjury and cowardice: 'some had perjured themselves in the name of political expediency, some got scared and changed their minds'.[19] When a third delegate moved to oppose the report, it became obvious that a concerted effort to challenge the platform was underway. Paddy Smith accused the dissidents of putting together 'an organised line-up' to exclude anyone who did not agree with them.[20] Hillery believed that Blaney had organised the dissidents: 'But I went down to the Ard Fheis and I had hoped just to sit on the platform, but when I went in, Blaney was there, who was a great organiser of stunts; all the length of the hall there were people waiting to speak, every one of them anti-Lynch.'[21] Blaney had managed to fill the speaking slots with his own supporters, 'a packed group antagonistic to the platform.'[22] He stole a march on the leadership, provoking confrontation with the party officers at the outset of the Ard Fheis; the leadership had expected the worst of the conflict to come later, in the course of the debate on Northern Ireland.[23] Chris Glennon of the *Irish Independent* acknowledged that the dissidents were a minority, but felt that weight of numbers alone did not guarantee success for Lynch that morning:

> At times during that dramatic Saturday confrontation between the pro- and anti-Lynch forces in the Great Hall of the RDS it seemed as if a form of revolution would take over the Ard Fheis. The rebels, well organised and in a major grouping near the platform, mounted and maintained a barrage of noise and comment that at times reached a decibel level higher than Mr Lynch's supporters.[24]

The dissident group gave vocal support to critics of the leadership and barracked delegates who sought to defend the government. Lynch's supporters responded with shouts of 'We want Jack'; scuffles broke out around the hall as punches were thrown and groups of angry delegates

hurled abuse at each other.[25] The rostrum for speakers was positioned on
the conference floor: it was the scene of several clashes between delegates,
and possession of the rostrum seemed to be the equivalent of seizing a
military strongpoint. Several ministers on the platform were visibly
alarmed at the organised demonstration against the leadership.[26] The party
leader turned to Hillery to confront the dissidents. When Smith moved
to close down the acrimonious debate, Lynch asked Hillery to respond on
behalf of the leadership. Hillery had not expected to address the Ard Fheis,
but realised that he would have to speak when he saw the uproar in the
hall:

> Then the chairman amidst protests said the discussion must
> end. My moment to speak was here and I had nothing
> prepared. I went straight into confrontation 'First we must
> deal with these people', and only stopped now and then to
> ask Jack 'Is that enough?' He said 'keep going'.[27]

Hillery spoke from the platform itself rather than the rostrum. He began
by warning delegates that they had to choose between Fianna Fáil and the
dissidents. But his speech was interrupted when Kevin Boland appeared
on the rostrum below as if to deliver a speech himself. Boland's appearance
triggered a storm of applause from his supporters, mixed with jeering and
catcalls; he shouted at the platform but his words were lost in the uproar.[28]
Hillery then continued his speech, undeterred by shouting and chanting
from Boland's supporters and by scuffles between delegates in the hall
below. He later recalled 'I shouted against their noise but on television it
appeared that I shouted in anger, as their sound was not caught by the
microphones which were turned away from them.'[29] Hillery delivered an
uncompromising message, telling delegates that the dissidents were the
enemies of Fianna Fáil and would not be allowed to stop the Ard Fheis
from deciding party policy:

> Our policy is Jack Lynch's policy, de Valera's policy, Seán
> Lemass's policy and we will continue that policy in spite of

any bully boys within or without the organisation. We can
have elections, we can have elections for our officers, but
we won't frighten Jack Lynch out of here by a few bully
boys. We can change our policy, but we'll change it there
[in the elections], and not over there [pointing at Boland
supporters]. And Fianna Fáil will survive as it did before.[30]

Meanwhile a crowd of Boland supporters below the platform chanted
'We want Boland, we want Boland'. Hillery fired back the most
memorable line of the Ard Fheis: 'You can have Boland, but you can't
have Fianna Fáil'.[31] The moment was immortalised by the assembled
journalists and TV cameras; Hillery's blunt rejoinder passed into political
folklore.

Hillery's speech did little to calm the uproar at the Ard Fheis, but then
that was not what he set out to do. Instead, it reassured the majority that
the leadership was capable of defending itself and took the battle to the
dissidents in aggressive, uncompromising terms. His intervention was
decisive in upholding the embattled leadership of Jack Lynch: not only the
delegates but also the media were left in no doubt that a vocal minority
would not be allowed to displace the party leader. Boland was carried
from the hall on the shoulders of his supporters, but it was Hillery who
won the day.[32] While there were further noisy demonstrations on the floor
later that day, the Taoiseach's supporters clearly had the upper hand. The
Irish Independent estimated that the dissidents commanded the support of
only about 550 delegates, with around 4,000 backing the leadership.[33]
This was obviously a rough assessment of the numbers on each side, but
the leadership certainly commanded the support of an overwhelming
majority. Lynch's presidential address on Saturday evening met some
heckling and shouts of 'Union Jack', but also drew sustained applause and
a standing ovation that drowned out all opposition by the end.[34] At least
one of the Taoiseach's opponents read the political runes correctly; Charles
Haughey took no part in the organised demonstration against the
leadership and spoke to Hillery that day to disassociate himself from the
dissidents: 'Even in the middle of that thing on the floor of the Ard Fheis,

he came over to me and he said, "I've nothing to do with this." I believe he hadn't.'[35] The party elections later on the same day confirmed the rout of the dissidents. Hillery and his colleague Joe Groome were re-elected as joint Honorary Secretaries of the party, defeating Boland's bid to regain his previous post. Blaney also lost out in the election for Honorary Treasurer to George Colley. All the opponents of the government's line on Northern Ireland disappeared from the key party posts.[36] The showdown at the Ard Fheis ended in a decisive victory for Lynch and a lasting setback for his most vociferous opponents. The Taoiseach's political skill and resilience were certainly crucial to his survival; but scarcely less important was Hillery's ability to confront and face down the dissidents. The Ard Fheis was a personal triumph for Hillery, who was widely regarded by the media as Lynch's most effective ally within the party.

The clash at the Ard Fheis underlined many of Hillery's strengths as a politician. While he was never a great parliamentary orator, he was a very effective platform speaker and was at his best speaking off the cuff without a prepared text. Hillery showed toughness and political courage in confronting the protesters in such a striking fashion; a more timid or less principled politician would have ducked the challenge entirely and stayed on the sidelines. While Hillery's political style was usually friendly and low-key, the uproar at the Ard Fheis brought out the combative side of his character and displayed to the full his ability to fight his corner in difficult circumstances. Hillery's natural instinct was to be conciliatory, but confrontation held no terrors for him if he felt it was necessary. It was to be his most famous speech, at least with the domestic Irish audience. His intervention would be replayed many times, usually by RTÉ's popular *Reeling in the Years* programme; it also became RTÉ's favoured TV clip to be recycled whenever there was a crisis in Fianna Fáil politics. His address to the UN, which attracted impressive international coverage, had much less impact in Ireland, probably because it was carried live only on radio by RTÉ. Hillery would have been amused had he realised that a generation not yet born in 1970 would gain their most striking impression of him from his authoritative intervention amid the tumultuous scenes at the Ard Fheis.

Boland attacked Hillery in the *Irish Independent* on the Monday after the Ard Fheis: 'I think Dr Hillery really lost control of himself when he called them bully boys'.[37] This comment was ironic considering Boland's volatile temper and his confrontational stand at the Ard Fheis; it was also entirely wrong. While Hillery's speech was not scripted in advance, it was not simply an off-the-cuff expression of anger or frustration. It was not a spontaneous outburst, but a composed and well-controlled performance. Hillery was obviously angry but his message was clear and coherent; it was also calculated and reflected weeks if not months of private reflection on the internal conflict within Fianna Fáil. He told John McColgan the following week: 'I had to do that deliberately.'[38] Hillery may have hoped that he would not have to speak at the Ard Fheis, but he came prepared to deliver a deliberate message. He believed that he was protecting Fianna Fáil from the undemocratic tactics and methods of a small minority. He recalled later that he did not act solely to support Lynch, but to marginalise the dissidents and break their influence within the party: 'I said that I was protecting the organisation from this subversion. I said what's down there now is like a rotten apple that will destroy the rest of the organisation.'[39] He was particularly angry at the militant tactics used by the dissidents, which he attacked as bullying and undemocratic. Hillery made a deliberate attack on the hardline nationalist minority at the Ard Fheis, which reflected his own political convictions and especially his belief that Fianna Fáil had to face up to the realities of the crisis in Northern Ireland.

Aftermath

The Ard Fheis reinforced Lynch's authority and secured his position as Taoiseach in the short-term.[40] The extensive media coverage of the Ard Fheis was hardly favourable to Fianna Fáil, giving maximum attention to the turmoil and internal division. But it was universally acknowledged in the print media that the Taoiseach would not be forced out by the dissident elements and that the danger to his leadership had receded.[41] Lynch was, for the first time, firmly in command of his party. This was

recognised by his predecessor Seán Lemass, when Hillery visited the
former Taoiseach, who was seriously ill in the Mater Hospital:

> I went to see him in hospital after that Ard Fheis, I had
> visited him before [as well]; and he said that Jack Lynch is
> in control of his party now. That was the day after the Ard
> Fheis. He never went around, Lemass, he was straight down
> the line with you.[42]

The Taoiseach's success in defeating or sidelining his leading opponents
owed much to Hillery's consistent support and particularly his dramatic
intervention at the Ard Fheis. Most of Lynch's leading opponents were
gone from the party by 1972. Boland took the most honourable course
of action in the light of his fundamental disagreement with his former
colleagues. He had already resigned his seat in November 1970 and he left
Fianna Fáil in 1971 to establish a new republican party, Aontacht
Éireann.[43] The new party made no impact in the 1973 general election
and the tumultuous Ard Fheis proved the final act of Boland's political
career. Blaney attempted to remain within Fianna Fáil as the government's
most prominent internal critic, but was expelled from the parliamentary
party in November 1971, following his abstention on an opposition
motion of no confidence in Jim Gibbons. Blaney was expelled from the
party itself in 1972.[44] He easily retained his seat in Donegal as an
Independent Fianna Fáil TD, but remained in the political wilderness and
never regained the power and influence he had enjoyed until 1970.
Haughey had no intention of joining his former allies in the wilderness.
He publicly accepted Lynch's leadership and rigidly followed the party
line. Haughey was able to ensure that, unlike the other ministers removed
in 1970, he remained a prominent member of Fianna Fáil, enduring a
temporary exile on the backbenches.

The government itself not only survived the arms crisis but also
became a much more effective and cohesive unit. Although Lynch soon
led a minority government due to resignations and expulsions from the
party, he was able to remain in office until he opted for a general election

in February 1973. The removal of Lynch's leading opponents from the Cabinet eliminated the division that had paralysed and distorted policy-making on Northern Ireland. The sustained attacks from external opponents and internal dissidents left the remaining ministers with little alternative but to hang together. 'The party's survival bewildered its opponents and amazed its friends' was Dick Walsh's comment on this period.[45] Hillery felt that the ability to surmount or contain internal divisions was the key to the government's survival:

> Perhaps the best-known meeting in the public mind was that year's Ard Fheis. But there were many meetings in private which were stormy. Outside they [the media] waited, but we always found a solution. The opposition must have been exasperated.[46]

Fianna Fáil's legendary survival skills were certainly demonstrated to the full in this period. But some ministers at least were motivated by higher concerns than simple survival; contrary to popular myth and some contemporary evidence, politicians are not always venal creatures obsessed with their own advancement. Hillery at least was deeply concerned to maintain Ireland's progress towards accession to the European Communities. He was conscious that the fall of the government, or even worse, its replacement by a militantly nationalist administration, could have damaged or even decisively derailed Ireland's efforts to enter the EEC. Moreover, both Hillery and Lynch were preoccupied with managing the conflict in Northern Ireland in a responsible way, seeking to de-escalate the violence in the North and prevent it from spreading to the entire country. Whatever the limitations of their approach, which focused primarily on nationalist grievances and aspirations, it did not require much imagination to realise the impact on the volatile situation in the province if some of their former colleagues got their hands on the levers of power; Hillery merely had to recall 'the ballad singing session style of government' which had been much in evidence around the Cabinet table in 1969.[47] Hillery's determination to keep the government in office was based to a large extent on genuine concerns with major policy issues, not on any desire to cling to power at all costs.

There was also a strong case to be made for keeping Lynch's government in power in the early 1970s on public policy grounds. There was no viable alternative to a Fianna Fáil government in 1970; coalition between Fine Gael and the Labour Party appeared a distant prospect, not least because Labour had not yet abandoned its opposition to coalition. Indeed, the two opposition parties were to reach agreement on a joint programme only after the general election was actually called in February 1973.[48] The fall of Lynch in 1970–71 would have resulted either in a new Fianna Fáil government dominated by his opponents or a party split followed by a general election, with highly unpredictable consequences. While many in the opposition parties would undoubtedly have found such an argument hard to digest, there is compelling evidence that the survival of Lynch's government served the public interest, not simply the interests of individual politicians, between 1970 and 1972.

Hillery's active participation in the internal party struggle of the early 1970s was significant not only for its immediate results but for what it allowed him to do in other areas of politics. The short-term political outcome was obvious – Lynch's government won the power struggle with the dissident nationalist group within the party. The 1971 Ard Fheis did not resolve the perennial debate about Fianna Fáil's policy on Northern Ireland in favour of unity by agreement; the policy would shift again to a more traditional nationalist line when the party was in opposition in 1975 and especially when Haughey became leader in 1979. But the internal struggle that culminated in the Ard Fheis did settle a couple of issues for good. Firstly, Lynch would not be removed as leader as a result of the arms crisis or his moderate line on Northern Ireland. Secondly, Fianna Fáil as a party would not, at any time throughout the Troubles, show ambiguity or covert sympathy with political violence, whatever position might be taken by individuals. Hillery's prominent involvement at the Ard Fheis underlined his prestige within the party and enhanced his stature among the public and the media. But more significantly, the government's position was stabilised to a large extent by early 1971; nobody really expected Lynch or his colleagues to succumb to an internal party *coup* after they had survived the turmoil of the Ard Fheis. The greater stability enjoyed by the government allowed Hillery to pursue discussions with British ministers, which he initiated in the summer of 1970. Anglo-Irish diplomacy and attempts at constructive engagement with Britain, not threats and bluster across the Irish Sea combined with secret arms deliveries across the border, would become the characteristic elements of the Irish government's policy on Northern Ireland. The government, with Hillery taking the lead in the European negotiations, was able to forge ahead with the process of accession to the European Communities. Hillery's involvement in the internal power struggle helped to safeguard policies to which he was deeply committed; his success as a party politician also opened the way for the most productive and influential phase of his career.

13.

The Troubles
1970–1972

Hillery was a leading advocate for peaceful, constitutional change in Northern Ireland once the crisis broke in August 1969. He represented an Irish government that was determined to contain the violence in the North and to prevent the conflict engulfing the whole island. Yet this did not mean that Hillery sought simply to ensure that violence was kept firmly on the northern side of the border. His consistent objectives were to re-establish peace within the North and secure justice for the Catholic minority – principles that he regarded as two sides of the same coin. He promoted more intensive engagement with Northern nationalists than any Irish foreign minister since the foundation of the state. Hillery also led the way in promoting diplomatic contacts between the two governments in the first two years of the crisis. Lynch increasingly took the leading role in Anglo-Irish relations from 1971 onwards, as the turmoil within the governing party subsided and his hold on power became more secure. Yet Hillery remained a crucial figure in establishing constititional nationalism as a viable political alternative in the face of increasing paramilitary violence.

The resolution of the arms crisis in Dublin was closely followed by a change of government in London. The election of a Conservative government led by Edward Heath in June 1970 triggered a bout of pessimism among nationalist politicians and officials in Dublin, as it was widely assumed that the Conservatives were less likely than Labour to press ahead with reforms in Northern Ireland.[1] Likewise there was elation among Unionists, who regarded the Tories as their traditional allies against nationalist demands.[2] Both unionist jubilation and nationalist gloom ultimately proved misguided, not least due to Heath's willingness to engage constructively with the Irish government. But in the short term the Conservatives appeared to justify nationalist fears by relying almost exclusively on a security response to contain the growing sectarian tension and violence.

It was not any change in strategy by the new British government, however, but the growing strength of the Provisional IRA, fuelled by the tactics of the British army on the ground, that did most to exacerbate the conflict. British troops had generally enjoyed a 'honeymoon' with the Catholic population following their intervention in August 1969; they were widely welcomed in Catholic areas as protectors of the minority against attack by loyalists.[3] But the province was fundamentally unstable by the autumn of 1969, and the army faced a task infinitely more complex and difficult than the missions for which it was trained.[4] The army was meant to maintain the peace and prevent open civil strife, but it was also obliged to support the 'civil power', namely, the security forces that were entirely discredited in the eyes of the minority. Moreover, the deployment of British troops presented the newly formed Provisionals with a golden opportunity to provoke a direct confrontation with the British state. The Provisional IRA began a bombing campaign early in 1970 and was prominently involved in organising riots against the security forces in Catholic areas.[5] The British response played into the hands of the IRA leadership. The commander of the British forces in Northern Ireland, General Sir Ian Freeland, authorised several heavy-handed security operations from the summer of 1970 onwards, which did much to alienate nationalist communities from the army.

The change of government in London coincided with the start of the Orange marching season. The annual parades by the Orange Order, especially the insistence of the Orangemen on following traditional routes through Catholic areas, inspired intense resentment among nationalists and presented an obvious risk of sectarian conflict following the events of the previous year. British ministers agreed on 22 June that provocative demonstrations by either side were undesirable, but decided against banning or rerouting the parades immediately, fearing a major confrontation between the marchers and the security forces.[6] The next fortnight saw instead the worst confrontation between nationalists and the British forces since the army had been deployed the previous August. The arrest of Bernadette Devlin near Derry on 26 June, following her conviction on charges arising from the Battle of the Bogside in the previous year, acted as the spark for a major outbreak of violence. Severe rioting broke out in Derry, as British troops were attacked with stones and petrol bombs; the soldiers responded by using CS gas to control the riot. The Orange parades ignited the conflict in Belfast. Orangemen marching down the Crumlin Road clashed with Catholic residents of the Ardoyne on the same day.[7] Hillery, who was warned by John Hume on the night of 26 June that the violence in Derry would spread throughout the province, organised representations to the British government for Devlin's release. Hillery phoned Ambassador O'Sullivan in London to warn him that the British should make some gesture immediately; otherwise any action would be pointless. O'Sullivan warned the Home Office that 'if they took no action today there would be a conflagration throughout the whole of the North.'[8]

The new Home Secretary, Reginald Maudling, received the warning but rejected it. He took the view that releasing Devlin would 'accentuate the trouble and make it worse'.[9] This assessment proved spectacularly wrong within 24 hours. There was widespread sectarian violence in both Derry and Belfast on the following day, 27 June, in which 96 people were injured. Six people were killed in Belfast, three of them in a gun battle between the Provisional IRA and loyalist paramilitaries at St Matthew's church in the Short Strand.[10] The incident provided a fertile recruiting ground for the Provisional movement, which took on the mantle of defenders of the nationalist minority.[11] Lynch appealed for calm, but the violence went from bad to worse in the first week of July. British forces began a security crackdown in west Belfast on 3 July, following arms searches in the Falls Road that developed into a confrontation with the local community. The move triggered an outbreak of rioting and open clashes between British soldiers and IRA gunmen. The military authorities imposed a curfew lasting 34 hours, which was implemented with considerable brutality by some elements of the security forces.[12] Most observers regarded the curfew as a key turning point in the relations between the Catholic population and the British army. The army, seen as protectors of the minority only the previous autumn, was perceived increasingly as an oppressive force on the side of the unionist establishment.[13] The heavy-handed security measures gave an invaluable propaganda weapon to militant republicans. Following the sectarian violence of the summer and the Falls Road curfew, the Provisional IRA emerged as a major force in Catholic areas and acquired the necessary support to sustain a new offensive against the British forces.

The Irish government faced severe pressure to respond effectively to the events in the North. Hillery responded initially by intensifying diplomatic contacts with the new British government. He met with the new Foreign Secretary, Sir Alec Douglas-Home on 29 June, expressing the 'grave concern' of the Irish government at the escalating crisis in Northern Ireland.[14] The minister also called in the ambassadors of the United States, Canada, West Germany, Italy and France to brief them on the situation in early July, seeking to generate diplomatic pressure on the British government. These diplomatic initiatives were essential, but also unlikely to achieve much in the way of immediate results. Lynch faced criticism from the opposition parties for his apparent inability to influence the rapidly deteriorating situation; more significantly, the events in the North appeared to vindicate the militant rhetoric of his opponents within Fianna Fáil. Hillery therefore moved to make a symbolic show of support for the nationalist minority. He visited the Falls Road on 6 July, the day after the curfew was lifted. His action was a direct response to the political pressures on Lynch: 'Jack came on the phone and in a worried way spoke of the need to do something in relation to the north of Ireland. The British army had raided houses in the Falls Road and did it with much brutality and roughness.'[15] Although Lynch did not ask him to do anything specifically, Hillery understood the Taoiseach's concerns and took the hint:

> I asked him to give me five minutes to think about it and I phoned back and said I would go to Belfast myself. He seemed very pleased and said 'you are taking an awful lot on yourself and I am very grateful to you'.[16]

Hillery went North secretly, giving no prior warning to the British Army or the Stormont authorities. McCann told Eamonn Gallagher to rent a car from Murray's, the car-hire firm, to take Hillery to Belfast. The only real difficulty arose in Dublin at the start of the journey, with a nervous employee from Murray's:

> When I emerged from the office building I found Gallagher quarrelling with the young woman who delivered the car. The problem was that she wouldn't hand it over to Gallagher without sight of his driver's licence; he did not have one. I showed her mine and we set out for Belfast with Gallagher at the wheel. At the border he waited until there were other cars and got in line in the middle. He said 'read the paper when they inspect us'. They made no problem for us.[17]

They reached Belfast without incident and Hillery toured the Falls Road the same afternoon. The visit allowed Hillery to meet with several community leaders and representatives of Northern nationalist opinion, including James Doherty of the Nationalist Party. The Foreign Minister also met William Philbin, Catholic Bishop of Down and Connor, at the

Europa hotel.[18] Perhaps more importantly, it enabled Hillery to gain first-hand knowledge of the situation on the Falls Road in the wake of the curfew:

> Eamonn met his contacts and we were guided into the Falls Road where I saw the British soldiers on duty with their guns. I met people who recognised me and some whom I knew from meeting them in Dublin. Those whom I met asked me to speak for them to the British government as they complained that their only approach to the [British] government was through their enemies in Stormont.[19]

What he saw and heard on the Falls Road reinforced Hillery's conviction that the British state had to guarantee equality of treatment for the minority immediately, not only by enacting necessary reforms but by restricting provocative Orange marches and generally curtailing the privileged position of the unionist establishment. He recorded his impressions in a private note immediately after his visit, drawing attention to the key role of the British government if any advance was to be achieved: 'My own belief is that the British need fierce pushing at this time and I am going to give it to them'.[20]

The visit was kept secret from the media until after Hillery's return to Dublin on the evening of the same day. He asked Hugh McCann to meet ambassadors in Iveagh House in his place; Pádraig Faulkner, the Minister for Education, also agreed to stand in for Hillery at other events during the day.[21] This ruse worked so well that Hillery heard an RTÉ news report on the car radio during the return journey that 'the Minister for External Affairs had been meeting ambassadors all day in Iveagh House'.[22] Hillery met the British ambassador, John Peck, immediately after his return to Dublin, giving a frank explanation of the pressures that had dictated his intervention. He told Peck that the position of the Irish government was seriously undermined by the British operation and Hillery had acted to relieve the pressures on Lynch; the visit was also essential to reassure the people of west Belfast.[23] Hillery then held a press conference, informing an astonished corps of journalists that he had just returned from Belfast. As he commented with some understatement, 'this was obviously news.'[24] He told the journalists that the people he had met in the Falls Roads did not want guns from the administration in Dublin, 'but intense diplomatic activity'.[25] An editorial in *The Irish Times* on the following day gave qualified support to Hillery's move and noted the widespread amazement that it had happened in the first place: 'If he had flown around the North Pole in one afternoon, he could hardly have caused more astonishment.'[26]

Hillery's move was undoubtedly influenced by a desire to be seen to 'do something' on the North, not least to counter allegations from Lynch's hardline opponents that he was abandoning Northern nationalists to British and unionist oppression. Yet it was not simply a public relations exercise driven by internal politics. Hillery wanted first-hand information about the situation on the ground in west Belfast. He was also deeply concerned that the actions of the British army would exacerbate fears among the Catholic minority and increase the prospect that they would turn to extremists.[27] His action was a move to maintain peace, by showing Northern nationalists that they were not isolated and dependent on the IRA for protection.

While Hillery's visit to the Falls Road could do little to change conditions on the ground, it did achieve some useful results. Firstly, his move provided reassurance to constitutional nationalists that the Irish government had not abandoned them, even if Dublin's ability to assist them was limited. Hillery's visit also underlined in an unmistakable fashion the Irish government's determination to act as the political guarantor of the interests of the minority. While the publicity generated by the visit was not entirely favourable, and was certainly unwelcome to the British government, Hillery's move illustrated that the Irish government had a vital interest in re-establishing peace and stability in Northern Ireland. His unscheduled visit to Belfast was fully consistent with his strategy of pursuing Irish objectives by exclusively peaceful and diplomatic means. While it did not conform to diplomatic protocol, his move was designed to reinforce the centre ground against the appeal of paramilitary extremism.

The unionist political class saw it in a very different light – as a one-man invasion by Dublin. Unionist politicians were outraged by Hillery's visit, complaining that it was an act of unwarranted interference by the Irish government, which would exacerbate tensions in the province. The move was condemned by Chichester-Clark, who rather ludicrously promised an investigation into how it had been allowed to happen in the first place. Ian Paisley had a ready explanation, accusing Chichester-Clark himself of complicity in the nefarious episode.[28] Hillery was unrepentant; the unionist criticisms merely served to strengthen the Irish government's position against its own dissidents. The British reaction was much more restrained and muted. In response to the protests of unionist MPs, Alec Douglas-Home delivered a measured rebuke in the House of Commons on 7 July, calling Hillery's action 'an error of judgement' and describing the lack of consultation in advance with the British government as 'a serious diplomatic discourtesy'[29]; but the Foreign Secretary was going through the motions rather than signalling any serious rift with the Irish government. There was no crisis in Anglo-Irish relations; indeed, contacts at ministerial level proceeded without even the briefest hiatus. Hillery left for London on 8 July for a meeting with Anthony Barber, the minister in charge of the British negotiations with the EEC, which had been arranged before the Falls Road curfew; not only did this encounter go ahead undisturbed by Hillery's unscheduled walk on the Falls, but Douglas-Home invited the Irish minister to call on him as well. Hillery accepted the invitation with alacrity, indicating that he would raise the issue of controversial Orange parades with the Foreign Secretary.[30]

Despite the unfavourable backdrop, the meeting itself was calm and friendly. Douglas-Home raised Hillery's visit to Belfast only in the most oblique way, commenting almost regretfully that 'I am afraid that I could not have said less in the Commons yesterday'.[31] Hillery criticised the security crackdown on the Falls Road as heavy-handed and unnecessary: the Foreign Secretary defended the actions of the British forces. While the two ministers did not agree about the security operation, it did not cause a serious row. The minister sought more rapid progress with the reforms, warning Douglas-Home that there was 'no sign to the man in the street that reforms were coming and that all the obvious evidence was to the contrary'.[32] Hillery was convinced that the Unionist government's commitment to reform was superficial and easily eroded by resistance from intransigent elements at Stormont. The Foreign Secretary took a conciliatory approach, reiterating that the British strategy was to deliver major reforms and that the British government recognised 'the necessity of removing injustice'.[33] Hillery reserved his strongest attack for the Orange Order, commenting that '[certain] Orange marches represent a taunting by intolerant people.'[34] He highlighted the ineffectiveness of British efforts to control or placate the Order. Maudling had appealed to the Orange Order to cancel all of their parades in July, but his appeal had been rejected: similarly Chichester-Clark had indicated that he would prefer if the parades did not go ahead this year, but the Order had ignored the wishes of their Prime Minister.[35] Hillery argued that the Orange Order had effectively rejected the authority of both the Stormont administration and the British government:

> Dr Hillery replied that the Orange Order needs a clear message that it is not going to run Westminster as it has run Stormont. They should be stopped in their tracks just once. They had defied the views of their own Prime Minister and Home Secretary.[36]

Despite his tough language, Hillery's solution was relatively moderate. He did not seek the cancellation of all Orange parades, but only the banning of parades that were clearly provocative to the minority. Douglas-Home suggested that legislation against incitement to hatred, which was being considered by Stormont as a result of pressure from the British government, might be the best way to contain bigotry and intolerance. Hillery replied bluntly that such a leisurely approach would not contain the escalating crisis but would succeed only in threatening the survival of his own government. He delivered a grim warning that further violence was inevitable if the British did not take immediate action to establish their impartiality between the two communities and to guarantee equality of treatment for Catholics:

> Dr Hillery said that legislation is not fast enough to solve the immediate problem and he doubted if he would be there if it is proposed to wait long enough for legislation. The situation in the North is totally abnormal as the [unionist] right wing is trying to determine the rate and extent of reform. This invites a violent reaction. It must be shown now that there is a higher authority than the Orange Order.[37]

Douglas-Home showed some sympathy with Hillery's case, commenting that he had experience of the Orange Order in his own constituency of Glasgow and promising to convey the Irish minister's views to the Home Secretary.[38] While Hillery neither expected nor received any commitment to limit the activity of the Order, he appreciated the conciliatory approach taken by Douglas-Home: 'I must say my feeling is that Sir Alec understood it and was nearer to my point of view than the Orange point of view.'[39] This was probably the best that the Irish government could have expected at a time when Douglas-Home was under pressure from unionist leaders and backbench Conservative MPs to denounce Hillery's visit to Belfast as an unwanted foreign intrusion.

Hillery was asked by British journalists immediately after the meeting whether he had been given a dressing down by Sir Alec: 'I was amazed to hear them ask if the Secretary of State had lectured me or rebuked me and all the time the tone was that of a superior race nettled.'[40] In fact this was exactly what the Foreign Secretary did not do – he was careful not to provoke a row with Hillery about the visit to Belfast and indeed expressed the hope that they would have further discussions about Northern Ireland on an ongoing basis. Hillery formed a high opinion of Douglas-Home's diplomatic skills and willingness to listen to the Irish case, regardless of the vocal hostility of unionist politicians and right-wing British journalists: 'His office was a calm oasis in the midst of all the self-righteous bullying of the ignorant men.'[41] Other British ministers were not so diplomatic or well briefed, as Hillery discovered in his subsequent meeting with Anthony Barber. Barber was friendly, but poorly informed about the situation in Northern Ireland. He suggested that the Orange parades could all go ahead without trouble if the Taoiseach made an appeal for calm.[42] The official record by the Department of External Affairs recorded judiciously that 'Mr Barber was not particularly well briefed on the Northern situation'.[43] Hillery recalled more bluntly that 'I met Barber afterwards, who did not seem to have a clue what I was at.'[44]

The objective of Hillery's diplomacy in 1970 was not to achieve immediate changes in British policy. Heath was publicly committed to supporting the unionist government and to implementing reform in Northern Ireland. Hillery had no illusions that Irish pressure would bring about a radical reorientation of British policy in favour of a united Ireland. He hoped instead to establish the right of the Irish government to be heard on Northern Ireland and to generate pressure from Westminster to bring in radical reforms quickly. Irish diplomatic efforts up to the summer of 1971 focused on overcoming key grievances of the minority, notably provocative Orange Order parades, the creation of gun clubs consisting of former B Specials and the slow implementation of reforms in housing and local government.[45] Hillery was successful in establishing the right of the Irish government to be heard in Whitehall. He had several meetings with Douglas-Home over the following year, in which the North was usually the main subject of discussion. The Foreign Secretary readily discussed the progress of the reform agenda in the North and acknowledged the legitimacy of the Irish government's concerns.[46] At a meeting with Hillery on 6 July 1971, Douglas-Home even held out the prospect of 'a solution of the Constitutional problem at some distant date', although he rejected any possibility of a time-scale for change in the constitutional status of Northern Ireland.[47] But Hillery's efforts to secure more rapid reform within Northern Ireland had little immediate influence on British policy. The Foreign Secretary was careful to avoid any commitments on policing, criminal justice and the vexed issue of parades, in part because such issues were not his responsibility but fell under Maudling's remit. Douglas-Home's caution, however, reflected above all British awareness of vehement unionist opposition to further concessions to nationalist demands. The British view, expressed by Douglas-Home to Hillery in July 1971, was that major reforms had been enacted and were working reasonably well.[48] Hillery believed that the reforms were too little and too late; full equality of treatment for the minority was an urgent necessity. He was deeply concerned about the increasing prestige enjoyed by the Provisionals within Catholic communities and was convinced with good reason that the British security response merely threw petrol on the flames.

The short-term impact of the ministerial meetings on the situation in Northern Ireland was certainly limited, but the ministerial talks were still valuable for the Irish side. Hillery's persistent diplomacy was designed to prevent the development of a political vacuum, which would be filled by paramilitary extremism. While he fell far short of what he hoped to achieve, nevertheless, his diplomacy secured some notable advances. The meetings between Hillery and Douglas-Home underlined an implicit acceptance by senior British ministers that the Irish government had a vital interest in Northern Ireland and would have to be involved in any solution to the conflict. The establishment of regular Anglo-Irish consultation about the North undermined unionist claims that developments north of the border were none of the Irish government's business. Finally the diplomatic contacts promoted by Hillery helped to prepare the way for direct talks between Lynch and Heath, which were scheduled for October 1971.

Yet the British government aimed above all to shore up the fragile position of moderate unionist leaders. Westminster's strategy was to keep Chichester-Clark in office, supporting his government against rebels within his own party and opponents such as Paisley.[49] The Conservative government sought to avert the prospect of direct rule, which would be the inevitable consequence of the collapse of the Stormont government or a takeover of the Unionist Party by extremist elements opposed to reform.[50] This order of priorities militated strongly against any effective British response to Hillery's demands for a more rapid transformation of the Northern state. The British strategy achieved incremental progress, though with painful slowness as far as Hillery was concerned. Chichester-Clark accepted the reform programme and secured the adoption of several important reforms, including legislation creating a new Housing Executive with guaranteed representation for the minority. But his position was undermined by intransigent opposition to reform by hardline unionists, notably Paisley, and by the escalation of the IRA campaign, which in turn reinforced unionist disaffection with the Prime Minister. The murder of three British soldiers in Belfast on 10 March 1971 dealt the final blow to Chichester-Clark's administration.[51] The embattled Prime Minister's response was to seek more British reinforcements; when Heath refused this demand, Chichester-Clark resigned on 21 March.

His departure did not change the basic features of the crisis in Northern Ireland. Brian Faulkner, who succeeded Chichester-Clark, was a more capable politician, but his room for manoeuvre was strictly limited. As a former opponent of reform who now advocated accommodation with the Catholic minority, his credentials were suspect on both sides of the community divide.[52] He also inspired deep distrust among Northern nationalists and within the Irish government. Hugh McCann accurately expressed the feelings of the political establishment in Dublin when he met the British ambassador on 22 March, the day before Faulkner's election as Prime Minister. McCann questioned Faulkner's sincerity in delivering reform and his ability to do so even if he had experienced a Pauline conversion to liberal unionism.[53] Peck saw no reason to doubt Faulkner's commitment to reform, but agreed that his prospects for survival were slim: 'He admitted, however, that if pushed, he [the ambassador] would give him about three weeks.'[54] Whatever their ambassador's view, British ministers were committed to supporting Faulkner, if only to hold back the dreaded spectre of direct rule. Faulkner sought to combine pragmatic acceptance of the reforms with an aggressive security policy. He attempted to remain in power by executing a balancing act between grassroots unionist demands for drastic action against the IRA and the British policy of reform. The Unionist leader's efforts to conciliate the minority were limited and ineffective; in July the

SDLP and other nationalist representatives withdrew from Stormont, in protest at Faulkner's refusal to hold a public inquiry into the deaths of two men in Derry, who were shot by the British army.[55] Faulkner's strategy ultimately completed the alienation of the minority without satisfying the unionist base.

A report from Eamonn Gallagher on 19 July 1971 noted that 'The North remains like a volcano but one whose eruptions follow no particular pattern.'[56] The next eruption was less than a month away. On 9 August 1971 Lynch received a personal message from Heath, informing the Taoiseach that internment without trial would be reintroduced in Northern Ireland on the same day.[57] Faulkner succeeded in persuading the British government to allow him to proceed with internment, ostensibly on the basis that it was necessary to defeat the IRA more quickly; in reality it had more to do with ensuring his own political survival in the face of unionist disaffection. British ministers had little faith in the likely success of internment but accepted it as the final alternative to direct rule.[58]

Operation Demetrius began in the early hours of the morning of 9 August; 464 people were arrested in the initial raids, with 347 being detained without trial.[59] The operation was entirely one-sided, involving the wholesale arrest of Catholics allegedly linked to paramilitary organisations. It was also based on flawed intelligence, as it transpired that many of those 'lifted' either had no connection with political violence or were not linked with the modern IRA.[60] Internment was a catastrophic blunder. The military action did little to curtail the activity of the Provisional IRA but, ironically, it did a great deal to undermine the authority of the Stormont government and to damage the reputation of the British army in Northern Ireland. The pre-dawn wave of arrests triggered an immediate upsurge in violence directed at the security forces; at least 24 people were killed between 9 and 13 August.[61] Internment dramatically heightened Catholic alienation from the British state, confirming the widespread suspicion within the minority that civil rights existed only for one section of the population. The army's action, intended to defeat the IRA, instead played directly into their hands. Lynch condemned internment as a deplorable attempt to maintain the unionist regime, which had 'long since shown itself incapable of just government and contemptuous of the norms of British democracy to which they pretend allegiance'.[62] As fighting raged on the streets of Belfast and Derry, Hillery went to London on another high-profile mission of protest.

The Irish Foreign Minister went personally to meet Maudling, instead of delegating the mission to O'Sullivan, to underline the force of the Irish government's objections to internment. Hillery's notes for the meeting with the Home Secretary, who was standing in for Heath, reflected his fear that the British action could undermine Irish efforts to contain the conflict and embroil the whole island in bloody civil war:

1. Am I dealing with a closed mind or is he willing to avoid a war in Ireland?
2. I see the Br. Govt desperately defending Orange Order dominance – is this their objective …
3. Govt in present form has failed; how much will they spend of British prestige, British lives, British money, to keep it there or be seen to be trying – and why? [63]

Hillery was appalled by the introduction of internment and did not bother to hide his anger at the ministerial meeting on 11 August. He told Maudling bluntly that the British government was pursuing a policy that could lead to war not only in the North, but also in Ireland as a whole. British policies that sustained unionist dominance in Ulster had led to the re-emergence of the IRA; internment was wrong and dangerous. The British 'have been backing unionism against the principles of their democracy.'[64] Maudling responded that Westminster was merely supporting the democratically-elected government in Stormont; the present situation in the North was 'a uniquely unhappy one', but he could not accept that the Orange Order was running Stormont. Hillery returned to the attack, arguing that people would no longer listen to the Taoiseach; the IRA was now a reality and the only way to remove them was to give political influence to constitutional nationalists.[65] Maudling urged a joint effort to suppress the IRA in the first instance, arguing that they trained and found refuge south of the border. Hillery replied that the IRA was as much the enemy of his government as of the British, but it was politically impossible for the Irish government to take severe action against the organisation in present circumstances; they could not appear to be acting in support of Stormont.[66] The only alternative to the present situation was to replace force with politics, and this could be accomplished only by power-sharing between the divided communities: 'The truth is that Stormont is finished and that the British are using vast resources to keep it alive. The obvious thing is to let Stormont die.'[67]

Hillery urged the British government to establish a power-sharing commission, including equal representation for each community, which would take over responsibility for the administration of Northern Ireland. Maudling was so alarmed at this suggestion that he sought to shut down any discussion of the idea – 'it would be better if this part of the conversation did not take place,' he commented.[68] Hillery persisted, arguing that urgent action was required and a commission would provide the basis for the two communities to work together; his priority was to create a strong political force representing the minority, with a guaranteed voice in the government of the province.[69] Maudling remarked that London favoured a strong opposition in Stormont, but Hillery commented that if the SDLP returned to Stormont while internment continued, it would be the end of them. He meant that they faced political oblivion but considering the level of nationalist outrage against internment the threat of physical extinction could hardly be ruled out.

Maudling inadvertently highlighted a key difference between the two governments when he commented that it was difficult 'to think about a political solution while violence continues'; the restoration of law and order had to be the first priority and full participation by the minority in the affairs of the province could be achieved once peace was restored. To Hillery, this way of thinking was woefully misguided: it was precisely the lack of a viable political project for nationalists that fed support for the Provisional IRA. He told Maudling that a power-sharing commission offered a political alternative to the Provisional campaign; there would be 'no sympathy' for the IRA if the minority were accorded meaningful political participation. Moreover a power-sharing arrangement could lead to eventual unity between North and South. The Home Secretary responded that any public suggestion of Irish unity at this stage would only exacerbate the situation; indeed, if there were to be any public disclosure that the point had even been raised, 'the British would have to deny that there was any such discussion.'[70] Maudling admitted with masterly understatement that 'Stormont has not been a great success,' but considered that any attempt at immediate constitutional change would lead to catastrophe. Hillery's case was summed up with his final warning that there had to be political progress, 'otherwise there is a grave danger of a major warlike situation developing'.[71]

The meeting exposed the key divergences between the two governments, which both aimed to contain the violence but could not agree on how best to do so. The British government was concerned to stabilise Faulkner's position and feared that a major political initiative would trigger not only the fall of his government but also a violent Protestant backlash.[72] The Irish side was gravely concerned by the apparent undermining of Lynch's peace policy and particularly worried at the popular support gained by the IRA among the minority as a direct result of internment. Neither side minimised the significance of the IRA threat by 1971, but Maudling presented an effective security response as the first priority, while Hillery regarded a political solution as indispensable if the IRA campaign was to be defeated. Hillery and Lynch were convinced that the British government would have to call the bluff of intransigent unionism and create a new political dispensation in the North, which guaranteed full political participation for the minority.[73] Irish ministers and officials believed well before August 1971 that reform within Northern Ireland was not sufficient to overcome nationalist alienation. Internment ensured that the Irish government would settle for nothing less than the abolition of Stormont; the end of single-party unionist rule and the establishment of an alternative power-sharing administration became the publicly proclaimed objectives of the Irish government.

Despite the public clash over internment, diplomatic activity between the two governments was intensified rather than abandoned. Sir John Peck met Hugh McCann on 23 August, informing the secretary that Heath was willing to bring forward the proposed summit with the Taoiseach. Peck regarded internment as a colossal error and told McCann that 'the Taoiseach and the minister were right about the effects of internment in the North.'[74] McCann's response expressed Irish frustration at British policy: 'I reminded the ambassador that they were also right in 1969 and 1970 and I suggested that perhaps it is about time that Whitehall should start listening to them rather than the spurious guidance they must be receiving from Belfast'. McCann was interested in the prospect of an earlier meeting, but warned that 'the Taoiseach could not come away empty-handed.'[75] Peck's approach signalled that a reassessment of British policy was beginning in the disastrous aftermath of internment. Senior officials in Whitehall were alarmed by the political fallout and advised their ministers to consider political initiatives to ease the crisis.[76] Heath proposed a two-day summit between the two leaders at Chequers for 6–7 September. Lynch, having delayed his decision until he consulted Hillery and other senior ministers, announced on 1 September that he had accepted Heath's invitation.[77] Hillery favoured acceptance of Heath's invitation and arranged for Donal O'Sullivan, the experienced ambassador in London, to accompany Lynch to the summit.[78] The invitation carried some political risk for the Taoiseach in the context of nationalist outrage over internment. Yet it amounted to formal recognition by the Prime Minister of the Irish government's legitimate interest in Northern Ireland. The briefing given to the media by the Foreign Office stipulated that the two leaders would discuss 'all matters affecting relations between the UK and the Irish Republic, including Northern Ireland, economic matters and entry into the EEC.'[79] But it was tacitly recognised on both sides that Northern Ireland would be the sole subject of discussion at the summit, with the other issues being postponed until the next meeting between the national leaders. Moreover, the summit met the compelling need for both governments to do something in the face of the escalating violence.

The Chequers summit marked a significant advance in Anglo-Irish relations, not so much for its content but due to the fact that it happened at all. The summit did not produce any dramatic breakthrough on Northern Ireland. It could not have done so against the grim background of the IRA campaign, internment and political deadlock at Stormont. Lynch and Heath had a wide-ranging discussion about the situation in the North, without reaching any substantive agreement; there was still a wide gulf between the two governments. Yet the summit was important as the first step in Anglo-Irish dialogue at the highest level about the major unresolved issue between the two countries. It was followed shortly afterwards by a tripartite summit, which also included Faulkner, at Chequers on 27 September 1971; this was the first meeting between the heads of government in Dublin, London and Belfast since 1925. The exchanges between Lynch and Faulkner were predictably unproductive and revealed little common ground other than opposition to violence.[80] Hillery gave John Hume a downbeat but essentially accurate summary of the tripartite summit when he met the SDLP politician on 1 October: 'it didn't do so good, but the fact of having the meeting was perhaps something.'[81] The situation in the North was deteriorating so rapidly that any dialogue, even with a much-distrusted figure like Faulkner, appeared preferable to none.

Shortly after the first Chequers summit, the British Foreign Office began to speculate that a rift had appeared between Hillery and Lynch. John Peck sent a telegram to the Foreign Office on 15 September, suggesting that the relationship between the Taoiseach and his Foreign Minister was showing signs of strain. Peck noted that 'Dr Hillery was present neither to wish the Taoiseach farewell to London nor to greet him on his return, notwithstanding that ordinary courtesy and political expediency would seem to require him to go through this normal routine'.[82] Whitehall was also informed that Hillery was 'incommunicado' in Clare for two weeks and would not return to Dublin until 23 September. The ambassador reported speculation in Dublin that Hillery was annoyed at Eamonn Gallagher's role as a leading adviser to Lynch. Peck also suggested that Hillery might be signalling his opposition to Lynch's participation in the summit with Heath. The ambassador even advanced a theory that Hillery was sulking in Clare to demonstrate his dissatisfaction with the Taoiseach:

> Dr Hillery's determination to resume an interrupted vacation in the countryside would be more comprehensible if he had observed the common civilities when his master returned from Chequers. Instead he has left the impression of an out-of-step minister having a fit of political sulks and taking considerable pains publicly to disassociate himself from the manner in which the Taoiseach conducts relations with ourselves.[83]

Peck, who was normally a shrewd observer of Irish politics, wisely concluded with a note of caution, telling his superiors that Hillery's behaviour might well involve no more than a 'temporary rift' with Lynch.

Peck's analysis involved a basic misunderstanding of the relationship between Hillery and Lynch. Hillery was a consistent advocate of negotiations with the British government and fully supported Lynch's decision to meet Heath. Hillery was in France when the Chequers summit took place and Lynch phoned his Foreign Minister from the Irish embassy in London to brief him on the outcome of the talks: 'He told me everything that happened at the meeting'.[84] Hillery then took a belated holiday in Clare, which had been impossible in August due to the political storm provoked by internment. It appears that a more flexible definition of civility and political routine prevailed in Dublin than in London. There were no essential differences between Hillery and Lynch on Northern Ireland. Both men firmly opposed any resort to force and stood for political change by peaceful means; both were deeply unhappy with most aspects of British policy in the North and maintained unification as a long-term objective. Peck may have been misled by speculation on the part of Irish journalists, especially the irrepressible Raymond Smith, that Hillery had opposed the Chequers summit. But Hillery had sought to promote negotiation between the two governments concerning

Northern Ireland since 1969; he had no objection at all to an Anglo-Irish summit that marked the logical culmination of his efforts.

Moreover, Hillery was keenly aware that the Taoiseach bore the ultimate responsibility for government decisions on Northern Ireland. He told John McColgan to ensure that Gallagher reported directly to Lynch: 'I am the Minister for External Affairs. But the North is the Taoiseach's responsibility. Tell Gallagher to report to Jack'.[85] Far from resenting Gallagher's influential role as an adviser to the Taoiseach, Hillery was at least partly responsible for it. The Foreign Minister never sought to set himself up as an independent operator on the national question, unlike some of his erstwhile colleagues. He worked closely with Lynch from the outset and was the Taoiseach's most valuable ally on Northern Ireland. Hillery's prominence both in August 1969 and July 1970 was dictated by his concern to preserve Lynch's moderate policy and maintain the relevance of constitutional nationalism. The real rift in 1971 was not between Hillery and Lynch, but between the policies of the Irish and British governments.

Yet Hillery undoubtedly played a very different role to the Taoiseach in Anglo-Irish relations. Hillery took the lead in articulating the grievances of the minority to the British government, and he was involved in a series of sharp encounters with British ministers, from Chalfont in August 1969 to Maudling two years later. This clearly affected the official British perception of Hillery; communications between John Peck and the Foreign Office showed a gradual change in the ambassador's view of the Irish Foreign Minister. Having regarded him, correctly, as a moderate ally of the Taoiseach in 1970, Peck increasingly saw Hillery as a more uncompromising figure within the Irish government by the autumn of 1971.[86] Hillery himself would not have been displeased by such a portrayal, but the reality was considerably more complex. Lynch deliberately employed Hillery as the government's point man on the North, especially at the most explosive moments of the conflict. Hillery's basic moderation and commitment to democratic nationalism made him a reliable representative abroad, while his willingness to confront British ministers reinforced the Taoiseach's position at home. This formed part of a wider pattern throughout Hillery's association with Lynch, as the

Taoiseach frequently called on him to rescue the government in difficult or unpalatable situations, from the curfew on the Falls Road to the 1971 Ard Fheis. This caused occasional irritation on Hillery's part, not least because Lynch usually gave him minimal warning before asking him to go into the breach.[87] But it did not amount to a serious disagreement between the two men, still less the policy rift imagined by British diplomats.

The diplomatic contacts between the two governments were overshadowed by the continuing violence. On 30 January 1972, soldiers of the Parachute Regiment killed thirteen men following a civil rights demonstration in Derry; another victim died later of his injuries. The paratroopers attempted to arrest demonstrators as they retreated into the Bogside after the march; the soldiers claimed that they came under fire from gunmen and responded in accordance with their rules of engagement.[88] This version of events was fiercely disputed by nationalist residents of the Bogside and remained a subject of bitter controversy for the following generation. The expert analysis conducted for the Saville Inquiry over a quarter of a century later found no evidence that any of those who died were carrying weapons or explosives.[89] The shootings generated a tidal wave of outrage and revulsion throughout nationalist Ireland. Bloody Sunday was a devastating blow to the prestige of the British army among Catholics, and it acted as a powerful recruiting agent for the IRA.[90] Anglo-Irish relations were plunged into their worst crisis since August 1969. There were massive protests in Dublin over the following week and public anger in the Republic reached a level not seen even in the autumn of 1969.

The government urgently needed to provide an alternative focus to prevent popular outrage from turning into support for the IRA. The measures adopted by the Cabinet reflected their anxiety to maintain the primacy of politics over paramilitary violence. Lynch immediately denounced the action of the British army as 'unbelievably and savagely inhuman'.[91] The Cabinet met in emergency session on 31 January, reaching a series of decisions that were intended to contain the crisis. The government demanded the immediate withdrawal of British troops from

Derry and other Catholic areas; the end of internment and a declaration of intent by the British government 'to achieve a final settlement of the Irish question and the convocation of a conference for that purpose.'[92] Ambassador O'Sullivan was recalled from London to underline the government's anger at British policies. The Taoiseach also pledged that the Irish government would support political action to bring about the end of Stormont by providing financial aid to nationalist parties committed to non-violence.[93] But the most prominent and high profile response authorised by the government was a renewed appeal to international opinion. There was disagreement within the Cabinet initially about the form this should take; George Colley proposed a general propaganda offensive against the British in which all ministers would participate. Hillery opposed this move and the Cabinet's decision gave him the central role in the Irish diplomatic response:

> The murders by the British Army caused the government to react very strongly and George came to the meeting with a proposal for all members of the government to travel abroad to speak against it. In the end control was established by me being given the task of visiting the UN and the US and Canada.[94]

Hillery's mission was to seek support from the foreign ministers of friendly governments and the Secretary-General of the UN for the Irish government's policy demands. He was attempting to internationalise Irish concerns, not only to exert the maximum public pressure on the British government, but also to reduce the danger that the Irish state would be drawn into suicidal conflict over Northern Ireland.

The urgency of his mission was underlined by events in Dublin in the first week of February. Bloody Sunday ignited passions that were, at least temporarily, beyond the control of the Irish government. Lynch made a broadcast to the nation, announcing his government's actions and proclaiming a national day of mourning for the victims; if this was designed to provide for a peaceful expression of the mood of national outrage, it did not fully succeed. Following a march through the city by tens of thousands of people on 2 February, the British embassy in Merrion Square was attacked and burned out, in a move orchestrated by a small minority, but watched with approval by a large section of the crowd.[95] Hillery was already in New York by the time the embassy was burned, but he needed no reminder that nationalist feelings at home were running high. He himself regarded Bloody Sunday as an act of murder and viewed it as the logical outcome of disastrous British policies in the North, based on upholding unionist rule and enforcing a security solution to the conflict. He was convinced, too, that the Irish government could not allow itself to be outflanked by the IRA in responding to the tragedy in Derry. It was no surprise that Hillery's public statements on his international tour made little concession to rhetorical moderation.

On 1 February, Hillery made the most vehement attack on British policy of his career. He told a crowded press conference at Kennedy Airport, just after his arrival in New York, that 'Britain was provoking a war against a nation which to a large extent is unarmed.' He was going to the UN and friendly governments 'to end the reign of terror which Britain is perpetrating on our people'.[96] His analysis of Bloody Sunday was stark: 'Death was the price of protest in Northern Ireland.' He hoped that 'friendly nations would turn Britain away from the lunatic policies which she is following.' Hillery issued a thinly veiled threat that made headlines at home, warning that if Ireland received no help from the West, his country might turn to the East: 'My orders are to seek help wherever I can get it.'[97] This was not an off-the-cuff remark, but a calculated statement. It echoed comments made by Lynch in Dublin on the previous day that Ireland would accept help from any nation in the world.[98] Hillery's statement was designed to raise the prospect that Ireland might be driven by British intransigence into the waiting arms of Soviet Russia. An alliance between Catholic Ireland and the Communist superpower certainly seemed a remote prospect to most observers, but it was not quite as unlikely as it might have appeared. The Soviet delegation had been one of Hillery's few reliable allies in his attempt to raise the crisis in Northern Ireland at the Security Council in 1969; there was little doubt that they would gladly attempt to exploit Britain's difficulties over the Irish question once again. Yet Hillery, who had just negotiated Ireland's accession to the EEC, was not about to propose a radical strategic shift in Irish foreign policy. He was seeking to alarm political elites in Britain and the United States, whose first preoccupation was the Cold War, by raising the unpleasant vista of Soviet co-operation with the Irish government on the issue of the North in various international bodies.

Despite his militant rhetoric, Hillery's comments did not mark any fundamental change either in his own views or the government's policy. He reiterated that the Irish government would never contemplate an invasion of the North; instead they sought assurances from the British that they would not maintain a unionist state by force of arms.[99] Hillery clarified the aims of his mission in a policy statement to another press conference at the United Nations building on the following day. He declared that the British army had become 'an instrument of coercion' to prop up the Stormont regime. He set out the core demands of the Irish government, including a clear declaration from Britain of its intention to achieve 'a just settlement of the Irish question', backed up by the convening of an all-party conference for that purpose.[100] He conceded that the reforms had eliminated formal inequalities between the two communities, but there was a wide disparity between the formal position and the reality on the ground: he emphasised that genuine participation 'cannot be accorded to the minority under the present regime'.[101] Hillery presented a power-sharing administration in the North as essential and argued that it could provide the foundation for the achievement of a united Ireland by consent.[102] He did not expect the British government to agree to constitutional change; Irish unity remained a long-term objective. But he expressed clearly the minimum requirements of the Irish government for further high-level talks with Britain: the end of Stormont and a new political initiative by Westminster. On this occasion, his aims were more realistic and achievable than the objectives imposed on him by a divided government in 1969. His tactics were also very different, focusing much more on diplomacy than on propaganda. Hillery did not plan to achieve Irish objectives by embarrassing Britain at the UN. He quietly ruled out a renewed appeal to the Security Council as soon as he arrived in New York. His initiative in 1969 had served its purpose and could not be repeated in the face of British opposition; it was unlikely that Lord Caradon's conciliatory approach would be replicated at a time of even greater tension between the two countries. He aimed instead to generate diplomatic pressure on Britain from friendly governments to change its policies in Northern Ireland. He was also determined to promote the Irish government's demands in the international arena, rejecting British policies and proposing an alternative political solution. This reflected his conviction that the latest crisis, like the underlying conflict itself, could be contained only by providing a political alternative to the IRA. Hillery's uncompromising rhetoric concealed the essential moderation of his position.

The subtle nuances of Hillery's position were certainly not appreciated by William Rogers, the US Secretary of State. Hillery's meeting with Rogers on 3 February was the first of his consultations with other foreign ministers in the wake of Bloody Sunday; it was also the most acrimonious and the least successful. The administration of Richard Nixon was firmly wedded to its alliance with Britain and had no intention of undertaking any initiative on Northern Ireland. The British ambassador to Washington, Lord Cromer, had lobbied Rogers on the previous day against giving aid and comfort to the Irish, and this intervention counted for much more with the Secretary of State than anything the Irish Foreign Minister had to say. Hillery urged Rogers to use his good offices to persuade the British government to abandon its reliance on a military policy and seek a political solution in the North; military action was an old-fashioned and self-perpetuating way to solve problems.[103] Hillery emphasised that he was not asking any government to criticise Britain publicly, but wanted their allies to use their influence with the British government privately. But Rogers refused to have anything to do with the conflict; the US government would not condemn the British nor would he put forward proposals for consideration by them. He categorically ruled out any action by the United States:

When the situation is almost uncontrollable we are asked to step into a problem that has gone on for 300–400 years. Eventually it has to be solved by the people concerned. Lord Cromer called on me when he heard you were coming. We are not in a position to intervene.[104]

The secretary asked Hillery why the Irish were opposed to direct discussions with the British. Hillery, who had been advocating such discussions for three years, replied that his government wanted meaningful talks, not fake discussions. Each time Irish ministers had discussions with the British government, military action by the British army triggered a new crisis. He commented that: 'I am afraid the kind of discussion we have had so far is "shoot you in the back as you go out the door". They act as if they are diminishing a nuisance.'[105]

Hillery expressed his genuine fears about a further descent into the abyss: 'If this goes on there will be some of our people in the South fighting with guns and bombs. We'll be put out of government.'[106] The Secretary of State was unmoved by this blunt assessment, commenting that he certainly could not tell the British government anything like that. Instead he urged Hillery to have direct discussions with the British: 'Get discussions started unconditionally. Say this is idiotic, Christians killing one another in the name of Christianity for over 600 years'.[107]

Rogers' ignorance about Northern Ireland was impressive. Apart from being confused about the historical timeline, he appeared to assume that the conflict was a modern religious war, showing almost complete ignorance of the political and cultural divisions between the two communities. Rogers also misinterpreted Hillery's purpose in coming to Washington. The Irish minister was seeking diplomatic assistance to contain the conflict, but Rogers feared that his guest was seeking overt US intervention against Britain and possibly even unofficial military assistance. Hillery later recorded his private opinion that 'Rogers thought I had come to look for guns.'[108] Hillery's arguments had no influence on the secretary, who had already decided his view of the Irish mission. Rogers was deeply uncomfortable discussing the conflict with the Irish Foreign

Minister at all and sought to avoid even the slightest hint that he might do anything in response to Hillery's visit. It was hardly surprising that the encounter produced no positive result at all. Moreover, Rogers' subsequent attempt to minimise the significance of the meeting threatened to undermine Hillery's credibility. The secretary briefed journalists that when he informed Hillery that the United States could not intervene, the Irish minister replied that he understood and was making no such request.[109] This comment was a clear misrepresentation of Hillery's position, suggesting that he made no request for diplomatic assistance to Rogers. Hillery was infuriated by this piece of spin: 'He said I didn't ask for anything. That was a knife in the back.'[110] The Department of Foreign Affairs later issued a statement directly contradicting Rogers' version of the meeting, without naming him as the source of the inaccurate report.[111]

The Irish Foreign Minister's transatlantic diplomacy had little success in the wake of Bloody Sunday. Hillery also met Mitchell Sharp, the Canadian Foreign Minister, in Ottawa; while their discussion was less acrimonious than Hillery's encounter with Rogers, the outcome was broadly the same. The Canadian government indicated publicly that it would not take sides in the conflict or pass judgment on British policies.[112] The recently elected Secretary General of the United Nations, Kurt Waldheim, was in Addis Ababa, but Hillery met his *chef de cabinet*, CV Narasimhan, on 2 February to seek the good offices of the UN in alleviating the crisis. When Waldheim returned from Ethiopia four days later, he announced publicly that he was willing to assist in resolving the conflict if both sides agreed to UN intervention.[113] The British reaction was swift and predictable; the Secretary-General was informed that the situation was an internal matter that 'did not lend itself to United Nations intervention.'[114] Although the Secretary-General himself was sympathetic to Hillery's request, the UN could do nothing in the face of British opposition.

Yet Hillery's visit was not entirely unproductive. He found greater sympathy for the Irish case among leading members of the US Congress. He toured Capitol Hill in Washington, briefing prominent legislators in

both Houses of Congress on the crisis, including Senator Edward
Kennedy and Congressman Hugh Carey.[115] Kennedy publicly called for
US intervention to mediate between Ireland and Britain; he also
compared Bloody Sunday to a notorious massacre of Vietnamese civilians
by American troops in 1968, claiming that it was 'Britain's My Lai'. While
Kennedy's proposal for mediation was instantly dismissed by the Nixon
administration, the Senator's intervention was significant for the future.
Irish diplomats helped to arrange a meeting between Kennedy and John
Hume in November 1972, forging a connection that would endure
throughout the Troubles.[116] Kennedy emerged as a leading member of a
powerful Irish-American lobby, supportive of the Irish government's
position on Northern Ireland, later in the 1970s; he remained a key ally
of successive Irish governments in Washington over the following three
decades. The Irish government had virtually no influence in Washington
in 1972 and its views could be ignored with impunity by the Nixon
administration. The department under Hillery's direction began to change
this dismal landscape, cultivating prominent Irish-American politicians
and briefing leading public figures on the official Irish response to the
conflict.

Hillery enjoyed considerably greater success in his tour of European
capitals. He deliberately did not ask other governments to take sides in the
dispute between Ireland and Britain, but urged them to exert private
diplomatic pressure on Britain to take political initiatives that might
resolve the conflict.[117] He was well aware that most EEC governments
were concerned that Britain complete its entry into the Community and
would not welcome anything that might interfere with the process of
accession. Yet the European foreign ministers were not indifferent to an
armed conflict on their doorstep, nor could they ignore a major
unresolved dispute between two neighbouring states that were just about
to join the Community. Hillery went to Paris on 8 February to present
the Irish case, and received a much more friendly reception from the
French foreign ministry than he had at the US State Department. Hillery,
accompanied by the Irish ambassador, Eamonn Kennedy, first met the
State Secretary of the foreign ministry, Jean de Lipkowski, at the Quai

d'Orsay, and later had discussions with Maurice Schumann. Both men expressed sympathy with the Irish government over the situation in the North and emphasised the traditional links of friendship between Ireland and France. They also expressed concern at the apparent deterioration in Anglo-Irish relations at a time when hopes were high in France and across Western Europe that both countries would be able to join the Community.[118] The French Foreign Minister sought to help Hillery without overtly taking sides in the dispute. After their meeting Schumann presented Hillery to the waiting journalists and read a carefully polished introductory statement.[119] Schumann affirmed that the French government had no wish to intervene in 'the internal affairs of a friendly and allied country'. Crucially, however, he added that when 'a difference as sad as the present one' divided two friendly countries, which were both close to joining the Community, 'then we have a right to listen with attention and sympathy – a sympathy which should be translated into words and into action'.[120] Schumann's statement was a masterpiece of constructive ambiguity; it did not commit the French government to doing anything in particular. But he did suggest a strong sympathy for the Irish case and underlined French concern at the crisis, while remaining within the confines of diplomatic protocol. Schumann's willingness to discuss Hillery's concerns with British representatives was a significant gesture; the French government discussed the conflict in Northern Ireland following a report from Schumann on the following day and its public response was also designed to be helpful to Hillery. The government's official spokesman indicated that French ministers would not say much publicly about the crisis involving Ireland and Britain but would seek 'to help each of them to be better informed about the feelings of the other'.[121] The French response essentially gave Hillery everything he wanted, even if French goodwill was expressed with a certain amount of Gallic ambiguity.

The favourable outcome of his discussions in Paris enabled Hillery to counter suggestions by Irish journalists, especially his friend Dennis Kennedy, that his tour was turning into a series of rebuffs by friendly nations.[122] Hillery continued his tour of EEC capitals over the following month. Not all European ministers were as helpful as Schumann, but none received Hillery with the barely concealed suspicion displayed by Rogers. He was in Rome on 10–11 February, meeting Aldo Moro; the Italian Foreign Minister had already made enquiries to British representatives about the situation in Northern Ireland. He told Hillery that the Italian government could not intervene publicly, but assured him that 'there were many ways of saying things privately and confidentially, and Italy has acted on these lines wherever it might help.'[123] Hillery then visited three cities in two days, putting the Irish case to the foreign ministers in Brussels, The Hague and Bonn on 16 and 17 February. He expressed satisfaction publicly with the outcome of his discussion with Pierre Harmel of Belgium, although Harmel made no public comment on the situation in the North following their meeting. The Dutch Foreign Minister, Norbert Schmelzer, emphasised on 17 February that the Netherlands would maintain neutrality on the crisis, but agreed to seek additional information from Britain on the situation in the North and to discuss Irish concerns with the British government.[124] Later on the same day in Bonn, Hillery received a friendly but non-committal response from Walter Scheel, the Foreign Minister, who was ill and met his Irish counterpart only briefly. Hillery had, however, a detailed discussion with Paul Frank, the State Secretary of the German foreign ministry, who was a close associate of Chancellor Willy Brandt. Frank commented that the situation in Northern Ireland was 'a source of preoccupation and worry to the German government'; he openly admitted that they would like to help, but were not sure what they could do, as 'in the midst of a conflict it was difficult … to tell others what to do.'[125] He believed that increased political co-operation between the members of the enlarged Community would allow greater scope for other governments to make their views on Northern Ireland known to the British.[126] Hillery commented that he did not wish to raise the issue formally within the common European institutions, as he believed that his private talks with other foreign ministers served to maintain diplomatic pressure on Britain without exacerbating the dispute between the two countries: 'For the moment it was very helpful to be able to discuss this matter with friends of ours who were also friendly to the British since this in itself maintained pressure for a non-violent solution.'[127] It was a revealing statement, which summed up the whole purpose of Hillery's diplomacy after Bloody Sunday.

Hillery was not exaggerating when he told Irish journalists in Brussels on 16 February that he had found in Continental Europe 'a far greater interest in the problems of Northern Ireland than in the United States or Canada'.[128] He could have added that he had found far greater sympathy for the Irish government's position and less automatic deference to British policy than in Washington or Ottawa. He had good reason to be pleased with the outcome of his quiet diplomacy among the EEC member states; several European governments initiated discreet enquiries to British representatives or expressed their concerns privately about the situation in Northern Ireland. The Irish Foreign Minister's diplomatic efforts generated increasing international pressure on the British government, especially from its partners in Western Europe. Hillery's measured tactics won him no plaudits among the 'hillside men' of extreme republicanism, but he did a great deal to establish a constructive, non-violent alternative for Irish nationalism in the aftermath of Bloody Sunday.

It is unlikely, however, that Hillery's diplomatic efforts had any dramatic impact on the British government. Perhaps more important than his international tour was the reality which underpinned it – that the Irish government was no longer willing to talk to London unless there was a major political initiative and a decisive change in policy. British ministers and officials had been reassessing their options in Northern Ireland well before the slaughter in Derry.[129] Bloody Sunday acted as a catalyst for far-reaching change in British policy. Heath and the leading members of his government accepted by February 1972 that securing the collaboration of the Irish government with any political settlement in Northern Ireland was essential if it was to command wide acceptance among Catholics. Peck informed Lynch on 18 February that the British were considering a new political initiative.[130] It soon became evident that any new initiative would require direct rule from Westminster. Heath told Faulkner on 22 March that the British government intended to take full control over security and criminal justice in the North, with the intention of phasing out internment on a gradual basis.[131] When Faulkner indicated that his government would resign rather than accept these conditions, Heath moved to impose direct rule. Stormont was prorogued on 30 March, initially for a year, and William Whitelaw was appointed as Secretary of State for Northern Ireland.[132]

The suspension of Stormont transformed the political landscape in Northern Ireland. Whitelaw announced a policy of 'reconciliation', releasing over half of the internees and initiating talks with parties across the political spectrum on the way forward for the North.[133] Heath's initiative also allowed the normalisation of Anglo-Irish relations. Lynch welcomed the fall of Stormont and the Irish ambassador returned to London. Hillery soon resumed his previous pattern of diplomatic engagement with the British government. He met Whitelaw and Douglas-Home in London on 27 April, initiating the first high-level talks between the two governments since Bloody Sunday. The discussions were considerably more cordial than some of Hillery's previous encounters with British ministers, not least because he welcomed many of Whitelaw's policies and wanted him to proceed more quickly in seeking a political solution.[134] But the fall of Stormont could not resolve the conflict itself; it barely provided breathing space from IRA and loyalist violence. Following a brief ceasefire in June, the Provisional IRA resumed its campaign on 21 July with one of the worst atrocities of the Troubles, killing 11 people and injuring 130 in a carefully co-ordinated spate of bombs in Belfast.[135] Hillery had just arrived in London for another meeting with Whitelaw when the news of Bloody Friday broke and was not certain that the British minister would even wish to go ahead with the meeting: 'But the day of the bombs I arrived and he was very disturbed, he didn't want to see me at all.'[136] Whitelaw, however, agreed to see him before returning to Stormont. Hillery, who was deeply shocked at the news from Belfast, expressed his horror at the IRA's action; he also emphasised the continuing need for consultation at a political level between Dublin and London if there was to be any hope of a lasting solution. Whitelaw readily agreed: 'it is absolutely essential that we keep in touch. He might encounter opposition from the majority side in the

North but he will ensure that Dublin is kept as fully informed as possible.'[137] Perhaps even more startling in the circumstances was that the two ministers discussed how to draw the IRA into politics in the North. Whitelaw and Hillery agreed that it was essential to find some way to get the IRA leadership into constitutional politics, although both men were rightly pessimistic that such a process could succeed in the short term.[138] This aspect of their discussion remained secret; but as the meeting concluded, Whitelaw indicated that he was happy for Hillery to brief the press that the two governments would remain in close contact. This was an act of considerable courage by Whitelaw, coming as it did immediately after the IRA bombing and in the face of the likely outcry from the unionist leadership at continuing contacts with Dublin.

The ministerial meeting on 21 July, even as Belfast was engulfed in flames, reflected the strengths and the limitations of the evolving relationship between the two governments. The fact that the meeting went ahead at all underlined the resilience of the diplomatic connections between London and Dublin by the summer of 1972. The two governments were developing an increasingly close and constructive interaction on Northern policy, despite past setbacks and continuing disagreements. But Bloody Friday gave a brutal demonstration that the conflict in Northern Ireland had passed far beyond the control of either government. A briefing note for Hillery, composed by officials of his department in July 1972 just before the resumption of the IRA campaign, gave an analysis of the situation that was as bleak as it was prescient. The note argued that Whitelaw had been given 'the impossible job of creating a new Northern Ireland'.[139] His task was impossible because it attracted positive support from neither community; the dominant current of opinion within unionism sought the restoration of Stormont, while a vocal section of the minority simply demanded a united Ireland. This meant Whitelaw would be unable to find a durable local administration to replace his own, and direct rule would continue for the foreseeable future. Foreign Affairs predicted that continuing British rule would be accompanied either by a deterioration of the situation or 'at best an uneasy stasis in which nothing progressive can be done'.[140] The document underestimated the resilience of the two governments in seeking to find a political solution, but it predicted with gloomy accuracy the general course of events over the following two decades. The Provisional IRA remained committed to a military insurgency, believing that further terrorist action would force a British withdrawal. A loyalist backlash also gained strength in 1972, as the UVF and the Ulster Defence Association (UDA) escalated their campaign, which mainly took the form of indiscriminate attacks on Catholics.[141] The IRA campaign failed to force the withdrawal of British forces, but nor could the British defeat the IRA militarily. The situation in Northern Ireland settled into a political and military stalemate. While the British government fully intended the suspension of Stormont to open the way for a power-sharing administration, their hopes were not to be fulfilled. Direct rule would last, with the brief exception of the Sunningdale power-sharing experiment in 1973-74, for the rest of the twentieth century.

John McColgan summed up the conflict in Northern Ireland with stark simplicity: 'It was hell and all you could do was, the less hell there was the better'.[142] The situation in Northern Ireland by 1972 was bleak, and the impact of official Irish initiatives on the streets of Belfast or Derry was minimal; yet the Irish government could legitimately claim to have prevented an even greater disaster. Hillery could not prevent the explosion of violence in the North, but he did much to contain the conflict so that it did not engulf the whole island. Crucially, he did not abandon the people of Northern Ireland to their fate. He was a central figure in maintaining a peaceful, democratic alternative to paramilitary violence. Hillery was consistently called upon at moments of crisis, to express the discontent of the Irish government with British policy and so head off nationalist demands for a more militant response. This was the role he played in visiting the Falls Road, following the introduction of internment and again after Bloody Sunday. Hillery genuinely believed that British policy in Northern Ireland between 1970 and 1972 was wrong and would have a disastrous impact on nationalist opinion.[143] He was not simply enunciating the government's line on issues such as internment, but expressing real anger at the one-sided and frequently brutal treatment meted out to Northern nationalists. He combined absolute opposition to IRA violence with sustained criticism of British policies in Ireland.

Yet Hillery also promoted a policy of constructive engagement with the British government, often at the same time as he was publicly attacking British ministers. The initiatives taken by Hillery between 1969 and 1972 did much to establish the right of the Irish government to act as a diplomatic guarantor for the interests of the nationalist minority and secured an implicit acknowledgement by British ministers that the Irish state had a vital stake in the future of Northern Ireland. He played a leading part in initiating the first real engagement between Dublin and London about Northern Ireland in a generation. Heath and Whitelaw accepted the reality by early 1972 that the conflict could not be resolved without the active assistance of the Irish government. British and Irish ministers were still far apart in their analysis of the problem, but developing a constructive engagement between the two governments was an essential beginning, which was achieved in the most unfavourable circumstances.

14.

Mr Europe

General Charles de Gaulle's visit to Ireland in the summer of 1969 marked an unexpected turning point in Ireland's relations with continental Europe and had equally unforeseen implications for Paddy Hillery. It was the end of de Gaulle's long career – following defeat in a constitutional referendum, the former leader of the Free French in the Second World War had resigned as President of France. De Valera held a reception for de Gaulle in the midst of the general election count in June 1969; Hillery missed his election count in Clare to attend the function. The General greatly enjoyed his time in Ireland, referring to his Irish ancestry and telling his hosts that 'his blood took him to Ireland at that time'.[1] It was a less enjoyable occasion for Hillery, who was still uncertain about the outcome of his election count and was understandably distracted by the unpleasant possibility of losing his seat.[2] Yet de Gaulle's resignation would have far greater significance for Hillery than the inconvenience of missing his election count; even as the Irish ministers entertained General de Gaulle, they could hardly have been unaware that his sudden departure opened up a new opportunity for Ireland's entry to the European Communities.

Accession to the European Economic Community (EEC) and its two associated organisations, the European Coal and Steel Community (ECSC) and Euratom, had been the policy of the Irish state since 1961. But Irish entry to the EEC was a virtual impossibility so long as de Gaulle dominated French politics. It was not that de Gaulle was hostile to Ireland – indeed the opposite was true; he previously assured Lynch that France under his leadership had no objection in principle to Irish membership of the EEC.[3] But de Gaulle had twice vetoed Britain's application to enter the EEC, in 1963 and 1967. The dominant view among Irish politicians and officials was that Ireland's external trade and overall economic position were so closely intertwined with the British economy as to make accession without Britain entirely unrealistic.[4] Lemass announced that Ireland was applying to join the EEC in July 1961, but the application was put on hold following the French veto on further negotiations with Britain in January 1963. The Irish application made no progress for most of the decade, as de Gaulle remained implacably opposed to British entry to the Community. The French President's opposition to British membership also presented, almost inadvertently, an insurmountable barrier to Irish accession. De Gaulle's abrupt resignation preceded Hillery's promotion to External Affairs by only a couple of months. Hillery would be a major beneficiary of the former wartime leader's dramatic exit.

A Community of Seven?

De Gaulle's resignation paved the way for enlargement but it did not guarantee Ireland's early entry to the Community. The attitude of the new French administration, headed by Georges Pompidou, was not yet clear, although there was increasing optimism that the change of leadership in France would facilitate the entry of the four applicant states, Britain, Ireland, Denmark and Norway. But a Community of Seven, consisting of the six original member states and Britain, emerged as a real possibility in the summer of 1969. The Action Committee for the United States of

Europe, led by Jean Monnet, called in March 1969 for the early admission of Britain to the Community and envisaged a delay in the entry of the other applicant states until British accession was accomplished.[5] This was a nightmare scenario for Ireland, as Irish exporters would be excluded from the British market by a tariff wall, while their main competitors would be able to operate within the external tariff.[6] Even more alarming from an Irish perspective were Monnet's comments at a press conference in Brussels on 16 July, where he declared that to negotiate with four countries at the same time meant 'certain failure'.[7] Monnet, a committed federalist and former head of the ECSC, was widely regarded as the founding father of the post-war European project and commanded considerable prestige within the Community institutions; viewed from official circles in Dublin, this merely made his pronouncements all the more menacing.

Lynch asked Hillery within days of his appointment to External Affairs 'to look at the situation'; this was a polite way of telling the new Foreign Minister to counter Monnet's proposal as effectively as possible.[8] Hillery moved decisively to kill off the proposed Community of Seven. Within a fortnight of his move to Iveagh House, he began intensive diplomatic lobbying of the six member states, with the dual aim of reasserting Ireland's interest in acceding to the Community and of garnering support against Monnet's proposal. Hillery first visited Brussels on 14 July to lobby the Commission and the Belgian government; he met Jean Rey, the President of the Commission, and Eduardo Martino, Commissioner for External Relations. Hillery emphasised Ireland's strong interest in achieving membership of the Community at the earliest opportunity and made clear the government's absolute opposition to a Community of Seven: 'Because of the close economic relations between Ireland and Britain, such a development would be a disaster for Ireland's economy'.[9] Rey was sympathetic, expressing his personal opposition to the idea of allowing British accession first; both Commissioners supported enlargement to a Community of Ten.[10] Hillery also secured the backing of Pierre Harmel, the Belgian Foreign Minister, in a meeting on the same day. Harmel confirmed that Belgium favoured the accession of all four applicant states and was hopeful that the governments of the Community would take a decision before the end of the year to open negotiations for enlargement.[11]

Yet the meeting with the Commission underlined that the Irish government had good reason to be concerned. Rey quietly urged Hillery to take his case to representatives of the member states, advising him to approach Dr Joseph Luns, the Foreign Minister of the Netherlands and President of the Council of Ministers, the most influential decision-making institution within the EEC. Hillery arranged to meet Luns in London on 15 July, along with a team of Irish officials; he argued strongly that the negotiations for all four applicants should begin together and that 'our accession should take place simultaneously with that of Britain.'[12] This formula became the consistent theme of Irish lobbying in European capitals over the following eleven months. Luns at first gave the impression that he was inclined to support dealing with Britain first, but changed tack when confronted with adamant Irish opposition to the idea. Hillery argued forcefully that such a move would isolate Ireland and devastate the Irish economy: 'In the end I gave him a lecture that the Commission and the Community had no right to treat a small country as they might treat us by doing that. He took it; he said he would bring it back to the Council'.[13] While Luns was non-committal on the eventual decision of the Community, he was impressed by the strength of the Irish case and undertook to bring it to the attention of the Council: 'He added that he would endeavour to see that our interests were taken care of'.[14] If Hillery's meeting with Luns was a notable success, even more important was the backing of West Germany, the economic powerhouse of the new Europe. On the following day the Irish Foreign Minister welcomed to Dublin a representative of the Federal Republic; Dr Gerhard Jahn was the State Secretary of the German Foreign Ministry. His message could not have been more favourable. Jahn assured Hillery on 16 July that the Federal Republic supported all four applications and believed that the Council should give 'the same answer to all four'.[15] Moreover, he commented that he saw 'no likelihood of France agreeing to the admission of Britain alone'.[16] As Hillery had chosen not to visit Paris on the basis that the attitude of the new French government to British accession was still unpredictable, Jahn's information was extremely valuable. Hillery's initial round of lobbying was highly successful, generating considerable support in European capitals for the Irish position.

The outbreak of the crisis in Northern Ireland delayed the tour of EEC member states that Hillery had hoped to undertake over the following months. But his prolonged mission to the United Nations in the autumn of 1969 opened up a valuable opportunity to forge diplomatic connections with the representatives of EEC states. Hillery quietly met Foreign Ministers from several member states while in New York, and received a generally positive response to the Irish appeal for simultaneous negotiations between the Community and all the applicant states.[17] Hillery's most productive encounter was with the French Foreign Minister, Maurice Schumann, at the French Mission in New York on 20 September. Schumann did not formally commit France to supporting enlargement, but expressed his hope that the Community's decision would be positive. More significantly, he assured Hillery that the French government would not consider dealing with Britain in advance of the other three applicants: 'This suggestion had been talked about but it had now been killed.'[18] Hillery was delighted by this categorical statement of French policy; the idea of a Community of Seven was certainly dead if it could not command French support. Schumann's positive comments on accession also provided a strong hint that the new French administration was willing to accept the enlargement of the Community.

The deliberations within the Community unfolded very much as the Irish government had hoped. The Commission in October 1969 endorsed the opening of negotiations with all four applicant states as soon as possible. The Council of Foreign Ministers did not immediately endorse enlargement, seeking to hammer out an agreement first on internal issues, especially the formulation of a definitive financial arrangement to support the Common Agricultural Policy (CAP).[19] The CAP provided for a common organisation of the agricultural market and a system of price support for the agricultural sector within EEC countries. The development of an enduring framework for the CAP was an essential

priority of the French government and resolving the issue was effectively
a precondition for French agreement to enlargement.[20] This was largely
achieved by the summit conference involving the heads of state or
government of the EEC countries in The Hague on 1–2 December 1969.
The summit agreed to establish a long-term financial arrangement for
the CAP and to move gradually to a system of funding based on the
Community's own resources.[21] This financial agreement opened the way
for enlargement. The governments also agreed to the opening of
negotiations between the Community and the applicant states, on the
basis that the four states accepted the Treaties establishing the European
institutions, the political objective of European integration and the
decisions taken by the Community since its foundation.[22] The decision to
open negotiations was based on the assumption that a successful
enlargement would involve all four applicant countries. The idea of
establishing a Community of Seven, even on a temporary basis, had
vanished virtually without trace. Irish diplomacy had secured a significant
success, although a long road still lay ahead to achieve membership; the
'tortuous path' described by Denis Maher, himself a participant in the
negotiations as an official of the Department of Finance, was still far from
complete.

The summit in December 1969 did not confirm a starting date for
negotiations, although there was an informal consensus within the
Community that the discussions would begin by the summer of 1970.[23]
Hillery sought to lay the groundwork for successful negotiations,
embarking on a diplomatic tour of the EEC states early in 1970. Hillery
and Hugh McCann visited all of the Community capitals, as well as
London and Copenhagen, between January and June 1970.[24] The aim of
the visits was to influence the evolution of the Community negotiating
position in Ireland's favour; the Irish representatives wished to allay any
fears among European ministers and officials that Ireland would not be
willing or able to meet the obligations of membership, while they
themselves still had strong concerns that Britain might be given preference
within the negotiations.[25] Hillery was determined to influence how the
Community dealt with the British application: 'our aim was start together,

finish together, consult at all stages'.[26] Hillery and McCann emphasised that the Irish government was willing to accept the full political and economic obligations of membership, including the long-term implications of increasing European integration; they also sought to establish as a guiding principle that it was essential for negotiations involving Ireland and Britain to begin simultaneously and end together.[27] The Irish representatives sought agreement too that they would be consulted on any decision in the Community's negotiations with other applicants, which affected the Irish position – this stipulation reflected their concern to maintain the benefits of the Anglo-Irish Free Trade Agreement (AIFTA) during and after accession to the EEC.[28] Hillery's diplomatic efforts generally achieved the desired result. The EEC governments were unanimously supportive of Ireland's application for membership. Crucially their representatives also acknowledged that negotiations with all the applicant states had to proceed on the same basis. The Community negotiators later agreed to consult each candidate country on the outcome of bilateral negotiations with other applicants.[29]

Yet if the Irish side secured almost everything they wanted in preliminary discussions with the EEC member states, effective consultation throughout the negotiations could not be achieved without the co-operation of the British government. Hillery met George Thomson, the minister in charge of British relations with the Community, on 10 December 1969 for a review of the Anglo-Irish Free Trade Area Agreement. He asked Thomson to keep the Irish fully informed on any issues affecting vital Irish interests that arose in the British negotiations.[30] Thomson agreed to deal openly with the Irish delegation, subject only to 'the inhibitions of negotiations'.[31] It was a generous concession by the Labour minister, which was greeted with ill-concealed dismay by some British officials and amazement by Hillery's colleagues:'George said,"Yes, ok we'll let you know what's going on." Haughey was sitting beside me and he couldn't believe me asking. He said,"Ask him again!"'[32] Thomson was as good as his word, agreeing to set up regular contacts at official level between the two sides. But Thomson lost office on the eve of the negotiations when Wilson was defeated in the general election of June

1970, and Hillery was obliged to repeat the process with the new Conservative government. Anthony Barber, who was initially given responsibility for leading the negotiations, became Chancellor of the Exchequer following Ian McLeod's death after only a month in office. Geoffrey Rippon succeeded Barber as Chancellor of the Duchy of Lancaster with responsibility for the European negotiations. When Hillery approached Barber to maintain the previous understanding in July 1970, official hostility on the British side to the arrangement surfaced openly. Sir Con O'Neill, the senior Foreign Office civil servant who was the head of the British team of officials for the negotiations, was firmly opposed to such detailed consultation with the Irish :

> Anthony Barber was there, I went to him – that's when Sir
> Con O'Neill showed his total disapproval of showing their
> hand to another country. So Barber said, 'If George
> Thomson agreed to it, I'll agree to it.' But then McLeod
> died and Anthony Barber was taken back for his position
> in government, so I had to go through my performance
> again with the next fellow [Rippon].[33]

Rippon, acting in defiance of official advice, stood by the commitment given by his predecessors; he kept Hillery fully informed on the progress of the British negotiations.[34] The Irish delegation benefited considerably from the close liaison with their British counterparts and Hillery worked closely with the British negotiators on some highly controversial issues, notably the Community proposal on fisheries.

'The chain of command is clear now; Deputy Hillery is next in command'

Despite Hillery's pivotal role in the preliminary discussions, it was not obvious in early 1970 that he would lead the negotiations for accession. The Department of Finance took charge of preparing a White Paper, *Membership of the European Communities – Implications for Ireland*, which was published in April 1970.[35] The White Paper outlined the likely economic consequences of entry to the EEC, asserting that the long-term gains outweighed any short-term losses for Irish industry, while agriculture would benefit significantly from EEC membership. The state paper also considered the constitutional and political implications of accession, concluding that a constitutional amendment would be required to enable the state to accept the obligations of membership and to allow Community decisions to have legal effect in Ireland.[36] The Department of Finance was preparing to manage the process of accession and was assembling a team of officials to handle the negotiations. Hillery himself did not expect to lead the delegation, believing that his work was largely done once he got Ireland to the conference table and secured agreement from the Community to negotiate with Ireland on an equal basis with its more powerful neighbour.[37] It was Lynch who made the key decision that Hillery should take charge of the negotiations. The Taoiseach acted in a characteristically indirect fashion; at a government meeting immediately after the publication of the White Paper. Hillery informed the Cabinet that RTÉ were looking for a minister to participate in a panel discussion on the White Paper with Dr Garret FitzGerald, then Fine Gael's spokesperson on Finance. Lynch's response surprised Hillery and infuriated Charles Haughey:

> Jack seemed to reflect for a while and then looking at me said, 'You do it.' Later that day in the Russell Hotel at lunch Haughey said it was typical of Lynch to do it like that. I did not understand his chagrin until it dawned on me that this could imply a much bigger decision: one that would mean I would be responsible for Europe and the negotiations. Charlie definitely saw it that way; he was correct and he was mad.[38]

Lynch's decision may well have been influenced by the imminent breakdown of his relations with Haughey; the final breach between the two men was less than a month away. But the Taoiseach was also aware that all the negotiating sessions were chaired by Foreign Ministers from

Community member states and he could point to the advantages of continuity, in allowing Hillery and his officials to finish the task they had started in July 1969; nor did Lynch show any sign of changing his mind when he appointed George Colley to replace Haughey at Finance early in May 1970. Whatever Lynch's motivation the decision made perfect sense. Hillery's good personal contacts with other Foreign Ministers would prove a useful asset in the negotiations, while the officials of External Affairs and particularly the Irish Mission in Brussels had already secured considerable expertise in dealing with Community institutions.

The Taoiseach announced publicly on 27 May 1970 that Hillery would lead the Irish delegation for the negotiations, although other ministers would take part in the discussions as required, to deal with issues affecting their departments.[39] As it transpired Hillery was the only minister to be directly involved in the negotiations. Lynch also confirmed that 'the broad co-ordination of the presentation of our case' would be in hands of the Department of External Affairs; he marginally softened the blow for Finance by noting that the department would continue to co-ordinate preparatory work in Dublin for the Irish application.[40] Some opposition politicians claimed to see a wider political significance in Lynch's announcement. The Labour TD Michael O'Leary commented mischievously: 'The chain of command is clear now; Deputy Hillery is next in command'.[41] George Colley, under pressure from his officials, asked Hillery if he would simply take the Department of Finance team for the negotiations. Hillery declined this request, which would have amounted to a vote of no confidence in his own department.[42] Yet the negotiating team at official level was a broadly based delegation, composed of senior officials from several major departments; the team was led by Seán Morrissey, assistant secretary of the Department of External Affairs; the core membership of the delegation also included Denis Maher (Department of Finance), Jimmy O'Mahony (Agriculture and Fisheries), Des Culligan (Industry and Commerce) and Seán Kennan, head of the Irish Mission in Brussels.[43] Officials from other departments also participated in the negotiations on a more infrequent basis. Hillery certainly benefited from the support of a group of capable and experienced officials. Yet the ultimate responsibility for key decisions in the negotiations rested with him as the political head of the delegation.

The Road to Accession

Opening the negotiations

'They did Collins and they will do you, Doctor' was the cheerful comment of the journalist Raymond Smith, as Hillery left Dublin for the opening of negotiations with the European Community.[44] Smith was a colourful, eccentric character, who enjoyed a long and distinguished career as a journalist with Independent Newspapers. Smith's throwaway remark brought home to Hillery the importance of public reaction in Ireland to the negotiations; it was a factor that he kept constantly in mind throughout the process, not least because the terms of Irish accession would ultimately have to be approved by referendum. The government agreed the negotiating position for the delegation in May 1970, shortly before Hillery was officially confirmed as leader of the negotiating team.[45] The brief was a lengthy and detailed document, which dealt with a wide range of issues that the Irish delegation would have to resolve if accession was to be achieved, from transitional measures for agriculture and industry to the legal arrangements for Irish representation within the Community institutions.[46] The document also set out areas of particular concern to Ireland, which might not be included in a formal treaty of accession, but were so important to Irish national interests that it was essential to raise them in the negotiations; in this context the retention of state aids to industrial development emerged as a key concern of the Irish government.[47] The Irish negotiating position required an extensive selection of concessions from the Community if it was even to come close to fulfilment. Hillery had no illusions about the difficulty of the task confronting him in translating the Irish government's objectives into reality, and in securing favourable enough terms to deliver public support for Ireland's accession. He never lost sight of the reality that the negotiations were a highly political process in which the Irish position would have to be communicated effectively to interest groups, the media and the public at home.

It was for this reason that Hillery initiated a detailed briefing operation for Irish journalists covering the negotiations. He became concerned about the lack of information being circulated to the media and important interest groups following a complaint from the Confederation of Irish Industries (CII):

> Aliaga Kelly was from the CII; he asked me to lunch and he told me they were getting no information from the Department of Industry and Commerce about our negotiating. The farmers' organisation was getting nothing from the Agriculture department. Any document that was prepared and presented to the Commission became their document; you would have no right to publish it.[48]

Hillery acted to circumvent the Commission's rule that all documents presented to it were to be treated as confidential. The need to communicate the Irish government's position was all the more acute as the Commission itself leaked like a sieve; the publication *Agence Europe* was usually particularly well informed about unpublished Commission proposals or initiatives.[49] Irish officials were taking the Commission's rules much more seriously than the staff of the Commission itself. Hillery's solution was straightforward – 'set up our own leaks'.[50] He instructed Robin Fogarty, a senior official in the Department of External Affairs who was a member of the delegation, to give representatives of the employers and the Irish Farmers' Association (IFA) full information on the Irish negotiations. More significantly, Hillery also told Fogarty to brief Irish journalists confidentially on the delegation's objectives and the progress being achieved in the negotiations.[51] Hillery ensured that he was easily accessible to the media, holding press conferences before ministerial meetings in Brussels, and hosting private lunches for groups of Irish journalists. It was the first time that collective news briefings were given to Irish journalists on a systematic basis.[52] Ministers such as Donogh O'Malley had skilfully used the media by briefing favoured members of the press, but it was Hillery who took the initiative in establishing official news briefings for groups of journalists on an organised basis. Hillery himself drove the process of informing the media on the detail of the European negotiations, while Fogarty gave weekly news briefings when the discussions were in session.[53] It was largely as a result of Hillery's initiative that reports by Irish journalists covering the negotiations were generally well-informed, detailed and frequently positive about the process of accession.

The negotiations between the Community and the states applying for membership were formally inaugurated on 30 June 1970 in Luxembourg; it was entirely a ceremonial session, devoted to opening speeches by the Foreign Ministers.[54] The most significant contribution was made by Pierre Harmel, Belgian Foreign Minister and current President of the Council, who outlined the conditions for accession to the Community. His essential message was that the applicant states were joining a moving train and could not change the overall direction of the journey. Harmel warned that all new member states would be obliged to accept the *acquis communautaire* – the established body of Community law and action; in practical terms, this meant that the applicant countries had not only to accept the Treaties and their political objectives, but also all the decisions made subsequently by the Community, including the resolutions of the Hague summit in December 1969.[55] Harmel clarified that the negotiations would operate on the basis that problems of adaptation for accession states had to be overcome through transitional measures and not changes in existing rules. Moreover, as a general rule the transitional arrangements would be limited in duration and would incorporate specific timetables.[56] Harmel also confirmed that the various accession treaties should come into force on the same day, and pledged that the Community would set up a procedure to allow for consultations between applicants and member states on matters of common interest, in conjunction with the bilateral negotiations on membership with each applicant state. This meant effectively that the Irish delegation would have the opportunity to comment on issues arising out of talks involving Britain.[57] These commitments by Harmel were a tribute to the success of Hillery's European diplomacy in the previous year and laid to rest lingering fears in the Irish political establishment that Britain might still be able to steal a march on the other applicants.

Hillery, in his own speech to the opening meeting, reaffirmed without reservation the government's acceptance of the political and economic objectives of the Community. He also drew attention to the specific issues that the Irish delegation would raise during the negotiations, including the preservation of incentives for industrial development, measures to prevent dumping of foreign goods on the Irish market and transitional measures for industry and agriculture.[58] Hillery regarded the Community's backing for ongoing consultation throughout the negotiations as a significant gain for Ireland. Otherwise, as Dennis Kennedy remarked, the occasion was important mainly because 'it marked the transition of Ireland's European policy, after nine years, from aspiration to negotiation.'[59]

The real business of negotiation began in the autumn of 1970. The Community delegation was led by the Foreign Minister of the member state that held the presidency of the Council, with the Commission playing a supporting role. As the presidency of the Council rotated between member states every six months, different Foreign Ministers took their turn to lead the Community delegation; the Irish team dealt first with Walter Scheel for West Germany, then with Maurice Schumann, Aldo Moro for Italy and Gaston Thorn of Luxembourg, on whose watch the negotiations were concluded. The Community established a broadly intergovernmental framework for the talks, reflecting the reality that the ultimate power of decision rested with the Foreign Ministers and the governments they represented. Yet the Commission played a central part in the negotiations. Jean-François Deniau, a newly appointed French Commissioner, led its negotiating team, while Edmund Wellenstein, a shrewd and experienced official whose involvement with the Community institutions went back to the 1950s, was the chief negotiator at official level.[60] Both men were deeply involved in the negotiations with Ireland and did a great deal to overcome difficulties that arose for the Irish delegation.

Hillery placed great importance on establishing strong personal connections with Deniau and Wellenstein; he was soon on excellent terms with the two negotiators. John McColgan recalled his minister's informal techniques in preparing for the negotiations with the Community representatives:

> I would bring the briefing notes into Paddy on the Thursday before the negotiating meeting on the following Monday. He said 'John, if I read all of that, I'll be as confused as they are.' He had a very good political appreciation of how to approach the negotiations.[61]

This did not mean that Hillery ignored his brief; throughout the negotiations he showed a very clear grasp of the key issues at stake. But he recognised that his time was best used in building informal relationships and resolving political problems with the Community negotiators. He met privately with Wellenstein before each negotiating session, and the two men went through each step of what they were going to agree before the formal ministerial meetings. Wellenstein was very sympathetic to Hillery's concerns, and the close collaboration between them was pivotal to the success of the Irish negotiations.

Irish lobbying influenced the format of the talks. The negotiations took the form of bilateral meetings at ministerial level or between officials – known as 'Deputies' by the Community – to thrash out various issues. The conclusions of each bilateral session were provisional until the other applicants were consulted and the final conclusions were adopted in multilateral meetings of the negotiators. The Commission team undertook to keep all applicant states fully informed on substantive and technical issues affecting the negotiations.[62] This format fulfilled the commitment given by the Community, largely at Hillery's instigation, for ongoing consultation with each accession state on issues that arose in bilateral negotiations with another applicant.

The first negotiating session involving the Irish delegation was held in Brussels on 21 September 1970, with Walter Scheel speaking for the Community. Hillery assured a press conference on the previous day that 'membership of the Community presented no great problem for

Ireland.'[63] This line reflected his concern to reassure the Community negotiators that Ireland would be able to meet the political and economic obligations of membership. Yet Hillery also signalled publicly that he expected hard bargaining on various key issues. He was particularly concerned about preventing any dilution of the benefits enjoyed by Irish agriculture in the British market under AIFTA, even in the short term, and about protecting the state's ability to promote industrial development. Hillery identified the protection of existing industrial incentives and the negotiation of special arrangements for manufacturing industries, which were seen as particularly vulnerable without tariff protection, as key priorities for the Irish delegation.[64] He also expressed grave concern at the Community's policy on fisheries, which was about to emerge as a major bone of contention for Ireland and would be the single most difficult issue of the negotiations. Ireland enjoyed in 1970 an exclusive fishery limit of twelve miles from its coast; while several European countries were allowed to fish in certain parts of this area, an inner six-mile zone was reserved exclusively for Irish-registered boats. The Council of Ministers moved to adopt a common fisheries policy in June 1970, which provided for common access to the fishery grounds of all member countries, subject to limited local derogations in certain circumstances. Even more damaging from an Irish perspective was the proposal to limit any derogation to fishing grounds within a three-mile zone, and to abolish exclusive national zones completely after five years.[65] Hillery was angry at this move, which he viewed as a pre-emptive strike by the French government to dictate conditions in advance of enlargement that the new member states would be powerless to influence: 'It was a dirty trick. The day after we said we'd accept all the decisions and regulations, they brought in this regulation about the right to fish up to the shore.'[66] Hillery protested publicly against the Council's decision; he also raised Irish concerns formally at the ministerial meeting on 21 September and again on 16 December.[67] But the Council pressed ahead, formally adopting the new regulations on fisheries in October 1970. The controversy over fisheries would lead to tense and protracted negotiations between the Irish delegation and the Community in 1971.

The discussions up to December 1970 generally focused on a full presentation of the Irish position with no real move to negotiate on potentially difficult issues. Dennis Kennedy accurately commented on 16 December that progress so far had been 'almost imperceptible'.[68] This was partly a product of the complex nature of the process, in which the Community delegation was obliged to conduct separate sets of negotiations with four applicant countries, while ensuring a unified response from the governments of the six member states.[69] At this early stage, the Irish delegation was content to focus on easily agreed issues, and was careful not to press the Community for concessions they might be refused on grounds of precedent for other accession countries.[70] Hillery confirmed in December 1970 that Ireland would accept a five-year transition period to allow industry and agriculture to adapt to the requirements of EEC membership, although the timetable for the reduction of tariffs and the implementation of the CAP had not yet been defined. The Foreign Minister also announced that the five-year period would be sufficient to enable Ireland to meet the same obligations as the existing member states with regard to the free movement of capital and labour, as well as the application of the principle of equal pay for equal work between men and women, which had not yet been implemented by the Community itself.[71] But a wide range of difficult issues remained to be settled in 1971, including the adaptation of Irish agriculture to the CAP, trading relations with the UK, transitional arrangements for industry, the Irish case for a strong regional policy and the unexpected problem of fisheries.

The Community proved willing to satisfy Irish concerns on many of the outstanding issues. The Irish delegation gained significant concessions in the run-up to the ministerial meeting in Luxembourg on 7 June 1971. The most striking success was achieved in agriculture. Irish officials sought to secure repayment by the Community from the beginning of the transitional period for the subsidies on agricultural exports and the market supports on various products provided by the Irish government. There was some caution on the Irish side about how to pursue this objective; an official report to Hillery in early June noted that 'We had to be careful in the negotiations in treating this matter least we appeared too "greedy" and we have rather played it down.'[72] But the Irish delegation raised the issue at a Deputies meeting early in the summer and was able to report 'broad agreement' with Community officials on 2 June. The ministerial meeting itself confirmed an important advance in the negotiations.[73] In response to a request from Maurice Schumann on behalf of the Community, Hillery accepted a revised timescale for the transition to a common market in agriculture, but he received much more far-reaching concessions from the Council negotiator. The Community agreed to finance the export subsidies and market supports provided by the Irish government from the date of Ireland's accession.[74] Ireland would have immediate access to the European Agricultural guidance and guarantee fund (FEOGA) without any phasing-in period. This agreement would relieve the Irish government of the considerable burden of around £30 million in export subsidies to farmers immediately on accession to the Community.[75] Ireland would gain many of the benefits of the Common Agricultural Policy from the first day of membership. The Community's price-support system would also operate within the new member states from accession, although a gradual timetable was laid down for bringing the prices paid to Irish farmers up to the common price levels in the Community. This process was to be achieved in a series of steps over the five-year transitional period.[76]

Hillery also secured an equally valuable concession on Anglo-Irish free trade during the transitional period, even if it was less immediately rewarding for the government. The Irish delegation sought consistently to ensure that the transitional arrangements introduced by the Community for Britain would not create any new barriers for Irish agricultural exports to the British market, which were free from levies or duties under AIFTA, or diminish the degree of free trade between the two countries even on a temporary basis.[77] Once again, the Community negotiators gave the Irish essentially what they asked for. Following a favourable recommendation from Community officials, Schumann agreed on 7 June that the degree of free trade already achieved between Ireland and Britain would be preserved during the transitional period.[78] This was a vital concession from an Irish perspective which removed the real fear that 'Ireland would have to go back to go forward in terms of free trade with Britain inside an enlarged Community.'[79]

If farmers were unmistakably the clear winners in this phase of the negotiations, there were also some advances for Irish industry. Hillery made the case over several months that Ireland was particularly vulnerable to 'dumping', the import of surplus goods from other markets at substantially reduced prices.[80] He sought agreement for the Irish state to take unilateral measures against dumping from countries both within and outside the Community during the transitional period; this demand was motivated by official concern that local industry might be damaged or even destroyed before the full range of Community controls came into effect.[81] The Council of Ministers conceded the Irish demand, agreeing that the government would be allowed to use national anti-dumping legislation during the transitional period; in exceptional circumstances the Irish state could act first against dumping and seek subsequent approval from the Commission.[82] This concession had a wider significance, as the Community implicitly acknowledged Ireland's exceptional position with regard to industrial development. The agreement marked an important precedent for later negotiations on the application of the Community's regional policy to Ireland.[83]

Regional development

The Irish Protocol

Perhaps the most fundamental obligation of membership was participation in the Community's customs union, which involved the abolition of tariffs and restrictions on trade between member states, as well as the adoption of a common external tariff to imports from states outside the Community. The Irish delegation agreed to the progressive dismantling of tariffs on industrial goods from Community member states over the five-year transitional period, while also seeking a series of interim measures to protect Irish manufacturing industry during the transition to full participation in the customs union.[84] The official concern about dumping was part of a much broader argument by the Irish delegation that Ireland faced special circumstances for industrial development due to its geographical position as a small island economy and as a result of 'the particular needs of Irish industry'.[85] Hillery emphasised on 7 June several distinctive factors affecting the Irish economy, notably an increasing population, the small size of the domestic market and the limited capital available for industrial expansion – all of which required exceptional measures to promote increased employment.[86] He made a strong case that Ireland should receive special consideration under the Community's regional policy, which was intended to overcome problems of regional underdevelopment and reduce social and economic imbalances between different regions of the Community. The Treaty of Rome provided that state aids, which distorted competition, were generally incompatible with the common market; but the Treaty also indicated that state assistance could be allowed to promote regional development. Otherwise the Community's regional policy was still largely aspirational in the early 1970s; progress in social and regional development lagged behind even the incremental advances towards economic integration.

The Irish negotiators aimed to protect the range of tax incentives for industrial development provided by the state; they were particularly eager to maintain the scheme for tax relief on the profits derived from exports up to the end of their legal shelf life in 1990. The problem, however, was that tax relief on exports were explicitly banned by Article 98 of the Treaty of Rome.[87] Another key issue, based on similar concerns, arose from the special concessions enjoyed by the car-assembly industry, where firms were allowed to import vehicles at reduced rates of duty in return for commitments to maintain a basic level of local production on a long-term basis. This allowed the state to channel imports through registered firms, usually those who had given such assurances of local employment.[88] Hillery argued on 7 June that it would be wrong to undermine any 'reasonable proposals aimed at stimulating industrial development in Ireland', highlighting export tax relief as a vital element in economic development.[89] The risk of increased unemployment was the key concern here. The loss of export tax relief would remove an important stimulus to industrial production for export. The removal of the favourable terms enjoyed by the motor-assembly industry could cause significant job losses among a large section of workers in the motor industry and in ancillary supply firms.[90] The Irish delegation sometimes referred to 'sensitive industries', which required special treatment in the negotiations. The loss of manufacturing employment as a result of accession was politically sensitive and figured prominently in the calculations of the Irish negotiators.

Hillery set out to maintain the industrial incentives wherever possible and otherwise to gain time for the reorganisation of the protected industries. He also sought to achieve Irish objectives by highlighting the disparities in wealth and industrial development between Ireland and the existing member states, placing the specific Irish demands within the context of fulfilling the Community's regional policy. The Irish negotiators sought a special protocol on economic development in Ireland, which would not only protect the existing industrial incentives in the short term, but also guarantee financial assistance from Community resources for Irish initiatives to promote economic development. The negotiations on industrial incentives and regional policy saw some tough bargaining between the Irish team and Community negotiators, although it did not attract the same level of public controversy as fisheries or indeed the dispute over sugar production that arose at the end of the negotiations. Hillery made the case for the retention of the export tax relief in a meeting with Deniau on 5 July 1971, but no agreement was reached.[91]

The Irish team enjoyed more immediate success in securing favourable terms to safeguard the motor-assembly industry. The Community initially proposed an extension of the existing scheme for seven years until January 1980, with some modifications in the meantime to allow for a gradual opening up of the market to EEC firms.[92] The Irish side was willing to accept the modifications to the scheme, but sought a longer transitional period before it was phased out. Hillery lobbied the Community negotiators for a more generous concession. He argued that the key issue was the safeguarding of employment, highlighting the political consequences of a bad decision: 'A wrong result here or on tax reliefs could swing the whole trade union movement against the common market'.[93] Hillery

secured a further ministerial meeting on 12 July to resolve the issue and
reinforce the Irish case for exceptional treatment under the Community's
regional policy. The Council conceded the Irish demand during a break
in the negotiating session, following an effective intervention by Franco
Maria Malfatti, the Italian President of the Commission, who acted as an
intermediary between the EEC ministers and Hillery. The Council agreed
that the scheme for the motor-assembly industry could be maintained for
twelve years from the date of accession, until 1 January 1985.[94] It was the
longest transitional period for an industry conceded to any accession state,
and allowed the Irish motor industry more time to adapt to the demands
of free trade and European competition. Moreover, the Community
negotiators explicitly accepted Hillery's argument that industrial
development in Ireland required special consideration under the
Community's regional policy; their spokesman asserted that the terms
presented to the Irish delegation were 'a first confirmation of our
recognition of the regional problems which we have as regards Ireland'.[95]

It soon became evident that the six member states were willing to
agree a protocol acknowledging Ireland's strong claims on Community
assistance for regional development, but considerably more reluctant to
approve the existing tax incentives employed by the Irish state. The future
of the industrial incentives, especially the highly controversial export tax
relief scheme, formed a key stumbling block in the negotiations. It was
generally accepted that the Commission would review all state aids to
industry after Ireland's accession. The Irish negotiators were determined
to ensure that firms benefiting from export tax relief before accession
would continue to do so after the review; they were equally concerned
that industries that signed contracts under the scheme after Ireland's entry
to the EEC should benefit from tax relief for as long as possible.[96] The
Community delegation, now led by Aldo Moro who had taken over from
Schumann as chairman of the Council of Ministers, maintained that if
the scheme was ruled out by the Commission, the Irish government
would have to renegotiate alternative arrangements with all the firms
involved. But Hillery, while accepting that the scheme might not continue
in the long term, argued that contracts had been signed with industrialists

and these commitments had to be honoured.[97] Michael Killeen, managing director of the IDA, warned Hillery that uncertainty about the tax incentives would give rise to damaging speculation and severely harm the IDA's efforts to attract industries to the country.[98] The discussions between officials, which had been highly successful in overcoming previous obstacles, could not resolve this central issue. It was left to Hillery to break the deadlock in direct negotiations with the Community representatives on 19 October 1971 when the draft protocol dealing with Ireland came up for discussion. Hillery addressed a formal ministerial meeting in Luxembourg on the morning of 19 October, essentially reiterating the Irish case; he then undertook private negotiations with Aldo Moro and Jean Francois Deniau solely on the vexed problem of industrial incentives.[99] Wellenstein, the senior Commission official involved in the negotiations, was also present throughout the day and played a major part in facilitating a favourable outcome for Ireland.

The negotiations on this occasion were prolonged and sometimes tense, with Deniau taking a hard line and at one stage threatening that Ireland might lose its protocol completely unless Hillery accepted the terms offered by the Commission.[100] The French Commissioner also warned that the Council of Ministers would decide to deny export tax relief on all new contracts if the Irish negotiator failed to settle immediately. This negotiating ploy failed to move Hillery:

> At one stage he went into the corridor and came back and said that he had sounded out three Ministers ... He said 'that's it, no more contracts from now.' And I said 'is that a decision?' and he said 'yes'. So I said 'I cannot negotiate any further', so he said 'that's a decision if you go to the Ministers'. Wellenstein at this stage said 'that's much too harsh' and led me back into the position of dealing with the situation at the review.[101]

Wellenstein took a more conciliatory approach. He assured Hillery that tax relief could still be given on a different basis, but the difficulty arose from the scheme giving relief on exports, as this involved discrimination against other Community countries. More significantly, Wellenstein agreed that contracts undertaken before any review had to be honoured: 'A contract is a contract and the law is the law. I don't like it, but if a contract is made there is nothing we can do to make you change it'.[102] The Commission representatives were willing to accept the validity of existing contracts, but at first refused to give any assurances about what would happen to the incentives once Ireland was accepted into the EEC. Wellenstein commented that the Commission, which conducted the review after accession, would include an Irish nominee; surely it could safely be left in their hands. But this was not enough for Hillery. He emphasised that the tax incentives were vital to industrial development, and he required certainty about their survival after accession. The Irish minister told Deniau that 'I could not possibly deal on this basis, that any vagueness would destroy our incentives and we could not give them up, and he accepted this.'[103] Following a six-hour meeting, Hillery secured assurances from the Commission negotiators that tax relief could be a major part of the incentive schemes and that, if any change was required in the export tax relief, industrialists could secure an equal benefit from an alternative scheme. Despite Deniau's sometimes abrasive approach, the Commission representatives undoubtedly wanted the negotiations to succeed and showed considerable flexibility in their dealings with Hillery. Wellenstein in particular did his utmost to help the Irish delegation. Hillery wished to make a statement to the ministerial meeting, interpreting the effect of the Protocol on the industrial incentives; he aimed to confirm publicly that the tax incentives would survive following Irish accession. Wellenstein helped to draft the statement and made several amendments to it, which were intended to avoid alarming the Ministers on the Council or jeopardising their support for the Protocol itself.[104] Aldo Moro also agreed to accept Hillery's interpretation of the draft Protocol.

When the ministerial meeting reconvened, the assembled delegates witnessed a decisive breakthrough in Ireland's negotiations. Hillery made his statement; he was able to note that the Community recognised the necessity for a system of tax incentives to promote industrial development in Ireland, although the form taken by the incentives might have to change. He emphasised that the Irish government would have to honour the commitments made previously, but would be ready to discuss any changeover to a new system of incentives.[105] Moro announced the Community's support for the Protocol, which would be annexed to the Treaty of Accession with Ireland. The Italian Foreign Minister assured the meeting that the articles governing state aids in the Treaty of Rome were flexible enough to allow the Community to take account of the particular needs of less developed regions.[106] The Protocol itself noted that the government's policy of economic development was designed 'to align the standards of living in Ireland with those of the other European nations and to eliminate under-employment'; it recommended that all means available to the Community, especially its financial resources, should be employed to support the objectives of industrialisation and economic development in Ireland.[107] Equally significant was the Protocol's carefully worded clause on state aids to industry, which recognised that in assessing the Irish industrial incentives, the Community would have to take into account 'the objectives of economic expansion and improvement of the population's standard of living'.[108]

The final clause of the Protocol was a definite indication that the Commission would interpret the Treaty in a flexible fashion and would not cut off the industrial incentive schemes abruptly. It was openly acknowledged that the Irish state would keep the existing incentives in operation until the review by the Commission.[109] Hillery could not obtain a categorical statement of the Community's position on the export tax relief in the future, mainly because a new Commission following enlargement would make the final decision. But he secured a clear understanding that all firms enjoying the benefits of export tax relief up to the time of the review would be entitled to retain the advantages of the scheme for the lifetime of the original legislation.[110] Moreover, the Community had also indicated that any new system of industrial incentives would be equally attractive and would allow the Irish government to maintain its policy of tax relief to promote industrial

development. The Community institutions more than fulfilled their side
of the bargain; the export tax relief was maintained for ten years after
Ireland's entry to the EEC, and was then replaced by an exceptionally
favourable tax regime for firms located in Ireland, with a corporation tax
rate of only ten per cent on the profits of manufacturing companies.[111]
The outcome was a considerable accomplishment for Hillery, who not
only secured a new lease of life for the existing incentives but gained
concessions of lasting importance for Irish economic development in the
late twentieth century.

   The adoption of the Protocol was arguably the most significant and
lasting achievement of the Irish negotiations for EEC membership. The
importance of the Protocol went far beyond the preservation of the tax
incentives. The Protocol recognised that the country as a whole, not
simply designated regions of it, deserved support under the Community's
regional policy.[112] It also marked an explicit commitment by the
Community to promote the social and economic development of the
Irish state. The agreement accorded Ireland a special position on the basis
of its later pattern of industrial development and its status as a small,
peripheral economy. The Protocol would give considerable leverage to
successive Irish governments in their constructive engagement with the
institutions of the Community. The acceptance of the Protocol was the
starting point of a sustained process of European support for Irish
economic and social objectives, which contributed greatly to a
transformation of the Irish economy and society over the following
decades.

Fisheries: Defending the crustaceans

If the agreement on the Protocol was the most enduring accomplishment
of the Irish delegation, the negotiations on fisheries were undoubtedly
the most difficult and protracted. Hillery opposed from the outset the
Council's move to abolish exclusive fishery zones and enforce equal access
to fishery grounds for all member states, which would be deeply
damaging to the livelihood of Irish inshore fishermen. He was almost
isolated at first in his criticisms of the policy; of the other applicants,

Britain was preoccupied with other issues, such as its contribution to the financing of the enlarged Community, and the Danish delegation was not greatly concerned with fisheries. Norway's position was very different, as it was affected by the proposed regulation more than any other country, but the Norwegian response did little to assist Hillery. The Norwegian government rejected the entire common fisheries policy, warning that Norwegian membership of the EEC would be endangered unless they retained exclusive fishing rights within the entire 12-mile limit. The Norwegian delegation refused to negotiate on the issue in conjunction with the other applicants, insisting that the EEC had to treat Norway as an exceptional case on fisheries.[113]

Meanwhile, public and political pressure was mounting at home to protect Irish fisheries. Hillery faced demands for action not only by the fishermen's organisations, which were understandably appalled at the regulation, but also from opposition politicians and backbench Fianna Fáil TDs:

> But it became the most obsessive thing in the country ...
> I remember Joe Leneghan, the TD from Mayo in the Dáil;
> he said 'the Frenchmen will be scraping the snails off the
> walls of the houses in Mayo'; not alone the fish, but even
> the snails! But the most unexpected people took it up and
> it became the essential thing of our national
> independence.[114]

Hillery was caught between the opportunism of the Council, which had conveniently adopted the regulations just after the applicant states had pledged to accept existing Community policies, and the intransigence of public opinion at home, which demanded the protection of Irish fishing rights. He publicly called on the Council to review the policy, arguing that it was designed for a Community of six and was unacceptable to the new member states. His favoured solution was for Ireland to retain its 12-mile fishing limit and to defer the development of a new fisheries policy until the Community was enlarged.[115] But Hillery got little support for his stand from the other applicants and, at first, his prospects of achieving any progress seemed bleak.

The British government stayed silent on fisheries in the early months of the negotiations.[116] But as their application for membership inched closer to success, British ministers became more alarmed by the domestic implications of the common fisheries policy. Jim Prior, the British Minister for Agriculture, visited Dublin in the spring of 1971 to meet his Irish counterpart, Jim Gibbons. Prior asked to meet Hillery, without specifying what he wanted to discuss: 'he came to see me, and as he left going out the door, he said "we will back you in this thing about the fisheries" – now that was in a whisper. So it was a great help to get it, because I was no longer alone.'[117] Soon afterwards, Rippon took up the issue in the negotiations and Heath raised British concerns about the fisheries policy in his meeting with Pompidou in May 1971.[118] The British delegation told the Community negotiators in June 1971 that the access provisions would have to be changed in an enlarged Community and that 'everyone should keep the status quo until the Community of Ten could work out a suitable policy.'[119] This line was almost identical to the Irish position, and echoed Hillery's arguments over the previous year. A meeting in Brussels between Irish and British officials on 30 June confirmed their common interests in rolling back key features of the common fisheries policy. The officials agreed that neither delegation would settle for 'a second-best solution', nor would they accept terms inferior to those offered to Norway or Denmark.[120] Hillery had no illusions that the British intervention on his side was motivated by altruistic concerns, but equally had no doubt about the importance of British support: 'They got into it then. Not for the love of us, but they had quite a lot of Conservative constituencies affected by the fisheries policy. It saved my life.'[121]

Anglo-Irish collaboration on fisheries greatly enhanced Hillery's bargaining position, although it did not bring an immediate settlement of the issue. The Community negotiators accepted in June 1971 that the proposal for equal access to fishing grounds would have to change due to enlargement, but resisted pressure from Ireland and Britain to maintain the status quo in the meantime.[122] The Council instead approved a revised proposal involving transitional arrangements for the accession states. Governments would be free to maintain a six-mile exclusive limit for five years, with the Council of Ministers making the decision on the fishing grounds that might require protection for the following five years.[123] This proposal, which was presented to the national delegations on 9 November 1971, was unacceptable to all four applicant states. The Norwegian Foreign Minister was particularly hostile to the plan, informing the Community negotiators bluntly that unless the equal access provision was abandoned, Norway could not join the EEC. Hillery did not go as far as his Norwegian counterpart, but he rejected the proposal emphatically. He told the Council of Ministers that fisheries were a valuable economic resource in Ireland, and the Community's plan threatened to dissipate this resource, aggravating Ireland's problems in achieving economic development.[124] Hillery deliberately cited the Irish protocol, negotiated with the Community in October, pointing out that the Council had explicitly recognised less than a month before the scale of Ireland's development problems. *The Irish Times* noted that while Hillery's language was diplomatic, the message to the Community was clear: 'He did not spell it out, but his meaning obviously was that the Community could not promise special help for Ireland in October, and then ask her in November to accept a proposal that would hinder her development.'[125] The session broke up without agreement after twelve hours of discussion.

When the negotiations resumed on 29 November, the Community produced a much-improved offer, which went well beyond the original, highly restrictive terms of the common fisheries policy. The new proposals envisaged a ten-year transitional period in which Ireland would have a six-mile limit exclusive to Irish fishing boats for all types of fishing; this would be extended to a twelve-mile limit for special areas and for certain types of fish.[126] Hillery welcomed the proposals as a notable advance, but argued that Ireland should secure the protection of a twelve-mile limit for its entire coastline. He also expressed strong reservations about the rigid time limit, seeking instead a more flexible review that would take into account the development of the fishing industry; Rippon shared this concern about the review procedure and both men sought a modification of the Community proposal. Anglo-Irish opposition had done much to force a more flexible approach by the Community, but it did not succeed in gaining further concessions this time. Deniau took the concerns of the applicants back to the Council, but to no avail; the French refused to allow any changes to the Community policy. The negotiations continued in a marathon session throughout the early hours of the following morning, without reaching a final agreement. A frustrated Rippon described the process as a 'pantomime', which was jeopardising European unity over fish.[127] Yet the latest offer from the Community provided the basis for a satisfactory resolution for both Britain and Ireland and a final settlement was not long delayed.

Hillery was not greatly disturbed by the protracted nature of the negotiations, seeing an advantage in drawing out the talks to gain the benefits of concessions offered to other applicants. Both he and Rippon were also concerned that they not be outmanoeuvred by the Norwegians, who were intent on holding out for a special deal until the last possible moment. Hillery consulted Per Kleppe, the chief Norwegian negotiator, in an attempt to co-ordinate their strategy for the negotiations, but Kleppe responded that he wanted a permanent arrangement for Norwegian fisheries and would not reach agreement without a special deal from the Community.[128] Hillery was disgusted with Kleppe and his unilateralist tactics:

> The Norwegian hung around the Charlemagne Building, with no intention of negotiating, smug and self-satisfied looking, would not give me a straight answer as to whether he wanted me to stay with him or not; gave the clear impression that he was waiting for a gift from the gods – the gods being the EEC and the gift being the special treatment for Norway mentioned at the early stages when the EEC thought they could hold their fisheries access regulation if they gave some concession to Norway … He gave the impression of being a tougher negotiator whereas

his whole attitude was that there was a gift to be got for
him if everybody else went home.[129]

Kleppe later attacked the other member states for 'giving in' to the
Community on fisheries.[130] But as co-operation with the Norwegians
was impossible, Hillery had to make a final decision and he did so on the
basis that he had extracted the maximum concessions possible from the
Community. When the negotiations resumed on 11 December, Rippon
signalled that he would accept the Community proposal in return for a
review of fisheries policy following the ten-year transitional period, which
took into account the economic and social development of member
states' coastal areas, as well as the condition of fish stocks. Hillery regarded
this move as being largely a face-saving device by the British, who were
accepting a very similar agreement to the one they had rejected on 29
November.[131] Nevertheless, it indicated that the moment of decision was
at hand. Having secured some further concessions on Irish fishery limits,
Hillery accepted the fisheries proposal on the basis that it was the
Community's last word on the subject.[132] Denmark and Britain also
reached agreement with the EEC, while Norway rejected the terms. The
breakdown in Norway's negotiations with the EEC proved temporary on
this occasion, but it provoked a memorable intervention from Raymond
Smith; at a late-night press conference attended by several Foreign
Ministers, the Irish journalist produced the immortal line – 'Is it true that
fish is now a dead duck?'[133]

   The final agreement allowed the Irish state to enforce the six-mile
limit for ten years and to maintain a twelve-mile limit for the full northern
and western coasts from Lough Foyle to Cork Harbour for the same
period; the twelve-mile limit also applied to the east coast from
Carlingford Lough to Carnsore Point for certain types of fish, including
shellfish.[134] The agreement guaranteed the maximum level of protection
for Ireland's in-shore fishermen along 70 per cent of the Irish coastline,
taking in about 90 per cent of the catch. Ireland and Britain had gained
almost everything they sought, at least in the short term. Hillery was
undoubtedly correct in commenting immediately after the agreement

that he had secured much better terms than he or the government as a whole had originally expected.[135] The settlement was in many respects a considerable success for the Irish negotiator.

But there was at least one significant drawback to the agreement – the absence of any definite guarantees for what would happen when the ten-year transition period expired. The review clause proposed by Britain did not give any real assurance of continuing arrangements to protect coastal fishing grounds after the end of the ten-year period.[136] This key aspect of the deal provoked mixed reactions within the fishing community. The Federation of Irish Fishing Co-operatives broadly welcomed many elements of the agreement, but expressed concern about the ambiguous nature of the review clause.[137] The fishing communities in Wexford and Donegal expressed more trenchant opposition to the terms as a whole, including the temporary nature of the agreement.[138] While some of the criticisms of the terms were unfair and unrealistic, the concerns in the fishing industry about the review clause proved well founded. It was true that both Ireland and Britain would be members of the Community when the review took place. But this simply meant that Hillery was relying on his successors a decade later to show the same ability to negotiate and win wider European support for Irish concerns as he had done in 1971. This was a gamble that did not work out in practice. Yet if Irish fishermen had genuine grounds for concern, Hillery had little choice but to accept a greatly improved Community offer in December 1971. His only other option was to stage a show of brinkmanship on the Norwegian model, which would have threatened Ireland's membership of the Community. Even in the unlikely event that the government allowed Hillery to embark on such a dangerous course of action, the Norwegian example did not augur well for its success. While the Norwegian government eventually signed the Treaty of Accession, its display of brinkmanship did not impress its own people; a referendum resulted in a rejection of entry to the EEC in September 1972 and Norway never joined the Community. While the agreement on fisheries was by no means ideal, especially in the longer-term, it was the best possible agreement that Hillery could have secured from the Community, especially with the staunch opposition of France to further concessions. Moreover if the agreement postponed rather than averted problems for Irish fisheries, it was still a dramatic improvement on the original *fait accompli* presented by the Council.

Final Negotiations

The deal on fisheries removed the last major obstacle to Irish membership of the Community. Most politicians and journalists assumed that it also opened the way for the formal signature of the Treaty in January 1972. Hillery was relieved by the settlement on fisheries and did not anticipate any further problems in the negotiations. But he had reckoned without the Irish sugar industry. The Irish Sugar Company, a major semi-state body, managed four sugar processing factories, in Carlow, Tuam, Mallow and Thurles. The Irish sugar industry was subsidised by the state; both the company and sugar producers looked forward to further subsidies from Europe. Their claims took centre-stage in the final days of the negotiations. The Sugar Company and the beet farmers, represented by the Beet and Vegetable Growers' Association (BVA), were deeply dissatisfied with the quota for sugar production offered by the EEC. The Community offered a sugar quota of 135,000 tons annually, which was slightly above the average production of the Irish sugar industry over the previous five years; producers were guaranteed a minimum price by the EEC for all quantities within the level of production set by the quota.[139] But as production in the Irish sugar industry was expanding rapidly in the early 1970s, the estimated level of production for 1971–72 was 170,000 tons. This triggered predictions of imminent catastrophe from both employers and producers. The Sugar Company and the BVA angrily rejected the original offer, claiming that acceptance of the quota would not only obstruct the industry's plans for expansion but would also lead to the closure of one or more of the sugar refining plants.[140] This claim was entirely wrong and was based on a fundamental misunderstanding of the Community's price-support system. The system of production quotas was a temporary measure by the EEC to control surplus production, which was intended to end by 1975. Moreover the quota did not mean an automatic limit on sugar production, but simply a limitation in the price guarantee offered by the Community. An additional 35 per cent of the basic production quota for each country also qualified for Community price-support, though at a reduced level to the original amount.[141] But reality was not allowed to stand in the way of a good argument, especially when the prospect of further European largesse was on the horizon.

The beet producers had recently joined forces with the farmers' association and the IFA gave vociferous backing to their cause. The IFA President, TJ Maher, fired a shot across the government's bows on 6 January 1972. He warned that it was essential to secure a maximum quota of 240,000 tons; otherwise the beet growers would suffer major losses, while at least 1,000 workers in the sugar factories would lose their jobs.[142] His assertion was wildly inaccurate. The figure of 240,000 greatly exceeded the existing level of sales and production capacity; such a dramatic expansion in production would have required substantial capital investment from the state, probably including the building of a new sugar factory.[143] But the government could not ignore the power of the IFA, whose support was vital in the forthcoming referendum. Hillery had already agreed to ask for a renewal of ministerial talks with the Community to review the sugar production quota. But he had well-founded reservations about the case presented by the farmers and the Sugar Company; he also knew only too well that the Community would not approve a dramatic hike in the Irish sugar quota just before the end of the negotiations. Hillery held a series of meetings with IFA representatives, trade union officials and officers of the Sugar Company in Dublin early in January, seeking to persuade them to agree a more realistic figure. He also met another IFA delegation, led by Maher, in Brussels on the eve of the talks, and urged them to give him a lower figure as a fall-back position in the negotiations.[144] This attempt to advise moderation fell on deaf ears:

> I did everything in my power to get a lower figure which
> would be reasonable to produce for the Community as I
> felt ashamed of going out with this high demand figure,

but the Sugar Company officer, Mr Daly, who was supposedly in Brussels for the purpose of bringing reality into the picture, totally agreed with the IFA and BVA group in my presence that 240,000 [tons] was a minimum and that you would have no industry in a couple of years without such a quota.[145]

The IFA officials also had no hesitation in highlighting the political implications of a failure to meet their demands. John Fardy, the representative of the sugar beet producers within the IFA, warned that 'they would become militant and vote against the Referendum at anything less than 240,000.'[146] IFA leaders and union officials took the same line, warning publicly that the inadequate sugar production quota represented a major obstacle to EEC membership.[147] Hillery feared that the last-minute row over sugar could have a decisive impact in the referendum, out of all proportion to its actual importance.

The government's concerns were heightened by the emergence of a vigorous campaign to secure a major improvement in the Community offer. A rainbow coalition of interests came together to demand better terms for the Irish sugar industry. A public rally was held in Tuam on 7 January, drawing support from about 2,000 factory workers, beet farmers and union officials. The organisers declared that the rally was intended 'to support Dr Hillery' in making his case at Brussels; it was actually designed to exert pressure on him to deliver the maximum quota demanded by the IFA.[148] The campaign also won the backing of prominent Catholic bishops. The Archbishop of Tuam, Dr Joseph Cunnane, addressed the rally in the town to support the demands of the sugar industry. His episcopal colleague, Thomas Morris, Archbishop of Cashel, addressed a similar demonstration held in Thurles.[149] Hillery now faced overwhelming pressure to secure a figure for the sugar quota that he knew to be unreasonable and unattainable. His solution was to negotiate the best possible deal in Brussels, while seeking to highlight the futility of threatening the entire process of Irish accession over dubious claims by the sugar industry.[150] Hillery first sought to lower public expectations in advance of the ministerial meeting on 10 January, briefing journalists that he had no chance of securing the quota sought by the IFA. This move was successful in shaping media coverage of the talks, although it had little influence on the farmers' representatives:

> [I] informed newspaper men and members of the delegation to say that there was no question whatever of getting any figure for sugar near what is being asked by the farmers. The Trade Union officials seem to recognise this but the farmers who were in with me stuck to the figure and were most adamant.[151]

The Foreign Minister realised, however, that he could not afford any appearance of weakness in the negotiations, whatever his private reservations about pursuing the issue at all. Hillery made a strong case in his opening statement for an increase in the quota, arguing that it would ensure the future viability of the Irish sugar industry; he also urged the Community to grant a quota of 240,000 tons annually.[152] This claim was strictly for public consumption; when the meeting was suspended to allow for private negotiations on the issue, Hillery sought to secure a more reasonable settlement. Having telephoned Lynch in Dublin to make sure of his approval, he suggested a figure of 170,000 tons as the minimum acceptable level for the Irish government. Even this more modest proposal was utterly unacceptable to the Community negotiators.[153] Both the ministers and the Commission representatives, who usually took a more flexible approach, warned Hillery that no major increase would be conceded, as it would undermine the principles governing the allocation of all the national quotas: 'all flatly told me to forget about any increase which would change the principles of measuring the quota'.[154] The intensive negotiations dragged on into the early hours of Tuesday 11 January, as the gap between the two sides narrowed but did not close. Hillery did have some success, securing a moderate improvement in the Community proposal, but not by nearly enough to satisfy the interest groups waiting outside. The Community negotiators made a final offer of a basic production quota of 150,000 tons. The official Irish report on the negotiations underlined that Hillery had reached the end of the road: 'They emphasised most strongly that this was their final offer and that there could be no going beyond it.'[155] Hillery played out the last act in the drama with considerable flair. He informed the Community delegation formally that he had no authority from the government to accept the proposal: he could only promise to bring the Community's final offer before the government and let the EEC have the government's decision as soon as possible.[156] The meeting broke up without agreement, apparently leaving the Irish negotiations unresolved and Ireland's membership of the Community in the balance.

Yet this was not the whole story. Hillery was engaging in his own game of brinkmanship, which was aimed firmly at the IFA and the Irish sugar lobby, not the Community. Hillery assured Deniau privately that the deal was acceptable, but warned him to maintain the suspense for a couple of days:

> I said to the negotiator from the Commission, 'I'll take that but don't tell anyone.' ... Then I came out, and the farmers' association were outside of course, and TJ Maher was there; I said, 'This is serious, we mightn't be able to join at all.' I frightened the life out of him. I was going back to the government, I said. I wouldn't take responsibility for this; they had made such a row.[157]

Hillery confronted his critics with the nightmare scenario that Ireland might fail to enter the EEC solely due to a dispute over sugar. This scenario was by no means fanciful, given the way the sugar quota had suddenly emerged as a major political issue at home. There was no real prospect that the government would reject the terms and abandon the substantial benefits of EEC membership, especially following the highly favourable terms secured by the Irish delegation on agriculture and regional development. Yet EEC membership would still be endangered if discontent among farmers caused the defeat of the referendum. Hillery's move was designed to exert pressure on the IFA to accept the compromise. It was a calculated gamble that paid off.

The Foreign Minister recommended the terms of the deal at a Cabinet meeting immediately after his return from Brussels; no decision was announced on 11 January, but the government publicly accepted the compromise two days later.[158] Hillery was correct in calculating that the prospect of the Irish negotiations failing at the final hurdle would concentrate minds wonderfully, especially in the IFA; farmers had too much to gain from the EEC to risk the benefits of the CAP over a dispute on sugar quotas. TJ Maher issued a statement accepting the agreement on 13 January. He covered his strategic retreat with a parting shot at the government, demanding that the state should support the maximum expansion of sugar production.[159] While the compromise was criticised by the ITGWU and the Labour Party, the Sugar Company also gave a positive response to the deal, which was far removed from the alarmist approach adopted by some of its managers only a few days before. The company announced that existing jobs would be maintained under the agreement, while the immediate prospects for the sugar industry appeared favourable.[160] Hillery had good reason to believe that the company had orchestrated much of the pressure on the government, not to ensure its survival, but to get the EEC to pay for the development of an expanded sugar industry. This alluring but unrealistic vision also had a strong attraction to the beet farmers and trade unions. Hillery's verdict on the sectional interests that had largely determined the government's policy in this instance was scathing: 'So all agreed that I should be forced to look for 240,000 and forced to fight for it. They were supported by two archbishops, Morris and Cunnane. It was a try-on to be ashamed of as a nation'.[161] Hillery, however, wisely kept his private views to himself. He negotiated a sensible compromise that met the essential needs of the sugar industry and contained the potential for negative fall-out from the issue in the referendum campaign.

The compromise negotiated by Hillery on the sugar quota resolved the final outstanding issue of the Irish negotiations. Lynch and Hillery signed the Treaty of Accession and the other legal instruments formalising

Ireland's entry to the European Communities in the Great Hall of the Palais d'Egmont in Brussels on 22 January 1972.[162] Ireland had secured membership of the EEC on remarkably favourable terms. The Irish delegation unquestionably enjoyed considerable goodwill on the part of the Community member states in the negotiations and benefited particularly from the flexible and accommodating approach of the Commission.[163] The expertise and initiative of the Irish officials also made an indispensable contribution to such a favourable outcome.

Yet Hillery played a central part in steering the negotiations to a successful conclusion. He established good personal connections with almost all EEC Foreign Ministers and members of the European Commission, which proved invaluable in overcoming difficulties over regional development and state aid to industry. A key theme running through the negotiations was the unavoidable linkage between the Irish and British negotiations. It was essential for the Irish delegation to make roughly parallel progress with the British application, not only because of the close economic relations between the two countries, but for wider political reasons linked to history and the effect on Irish public opinion. Hillery managed this difficult but vital relationship skilfully, not only securing simultaneous negotiation of the two applications from the outset, but also maintaining roughly equal progress with the British throughout the process. He achieved this feat by maintaining excellent relations with his British counterpart and collaborating closely with the British delegation on various issues; Irish national interests were well served by such collaboration, not least in overcoming the key obstacle of the Council's fait accompli on fisheries. While an exceptionally able group of Irish officials carried out much of the detailed negotiation, Hillery was centrally involved in resolving the most difficult issues, from industrial incentives to the sugar quota. He combined a conciliatory style with unwavering tenacity in pursuing Irish objectives; this combination of diplomacy and persistence made him a highly effective negotiator. Hillery gave overall direction to the Irish negotiations and managed the process with determination, patience and considerable tactical skill.

15.

The Last Campaign

The signature of the Treaty of Accession did not guarantee Irish membership of the EEC. The referendum lay ahead and the battle for public opinion had still to be won. Hillery certainly did not take the electorate for granted and was deeply concerned that the referendum might be defeated. He was justifiably proud of the terms that the Irish delegation had negotiated and knew that a rejection of the Treaty would effectively be a negative verdict on his own performance as the chief Irish negotiator. But Hillery's concerns about the outcome were dictated primarily by his deeply held conviction that a No vote would be a catastrophe, which would isolate Ireland on the periphery of Europe and leave it at the mercy of British policy: 'If I was worried at all at that time, it was that the stakes were so high. If we didn't get in and Britain got in, we were pauperised, we were destroyed.'[1] Hillery believed that failure by Ireland to accept EEC membership at the same time as its larger neighbour would not only mark the loss of a historic political opportunity, but would reinforce Ireland's economic dependence on Britain in the most unfavourable conditions imaginable. This view was based on the uncomfortable reality that almost two-thirds of all Irish exports in 1970 went to the United Kingdom. The external tariff of the Community would cut Ireland off from the crucial British market, while the gradual progress towards free trade would be stopped in its tracks. Ireland would be forced to negotiate the terms of its trade with a British state, which had the full influence of the EEC behind it. While Hillery had collaborated closely with the British negotiating team in 1971–2, he had a vivid recollection of official intransigence on the British side in reviews of the Anglo-Irish Free Trade Agreement. He retained a healthy suspicion about the willingness of the British establishment to exploit the level of Irish dependence on the British market. 'The British would want the advantage. I didn't want them across the table from me [in the EEC].'[2] Hillery, like many other supporters of Irish accession, hoped that membership of the EEC would reduce Ireland's dependence on Britain and compensate for the political and economic imbalance between the two countries.

The government began preparations for the referendum well before the end of the negotiations. The Third Amendment to the Constitution Bill was introduced in the Dáil in November 1971; the Bill enabled the Irish state to enter the European Communities and provided that Community legislation or decisions would have the force of law within the state. The original amendment would also have allowed the state to adopt all laws or measures 'consequent on membership of the Communities'.[3] Hillery hoped that the referendum would authorise not only the ratification of the Treaty of Accession, but also subsequent amendments to the European treaties.[4] If adopted, his approach would have had far-reaching consequences; it would have meant only a single referendum, with later treaties being ratified by the Oireachtas. But Fine Gael objected strenuously to this proposal, arguing that it gave dangerously broad powers to the government. Liam Cosgrave, the Fine Gael leader, and Garret FitzGerald proposed an amendment to clarify that the legal changes involved would be only those 'necessitated by the obligations of membership'; this was a much narrower definition, designed to ensure that the referendum would involve only the minimum changes necessary to provide for membership of the Community.[5] The government could not risk undermining Fine Gael's support for the referendum itself. Colley accepted the Fine Gael amendment in the Dáil on 25 January, although he wrongly claimed that it would make no difference to the Bill. The Dáil approved the legislation, with both Fianna Fáil and Fine Gael in favour, by a massive majority on 26 January 1972.[6]

The government also produced a White Paper, on *The Accession of Ireland to the European Communities*, which was presented to the Oireachtas in January 1972. As its title suggested, the White Paper provided a comprehensive and accurate description of the terms for Ireland's accession.[7] It also presented a strong case for Ireland's membership of the EEC; the White Paper concluded that there was no realistic alternative to membership and 'the national interest and welfare of our people would best be served by joining an enlarged European Economic Community.'[8] Although some attention was given to the political objectives of the Community, the White Paper concentrated heavily on the economic benefits of accession and the economic risks of isolation from Europe. Hillery sought to redress the balance in his contribution to the debate on the terms of entry in the Dáil on 23 March 1972. Having announced to the assembled Deputies that the referendum would be held on 10 May, Hillery argued that 'in this national debate we should ask ourselves what the Community is all about.'[9] The EEC was born 'out of the devastation of the last World War' and was based on the ideal of achieving unity among the people of Europe, which would make war between European nations impossible in the future. The founders of the Community sought to achieve the constant improvement of the living and working conditions of their people.[10] Hillery told the Dáil that it was vital to 'appreciate fully the nature of this Community' that Ireland had the opportunity of joining. He put a rhetorical question to his colleagues and opponents: 'I would like to ask: surely the ideals I have mentioned, the objectives set, the tasks they have undertaken are ones that we in Ireland fully sympathise with and can support?'[11] He argued passionately that the Community had created freedom, peace and prosperity in Western Europe; enlargement offered a unique opportunity to extend the benefits of European integration to

Ireland.[12] Hillery made no attempt to conceal the essentially political vision that underpinned the European project, even if the remit of the institutions was still restricted to economic integration. The opposite was true – he forcefully promoted the political values that drove the movement for closer European union.

Hillery had never lost sight of the need to build public support for EEC membership during the negotiations. He laid the groundwork for a successful referendum campaign by regularly briefing key interest groups such as the IFA and the Confederation of Irish Industries on the progress of the negotiations. The media operation co-ordinated by Fogarty also played its part in disseminating information about the EEC and creating a broadly favourable context for the referendum. An EEC Information Service was established within the Department of Foreign Affairs, which was designed to provide public information about Community institutions and the terms of accession secured by Ireland.[13] The line between information and positive advocacy by government departments became blurred to the point of invisibility as the referendum drew closer. This did not bother Hillery; he told the Dáil on 23 March that he would spare no effort to secure a favourable popular verdict: 'Anybody whom I can influence to vote "yes" for membership to Europe, I will do so.'[14]

The first task facing Hillery was to organise the government's campaign and to rally the Fianna Fáil organisation behind the cause of accession to the EEC. The Foreign Minister acted as national director of Fianna Fáil's campaign, which adopted the slogan of 'Into Europe'. Hillery worked closely with Senator Neville Keery, a member of the party's national executive from Dún Laoghaire. Keery took leave from his job in Trinity College to take up a post in Fianna Fáil's head office, working primarily on the European referendum.[15] He was later deeply involved in two further referendum campaigns, the lowering of the voting age to 18, and the removal of the special position of the Catholic Church in the constitution, which were passed in December 1972. Keery played a key role in the 'Into Europe' campaign. He acted as a full-time campaign organiser; he also wrote speeches for Hillery and other ministers during the referendum. Hillery came to have a healthy respect for Keery's efficiency, particularly regarding speeches written to address public concerns about the EEC: 'I would come back from a meeting and give them stuff to type a speech. I would give something to Fogarty and it would take several days; I gave Neville the same subject and he would have it back the next morning.'[16]

Hillery recognised that while the government had been committed to accession for over a decade, Fianna Fáil might not necessarily regard the advance towards European integration as a natural fit with its republican traditions.[17] He set out to persuade elected representatives that Europe would be a popular cause, and to mobilise Fianna Fáil's organisation in favour of the Treaty. The key decision of the early phase of the campaign was to hold 'Into Europe' conventions in every constituency. All the elected representatives were asked to attend their local convention and each constituency was required to appoint a director of elections by the time the convention was held. Each convention was addressed by a minister and sometimes also by an expert guest speaker. The planning for the campaign began in the autumn of 1971 and the conventions were rolled out from January 1972.

Hillery soon found that motivating TDs to get out and canvass for Community membership was no easy task. This was not generally due to any reservations about EEC membership among the parliamentary party, but to a widespread lack of knowledge about the Community and uncertainty about the response of their electorate. While many of his colleagues held back from the fray initially, Hillery started campaigning almost as soon as the ink was dry on the Treaty of Accession. His first speech of the campaign was given on 28 January to the Denis Lacey Cumann in Clonmel. He told party activists that accession would mean that Ireland would in future export 'goods, not people'; a decision to opt out of the Community would destroy the export industries and compel thousands of Irish people to emigrate to other European countries.[18] This was an early expression of a theme prominently emphasised by Hillery and other leading figures in the pro-EEC campaign – there was no viable economic future for Ireland outside the Community and membership was dictated by economic reality. This was not simply a good political argument, but unquestionably reflected Hillery's genuine beliefs. He returned to the same theme at an 'Into Europe' convention organised by Fianna Fáil in Dublin North-East on 6 March. Hillery voiced his own central concerns about EEC membership – joining the Community was essential to avoid economic isolation and permanent subordination to Britain. He warned that it was vital for Ireland to have access to the British market, but if the Irish people rejected membership then the government would be obliged to accept whatever crumbs were dropped from the Community table: 'If we were to negotiate for a trade agreement with the enlarged EEC which included Britain, we simply could not force them to give us a special deal. What we could negotiate would be largely on their terms'.[19] This was Hillery's personal nightmare scenario, not without good reason, but it also reflected the most compelling argument deployed by the pro-EEC campaign; in effect there was no economic alternative to accession. Although opponents of the EEC vociferously rejected this argument, they were never able to demonstrate that a viable alternative to membership actually existed.

While Hillery's speeches to Fianna Fáil meetings served the dual purpose of motivating activists and attracting press coverage for his message, securing the active participation of the TDs in the campaign was crucial to bring out the party's loyal core vote; it was also indispensable in delivering a good turnout, which was widely regarded as essential for the pro-EEC side. George Colley claimed shortly before the referendum that Fianna Fáil timed its campaign to peak just before the vote, while the anti-EEC campaign made a grave mistake in allowing their campaign to peak too early.[20] If this occurred it happened more by accident than by design. Many TDs on the government side were initially confused or uncertain about the referendum. Hillery asked Lynch to call a meeting of the parliamentary party, invoking the authority of the Taoiseach to mobilise the TDs:

> It was a strange campaign, the TDs didn't know what all
> this was about. ... They didn't want to go out. That's why
> I said to Jack, 'Bring them all in and ask every one of them

what did you do in your own constituency.' It was very
hard to explain to people. But they got out then and found
that this subject was known and people wanted it.[21]

Lynch and Hillery warned TDs of the high stakes involved in the decision,
both for the government that had negotiated the terms of entry and for
the country. In the final weeks before the referendum, all TDs, including
ministers, were instructed to organise the local campaign in their
constituencies, bringing out local activists for intensive door-to-door
canvassing.[22] Whether due to effective organisation by the campaign
committee, pragmatic calculation of the benefits involved or genuine pro-
European sentiment, the party organisation moved decisively behind the
pro-European campaign in the run-up to the referendum. The tone of the
party's campaign focused strongly on the political implications of the
decision, as well as the economic advantages. Fianna Fáil ministers and
TDs called upon supporters to 'vote with the people you trust' and
emphasised that the government would maintain control over the extent
of Irish involvement in future European integration.[23] The campaign drew
a generally favourable response, especially from Fianna Fáil supporters.
Indeed the canvass returns in many constituencies were so favourable that
Hillery did not fully believe them, and other ministers publicly expressed
concern that they might lead to complacency among the party's
supporters.[24] These fears proved unfounded. The Fianna Fáil campaign
was highly effective and contributed significantly to the decisive result in
favour of the EEC.

The balance of forces in the referendum was heavily weighted towards
the pro-EEC side. Fianna Fáil and Fine Gael both supported accession to
the Community. Garret FitzGerald was a particularly forceful and
eloquent advocate for EEC membership; indeed he came to be regarded
by many journalists as the leading public face of the Yes campaign. Hillery
was not disturbed by FitzGerald's prominence in the campaign. He
appreciated the advantages of having such a prominent opposition figure
making the case for membership.

I was glad of anybody speaking for it. I was glad of Garret informing the public. He filled an awful lot of space and he was very enthusiastic and committed. So I didn't feel there was any harm there at all, it was good and anybody else that spoke in favour was welcome.[25]

The strength of interest group support for entry was also impressive. Perhaps most important was the fervent backing of the IFA, whose quibbles over the sugar industry were long forgotten. The farming community formed the largest single occupational group strongly in favour of entry to the EEC.[26] The employer organisations also supported accession, while the trade union movement was divided. The ITGWU actively supported the No campaign, while the WUI backed entry to the Community. The Labour Party took a leading role in the No campaign, but was by no means united with a substantial minority of Labour representatives and supporters favouring accession. The fractured segments of the republican movement seized many of the headlines on the anti-EEC side; Official and Provisional Sinn Féin both ran separate and vociferous campaigns against the EEC. The Common Market Defence Campaign was launched in July 1971 to co-ordinate the No campaign, but could do little to unify the disparate elements opposed to the EEC.[27]

The republican opponents of the EEC attempted to make partition a key issue in the campaign. On 8 February the president of Conradh na Gaeilge, Maolsheachlainn Ó Caollaí, wrote to Hillery on behalf of a group of republican internees in Long Kesh; the prisoners attacked the Irish government for failing to allow the people of Northern Ireland the opportunity to vote in the referendum and claimed that their rights as citizens would be forfeited under the terms of entry to the EEC.[28] The republican opponents of membership alleged that by signing the Treaty of Accession the Irish government had accepted partition and given formal recognition to British jurisdiction over the six counties. Hillery did not reply to the letter, and Ó Caollaí published it on 28 March in a statement alleging that the government's refusal to open the referendum to all the people of Ireland was 'an act of treachery'.[29] Hillery did not ignore the challenge, but responded publicly in a speech in Dublin on 25 April. He deliberately sidestepped the emotive issue of votes for the internees and instead refuted the central contention made by hardline nationalist opponents of accession. He denounced as 'completely untrue' the allegation that EEC accession somehow involved formal acceptance of partition.[30] He pointed out that the claim was based on nothing more than Irish signature of the same treaty as the United Kingdom of Great Britain and Northern Ireland; Ireland had signed many international treaties to which Britain was also a party and none of these treaties involved implications for territorial claims made by either state. Hillery argued instead that an enlarged EEC, including both North and South, would promote unity in the long term by removing some of the economic and trade barriers to a united Ireland. But if Ireland stayed out of the Community, then partition would become further entrenched and 'the Border, in effect, would become the international frontier between the Republic and the EEC.'[31] It was an effective response to a spurious claim, although Hillery was certainly too optimistic in suggesting that EEC membership would promote economic integration on the island of Ireland.

Hillery was the most active and effective campaigner on the government side. He spoke at a series of public meetings throughout the country, setting a frenetic pace that was intended to serve as an example to fellow ministers and TDs. He told a local meeting on 12 March in Westport, County Mayo that attempts were being made 'to frighten people into blind opposition to the EEC', by giving a distorted impression that there would be a general upsurge in food prices following accession.[32] He acknowledged that certain food prices would go up, but only where fixed Community prices to farmers exceeded what Irish farmers were already getting for various products. He took the opportunity to point out that higher consumer prices on some items were a direct result of the increased prices that Irish farmers would receive due to Community policies. Then in a speech later on the same day in Ennis, he portrayed the entry to the Community as a gateway to foreign investment: 'A "yes" vote in the referendum is a vote to bring industry to the Irish people; a "no" vote is a vote to send Irish people to where the industry already is.'[33] He

returned to the same theme in Killarney on 23 April, rejecting claims by
the Labour leader, Brendan Corish, that membership of the EEC would
trigger major job losses in manufacturing industry. Hillery argued that
some failures in business were an inevitable part of economic activity, but
expected a net increase in employment for Irish industries within the
Community.[34] He emphasised that the EEC would transform Ireland's
economic opportunities for the better, while seeking to refute key claims
made by the anti-EEC campaign on price increases and threats to
employment.

Yet his campaign, unlike some later efforts by his successors in
subsequent European referendums, was not all about money – or even
about the purely economic benefits of EEC membership. He also focused
on broader arguments that reflected his personal commitment to
internationalism and the European project. He made a speech to a party
meeting in Dublin on 2 May, declaring that a vote against Europe was 'a
denial of Irish traditions'.[35] He pointed to Ireland's close historical links
and shared cultural heritage with continental Europe. Hillery portrayed
Irish accession to the EEC as an historic opportunity, which would enable
Ireland to take its rightful place in Europe and participate fully in a unique
international project:

> Not to join in this great and unique endeavour would be,
> in effect, to turn our backs on Europe, to abandon what is
> really a part of ourselves. It would be to renege on what is
> most worthy in our past and to sacrifice the hopes and
> aspirations which we have for ourselves and more
> importantly for our children.[36]

Hillery was seeking to reassure wavering voters that Irish national
traditions were fully consistent with European integration. Yet he was also
expressing political convictions which would come to the fore when he
left Irish politics for a wider European stage; he fully shared the ideal of
greater European unity promoted by the founding fathers of the
Community.

As the referendum drew closer, Hillery was as concerned about apathy and lack of interest among the electorate as he was about the No campaign. He took the lead for the government at several press briefings in Dublin during the final three weeks of the campaign; he told journalists he was confident of a majority for entry, but concerned about getting this majority to the polls on 10 May.[37] He constantly drove home the message that the stakes were much too high for complacency. He declared at a press conference on 29 April that the referendum was 'a vote for freedom' and compared it to the decision by the Irish people 'to be free from Britain half a century ago'.[38] The move to invoke the struggle for national independence to support accession to the EEC was designed to motivate nationalist voters, particularly Fianna Fáil supporters, to come out and vote for accession on 10 May. Yet it was not a cynical ploy; Hillery was firmly convinced that participation in the European project was a golden opportunity to overcome Ireland's dependence on Britain and provide a wider stage for a small nation state. Hillery's commitment to European ideals was entirely compatible with his nationalism.

The final week of the campaign saw clashes between Hillery and the anti-EEC campaign in his own constituency. The most memorable confrontation, which was reminiscent of the scenes at the Fianna Fáil Ard Fheis, came in Shannon two days before the vote. Members of the anti-EEC campaign claimed that the Irish government was about to give US planes landing rights in Dublin, abolishing Shannon's status as the sole transatlantic gateway to Ireland. Any threat to Shannon's special status provoked intense opposition in Clare, where the airport and the Shannon industrial zone provided an important source of employment. In fact, the government was resisting American pressure to give their planes landing rights in Dublin. Hillery himself staunchly defended Shannon's position in a meeting with William Rogers in October 1971.[39] Indeed, Hillery's forceful approach in discussions with US representatives about various issues, notably the crisis in Northern Ireland after Bloody Sunday, earned him unfavourable reviews from American officials. The US ambassador to Ireland, John Moore, reported to the State Department following the conclusion of Hillery's term as Foreign Minister in January 1973 that 'Hillery tended to be cold, inaccessible and not especially interested in relations with the US – except when he had something to ask.'[40] This one-sided assessment reflected the frustration of US diplomats with Hillery's line on Northern Ireland and his resistance to American pressure over Shannon. It was deeply ironic that Hillery was attacked during the referendum campaign for being too accommodating to the US government.

Hillery went to a meeting at the airport on 8 May, aiming to refute the claim that the government was about to abandon Shannon and to reassure the workers at the airport that their jobs would be safe if Ireland joined the EEC.[41] But before he arrived, the Common Market Defence Committee, including trade unionists and members of Sinn Féin, undertook a pre-emptive strike, setting up their own public address system and warning the assembled workers not to be deceived by the pro-EEC campaign. Rory Cowan, an ITGWU official, was addressing the workers when Hillery arrived and refused to give way.[42] When Hillery began to speak anyway, he immediately clashed with Cowan and the two men had a brief impromptu debate. But the real fun began when Hillery laid into his opponents in no uncertain terms. He declared, accurately enough, that the landing rights issue had nothing to do with the EEC, and denounced the Defence Committee for making false statements to frighten the airport workers. He expressed confidence that the workers would not be manipulated by the opposing campaign: 'No cowards or nondescripts could go in behind the polling booths on Wednesday and prevent Shannon Airport workers from being heard'.[43] His speech triggered shouts of outrage and some vigorous heckling from the group of anti-EEC campaigners. But he took full advantage of his microphone to make himself heard, singling out the demonstrators: 'If you listen to those people you will have no Shannon. They would rather see the grass grow over the airport as part of their campaign to bring about chaos.'[44] It was hard to say who won the exchange, but Hillery certainly made his point, and the raucous scenes did few favours for his opponents. He deliberately took an uncompromising line, seeking to portray his opponents as irresponsible extremists who would not hesitate to disrupt a public meeting – or threaten the future of an airport. This was hardly fair to mainstream opponents of the EEC, but Hillery was happy to exploit the counter-productive tactics of the more extreme elements within the No campaign. Hillery regarded both elements of Sinn Féin as a major political liability to the No campaign and was delighted with anything that publicised their opposition to the EEC.[45] He was not at all displeased when a group of republican activists sought to challenge him on his own ground, following him around Clare during his speaking tour of the county in the final days of the campaign: 'I remember they followed me around Clare. I lost my voice in one place, but it came back when they came. But I had a great microphone and shouted them down. They were enjoying themselves, I think. I was delighted.'[46] The demonstrators may have enjoyed the occasion, but he was winning the votes.

The outcome of the referendum on 10 May far exceeded Hillery's expectations. The verdict was decisive, giving a landslide victory to the Yes campaign. The Yes votes accounted for 83 per cent of the total poll, with only 17 per cent voting No. Accession to the EEC was approved by a majority of almost five to one. Moreover the vote produced a record turnout for a referendum of 71 per cent.[47] Every constituency in the country returned a clear majority for entry to the Community. Hillery was elated with the result but surprised by the margin of victory:

> I didn't expect such a big number, 83 per cent. Early on I met Barry Desmond, who was Labour but against Labour policy [on the EEC]; we met at the installation of a bishop for the Church of Ireland in Killaloe, I think, and he said, 'You're going to win this.' The fact is, if you didn't you were gone. The country was in an awful state if it didn't get into the common market. The stakes were so high I wouldn't cheer until it was done, you know.[48]

The Yes campaign was well funded and highly effective in presenting its core message that there was an overwhelming economic rationale for accession to the EEC. The opponents of the EEC suffered from inadequate funding and repeatedly attacked the government's use of taxpayers' money to promote the referendum.[49] The financial imbalance between the two sides was certainly exacerbated by the government's ability to employ the resources of the state to support its campaign. But lack of financial resources was not the only problem facing the anti-EEC campaign; equally damaging were the divisions within their own ranks and the extremist rhetoric used by hardline nationalist elements on the No side. Perhaps most significant was the inability of the No campaign to provide a plausible alternative to Irish membership.[50] The decisive endorsement of EEC membership ultimately reflected the political and economic realities of Irish society in the early 1970s.

Hillery's skilful management of the negotiations marked his most significant contribution to the decisive outcome of the referendum. But he was also a central participant in the successful pro-European campaign. He acted effectively to mobilise the government's supporters and treated the referendum with the same urgency he would have given a general election campaign in Clare. He set out to persuade the electorate on the merits of accession, rather than assuming that the predominant political and interest group backing for the EEC would inevitably produce a positive result. The referendum campaign underlined his pivotal position in the government and enhanced his status as one of the leading figures on the Irish political landscape. It was not widely known, even to Hillery himself, that it would be his last campaign in Irish politics.

Within days of the referendum result, speculation emerged in the Irish media that Hillery would become Ireland's first European Commissioner.[51] Each state within the Community was entitled to nominate a member of the Commission, subject to the formal approval of the other governments. While the Commission lacked the power enjoyed by the Council of Ministers in the early 1970s, it played a crucial role in the initiation of European policies and legislation. Hillery did not initially consider himself the likely nominee. As the Commission occupied a clearly subordinate position to national governments and was often regarded as more of a European civil service than a political institution, he expected that an economist or civil servant would be the most likely choice.[52] But by the autumn of 1972 it became clear that the incoming

Commission would be a highly political body, consisting mainly of prominent political figures from member states; an authoritative Irish voice on the Commission appeared all the more necessary, with regional development and the Community's plans for economic and monetary union on the agenda.[53] The Community had decided in 1970 that economic and monetary union should be achieved within ten years under the terms of the Werner report; this timetable proved wildly optimistic, but this was not yet apparent in 1972. Once it became evident that the nominee would be a leading politician, Hillery was the obvious choice. He had been a forceful representative of Irish interests in the negotiations and an equally effective advocate of entry to the Community. Moreover, he had an impeccable record of loyalty to the government and to Lynch's leadership, which was no less important in determining who secured such a key position. Lynch, however, took some time before making the appointment, probably because he was uncertain about allowing Hillery to leave the government. He cautiously sounded out his Foreign Minister, without actually offering him the job:

> Jack phoned one day; he asked, 'If I offered you the job in Europe, would you take it?' I said yes; I hadn't been thinking of it myself, but you had to say yes or no, so I said yes. And he said, 'Well I'm not offering it to you, I'm only wondering what you'll do if I offer it!' I was as mad as anything and told him so.[54]

Hillery undoubtedly wanted the appointment as a Commissioner. He had no interest in seeking to rise further up the greasy pole in Irish politics and saw the Commission as a new and attractive opportunity.[55] He did not lobby actively to secure the nomination; he had no need to do so, considering the strength of his claim on the position. Erskine Childers was also interested in the position, but had little chance of getting it once Hillery declared his interest. The Foreign Minister was the clear favourite for the nomination from the outset.[56] Lynch did not speak directly to Hillery again; but the Taoiseach had made up his mind by mid-August.

When Cearbhall Ó Dálaigh, the Chief Justice, was appointed on 15 August as the first Irish member of the European Court of Justice, journalists were also briefed by 'reliable sources' that Hillery would become the Irish Commissioner, although no official announcement was made.[57] The decision was confirmed while Hillery was out of the country, attending the UN General Assembly in New York. Lynch announced on 26 September that the government would nominate Hillery as a member of the Commission on Ireland's accession in January 1973.[58] The approval of Hillery's nomination by the other member states was a formality. The Council of Foreign Ministers formally appointed the new Commission, including Hillery, on 18 December 1972. More fortuitously, Hillery also became one of the five Vice-Presidents of the incoming Commission, due mainly to the Norwegian decision to reject membership of the EEC.[59]

The government's nomination did not mean an immediate break with Irish politics. The Taoiseach asked Hillery to remain as Foreign minister until the end of the year, mainly to complete the necessary legislation to allow Irish membership of the Community. The Department of Foreign Affairs produced the European Communities Bill, which was designed to make the European Treaties and the weighty volume of European legislation legally binding within the state; it also authorised ministers to make regulations giving full effect to Community decisions.[60] Hillery piloted the Bill through the Oireachtas between October and November 1972, accepting some opposition amendments on points of detail, but brushing aside claims by Richie Ryan of Fine Gael that the Bill as drafted was in breach of the Constitution.[61] The approval of the legislation enabled the Irish government to ratify the Treaty of Accession formally in December. This concluded the final act of Hillery's memorable term as Foreign Minister. Brian Lenihan was appointed to succeed him in Iveagh House on 29 December, the same day that Hillery was formally notified by the European Community of his appointment as Vice-President of the Commission.[62]

The European referendum was a decisive turning point in Hillery's political career. It meant the end of his participation at the highest level of Irish politics. He would never hold office in an Irish government again after 1972. Moreover after 21 years in the Dáil he was no longer a TD for Clare; he resigned his seat in January 1973 to take up membership of the Commission. There was widespread speculation that his time in Brussels was merely a temporary interlude, to be followed in due course by his triumphant return to the Irish political scene as Jack Lynch's anointed successor. The political columnist John Healy even claimed in October 1972 that the succession was virtually decided in Hillery's favour: 'while others may have ambitions and may press them, as of now it is a no-contest'.[63] This speculation appeared perfectly plausible at the time, but proved well wide of the mark. Hillery made a definite decision to leave Irish politics when he accepted appointment to the Commission: 'I made up my mind that it was time to give up politics and leave the Dáil.'[64] He had no intention of returning to party politics in Ireland and still nurtured an almost wistful desire to resume full-time medical practice after his time in Brussels. While this hope was destined never to be realised, Hillery's decision to accept membership of the Commission marked a permanent break with Irish politics. It was a deliberate decision that he never came to regret.

16.

Commissioner

The European Commission that Hillery joined in January 1973 was unmistakably the junior partner within the Community institutions. The real power rested with the national governments represented on the Council of Ministers. Moreover, there was no real advance in the influence of the Commission during Hillery's four-year term; instead, any political developments that did occur reinforced the power of the nation states. The European Council developed by 1974 from occasional summit meetings between the leaders of the nine member states. The Council, which involved regular meetings between the national leaders, became the most powerful institution within the Community.[1] The emergence of the European Council underlined the dominant position of the national governments. The French government in particular retained a Gaullist suspicion of the Commission and was determined to resist any significant erosion of the power of the nation states. The European Parliament was the least influential of the European institutions in 1973; it had no legislative functions and was essentially restricted to a consultative role.[2] As a former Foreign Minister, Hillery had a good appreciation of the balance of power within the Community and knew that the Commission's ability to effect change would be strictly limited unless it secured the support of the national governments.

The first task of the new Commission, headed by former French finance minister François-Xavier Ortoli, was to share out the portfolios among its members. Hillery had a definite idea of what he wanted and succeeded in getting it. Lynch and his economics adviser, Martin O'Donoghue, urged Hillery to seek the Regional Policy portfolio, but he opted instead for Social Affairs. Regional development was a key priority for the Irish government, which stood to gain more from a strong regional policy than any other member state. Yet Hillery calculated that taking charge of a key Irish national interest was ill advised; it would compromise his impartiality and undermine his ability to influence his colleagues.[3] He had also received well-founded information that the area of regional policy would be slow to develop, not least because no progress had yet been made in establishing a Regional Development Fund to assist less developed areas: 'Certainly, Deniau, when I spoke to him in Dublin, didn't think that regional policy would come in our time.'[4] Yet the previous history of Community action on Social Affairs did not inspire much confidence either. There was no coherent European social policy in 1973, and social issues traditionally took second place to the economic demands of removing trade barriers and developing the common market.

But Social Affairs had a couple of major advantages in Hillery's eyes. The European Social Fund was already in operation, even if it was severely under-resourced by member states. More significantly, the Paris summit of the national leaders in October 1972 declared that they attached as much importance to 'vigorous action in the social field' as to the achievement of economic and monetary union.[5] President Pompidou called for priority to be given to social reforms, as a means of achieving tangible results that would generate public support for the European Community. But the strongest impetus for action on social issues came from the West German Chancellor, Willy Brandt, who led a Social Democrat–Liberal coalition. Brandt proposed a new initiative on social policy that formed the basis for the declaration adopted by the summit.[6]

The heads of state and government invited the Community institutions to develop a social action programme by 1 January 1974. The new Commission would play a key part in developing a European social policy and Hillery saw the potential in the previously neglected area of Social Affairs (DG–V). He asked for the portfolio at his first meeting with Ortoli.[7] The Commission decided the distribution of portfolios at its first meeting on 6 January 1973, and the outcome was not entirely predictable, as Hillery's hopes of securing Social Affairs depended on how disputes over other portfolios were resolved, especially a clash between the British and German nominees over DG-I, the prestigious External Relations post.[8] Ortoli engaged in a complex series of negotiations to reconcile the differing claims of his colleagues.[9] Following six hours of private discussions, the make-up of the Commission was decided without internal bloodletting. Hillery became the new Commissioner for Social Affairs. The Regional Policy portfolio went to George Thomson, the former Labour minister who had agreed to consult with the Irish side in the European negotiations; the other British nominee, Christopher Soames, secured the External Relations post.

Hillery's first three months in Brussels were among the most traumatic of his career. This reflected in part the difficulties of acclimatising to a new position in a profoundly different cultural and political milieu, with the additional challenge of operating to a considerable extent in a foreign language. French was the working language of the Community. All the Commission documents were produced in French and full-scale translation services were not yet available immediately after the accession of the new member states. While interpreters were used at meetings of the Commission itself and the European Parliament, many official meetings were still conducted entirely through French at the beginning of 1973. But Hillery already had a working knowledge of French and quickly set out to become fluent, asking officials of DG-V to speak with him only in French and selecting French-speaking secretarial staff.[10] The initial difficulties involved in adapting to a different language and a new working environment did not greatly disturb him. The major problem concerned the working of Hillery's own *cabinet*.

Each Commissioner had the right to choose a core group of staff, who worked directly with him and supervised the implementation of his key policy priorities. Hillery appointed Robin Fogarty as *chef de cabinet*, with Edwin FitzGibbon, a diplomat who had served in the Irish Mission to the Community, acting as deputy. John Feeney, who had covered the negotiations as economics correspondent for RTÉ, also joined Hillery's team to take charge of press relations.[11] Hugh McCann recommended Fogarty, who had been a prominent member of the Foreign Affairs team in the Irish negotiations and had very ably co-ordinated the department's liaison with the Irish media and interest groups.[12] Hillery generally chose the members of his *cabinet* well and benefited greatly from their expertise and support. He established lifelong personal friendships with almost all of his staff, who generally regarded him with deep affection and respect. Fogarty proved a striking exception on all counts.

Fogarty was an able and intelligent official; but he was also abrasive and utterly lacking in social skills. He failed completely to adapt to working life in the European Commission, not least because he was unable to learn French.[13] More seriously, he showed an absolute inability to interact constructively either with his nominal colleagues in the *cabinet* or with Hillery himself. Hillery's relations with Fogarty began to deteriorate within days of the new Commissioner's arrival in Brussels. As Hillery had been dealing with the legislation to confirm Ireland's accession to the EEC, he had been unable to go to Brussels himself to prepare for the changeover to his new job in January. Instead, in October 1972 he assigned Fogarty to liaise with the Commission concerning arrangements for staffing and the running of his office when Hillery took over in January. He arrived only on 5 January after his plane was first diverted to Frankfurt because of fog; when Hillery went to the Commission's offices at the Berlaymont building, he discovered that virtually no preparations had been made and his office was 'a shambles'.[14] There were mitigating circumstances for the initial confusion, as it was not yet clear which portfolio Hillery would hold and the Commission was in a state of flux due to the ongoing process of incorporating officials nominated by the new member states. But it soon became evident that Fogarty intensely disliked most senior officials in the Berlaymont. He regarded his continental colleagues with grave suspicion, while he was contemptuous of the other Irish members of the *cabinet*. An Irish civil servant who was later a member of Hillery's *cabinet* believed that the language barrier was a key problem: 'The Chef de Cabinet meetings were all in French. Robin didn't have a clue what was going on. Then he got paranoid and decided they were all talking about him.'[15] An Irish journalist, who knew Fogarty well, had a more succinct explanation: 'Robin felt he was surrounded by fools'.[16] When he started to treat his new boss as one of the many fools he had to deal with, it was hardly surprising that their working relationship came to an abrupt end.

The new Commissioner's disillusionment with Fogarty was rapid and complete. Hillery kept a diary during his time in Brussels, which was not comprehensive and was often interrupted, probably by the pressure of events. But transcripts from his diary in the early months of 1973 give a vivid portrayal of the collapse of his working relationship with his *chef de cabinet*. Hillery noted his bafflement at Fogarty's behaviour on 8 January: 'Mr Fogarty is worried. He speaks of going deeper into the morass but I find it hard to get a clear picture from him of the real difficulty. It is partly emotional'.[17] Then on 30 January Hillery confided to his diary that 'Mr Fogarty does not have any French so the situation is impossible'.[18] He had some sympathy with the Irish official's inability to master a foreign language, which was probably why their association lasted as long as it did. But Hillery's bemusement soon turned to anger. His diary entries for 9 February noted:

> During the past week there have been events which bothered me. One is the unavailability of Mr Fogarty to me as Commissioner. He has taken on a life of his own in the work itself and obviously seems to deal with it without thought to anyone else.[19]

Hillery was frustrated that he found himself attending meetings of the Commission on his own, without support from any member of his *cabinet*, as Fogarty failed to attend himself and did not brief anyone else to do so. Fogarty also attacked Emile Noël, the French Secretary-General of the Commission, warning Hillery that Noël should be sacked: 'He came rushing to me several times – Noël had too much power, was cynical, had to be curbed.'[20]

The final straw came in the middle of February, when Hillery was in Luxembourg at a meeting of the Commission. Fogarty told Hillery that he had an appointment with the Minister for Labour in Luxembourg, but did not pass on the details to the Commissioner's private office or give Hillery a list of appointments for that week. It later transpired that the meeting with the minister was not scheduled for that date at all. A farcical scene ensued in which Hillery left the Commission meeting early to keep his appointment with the minister, only to find that his Flemish driver had been given no information about it and had no idea where to go.[21] This provoked the final rupture in a relationship that was already strained to breaking point. Hillery was furious at Fogarty's ineptitude and told him bluntly to get his act together. Fogarty in turn questioned the Commissioner's ability to run his own office and threatened to resign from the *cabinet*. If Fogarty hoped to force Hillery into backing down, he had seriously misjudged his man:

> He said he was being blamed just because I could not run my private office. This was insolence in the first place and in the second it was untrue, because neither of the people in my private office had been told of the arrangements. ... He said he would have to withdraw and I said 'alright'. Then he said 'I'm serious' and I replied 'I am too. You have withdrawn, I have accepted, now you are out, it's over.'[22]

Hillery immediately phoned Ed FitzGibbon in Brussels and asked him to take over as head of the *cabinet*. Both FitzGibbon and John Feeney, who was in Luxembourg, tried to dissuade him from removing Fogarty but

Hillery was adamant. He was convinced that he could not retain an official who had offered to resign without destroying his own authority: 'On reflection they both saw that I could not have a person who threatened to resign. Otherwise he would be impossible to handle'.[23] In any event he had decided that Fogarty had to go; the working relationship between them had collapsed in the most dramatic fashion. The official hardly had any rational basis for complaint. He miscalculated by offering to resign and Hillery took him at his word.

The removal of Fogarty allowed Hillery to reorganise his *cabinet*. FitzGibbon took over as *chef de cabinet* by 22 February, although Fogarty's departure was not confirmed publicly until the end of March. Hillery asked Hugh McCann to find an alternative post for his former adviser and allowed Fogarty to remain in Brussels, as a semi-detached member of the *cabinet* until Foreign Affairs was ready to accommodate him.[24] Fogarty, however, conducted press briefings against his former boss with Irish and British journalists; he spread an inaccurate rumour that Hillery had no interest in his work in Brussels but was planning to return to Dublin, with the intention of taking over the leadership of Fianna Fáil. The Commissioner wanted McCann 'to get him out of this place and let him do his talking in Dublin.'[25] Fogarty left Brussels at the end of March. His career did not suffer as a result of his precipitate departure from the Commission; soon afterwards he was appointed as an ambassador and later served as the Irish envoy to Bonn.

Hillery lost no time in replacing him, and this time made sure to choose an official whom he already knew and trusted. He met John McColgan in the Savoy hotel in London and asked his former private secretary to join him as deputy head of the *cabinet*. McColgan, who was press counsellor to the Irish embassy in London, was happy to rejoin Hillery, although he commented that he would 'have to sort it out with the department'.[26] Hillery did, and McColgan took up his new post in Brussels on 1 May 1973. In the meantime, the new Commissioner completed the line-up of his key staff. Jean-Claude Eeckhout, a Belgian official who had worked closely with Hillery's predecessor, Albert Coppé, became a member of the *cabinet*. Eeckhout's considerable experience of

the inner workings of the Commission proved a valuable asset to Hillery.[27]
Enrica Varese, an Italian member of the previous *cabinet*, also joined
Hillery's team. Varese was a feminist with a strong commitment to radical
social reform. She played a major part in drafting and implementing the
social action programme. Another Irish addition to the *cabinet* was Marcus
McInerney, previously a lecturer in agriculture, who joined Hillery's staff
on a temporary basis in February 1973.[28] Evelyne Pichon, a
Frenchwoman who had worked for the Irish mission in Brussels, and
Ludmilla Arco, who enjoyed Commission experience going back to her
time in the *cabinet* of the first President, Walter Hallstein, managed Hillery's
private office. Joe Carroll, who had covered the negotiations as a journalist
for the *Irish Press*, acted as the official spokesperson for Hillery's
directorate. The reformed *cabinet* gave Hillery a highly effective and
dedicated team, who played an indispensable part in guiding him through
the bureaucratic labyrinth of the European Commission.

He badly needed such official support, as the Social Affairs Directorate,
DG-V, was poorly organised and suffered from lack of leadership at official
level. Social Affairs was an underdeveloped portfolio, in part because it
had previously been held by less dynamic or effective members of the
Commission, but also due to the lack of support among national
governments for joint action on social issues.[29] Fogarty was not solely
responsible for the problems confronting the new Commissioner in the
first months of his term. Hillery confided his fears about his new
department in his diary: 'DG-V is not functioning properly. It is like the
Department of Education when I first went there'.[30] The comparison
with the Department of Education in the late 1950s was understandable,
but not entirely accurate. Hillery had a similar mountain to climb in
overcoming resistance to change among stakeholders and implementing
a programme of radical social reforms. But there were also marked
differences; a group of officials in the Department of Education favoured
a break with the previous conservative consensus and provided invaluable
backing for Hillery. But the situation in DG-V was very different. Hillery
had been accustomed to the Irish civil service, where he generally found
that officials gave full commitment to implementing the instructions of a

minister. But it quickly became apparent that many Commission officials did not feel any such commitment to the views of an individual Commissioner. The Commissioner had no say in their appointment and there were rarely ties of nationality or culture between Commissioners and their officials. Moreover most officials below the top level knew that their careers would continue while Commissioners came and went.[31] The impact of enlargement also cut both ways; officials from continental countries had to get accustomed to working with Commissioners from the new member states, while some Irish and British officials struggled to adapt to the working environment in the Berlaymont. The end result was that the impetus for change in Social Affairs was largely external and had little to do with the internal dynamics of DG-V. Yet on this occasion the momentum for change was much more powerful, as it came from the national leaders, especially Brandt and Pompidou. They had demanded a social action programme and Hillery used this crucial advantage to the full, both within the Commission and later in his negotiations with national governments. The challenge was to transform the vague ideals of the Paris summit into reality.

As Hillery did not inherit a proactive directorate, he relied heavily on his *cabinet* to devise and implement the reforming plans sought by the Paris summit. He was consistently preoccupied throughout his career with the need to ensure the effective organisation of his own office. He disliked constant interruptions to his own work; he also placed a high value on harmony among his staff, which was undoubtedly one of the reasons that he refused to tolerate Fogarty. He was particularly concerned to avoid unnecessary meetings with officials, who wished to divert his attention to minor problems that they could cope with themselves. As it turned out, these concerns proved largely unfounded due to the presence of the extremely capable Evelyne Pichon, who acted as gatekeeper for the Commissioner: 'In the event Evelyne proved to be all I needed in this area. She disciplined the entries to the office.'[32] But the bureaucracy in Brussels created its own challenges, not least as a result of the sheer volume of paper generated by the Commission. Each *cabinet* was bombarded with an extensive range of documents, both from other Commissioners and from their own directorate. Hillery established a highly structured system to prevent himself and his staff being lost in the paper jungle.[33] He asked each member of the *cabinet* to take responsibility for a different area of his work as Commissioner. Then as all documents arrived in triplicate, he told his staff that one copy should go to the *chef de cabinet*, one to the staff member dealing with the relevant area and one to the archivist.[34] This guaranteed that two officials were dealing with each issue and had the additional benefit of ensuring that the office was not overwhelmed by paper. The only change to the system came with the voluminous material received from DG-V, which Hillery usually had to see personally. This system was based on an 'organigram', which allocated definite functions to each member of the *cabinet*. When Ed FitzGibbon first saw the list of responsibilities he wryly commented to Hillery, 'There is no room for the flu there, Minister.'[35] A tightly-structured system succeeded in keeping the Commission's paper mountain at bay. Hillery's *cabinet* soon overcame its initial problems, operating in a highly effective and integrated way; his team made a vital contribution to the far-reaching social reforms introduced over the following three years.

While Hillery was establishing himself in Brussels, there was a change of government in Dublin. Lynch called a general election early in February, hoping to capitalise on his government's remarkable recovery since the arms crisis. But Fine Gael and Labour combined to offer a joint policy statement to the electorate, offering the real prospect of an alternative government. Hillery played no active part in the election, agreeing with the Taoiseach that it would be inappropriate for a Commissioner to get involved openly in a national campaign.[36] Yet he was not totally disengaged from Fianna Fáil politics. He quietly helped his cousin Brian Hillery in his first attempt to be elected to the Seanad. He supported Brian's efforts to secure a nomination; although the younger man did not win the election in 1973, he was elected to the Seanad four years later. Hillery returned home to vote in the election on 28 February and witnessed Fianna Fáil's first election defeat in sixteen years. The party's first preference vote remained solid, but the steady transfer pattern between Fine Gael and Labour was enough to give victory to the national coalition. Hillery was disappointed by the result, but not greatly disturbed by it. His decision to leave Irish politics looked even better in hindsight than it had at the time.

The new government, led by Liam Cosgrave and with the Labour leader, Brendan Corish, as Tánaiste, took office on 14 March 1973. Hillery watched the Cabinet appointments that concerned him directly with considerable interest:

> The news from Ireland is that the new government has been formed. Mark Clinton is the new Minister for Agriculture, of which I am glad because he is competent. The Minister for Labour is Michael O'Leary … Foreign Affairs is Garret – the Lord deliver us! Richie Ryan has Finance.[37]

Although they were divided by party allegiance, Hillery was on good terms with several of the new ministers. He had been friendly with Mark Clinton for over twenty years, since the Fine Gael man had worked at Peamount and urged a young assistant medical officer to let his name go before a selection convention. He also got on well with Garret FitzGerald. Hillery's humorous reaction to FitzGerald's appointment was provoked by a vivid recollection of the new Foreign Minister's time as a highly effective but loquacious opposition spokesman across the floor of the Dáil. Hillery set out to establish constructive relations with the new Irish government and generally succeeded in doing so. He met FitzGerald in Brussels within a couple of days of his appointment and the two men established a friendly working relationship, which endured for the rest of Hillery's term in the Commission.[38] He also provided discreet but regular briefings to the Irish ministers on key national interests in Europe, especially protection of the CAP and the development of regional policy.[39] While members of the Commission were obliged to be independent of all national governments, an obligation that Hillery took seriously, there was also an informal understanding that they looked out for national interests and kept their national representatives informed about developments in the Community.

The ministers with whom Hillery interacted most frequently over the next four years, with the exception of FitzGerald, were Labour politicians; Michael O'Leary, the new Minister for Labour, and Frank Cluskey, who acted as Parliamentary Secretary at the Department of Social Welfare. Cluskey held delegated authority over Social Welfare and also took responsibility for European social policy outside the remit of the Department of Labour. Cluskey worked closely with Hillery on various elements of social policy and influenced the final shape of the social action programme in the autumn of 1973. Hillery liked and respected Cluskey and they generally got on well, despite some inevitable political differences. The Commissioner's relations with O'Leary were much more turbulent, featuring occasional clashes at the European Parliament where O'Leary often criticised the Commission for doing too little on social policy.[40] An Irish official in Brussels summarised the situation simply: 'Paddy couldn't stand O'Leary at all. He got on extremely well with Frank [Cluskey]'.[41] The differences between Hillery and O'Leary were more about political tactics than policy; both wanted a strong European social policy, but neither believed that the other was doing enough to achieve it. Moreover, both were competing to establish their superior credentials on social policy, with Hillery having a distinct advantage, as he was promoting Community action in the area for the first time. Yet despite the tension with O'Leary, Hillery generally maintained positive relations with the coalition government and worked constructively with them to protect Irish interests in the Community.

Social action programme

The Social Affairs directorate had traditionally been concerned with providing social support for the economic objectives of the Community. The Social Fund originally provided support for the resettlement and retraining of workers affected by economic changes.[42] The Community's social policies were, in practice, largely about picking up the pieces after the job losses caused by industrial changes. This began to change in 1971, when the Council of Ministers agreed to restructure the European Social Fund, to provide assistance to workers directly affected by the implementation of Community policies. The new Fund gave greater scope for the Commission to take the initiative in deciding who to help.[43] The newly established flexibility of the Fund gave Hillery greater freedom of action and was an important asset in providing funding for more ambitious social projects. Yet despite the advantages conferred by the reform of the Fund, by 1973 neither the Commission nor the Community as a whole had developed a viable social policy to meet the widespread demand voiced by trade unions, women's groups and even national leaders, for joint action to deliver practical and visible benefits to the people of Europe. Hillery's central priority was to develop a wide-ranging European social policy, which would fulfil the general aspirations expressed by the Paris summit 'to give Europe a human face' and demonstrate that the Community was more than just an economic organisation.

While the social action programme was intended to make a real difference to the lives of ordinary Europeans, Hillery was keenly aware that the reform proposals would have to secure broad support within the Commission and from national governments jealous of their sovereignty. He warned his *cabinet* that they had to set realistic and achievable goals for the programme. This meant reining in the enthusiasm of senior staff in DG-V who sought rapid integration of social policies across the member states regardless of the attitudes of national governments.[44] Hillery was privately concerned at 'the excited and fantastic views of the some of the staff', who came up with impractical schemes for extending the remit of the Community. He feared that attempts by Commission officials to restrict the power of national governments in social policy would backfire disastrously: 'It was a kind of disease expecting to unify Europe quickly and take power from the national governments as if they did not want the power ... It was a talk shop and few seemed to know how achievements were won.'[45] He told Ed FitzGibbon to take charge of drafting the programme within DG-V, giving his new *chef de cabinet* broad guidelines on the major proposals to be included. Hillery wanted to include plans to provide employment opportunities for people with disabilities and to protect migrant workers; he was also concerned to overcome legal discrimination against women in pay and working conditions, which was still a reality of life in several European countries, including Ireland.[46] These ideas became key elements of the programme put before the Commission and the national governments. The programme went through several drafts; the final text was hammered out between Ed FitzGibbon and Jean Degimbe, a senior member of Ortoli's *cabinet*.[47] Hillery presented the draft programme to the Commission early in April 1973 and publicly suggested that it would become Community policy by the end of the year, in line with the declaration of the Paris summit.

The key areas outlined by the programme included full and better employment, the improvement of living and working conditions, and greater participation by workers and management in the economic and social decisions of the Community.[48] The promotion of employment was a key element of the programme, which envisaged the payment of EEC grants to encourage the creation of employment and fund retraining programmes; the draft programme proposed a major upgrading of vocational training, Community assistance to employees with disabilities and equality of treatment for migrant workers. The proposals on working conditions involved the establishment of minimum standards of social protection and the abolition of job discrimination against women. The plan also envisaged the introduction of worker participation in industrial enterprises and the development of improved structures for participation by the 'social partners' in decision-making at European level.[49] The draft programme set out an ambitious vision for a comprehensive European social policy.

It was hardly surprising that a radical social action programme faced opposition within the Commission, despite its formal commitment to joint action on social policy. Christopher Soames, the British Conservative who was Commissioner for External Relations, was sceptical about any measures to improve the working conditions of marginalised groups, but this view at least commanded virtually no support within the college. Hillery was in turn amused and appalled by Soames' bombastic political style: 'Soames even made a most offensive joke about the handicapped one day but he did not realise it was offensive. It was the way he saw things and he was in such matters very near the early teenager in what he thought was funny'.[50] Altiero Spinelli, the left-wing Italian Commissioner for Industry, was a more surprising critic of elements of the programme, while warmly supporting it in principle.[51] The most dangerous obstacle to Hillery's plans came from several Commissioners who accepted the need for a European social policy in theory, but sought to dilute the programme in practice, not least because the new social policies would intrude on their own turf. The level of hesitancy and outright scepticism at the proposed reforms could be gauged from the fact that the Commission deferred a decision when Hillery first presented the programme in early April. Several members argued that certain proposals, especially relating to employment policy, were unrealistic and likely to provoke opposition in the Council of Ministers; journalists were then briefed, inaccurately, that the opposition to the programme was motivated by concerns that it was not ambitious enough.[52] In fact the opposite was true. Hillery lobbied his colleagues extensively in support of the programme, speaking to each member individually before the various meetings on the issue.[53] Ortoli, who was concerned above all to maintain the unity of the Commission, suggested that further study was required on some aspects of the programme. The outcome was a qualified success for Hillery. He agreed to produce broad policy guidelines for the programme, which would be presented as a discussion document to the Ministers on the Social Affairs Council. This apparent tactical retreat gave Hillery almost everything he wanted. The Commission approved the guidelines, which maintained almost all the key principles of the original proposal, with only minor amendments, on 18 April 1973.[54] The social action programme had passed the first hurdle, but a more difficult struggle lay ahead.

The Council of Ministers made no decision on the guidelines at their meeting in May 1973, but no opposition to the programme materialised and Hillery was able to proceed with the development of the proposals. He made a series of visits to European capitals throughout 1973, lobbying governments to support the social action programme and briefing key interest groups on his proposals. He was particularly concerned to involve the trade unions in the planning of the social reforms; he identified the unions as his department's key constituency and set out to mobilise broad trade union support for his plans. Hillery established personal connections with union leaders across the Community in his first year in office. He visited Bonn as early as February 1973, discussing the proposed social action programme with Hans Vetter, the powerful head of the West German trade union confederation, the DGB. Vetter was supportive and took a strategic view of how to secure a progressive European social policy; he urged Hillery not to be rushed into producing an inadequate programme by pressure from ministers or European officials, but to 'take our time deliberately to produce a good programme ... '.[55] Hillery also opened discussions with trade union leaders in Belgium, Luxembourg, Italy and France early in his term as Commissioner. He gradually developed friendly connections with trade union peak organisations in all the member states. Ireland was no exception. Hillery's success in building a constructive relationship with the ICTU would prove a useful asset in the subsequent struggle with the Irish government over equal pay for women. His increasing success in developing a constructive dialogue with national trade union organisations did not command universal approval among their governments; he discovered official unease within the French government at such an active approach by a Commissioner:

> I went to Paris, I asked for appointments with all the trade unions, I think there were nine of them. I spent a whole day interviewing them in French. Later at some reception, the French ambassador [to the Community] said, 'You were in Paris – that's very good, very good. – I'm not sure the President would like it if you went too frequently.'[56]

The apparently minor episode underlined acute French sensitivity about the prospect of an over-mighty Commission. This elegant warning did not deter Hillery from maintaining his contacts with French trade unions. He needed no reminder that the success of his social initiatives ultimately depended on maintaining political support, not only from national governments but also more broadly from institutions of civil society.

The Irish Commissioner also forged links with the British trade union movement, although such contacts were more difficult because the British Labour Party and much of the union movement opposed EEC membership in the early 1970s. Hillery's contacts with the British union leaders often took the form of private meetings, unknown even to other members of the Commission. He arranged a private meeting in June 1973 with Vic Feather, general secretary of the British TUC, and Jack Jones, the influential head of the Transport and General Workers Union, at a European trade union conference in Rome, to discuss the social action programme. The meeting in June 1973 provoked reports in the Irish media claiming that Hillery had received a 'personal rebuff' from the British trade union leaders. The confusion arose from leisurely timekeeping and rhetorical overload by Italian trade unionists:

> I noticed that the meeting was not called to order for ages after the appointed time. The speech of one secretary general was very long. I left after about an hour as we had arranged to meet, but Feather and Jones were on the podium as fraternal delegates, so they could not get away until he finished, which was something like three hours after he started. I remember waiting for them, we had lunch in the Piazza Navona in Rome. Then *The Irish Times* had a bit of news that I had been 'snubbed by the British trade unions!'[57]

Despite this inauspicious start, Hillery opened a line of communication to the British union leaders and developed strong connections with the TUC. He had regular meetings with Len Murray, Feather's deputy and eventual successor as head of the TUC. Murray greeted Hillery at their first meeting with the catchphrase 'What can we do for you? What can we do to you?'; he told Hillery it was the question they asked about the people they were dealing with.[58] Hillery was only too familiar with the confrontational model of industrial relations, which had been developed to a fine art in Britain, from his own experience as Minister for Labour. He met trade unions and employers separately in Ireland and Britain to brief them on the social action programme. He followed a very different practice in several continental states, where the concepts of social partnership and consensus in economic decision-making were firmly established; in Denmark he met management and unions jointly to explain the programme.[59] Hillery's extensive consultations in 1973 opened up a constructive dialogue between national trade union movements and the Community; more significantly in the short-term, his lobbying helped to maintain the momentum for major social reform and to stimulate trade union support for his efforts to create a European social policy.

The consultations were not simply window dressing to legitimise decisions that the Commission had already made. Hillery's discussions with national governments and trade unions influenced the final shape of the social action programme. The most notable development was the result of an initiative by Frank Cluskey, who saw the opportunity to secure Community support for coherent action against poverty.[60] When Hillery met Cluskey and Corish in Dublin on 3 September 1973, Cluskey proposed the inclusion of pilot projects targeting poverty in the programme, inspired in part by the example of anti-poverty initiatives launched by Lyndon Johnson's administration in the United States during the 1960s. Tony Brown, who served as special adviser to Cluskey, recalled that the Irish representatives were pushing an open door:

> Frank realised that it was not likely to be feasible to establish some huge programme, but what he wanted to do was to get the issue onto the agenda and to set up a programme and begin to get things done. Hillery said, 'Yes, that's a good idea, but we're moving very quickly now. I want this document to go to the Council in December; can you provide me with something to work on quickly?' Cluskey and Corish said they would. So on the following day Cluskey told me and Flor O'Mahony [adviser to

Corish] and two or three civil servants to draw up a document.[61]

Cluskey's advisers drafted a short document outlining ideas for a poverty action programme, including pilot schemes to combat poverty in selected areas. Tony Brown delivered the proposal to Hillery's *cabinet* in Brussels on 11 September.[62] Hillery backed the initiative strongly and a revised version of the proposal was included in the social action programme approved by the Commission.[63]

Hillery presented the final draft of the social action programme to the Commission in the last week of September. His proposals set out 40 different recommendations for Community action on social issues, with the ultimate objective of achieving a social union as well as an economic Community.[64] A wide range of new initiatives to expand and upgrade vocational training formed a central part of the programme. These measures included proposals for a European Centre for Vocational Training and the introduction of general training incentives, involving income supplements to unemployed workers undergoing training or retraining.[65] The programme sought a far-reaching expansion of social policy to provide effective assistance for migrant workers, people with disabilities and 'the chronically poor'.[66] The most significant reforms affecting wages and working conditions were the implementation of equal pay for equal work between men and women, the introduction of a 40-hour working week across the Community and the adoption of four weeks' paid holidays for workers. Proposals for expanded health and safety programmes as well as a new Foundation to conduct research on living and working conditions were also included.[67] The programme proposed new legislation to protect workers from arbitrary dismissal, the development of formal worker participation in decision-making by industrial enterprises and enhanced procedures for consultation with the social partners at European level.[68] The European social policy proposed by Hillery was radical, wide-ranging and ambitious. It was also expensive – while the existing Social Fund amounted to less than 100 million units of account in 1973, the total cost of European social projects, including

the social action programme, would come to about 550 million units of
account in the 1976 budget. The high cost of the programme increased
the prospect of internal opposition within the Commission and inspired
speculation among Irish journalists in Brussels that Hillery would be
unable to get approval for his social programme at all.[69]

Yet Hillery held considerable political leverage in winning support for
the substance of his proposals, whatever financial limitations might be
imposed on the programme. While some members of the Commission
were unenthusiastic about the more radical elements of the programme,
they could not block it due to the mandate given by the national leaders.
Hillery constantly reiterated that the Paris summit had given a mandate
for Community action and the Commission could not be seen to be
dragging its feet. The debate was about what kind of social action
programme the Commission would eventually come up with. Ed
FitzGibbon recalled that 'it was a battle to get it through'.[70] Another Irish
official in attendance at the meetings remembered that cultural and
language differences within the Commission produced some bizarre and
hilarious exchanges:

> The social action programme was being discussed. Spinelli
> was waxing lyrical about how the trade unions wanted to
> be brought on-side, he went on for about a quarter of an
> hour about the need to bring them in and he said – 'They
> want to be sucked …' and Soames said in a very tired voice
> – 'Don't we all, dear boy, don't we all.'[71]

On a more serious level, there were undoubtedly concerns within the
Commission at the cost and feasibility of Hillery's proposals. He sought
to overcome such reservations by proposing to implement the programme
on a phased basis; the actions given the highest priority would come into
effect immediately, while a second tranche would be implemented in
1974–6 and the remainder would be introduced over the following three
years.[72] The Commission broadly accepted the logic of this approach,
although it also reduced the number of projects identified by Hillery as

immediate priorities from fourteen to seven, with four more projects to be implemented in the short term.[73] Following a protracted debate within the college, Hillery eventually prevailed. The Commission approved the social action programme on 24 October 1973. He secured the backing of the European executive for far-reaching social reforms, at the price of some concessions over the phasing-in of the programme.

Hillery moved swiftly to mobilise public support for his plans, holding a press conference in Brussels on the day after the Commission's decision. He gave a relaxed and authoritative performance, buoyed up by the positive verdict from his colleagues. He made a deliberate pitch for the backing of the trade unions, identifying himself unequivocally with the cause of organised labour:

> A Minister for Labour, which I regard myself as being equivalent to ... should be on the side of the workers. The management side is able to take care of themselves. When working on human problems, one must respond to the anxieties and insecurities of the workers, and so we took more notice of trade union representations.[74]

His striking public declaration that he was on the side of labour was designed to overcome the initial scepticism of trade union leaders, who had heard promises of action on social issues from the Community many times before, only to be disappointed by the inability of the Commission to produce a viable plan or by gridlock within the Community institutions.[75] But he had tangible evidence to convince trade union leaders that it was different on this occasion; the Commission had developed a far-reaching programme of social reform and was putting it to the Council of Ministers. Irish union leaders who recalled his term as Minister for Labour, when he staunchly opposed union demands for wage increases, might have enjoyed a wry smile at his declaration that he was 'on the side of the workers'. Yet Hillery could reasonably maintain that the situation was entirely different; he was no longer attempting to manage industrial strife, but to introduce a comprehensive European social policy.

The Commissioner's press conference also had another intended target: the Social Affairs Council, consisting of the ministers who would ultimately decide the fate of his social action programme. He had to strike a difficult balance – it was vital to promote the programme effectively, not least because public support would greatly increase the prospect of its adoption by the ministers, but equally he had to avoid the appearance of dictating to the Council. Hillery expressed confidence that the Council would adopt the social action programme, but added the classic qualification: 'I don't think a pessimist would get very far in this job.'[76] Having pointed out that he was working on the basis of a political mandate given by the heads of state and government, he proceeded to lay down a quiet but explicit challenge for the Council: 'They now have a draft programme which is a full response to the political realities of the day. It will fully test the will of the council.'[77] He managed a skilful balancing act, exerting subtle pressure on the Council to adopt his plans, while avoiding any suggestion that he was usurping their authority to make the final decision.

Despite the green light given by the Paris summit, getting the social action programme approved by the Council was no easy task. The international economic outlook deteriorated dramatically in the autumn of 1973, due mainly to the Arab–Israeli conflict and the resulting turmoil in the Middle East. Following the outbreak of war between Israel and its main Arab enemies, Egypt and Syria, in October 1973, the Arab oil producers, represented by OPEC, enforced a cut in oil production, acting in solidarity with their Arab neighbours. Then in response to the rapid dispatch of US military aid to Israel, Saudi Arabia went further by imposing a complete embargo on oil sales to the United States and the Netherlands, combined with a sharp cut in oil supplies to other developed countries.[78] The first oil shock had a devastating impact on European economies, driving up inflation and threatening employment throughout the developed world. The oil crisis contributed greatly to the emergence of 'stagflation' – the combination of high inflation and sluggish economic growth that afflicted much of the developed world by the mid-1970s. The crisis plunged the Community into economic and political turmoil, threatening all the constructive policy developments that the national leaders had contemplated benignly in the golden glow of economic prosperity. Tony Brown believed that 'the whole concept of social policy development was imperilled.'[79]

Hillery had only just secured the approval of the Commission for the social action programme when the effects of the oil crisis began to be felt throughout Europe. Any hesitation on his part at this stage would have had fatal consequences, not just for the programme itself, but for the whole project of a European social policy. He kept his nerve and ensured that his reforming plans were not derailed by the abrupt economic slump. He maintained quiet pressure on the national governments to honour their commitments, continuing his consultations with Social Affairs ministers and operating on the basis that the Council would keep to the original timetable for adopting the programme. He combined private persuasion with effective public promotion of the social reforms. Hillery issued a public statement on 20 November during a visit to Utrecht, in Holland, declaring that the Community would be judged by its success in developing a real social policy. He commented that the Council meeting in December would 'determine the outcome of social union, which was an essential objective in its own right, and an essential part of the concept of European unity'.[80] He hammered home a similar message in his address to the European Parliament on 10 December, which occurred strategically on the eve of the Council meeting. Hillery acknowledged that the oil crisis threatened jobs and living standards throughout the Community. But he also told the MEPs that the poor would suffer most from the economic effects of the crisis and urged the Council to adopt the social action programme.[81] Hillery's shrewdly calculated tactics in the run-up to the Council meeting maintained the political momentum for the development of a European social policy and helped to create public expectation that the Council would do the right thing by approving the social action programme.

Sharp divisions within the Council itself, especially between wealthy countries and poorer member states such as Ireland, complicated the process of agreeing a European social policy. Michael O'Leary, speaking at a weekend seminar organised by the Irish Council of the European Movement in Dublin, strongly criticised Hillery's plans on 27 October. The Irish minister claimed that the social programme was much too limited and did not go far enough towards ensuring full employment; he was particularly concerned that it did not deliver sufficient resources to overcome regional imbalances within the Community.[82] O'Leary's pronouncements lacked much sense of realism in the drastically altered economic circumstances facing the Community by October 1973. Hillery refuted without much difficulty the Irish minister's arguments that the social action programme had already been significantly watered down even before it reached the Social Affairs Council. Yet both O'Leary and Cluskey raised a legitimate concern, which was by no means restricted to Ireland, that the Council might rubber-stamp the programme, without giving poorer member states the resources they needed to implement it. The Irish and Italian ministers sought to ensure that the Community made an unequivocal commitment to find financial resources that would match policy recommendations.[83] As this money could only come from the wealthy states, especially West Germany, which was already the long-standing paymaster of the EEC, the cost of paying for the programme emerged as a key sticking point that threatened to block agreement within the Council.

The Social Affairs Council gave its verdict on 11–12 December 1973, following a marathon negotiating session that went on into the early hours of the following morning. The list of immediate priorities for joint action, submitted by Hillery as part of the programme, was amended by the ministers to reflect national political concerns. But the revised list of political priorities was broadly satisfactory to Hillery, incorporating most of the key points he had sought. Any items dropped from the priority list remained in the programme itself and Hillery retained the freedom to introduce detailed proposals to implement them.[84] The Council added the proposal for pilot schemes to combat poverty to the priority list, in a move instigated by the Irish delegation, but fully supported by Hillery. The only real setback Hillery suffered was the disappearance of his proposal for income support to workers undergoing training. As Germany was the only member state to have a comprehensive scheme offering income support for workers in training, he had aimed to secure the introduction of such schemes in all member states, with Community funding to assist the poorer countries. But an Irish official in his *cabinet* told journalists shortly afterwards that it was 'an important, costly point which did not come off'.[85] The cost of the proposal was the crucial stumbling block; it was simply too expensive to get through the Council. Hillery had no doubt that it was a decisive setback for the project and publicly expressed his disappointment at the decision; he was unhappy that Ireland and Italy did not fight harder for Community support for workers in training, as they would have had most to gain from the scheme.[86]

The financing of the programme as a whole proved the most contentious issue and at one stage threatened to cause the Council to break up without full agreement – which would have been a devastating blow to Hillery's plans. The Danish President of the Council suggested that the controversial question of financing the programme could be referred to the summit of national leaders in Copenhagen later in the same week. But the ministers rejected this option and agreed instead that the resources should be found through a restructuring and extension of the European Social Fund.[87] The meeting dragged on throughout the day and well into the night, dominated by constant reminders of the crisis engulfing Europe. The Danish government lost a key vote on the day of the Council itself. The Danish ministers discovered in the middle of the afternoon that their government had been defeated in parliament over austerity measures imposed as a result of high fuel prices; there was a short adjournment while they were briefed on the events in Copenhagen, before a shaken Danish President resumed the meeting. Tony Brown had no doubt of Hillery's pivotal part in preventing the breakdown of the negotiations: 'Hillery's role in that Council meeting was extraordinary in terms of holding the thing together, particularly when the Danish crisis happened.'[88] Hillery conducted a series of bilateral talks with the national delegations to resolve the remaining differences between them. The Council finally approved the social action programme around 3.30 on the morning of Wednesday 12 December.[89] The programme agreed by the

ministers contained almost all of the key priorities sought by Hillery, with
the important exception of the ambitious vocational training scheme. The
decision amounted to approval in principle for the vast majority of the
reforming plans that he proposed. The social action programme came into
effect following a formal resolution passed by the Council on 21 January
1974, which embodied the decisions made at the nocturnal meeting in
December.[90] While the challenge of compiling specific directives to
implement the programme still lay ahead, Hillery had obtained the crucial
stamp of legitimacy for his reforming plans from the member states.

The frequently tortuous process that led to the negotiation and
eventual acceptance of the social action programme was a triumph for
Hillery. He determined the shape of the original programme, ensuring
that it was a radical but attainable charter for reform. He played the crucial
part in securing the sometimes grudging consent of his colleagues on the
Commission, getting his plans through the protracted internal debates of
the college essentially intact. Yet Hillery's most vital contribution was to
be found in his painstaking negotiations with national governments and
his apparently endless round of consultations with key interest groups,
particularly the trade unions. He secured the adoption of the social action
programme at a time when delay would almost certainly have been
disastrous; a Community social policy, universally regarded as a vital
necessity in 1972, would increasingly have appeared an impractical luxury
in the harsher economic climate of the mid-1970s. Other cherished
aspirations fell by the wayside in the same era, none more illustrious than
economic and monetary union, which was quietly abandoned for almost
two decades. The same could easily have happened to social reform. It
was due above all to Hillery's determination and political skill that the
ideal of a European social policy became a reality despite an increasingly
unfavourable economic and political backdrop.

17.

Social Reform

The implications of the oil crisis for social policy were ominous. The consensus that had underpinned European social reform was increasingly threatened by the economic recession. John McColgan recalled the impact of the abrupt change in the economic climate: 'Once the oil crisis came in, it made it much harder to get any enthusiasm for social policies. It was wickedly disappointing.'[1] The prospects for further social advances were also affected by changes at the highest level of European politics. Georges Pompidou died in April 1974; he was succeeded as President of France by Valéry Giscard d'Estaing. Pompidou's death was a bitter blow to Ortoli, who had been a close ally of the former President but had no influence with his successor.[2] Hillery was more disturbed by the second political shock of 1974. Willy Brandt resigned as Chancellor of the Federal Republic of Germany on 6 May, following the arrest of his close personal aide, Günter Guillaume, who was an East German spy.[3] The leading national advocates of giving Europe 'a human face' had been removed from the scene. Hillery admired Brandt and was worried at his abrupt fall from power. He told Michael Foot, who had recently become Employment Secretary in Britain, a fortnight after the Chancellor's resignation, that the EEC had been 'too much of an economic Community and Brandt, who was a force in humanising it, had now disappeared from the scene'.[4] The new Chancellor, Helmut Schmidt, was firmly supportive of European integration, but was more critical of the Commission than his predecessor, and was concerned to limit the impact of the economic crisis on West Germany. The German government took an increasingly restrictive approach to Community spending, generally casting a jaundiced eye on new spending proposals from the Commission.[5] The effect of the transition to new leaders in France and West Germany was less than it might have been a year earlier, largely because Hillery had already secured the formal backing of the Council for the social action programme. He also acted decisively to implement the key elements of the programme in 1974, operating on the principle that he had outlined to his press conference in Brussels the previous October: 'My experience in politics shows that it is best to do what you can now, and not wait until later.'[6] He ensured that several draft directives were submitted to the Council even before the programme was formally approved. Hillery took full advantage of the narrow window of opportunity, provided by continuing political support for social reform, before it disappeared in the wake of increasing economic turbulence.

Hillery reshuffled his *cabinet* in the summer of 1974, just as the implementation of the programme was beginning. The Department of Foreign Affairs sought John McColgan's services in May 1974, asking him to take up a senior position in the Northern Ireland section. McColgan offered to stay in Brussels, but Hillery urged him to accept the offer, advising his friend to think of his career. McColgan retained an enduring memory of Hillery's generosity:

> He said 'Garret was looking for you, John.' I said I would be happy to stay with him. Paddy replied, 'Well, that's very nice to hear, John, but you are a young man and you are at the beginning of your career. You have done what I wanted you to do for me, it's plain sailing now. Do what's best for

you.' It was the most generous response I ever heard from an Irish minister.[7]

John McColgan decided to return to Dublin with Hillery's blessing. The exchange highlighted not only Hillery's generosity but his confidence that he had mastered the intricacies of the European Commission. Hillery was an expert practitioner in the European corridors of power by the summer of 1974. McColgan helped to stabilise the *cabinet* after Fogarty's acrimonious departure. Hillery knew that his *cabinet* was now working well and was confident, rightly as it turned out, that it could absorb changes in personnel without difficulty.

He succeeded in finding an equally capable replacement for McColgan, making a creative choice from outside the ranks of the Irish civil service. Hillery immediately approached Neville Keery to take over the key position of deputy *chef de cabinet*. Keery, who had contested the 1973 general election unsuccessfully for Fianna Fáil, already worked for the Commission; he had been appointed as Deputy Director of its Dublin office in 1973. The former Senator readily agreed to join the *cabinet* in May 1974, and he remained with Hillery in Brussels until the end of his term. At the same time as McColgan's departure for Dublin, Marcus McInerney accepted promotion to a post within the Directorate General on Agriculture. Seán Ó hEigeartaigh, a Cork man who had previously been an official of the Department of Finance, replaced McInerney in the *cabinet*.[8] Both of the new members performed key functions within the *cabinet*. Ó hEigeartaigh became its expert on agriculture, although his activity also extended to other policy areas; agriculture was always an area of vital concern to Irish governments and Hillery was a consistent defender of the CAP at meetings of the Commission. Keery took responsibility for dealing with Hillery's interaction with the European Parliament and preparing draft speeches for his public appearances.[9] Keery's political background and administrative expertise made him a valuable addition to Hillery's staff. The broad range of expertise and ability within his *cabinet* served Hillery's purpose admirably. While his main focus was undeniably the social action programme, he was concerned to make an informed contribution across the whole range of the Commission's activity.

Despite the impact of the economic crisis, the approval of the social action programme opened up the most productive and influential period of Hillery's term as a Commissioner. The reforms were to be implemented in three stages, with the first segment to be acted on immediately. The first seven policy measures included aid to migrant workers and employees with disabilities, health and safety measures, a directive regulating mass redundancies and equal pay for equal work between men and women.[10] The Council adopted all seven of these initiatives by the summer of 1975. The second phase of Hillery's plans contained a series of initiatives, identified as 'priority actions' by the Commission, which were to be put before the Council for decision between April 1974 and December 1976.[11] Many of these reforms were also approved before the end of Hillery's term. The final element of the programme was the most aspirational; it was composed of 'other supporting actions' and included a wide variety of proposals that were seen as valuable, but not urgent priorities.[12] Several of these items took the form of studies on different areas of social policy, which were implemented over a longer period.

Hillery accepted the phased nature of the programme as a political and financial necessity. The Commission had determined the order of the policies based mainly on their feasibility; this selection was modified by the Council to reflect national political concerns and financial constraints dictated by the oil crisis. Although he did not entirely agree with the order of priorities set by the Social Affairs ministers, Hillery recognised the opportunity to secure the rapid implementation of reforming plans, which had been identified as priorities by the national governments. He secured the agreement of the Council in June 1974 to provide financial assistance from the Social Fund to migrant workers and employees with disabilities.[13] This marked a significant departure from the original purpose of the Fund, which had been used essentially as an emergency service to assist unemployed workers in areas affected by industrial decline or Community economic policies.

The Commission's proposals on health and safety were useful but modest. The Council agreed in June to establish an Advisory Committee on safety and health protection at work, which would assist the Commission in preparing regulations on health and safety in the workplace and contribute to the formulation of Community policies in the area.[14] This move was combined with an expansion of EEC regulation in the mining industries; the competence of the Mines Safety and Health Commission, which had previously been restricted to coal mining, was extended to oversee measures for the safety of workers in all mineral extracting industries.[15] The two decisions sailed through the Council, not least because they had minimal financial implications. The initiatives were significant mainly as a portent of things to come, reflecting the first moves towards intervention by the Community to protect occupational health and safety.

Hillery's plans for new European research centres were equally uncontroversial. He secured the establishment of a specialised unit, the European Centre for the Development of Vocational Training, which was intended to promote the co-ordination of training standards and qualifications between member states.[16] The Centre's mission was to conduct research and disseminate information throughout the Community on vocational training. The Council approved the proposal in February 1975, deciding to base the new Centre in West Berlin.[17] The Centre had obvious potential as a research unit and offered a useful forum for the trade unions and employers represented on its board of management. A similar proposal from the Commission saw the creation of the Foundation for the Improvement of Living and Working Conditions, which was designed to conduct research and promote the exchange of information on social, labour and environmental problems within the EEC.[18] The Foundation was the first new European institution to be based in Dublin; it was established in 1976, with a wide remit involving the development of studies on ways of humanising work, health and safety, worker participation, pollution and urban renewal.[19] These initiatives were undoubtedly worthwhile and could be expected to offer long-term benefits in their contribution to European policy-making. But journalists were not slow to point out that the new foundations would do little to combat increasing unemployment and offered few immediate benefits, except perhaps to the people of Dublin and West Berlin.[20]

The initiative to regulate mass redundancies had more effect in the short term, although it also secured consensus among the member states without great difficulty. The Commission's proposal set out to ensure that collective redundancies could not be undertaken in an arbitrary fashion, or without any consultation with workers' representatives and public authorities. This was achieved by securing the harmonisation of national laws on mass redundancies.[21] This moderate measure of worker protection was generally accepted by the member states, although there was some disagreement over the minimum number of redundancies that would attract protection under the directive.[22] The dispute was resolved by setting a series of minimum numbers depending on the size of the firm, starting with ten workers in a company with less than one hundred employees.[23] The Social Affairs ministers approved the initiative in December 1974. The directive required employers to give thirty days' notice of any collective redundancies to workers' representatives and to the local public authorities; the employers were obliged to initiate consultations with workers' representatives before undertaking collective redundancies.[24] The Council also adopted another proposal initiated by the Social Affairs directorate in 1974, which protected the entitlements of employees in the event of commercial mergers or takeovers.[25] The initiatives gave credibility to Hillery's claim in October 1973 that he was on the side of labour, and marked the beginning of Community activism to enhance the rights of employees.

Many of these reforms were uncontroversial, sometimes due to their modest cost or because most member states were already moving in the same direction, as had been the case with the regulation on mass redundancies.[26] Several of the initiatives did not offer significant advances in the short term, even if they had valuable potential over a longer period. Yet this was certainly not true of all the Commission's proposals. The reforms promoted by Hillery on equal pay and equal treatment for women had a far-reaching impact on member states in the short term. A new poverty action programme and his initiatives to enhance the status of migrant workers were less dramatic, but equally important in establishing Community policies to assist underprivileged social categories for the first time.

Equal pay

Equal pay between men and women for equal work was the reform with which Hillery was to be most associated, especially in his own country, not least because the Irish government made an inept and unsuccessful attempt to delay its introduction. The EEC had long since accepted equal pay in principle, but had shied away from enforcing it in practice. The principle of equal pay between men and women was recognised by Article 119 of the Treaty of Rome, but had not been implemented by several European states, including Ireland and Britain. Hillery submitted a draft decision on equal pay to the Social Affairs Council in December 1973. This was only the initial step in the usual process of consultation within Community institutions, as Hillery sought to build consensus for his plans. He secured the backing of the European Parliament and the Economic and Social Committee for the proposal in 1974. The Council agreed the draft directive on equal pay on 17 December 1974.[27]

The directive established minimum legal protection for women with regard to their right to equal pay, requiring the establishment of legal equality in pay structures between men and women across the Community. The decision set out to secure 'the elimination of all discrimination on grounds of sex with regard to all aspects and conditions of remuneration'.[28] The initiative had wide-ranging implications for member states that had done little to prepare for equal pay, requiring the abolition of discrimination in national laws relating to pay and the removal of formal inequalities in pay scales. Collective agreements and individual contracts of employment that did not reflect the principle of equal pay were to be amended or declared null and void. The directive also protected workers who took legal claims for equal pay through the courts, preventing the dismissal of female employees as a reaction to complaints or legal proceedings aimed at enforcing compliance with the new legislation.[29] The member states were obliged to introduce national legislation to ensure full compliance with the directive and to implement the initiative within a year of its introduction. The directive was formally issued on 10 February 1975, under the Irish presidency of the EEC; it was signed by Garret FitzGerald, as President of the Council of Foreign Ministers.

Yet before the end of the year, Ireland would be the only member state seeking to postpone the introduction of equal pay. This was particularly ironic, as Michael O'Leary had piloted national legislation through the Dáil in July 1974 that provided for the enforcement of equal pay in Ireland by 1 January 1976, over a month before the deadline set by the Community.[30] It even appeared briefly that Ireland was slightly ahead of the rest of Europe in vindicating the rights of female workers. This illusion was soon dispelled. The Irish government faced strong pressure from the FUE and other employers' organisations to defer equal pay at least until 1978. The employers based their case primarily on the economic recession triggered by the oil crisis, arguing that the rapid introduction of equal pay would be disastrous for manufacturing industry in the prevailing economic circumstances. The Irish economy was unquestionably undergoing a severe crisis, driven by unfavourable international and domestic conditions; unemployment in Ireland reached 10.5 per cent in January 1976, the highest level of any EEC country. A coalition of business lobby groups mounted a campaign warning of dire consequences if equal pay was implemented immediately, claiming that 5,000 jobs could be lost if the legislation came into effect as planned.[31] Hillery was sceptical of these prophecies of doom and determined to defend his initiative. He categorically reiterated the Community's commitment to equal pay shortly after the directive was approved. He told a news briefing in Dublin on 28 February 1975 that the new directive was binding on all member states and could not be set aside unilaterally by a single country: 'The law is now there and it has to be implemented.'[32] The employers' case secured considerable support in Ireland, but it suffered from at least two key flaws that Hillery rapidly exploited. He pointed out that the entire argument for postponing equal pay rested on an assumption that some industries could survive only by maintaining lower wages for the female section of their workforce; trade unions rejected the general argument that raising wages would lead to the collapse of industries, and he saw no reason why it should be any different for female workers. Moreover, while the economic conditions were far from favourable for any new initiative on pay, there was no ideal time to introduce pay increases, and indeed, there was no guarantee that conditions would be any better in two years.[33] Hillery was responding directly to the complaints of Irish employers, but his press conference was also a shot across the government's bows. He delivered an equally uncompromising message on 13 June to female leaders of the European Trade Union Confederation in Dublin Castle, assuring the meeting of female trade unionists that measures to establish equality for women would not be sidelined as a result of the recession. He suggested that equal treatment of women was a defining issue for the Community itself: 'We must ask ourselves what kind of Community we want to build. Is it to be one in which the situation of underprivileged groups is to be improved only in times of prosperity when the well-off have a bit extra to throw away?'[34]

Hillery's warnings did not deter his counterparts in Dublin, who either did not take him seriously or were more afraid of the domestic backlash to equal pay than the reaction of the European Commission. The Minister for Finance, Richie Ryan, told the FUE in September that the legislation would be reviewed if employers and trade unions could agree that jobs would be lost under equal pay.[35] This was a definite signal that the government was preparing a U-turn, despite the new European directive. Then, in December, the Labour Court upheld an agreement between the Federation of Irish Footwear Manufacturers and two unions representing factory workers in the footwear industry, providing that negotiations for equal pay should be delayed until July 1976. The Court found that the immediate application of equal pay could cause the loss of up to 700 jobs in the industry.[36] The footwear industry, which had a substantial proportion of female employees, undoubtedly faced real difficulties in adapting to the directive. The Commission accepted that the industry deserved special consideration and Hillery was willing to recommend assistance for the industry from the Social Fund to ease the transition.[37]

But instead, the report by the Labour Court provided a political fig leaf to justify a full-scale reversal of the government's position. Cosgrave announced in the Dáil on 17 December 1975 that the government would be amending its own legislation to postpone the implementation of equal pay.[38]

The government itself was divided over equal pay. Richie Ryan sought the exclusion of the public sector from equal pay for two years, combined with a temporary exemption for private sector firms. The Taoiseach's department favoured an across-the-board exemption for Ireland until December 1976.[39] Michael O'Leary resisted proposals for a blanket exemption from equal pay; he persuaded the government that an attempt to exclude the public sector from the directive would be futile and politically damaging.[40] But his solution for the private sector proved equally controversial and ultimately unattainable. The Minister for Labour sought to allow firms to defer equal pay for up to two years, wherever 'the viability of companies or the maintenance of employment would be put at risk.'[41] His draft legislation provided for a temporary opt-out by individual companies, if the employers and trade unions negotiated an agreement to postpone equal pay. The government essentially adopted O'Leary's approach for the private sector and agreed on 7 January 1976 to apply for a partial derogation from the equal pay directive.[42] The proposed derogation was justified as a measure to protect employment under Article 135 of the original Treaty of Accession. The Cabinet did not seek an exemption for the public service, which maintained a higher salary scale for married men than it did for women and single men, as well as pay discrimination based on gender in certain grades. Instead the government announced on 21 January 1976 that discrimination in salary scales based solely on gender would be abolished immediately; but the unequal pay scales linked to marriage would be maintained, with the proviso that married women would be placed on the same salary scales as married men.[43] This merely substituted discrimination by marital status for discrimination based on gender. O'Leary informed the Dáil on 12 February 1976 that the amending legislation would apply only to a minority of workers in the private sector.[44] If this was correct it was difficult to understand why the Cabinet proceeded with such a confused and half-baked measure in the first place. It was a muddled compromise, which made little practical sense and would have ensured that female workers were still subject to pay discrimination.

But the final decision on the deferral of equal pay in Ireland rested not with the Irish government, but with the Commission, and specifically, with the man who had introduced the directive in the first place – Paddy Hillery. The Commission would decide collectively on the Irish request, but Hillery's views carried particular weight, as he had secured the passage of the European legislation and was responsible for overseeing its implementation. Supporters and opponents of the Irish derogation descended on Brussels and Strasbourg to besiege the Commission and the European Parliament before the directive came into effect on 12 February 1976. The Irish Commissioner suffered from no shortage of advice on what to do, much of it given publicly by outraged trade unionists and advocates for women's rights. The ICTU publicly condemned the government's 'incredible decision' on equal pay and made strong representations to Hillery to maintain the original policy; their submission denounced the government's amending legislation as 'a serious infringement of civil liberty and human rights'.[45] Hilda Tweedy, chairperson of the Irish Council for the Status of Women, led a delegation of activists from women's groups to lobby Hillery directly against the government's policy.[46] Yet he also faced considerable pressure to allow the derogation. Representatives of the main Irish employers' organisations lobbied the Commission to defer equal pay, while the government itself made its case for the derogation early in February.

The Irish request appeared to present a difficult dilemma for Hillery, as it placed him on the front line of a potential battle between his own country and the Commission. He had taken an oath to serve the interests of the Community independently of national governments, but his reappointment to the Commission was entirely in the gift of the Irish government. Yet the Irish application also threatened to undermine a policy he had promoted and a cause to which he had become deeply committed. Hillery did not tell even the senior members of his *cabinet* what he intended to do. But his private view of the Irish request was clear from the outset; the directive on equal pay had been approved by the Council and accepted by the member states; the European legislation could not legally be changed or deferred at the instigation of a single government.[47] Even if the Commission could find a legal loophole for Ireland, he was convinced that they should not do so: such a concession would undercut the principle of equal pay and render futile the work done by Hillery in securing the directive in the first place.[48] While he did not comment publicly on the proposed derogation until after the Commission made its decision, Hillery had no intention of undermining the policy that he himself had introduced.

Garret FitzGerald and the Attorney General, Declan Costello, met Hillery in Brussels on 5 February to present the Irish application.[49] Hillery was accompanied by Ed FitzGibbon and two legal advisers, Jean-Pierre Delahousse, the acting chief adviser to the Commission, and Marie-José Jonczy, a member of the Legal Services directorate who worked closely with Social Affairs. The role of the officials was not so much to defend the principle of equal pay as to explain the legal barriers to the Irish application. Hillery gave the Irish representatives little hope of a favourable verdict; he ensured that they were fully briefed on the obstacles facing their application and suggested that the Irish government should consider instead an alternative approach to the Commission for economic aid.[50] FitzGerald and Costello were courteous and correct in their dealings with Hillery. They were not seeking to negotiate a solution and neither man attempted to put any pressure on the Irish Commissioner. The Attorney General had already advised the government that individuals would have the right to sue the state under the directive in the absence of a derogation.[51] Costello acknowledged on 5 February that the amending legislation would be in conflict with Community law; the logical implication was that if the Commission refused the Irish request for a derogation, the amendment became redudant. The meeting passed off amicably and was low-key until close to the end, when Hillery invited the officials to comment on the legal implications of the Irish request.[52] Delahousse was an outstanding orator, whose legal opinions were usually delivered with a rhetorical flourish. Hillery was well aware that the flamboyant Frenchman would be critical of the Irish application, but even he did not anticipate the verbal pyrotechnics that followed:

> It was dramatic – the Frenchman started by making a great eulogy of Garret, he had a great love of Europe, he was a great European – Garret was floating in the air by the time he finished. But then he said 'now you want to do this dreadful thing to women.' He couldn't allow them to get out of this directive, which had made progress for the first time.[53]

Jonczy also criticised the government's attempt to delay equal pay, in a more restrained but equally definite fashion.[54] Hillery did not orchestrate the contribution by the officials; indeed FitzGibbon maintained that 'we never envisaged the theatrical performance that we got from Delahousse'.[55] Yet the Commissioner gave the officials considerable latitude to express views that went well beyond purely legal considerations. He certainly wished to impress on the Irish representatives the depth of opposition within official Europe to the proposed derogation. The meeting gave a reliable indication of the likely fate of the Irish application.

The decisive meeting of the Commission occurred on Wednesday 11 February in Strasbourg, the day before the equal pay directive came into effect. It was common practice for the Commissioners to reach an interim conclusion, known as an 'orientation', followed by a final decision at a subsequent meeting; this was how they dealt with the Irish application. Hillery advised Ortoli that the Commission should take an interim position, rejecting the application for a derogation and 'expressing a strong preference for solutions of an economic nature.'[56] Hillery favoured additional financial assistance for Ireland, particularly from the Social and Regional Funds, to alleviate the worst effects of the economic crisis. He sought to uphold the directive, while holding out the prospect of aid to relieve Ireland's genuine economic difficulties. The Commission unanimously adopted Hillery's recommendation on 11 February. The Commissioners adopted an 'orientation' that rejected any departure from the principle of equal pay for equal work.[57] They decided to establish a task force of five members, headed by Hillery, which would examine possible financial solutions to the problem, while a working party of officials was also set up to assess the economic costs of refusing the exemption. The Commission delayed its formal response to the Irish government, allowing time for the group to have discussions with Irish officials.[58] But the crucial decision to refuse the Irish derogation was taken on 11 February. The Commission issued a statement, announcing that 'it would not be appropriate to withdraw from women their right to equal pay'. The statement acknowledged the severity of Ireland's economic difficulties, but warned that retreating from equal pay was not an acceptable solution.[59] The Irish government's legislation, which was debated in the Dáil for the first time on the same day, was essentially dead on arrival in Leinster House.

The scene was set for confrontation between the government and the Irish Commissioner. Hillery made his first public response to the Irish application on the afternoon of 11 February. He decided what to say at an unusual forum for a senior politician – the ice skating rink in Strasbourg. There was considerable speculation among the Irish press corps that the derogation was about to be rejected, and several journalists contacted Hillery to seek his response to the government's move. He often sought time for quiet reflection before taking a major decision and found it at the skating rink in the company of his young daughter:

> A journalist [from RTÉ] asked me what did I think of this [the Irish application] and I said to him, 'Come back to me'; I wanted to think, because it was the Irish government. I went skating, on the blades, for an hour; I usually went golfing when I wanted to figure something out. So I came back after skating, and I always remember Neville Keery was in a little office beside me – it was all temporary offices then in Strasbourg – and I got on the

phone to the journalist. I made a sad speech about the Irish government looking for so much from Europe, from all the other members, and now here's something that they don't want to do themselves. I could see Neville's face was dropping, I could see him through the door.[60]

Hillery gave a radio interview to RTÉ indicating the Commission's intentions and criticising the government's move. He expressed regret that Ireland, which had so recently called on the Community to expand its social policy, had become the first state to seek a derogation from the equal pay directive.[61] He emphasised that it was not his decision alone but the unanimous verdict of the Commissioners. This was entirely accurate. The Commission under Ortoli acted as a college, at least in its formal decision-making, even if this did nothing to restrain the culture of media briefing and intensive self-promotion by some Commissioners. Moreover, it was never likely that the Commission would retreat from such a key directive, especially when it had been hard won by Hillery's efforts after a long period of inaction. Yet Hillery was primarily responsible for the swift and decisive action taken by the Commission to protect the equal pay directive. He could have sought a compromise that gave the Irish government part of what they wanted, or kept his head down and attributed the decision entirely to the opposition of his fellow Commissioners; instead he chose to make a public stand in defence of equal pay.

Irish journalists covering the events in Strasbourg were in no doubt about Hillery's crucial role in securing the rejection of the government's initiative, and several concluded that he had guaranteed his own departure from the Commission at the end of the year. Walter Ellis, the European correspondent of *The Irish Times*, commented just before the Commission's decision on 11 February that Hillery 'must be aware that, if he causes the government embarrassment in the Community, he can be virtually assured of an exit from the Commission'.[62] Michael Mills drew the same conclusion in the *Irish Press* on the following day: 'Dr Paddy Hillery's criticism of the government yesterday ... is not expected to enhance his chances of being reappointed as an EEC Commissioner when his term of office expires at the end of this year.'[63] Hillery himself did not expect to be appointed for a second term in any event. He believed that Liam Cosgrave was unlikely to forego the opportunity to confer such a desirable appointment on one of his key allies in Fine Gael.[64] Regardless, concerns about his own political future did not loom large in Hillery's thinking; if they had, his actions would have been inexplicable. He undoubtedly wanted to underline his independence as a Commissioner, both to his colleagues and to the Irish government; yet even this did not explain the stand he took in February 1976. The lobbying by representatives of the women's movement in Brussels and Strasbourg was undoubtedly influential, especially in highlighting the extent of the domestic opposition to the government's move.[65] The case made by feminist activists reinforced Hillery's determination to block the derogation and enabled him to argue that women in Ireland were critical of the attempt to delay equal pay. Hillery had dedicated himself to the achievement of his social reform agenda for the previous three years, and he was particularly committed to the elimination of inequalities affecting the place of women in European society. The Irish government's move threatened to undermine the objectives he had cherished most since he moved to Brussels in January 1973. He was determined to uphold the principle of equal pay for equal work and was willing to risk conflict with the Irish government to do so. His stand reflected his character both as a man and as a politician; he consistently refused to compromise on issues that reflected his deepest personal convictions. The same stubborn determination that had driven him in his private conflict with the Irish bishops in the 1960s and his very public clash with the Fianna Fáil dissidents at the 1971 Ard Fheis surfaced once again in the controversy over equal pay. Ed FitzGibbon, who was at Hillery's side throughout the controversy, believed that 'he would not want to be remembered as one who compromised on a basic principle.'[66] John McColgan summed it up more simply: 'It was because Paddy believed in it.'[67]

The reactions to Hillery's stand in Dublin varied dramatically, even within the government itself. He returned to Dublin as usual at the weekend and deliberately arranged a series of meetings with Irish ministers:

> I immediately made appointments in Dublin, went straight into the middle of them. To give Garret his due, he wasn't angry. But O'Leary was smarting and he said, 'you'll never be appointed again.' There was no question that I would be appointed anyway.[68]

O'Leary certainly responded sharply to Hillery's criticisms of the government, commenting pointedly that the Commissioner had 'belonged to a party which was not exactly a trailblazer' for women's rights. Yet the Minister for Labour also accepted the validity of the decision and acknowledged Hillery's right to comment publicly on the issue, while challenging the Commission to propose alternative measures for the protection of employment.[69] A statement from the Government Information Service also sought clarification on the Commission's view of the alternatives available to the Irish state to finance the full implementation of equal pay. This might have given space to resolve the controversy without further acrimony, but at least one leading member of the government was not reconciled to the rejection of the exemption.

Richie Ryan entered the fray the following weekend, just as the controversy appeared to be winding down. Ryan vehemently attacked Hillery, in a speech supposedly given to a Fine Gael meeting in Slattery's pub in Terenure on Saturday 14 February. It soon emerged that he had never actually delivered the speech. There was no party meeting in Slattery's that night, and he had simply issued the statement to the newspapers.[70] Ryan declared that the inability of the Irish economy to pay for equal pay was being dishonestly overlooked. He proceeded to identify Hillery and the Fianna Fáil members of the European Parliament as the villains of the piece, with a walk-on part for malignant EEC bureaucrats:

> Ireland's name on the international scene has been damaged by the irresponsible antics of the Fianna Fáil-

appointed Commissioner to the European Communities
and the Fianna Fáil members of the European Parliament,
who have abused their position in Europe to damage
Ireland's reputation.[71]

Ryan extended his scattergun onslaught to include the Commission,
arguing that all those 'clamouring for instant implementation of equal pay,
be they Fianna Fáil opportunists or EEC bureaucrats' should put their
money where their mouths were.[72] He warned that the government was
strongly opposed to the imposition of additional taxation 'to meet the
dictates of Brussels or the insincere and opportunist propaganda of Fianna
Fáil'.[73] It was an extraordinary performance by any standard. Ryan's attack
highlighted the resentment among some ministers that Hillery had not
simply acted as a loyal agent of the Irish government in Brussels and took
no account of the obligation accepted by each Commissioner to act
independently in the interests of the Community. But an even more
serious blunder was the entirely inaccurate allegation that Hillery had
dictated the Commission's decision, acting malevolently in the interests of
Fianna Fáil. The other Commissioners were presented as unwitting
puppets dancing to Hillery's tune. Ryan's statement did no harm at all to
Hillery, but damaged his own standing and revived a controversy that was
deeply embarrassing for the coalition.[74] The minister's embarrassment was
compounded when the *Sunday Press* gleefully publicised the fact that he
had given the speech to 'a non-existent Fine Gael meeting'.[75] The incident
was a self-inflicted wound of considerable proportions.

The Irish minister had effectively thrown down the gauntlet to the
Commission. Hillery was in Dublin for the weekend, but wisely declined
to comment on Ryan's statement. He had no need to do so, as the
Commission moved to respond on his behalf. Ortoli was furious at Ryan's
statement, regarding it as an attack on the Commission as a whole.[76] Ryan's
comments to journalists in Brussels on Monday 16 February, in the margins
of a meeting of EEC finance ministers, merely added fuel to the flames. He
called on the Commission either to grant the exemption from the directive,
which was clearly his preferred solution, or to supply the full cost of

implementing equal pay in Ireland.[77] Ryan's hostility to equal pay, which he presented as an unreasonable imposition by an external body, was revealed in stark terms: 'If the EEC wants to force on us a policy which will cost the Irish taxpayer more money, then the EEC must supply the revenue.'[78] He neatly ignored the reality that the directive had been approved by the Council of Ministers during the Irish presidency of the EEC and signed by none other than his Cabinet colleague, Garret FitzGerald. The finance minister also stood by his earlier attack on Hillery, assuring journalists that it had not been delivered in the heat of the moment: 'I am a very cool man'.[79] Ryan's performance did little to mollify Ortoli. When the Commission met on Wednesday 18 February, Ortoli led the condemnation of Ryan's statement and all the members, except the absent Finn-Olav Gundelach, expressed support for Hillery.[80] The Commission unanimously confirmed its position that no legal exception could be made to the principle of equal pay, although its members also expressed willingness to 'help Ireland to overcome its problems by other means.'[81] A spokesman for the Commission issued a firm rebuke to Richie Ryan, emphasising that under the Treaty of Rome, the Commissioners could 'neither seek nor take instructions from any government'; he noted pointedly that all member states had undertaken to respect this principle. The statement concluded with a ringing endorsement of Hillery's actions: 'In these circumstances, the Commission cannot accept that doubt is thrown on the conditions in which Dr Hillery has performed his duties and it wishes to declare its total solidarity with him.'[82] Such a collective rebuke from the Commission to a government minister was very rare for its time; it happened only twice during the term of the Ortoli Commission. Ryan's attack was not only futile, but counterproductive. The Commission united around Hillery in an exceptionally strong show of solidarity.

There was also considerable support in Ireland for Hillery's stand on equal pay. Both the *Irish Press* and *The Irish Times* published leading articles denouncing Ryan's statement and backing Hillery. While the support of the *Irish Press* was to be expected, the editorial in *The Irish Times* was, if anything, even more damning for the finance minister, describing Ryan's intervention as 'silly and petulant'.[83] The leadership of the trade union movement welcomed the Commission's decision on equal pay, so, too, did the Irish Council for the Status of Women. Moreover, there were some dissenting voices within the ranks of the government parties. Barry Desmond, Labour TD for Dún Laoghaire, issued a personal statement on 11 February not only welcoming the decision itself, but also endorsing the comments made by Hillery, whom he credited with having 'put this issue in its true perspective.'[84] There was also unease within the Cabinet at the equal pay debacle, with several ministers quietly disassociating themselves from Ryan's intervention at meetings with their European counterparts.[85] Moreover, at least one minister signalled his concern at a meeting of the government itself; Garret FitzGerald told the Cabinet on 4 March that 'he had found some hostility in EEC circles (because of the recent speech of the Minister for Finance criticising Commissioner Hillery) ...'[86] Following the Commission's unequivocal support for Hillery, the government implicitly accepted that it had lost the battle to postpone equal pay and focused on securing substantial EEC support to subsidise the implementation of the directive. Walter Ellis commented on 3 March that 'the campaign for a wide-ranging derogation is dead.'[87]

This did not mean that the dispute was over. A gaping hole emerged between the Irish estimates for the cost of implementing equal pay and the Commission's assessment of the necessary aid. The team of officials appointed by the Commission met an inter-departmental group of Irish civil servants in Dublin on 19 February. The Irish delegation proposed the establishment of a special fund of £20 million, to be financed entirely by the EEC, to assist Irish industries in meeting the cost of equal pay.[87] Moreover, the representatives of the Irish employers claimed that the direct cost of equal pay to manufacturing industry would amount to at least £25 million. The Commission working party believed that the alternative proposals offered by Irish officials and employer representatives were based on grossly inflated figures; the Community officials were also frustrated that their Irish counterparts declined to give precise estimates for the cost of implementing equal pay in the private sector.[89] The working party suggested that the maximum cost of any Community initiatives to assist Irish industry should not exceed £5–6 million annually

up to December 1977.[90] The glaring disparity between the two estimates
had a straightforward explanation. The Commission was willing to open
up possibilities for additional funding to assist specific sectors or initiatives
to alleviate unemployment, while the Irish government and employers
sought to obtain the entire cost of implementing the equal pay directive.
The working party's scepticism about the government's case was well
founded. A briefing note prepared in the Department of the Taoiseach
for a government meeting on 20 February acknowledged that the official
proposals for assistance would have to be refined, as they lacked
consistency and 'were originally formulated as a rush job'.[91] The working
party recommended that the Commission should provide additional aid
to Ireland through various Community policies, especially the Social
Fund; but the Irish government would have to submit a series of specific
projects for approval under existing rules.[92] This meant that the Irish state
would have to contribute to the initiatives on a 50:50 basis to secure
additional funding from the Community. The requirement for matching
funding drew strong opposition from the Department of Finance, which
opposed any proposals involving further Exchequer spending or
borrowing.[93] The Irish position amounted to a demand that the
Commission pay for the implementation of European legislation. Such a
blanket application drew predictable hostility from the Commission; it
also threatened to alienate members of the college who had previously
been sympathetic to Ireland's economic problems.

When Hillery opened the final discussion on the Irish application
during a two-day meeting of the Commission on 4–5 March, he found
that his colleagues were increasingly exasperated with the Irish
government:

> Ortoli very quickly came in and he was totally changed
> because he said that he had told Garret straight that the
> Irish dossier was 'très mauvais', terrible from beginning to
> end. He advised him to calm it down as Ireland was getting
> into a very bad position vis-à-vis the Community … Finn
> followed up that we should have closed the door the first

day [11 February] and that we must in no way give the
impression that we will pay for the implementation of
Community legislation.[94]

Hillery was equally unhappy with the attitude of the Irish government,
but had a more immediate concern, notably that the new-found
intransigence among the Commissioners might lead them to reject any
possibility of aid to Ireland:

> [It was] an extraordinary, tough attitude of the
> Commission, which I was afraid of the first day [4 March],
> but I think it was due mainly to Richie Ryan's outburst,
> plus I think the fact that the Irish government is pretty well
> unpopular all round.[95]

The Commission's final decision was unequivocal; the members rejected
the Irish application and refused to consider the idea of direct
compensation to Ireland for implementing equal pay. But the
Commission left open the possibility that they would consider favourably
more limited submissions for financial assistance.[96] Hillery privately
advised Irish ministers and officials to develop more modest proposals for
aid to specific projects that could attract Community support under the
Social Fund. The government belatedly inched closer to this approach
following the formal rejection of the derogation. The Cabinet agreed to
propose several options for EEC aid to the Commission in April 1976.[97]
The Irish proposals focused mainly on obtaining additional assistance from
the Social Fund and on modifying the regulations governing the Fund to
secure direct support for maintaining employment in the manufacturing
industry.[98] The demands for a partial exemption from equal pay or full
reimbursement of the economic cost of the directive were quietly
dropped. The Irish government accepted that it could neither postpone
equal pay nor force the Community to pay for it; following the end of the
dispute, the Commission agreed to grant increased aid to Ireland under
the Social Fund.

The dispute over equal pay resulted in a considerable victory for Hillery and an embarrassing capitulation for the Irish government. The amending legislation for the private sector lapsed following the Commission's decision and equal pay for equal work became a legal obligation immediately. The government later moved to end the marriage differentials in the pay of public servants, which had been part of its attempt to delay the full introduction of equal pay.[99] Hillery's stand succeeded in protecting the European directive and establishing the principle of equal pay throughout the Community from February 1976. This was achieved at a personal cost to Hillery himself. While the prospects for his reappointment by the national coalition were never favourable, there is little doubt that the public clash with the government over equal pay sealed his fate. A more conventional politician would have hedged his bets and dodged the conflict; Hillery undoubtedly wanted to remain in the Commission, but was more concerned to safeguard his policy achievements and defend an initiative in which he genuinely believed.

Equal Opportunities

The controversy over equal pay became the most enduring public memory of Hillery's term as Commissioner for Social Affairs. Yet his commitment to equality between men and women went far beyond the issue of pay. He secured the Commission's approval in February 1975 for a draft directive on equality of treatment for women; his proposal sought to eliminate all legal and administrative measures that discriminated against women at work on the basis of gender, marital or family status.[100] The draft directive was an ambitious reforming initiative, which sought not only to establish equal treatment for women in access to employment, vocational training and working conditions, but also to abolish established inequalities in the level of social welfare benefits between men and women in most member states. Hillery's proposal included a requirement to provide an equal level of social security benefits for men and women, which was to be introduced gradually over several years.[101] This reform proved particularly controversial among national governments, while the far-reaching character of the overall package generated more suspicion than enthusiasm at a time of economic recession.

Hillery attempted to guide the proposed reforms through the Community institutions during the Irish presidency of the EEC. But he suffered a significant setback in June 1975, when he presented the draft directive to the Social Affairs Council. Michael O'Leary, who chaired the meeting on 17 June, and Frank Cluskey were generally supportive of Hillery's plans, but this had little effect in the face of strong opposition from the represntatives of Britain and West Germany. There was disagreement over almost every aspect of the proposal, but the reform of social security benefits aroused the strongest opposition.[102] The British Social Security Secretary, Barbara Castle, who was attending her first ministerial Council, led the opposition to the equalisation of social benefits. Castle declared that she was entirely in favour of providing equality of treatment for women, but argued that the directive had been prepared too hastily and the Commission had not fully considered the financial consequences of its proposals. She claimed that the cost to Britain of giving both men and women the same benefits would be £1,400 million annually.[103] Several other politicians echoed Castle's argument that the Commission had not done its homework on social security. Walter Arendt, the German Minister for Labour, objected to any proposals that involved expenditure beyond what was already agreed. The meeting started at 10 in the morning and concluded at 11.30 that night, having achieved virtually no progress on the equal opportunities directive.[104] The Council eventually agreed to refer the draft proposal to the Committee of Permanent Representatives for more detailed assessment. Hillery was deeply unhappy with the outcome and was scathing about O'Leary's chairing style:

> It was acknowledged by all to be the very worst operated
> meeting that anyone had ever attended. He didn't
> understand how to run a meeting and he didn't understand
> the subject matter. Barbara Castle was there for her first
> visit and at a given moment she said 'this is no way to run

a tea party'. As I said to the Irish delegation, now I know the difference between Labour and the Conservatives in Britain because Soames said this is no way to run an 'effing' railway.[105]

Hillery was not alone in his opinion that O'Leary managed the meeting poorly; the Dutch and German delegations also complained that his handling of the meeting was erratic.[106] Tony Brown, who was a member of the Irish delegation, took a more favourable view, seeing an element of calculation in O'Leary's management of the meeting: 'He was prepared to have a chaotic meeting provided he got the results out of it.'[107] The meeting was undoubtedly chaotic, but the failure to achieve tangible progress on equal opportunities reflected the sharp divisions among the ministers and the strong resistance to Hillery's initiative more than O'Leary's political style. The representatives of Britain and West Germany were simply not willing to accept such far-reaching and costly reforms in the prevailing economic circumstances. The national governments increasingly regarded economic decline and male unemployment as more central priorities than social reform or enhancing employment opportunities for women.[108]

The rebuff by the Council proved a temporary setback. Hillery recognised that he had to adapt to unwelcome political and economic realities if he was to win over the national governments. In practice this meant delaying equality in social welfare to pave the way for the acceptance of equal opportunities in employment and working conditions. The Commission produced a revised version of the directive, which endorsed the principle of equal treatment in social security, but deferred the actual implementation of equal benefits until a further decision was taken by the Council. Hillery kept most of the other elements of the original proposal, although a section referring to equality of access to all levels of education was watered down so that it referred only to vocational training.[109] He undertook extensive lobbying in European capitals to smooth the passage of the amended directive. His most important visit was to Bonn in October 1975, where he met Arendt, who had reservations about enforcing equal access for private sector employment through the courts. The legal enforcement of equal treatment for women in both the public and private sector was a central plank of the directive, and any compromise on this principle would have been a crippling blow to the initiative. Hillery succeeded in overcoming Arendt's objections about legal enforcement of the directive, and the German minister agreed to support it.[110] The Commissioner presented the revised directive to the Social Affairs Council in December 1975.[111] On this occasion nobody could accuse Hillery of not doing his homework; his assiduous lobbying paid off, and the directive was formally approved on 9 February 1976.

Despite its troubled birth and the major compromises involved in bringing it into being at all, the directive on equal treatment was a major landmark in the achievement of legal equality between men and women in the workplace. The directive established the principle of equal treatment with regard to employment and working conditions, banning discrimination on the basis of gender; legal inequalities linked to marital or family status were also outlawed.[112] The initiative prohibited discrimination against women in access to employment and promotional opportunities; it also gave a legal guarantee of equal access to vocational training. The directive required that men and women would be guaranteed the same working conditions without discrimination based on gender.[113]

The adoption of the initiative as the policy of the Community had a wide-ranging impact on member states. National governments were legally obliged to abolish all laws or regulations contrary to the principle of equal treatment; individual contracts of employment and professional codes of conduct also had to be revised to remove discrimination against women. The directive came into effect within 30 months of its adoption by the Council.[114] The lengthy prologue to the implementation of the legislation underlined the continuing reservations of some member states about the abolition of gender discrimination.

Hillery promoted wide-ranging and influential initiatives to transform the legal position of women. He secured the adoption of reforms establishing legal equality between men and women in the workplace for the first time. The social action programme guaranteed not only the abolition of discrimination in pay, but also equality of treatment in working conditions and equal access to employment. Some of his most ambitious initiatives, such as equality in social welfare, did not become a reality until after he left office. Yet by the end of his term, equal pay was well on the way to becoming a practical reality and European legislation on equal opportunities was accepted despite the visible lack of enthusiasm by several member states. Hillery's reform agenda also left its mark within the Commission itself. In June 1976 he initiated the establishment of a section within DG-V dedicated to women's rights; the new section was designed to draft further proposals for reform and to monitor the implementation of existing European legislation, notably the directive on equal pay.[115] The section was the principal institutional legacy of his term as a Commissioner. It was due in no small part to Hillery's initiatives that the Community emerged as the legal guarantor of gender equality in Europe.

Expanding social policy

While Hillery was publicly identified above all with the cause of women's rights, his objectives extended far beyond a single issue, important as it undoubtedly was, to the creation of effective Community action across the whole range of social policy. He consistently sought to widen the scope of the Community's social policy so that it offered adequate protection to marginalised social groups. Hillery focused initially on incremental measures to assist the rehabilitation of workers with disabilities and to offer support from the Social Fund to migrant workers. But as the recession worsened he sought to use the resources of the Fund to alleviate the worst effects of growing unemployment. He also promoted a viable European anti-poverty programme for the first time. Hillery found an important ally in Frank Cluskey, who acted as Corish's Parliamentary Secretary but was much more influential than his title suggested, taking the lead on a wide range of social issues. Cluskey was fiercely critical of the EEC's efforts on social policy for much of Hillery's term; the Labour TD publicly attacked both the failure of member states to finance the Social Fund adequately and the Community's traditional preoccupation with economic rather than social concerns.[116] None of this bothered Hillery, not least because Cluskey was frequently expressing views that were very close to his own. The two men, although very different in their backgrounds and coming from opposing political traditions, shared essentially the same social vision. Cluskey consistently argued that the Community's social policy had to take its rightful place on an equal footing with economic concerns; he demanded social initiatives that were not supplementary to economic priorities, but were designed primarily to solve problems of social deprivation.[117] Hillery was at one with Cluskey in widening the scope and influence of European social policy, and the two men formed a formidable alliance on social issues.

The first notable effect of the collaboration between Hillery and Cluskey was the extension of Community assistance for people with disabilities. The initial EEC action programme for disabled workers, which was approved by the Social Affairs ministers in June 1974, was an innovative measure; it was the first Community initiative to support the rehabilitation of people with disabilities. The action plan sought to promote the rehabilitation of workers with physical or mental disabilities who had the capacity for employment in the open labour market. The Community provided funding under the scheme for short-term demonstration projects to enhance the facilities for vocational rehabilitation, and for longer-term efforts to prepare people with disabilities for conventional employment.[118] The initiative was designed to encourage the full integration of people with disabilities into society; it was intended as a first step towards a common European approach to achieve 'social integration for all mentally and physically handicapped people'.[119] But the initial plan was limited in its scope. Cluskey raised concerns that the programme would not finance training facilities for workers with severe disabilities who were unable to find employment in the open labour market. This shortcoming was particularly damaging from an Irish perspective, as most Irish organisations working in the area concentrated their efforts on preparing people with disabilities for sheltered employment and so did not qualify for EEC funding. Hillery agreed to extend the programme to include support for rehabilitation in sheltered workshops and backed Cluskey's efforts to secure immediate funding for sheltered employment; the Social Affairs ministers agreed in June 1974 that sheltered workshops would qualify for assistance straightaway from the Social Fund.[120] This was a valuable advance for people with severe disabilities and an important extension of the Community's original plan.

Poverty

An equally significant accomplishment was the development of a European action programme to combat poverty. The initiative for joint action on poverty was the most tangible legacy of the collaboration between Hillery and Cluskey. The ideas included by the Commissioner in the social action programme were influenced by Cluskey's original proposal in September 1973. Hillery presented the poverty action programme to the Social Affairs Council in June 1975; his proposal stipulated that individuals or families were affected by poverty if their resources were so inadequate 'as to exclude them from the minimum acceptable way of life of the member state in which they live'. The initiative envisaged Community support for pilot schemes to combat poverty in selected areas and similar backing for studies of poverty as a key problem facing the EEC.[121] The programme indicated several distinct types of pilot scheme that could attract support from the Social Fund. The potential projects included the regeneration of a specific district severely affected by poverty; assistance to a clearly defined group, such as the children of poor families; the creation of new services for the poor; and making existing services for the whole population of a given country more responsive to the needs of the poor.[122] It was an ambitious proposal, which aroused strong opposition from the West German delegation, when it came before the Council on 17 June 1975.

Hillery hoped that the action programme would be adopted as the initial stage of a joint Community approach on poverty. The Commission proposed a budget of 5.25 million units of account over a two-year period (1975-76).[123] But Arendt opposed any attempt to approve additional funding for the poverty programme. The German government was reluctant to commit more resources to the Social Fund, at a time when it was providing the most substantial share of the newly created Regional Development Fund and contributing heavily to other areas of the Community budget. This was not an isolated episode; Hillery encountered increasing opposition among the German political establishment to any expansion of their traditional role as the paymasters of the Community.[124] The initiative secured the full support of all the other ministers present and Cluskey made a passionate appeal to the Council to adopt it.[125] The German delegation insisted, however, that the money required for the first year of the new projects would have to be drawn from the existing Community budget. Arendt also suggested that the Commission should fund the anti-poverty programme in the following year from savings elsewhere in the budget for 1976.[126] Hillery immediately rejected this attempt to tie his hands on the allocation of funding for the following year, especially as the draft budget presented by the Commission had not yet been approved by the member states:

> I refused absolutely to say that we could have savings at all on the '76 Budget and also I said I didn't know what that Budget would be. If the Minister could tell me that the draft Budget put up by the Commission will be adopted, then I might be able to answer.[127]

But the German representatives were adamant that they could not support any increase in the allocation for the following year; they had gone as far as they could in agreeing to the use of existing funding for the new poverty action programme. Hillery commented in his diary: 'The Germans had their way, saving money'.[128] The Council agreed the allocation of 2.5 million units of account for 1975 only, with the proviso that the money had to be committed by the end of the year. Hillery's directorate found the money for the programme from savings and switching resources from other areas.[129] The Council decision authorised Community assistance for pilot schemes that would develop new methods of helping people affected by or threatened with poverty; support would also be available for pilot studies designed to improve official understanding of the nature and scope of poverty in the EEC.[130] The projects were funded on the basis of matching 50 per cent contributions from Commission funds and national resources. The Commission succeeded in financing the programme for the first two years and it was renewed in 1977. Despite the significant financial limitations imposed by the Council, the passage of the initiative itself was a considerable achievement; it was a striking illustration of what former political opponents could achieve by working together at European level. The decision marked the first definite policy commitment by the Community to joint action against poverty, even if it was not backed up by the devotion of adequate resources to the pilot projects.

The deteriorating economic conditions in several member states encouraged a certain amount of political schizophrenia on social policy. Economic decline made national governments more receptive to joint action to tackle the scourge of unemployment, but also reinforced the reluctance of wealthy states to commit scarce resources to social programmes. This contradiction was apparent in the fate of Commission proposals on unemployment. Hillery presented an initiative to the Social Affairs Council in June 1975 for the retraining of young workers under the age of 25, who were unable to find employment due to the recession. This involved using the Social Fund to finance projects facilitating the employment and professional mobility of unemployed young people. The proposal gave priority to projects supporting young people who were seeking their first job.[131] The Council approved the proposal for the retraining of young workers on 17 June, but once again did not provide any additional funding for the initiative.[132] The training programme for young people was instead funded from an allocation of £22 million left over from the Social Fund's budget in the previous year.[133]

Both Hillery and Cluskey sought to transform the Social Fund, which traditionally functioned as an 'ambulance operation', rescuing workers from collapsing industries for retraining.[134] They collaborated closely, working to extend its original restricted remit to provide support for underprivileged social groups. The initiatives to support people with disabilities, migrant workers and the unemployed underlined the gradual transition in the character of the Social Fund. Hillery was determined to make the Fund a key instrument of European social policy, which would underpin the reforms in the social action programme. The two men had considerable success in transforming the functions of the Fund, but found that securing adequate resources to finance social reform was a much more formidable challenge.

Equality for immigrants

Equality of treatment for underprivileged social categories was a key theme of Hillery's reform agenda. Few social groups faced greater disadvantages than migrant workers, especially foreign workers who sought to escape economic deprivation in their native countries by making a new life in the Community. The problems of migrant workers in the EEC became a key preoccupation for Hillery and his close advisers almost from the outset of his term. There were over six million migrant workers in the Community in 1973; immigrants made up 4 per cent of the total population of the EEC. Over three-quarters of all migrant workers were from 'third countries' – states outside the Community.[135] West Germany had the highest level of immigration, with particularly large numbers of migrant workers from Turkey and Yugoslavia. While immigrants who were citizens of EEC countries enjoyed equality of treatment in social security benefits and conditions of employment due to a Community regulation in 1968, migrant workers from 'third countries' had no such protection under European law.[136] The immigrant population drawn from outside the EEC experienced social and economic conditions that were greatly inferior to those enjoyed by the native population. The social action programme acknowledged that discrimination against migrant workers was 'particularly widespread', highlighting the lack of reception centres, advisory services and educational facilities for immigrants and their children.[137] Migrant workers usually undertook jobs rejected by the local labour force, faced discrimination in vocational training and were excluded from many social security benefits. The programme identified discrimination against immigrants as a key social problem and argued that 'there is an urgent need for the Community to assume its overall human responsibilities towards the whole migrant population, irrespective of its country of origin.'[138]

Equality of treatment was the central principle of the action programme for migrant workers that Hillery presented to the Commission in 1974. He believed that the exclusion of third country migrants from most of the benefits of the Community was unfair and increasingly intolerable.[139] The programme, which was drafted by Hillery's *cabinet*, proposed a transformation in the social, economic and political status of immigrants. Discrimination between foreign workers and Community nationals in social security would be abolished; migrant workers would secure equality of treatment in wages and working conditions. The programme also set out to guarantee access for foreign workers to social services and vocational training.[140] Hillery sought to apply the principle of the free movement of labour, enshrined in the Treaty of Rome, to all migrant workers. But the most radical element of the programme was political – it proposed to give migrant workers from 'third countries' full political rights in local elections. Hillery knew that immigrants had no political power and intended to give them votes in local elections to ensure that politicians would take notice of them.[141] This was an entirely logical idea; it was also politically explosive in several European countries, notably West Germany.

The initiative triggered considerable opposition within the Commission; the move to give migrant workers political rights proved particularly controversial. Ortoli turned to Hillery in a meeting on the initiative and exclaimed, 'There could be a Turkish major of Lille!'[142] Several other Commissioners also sought to rein back the programme for migrant workers. The proposal went through a lengthy process of redrafting, in which Hillery made some concessions but managed to maintain most of his original plans. The Commission agreed to recommend the extension of political rights to migrant workers in local elections by 1980. The final proposal envisaged that social security benefits would be provided to foreign workers, while a uniform system of family benefits and non-contributory schemes was to be introduced for Community citizens. Immigrants from 'third countries' would be accorded the same protection against arbitrary dismissal as their EEC counterparts.[143] The Commission approved the final version of the action programme on 18 December 1974. Hillery noted the outcome with relief in his diary: 'The programme for migrants was finally through the Commission today and there is a great sense of achievement in the cabinet. Edwin and Ms Veressa [sic] have worked with it all the time and it is a great achievement for them … '.[144] It was also a notable success for Hillery, who had persuaded a hesitant Commission to back a far-reaching transformation of the status of migrant workers within the Community.

The initiative proved a bridge too far for several national governments. Winning the support of the Council for a viable policy on the rights of migrant workers was a formidable challenge in itself, especially in an era of rising unemployment and growing economic insecurity; securing equal political and social entitlements for foreign workers proved impossible. Hillery's original proposals were greatly watered down due to pressure from national governments. The Council approved a resolution on the action programme for migrant workers and their families in February 1976.[145] The Council agreed to 'encourage the achievement of equality' for 'third country' migrant workers in living and working conditions, wages and economic rights.[146] But the ministers adopted few definite commitments on social equality to match this general statement of principle. Moreover, Hillery's proposal to give political rights to migrant workers was sidelined by the Council. Yet the action programme had some effect; the resolution endorsed measures to improve the social and economic conditions of migrant workers through the upgrading of national employment services and improving facilities for the reception of immigrants in host countries.[147] But overall, the outcome was disappointing. The British Labour government took the lead in blocking many of the reforms sought by Hillery.[148] No further progress was achieved in upgrading the position of migrant workers before the end of Hillery's term.

The initiatives proposed by Hillery to enhance the status of immigrants within the EEC were among the most ambitious and controversial elements of the social action programme. Much of what he sought to achieve proved impossible, as various aspects of his plans proved too radical for national governments and even for some members of the Commission. While his more ambitious objectives fell far short of realisation, Hillery did succeed in achieving incremental advances for migrant workers and, perhaps more importantly, put the issue of equal treatment for third country workers firmly on the Community's agenda.

The relatively limited short-term impact of Hillery's efforts in some areas, notably the advancement of the status of migrant workers, reflected the reality of conflict between his radical objectives and the increasingly inhospitable economic and political climate. He sought to secure a far-reaching and comprehensive European social policy; this ambition could not be fully realised, due mainly to the ravages of the oil crisis and the subsequent economic decline. But Hillery promoted effective Community action on social issues for the first time. The scope of European social policies widened dramatically beyond their traditional ambit of facilitating economic integration. It was due above all to Hillery's initiatives that a progressive social policy at European level became a reality in the mid-1970s. The development of wide-ranging social legislation affecting most aspects of European life was still in the future, but the later evolution of European social policy owed much to Hillery's pioneering efforts in the 1970s.

The wide-ranging role of European Commissioner gave Hillery the greatest freedom that he had enjoyed as a public figure. While he was ultimately accountable to his colleagues on the Commission, he had the advantage of a clear political mandate from the national leaders to give Europe 'a human face'. He benefited, too, from the previous underdevelopment and weakness of the Social Affairs area; as a new Commissioner, he inherited a vacant political space and took the opportunity to put his own imprint on the social policy portfolio. He proved adept at mobilising support for social reform within the European institutions and from national governments. Hillery also enjoyed greater independence than before, due to the collegiate style adopted by Ortoli, who was neither an experienced politician nor a dominant leader. In another sense too, Hillery had far greater freedom to give expression to his own political values, notably his belief in equality of opportunity and his sympathy for marginalised or under-represented social groups. There is no doubt that he was acting in accordance with his most firmly held convictions throughout his term as Social Affairs Commissioner. Hillery's commitment to the expansion of social and economic opportunities for the underprivileged had remained consistent since his time as a reforming Minister for Education. But on this occasion he had the opportunity to express his egalitarian ideals on a wider stage, unimpeded by local constituency concerns or domestic party politics. His ability to translate his beliefs into action left an enduring legacy of social reform both in Ireland and more widely within the European Community. Hillery's service as a Commissioner was arguably the most creative and innovative period of his career.

18.

President by Consensus
1976

The retirement of Éamon de Valera in 1973 at the end of his second term as President of Ireland marked the beginning of an unlikely chain of circumstances that led to Paddy Hillery's inauguration in Dublin Castle at the end of 1976. The intervening period saw unprecedented tension between successive Presidents and the government, which contributed to an exceptional level of instability surrounding the presidency itself. The coalition government co-existed uneasily with two presidential incumbents drawn originally from Fianna Fáil. De Valera's immediate successor, Erskine Childers, who had a troubled relationship with the government, died in office in 1974. The relations between his successor, Cearbhall Ó Dálaigh, and Cosgrave's government were much worse and soon led to a major political crisis. The tension between the executive and the head of state came to a head in October 1976 when Ó Dálaigh resigned as President in a blaze of controversy. The crisis brought leading representatives of his own party to Hillery's door in the autumn of 1976, with a virtually unanimous demand from the Irish political establishment that he should accept the office of President.

The presidency in the 1970s was essentially a ceremonial office: as executive power was vested in the government, the head of state was important almost entirely as a symbolic figurehead for the Irish republic. Brian Lenihan light-heartedly referred to the office as a 'totem pole', a sort of ancestral symbol to which members of the tribe could pay homage.[1] Both Childers and Ó Dálaigh were frustrated by the constitutional and political constraints on the role of the President. Hillery was well aware of the severe constraints surrounding the office and he had no intention of becoming President.[2] Yet speculation emerged that he might seek the presidency as early as 1973, inspired partly by rumours that he was unhappy in Brussels following the breakdown of his relations with Fogarty.[3] Following de Valera's retirement, Fianna Fáil faced the apparently daunting prospect of contesting a presidential election only months after losing office to the Fine Gael–Labour coalition in February 1973. There were reports in the Irish media that Hillery might return from Brussels to become the party's presidential candidate.[4] Hillery himself refused to consider it and moved swiftly to close down speculation that he might be about to return to Irish politics. He told Irish journalists in Brussels on 26 March that he accepted appointment as a Commissioner on the basis that it was a commitment for four years; 'I do not regard it as a gambit for political advantage at home'.[5] Hillery was fully committed to the Social Affairs portfolio and had already decided that he did not wish to return to Irish politics. As it turned out, drafting Hillery was not necessary to win the election. The party turned to Childers, who unexpectedly defeated O'Higgins in June 1973. But it was fortunate that Hillery at least had a clear vision of what he was doing. It would have been deeply damaging to Ireland's reputation among the original Six for the first Irish Commissioner to abandon his post after only three months in office.

Yet the next presidential vacancy saw the beginning of a series of political advances from Fianna Fáil, which increased in volume and intensity over the following years. Childers died suddenly in November 1974. Neither the government nor the opposition wanted another election and a consensus rapidly emerged that an agreed candidate should be found to succeed him. Lynch's opponents within Fianna Fáil hoped that the party leader could be moved upstairs to the presidency, but Lynch had no intention of going to the Park and set out to find an agreed candidate to forestall his internal critics. Hillery's name was floated by elements within Fianna Fáil as a potential candidate, but he firmly resisted suggestions that he might become President. He told both Brian Lenihan and Sylvester Barrett 'to make it quite clear to any meeting that I am not available'.[6] He was determined to serve his full term as Commissioner and see through the social action programme. Lynch had few illusions about his former colleague's position, but nevertheless he phoned Hillery in Brussels on Wednesday 27 November to discuss the presidency.[7] He first asked Hillery on behalf of Fianna Fáil if he would be the presidential candidate, although it appears that it was essentially a *pro forma* request and Lynch already knew the answer. Hillery's response was emphatic:

> When Childers died, Jack contacted me. He said: 'The party wanted to know would you go for the presidency, but I don't think you would want to'. I said 'I don't'. Then Jack asked, 'Would you ask Cearbhall Ó Dálaigh?'[8]

Lynch had anticipated Hillery's refusal and sought to enlist his help in persuading Ó Dálaigh to stand as an agreed candidate for the presidency. Cearbhall Ó Dálaigh was an eminent lawyer who had served as a liberal Chief Justice, and was the first Irish member of the European Court of Justice.[9] He had twice been an unsuccessful Fianna Fáil election candidate, but was best known for his distinguished career as a judge.

Hillery agreed to approach the judge to transmit Lynch's message, although he had no intention of placing any pressure on Ó Dálaigh to accept.[10] Hillery respected Ó Dálaigh without knowing him particularly well. Lynch's choice of Hillery as an intermediary had more to do with the need to keep the approach secret until Ó Dálaigh accepted it, as any premature leak of Ó Dálaigh's name might destroy his prospects of being an agreed candidate between Fianna Fáil and the government parties. It was assumed that the Irish Commissioner in Brussels would be able to contact the judge in Luxembourg urgently and quietly. In fact this did not prove a straightforward undertaking. When he received Lynch's call on 27 November, Hillery first scribbled a note to Ed FitzGibbon, which reflected the secretive nature of the request from Dublin: 'Can you get me Cearbhall Ó Dálaigh's number. I must get him tonight, but don't let this be known.'[11] But as it was already evening, most of the staff had gone home, and FitzGibbon was out of the office on business. Neville Keery was the only member of the *cabinet* still in the office and he ransacked various address books in a vain search for Ó Dálaigh's number; similar attempts to contact the Court of Justice or to find a home number for the judge in the Luxembourg directory were unsuccessful.[12] Hillery eventually turned to Emile Noel's office for help; it was Noel's assistant, Franz De Koster, who succeeded in finding the judge's phone number. Hillery contacted Ó Dálaigh on Thursday morning to give him Lynch's message and the judge asked for some time to consider his position:

> He asked for 24 hours to consider it and then phoned. He was reluctant, but in view of the times that were in it he accepted and I told Jack. De Koster always looked at me in a special fashion from that day forward; the kingmaker from Ireland![13]

While Ó Dálaigh was approached by Hillery at Lynch's instigation, the judge was quickly accepted as an agreed candidate by all the major parties. Ó Dálaigh was nominated unopposed as the fifth President of Ireland in December 1974. Hillery's role in Ó Dálaigh's elevation to the presidency remained a closely-guarded secret, but it was widely known in Leinster House and the European institutions that the Irish Commissioner had resisted political pressure to become President himself. The members of his *cabinet* fully supported his stand; Keery sent him a brief note on 27 November, which concluded simply: 'Keep saying No!'[14] Lynch was greatly relieved by the outcome and warmly thanked Hillery for making the approach to Ó Dálaigh: 'he was very grateful to have me, the right man in the right place at the right time because he wanted to be able to say that Ó Dálaigh had been consulted'.[15] Hillery too could have been forgiven for breathing a sigh of relief with Ó Dálaigh's inauguration. He had firmly declined the entreaties of his former colleagues and hoped that was the last he would hear about it.

The new President remained in office for less than two years. While considerable tension emerged between Ó Dálaigh and leading members of the coalition over the role of the presidency, his departure from office was provoked by a clash with the Minister for Defence, Paddy Donegan, concerning the government's security policy. Following a dramatic escalation of the IRA's campaign in the Republic, which reached its peak with the murder of the British ambassador, Christopher Ewart-Biggs, in July 1976, the government secured additional legal powers to confront the IRA. Ó Dálaigh, acting strictly in accordance with the Constitution, referred the new Emergency Powers legislation to the Supreme Court to test its constitutionality. Donegan made an angry and semi-coherent attack on the President's action at a military function in Mullingar on 18 October 1976; he denounced Ó Dálaigh as a 'thundering disgrace' – which was probably the polite version of the minister's actual comments.[16] Even more provocative was Donegan's explosive comment that 'the Army must stand behind the State', which was regarded by Ó Dálaigh as a clear insinuation that the President, as formal commander-in-chief of the Defence Forces, did not stand behind the state.[17] While Donegan offered his apologies to the President almost immediately, Cosgrave was adamant that the minister should not be forced to resign; the government defended Donegan's position in the Dáil against a motion of censure put down by Fianna Fáil.[18] The outcome was entirely predictable, but apparently not foreseen by the Taoiseach. Ó Dálaigh resigned on 22 October, arguing that the essential relationship between the President and the Minister for Defence had been irreparably breached and that his decision was the only way to protect the independence and dignity of the presidency.[19]

The President's resignation came on the same day as the news broke that Hillery would not be reappointed as European Commissioner. He had been told officially only the previous week. Cosgrave informed

Hillery by letter on 15 October that the government's nominee to the Commission for the next four-year term would soon be decided. The Taoiseach proceeded to thank Hillery in valedictory style for keeping the government well informed on matters of particular interest to Ireland and for his 'courtesy and attention' when Cosgrave visited Brussels.[20] Although it was not explicitly stated, the clear implication was that Hillery would not be the government's choice. Cosgrave had decided to nominate his close ally, Dick Burke, the Minister for Education, whose appointment was already the subject of widespread speculation by Irish journalists. The decision not to reappoint the outgoing Commissioner was widely expected and certainly came as no surprise to Hillery himself. He had never expected Cosgrave to re-nominate him and knew that his clash with the government over equal pay rendered his departure from Brussels inevitable.[21] Hillery was disappointed at the decision, but he never expressed any resentment subsequently at Cosgrave's action; the former Fianna Fáil minister was well aware of the winner-takes-all nature of Irish politics. But Hillery was annoyed at the offhand way in which he was informed of the decision and even more irritated that the Taoiseach had thanked him for helping the Irish government, which Hillery was specifically precluded from doing by his oath as a Commissioner.[22] He issued a polite but pointed reply to Cosgrave on 28 October. Hillery noted that he had always kept in contact with national governments to draw their attention to the obligations of Community policies, while maintaining his freedom of action: 'These contacts, naturally, did not prejudice in any way the Commission's independence of action.'[23] The episode reflected Hillery's scrupulous concern not only to maintain his obligations to the Commission, but also to be perceived as independent from the Irish government.

The outgoing Commissioner decided to break the news of his impending departure himself; this would allow him to control the timing of the announcement and ensure that his achievements over the previous four years received some attention in the media before the new nominee was announced.[24] His statement was carefully crafted by Ed FitzGibbon and Neville Keery. Hillery made the announcement in Brussels at noon on 22 October, some hours before Ó Dálaigh's resignation. He informed journalists that the Taoiseach had 'appeared to indicate' to him that he would not be considered for reappointment to the incoming Commission. Hillery wished his successor well 'in the important task he or she may have'.[25] The statement was an elegant response to Cosgrave's letter and Hillery took mischievous pleasure in the subtle dig buried in his good wishes. There was no chance of a woman being appointed but Hillery's suggestion that his successor might be either male or female highlighted his own commitment to equality and the government's embarrassment over equal pay.

Yet not everything worked out as Hillery and his advisers had planned. Ó Dálaigh's abrupt resignation dominated the headlines and naturally overshadowed the news of Hillery's departure from Brussels.[26] Moreover, the entirely accidental coincidence fuelled widespread speculation among politicians and journalists that Hillery would now seek the presidency.[27] Several conflicting political agendas drove the search for a new President. The government's agenda was straightforward – its leaders sought to avoid an election, which they would certainly lose after the fiasco that led to Ó Dálaigh's resignation. Fianna Fáil's strategy was more complex and ambiguous, not least because the opposing factions within the party sought to achieve very different outcomes. Haughey's supporters within the parliamentary party wanted Lynch to accept the presidency, opening the way for their man to complete his long-awaited political comeback by taking over the leadership. Haughey avoided association with this move by calling for a contested election, which the party was favoured to win. Lynch sought to find an alternative Fianna Fáil candidate who would be acceptable to the other parties.[28] Hillery's own agenda was simple – he did not want to become President. He was happy to return to medical practice in the short term. He was not about to retire from public life but had no desire to return to domestic Irish politics. He hoped instead to contest the first direct elections to the European Parliament, which were scheduled for 1978.[29]

But within hours of Ó Dálaigh's resignation, sources both within Fianna Fáil and the government were briefing journalists that Hillery was the obvious successor. His immediate reaction to this prospect was unambiguous: 'It is very flattering but I would not like to spend seven years a prisoner in the Phoenix Park especially from the point of view of my children.'[30] He spoke to Lynch directly a few days after Ó Dálaigh's departure, seeking to remove himself definitively from the running: 'So I went to see Jack and I told him I didn't want to be involved. I wanted him to keep me out of it.'[31] Hillery also told Lynch that he had no interest in succeeding him as party leader or Taoiseach:

> I told him I did not want to succeed him, I did not want
> to be President, but that I would like to be a member of the
> European Parliament when it comes for direct elections. I
> told him that between succeeding him and being President
> I would think succeeding him was less desirable from my
> point of view. He said he would try to avoid my having to
> do either and would envisage both of us, him and me,
> being in the Parliament together.[32]

Initially, at least, Lynch was as good as his word. On Monday 25 October, he announced that Fianna Fáil would nominate a presidential candidate, but that Hillery had 'mentioned no interest in the presidency'. Lynch commented that his former colleague was interested in 'a continuing role in Europe' and would be 'an excellent parliamentary representative of Ireland' in the European Parliament.[33] He even told journalists that any attempt by the party to 'draft' Hillery as a candidate was unlikely, as the candidate was most likely to be a serving politician and member of the parliamentary party. Indeed, sources within the party named Joe Brennan, Lynch's deputy leader, or Vivion de Valera, the former President's son, as likely candidates to succeed Ó Dálaigh.[34]

Lynch, however, maintained this position for only about three days, largely due to pressure from his own party. The trigger for the renewal of party pressure on Hillery was an unguarded and apparently innocuous conversation that he had with Brian Lenihan. Hillery had spoken off-the-record to Dennis Kennedy the previous weekend, disagreeing with Fianna

Fáil's recent decision to ally with the French Gaullists in the European Parliament. Hillery believed, probably correctly, that the Fianna Fáil group had ended up in an alliance with the Gaullists because they had left themselves with no other option; Labour had joined the Socialist group, while Fine Gael were accepted by the Christian Democrats. He regarded the social democratic parties in the Parliament as Fianna Fáil's natural allies and was disappointed that his old party had not moved more decisively to link up with them from the outset.[35] The fact that Hillery made such comments at all, even though they were not intended for publication, underlined that he was keenly aware of the future potential of the European Parliament and hoped to be a member of the assembly in the near future.

But events now took a very different turn. Hillery's private conversation with Kennedy was overheard by Raymond Smith, who wrote a story for the *Irish Independent* highlighting Hillery's dissatisfaction and suggesting that he might move to forge an alliance between Fianna Fáil and the Socialist group in the Parliament. Hillery was worried at the reaction of the Fianna Fáil MEPs and wanted to assure Lenihan, who was the leader of the Fianna Fáil group in the Parliament, that he was not attempting to take over the other man's leadership role.[36] He phoned Lenihan, who was in Luxembourg, on Thursday 28 October to clarify what had happened; Lenihan was not disturbed by the story and cheerfully dismissed his former colleague's concerns. But Hillery unwisely allowed himself to be drawn into a discussion about the presidency. The conversation that followed was comical in many respects, but had serious consequences for Hillery:

> Lenihan ... then asked me was I sure about the presidency, and I said I was, and that Jack knew what I wanted and I also said to him if they want a contest, which they say they do, they cannot have either Jack or me as candidate; but then I added, 'don't lose the presidency'. I said I didn't think Vivion Dev could win it. So he said, 'I get the message' and I said, 'You don't get any message. What I

want is to stay in private life [for now] and go into the
European Parliament if possible.[37]

Hillery's account of the discussion gives the impression that the two
participants were like ships passing in the night. His recollections suggest
that Lenihan misinterpreted his political commentary as a coded message
that Hillery wanted to go for President. But it is also probable that
Lenihan, who was noted throughout his career for his unwavering loyalty
to the party, leaped at any opportunity to secure Hillery as Fianna Fáil's
candidate and virtually guarantee that the party would be able to
nominate the next President.

As soon as Lenihan returned to Dublin, he immediately spread the
word that Hillery was available among Fianna Fáil TDs and political
journalists. The next few days saw a sudden resurgence of speculation that
Hillery would be the Fianna Fáil nominee. Dick Walsh reported in *The
Irish Times* on Friday 29 October that Hillery 'more than ever seemed
likely to become the next President of Ireland' and that the decision of the
Fianna Fáil parliamentary party was the only remaining hurdle for his
candidacy.[38] Frank Dunlop, Lynch's press secretary, phoned Ed FitzGibbon,
asking Hillery to contact Lynch urgently. Lynch now faced pressure from
two diverse and mutually antagonistic sources, which led him to withdraw
from his previous commitment to keep Hillery out of the frame.
Haughey's supporters made a renewed effort to promote Lynch himself
for the presidency. At the same time senior government ministers privately
briefed journalists that neither Fine Gael nor Labour would oppose
Hillery's candidacy if he was nominated by Fianna Fáil.[39] Lynch spoke to
Hillery three times over the following week. Hillery was told first that
the party now expected him to go forward, but he still resisted the attempt
to draft him. Hillery's recollection indicates that Lynch's second
intervention was decisive:

> The next thing Jack was on – 'Lenihan says you'll go'. I
> said no, I just told you the opposite. 'No, no, he's spreading
> it all over the Dáil'. Of course the government took it up

and Jack phoned again: 'I'm in trouble' he said 'I really need
this', putting me in a position where I couldn't refuse.[40]

Lynch's appeal to his former colleague and friend proved crucial in
changing Hillery's mind. The party leader informed Hillery on 3
November that the front bench would propose his selection as the
presidential candidate to the parliamentary party; by then the deed was
done and Lynch was sure that Hillery would accept the nomination.[41]

Hillery finally accepted the approach to go forward for the presidency,
which he had previously rejected on at least two occasions. It was a draft
in the purest sense of the term; a candidate was selected who was not
only unwilling to seek the nomination, but also profoundly reluctant to
accept the position at all. Hillery was to some extent the victim of his
own success. While Lenihan may have triggered the final bout of
speculation concerning Hillery's candidacy, the demand within the party
for him to stand was very real and was rooted in practical politics and
selfish political calculation. Influential elements within Fianna Fáil
favoured his elevation to the presidency, in part due to a genuine
recognition that the outgoing Commissioner was a very strong candidate
and would be well placed to win the election in the unlikely event that
the coalition chose to oppose him. Yet there were other, more devious
motives for prominent figures in the party to promote Hillery for the
Park. Denis Coghlan, political reporter with *The Irish Times*, drew
attention to one such motive when he commented on 9 November that
'ambitious Front Benchers saw Dr Hillery as a stumbling block to a nice
well-paid seat in the European Parliament.'[42]

The possibility of Hillery taking a seat in the European elections may
well have been unpalatable to some of his former colleagues, but a much
more undesirable prospect to ambitious members of the shadow cabinet
was the return of the former Commissioner to the Dáil, where he could
potentially succeed Jack Lynch within a couple of years. The fact that
Hillery had no ambition to become Taoiseach was not widely known and
even if it had been, it would have been regarded with incredulity by the
leading contenders to succeed Lynch. Hillery himself felt that such

ambitions motivated much of the pressure within Fianna Fáil for his elevation to the presidency: 'There were people maybe who wanted me to be President, out of the way ... so that I wouldn't be Taoiseach. I often think that, I've never said it [publicly], but I think that's what they were working on'.[43] Whatever the motivations of those demanding Hillery's nomination, it is certain that he faced overwhelming pressure to accept the presidency within a week of Ó Dálaigh's resignation.

Following Hillery's decision to accept the nomination, Fianna Fáil moved swiftly to select the Commissioner as their candidate on 3 November. There was, almost inevitably, some further intrigue within the party before the issue was resolved, as Haughey's supporters still demanded a contested presidential election. Lynch regarded it as a minor local difficulty: 'according to Jack, Haughey had some little intrigues and caucus going, trying to use the situation for himself.'[44] Haughey's supporters proposed Joe Brennan as the party's nominee instead of Hillery on the basis that an electoral contest was desirable and that the government would not oppose Hillery. Haughey's motivations were ambiguous; he may have been attempting to block Hillery, or simply to embarrass Lynch by proposing the party's deputy leader for the nomination, but this piece of posturing did not affect the outcome. Hillery decisively won the vote within the parliamentary party, by 55 votes to 15 for Brennan.[45] He derived little satisfaction, however, from winning a vote for an office that he did not want. The reality was that Hillery's accession to the presidency was assured once he allowed his name to go forward. His candidacy commanded almost universal approval within the political establishment in Dublin. Hillery's selection inspired enthusiasm among many Fianna Fáil TDs, while he was an acceptable choice to Fine Gael and Labour. Fianna Fáil nominated him formally on 6 November and it was evident even before his nomination papers were lodged that he would be the sixth President of Ireland; both government parties had already announced that they would not contest the election. Hillery was declared elected as President when nominations closed on 9 November 1976.[46] The ease with which Hillery was elected testified to his non-partisan public appeal and the widespread respect he enjoyed from politicians of all parties. Yet

Commissioner Hillery catches up on the news.

Hillery at his desk, Brussels.

Hillery at a meeting of European ministers, *c*.1973.

Hillery with James Bond, Portmarnock, 1976.
The four golfers are (l–r) Commandant Joe O'Keeffe, Paddy Hillery, Sean Connery,
Gerry McGuinness.

Greeting the crowd at Miltown Malbay on his first official visit following his election
as President, 1977

Welcome home to Miltown Malbay, 1977.

The Papal visit, October 1979: President Hillery and Pope John Paul II.

The Hillery family at Áras an Uachtaráin, during the spring of 1980: (l–r) Maeve, Paddy, John and Vivienne.

Courtesy of Dr Maeve Hillery

Paddy with Maeve, Áras an Uachtaráin, during his second term.

Hillery at the Fulbright golf competition at the K Club, 1998: (l–r) Maeve, Paddy, Elaine Dobbin, Craig Dobbin and Prof John Kelly.

Courtesy of Prof John Kelly

the speed and smoothness of the process also underlined the extent to which Hillery was rescuing both the government and the leadership of Fianna Fáil from a difficult political dilemma. Hillery's unopposed election provided a rapid and relatively painless resolution of the crisis surrounding the presidency since Ó Dálaigh's resignation.

Hillery's eventual decision to accept the party nomination and, in effect, the presidency itself, was driven primarily by the values that shaped his political life. Hillery had a strong sense of loyalty to institutions in which he served, from departments of state to the European Commission and later the presidency. This loyalty certainly encompassed Fianna Fáil as an organisation and many (though emphatically not all) of its leading members. Yet it was not primarily loyalty to the party that motivated Hillery in 1976. He was too sophisticated and experienced a politician to believe that appeals to party loyalty constituted the last word in political debate. Dennis Kennedy, a friend of Hillery as well as a perceptive political observer, recounted a conversation he had with the Commissioner just after Jack Lynch's approach to him:

> I told him I thought he would be mad to accept. He was just three years into the new world of the European Community and was loving it. Seven years in the Park was a life sentence as far as his career was concerned. But Hillery said, 'Dennis, you don't understand. When someone asks you to be President of Ireland, you can't refuse.'[47]

Hillery's response should not be taken too literally. He had refused several previous approaches to become President. But there was an underlying truth in his comment to Kennedy. This approach was very different from previous efforts to draft him as a Fianna Fáil candidate, which were dictated solely by the party's electoral interests and often not pursued with any great vigour by the party leader. On this occasion, Lynch made a serious approach to his former colleague; Hillery's personal regard for Lynch was undeniably a factor in his decision. More significantly, it was apparent that the presidency itself was being offered to Hillery; his candidacy commanded the implicit support of the entire political establishment. Hillery was a patriot and a mainstream nationalist who believed deeply in the development of the independent Irish state and sought to serve the institutions of the state to the best of his ability. The presidency had now been plunged into crisis; he had the ability to resolve the crisis and stabilise the institution. In the circumstances, refusing to accept the highest office in the state would have run directly counter to his core political beliefs – patriotism, institutional loyalty and his compelling sense of duty to both the party and more importantly the state itself.

Commentators and journalists would later argue that, by his fateful decision to accept the presidency, Hillery lost the glittering prize that might have been within his reach – the opportunity to serve as Taoiseach in succession to Lynch, who would soon regain office.[48] Certainly Hillery was one of the most experienced figures in Irish politics in 1976, and at 53 he was still young enough to look forward to further political achievement if he returned either to the Dáil or even the European Parliament. Lynch himself expected Hillery to succeed him and quietly indicated to the other man that he favoured him as his successor, provided that the transition occurred at a time of his own choosing.[49] There is no doubt that the prospect of his securing the top job in Irish politics vanished for good when Hillery agreed to accept the presidency. But the disappearance of this prospect did not disturb Hillery; he knew what he was giving up when he agreed to accept the party nomination in November 1976. He simply did not want to be Taoiseach and lacked the fierce personal ambition to secure the top job that guided many of his contemporaries, especially Haughey and Colley. Hillery told Lynch in November 1976 that he would prefer to be President than a candidate for the leadership of Fianna Fáil, although he was not enthusiastic about either alternative: 'it became clear that either I became President or I fall into the succession race to succeed Jack and I must say I told him that I would not want to succeed him as leader of the Party and probably after as Taoiseach.'[50] Even if he had never become President, he had already decided not to return to the Dáil or to the top tier of Irish politics. Hillery was not unwittingly sacrificing a long-term aspiration to become Taoiseach, but making a personal decision not to re-engage in frontline party politics.

Yet Hillery was making a genuine sacrifice in taking up a position that he did not want. He resigned from the European Commission on the eve of his inauguration as President on 3 December 1976; while the term of the outgoing Commission was about to elapse within a month anyway, Hillery was disappointed that he was unable to attend the final meeting of the Social Affairs Council on 9 December, which considered several outstanding elements in the social action programme, especially his proposals to improve the position of migrant workers.[51] He left behind the position where he had reached the height of his political career and moved to a largely symbolic office, which was greatly inferior in practical terms, even if it was nominally more important. Hillery reluctantly gave up not only the very real prospect of serving in the European Parliament, but also the future opportunity to influence policy within the European institutions, whose importance and potential he had recognised much sooner than most Irish politicians. He abandoned, too, any possibility of maintaining an active political career; nobody who held the highest office of the state had ever returned to mainstream politics. Moreover, his decision finally put paid to his cherished ambition of returning one day to medical practice, which had briefly appeared a viable possibility in the autumn of 1976. *The Irish Times* certainly depicted his position accurately in its headline on 9 November, the day that Hillery was confirmed as President-elect: 'For Hillery, loyalty has had its price as well as its reward'.[52] It is difficult to say definitively whether he made the right decision, but it is evident that Hillery made a difficult choice primarily on the basis of altruistic concerns, when self-interest would have dictated a very different verdict.

19.

Steadying the Ship
1977–1979

When Paddy Hillery was inaugurated as President of Ireland on 3 December 1976, he emphasised in his first presidential address the necessity for Irish society to protect personal liberty within the framework of the rule of law.[1] It was a message with obvious relevance to the challenges confronting the Irish state in the mid-1970s, notably the threat of terrorist violence and the implications for civil liberties of the government's tough response. Yet Hillery's message had clear application also to the controversy that led to his own election. The new President's address contained a thinly veiled rebuke to the government, as he paid a warm tribute to his predecessor, Cearbhall Ó Dálaigh. Hillery had publicly praised the former President's stand shortly after he himself was nominated to succeed Ó Dálaigh. He commented in a radio interview with RTÉ on 7 November that the former President had been right to resign and had displayed 'great courage' in pursuing his constitutional responsibilities. Hillery openly declared that he had been nominated to vindicate the constitutional position of the President and repudiate the coalition government's attitude towards the office.[2] This blunt statement caused some irritation within the Cabinet, but the relief of avoiding an election campaign no doubt eased any transitory discomfort that Cosgrave may have experienced. Hillery was genuinely outraged by the treatment of Ó Dálaigh and the episode helped to shape his priorities as President: 'It was in carrying out his constitutional functions that he suffered the insult for which he had no redress but to leave office. In any other country the insulter would have been the one to resign.'[3] Hillery certainly set out to stabilise the office after the crisis triggered by Ó Dálaigh's resignation. But he was also determined to establish the independence of the presidency and assert the right of the incumbent to fulfil his constitutional duties without interference from the government. These two central concerns largely dictated Hillery's actions throughout his two terms as President.

The new President was keenly aware of the symbolic and ceremonial nature of the office that he had inherited. The functions assigned to the President by the Constitution were usually formal powers, which could be exercised only on the advice of the government or the Taoiseach. The President formally appointed the Taoiseach but did so solely on the nomination of the Dáil; similarly, ministers were appointed by the President on the advice of the Taoiseach. There were only two significant powers that the head of state might exercise with any degree of independence. The President, after consultation with the Council of State, could refer bills passed by the Oireachtas to the Supreme Court to test their conformity with the Constitution. The head of state could also, in his absolute discretion, refuse to dissolve the Dáil on the advice of a Taoiseach who had ceased to retain the support of a majority in Dáil Éireann.[4] The Constitution also imposed significant restrictions on the presidency as an institution. The President required the formal approval of the government to leave the country; any address or speech by the President to the nation also had to be approved by the government. The

Constitution underlined in unmistakable terms that power rested with the government and the national parliament, not with the President.

Yet the constraints surrounding the presidency in the 1970s were political as well as constitutional. All the major parties shared a political consensus that the presidency was not merely outside party politics, but above politics in principle. This political perception dictated that the President had only formal or ceremonial functions and was not expected to undertake a wider public role, which might detract from the government of the day.[5] In effect, the conventional political consensus surrounding the presidency contemplated an office that was symbolic, silent and almost entirely powerless. Hillery himself shared this view to some extent; he fully accepted the limits set by the Constitution and was concerned to avoid conflict with the government.[6]

He was equally determined, however, to ensure that the presidency was firmly independent of the government and that the constitutional role of the office was respected. Hillery had neither the inclination nor the opportunity to expand significantly the role and profile of the presidency. As an incumbent selected by consensus among the political elite, Hillery, through no fault of his own, lacked the mandate given by a popular vote. He would have preferred to contest an election, but could hardly be blamed for the government's failure to run a candidate against him. Yet even an elected candidate would have enjoyed little scope to expand the role of the presidency in the face of the overwhelming political consensus that it should operate essentially as a symbolic, non-political office. Both Childers and Ó Dálaigh had attempted to expand the public role of the presidency and had been firmly rebuffed by the government. Hillery was a very experienced politician who had no illusions about the futility of challenging the political constraints surrounding the presidency in the 1970s.

The new President did not anticipate, however, the personal and political isolation of the office. He found the abrupt transition to Áras an Uachtaráin difficult and frustrating: 'It was extraordinary. I was suddenly isolated and silent. That big house was awful. It was a big, lonely old house'.[7] Peig O'Malley, who served as Hillery's private secretary throughout his time as President, believed that it took several months for him to adjust to life in Áras an Uachtaráin. The shock of the transition was particularly marked because he was living and working in the same place for the first time; he could no longer go home and leave the problems of his workplace outside his front door.[8] While he certainly adjusted to the new working environment in time, Hillery always disliked the restrictions on his privacy imposed by the dual function of Áras an Uachtaráin as the home and office of the President. Moreover, the physical isolation of the Áras, located in the middle of the Phoenix Park, the largest public park in Western Europe, created further difficulties, not least because Hillery's wife and children were also living in the Áras.

Hillery's sense of isolation was heightened by lingering tension with Cosgrave's government, which was inflamed by official delays in meeting even relatively simple requests by the President. He found that he had to consult two government departments and the Gardai to agree transport arrangements for himself and his family. He proposed that he would use his personal car, with a Garda driver, for official functions in or around the Dublin area as well as all private engagements; this meant that it would become a state car, with the maintenance and running costs covered by the state. Hillery hoped to make use of an official state car, a Mercedes, only for long journeys and ceremonial occasions in Dublin.[9] This apparently straightforward proposal, which was entirely in line with the practice of the previous two Presidents, immediately ran into bureaucratic hurdles, as officials of the Department of the Taoiseach either did not understand or did not agree with the President's proposed solution. Hillery also sought to arrange an additional Garda car to provide transport for his children and to look after the transport needs of the household staff in the Áras. The Secretary to the President, Máirtín Ó Flathartaigh, made an initial proposal outlining Hillery's wishes to the Department of the Taoiseach on 8 December 1976. The President's request was processed at a leisurely pace; there was no response at all until 15 February. Then Ó Flathartaigh was informed verbally by Brian McCarthy in the Department of the Taoiseach that it was proposed to sanction the use of the President's private car – provided he paid for all the expenses of running it himself; no provision at all was made for the transport of staff to the Áras.[10] Hillery regarded the official response as inadequate and even insulting – his instruction to the Secretary was terse: 'This seems to me to be asking junior officers for permission to drive my own car. Tell them to go to hell'.[11] To complicate matters further, it emerged that the Department of Justice had to sanction an additional Garda car to transport Hillery's children and the domestic staff; the department did approve the request but failed to tell the Garda Headquarters, so nothing was done about it for three months.[12]

This cavalier response infuriated Hillery, who suspected that political bias was at work. He complained directly to a senior official in the Department of the Taoiseach on 28 February 1977, raising the possibility that his requests were being deliberately frustrated: 'it seemed to him that there is a policy of hostility towards him (on the part of the government).'[13] This suspicion was almost certainly unfounded; it was apparently ineptitude rather than malice that lay at the root of the problem. Hillery's solution was simple but effective – he threatened to move out of Áras an Uachtaráin unless the situation was resolved:

> The President concluded his conversation by saying that if the difficulties of living in an isolated place like the Áras were not recognised (by the government) he would make his own arrangements to live elsewhere and would use the Áras merely as his office.[14]

This presidential threat had the desired effect. The Department of the Taoiseach approved the transport arrangements sought by Hillery in March 1977; an additional car and driver was duly provided to take Vivienne to school and to transport the domestic staff.[15] It was an apparently minor incident, but it graphically underlined the low political status of the presidency; the head of state could not even compel rapid action from officialdom for his own transport requirements. The dispute reflected Hillery's frustration and his sense of isolation shortly after taking over as President. The episode could have had wider consequences if Hillery had followed through on his threat to move out of the Áras. His warning that he might use the President's traditional residence solely as his office was a product of frustration and a tactic to exert pressure on the government rather than a serious statement of intent. Yet it might well have been better for him if he had moved out of the Áras, regardless of the outcome; the move would have caused dire political embarrassment to the government, but the controversy would also have marked out Hillery's presidency in a distinctive and positive fashion. He could easily have portrayed the move as a progressive step by a working President who was leaving behind some of the traditional shackles of the office.

Hillery soon found that his freedom of action was constrained not only by constitutional requirements but also by harsh financial realities. His initial impression of the presidency was that 'there was no staff, no money'; he was not far wrong.[16] The institutional support for the office of President was limited to the point of emaciation. The head of state had only a small office staff, including the Secretary to the President, his assistant, the private secretary to the President and three typists. Moreover, the President's salary and allowances were governed by the Presidential Establishment Act, 1973; any change in the remuneration of the head of state required legislation. This meant in practice that such changes happened very rarely; the personal salary of the President was the same in 1973 as when the office was created thirty-five years earlier.[17] The salary and allowances were increased significantly for the first time shortly before de Valera's retirement in 1973 and the President's salary was fixed at 10 per cent more than the remuneration enjoyed by the Chief Justice. But this legislation, which was mainly concerned with providing a reasonable salary for the head of state, did little to finance an adequate infrastructure to support the office itself. The additional presidential allowance of £15,000 in 1976 was intended to cover not only the day-to-day expenses of running the house and the salaries of the household staff, but also the costs of official entertainment incurred by the President, including hospitality for visiting heads of state.[18] The allowance was pitifully inadequate to support virtually the entire range of activities undertaken by the President in his official residence. Successive governments had adopted such a minimalist position in supporting the presidency that the office was in effect turned into a 'totem pole' rather than a significant institution of the state.

Shortly after Hillery's inauguration, he initiated efforts to enhance the financial resources allocated to the presidency. He raised with Liam Cosgrave the need for an increase in the presidential allowance. Cosgrave accepted that an increase was justified, but no immediate action was taken.[19] The imminence of a general election made any early review of the President's establishment unlikely. Hillery himself took action in the meantime. He was shocked at the low level of the salaries paid to the household staff and moved to double their salaries shortly after his appointment; the additional payments exceeded the official allowance and Hillery dipped into his own salary to supplement the payments to the staff.[20] Fortunately for the government and indeed the entire political establishment, this did not become public knowledge; nothing could have underlined the miserly scale of state support for the presidency more visibly than the head of state acting personally to subsidise the salaries of his staff.

The general election in June 1977 brought a Fianna Fáil landslide; Jack Lynch made a triumphant return to power with the largest overall majority in the history of the state. Hillery's friendly personal relationship with Lynch eased the tension with the Department of the Taoiseach that had marked the first months of his term.[21] The President made a renewed approach to the new government, which yielded some positive results. Peig O'Malley reminded the Department of the Taoiseach on 27 July of the President's approach to Cosgrave and highlighted the meagre nature of the presidential allowance.[22] The senior officials of the Taoiseach's department agreed that a considerable increase was justified and Daniel O'Sullivan, secretary to the government, recommended on 5 August a doubling of the allowance to €30,000. Lynch agreed in principle with this proposal, but was reluctant to sanction a major increase in the short term; he was concerned that the necessary legislation to enhance the allowance neither precede nor coincide with the forthcoming talks on the national pay agreement, fearing that it would undermine the government's calls for pay restraint.[23] The Taoiseach's caution was understandable, but threatened to delay indefinitely any improvement in the President's establishment. Hillery suggested an alternative approach that did not involve legislation. When the President met Lynch on 27 October 1977, they discussed the allowance and Hillery proposed that a government department should take over the payment of all staff working for the President.[24] Lynch approved this solution, which was implemented soon afterwards; the wages of the household staff in the Áras were no longer taken from the presidential allowance but were instead paid directly from the budget of the Board of Works.[25] This move resolved the immediate problem; it paved the way for a substantial increase in the staff salaries and a moderate improvement in the funding allocated to the presidency.[26] Lynch's government also agreed to provide an allowance for a clerical officer to act as a private secretary to Maeve Hillery on a part-time basis.[27] But the thorny issue of the presidential allowance itself was not resolved. The allowance remained inadequate even after staff salaries were removed from it and the opportunity to improve it to a reasonable level was lost.

While Hillery secured some modest advances in the level of state funding for the presidency in 1977, the support structure for the office was still severely underdeveloped. Moreover, successive governments maintained a strictly minimalist approach to financing and supporting the presidency. Fianna Fáil had fiercely criticised the national coalition for its treatment of Hillery's predecessor. But the party's return to power brought no fundamental change in the official neglect of the presidency, which was hardly less scandalous, though much less noticeable, than Paddy Donegan's treatment of Cearbhall Ó Dálaigh. Hillery later commented on his former party's priorities in office: 'It was up to FF to save the presidency and they should have taken some care of it after the resignation. But they went about their business which did not include the protection of the office.'[28] While Lynch approved some incremental improvements in the funding for the presidency, the minimalist pattern of the past persisted well into the 1980s. The head of state's salary was adjusted upwards from time to time in line with pay increases for members of the judiciary, but the presidential allowance was not increased at all in this period. Although the Department of the Taoiseach had acknowledged the case for increasing the allowance in 1977, no official action was taken to promote the necessary legislation and the level of the allowance remained unchanged for the rest of Hillery's term as President.[29] The prospect of enhanced support for the office steadily receded with the second oil crisis and the sharp economic decline that followed in the early 1980s. But even before the grim recession of the 1980s, the dominant political approach towards the highest office in the land essentially amounted to benign neglect. It was not until April 1991, several months after Hillery's retirement, that the Dáil approved legislation to provide an allowance of £100,000 for the President.[30]

Yet Hillery himself made a couple of tactical mistakes that contributed to his misfortunes as President. He could have sought guarantees from the leaders of the three major parties before taking up office that the necessary resources would be provided to allow him to function effectively as President. It is likely that Hillery missed his most favourable opportunity to secure adequate institutional support for the office even before his inauguration. Then, as the newly elected President, Hillery could have ensured that his officials immediately made a formal proposal for a substantial increase in the presidential allowance. The Department of the Taoiseach expected such a proposal in the summer of 1977, but it never materialised.[31] Hillery instead preferred to deal with the matter informally at official level and through his personal meetings with Jack Lynch. This approach undoubtedly brought some gains, not least for the staff in the Áras, but it also allowed the government to escape with some running repairs instead of a more lasting upgrade of the President's establishment. A formal proposal detailing the traditional underfunding of the office would not have guaranteed a favourable outcome, but it would have made it more difficult for successive governments to wriggle off the hook quite so easily. Yet this prospect should not be exaggerated: Hillery required the backing of leading politicians to upgrade the office and this was generally striking by its absence in the late 1970s. It was the complacency and indifference of the majority of the political elite that determined the level of official support for the presidency. The highest office in the state was poorly resourced and supported from the beginning of Hillery's term until his retirement because it hardly featured at all as a priority for the large majority of active politicians.

The severe limitations on the resources allocated to the President's office imposed additional pressures on Hillery himself and the small group of office staff in the Áras. Peig O'Malley recalled the challenges faced by the President's office: 'Because of the lack of staff, we had to turn our hands to everything. I almost felt that you had to have danger money to work for a President, especially as if there was any mistake it would be front-page news'.[32] The role of Secretary to the President was crucial in such a small office; the head of the office bore a dual responsibility to manage the work of the staff and act as private secretary to the President.

The new President benefited initially from the support of one of the most experienced figures in the civil service. Máirtín Ó Flathartaigh had previously served in the Taoiseach's office and as a senior official in the Department of Education; he headed the President's office under de Valera, Childers and Ó Dálaigh.[33] Ó Flathartaigh was close to retirement by the time of Hillery's election, but stayed on as Secretary beyond the normal retirement age to oversee the transition to the new incumbent. He provided a valuable element of continuity in the first year of Hillery's term.[34] When Ó Flathartaigh retired in August 1978, Hillery selected Micheál Ó hOdhráin, an assistant secretary in the Department of Education, as his successor.[35] The President's choice caused some tension with the Department of the Taoiseach, which had its own candidate for the post, Bertie O'Dowd. Jack Lynch proposed O'Dowd for the position, while the outgoing Secretary strongly recommended Micheál Ó hOdhráin. Hillery liked and respected O'Dowd, but chose Ó hOdhráin for the post even though he hardly knew him at all.[36] The selection reflected Hillery's concern to establish the independence of the presidency: 'I said, "I am going to get someone outside [the Taoiseach's office], like Dev did, he got Máirtín Ó Flathartaigh." I wanted to be independent of the Taoiseach's office and you can't, they control the money. You can't beat City Hall.'[37] Hillery sought consistently to underline the President's independence, and over time, he would demonstrate in no uncertain terms that it was possible for the office to be independent of the government. Yet it is not at all clear that he was right to allow his legitimate wider concerns to influence the choice of Secretary.[38] Micheál Ó hOdhráin was a diligent and conscientious public servant. His career had been spent entirely in Education, where he had risen through the ranks to become assistant secretary in charge of the higher education section within the department.[39] He was highly regarded in the department both as an official and a scholar, who had a particular interest in the Irish language. Ó hOdhráin, however, lacked his predecessor's detailed knowledge of the bureaucratic maze in which the President had to operate. The new secretary confronted a very difficult challenge in managing the President's office without any real support structure or the official connections enjoyed by his predecessor.

Despite the political and financial constraints on his activity, Hillery gradually adapted to the demands of the office. He sought primarily to stabilise an institution that had been shaken by recent controversy. Hillery undertook a full schedule of engagements, attending a wide range of events in local communities throughout the country; he attended functions organised by national schools, universities and community groups on a regular basis throughout his time as President. He also opened various public events with an international dimension, such as the meeting in Dublin of the World Medical Assembly in September 1977, and the annual conference of the Irish Section of European Journalists in the following month.[40] But much of Hillery's activity went unreported by either the print media or RTÉ. This was partly due to the reality that many of the local events attended by the President were not seen as newsworthy by the national media. Yet this was not the whole story; the President's office did not promote Hillery's activity in a systematic way, nor did it seek to develop news stories around his busy schedule.[41] Hillery himself did not seek publicity, and he was wary initially of drawing media attention towards the presidency at a time when he was working to stabilise the office within its political and constitutional constraints: 'I saw my task as one of restoring the presidency after the early death of Erskine and the resignation in the face of insult of Cearbhall Ó Dálaigh, followed by the attempts of the politicians to avoid elections.'[42]

Hillery's first priorities were to restore stability to the office and establish its independence, not to promote the presidency publicly. Yet as it became clear that much of the work he was doing had passed unnoticed, Hillery became more concerned about developing a public profile for the presidency; he found, however, that his ability to do so was strictly limited. The Áras had no press officer delegated to deal with the media and successive governments proved unwilling to appoint one or to provide money for Hillery to do so.[43] Hillery occasionally raised the matter with the government, beginning in 1979 when he asked Charles Haughey just after his election as Taoiseach if he would sanction the appointment of a press officer for the Áras. The new Taoiseach declined the request, and no official action was taken for the following decade.[44] The absence of a dedicated press officer undermined Hillery's ability to deal effectively with the media and severely limited the public profile of the presidency.

Hillery was also an active President at an international level. He undertook his first state visit within two months of his election, travelling to West Germany in February 1977. Hillery's state visits secured greater coverage in the Irish media than his engagements at home; it was striking that his international activity generated as much interest in the European media, where he was well known as a highly influential Vice-President of the European Commission, as in the Irish press corps. He accepted a request for an interview from the French magazine *L'Express* shortly after taking up office; he also gave a lengthy interview to the German Press Agency in January 1977 before his state visit to West Germany.[45] Hillery's background as Foreign Minister and a European Commissioner gave him a knowledge and appreciation of international affairs matched by few of his predecessors, with the exception of de Valera. Hillery undertook seven state visits during his first term, including the first visit by a serving Irish head of state to India in January 1978; he also visited Luxembourg (September 1978), Bahrain and Tanzania (1980), Denmark (June 1983) and Japan (September 1983).[46] He also made a wide range of official trips abroad, including two provoked by the high mortality rate of the occupants of the throne of St Peter. Following the death of Pope Paul VI, Hillery attended the enthronement of the new pope, John Paul I, in Rome on 3 September 1978.[47] The new Pontiff died suddenly on 29 September only 33 days after his election. The President was back in the Eternal City on 22 October for the enthronement of the Polish Cardinal Wojtyla as Pope John Paul II.[48] The new pope would visit Ireland within a year of his accession, undertaking the most memorable state visit of Hillery's term and inadvertently triggering the most controversial episode of Hillery's presidency.

The pattern of Hillery's presidency was set in the first two years of his term. He was a hardworking and conscientious head of state from the outset, even if much of his activity at home was overlooked by the media and largely invisible to the public. While Hillery ultimately adapted well to the demands of the office, he was deeply frustrated by the essentially powerless character of the institution. He had never sought power for its own sake, but the promotion of reforming policies was at the heart of his career, from comprehensive schools to equal pay. The lack of political substance in the presidency was the most fundamental reason he had not sought the office in the first place: 'There are no policies to carry out. So one could not wish to be in a job where your talents have no place and the capacity to please by personality or stunts might be more useful'.[49] Hillery developed a low-key method of operation, which generally avoided self-promotion and fulfilled the obligations associated with the office without attempting to expand its public role. This approach was in part a reflection of his own political style and his preference for not seeking the limelight unless it was clearly necessary, but the importance of the context in which he operated should not be ignored. Hillery's low-key style as President was at least as much a response to the severe constraints on his freedom of action and the instability that preceded his term of office as a reflection of any personal preference. Hillery's style and working practices as President were well suited to the demands and restrictions of the office in the 1970s.

20.

Conspiracy and Rumour
1979

I always think of rumours as the shark. You know, the shark
is millions of years old, but it's so effective, it hasn't changed
because it's able to deal with everything that came its way
over the years. The rumour is the shark in politics.[1]

This was Hillery's verdict many years later on the events that might
have ended his presidential term prematurely. The visit by Pope John
Paul II in the autumn of 1979 triggered the most controversial and
traumatic episode of Hillery's presidency. Hillery was obliged to respond
publicly just after the papal visit to the false rumour that he would resign
his office because his marriage was about to collapse. The story was
entirely fictional, but the full details surrounding the rumours have never
emerged. Various theories were advanced to explain the rumours then
and later; perhaps the most intriguing was the notion that the KGB
instigated the rumours in the European media to embarrass the pope and

promote the Soviet Union's international agenda. But the origins of the rumour were to be found in the shark-infested waters of Irish politics.

The visit of Pope John Paul II to Ireland from 29 September to 1 October 1979 was an extraordinary event, which provoked a massive outpouring of emotion in an overwhelmingly Catholic country.[2] The pope's open-air Mass in the Phoenix Park on 29 September attracted a crowd of over 1.25 million people. John Paul also drew huge crowds in Drogheda, Galway, Knock and Limerick. Almost half a million people turned out in Limerick on 1 October to hear the final homily of his visit, emphasising the need to maintain traditional Catholic values.[3] The papal visit saw a national celebration of Ireland's historical and cultural attachment to the Catholic faith.

The papal visit coincided with the second oil crisis, which had triggered an international economic downturn. This would become a full-scale recession in the early 1980s. The escalating levels of public debt were already evident to the political class by 1979, although it would be several years before any effective remedial action was taken. Pope John Paul's visit also occurred against the background of intensive speculation and intrigue surrounding the leadership of Fianna Fáil. Jack Lynch's position was increasingly precarious, following a major setback for Fianna Fáil in the first direct elections to the European Parliament in June 1979. Lynch had privately decided to retire by 1980, but a group of backbench TDs, drawn mainly from the new generation of deputies elected in 1977, were orchestrating a heave to force him out immediately. The backbench manoeuvres to destabilise Lynch were covertly promoted by Haughey, who had been restored to the Cabinet as Minister for Health and Social Welfare.[4] Haughey had bided his time after his disgrace in 1970 and painstakingly built up support within the party organisation. George Colley, Minister for Finance since 1977, was Lynch's chief lieutenant and enjoyed the support of the party establishment. But Haughey was convinced that his hour had come and his calculations were ultimately proved right. Lynch's impending departure was an open secret by October 1979 and the struggle for the succession was already in progress. The leadership struggle within the governing party was not restricted to the corridors of Leinster House or the Coffee Dock in Jury's Hotel, where dissident TDs met to discuss Lynch's removal. The battle for the succession also extended its tentacles to Áras an Uachtaráin and the offices of the international media in Washington, London and Bonn.

The rumours about Hillery's private life began to circulate among the Irish and international media over a month before the pope's visit. The rumours continued to flourish in Leinster House and the Irish media for some time after Hillery's emphatic denial in October 1979, eventually dying down only in the early months of 1980.[5] There is no doubt that the rumours were carefully orchestrated from the beginning. The basic story itself remained remarkably consistent over several months: – the President of Ireland would resign because his wife was about to end their marriage, due to his extra-marital affairs with two unnamed women.[6] The story was embellished with the suggestion that Maeve Hillery was taking a case for a legal separation against her husband. A boat trip taken by the President to the Isle of Man in March 1979 was also fed into the rumour mill. It was suggested that Hillery had failed to secure the government's permission to travel outside the jurisdiction of the state.[7] While it was not always stated explicitly, the unmistakable subtext was that the covert boat trip provided a convenient opportunity for an affair. The rumours circulated widely in the early autumn of 1979, reaching journalists in Bonn, London and other European cities, who were preparing to cover the pope's visit to Ireland.[8]

The story itself was a work of fiction; it was not a case of unfounded malicious gossip, but a deliberate invention designed to smear a leading public figure. Hillery had no intention of resigning his office; indeed he later went on to serve a second term. The vicious innuendo about his marriage was entirely untrue. Paddy and Maeve Hillery had been married for 24 years in 1979; they would celebrate 50 years of marriage in 2005. The suggestion that the President had entertained a mistress at the Áras was not only untrue but also transparently absurd; maintaining a secret liaison in the President's official residence, with its complement of domestic staff and security officers, would indeed have been an extraordinary achievement. In any event conducting such a clandestine relationship would have been entirely alien to Hillery's character and personality. The story was based on a deliberate misrepresentation of Hillery's friendly relationship with two female staff members in his *cabinet* in Brussels. No enterprising journalist was ever able to produce a scintilla of evidence to suggest an extra-marital affair, despite efforts by at least one Irish editor to investigate the allegations in Brussels.[9] Even the story about the boat trip was inaccurate; Hillery had secured the authorisation of the government for the voyage to the Isle of Man, so it was scarcely a covert expedition for illicit purposes. The rumours can fairly be described as a devious concoction of lies, distortions and malicious innuendo. The most notable feature of the story was that it did not change fundamentally over several months, even though it was extensively disseminated among hundreds of journalists. It was also striking that it did not end with Hillery's denial in October 1979 but continued to circulate until January 1980. It was then allowed to fade away, suggesting that it had served its purpose.

The rumours first came to Hillery's attention in September 1979. A former classmate from UCD, Joan McCarthy, wrote him a letter warning that *Hibernia*, a weekly political magazine edited by John Mulcahy, was going to publish a story about the alleged break-up of his marriage: 'She wrote me a letter and as far as I was concerned it was out of the blue. In fact I laughed [at it]. *Hibernia* was going to publish this thing that I had women in the Áras.'[10] Hillery's initial reaction was that the story was simply ludicrous and would not be taken seriously. He could not see how anyone would believe that the President, who lived in the full glare of public and media scrutiny, would be able to conduct a clandestine affair, still less to keep a mistress in the Áras. But the potential story in *Hibernia* was far from an isolated incident. The President soon received shocked messages from close friends and relatives who were very disturbed by the rumours that he was on the verge of resigning because his marriage was about to collapse.[11] The story rapidly gained momentum during the weekend of the papal visit itself. The exceptional level of interest among international newspapers at the pope's decision to visit Ireland so early in his pontificate and the presence of approximately 2,000 journalists in

Dublin to cover John Paul's visit provided fertile ground for the rumours. Raymond Smith, who liked and admired Hillery, left a colourful description of how the story swept through the massed ranks of the media:

> Some newsmen will grasp at any straw in the wind – if there is not something concrete to go on. Dublin Castle became a hotbed of rumour and counter-rumour once the Big One began circulating – that is the 'story' about the private life of President Hillery and alleged 'difficulties' in his marriage. ... Then, however, like a prairie fire word got around that the man from Le Soir [Belgian newspaper] had actually filed a story for his newspaper and that it was going out that afternoon. [12]

Smith gave no credence to the rumours and believed that other Irish journalists were equally sceptical, while foreign journalists proved much more credulous – or in the case of British tabloids, more eager to pursue the story regardless of its veracity. But this recollection of events was not entirely accurate. An Irish weekly, *Hibernia*, was one of the news outlets prepared to break the story, along with at least one British daily newspaper.[13] While most Irish journalists did not believe the rumours, they were caught up in the frenzied atmosphere generated by the story. *Le Soir* did not break the story and it is not at all clear that its correspondent ever intended to do so. But the story naturally spread well beyond the assembled press corps; knowledge of the rumours was widespread in official circles in Dublin during the weekend of the papal visit.[14] The pervasive character of the rumours eventually forced Hillery to act.

While Hillery was well aware of the rumours by the time the pope landed in Ireland, he managed to ignore them for the duration of the visit, going ahead with his official duties as if there were no subterranean rumblings about his private life. The President was a central participant in the official ceremonies that marked the papal visit. He was present at Dublin Airport along with the Taoiseach to greet Pope John Paul II on the morning of Saturday 29 September. Hillery, accompanied by Maeve, attended the open-air Mass in the Phoenix Park later that day, sitting directly under the podium where John Paul celebrated the service.[15] The pope then called to the Áras for an official meeting with the President on Saturday evening around 9pm.[16] Finally Hillery and his wife saw the pope off from Shannon Airport on Monday 1 October; the President gave a short farewell address before Pope John Paul boarded an Aer Lingus jet for Boston, his next destination. Hillery assured the Pope of the enduring affection of the Irish people and expressed the hope that his forthcoming address to the United Nations would be 'taken to heart by world leaders'.[17] But the rumours had not gone away. While most editors were not yet willing to rush into print with such an unconfirmed report, it was only a matter of time before the story appeared in some form. At least two publications, *Hibernia* and the *Daily Mirror*, were ready to publish the story on Thursday 4 October.[18] The reality of imminent publication compelled Hillery to take action.

The two days following the pope's departure saw frenzied behind-the-scenes activity in Dublin, as journalists rushed to check the story, leading politicians urged the President to deny it immediately and last-minute consultations occurred between the Áras and the Taoiseach's office to decide what to do. Maeve Hillery left for a pre-planned holiday in Spain immediately after the pope's departure. This was not at all unusual, as Mrs Hillery often spent time at her holiday home in Spain while her husband was preoccupied with official business.

Meanwhile, the Government Information Service (GIS) was deluged by queries from journalists about the President's impending resignation; one weekly magazine estimated, probably correctly, that the GIS received over a hundred media queries in the space of 24 hours.[19] The Áras also received numerous phone calls from journalists seeking information on the story and warning that reports might be published.[20] Lynch called Hillery personally to discuss how to contain the rumour: 'Jack phoned – he said, what's happening? I said "there's nothing in it, Jack". He said, "we'll have to deny it, it's very strong"'.[21] Lynch offered to brief the editors of RTÉ and the three major daily newspapers on the President's behalf, but Hillery insisted on speaking to the editors personally. Lynch was concerned that the presidency would be dragged into further controversy if Hillery made a statement, but Hillery warned him that silence from the Park would be misinterpreted and journalists would conclude that the President had something to hide.[22] Hillery also spoke to the leading members of the opposition, Garret FitzGerald, now leader of Fine Gael, and Frank Cluskey, the leader of the Labour Party, on 3 October. He assured them that the story was entirely false and indicated that he would have to speak out publicly. Both politicians expressed sympathy with Hillery's predicament and Cluskey was particularly forceful, warning him to challenge the rumours without delay: 'This is very serious, Paddy. You have to deny it.'[23] Hillery agreed that he would have to challenge the story publicly, but hoped to do so without becoming the centre of a media circus. The President himself took the final decision to go public on the afternoon of Wednesday 3 October.[24] He did not intend to have a press conference at all initially, but aimed to brief the editors that the story was false and issue a statement clarifying that he had no intention of resigning. After some hesitation, the Taoiseach agreed that Hillery should deal with the media directly, although both men still hoped that briefing the editors would suffice to quell the rumours.

The editors, not surprisingly, saw things differently when they were called to Áras an Uachtaráin at about 4.30 p.m. on Wednesday 3 October. Hillery had a private meeting with the four editors, including Wesley Boyd, Head of News in RTÉ, Aidan Pender, editor of the *Irish Independent*, Tim Pat Coogan of the *Irish Press* and Douglas Gageby of the *The Irish Times*. The meeting lasted about 30 minutes and did not proceed as Hillery had hoped. He told the editors that the rumour was entirely unfounded and read the statement that he intended to issue.[25] But the editors were reluctant to take the responsibility for briefing other journalists on the story. They advised the President to hold a press conference for all the political correspondents; they argued that it was the best way to kill the rumours for good.[26] Hillery was angry at the editors' response, feeling that they were simply passing the buck and forcing him into a full–scale media event that he did not want. His anger was still evident in an interview for this book 27 years later: 'The editors were a miserable lot, they took no responsibility. I have nothing but contempt for them still, they wouldn't take it on themselves to believe me. "Ah," they said, "you'll have to talk to the journalists." So that's how it became a press conference.'[27]

Hillery's anger was entirely understandable; holding a press conference meant that he would have to face the assembled journalists and answer the inevitable questions about his marriage and personal life. It was always unlikely, however, that the editors would agree to take responsibility for containing the story. In the post–Watergate era, accusations of a cover–up would rapidly ensue, and the editors took the path of least resistance in passing the story onto their political correspondents. Hillery's outrage did not impair his sharp political judgement. He recognised that he had no alternative but to go ahead with a press conference for the political journalists once the proposal was made; otherwise it would appear that he was evading legitimate questions about the story.[28] The political correspondents for RTÉ and the major daily newspapers were immediately invited to a formal news briefing at the Áras, which took place at about 7.30 on the same evening.

The press conference that followed was unprecedented in the history of the presidency. Formal news briefings or large–scale media events involving the President were rare enough in any event until the 1990s. But the press conference on 3 October 1979 was like none other held by an Irish President before or since. It was the most dramatic and sensational media briefing given by an Irish head of state. The briefing was attended by seven political journalists, Dick Walsh (*The Irish Times*), Michael Mills (*Irish Press*), Chris Glennon (*Irish Independent*), Joe O'Malley (*Sunday Independent*), Seán Duignan (RTÉ), Liam O'Neill (*Cork Examiner*) and Maurice Hickey (*Evening Herald*). It was hardly surprising that no journalist from *Hibernia* was invited.[29] At the outset Hillery issued a short formal statement, which emphatically dismissed any suggestion that he was about to resign:

> In recent days, it has come to my attention that there were
> rumours circulating as to the possibility of my resigning as
> President. There is absolutely no foundation, whatever, for
> such rumours. I am not resigning.[30]

Hillery's categorical denial was designed to direct the focus of the media
firmly to the issue of his supposed resignation, rather than the equally
false rumours about his private life: 'I went in and I said to them "I have
only one statement, that is I am not going to resign". That was the big
thing, they had a structure that way [for their stories]; it was the serious
thing, that I was going to resign.'[31] The President's statement obviously did
not prevent questions about his marriage, but it gave the journalists a
framework for their stories that was about politics rather than alleged
personal scandal. Hillery nevertheless faced a series of questions about his
personal life, which sought to probe the rumours of a rift in his marriage
due to 'suggestions of an alleged liaison with a third party', as the *Irish
Press* delicately described it.[32] He firmly dismissed the rumour that his
marriage was about to collapse and specifically denied involvement in an
affair with any other woman. When he was asked about suggestions that
a legal case concerning his marriage was imminent, he denounced the
rumour of legal action as 'absolutely without foundation'.[33] Hillery
reiterated several times that there were no difficulties in his marriage and
asserted that 'There is no problem, no reason at all, why I should not stay
in the presidency'.[34]

Seán Duignan, political correspondent with RTÉ, asked the question
that preoccupied many of the journalists – why was the President denying
rumours about his office and his marriage in such a public fashion?
Hillery responded honestly that he had been compelled to act by the
pervasive nature of the story; 'the rumours have persisted and I have heard
it from people who have heard these rumours, growing stronger and
stronger. There is nothing I can do about it, except to say there is no
reason why I should resign.'[35] He also emphasised that he was attempting
to protect the constitutional position of the President, and believed that
it was essential to 'put on record his intention of remaining in office'.[36]

Hillery was undoubtedly concerned that the office of the presidency be protected, as it had already been embroiled in considerable controversy and instability during the brief terms of his two predecessors. He also saw the political value of appealing to the media and the wider public to protect the institution of the presidency; this theme was soon taken up by supportive elements in the media, especially the *Irish Press*. Despite his unhappiness at having to undertake the press conference at all, Hillery gave a controlled and dignified performance, dealing courteously and reasonably with the questions raised by the political journalists.

The drama of the occasion was enhanced when the press conference was interrupted by a phone call for the President. In a further twist to the saga, the call was from Maeve, who was replying to a message that her husband had left earlier that day. As there was no direct phone link at her holiday spot, Hillery had left a message for his wife to phone him urgently; he had not been able to consult her before speaking to the editors.[37] When she did so, Hillery briefly left the press conference to tell Maeve that he was issuing a public statement to deny the rumours. When he returned to the briefing, he informed the journalists that 'his wife strongly supported' his action in challenging the rumours.[38] He wisely did not add that on being told he was giving a press conference, Maeve had commented cheerfully, 'give them my love!'[39] Mrs Hillery's supportive phone call highlighted the extraordinary nature of the whole episode. In a later era of spin-doctors and instant rebuttal, the phone call would have been taken as a pre-arranged device to influence the media coverage. In fact, Hillery's decision to go public had been made at such short notice that he was genuinely unable to reach his wife before speaking to the press. It reflected the level of consternation caused by the rumours that Maeve Hillery was briefed on the situation in the middle of the President's press conference.

The story itself caused a public and media sensation. While the rumours were widely known in political and journalistic circles in Dublin, the vast majority of the public were entirely unaware of the story until Seán Duignan's report on RTÉ's nine o'clock news bulletin. RTÉ had a special current affairs programme ready to go out if the President resigned. The presenter, Brian Farrell, and the production team were on stand-by in the studio for several hours, waiting for definite news to come out of Áras an Uachtaráin. The programme was cancelled when Hillery confirmed that he was not resigning, but the fact that it was all set to go reflected the febrile atmosphere in Dublin at the time. Duignan's report was sensational enough; it broke the story publicly for the first time and carried the President's statement that he had no intention of resigning, as well as his denial of any marital difficulties. The RTÉ report marked a dramatic end to an excruciatingly difficult and embarrassing day for Paddy Hillery. It was no less uncomfortable for the President the following morning, when the story attracted massive media coverage in all the national newspapers, with banner headlines announcing Hillery's statement and front-page articles faithfully recounting every detail of his press conference.[40] Most daily newspapers also ran follow-up articles on 5 October, outlining the political response to Hillery's statement and discussing the more controversial elements of his career before the presidency.

Yet the general media reaction to the story appeared to vindicate Hillery's decision to issue a public statement and speak openly to the press. The reports by the political journalists were detailed and professional, but not in any way critical of Hillery. The correspondents took Hillery at his word and reported his comments verbatim. There was no attempt to go beyond the details provided by the President into lurid speculation about his personal life. The conventions of the time undoubtedly affected the relatively restrained way in which the story was reported. The journalists probably also realised that the story was sufficiently sensational in its own right without any additional embellishment. Some of the correspondents expressed sympathy for Hillery's predicament once the rumours had gained momentum; Michael Mills, political correspondent of the *Irish Press*, remarked that 'The President's decision to call in political correspondents to deny specific rumours about his resignation, and particularly his marriage, cannot have been an easy one'.[41]

Moreover, the editors of the major daily newspapers gave over-whelming support to the President. The *Irish Press* nailed its colours to the mast in an editorial on 4 October entitled 'Dr Hillery's Statement'. Tim

Pat Coogan declared that the President had taken 'an unusual and courageous step' in confronting the rumours about his private life; he had acted to maintain public confidence in the presidency and protect the dignity of the office itself. The editorial concluded with a ringing endorsement of Hillery's position: 'Dr Paddy Hillery is the President of Ireland and as such a slur on him is a slur on all of us. He needs our support at this time.'[42] The unqualified backing of the *Irish Press* was to be expected; the newspaper still maintained its connections with Fianna Fáil and Hillery enjoyed friendly relations with many of its journalists. But the other leading daily newspapers were equally unambiguous. The *Irish Independent* proclaimed that the President had acted 'firmly, courageously and correctly' in dismissing the rumours; the editorial expressed regret that Hillery had become 'the target of some rumour-factory' and proclaimed that he should be 'allowed to perform his duties without the attentions of malicious or idle gossip-mongers'.[43] Perhaps most striking was the line taken by *The Irish Times*, which had fiercely criticised past Fianna Fáil governments of which Hillery was a prominent member. But on this occasion Douglas Gageby's editorial offered unequivocal support to the President. Gageby elegantly commented on the unprecedented nature of Hillery's statement, noting 'It was an unusual step; these are unusual times.'[44] The editor of *The Irish Times* portrayed Hillery as a worthy occupant of Áras an Uachtaráin, who compared favourably with his distinguished predecessors from Douglas Hyde to Cearbhall Ó Dálaigh: 'Dr Paddy Hillery is worthy to take his place in the ranks with these imposing figures. He and his wife and his whole family deserve the sympathy and understanding of all citizens. Public life can be hell'.[45]

The leading figures of the political establishment also rallied behind the President following his press conference. Jack Lynch publicly endorsed Hillery's intervention on 4 October, when a spokesperson for the government confirmed that 'The President has had the Taoiseach's full support in the action he took.'[46] Similarly, Frank Cluskey explicitly supported Hillery's position, affirming that 'Naturally, I accept the word of the President.' The President also received the support of Garret FitzGerald, who did not comment directly on the statement but confirmed that he was fully aware of Hillery's intention to speak out publicly.[47] The initial public reaction was also strongly favourable towards Hillery. When he arrived to open a conference held at the Central Remedial Clinic in Clontarf on Thursday 4 October, he received a standing ovation from the delegates; it was his first public appearance since the rumours broke, and it left journalists who were covering the story in no doubt of the popular backing for the President.[48] Hillery's decision to challenge the rumours publicly was a calculated gamble; his dramatic intervention generated more publicity for the story in the short term, but also ultimately defused the crisis by confronting the rumours openly and garnering widespread support for his position.

The necessity for Hillery's public intervention was soon questioned, not least by some journalists who had been eager to publish the story in the first place. Darach MacDonald argued in *Hibernia* on 11 October that the President had overreacted, making a key miscalculation in speaking to the editors and journalists when a single sentence from the GIS might have achieved the same objective. MacDonald even claimed in Shakespearean vein that 'As it was, it appeared that "he doth protest too much"'.[49] It is difficult to take *Hibernia's* commentary too seriously, however, as its attempt to break the story on 4 October was a key factor in provoking Hillery's action and MacDonald's original story on that date had been comprehensively upstaged as a result of the President's statement. But others expressed a more general unease at the media intrusion into the private life of a public figure. Raymond Smith questioned whether Hillery had been badly advised, either by the government or the editors, in denying the rumours in such a public forum, and especially in commenting at all on allegations of an extra-marital affair.[50]

Michael D. Higgins, the left-wing chairman of the Labour Party, made the hardest-hitting critique of the entire episode on 4 October. Higgins extended his sympathy to Hillery and his family following 'the unwarranted intrusion on their privacy'. But Higgins also raised a wider issue of principle, condemning 'the petty invasion of the private world of a political figure' and rejecting the idea that 'the private life of a political figure affects his public political probity and acceptability'.[51] Hillery avoided this issue of the distinction between public values and private morality by directly challenging the truth of the rumours, but some politicians and journalists believed that he should simply have refused to discuss his private life. This course of action would probably have commanded strong public support; but it also carried the obvious risk that the rumour about his marriage would then be generally believed, even if it was accepted that no political consequences flowed from it. Moreover, the rumour was carefully crafted to ensure that it was virtually impossible for Hillery to dismiss reports of his resignation without provoking further questions about his personal life. It appears that Hillery was confronted with a narrow range of deeply unpleasant choices and he chose the least damaging option for his own reputation, his family and the presidency.

The press conference ended the crisis that had suddenly engulfed the presidency in the autumn of 1979. Hillery's public intervention did not, however, immediately quash the rumours about his private life. His public statement caused the rumours about his resignation to recede in the short term; even *Hibernia*, the only Irish newspaper that gave some credence to the story, acknowledged on 11 October that 'The Gale Force rumours against which President Hillery dramatically reacted a week ago today have abated for the moment'.[52] But the story was not yet finished. The editor of *The Irish Times* attempted to investigate the rumours in Brussels; Gageby put pressure on John Cooney, the paper's European correspondent, to probe the truth of the rumours shortly after the story broke. Cooney initially stalled for time, telling the paper's editorial staff that he was about to go to Madrid to cover the Spanish application for membership of the EEC.[53] But on his return to Brussels, Cooney faced further pressure from a senior executive at *The Irish Times*, who reiterated that Gageby wanted the story checked out. Cooney flatly refused to do so: 'Look, I am out here as a European correspondent. I know the two women concerned and I don't believe there's anything in it. I am a journalist, not a private investigator.'[54] The effort to investigate the rumours came to nothing – not surprisingly, since there was nothing to investigate, beyond the suspicious origins of the story itself.

But the rumours were revived towards the end of the year, as the struggle for the leadership of Fianna Fáil reached its height. It soon became apparent that the rumours were inextricably linked to the battle for the succession to Jack Lynch. Haughey's supporters intensified their efforts to undermine Lynch in November 1979; the Taoiseach decided to resign early in December. It was no accident that the rumours were revitalised just as Haughey made his final bid for power. Lynch privately warned Hillery, his most effective ally in previous internal battles, of his intention to resign. As Ireland held the presidency of the EEC for the final six months of 1979, a summit meeting of the European Council was held at Dublin Castle on the first weekend in December and Hillery hosted a dinner for the European leaders in the Áras. Lynch called the President aside for a brief word, in a fashion that vividly illustrated the conspiratorial atmosphere of the time and his distrust even of senior Cabinet members:

> Jack was there, he was President of the European Council and he had Michael O'Kennedy, who was Minister for Foreign Affairs, with him. At a certain moment I was away from the group and Jack came over and very quickly said 'I'm resigning tomorrow'. It was said in a way that no one could hear it. So he didn't trust O'Kennedy obviously, to say it near him.[55]

Lynch announced his resignation on 5 December 1979, bringing the date of his departure forward because he was advised that Colley had the votes to win the leadership. Hillery was dubious about the wisdom of Lynch's decision to go before Ireland's presidency of the EEC had concluded and was privately critical of the inept tactics of Colley's supporters: 'He told Jack he had plenty of votes; he had all the votes. Jack told me that later. I think he was timing it to suit George. As I said afterwards, George couldn't count.'[56] Lynch's final gamble miscarried. The party establishment gravely underestimated Haughey's support among the backbench TDs. Haughey won the vote, narrowly but decisively, on 7 December, securing 44 votes to 38 for Colley.[57] The most formidable and controversial politician of his generation was elected as Taoiseach by the Dáil four days later, with the reluctant support of his defeated opponents within Fianna Fáil.

Haughey's final ascent to power was accompanied by a resurgence of the rumours about Hillery's private life. Senator Brian Hillery, the President's cousin, warned him in December 1979 that the story was still circulating at an official level in Dublin. The younger man was attending a diplomatic function when the wife of a foreign diplomat recounted the rumours about the Presidents private life.[58] Hillery was also informed that an official of the Department of Foreign Affairs had spoken openly about the rumours, which were circulating within the department.[59] Brian, who was very close to the President, was deeply concerned about the rumours, and immediately informed his cousin of both incidents.[60,61] More significantly, the rumours took flight once more within the media at the culmination of the Fianna Fáil leadership contest. Several journalists contacted the President's office just before and after Haughey's election as Taoiseach to ask if Hillery was resigning to join the new government. Hillery himself recorded the revival of the rumours in a private note, which was taped and transcribed at the time: 'Today the 13th of December. I heard some talk yesterday and the day before, that I was resigning again today and joining the government so the thing reached a crescendo during the day and the newspapers were on again and again and again'.[62] It was in the midst of the second spate of rumours that Hillery received Haughey for his formal appointment as Taoiseach.

The new Taoiseach was in ebullient form when he came to the Áras on 11 December to receive the seals of the office. It was an amicable encounter; relations between the two men had been reasonably good when they served together in the government and Hillery had rarely come into direct conflict with Haughey even after the other man's dismissal in 1970. Hillery invited the new Taoiseach to join him for a cup of tea while they signed the papers and they talked privately for a few minutes. Haughey commented that he hoped to meet the President once a month, as Lemass had with de Valera. They also discussed Haughey's decision to appoint Máire Geoghegan-Quinn as a Cabinet Minister – she would become the first woman to serve in the Cabinet since the Treaty. Hillery favoured greater promotion of women in public life and commented that 'I had done everything I could to promote them when I was in Brussels, but these efforts had been used against him to fuel the rumours about his private life.[62] Haughey commiserated with Hillery about the rumours, telling him 'these things take on a life of their own and that I had done the right thing, dealing with it through the Press.'[63] But, oddly, the conversation did not stop at polite expressions of concern. The new Taoiseach commented that he too had been the victim of false rumours, which he described for Hillery's benefit – 'such as Gallagher made £200,000 available and anybody in the red in the bank was offered help.'[64] Hillery could not have known that such reports, so casually dismissed by Haughey, would be investigated in the 1990s by various tribunals of inquiry. The investigations discovered that Haughey received lavish personal donations from wealthy businessmen, including property developer Patrick Gallagher, to clear the Taoiseach's debts and support his ostentatious lifestyle; he also secured a settlement with Allied Irish Banks in January 1980, which wrote off a substantial part of his outstanding debt to the bank.[65] Perhaps because Haughey was still jubilant at his long awaited victory over his enemies within Fianna Fáil, he was careless in his remarks to the President. The new Taoiseach commented cheerfully that 'all the talk was about you, not about me.'[66] Hillery found this remark surprising, but was even more amazed by what followed:

> When I spoke to Haughey and asked him if the govern-
> ment would finance a press officer for the President, he
> said 'It is all over now'; and I wondered how he could say
> that in relation to generalised rumours which were without
> foundation and which were spread with a very clear
> structure and repeated in the same words some time later.[67]

Hillery's conversation with Haughey left the President with a strong suspicion that the new Taoiseach had instigated the rumours. He later became convinced that Haughey had orchestrated the campaign through the media to further his own agenda: 'He was talking about the gossip about me and he said it was all over now anyway. So he was a clever man, but I was surprised he said it, you know. It was a giveaway. I suppose he was excited'.[68] Whatever the reason for Haughey's unguarded remarks to the President, the rumours certainly began to recede following his election as Taoiseach.

The second flurry of rumours reached its height in mid-December and persisted into January, with the additional twist that Hillery was postponing his resignation until March 1980.[69] On this occasion Hillery refused to make any public reaction to the rumours. He told Mícheál Ó hOdhráin in December that 'if anybody phones up about rumours to say that he was instructed not to answer that question in any form until 1984.'[70] Instead, Hillery met separately with two editors, Tim Pat Coogan and Aidan Pender, in January, seeking to end the speculation about a presidential resignation once and for all. Both editors were sympathetic and indicated that they gave no credence to the story. Pender told the President that the *Irish Independent* had ignored the renewed speculation in December and that Hillery had handled the situation properly. Coogan urged him to develop a positive profile for the presidency, which would allow him to leave the rumours behind.[71] In any event, the rumours gradually faded away in early 1980, as most journalists realised that the story was essentially a fabrication. Hillery continued with his public engagements, undertaking state visits to Tanzania and Bahrain in February 1980.[72] The timing of the visits was designed to move the focus of the media away from the rumours and towards the mundane business of the presidency. This tactic was largely successful; the furore about the rumours died out completely by the early spring of 1980.

The origins of the rumours attracted almost as much as media attention as the story itself. Tim Pat Coogan made a thinly veiled accusation against the British intelligence services, in his editorial defending the President on 4 October 1979:

> There has been enough speculation in the past week
> without adding further fuel to the fires, but it is surely not

impermissible in this context to enquire whether or not the 'dirty tricks brigade' which has played such an inglorious role in Northern Ireland may not have taken a hand at creating political embarrassment at a time when the government is engaged on negotiations of the utmost importance and delicacy concerning the North and after we had done so well nationally in handling the papal visit.[73]

This theory had some superficial plausibility at a time when Anglo-Irish relations were at a low ebb following a series of bloody atrocities by the Provisional IRA and difficult negotiations between Lynch's government and Margaret Thatcher's administration on security co-operation. But it made no sense for the British government or its security services to indulge in rumours about the private life of the President of Ireland; undermining the institutions of the Irish state was not only pointless, but also actively damaging to the British agenda of securing more effective cross-Border co-operation against the IRA. Discrediting Hillery personally made even less sense; he was a largely powerless, ceremonial head of state, who had also been a firm opponent of republican violence during his term as Foreign Minister – a fact of which successive British ministers were well aware.

A more dramatic conspiracy theory was sketched out two years later by Gordon Thomas, a prolific British author living in Ireland. Thomas claimed in an article for the *Sunday Independent* in April 1981 that Department D of the KGB was responsible for spreading the rumours about Hillery's private life. It was alleged that Soviet intelligence chiefs aimed to bring down the President in the midst of the pope's visit to Ireland. The KGB aimed to strike a double blow against the West; toppling Hillery would wreck the papal visit and destroy any prospect that Ireland might join NATO.[74] The KGB feared the influence of the pope as the leading global symbol of religious anti-communism and hoped to embroil John Paul in a scandal at an early stage in his pontificate. Thomas's scenario of KGB involvement deserves recognition as the most unlikely conspiracy theory about Irish politics in Hillery's lifetime. The notion that senior

KGB officers invested substantial time and effort in manufacturing rumours about the private life of the President of Ireland is simply ludicrous. Hillery himself regarded the KGB conspiracy theory as highly entertaining and shared his amusement with Alexei Nesterenko, the Soviet ambassador to Ireland:

> The President gives a cocktail party at Christmas for the ambassadors; there was a group photograph. But there was a stern looking Russian ambassador at the time; he held up his glass to me privately and said 'To the victim of the KGB!'[75]

Hillery was firmly convinced that the source of the rumours lay not in Moscow or London, but in Leinster House.

The witness who knew most about the episode – Hillery himself – did not add to the speculation; he could not do so while he remained President, and he generally avoided commenting on a very painful and difficult period even in his retirement. But he formed a clear view of what had happened from his observations and from private discussions with friends and sympathetic journalists in 1980. Hillery was certain who had instigated the rumours: 'The thoroughness of it was Haughey. I had a letter from a friend in the army, our own army. We were together as children and he got very high rank, he's retired now. I had a letter from him to say that the origin of the rumour was not Russia, it was far nearer to home'.[76] Hillery also had a private conversation with Dennis Kennedy in January 1980, which reinforced his suspicions about the source of the rumours:

> I had a long conversation with Dennis who is quite clear that this was organised and also quite clear from something that was said to him by a Fianna Fáil man ... and by a Fianna Fáil man to Gageby, that this has been done by Fianna Fáil.[77]

This information from Kennedy, a highly respected journalist who was also a personal friend, did not specifically identify Haughey as the culprit.

But it dovetailed with reports that Hillery was receiving from friends and associates. His close friend Norman Butler warned the President shortly before Christmas 1979 that 'the rumours came from the centre of Fianna Fáil'.[78] Hillery's belief that leading figures within Fianna Fáil had played a central part in spreading the rumours was also reflected in private correspondence with his relatives around this time.[79]

While it is always difficult to unearth evidence about the origins of a political rumour, it is very likely that Hillery's suspicions were well founded. Haughey had cultivated connections with prominent journalists since the 1960s and he commanded the support of a loyal corps of allies, including civil servants and party activists with ready access to the media. He unquestionably had the capacity to generate such a story. There is little doubt either that he had a powerful motivation to do so. Hillery was not entirely certain about the motive for Haughey's ruthless tactics, but thought that he was seeking to divert the attention of the media from his own bid for power:

> I tried to understand it in terms of Haughey afterwards; did he want to get in as Taoiseach without all the attention being on him? He used distraction a lot in political life. That would have justified the rumours, you know, take the tension off him. ... Journalists would say 'a source high in Fianna Fáil'. It was always one of Haughey's messengers.[80]

In fact, Haughey's motivation appears much more compelling than undertaking a simple diversion, although that may have been an element in his calculations. If the rumours forced Hillery to resign, then severe pressure could be brought to bear on Lynch to take his place as President. An enforced move to the Park by Lynch would leave the way clear for Haughey to fulfil his cherished ambition of leading the government. This was not a flight of speculative fantasy, but very much in the realm of practical politics. It was significant that *Hibernia* raised this possibility in its story on 4 October 1979, which suggested that Hillery was about to resign: 'Jack Lynch would once again be presented with the opportunity of opting out of active politics and going to the Park. In that case, of course, the battle for the Fianna Fáil leadership would be joined at last.'[81] It was Haughey who would benefit from the opening created by Hillery's resignation. This was not the first time that Haughey's supporters had attempted to force Lynch into running for President; a more overt attempt to move the party leader upstairs had been made in 1976, before Hillery agreed to accept the party's nomination for the presidency. Moreover, Hillery's enforced resignation in the middle of the papal visit could be expected to inflict lethal collateral damage on Lynch. The Taoiseach would be in charge as a personal scandal engulfed the presidency, at the very time that the country was receiving the leading figure of international Catholicism and the most famous world leader to visit Ireland since John F. Kennedy in 1963. Even if the fall-out was not immediately fatal to the Taoiseach, Haughey's succession could not have been long delayed if such a fiasco had occurred. Finally, the campaign of rumours might also discredit Hillery so thoroughly that he would never be able to re-enter party politics as a rival to Haughey. It was not coincidental that the rumours gained strength just as the struggle for the leadership of Fianna Fáil began in earnest. It was also significant that the story faded into the background once Haughey was safely installed as Taoiseach. Haughey was one of the few Irish politicians with the ability and media connections to start such rumours. He was also the only leading figure with such a compelling motivation to do so.

The most damning verdict on the conspiracies and rumours that dogged the presidency in 1979 was pronounced by Michael D. Higgins, who commented that 'it is clear that the most offensive aspects of Irish political culture are being resurrected at a time of major social, political and economic problems'.[82] Hillery himself privately recorded his anger and frustration at 'being a prisoner and having to listen to the gossip'.[83] The political and financial constraints surrounding the presidency, illustrated especially by the lack of a press officer at the Áras and the traditional convention that the President should stay out of political controversy, greatly complicated Hillery's efforts to defend himself. Such conventions did not serve the office well in an era that saw the development of an increasingly competitive and diversified mass media and the emergence of political spin doctoring – both developments which would become more marked throughout the 1980s. Yet if there was negative fall-out from the rumours, it was not all a case of doom and gloom.

Hillery succeeded in defending his reputation and eventually in seeing off the rumours by speaking out publicly; it was a brave and ultimately well-judged move, which generated strong popular and media support for his position. He was the target of a cunning and unscrupulous smear campaign, conducted with skill and deviousness in the international as well as the Irish media. But Hillery was neither forced to resign nor was he discredited by the rumours. Perhaps more significantly, his actions in 1979 served to protect the institution of the presidency. Hillery was the third President to assume the office since de Valera's retirement in 1973; his immediate predecessor, Ó Dálaigh, had resigned in a blaze of controversy involving the government of the day. If Hillery had been forced to resign in October 1979, the presidency itself would have entered uncharted and hazardous territory. The office would have been severely damaged by scandal, controversy and instability. Whether the presidency would have survived at all is probably questionable, but even if it had the authority and credibility of the office would have been greatly diminished. Hillery's survival in October 1979 was essential in restoring stability to the presidency.

21.

Guardian of the Constitution
1980–1982

The sixth President of Ireland took up his office with few illusions about the political limitations on the institution that he had inherited. Yet Hillery had not anticipated the extent to which the President was a hostage to the political priorities of others. Jack Lynch was wary about the timing of any major increase in the presidential allowance, as it might prejudice the negotiations for a national wage agreement. The unequal balance of power between the President and the Taoiseach became even more marked when Charles Haughey succeeded Lynch in December 1979. It soon became evident that Haughey regarded the President as a potential competitor, who might detract from the position of the Taoiseach. It is difficult to know whether Haughey's concerns were due to political calculation or straightforward vanity, or perhaps most likely a mixture of the two, but the effect was to intensify the existing constraints on the role of the President. Haughey's actions also contributed to a further deterioration in his relations with Hillery, which had already been soured by Hillery's suspicions over the source of the rumours in 1979.

The first indications of a different and more turbulent relationship between the new Taoiseach and the President emerged in the spring of 1980. Haughey's department advised Hillery in April 1980 not to attend the inauguration of Dr John Armstrong, who had recently been elected as the new Church of Ireland Archbishop of Armagh, on the basis that Haughey wished to go to the ceremony personally. Bertie O'Dowd informed Micheál Ó hOdhráin on Haughey's instructions that 'An Taoiseach felt there should be one representative at the ceremony and that An Taoiseach himself was anxious to go'.[1] Hillery was at a loss to understand why the issue arose at all:

> Charlie wanted to do the Armstrong ordination himself. I told him I only went to these things from a sense of duty. I didn't know what the fuss was about between the officials if I went. I feel the new bishop is working with Charlie on this because when he was on television, one of the reasons for hope in North, he said, was the new Taoiseach in Dublin, which was a bit hard on the old Taoiseach but it was strange as well.[2]

The issue certainly arose because the President took precedence over the Taoiseach if both attended the same ceremony. Hillery was surprised by Haughey's intervention, but not greatly disturbed by the prospect of missing the ceremony. The President decided not to attend Armstrong's installation on the basis of Haughey's express wishes and the suggestion by the new archbishop himself that he would prefer to meet Hillery after his inauguration.[3] Hillery was not unduly worried by the incident, but it proved an ominous portent for his future interaction with the new Taoiseach.

A much more serious controversy arose later in the same year, which exposed Hillery to severe criticism and dragged the presidency into a damaging public dispute. The President's office received an invitation from the British Legion for a Remembrance Day service in St Patrick's

Cathedral on 9 November 1980. It was the first time that the President had been invited to attend such a service. The Remembrance Day service in Dublin traditionally commemorated Irish members of the British armed forces who had died in the two World Wars, but Dean Victor Griffin, who was conducting the service, had broadened the ceremony to encompass all Irish soldiers who had fallen 'in the cause of justice and peace', including those who had perished on United Nations' peace-keeping missions.[4] As the British Legion consisted of veterans of the British Army, however, the invitation still raised sensitive political issues for the Irish head of state, not least at the height of the Troubles in Northern Ireland. It would have caused no great surprise had Hillery politely declined the invitation; the worst that could be said was that he was reluctant to break new ground. But what actually happened was a great deal worse and underlined with painful clarity the essentially subservient position of the President relative to the Taoiseach.

Micheál Ó hOdhráin correctly sought the advice of the Department of the Taoiseach concerning the President's response to the invitation. The advice from the Taoiseach's department was that it would be inappropriate for the President to attend or be represented at memorial services for the armed forces of other countries; a suggested reply to the British Legion was included along the same lines.[5] The secretary promptly dispatched the reply to the Legion under his own name without referring it to the President. Hillery himself knew nothing about the official response until it was headlined in all the major newspapers:

> I was having my breakfast, having seen Vivienne off to school and the news came on and it was in the papers, there was a letter sent by the President to the British Legion; and it was a letter insulting them. I remember the *Evening Herald* had two journalists working on it. It was the first I heard of it.'[6]

It would not be the last that Hillery heard about it. The official response ignited a firestorm around the President. The British Legion reacted

angrily and the interpretation put on the affair by their representative
inflamed the controversy. Lieutenant-Colonel D. H. Boydell, the president
of the Legion in Ireland, told journalists that the reason for the President's
decision not to attend the service was that he 'did not attend the
ceremonies of foreign armies'.[7] Boydell also commented that Hillery's
response was 'a snub' and indicated that he would not be invited to the
ceremony again. Dean Griffin too expressed shock at the tone of the
President's response and was amazed that Hillery would have issued such
a letter – not without reason, since the President had done nothing of
the sort.[8] It later emerged that the explosive reference to 'foreign armies'
was not included in the Secretary's response, which had been paraphrased
by Boydell. The Legion's representative commented shortly afterwards
that he had sought to paraphrase the official response fairly, but had not
realised the emotive connotations of the terminology he used.[9] But by
then the damage was done. Indeed, even without the further twist
provided by Boydell, the actual reply was quite bad enough. The official
response was deeply offensive towards the relatives of those who were
being commemorated, provocative to the British Legion and insulting to
Irish veterans of the British Army.

The incident was headlined in the national newspapers as a snub by the
President to the British Legion and the Remembrance Day ceremonies.
The Irish Times ran two highly critical stories and delivered a stinging
rebuke to Hillery in an editorial headed 'The President's "No"'.[10] While
the editorial allowed that Hillery had probably been 'the victim of
circumstances', it also mercilessly dissected the official response as
'ridiculous and inaccurate' and commented portentously that 'Dr Paddy
Hillery is not a lucky President'.[11] Hillery could take little solace from the
coverage in the other daily newspapers. The traditionally supportive *Irish
Press* devoted extensive space to the Legion's complaint against Hillery
and its editorial on 11 November declared that the row was 'unfortunate
and let's face it, disedifying'. The editorial did attempt to offer a muted
response to criticisms of the President, describing Hillery as 'the soul of
courtesy'; the *Irish Press* also reminded its readers that 'we live in the era
of the H-Blocks and Castlereagh' and regrettable incidents of this kind

were likely to continue as long as British soldiers maintained the border.[12] The *Irish Press* editorial was more of a digression into traditional anti-partition rhetoric than a defence of the President and did little to conceal its embarrassment over the discourtesy and tactlessness of the official response. Hillery himself was appalled both at the reply itself and the critical press coverage. He feared that the incident might affect the excellent relations that he enjoyed with Protestant church leaders. He made no public comment on the controversy; despite the outcry this was probably a shrewd move, as a statement from the President would merely have prolonged the public dispute. Instead, Hillery privately contacted leading Protestant clergy, including Dr Henry McAdoo, Archbishop of Dublin, to explain the blunder and clarify his position: 'But there was war. I was friendly with all those leaders and I rang up the then archbishop to tell him that this was a mistake, it wasn't an intended slight by me.'[13] Hillery succeeded in reassuring the Protestant church leaders that he had been misinterpreted, but it took longer to calm the public controversy, not least because the government made no attempt to assist the President.

Hillery's embarrassment was intensified by a comment from Seán Moore, the minister of state who represented the government at the ceremony. Moore, a junior minister at the Department of the Taoiseach, told journalists on 10 November that he had represented the Minister for Defence 'at what were strictly religious ceremonies as far as I was concerned. It was simply a religious service in memory of Ireland's dead'.[14] This raised the obvious question of why, if it was strictly a religious ceremony, the Taoiseach's department had advised the President not to attend in the first place. Moreover, Haughey's press advisers sought to disassociate the Taoiseach entirely from the dispute and had no hesitation in cutting the President adrift. An official spokesman reaffirmed the government's intention to be represented at future ceremonies: 'We will continue accepting invitations to Remembrance Day services because they are held in memory of those thousands of Irishmen killed in two World Wars'.[15] The President had been given advice that was almost exactly the opposite of the government's public line. The Taoiseach not only failed to make any effort to ease the President's predicament but instead greatly exacerbated it. Hillery was furious at the government's response and concluded that Haughey had left him to take the flak: 'Haughey had a representative there. But anyway, when he was questioned they made no attempt to save my skin, he said it was only a religious function. He was protecting Haughey from having recognised them at all, you see, by sending him.'[16] Hillery felt that he was helpless to deal with the chorus of disapproval due to the lack of a press officer in the Áras itself and the refusal to assist him by the government's media managers.[17] He was particularly angry that the government contributed to the false impression that it was the President's decision alone not to attend the ceremony: 'That's when I felt I was dropped through the trapdoor. Here was I refusing to go to a simple religious service. It made me look very bad.'[18] Hillery was undoubtedly right in believing that he had been deliberately left alone to deal with a controversy not of his own making.

Having dragged Hillery through the mill of public controversy and done some damage to the public standing of the President, the media outcry gradually subsided. It is very likely that Hillery would still have declined the invitation if the decision had been left to him. As the Irish head of state, he was certainly reluctant to attend what had traditionally been a British military commemoration. This did not spring from any hostility to commemorating the Irish soldiers who had perished on the British side in the two World Wars. Hillery later agreed to participate in a general ceremony of commemoration for all Irish soldiers who had died in the British or Irish armed forces, which was initiated during his second term as President.[19] There were real political sensitivities in 1980 surrounding the British Army's role in Northern Ireland and Hillery placed a high value on keeping the presidency out of political controversy. But Hillery would certainly never have authorised a reply that was discourteous to the British Legion, still less one that insulted former Irish war veterans or their families; neither his innate decency nor his political instincts would have permitted such a blunder. Very few of the main participants in the affair, with the exception of Hillery himself, emerge with any credit. The secretary undoubtedly made a mistake in sending the official response at all without clearing it with Hillery. Peig O'Malley regarded it as an uncharacteristic error on Micheál Ó hOdhráin's part, and suggested that secretary's mistake arose from undue deference to the Department of the Taoiseach: 'I was surprised; Micheál was usually very careful. Maybe he didn't want to change something from the Taoiseach's department'.[20] The Department of the Taoiseach bore a fair share of the responsibility for providing such ill-judged and provocative advice in the first place. Lieutenant-Colonel Boydell criticised the President publicly without knowing all the facts, or even interpreting the facts that he did know correctly, although his anger was certainly understandable. Haughey and his closest associates behaved worst of all. Even if the Taoiseach knew nothing of the advice offered by his department (an unlikely scenario), he was still formally responsible for such official advice to the President. Once the story broke, Haughey not only failed to contain the fiasco that his department had helped to create, but he allowed his associates to aggravate Hillery's predicament with selective news briefings.

The Remembrance Day controversy showed the weakness of the President's position relative to the power of the government. The episode reflected the extent to which the presidency could become simply a pawn in the political game played by the Taoiseach of the day. It underlined too, not for the first time, how even a capable and experienced President could be virtually helpless in defending himself or the institution from sustained press criticism without effective assistance from the government. Hillery recorded his personal view after his retirement on the treatment of the presidency by successive governments in this period: 'Generally Presidents have in recent years been treated shabbily because of being without power.'[21] His assessment of the traditional place of the presidency in Irish politics was entirely accurate and owed much to his recollection of the Remembrance Day controversy. The episode marked a further turning point in Hillery's relationship with Haughey, which deteriorated rapidly in the wake of the controversy. The relations between the two men had generally been friendly, though never particularly close, before Haughey's dismissal in 1970. After the arms crisis Hillery combined a wary respect for Haughey's considerable ability, with distrust of his conspiratorial political methods. Yet the controversy in 1980, following closely on the rumours about Hillery's private life during the previous year, permanently marked the personal relationship between them. For the rest of his term Hillery's interaction with Haughey would be correct, but also cold and distant, marked by a consistent suspicion of Haughey's schemes and methods. Hillery's experience of his former colleague's political style would prove a useful asset as he confronted the most important and difficult decisions of his presidency in a time of extraordinary political instability.

Hillery played a low-profile but vital role as a stabilising influence in the highly contentious politics of the early 1980s, dominated by the bitter rivalry between Fianna Fáil under Haughey and Fine Gael led by Garret FitzGerald. The early 1980s was a time of unprecedented political instability, with three general elections within eighteen months. The first of those elections, in June 1981, resulted in a narrow victory for FitzGerald, who took office at the head of a fragile Fine Gael–Labour coalition that lacked a majority in the Dáil and relied on the support of three left-wing Independents. FitzGerald's first government collapsed suddenly after less than seven months, losing a key vote on the budget in January 1982. The second election of the troika in February 1982 brought Haughey back as Taoiseach, despite rumblings of discontent at his leadership within Fianna Fáil itself. Haughey, too, led a minority government, sustained by the support of the Independent TD Tony Gregory and less reliably by Sinn Féin the Workers Party. This time, the government lasted for nine months until Haughey lost a vote of confidence in the Dáil and a third election followed in November 1982. On this occasion FitzGerald was able to form a more durable administration commanding a majority in the Dáil.

Hillery's most significant and controversial decision as President was taken in January 1982. It was a quirk of the Irish political system and the place of the presidency within it that his key decision was to do nothing – to resist demands to intervene in the process of government formation. As President, Hillery had only a ceremonial role in the formation of the government, formally appointing the Taoiseach on the nomination of the Dáil and presenting the ministers with their seals of office on the nomination of the Taoiseach. He did not, unlike heads of state or monarchs in some other European states, have any role in facilitating the appointment of the head of the government, either directly or through the appointment of an intermediary to identify potential prime ministers. Nevertheless, the political instability of the early 1980s encouraged attempts to involve the President in party politics and to draw Hillery into using the powers of the office to benefit the competing party leaders. One of the few positive powers held by the President was the right under Article 13.2.2 to refuse a dissolution of the Dáil to a Taoiseach who had ceased to command the support of a majority in the Dáil. The refusal by the President to dissolve the Dáil in such circumstances would lead to the immediate resignation of the Taoiseach and allow the formation of an alternative government from within the existing Dáil. This hitherto obscure provision began to attract keen attention from various political figures at the beginning of 1982, but especially from the leading members of Hillery's former party.

The pressure on the President to smooth the way for Fianna Fáil's return to power began well before the defeat of FitzGerald's government in January 1982. Haughey, then leader of the opposition, floated the idea to Hillery in a deliberately casual fashion at a social function a couple of months before the vote on the budget. Hillery wryly recalled Haughey's *modus operandi*:

> One night … in the National Concert Hall, CJH sidled up to me (which he only did when he had some need of me) and said 'did you know that the President can refuse an election?' I replied that I was well aware of it. Long before, I spoke to Dev about this power of the President. Dev was President then and he said it would be a very foolish President who would do that.[22]

Hillery made no comment on Haughey's approach either then or later, but it alerted him to the Fianna Fáil leader's likely strategy if the government was to be defeated unexpectedly: 'That immediately put it in my mind, what this man is thinking now, how he can avoid an election.'[23] Hillery was surprised by the maladroit nature of Haughey's approach, which clearly revealed his plans. 'Haughey, I could never understand him, you know. He was a clever man. But the foolishness of coming up and telling me that there was something in the Constitution – that he would think I wouldn't know that. There was a stupidity in his vanity.'[24] While the President kept his own counsel on the matter, Haughey's initial approach gave Hillery the opportunity to consider his response if the Taoiseach was forced to seek a general election.

That occasion was not long in coming. The budget presented by John Bruton, Minister for Finance in the coalition government, sought to impose VAT on children's clothing and footwear for the first time. This move earned the budget an unenviable place in Irish political folklore. More immediately, it helped to cause the defeat of the government, which lost the backing of two key Independent supporters, Jim Kemmy and Seán Dublin Bay Loftus; the coalition lost the key division on the night of 27 January 1982 by a single vote. Following the unexpected fall of FitzGerald's government, Hillery was confronted with urgent demands from Haughey to refuse the dissolution of the Dáil, which was sought by FitzGerald as the outgoing Taoiseach. This action would have forced FitzGerald to resign immediately and allowed Haughey to form a government, if he could secure a majority, without facing a general election. After the coalition government was defeated in the Dáil, the Fianna Fáil front bench immediately issued a statement calling on the President not to dissolve the Dáil, but instead to allow Fianna Fáil to form a government.[25]

Hillery decided almost immediately not to exercise his powers under Article 13.2.2 and to grant the Taoiseach's request to dissolve the Dáil. His decision was dictated largely by pragmatic political considerations. If the President effectively prevented a general election, he had to be sure that a new government could be formed or his action would provoke a political and constitutional stalemate. Hillery recently recalled his thinking at the time:

If I refused an election, the Taoiseach must resign, he has to go – there is no Taoiseach, and if the Dáil cannot produce a Taoiseach, where are we? Then I did the count, and I think it worked out that the man from Limerick, Jim Kemmy, swore he would never vote for Charlie Haughey and he was voting against [VAT on] the children's shoes. So my sums told me that you could get a Dáil with no Taoiseach and therefore nobody to go to the President for a dissolution.[26]

Hillery's reasoning was sound. Jim Kemmy, an Independent socialist TD from Limerick, was critical not only of the specific tax on children's footwear, but also of the general policy orientation of the budget, which he considered too conservative.[27] Kemmy, however, was even more hostile to Haughey and later voted for FitzGerald as Taoiseach in the new Dáil after the general election. Loftus' position was less clear, but it was far from certain that he would be willing to support a new Fianna Fáil government. Hillery had good reason to fear that any intervention by the President would create a political crisis rather than solving one.

Hillery was also determined to avoid embroiling the presidency in party politics, which would be an inevitable result of a decision to refuse the dissolution of the Dáil. He was particularly concerned to prevent any attempt to influence his decision on a vital issue where the Constitution gave full discretion to the President. Hillery was convinced that as the Constitution did not permit the President to assist in the formation of governments, any discussion with party leaders on the formation of an alternative government was inappropriate: 'I felt it was of the first importance not to consult or discuss with anyone'.[28] He also believed that the President was not obliged to offer any justification for his decision under Article 13.2.2, which was taken at his own discretion. But the events that followed were not simply about respecting the formal principles of the Constitution. Hillery's concern to protect the presidency from attempts to draw the office into party politics was central to the events that unfolded on the night of 27 January 1982. He anticipated efforts to influence his decision and took steps to forestall them:

> When the Dáil voted down the budget I felt instinctively
> it was an occasion when one might consider this and more
> important I felt there would be need to stop any outsider
> trying to interfere with the President as he came to his
> decision. I explained to the ADC [aide de camp] on duty
> that I would not speak to anybody but the Taoiseach that
> night no matter who phoned.[29]

Hillery's instructions to the junior ADC to the President, Captain Oliver
Barbour, who was on duty in Áras an Uachtaráin on the night of 27
January, were designed to head off the expected demands for intervention
from Haughey and his associates.

The political pressure that Hillery had expected was not long in
coming and proved even more relentless than he had anticipated. The
Unit Journal maintained by Captain Barbour tells its own story: eight calls
were made to the Áras that night, either by Haughey himself, his political
secretary Catherine Butler, or by close political associates, including Brian
Lenihan and Hillery's former colleague in Clare, Sylvester Barrett.[30] A
series of other, less well-known individuals also contacted the Áras from
various parts of the country in an effort to influence Hillery – and it is
fair to assume that not all of them were calling on their own initiative.
One of those who sought to speak to Hillery was none other than Seán
Dublin Bay Loftus, the TD who had voted to bring down the government
but was now desperate to avoid an election. Dublin Bay Loftus urged the
President not to dissolve the Dáil, but instead to meet with the Council
of State and to convene a meeting of both Houses of the Oireachtas to
form 'a National government'.[31] This highly eccentric suggestion was
passed on to Hillery and politely ignored, not least because it was both
unconstitutional and fanciful. The Council of State had no role in advising
the President on the exercise of his power to refuse a dissolution of the
Dáil, while any attempt by the President to instigate the formation of a
national government had no basis in the Constitution and would have

provoked almost universal condemnation.

In any event, Hillery refused to speak to anyone who called Áras an Uachtaráin that night, and remained determined to avoid discussing his decision on a constitutional matter with any politician other than the Taoiseach: 'The only one that could come in there was the Taoiseach to resign or to call for an election. So I had to create a situation where I did not speak to anybody trying to promote this idea'.[32] Hillery was not only concerned about becoming involved in a messy political controversy, but also about protecting the office of the presidency from political scandal and guarding against the perception that Haughey was able to influence the President's decisions.

Hillery was successful in deflecting most of those who sought to exert influence on him without great difficulty. Capt Barbour told Dublin Bay Loftus that the President was not available and the Independent TD did not attempt to contact Hillery again. Haughey was not so easily deterred. The Fianna Fáil leader made his first call to the Áras at 8.15 p.m., announcing that he was available to form a government and wanted the President or his secretary to contact him. Haughey's message was direct and to the point: 'I do not wish the Dáil to be dissolved'.[33] As Hillery had no intention of contacting Haughey, Catherine Butler made a further call to reiterate Haughey's desire to speak to the President or his private secretary; on this occasion she was informed that neither Hillery nor the secretary were available.[34] Brian Lenihan and Sylvester Barrett were then enlisted to join the Fianna Fáil chorus serenading Hillery. The two TDs sought to meet Hillery, on the basis that 'they wish to see the President on a private matter'.[35] The nature of the 'private matter' they wished to discuss with Hillery was left unspoken but required no great powers of deduction on the night that the government had fallen; they too had no success in speaking to Hillery. Lenihan then made two further calls to the Áras to check whether his and Haughey's messages had been passed on to the President; he was assured that they had been but that the President was not available.[36] At this stage an impatient Haughey decided to turn up the volume. The Fianna Fáil leader declared his intention to call up to the Áras personally to see the President. Haughey's message to Captain

Barbour was blunt and uncompromising:

> I am leader of the largest party in the Dáil. I wish to speak
> to the President on a constitutional matter and it is urgent.
> I propose to call to the Áras at 22.30hrs to see the
> President. Please inform the President I will wait for his
> answer.[37]

Hillery now made his only direct intervention of the night, seeking to
relieve the pressure placed on the young officer by Haughey and his
associates:

> When it got very hot and Haughey was threatening, I said
> 'tell him I do not think it appropriate to speak to him'; that
> was the only message I delivered.[38]

Hillery was willing to go further if necessary to prevent Haughey calling
up to the Áras: 'I told them, "Bar the gates!"'[39] It was a striking example
of how angry Hillery was and how determined to prevent even a
perception that Haughey was able to interfere in the President's decisions.
Barring the gates to Haughey proved unnecessary, although the Fianna
Fáil leader did make further efforts to speak to Hillery, reiterating that he
wished 'to speak to the President at the earliest possible moment with a
view to forming a government'.[40] By this time Hillery had enough – he
made no response at all; the log records only a terse statement 'President
informed'.[41]

Meanwhile, Garret FitzGerald did not go immediately to the Áras after
losing the vote, giving Haughey and his cohorts a larger window of
opportunity for their opportunistic lobbying. Hillery was surprised at
FitzGerald's late appearance: 'Garret complicated the situation by
disappearing. I don't know where he went. He didn't come immediately.'[42]
FitzGerald was delayed because the necessary papers for dissolving the
Dáil were not yet ready. Micheál Ó hOdhráin, whose participation in the
process was essential, was attending a performance of *Mr Joyce is Leaving*

Paris at the Peacock Theatre, and the Taoiseach's assistant private secretary was hastily dispatched to find him. An usher had to locate him in the dark of the theatre with a flashlight while trying to avoid interrupting the play.[43] In the meantime, FitzGerald set out for the Áras, but stopped some way short of the gates to await Dermot Nally, secretary to the government, who was bringing the required documents: the necessary papers were eventually transferred at an impromptu rendezvous in the Phoenix Park, not far from Dublin Zoo.[44] But when FitzGerald did arrive shortly after 10 p.m., Hillery had no hesitation in granting the Taoiseach's request for a dissolution of the Dáil. He was still angry at the barrage of phone calls and told FitzGerald of the attempts to influence his decision by prominent Fianna Fáil politicians. The general election was called for 18 February 1982.

The phone calls by leading Fianna Fáil politicians to the Áras on the night of 27 January did not long remain a secret. Several journalists referred to the story over the following weeks, including Tom Brady of the *Irish Independent* and Geraldine Kennedy in the *Sunday Tribune*. Haughey resolutely denied any involvement in the affair: it was soon brushed aside in the excitement of the general election campaign and the speculation over Haughey's ability to form a viable government.[45] But the story was like a dormant volcano, which was apparently placid for almost a decade, but then erupted during the campaign for Hillery's successor in 1990, with devastating consequences for Haughey and particularly for his close ally Brian Lenihan. Nobody in 1982 could foresee the dramatic impact of the affair: in the meantime, the election that Haughey had tried to prevent gave him the platform to return to power. Fianna Fáil fell three seats short of an overall majority, but Haughey outmanoeuvred his internal opponents and succeeded in forming a minority government with the votes of Tony Gregory and the three TDs from Sinn Féin the Workers Party.

Hillery made no public comment on the events of 27 January, nor did he attempt to draw attention to the phone calls privately or to leak the details of what had happened. He operated within the conventional political consensus surrounding the office, which dictated that the

President should stay rigidly outside normal politics. Even journalists would have been shocked (as well as delighted) in 1982 if the President had sought covertly to brief the media. But Hillery was undoubtedly very angry at the actions of Haughey and his associates. He commented later: 'I was angry, they should know better than that – phoning the President to tell him what to do. It was part of the gang mentality'.[46] He was also concerned about the army officer who had taken the brunt of the pressure from Haughey. Hillery took the exceptional step of calling in the Army Chief of Staff, Louis Hogan, to ensure that Captain Barbour's career was not damaged by the affair.[47] Hillery correctly anticipated Haughey's return to power and acted to guard Captain Barbour against possible retribution for following the President's orders.

> I brought him in to protect the young officer and to say that everything that was done was done under my direct orders to the young officer. Louis, he was a Clare man, he assured me that the young man would be safe and that he would put it on his record. Haughey was very angry; you know, Haughey couldn't tolerate people not doing what he wanted.[48]

Hillery's prompt action to safeguard the officer's career underlined his keen appreciation of how Irish politics worked in the 1980s. He was well aware that a senior politician could wreck the career of an unduly independent public servant. Hillery also knew how Haughey worked, having a much greater knowledge of the Fianna Fáil leader than many of his allies and opponents. He was by no means entirely critical of Haughey, recognising his considerable ability, but by the same token the former Fianna Fáil minister had no illusions about Haughey's ruthlessness and his willingness to settle scores with those who displeased him. Hillery ensured that the captain would be fully protected for playing his part in safeguarding the presidency on 27 January.

Haughey himself preferred to forget the events of January 1982. When he formed his second government in March and received the seals of office from the President, he made light of the phone calls in his meeting with Hillery. The President left a revealing account in his private papers of their first meeting since the night of the phone calls:

> Haughey came to see me to be appointed Taoiseach after winning the vote in An Dáil and referred to the phone calls before the dissolution in a dismissive way [as] 'that nonsense' and moved his hand as if he were throwing away a piece of paper. I did not comment. By now I had come to realise that he had developed the practice of creating his own reality, deciding what reality was and what would be dismissed. A later stage would be to deny the very happening at all of the calls or his part in it. This was no madness. He convinced himself first and never yielded to any other version of events. It was part of his fighting arsenal.[49]

This was certainly a reasonable account of how Haughey subsequently dealt with allegations of involvement in the phone calls, issuing a blanket denial that either he or any other leading figures in Fianna Fáil had anything to do with it.[50] Hillery himself did not wish to raise the issue again and the affair faded out of public sight apparently for good, until it resurfaced in dramatic fashion in 1990.

Haughey's new government lasted only slightly longer than the previous coalition. His administration was damaged by bitter faction-fighting within Fianna Fáil over his leadership and by continuing economic instability, as the government failed to bring a spiralling level of public debt under control. Haughey's second government was hugely controversial, featuring several scandals, notably the illegal phone tapping of two journalists, Bruce Arnold and Geraldine Kennedy, by the Minister for Justice, Seán Doherty.[51] Following a withdrawal of support by Gregory and the Workers Party, the government lost a vote of no confidence on 4 November 1982. Haughey was now in the same position as FitzGerald nine months previously. As the outgoing Taoiseach he was obliged to seek a dissolution of the Dáil from the President, while some of his opponents, especially within Fianna Fáil, hoped that Hillery might refuse to dissolve the Dáil and give them an opportunity to put forward another candidate for Taoiseach. Certainly Haughey feared exactly this scenario. Hillery recalled that Haughey was unusually nervous when he met the President for the second time in nine months:

> When he arrived at the Áras he was very tense and not sure of what I would do. He asked Micheál Ó hOdhráin 'what happens now, what happens now?' It seemed that he feared a refusal and there were several in his party who felt that if I refused him a dissolution they could get rid of him.[52]

If Hillery had refused the Taoiseach's request to dissolve the Dáil, it would certainly have triggered an immediate move against Haughey within Fianna Fáil. Haughey would have been forced to resign as Taoiseach and the party could have put forward another candidate for approval by the Dáil. While there was no direct approach to the President by any of Haughey's leading rivals within Fianna Fáil, Hillery was discreetly made aware that some of the party's TDs saw a golden opportunity to remove Haughey: 'There was a group within Fianna Fáil, and they communicated to me in some way, one of these whispers at cocktail parties; it was a chance for them to get rid of Haughey. It was a mighty stroke, they had worked out what I could do.'[53]

Neither Haughey's fears nor the hopes of his opponents were to be realised. The President granted the Taoiseach's request, paving the way for the third general election in eighteen months. Hillery's rationale was straightforward: 'Again, my job was to take care of the presidency and I didn't do what they hoped for'.[54] It was virtually impossible for Hillery to do anything else: having granted FitzGerald's request to dissolve the Dáil, he could hardly refuse the same request from Haughey. Such a manoeuvre would have been entirely inconsistent with his previous stand, and would have triggered a political crisis. Hillery had no intention of embroiling himself in the internal politics of Fianna Fáil or of becoming a de facto arbiter in the conflict between Haughey and his opponents. Moreover, there was no guarantee that an alternative Fianna Fáil leader could command a majority in the Dáil. In the circumstances Hillery's action was both principled and sensible.

While the plans of the Fianna Fáil dissidents did not bear fruit, Haughey was removed from office, at least temporarily, by the electorate. The election on 24 November brought FitzGerald back to power, at the head of a Fine Gael-Labour coalition. While Fianna Fáil remained the largest party, Fine Gael enjoyed its best ever result, taking seventy seats in the new Dáil; FitzGerald was able to form a majority government with the Labour Party.[55] The new Fine Gael-Labour coalition proved reasonably durable, lasting until 1987, though it was not to be a happy experience for either party.

When politicians and commentators subsequently debated the President's actions in 1982, the debate usually focused on the attempts of Haughey and his leading associates to influence the President and often shed more heat than light on what had actually happened. It is now known beyond any doubt that Haughey exerted pressure on the President to prevent an election and allow instead the formation of an alternative government in January 1982. Hillery took a principled stand in defending the right of the President to make decisions on a constitutional matter without interference by party politicians. The events of 1982 underlined Hillery's independence in resisting very considerable pressure from the leading members of his old party. But the question is rarely asked – was Hillery right in 1982? An argument can certainly be made that the country would have benefited from fewer elections, less opportunistic electoral campaigning and more stable governments at a time of severe economic crisis. But it was not the responsibility of the President to deliver stable government, still less to prevent elections when the government of the day lost the confidence of the Dáil. Moreover, it is very likely that a decision by the President to prevent an election in January 1982, without any guarantee that an alternative Taoiseach could be elected, would have aggravated the political crisis rather than alleviating it. Hillery's concern for the office of the presidency itself was also well founded: open intervention by the President in party politics, in response to demands from the most controversial political figure of his generation, would have damaged the institution of the presidency and increased public cynicism about politics and politicians. Hillery's decisions in 1982 showed not only consistency of purpose but also better political judgement than many active politicians. Hillery set out to protect the presidency in 1982, but his actions also guaranteed that the political system would continue to function normally in an era of considerable instability and that politicians were not allowed to bypass elections if they voted to bring down a government. Hillery ensured that the presidency served as a stabilising influence and not a further source of division in the volatile and vitriolic politics of the early 1980s.

22.

Second Term
1983–1990

The achievements of Hillery's first term as President are easily overlooked. While the public role of the President did not change very much in a seven-year period, Hillery provided stability to the institution itself and acted as a quiet stabilising influence within the wider political system in the early 1980s. The independence of the presidency from party politics or factional struggles within parties had been firmly established. Nobody in 1983 would snipe at Hillery as a Fianna Fáil President, as Richie Ryan had attacked 'the Fianna-Fáil appointed Commissioner' seven years earlier. Hillery had achieved what he set out to do when he was elected unopposed in December 1976. Yet he felt a much greater sense of frustration than accomplishment; he had not enjoyed serving as President and particularly disliked the isolation imposed by the office. He looked forward to the end of his term in December 1983 and fully expected that it would also see the end of his public career.[1] Hillery was sixty in May 1983. He had no further political ambitions and intended to retire from public life.

If Hillery's personal preferences had been the sole consideration, he would certainly have retired in 1983. He vividly recalled his feelings in an interview with Joe Carroll in 1991: 'At the end of the last year of the first seven years I was longing for the day … I felt it was an achievement to have done seven years. I was looking forward to taking up some new life'.[2] But the most prominent figures in the Irish political establishment made strenuous efforts to persuade him to stay on. Haughey and FitzGerald, in complete agreement for once, both strongly urged Hillery to nominate himself for a second term. Neither the government nor Fianna Fáil wanted a presidential election, especially after three general elections in the space of eighteen months. Moreover the country was experiencing the most severe recession since the 1950s, with a rapid rise in unemployment and persistently high levels of public debt; in the grim economic circumstances the President was urged to serve another term and avoid an unnecessary and unwanted election. Hillery at first resisted this pressure, telling the politicians that he was determined not to seek re-election. He was unmoved when he received a joint approach from all three party leaders, FitzGerald, Haughey and Dick Spring, the new leader of the Labour Party who was the Tánaiste in the coalition government. Hillery met the three politicians at a social function in McKee barracks and told them that he wanted to retire from the presidency.[3] When he was asked was there anything he wanted from the government, he replied bluntly 'all I want is out'.[4] He did point out to the Taoiseach, however, the pressures on the head of state to fulfil his responsibilities with hopelessly inadequate funding and an understaffed office:

> I could not have been more definite that I wished to go and I even said to FitzGerald that he should consider the state of affairs when an incumbent did not wish to stay. This did not bring any offers but once when both he and CJH had been with me together and CJH left later than him, CJ said 'You could get anything you want off him

now'. I suppose CJH was trying to help me see the opportunity to get extra services (e.g. somebody to deal with the Press) but I did not see it as an opportunity to get what I wanted and stay. I wished to leave.[5]

Hillery was adamant that he would not run again and the party leaders failed to convince him to change his mind. He was not simply reluctant to accept office again on this occasion, but fully intended to bring about the end of his public career.

Yet this was not the end of the story. The party leaders continued their efforts to cajole Hillery into seeking a second term. Haughey visited the Áras in late September 1983 to make the case for the President to run again.[6] Hillery once again rejected this approach, perhaps not surprisingly in view of his chequered relationship with Haughey. But over several weeks in the autumn of 1983 he reluctantly came around to the idea of seeking re-election. His deeply-rooted desire to serve the country to the best of his ability, which had been a significant element in persuading him to accept the office in the first place, came to the fore in the face of the unanimous demand from the representatives of all the major parties in the Dáil.[7] He had agreed to accept nomination in 1976 in response to a personal appeal from Jack Lynch; seven years later the demand for Hillery to remain in office was more broadly based, and came as much from his former opponents in Fine Gael and Labour as it did from Fianna Fáil. This all-party appeal made a compelling case for him to continue in office. Hillery's sense of public duty meant that he found it difficult to reject such appeals definitively. Hillery eventually decided to go forward once again; he recorded in his private papers that 'I changed my mind against my better judgement and against my feelings.'[8]

There was another, more pragmatic factor which may have contributed to Hillery's decision to accept a second term. He believed that he had secured guarantees from the three party leaders that adequate funding would be available for the presidency if he served a second term. He told John McColgan that he had agreed to go forward again only on the basis that increased resources would be provided. He told them, 'If you give me the money to do the job, then I'll do it'. They agreed, no problem. But then the money never came. He felt he was treated shabbily by politicians of all parties.[9]

In fact, Hillery's discussions were not entirely fruitless; the government authorised a considerable increase in the President's travel allowance shortly after he agreed to run again. But crucially, neither the government nor the opposition was willing to propose an upgrading of the presidential allowance, which remained at a derisory level throughout Hillery's second term. Whatever assurances he secured from the party leaders counted for little in the face of the economic crisis and the lack of political importance attached to the highest office of the state.

Once Hillery had decided to go forward again, the rest of the process was essentially a formality, to an even greater extent than seven years before. Hillery nominated himself for the presidency and was re-elected unopposed in November 1983. He registered a unique historical record in becoming the only President of Ireland to be elected unopposed for two terms. It was a tribute to his success in stabilising the office after the turbulence surrounding the presidency in the 1970s.[10] It was a distinction he would happily have done without. He ruefully remarked to friends that 'It's the only job where you get another seven years for good behaviour.' Hillery was inaugurated for the second time on 3 December 1983; it was a low-key ceremony, which was scaled back by the government as part of the financial measures designed to control the national debt.[11] Hillery's decision to go forward for a second seven-year term was an act of considerable self-sacrifice, which conflicted sharply with his personal wishes and was dictated primarily by his sense of public duty.

The second term followed a broadly similar pattern to Hillery's first seven years in the Park, although the political controversies of the first term were largely absent. His presidency was characterised by low-key diligence in fulfilling his public duties, combined with minimal visibility in the national media. He attended numerous community and local events throughout the country, and sought to promote groups and causes that he considered worthwhile.[12] He was particularly interested in the efforts of groups working to overcome drug addiction, visiting several rehabilitation projects for addicts in Dublin on a regular basis. Hillery also sought to support charities involved in providing emergency help and accommodation for the homeless; he opened a new homeless centre for the Simon Community on the South Quays.[13] Hillery was interested in promoting better services for young people and he was consistently supportive of the work of the National Youth Federation. The head of the Federation acknowledged Hillery's 'whole-hearted support for youth services throughout the 14 years of his presidency' when he opened the Federation's national office and resource centre in his last official engagement in Dublin.[14] Hillery was disappointed at the almost complete absence of media coverage for speeches that he made at such events, although he was no longer greatly surprised by it: 'I got used to it, the press wouldn't print anything for me. The photographers were great; they were much admired abroad [on state visits]. But there was no way I could get a speech into a newspaper or into Radio Éireann.'[15]

While he had rarely sought to promote himself aggressively, Hillery was shocked at the low level of media interest in his activity as President. As Foreign Minister and later European Commissioner, he had enjoyed good relations with most journalists after a tentative start.[16] But he was well aware that the media could not be held solely responsible for the minimal public coverage of his schedule. Throughout his career, Hillery's personal shyness and dislike for overt self-promotion had never particularly harmed his relations with the press, but as European Commissioner and still more as Foreign Minister, he made news on a consistent basis. The presidency presented a very different challenge. The constraints on his role as President ensured that his ability to pursue newsworthy public initiatives was virtually non-existent, and the lack of policy or real political importance in the office meant that the personality and style of the office-holder became much more important. Hillery was reluctant to give in-depth interviews to individual journalists that might compromise his or his family's privacy.[17] Yet the effective promotion of the presidency within the media was not inhibited only by Hillery's low-key personal style. There were more significant practical obstacles with which he was all too familiar. The endemic weaknesses in the institutional support structure for the presidency – the understaffing of the office, the painfully inadequate presidential allowance and the absence of a press officer in the Áras, remained a crippling reality throughout his second term. The President's staff were usually overworked, preoccupied with the daily pressures of running the office and none had any expertise in dealing with the media.[18] The lack of any dedicated provision for dealing with the media was the most damaging weakness in the President's office and made the Áras seem a relic of the forgotten past, when public figures had no need of press officers or media managers. More importantly, it meant that on a practical level there was no concerted effort from the Áras to promote the presidency in a proactive way or to identify aspects of Hillery's schedule that might be newsworthy. There was no real prospect of substantial press coverage of the President's daily activity, at least within Ireland, without such a proactive effort.

The failure by successive governments to provide press support for the head of state was influenced by an outdated official view that the President, as a ceremonial figurehead who was above politics, had no need for regular interaction with the media.[19] Official reluctance to finance a press office for the Áras was reinforced by financial constraints in the difficult economic conditions of the 1980s. But it still marked an extraordinary neglect, in practical terms, of the highest office in the state; not only the Taoiseach, but government ministers had employed press officers since the 1970s, but somehow it was not considered either appropriate or urgent to provide one for the President. It was all the more inexplicable in the light of the media frenzy that had engulfed Hillery in October 1979 at the height of the rumours about his private life. This official failure left Hillery in an unenviable position; he could neither generate media interest in his considerable day-to-day workload, nor deal effectively with press queries about apparent gaffes, such as the controversy over the Remembrance Day service in 1980. Even more damaging was the perception, which took root within sections of the media, that he was a virtually invisible President. Hillery discovered that much worse than having an adversarial relationship with the media, as some politicians did, was being treated with relative indifference.

Moreover, as his presidency became an accepted feature of the political landscape, Hillery's low-key style was ridiculed in some sections of the media. Gene Kerrigan cast a jaundiced eye on Hillery's presidency in an article for *Magill*, the satirical magazine published by Vincent Browne, in June 1983. Kerrigan's assessment of Hillery's career before his election as President was balanced and by no means unfavourable, but his commentary drew attention for his portrayal of Hillery as an inactive first citizen who was preoccupied mainly with playing golf: 'One way or the other, with a handicap of 7 the President of Ireland has the lowest handicap of any European head of state. So the past six and a half years haven't been entirely wasted.'[20] Kerrigan's commentary was unfair and ignored Hillery's considerable work rate in promoting community groups and projects for the marginalised, not to mention his crucial role in establishing the independence of the presidency in the face of political interference, which was widely known in media circles even as early as 1983. The profoundly inaccurate portrayal of Hillery as an amiable, golf-playing gentleman who had accepted the presidency as a retirement post gained considerable currency in the national media during Hillery's second term and continued to influence public perceptions of his presidency after his retirement. Hillery's entire period as President was presented by critical elements in the media as a period of inertia and invisibility.[21] Yet this portrayal of Hillery was by no means a universal phenomenon. James Downey, a very experienced political journalist, gave a more serious and balanced assessment in the *Irish Independent* on the eve of Hillery's retirement. Downey acknowledged the low-profile nature of Hillery's presidency, but noted that he had attended countless community functions and promoted worthy causes: 'For this he has received little thanks and less publicity.'[22] Downey also drew attention to the formidable political and constitutional constraints surrounding the presidency and succinctly concluded: 'The scope for independent action is almost nil.'[23] This perceptive contemporary analysis went to the heart of the difficulties confronting Hillery throughout his time as President.

Patrick Hillery was a public figure accustomed to wielding considerable executive power and taking independent action over a wide area. As Foreign Minister he worked closely with Jack Lynch, but enjoyed considerable autonomy in his own sphere, particularly in managing Irish accession to the EEC. Hillery's freedom of action was even more marked in the Commission, where the diffident Ortoli provided little overall direction and allowed Hillery a free hand in developing a wide-ranging agenda of social reform. But the presidency of the 1970s was hedged around with a dense thicket of constraints, created not only by the constitutional requirements, but also by political custom and practice. The traditional political view of the office was powerfully reinforced by severe financial restrictions. While the presidency was primarily an office of symbolic importance, Hillery lacked the resources to use the symbolism of the office effectively in promoting causes he favoured or groups whose aims he wished to support. The harsh reality of the Hillery presidency was that he had virtually no freedom of action at all outside the narrow formal powers given to the President by the Constitution.

Hillery exercised those formal powers conscientiously. The President called the Council of State into session four times to consider the referral of legislation to the Supreme Court and referred three of these Bills to the Court to ensure that they were in conformity with the Constitution.[24] The result in two cases certainly confirmed the President's judgement in referring them in the first place. The Housing (Private Rented Dwellings) Bill, 1981 sought to maintain rent control for tenants who had benefited from it before the relevant legislation was struck down by the Supreme Court; a key section of the new Bill was found to be in breach of the Constitution by the Supreme Court and it had to be redrafted by the government.[25] The Electoral (Amendment) Bill 1983, which gave the vote in Dáil elections to British citizens resident in Ireland, also required amendment in line with a ruling by the Supreme Court. The final measure referred by Hillery was a Bill regulating adoption. This legislation was approved without difficulty; in this case Hillery was influenced less by any fear that the Bill might be unconstitutional and more by his concern to establish legal certainty in the area of adoption.[26] As the father of an adopted child himself, Hillery had first-hand experience of the concerns of adoptive parents and was determined to ensure that the law on adoption had a firm constitutional basis. It was one of the few occasions during his presidency when he was free to act in accordance with his own humane instincts on an issue of public policy.

There was no further pressure on Hillery after 1982 to use the sole power that lay within his absolute discretion, the right to refuse a dissolution of the Dáil if the Taoiseach no longer commanded a majority. The political instability of the early 1980s gradually receded, although no government of the decade survived for the full parliamentary term. Garret FitzGerald remained in office until 1987; Hillery generally got on well with the Fine Gael leader, who, unlike some of his predecessors, visited the Áras regularly to brief the President on the activity of the government.[27] FitzGerald sought Hillery's advice on various occasions, notably concerning the changeover of power in 1987, when it was not clear that the Dáil would be able to elect a Taoiseach.

The Fine Gael–Labour coalition broke up in January 1987 and the ensuing general election brought mixed fortunes for both FitzGerald and Haughey. Fine Gael lost ground heavily to the new Progressive Democrat (PD) party led by Des O'Malley, while Fianna Fáil again failed to secure an overall majority. It was evident that FitzGerald had no prospect of returning to office, but it was far from certain that Haughey could secure a majority in the Dáil. FitzGerald therefore consulted Hillery, considering that the President might have a vital role to play if a deadlock emerged when the Dáil convened on 10 March.[28] Hillery advised the outgoing Taoiseach on the course of action to follow if all candidates for the office were defeated in the vote. Hillery urged FitzGerald to avoid any suggestion that he would seek the dissolution of the Dáil, which had just been elected; instead, he should announce that he would discuss the situation with the President and go to the Áras for consultations with Hillery. While FitzGerald would resign after the defeat of his nomination, he would remain as a caretaker Taoiseach until the Dáil elected his successor; he would also make informal efforts to resolve a statemate.[29] Hillery's tactical approach was intended to exert increasing pressure on the Dáil to resolve the deadlock. It would also ensure that the President would not have to invoke Article 13.2.2 of the Constitution, which would only arise if the outgoing Taoiseach sought a further election. FitzGerald followed Hillery's advice and prepared two alternative speeches to be delivered after the decisive vote on 10 March, one simply announcing his resignation if Haughey was elected Taoiseach and the other outlining his intention to proceed in accordance with the advice of the President if no candidate was elected.[30] Hillery's approach carefully avoided any direct personal intervention in the process of government formation; he would act only through the outgoing Taoiseach. If the scenario outlined by Hillery had materialised, however, it would have broken new ground by establishing that the President could play a legitimate role in resolving a post-election deadlock, even in the most indirect and circumspect fashion. As it turned out, Hillery's planning proved unnecessary. When the Dáil met on 10 March, Haughey won on the casting vote of the Ceann Comhairle and took office as Taoiseach once again at the head of a minority government.[31]

Haughey remained in office for the final three years of Hillery's second term. The Taoiseach's contacts with Hillery were formal and distant, although there were no major clashes between the two men. Haughey adopted an increasingly presidential style, which tended to sideline the actual incumbent. His concern not to be upstaged by the President on major cultural or sporting occasions was also still very much alive. When the Irish soccer team enjoyed unparalleled success at the World Cup in 1990, Haughey's finely tuned instincts for self-promotion immediately kicked in. Hillery planned to attend the match between Ireland and Italy in Rome along with his son. John Hillery recalled what happened next:

> When Ireland were playing Italy in the quarter-finals of the World Cup, he said 'we'll go' and I said 'great'. Next week he came back to me and said that the government told him he couldn't go. Of course we all know why![32]

Haughey was a constant presence at major Irish sporting successes throughout his final term as Taoiseach, from the Tour de France to the

World Cup. He was not willing to relinquish his starring role as the spectator-in-chief to another and theoretically more prestigious office-holder. It was a minor episode compared to some of the previous clashes between Hillery and Haughey. Nevertheless, it underlined the severe constraints on the position of the President, at least up to 1990, and the extent to which they were open to abuse by the government. It is unlikely that when de Valera inserted the provision requiring the President to secure the agreement of the government to travel abroad, he anticipated that it would be used to prevent the head of state attending football matches lest he upstage the Taoiseach.

Haughey unwisely called a general election in 1989, hoping finally to secure the long-awaited overall majority; instead, Fianna Fáil lost three seats and forfeited any chance of retaining power as a single-party government. When the 26th Dáil assembled on 29 June, all the nominations for Taoiseach were voted down and for the first time since its foundation the Dáil failed to produce a majority for any candidate. This was the political impasse that Hillery and FitzGerald had anticipated two years earlier, but the President had no role in resolving it. His participation on this occasion was entirely ceremonial; his advice was not sought at any stage and he simply accepted Haughey's formal resigna-tion.[33] Haughey soon formed an alliance with his former opponents in the Progressive Democrats and the new coalition government was elected on 12 July. It was striking that the President was essentially a distinguished bystander as the crisis was resolved by the professional politicians. Hillery's discussions with FitzGerald in 1987 had no sequel, and the crisis two years later merely highlighted the strictly ceremonial role of the President in government formation.

Hillery enjoyed only slightly greater scope in fulfilling the international obligations of his office. He maintained his interest in international affairs and European integration throughout his time as President. He undertook a wide range of state visits in his second term, including Australia and New Zealand in 1985 and China in 1988.[34] Hillery also made several official visits to other European states, including the Netherlands, Austria and Italy. He enjoyed most of the state visits he conducted; he was an old hand in the field of international diplomacy. But there was no real opportunity for the President to express his own views publicly either in the course of state visits or when receiving foreign heads of state at the Áras; his speeches were usually drafted by officials and always vetted by relevant government departments before their delivery.[35] Hillery had consistently put his own stamp on official drafts as a minister, but as President he lacked the same latitude to do so. He still sometimes redrafted material he received from officials, but he was very conscious of the requirement to stay within the confines of government policy, and so his prepared speeches tended to be bland and unremarkable.[36] Yet there were some exceptions to this pattern, especially when Hillery was required to speak off-the-cuff without an official text. During his visit to China, the Irish delegation was taken by surprise on the morning of Hillery's departure when the representative of the People's Republic made a formal farewell address to the President. Hillery made a spontaneous reply thanking the Chinese government and was congratulated by Dermot Nally, who asked if he had spent the night preparing the speech. Nally was disbelieving when Hillery told him that he had not been prepared at all and had considered his response only when the Chinese minister was actually speaking.[37] It was not only Hillery's talents as a politician but his natural warmth and humanity that served him well on this occasion. More opportunity for unscripted, informal interaction with other public figures and journalists would have served him and the presidency considerably better than official constraints that belonged to a different era. The friendly, relaxed and affable man that the Irish public knew was strikingly at odds with the reticent public persona of the President. Yet on official visits abroad, Hillery's own convictions occasionally broke through the reticent official demeanour that he usually felt obliged to maintain.

The President's personal convictions certainly came to the fore on the most memorable overseas trip of his second term, when he visited the institutions of the European Community in October 1987; it was the first time that he had returned as head of state to his old stamping ground in Brussels. John Healy commented jokingly in *The Irish Times* that, as an old European hand, Hillery needed 'the European Fix and Europe duly obliged this week'.[38] Yet the visit was outstandingly successful. Hillery, and Brian Lenihan, now the Foreign Minister, were warmly received by the European Commission. Jacques Delors, the French President of the Commission, organised a detailed briefing for Hillery in the Berlaymont on 15 October that went well beyond the routine courtesies accorded to any visiting head of state.[39] Delors and other members of the Commission treated the meeting with Hillery and Lenihan as an important part of their preparations for the Copenhagen summit in December 1987, which would take decisions on the implementation of the Single European Act. The Irish position was to combine firm support for the Act, which would establish a single European market by 1992, with a strong case for the doubling of regional and social funds to allow poorer member states to adapt to the demands of the single market. As a former Social Affairs Commissioner, Hillery was ideally placed to make this case and he did so quietly but effectively throughout his five-day visit. The Commissioners were happy to discuss Community policy in detail with one of their former members and the briefing turned into a wide-ranging discussion of the political and technical issues to be resolved before the Copenhagen summit.[40] Hillery emphasised Ireland's interests in maintaining the CAP and expanding the social fund, but also underlined his confidence in the Commission's ability to protect the position of small states, referring back to his own positive experience of the understanding shown by European negotiators towards Ireland's problems during the process of accession.[41] The Commission was supportive of Ireland's case, and Delors emphasised his commitment to balancing the liberalism of the internal market with a major increase in Community support for poorer countries. Hillery enjoyed the encounter, which was undoubtedly useful for the Irish government in its efforts to expand the resources allocated to Ireland under the social and regional funds.

If the discussion with the Commission was perhaps the most important element of Hillery's visit, it was his address to the European Parliament that garnered the most public attention. He had an unusual stroke of good fortune here – a one-man protest by the Reverend Ian Paisley, which merely drew further media attention to Hillery's address. Paisley, who was then an MEP for Northern Ireland and the leading advocate of intransigent unionism, hoped to gain publicity for himself and highlight his claim that the Irish government had failed to confront the IRA. Hillery, who was invited to address the Parliament in Strasbourg on Wednesday 14 October, was warned beforehand by John Hume, also a member of the Parliament, that Paisley would attempt to disrupt his speech:

> I met John Hume – he said 'Paisley is going to cause you trouble.' John was worried about it. So I met the President of the Parliament at the time, Lord Plumb, he was an Englishman; he was most efficient. He asked could he see me, we had coffee in the morning before going down to the Parliament. His mind was made up – he knew Paisley was going to make a fuss and he was going to deal with it.[42]

Lord Plumb was as good as his word. The protest began even before Hillery started to speak but ended almost as quickly. As Plumb welcomed him to the Parliament as the President of Ireland, Paisley shouted 'not of the whole of Ireland'. Hillery received a standing ovation before he spoke; then as he began his address, Paisley heckled him and brandished a banner bearing the slogan 'IRA murders – extradite the IRA now'.[43] Other members of the Parliament turned angrily on Paisley and Plumb moved swiftly to have him ejected, warning him to be quiet or leave the chamber. As the ushers moved in to enforce his departure, Paisley went quietly, having secured his moment on television and the evening news bulletins.[44] Hillery was undisturbed by Paisley's protest: 'He was shouting and I spoke in Irish – until they got rid of him! Then the ushers got around him and they got him out and I made the speech'.[45] Paisley did Hillery an unexpected favour, guaranteeing more extensive press and TV coverage of the President's speech both in the Irish and European media.

Fortunately Hillery's speech deserved the attention it received – it was probably the best and most memorable address of his presidency. He emphasised Irish national interests as expected, warning that any attempt to dilute the CAP could breach the Treaty of Rome and underlining the importance of a significant expansion in the social and regional funds.[46] But Hillery also delivered a whole-hearted endorsement of European integration, recalling his own experience as Ireland's first Commissioner:

> As a vice-president of the Commission I felt that in pursuing the Community interest I was also pursuing the interests of the individual member states, including my own country's interests, which lie ultimately in a strong and united Europe. I address you in the same spirit today, as an Irishman and a European.[47]

He challenged national governments explicitly to support Delors' plans to develop greater social and economic cohesion throughout the Community. Hillery also emphasised the importance of the Parliament itself as an essential element in the ongoing process of European integration, supporting the expansion of its powers within Community decision-making. This passage was not simply a routine courtesy to the assembly he was addressing, but an echo of Hillery's personal aspiration, long since abandoned, of serving as a member of the Parliament. Moreover, he articulated a memorable metaphor for the long-term project of European unity: 'We are like the craftsmen of old who spent their lives on the construction of cathedrals which they knew they would not live to see completed'.[48] The comparison certainly flattered his audience, but his own identification with the cause of European unity was more significant in drawing an overwhelmingly favourable response from both MEPs and journalists. Hillery was interrupted by applause several times and his address was received with enthusiasm by the assembled MEPs.

The substance of the speech was overshadowed, however, by an accident which occurred just after he finished speaking; as he left the chamber, a TV spotlight fell from the ceiling and crashed on top of a desk normally occupied by an Italian MEP, who had fortunately just left.[49] The accident triggered a security alert, as alarmed security guards surrounded Hillery and Lord Plumb, fearing that a bomb had just exploded. Hillery

quipped to the British MEP: 'That wasn't a bad performance, a standing
ovation when I started and bringing the House down when I finished'.[50]
The joke was too good to remain secret; a gleeful John Healy printed it
in his column three days later. But Healy also acknowledged that 'it was
a good week for Ireland' and praised Hillery's speech to the Parliament.[51]
Hillery's address and indeed the visit as a whole offered valuable support
to Irish diplomatic efforts within the Community and underlined Ireland's
determination to be at the heart of European integration. The visit also
marked a rare public relations success for Hillery as President. This was
achieved not by media manipulation but because Hillery was able to find
his own voice as President. While Hillery's speech had a strong input from
the Department of Foreign Affairs and was fully in line with government
policy, it also bore his distinctive personal imprint. The address reflected
his genuine commitment to the European project and his sympathy with
the ambitious reforming objectives of the Delors Commission.
Unfortunately, the public relations success of his visit to the European
institutions was an isolated event rather than a presidential milestone. Yet
if Hillery's European visit was the exception that proved the rule, it was
at least a memorable one.

Hillery was a hardworking and effective President, who carried out
fully the public duties of the office and exercised his constitutional
functions with absolute impartiality. He operated, however, within the
traditional consensus that the office was essentially ceremonial and
powerless. This consensus was accepted by the government, the main
opposition parties and the civil service until the late 1980s. The traditional
way of doing business suited everyone, except the President himself.
Hillery accepted the constraints imposed on him throughout his two
terms, in part because he had little choice due to the limited resources
available to the President's office and the constitutional restrictions on his
freedom of action. But he was also personally averse to seeking out the
limelight and reluctant to challenge the official constraints on the office
for fear of involving the presidency once again in damaging controversy.
It is apparent in retrospect that his fears of dragging the office into public
controversy, which were entirely justifiable following the instability

surrounding the presidency in the 1970s, were exaggerated by the mid-1980s; arguably occasional controversy would have done the public image of the presidency no harm at all.

Nevertheless, Hillery's lengthy tenure of the office was marked by some important achievements. He took over the presidency at its lowest ebb since its establishment, at a time when it had become little more than a political football to be fought over between government and opposition. He quietly removed the office from the arena of party politics. He also restored stability to the institution by showing that persistent conflict between the presidency and the government was not inevitable. Much more significant was Hillery's undoubted success in establishing the independence of the presidency from all other institutions and from the governing party of the day. The political independence of the presidency was Hillery's finest accomplishment and the most valuable legacy that he left to his successor.

23.

Deciding the Succession

Hillery's term of office ended as it had began – in a controversy not of his making. The presidential election of 1990 was the most dramatic and controversial since the office was founded. It also produced several historic milestones, resulting in the election of the first woman to hold the office and the failure of Fianna Fáil to win the presidency for the first time. Moreover, the fall-out from the presidential election almost brought down the government – a unique occurrence in Irish political annals – and did provoke the fall of the deputy prime minister.

The campaign itself unfolded more like an adventure story than a conventional Irish election. It had all the necessary ingredients for a highly successful political thriller: incriminating tapes; skeletons tumbling out of cupboards; accusations of smears and black propaganda; and desperate last-minute attempts to save an embattled government. If the election was important especially for its outcome, much of the political theatre was provided by events eight years in the past, which had apparently been long forgotten by all except the main participants and a small group of hardened political anoraks. In fact, the campaign seemed to show that some of the leading participants themselves either had difficulty remembering or would have preferred to forget what had happened previously. The unresolved controversy surrounding the phone calls to the President on the night of 27 January 1982 re-emerged unexpectedly, with devastating consequences for the front-running presidential candidate, Brian Lenihan. The outgoing President, who had been at the centre of the storm in January 1982, watched the race for the succession with disbelief and occasional distaste. Hillery kept his feelings about the election to himself, and steadfastly refused to be drawn into the campaign. He was essentially ambivalent about the campaign and its eventual outcome.

The election for Hillery's successor inevitably drew attention to his own record for the previous two terms. Two of the three candidates were implicitly critical of Hillery and all three aspirants to the Park sought to distance themselves from his record as President, although none attacked him directly. This aspect of the election attracted relatively little attention then or later because of the sensational developments that dominated the final weeks of the campaign. In part, the tactics of the candidates represented a natural political reaction to the longevity of Hillery's term in the Park – the candidates had to distinguish themselves from a sitting President who had already served for over thirteen years. But the campaign also reflected a gradual change in public and political perceptions of the presidency. The dominant view of the presidency in the 1970s, as an office that was essentially ceremonial and almost entirely powerless in real terms, was no longer universally accepted. Instead, a very different vision of the presidency was gaining ground, which promoted effectively by Mary Robinson's campaign in 1990.

Robinson, a barrister and former member of the Seanad, was approached to stand for the presidency by the Labour leader, Dick Spring, and agreed to do so on the basis that she would run as an Independent with the support of the Labour Party.[1] Robinson's candidacy was launched on 1 May 1990 with the backing of Labour, the Workers Party, trade union representatives and members of the women's movement.[2] Yet from the outset, Robinson's campaign sought to reach far beyond the narrow confines of support for the Irish Left. Robinson's language and political style were carefully crafted to appeal to the middle ground; in the words of her media adviser, Eoghan Harris, she presented herself 'as a "democratic" candidate rather than a liberal candidate and never as a liberal left candidate'.[3] But there was also a definite message behind the reassuring rhetoric. Both Spring and Robinson set out to redefine the role of the presidency, making the case that a newly-elected President could highlight social injustice and promote respect for individual rights, especially the rights of women and minorities.[4] Robinson referred to the need for a 'working President', who would act to empower community groups throughout the country. This message contained an implicit but clear criticism not only of Hillery's presidency but also of the practice adopted by all previous incumbents since 1937. Hillery later commented wryly that an obvious implication of Robinson's argument was 'that former Presidents did not work'.[5] This was an understandable conclusion by a sitting President exposed to the critical scrutiny of his potential successors. Yet it appears that Robinson's message was not a criticism of Hillery's low-key style but a rejection of the traditional conventions governing the presidency and a challenge to the political establishment that had maintained those stifling restrictions. Her campaign undoubtedly tapped into a growing impatience with the traditional consensus surrounding the presidency, which was expressed particularly by journalists, but found considerable support among the public.

Robinson's campaign was not alone in seeking to differentiate its candidate clearly from the sitting President. Fine Gael sought to do so in a much less effective way. The main opposition party nominated Austin Currie, the former SDLP politician who had recently become a Fine Gael TD, as its candidate in September 1990. Currie had been a prominent and effective advocate of the civil rights movement in Northern Ireland and a leading member of the SDLP in the 1970s. But his public profile and electoral appeal in the Republic were extremely limited. He had reluctantly agreed to be a candidate only after more eminent public figures, including Garret FitzGerald, declined to go forward.[6] Fine Gael had no coherent vision of what their candidate might do if elected, merely a vague sense that promising some sort of change was desirable. The party tried to develop the theme of 'a new style of presidency', which would apparently be more open and active than the current practice.[7] What this actually meant was never clearly defined. The implied critique of Hillery got little public attention, as Fine Gael's campaign was fatally flawed from the start and Currie's candidacy failed to attract the support even of the party's core vote.

The attitude of Hillery's former party to the President during the campaign was more cautious and equivocal; as the party had provided every holder of the office except the non-partisan Douglas Hyde, Fianna Fáil could not credibly promise significant change in the role of the presidency and Haughey certainly had no desire to expand the office. But Fianna Fáil, too, showed some concern to distance its campaign from the incumbent. The governing party's standard-bearer was an immensely experienced politician and a personal friend of Patrick Hillery. Brian Lenihan had been a Cabinet Minister since 1964; he had served in nine different governments and by 1990 was Haughey's deputy, acting as Tánaiste and Minister for Defence.[8] He had recently suffered serious health problems, which had required a liver transplant at the Mayo Clinic in 1989. Lenihan was a hugely popular figure within Fianna Fáil, who was also liked and respected by politicians of other parties. He easily secured the party's nomination in September 1990 and most opinion polls gave him a commanding lead in the race to succeed Hillery.[9] Lenihan's initial appeal for support was more conservative than the other two candidates; he told the Fianna Fáil parliamentary party on 17 September that executive power belonged solely to the government and he would not seek any expansion in the formal powers of the presidency. But Lenihan also commented that he saw 'plenty of scope for an enhanced presidency within the existing constitutional parameters.'[10] Moreover, early in the campaign Lenihan described the presidency as a 'PR job', suggesting that he had the necessary skills and experience to develop the public relations aspect of the office more fully.[11] Lenihan's remark passed by without much notice in the media, but Hillery saw what his former colleague only hinted at: 'I took this to mean that Brian saw a gap in my handling of the media: a gap that if filled would make the holder of the office much more visible and popular.'[12] While Lenihan's comments were mild to the point of blandness and certainly did not bother Hillery, the candidate's line reflected a wider unease within Fianna Fáil about how to engage with Hillery's legacy as President.

The Fianna Fáil backroom team had commissioned qualitative research showing that Hillery was regarded as a low-key President and were concerned that Lenihan would be seen to be offering more of the same.[13] This concern was entirely legitimate in the light of Robinson's appeal for change, but the party faced a dilemma entirely of its own making. It was impossible to defend Hillery's record without indicting the leadership of Fianna Fáil itself, as well as the political establishment as a whole. The presidency had been neglected and denied adequate resources by successive governments since the 1970s; Haughey was not solely responsible for this trend, but he had done little to change it. Moreover, he had adopted an increasingly presidential style that further marginalised the institution of the presidency. To make matters worse, it was impossible for Fianna Fáil to highlight the real strengths of Hillery's tenure – his success in restoring stability to the office and asserting its political independence. Hillery had shown courage and principle in protecting the office from political interference in the early 1980s. But this was not something that Lenihan could acknowledge without revealing Haughey's central role in the failed attempt to drag the President into party politics. Fianna Fáil's campaign was caught in an insoluble dilemma – Lenihan's supporters could neither defend Hillery's record effectively nor criticise him; they could not credibly counter the perception that Lenihan was the candidate who would maintain the status quo. By a neat historical irony Haughey's manoeuvres almost a decade earlier had turned the presidential election into a minefield for his party and his candidate. In the circumstances it was hardly surprising that Fianna Fáil ran an uninspired, conservative campaign, which focused overwhelmingly on promoting Lenihan's impressive ministerial record and relied on his undoubted personal popularity.[14] This tactical approach at least had the advantage of sidestepping the tricky issues surrounding the party's ambivalent relationship with Hillery; in a more conventional contest it might well have been enough to secure Lenihan's election. But the struggle to succeed Hillery defied conventional wisdom from the beginning.

The outgoing President later described the election for his successor as 'a weird experience'.[15] This was only partly due to the curious sensation of being a spectator, unable to participate in any shape or form, in an election for an office that he had held for fourteen years. Outgoing incumbents in other republics, including the United States and France, had the luxury of being able to comment openly on the campaign and could endorse a potential successor if they wished; no such option was available to Hillery due to the constraints of the Constitution. Yet the restrictions inherent in the office did not disturb him on this occasion, as he had no intention of being drawn into the election. Hillery's feelings reflected especially the extraordinary events of the campaign itself and his long-standing personal connections with some of the leading participants. While Hillery's relations with Haughey were formal and frequently tense, he enjoyed a relaxed and friendly relationship with Brian Lenihan. Hillery had known Lenihan for almost thirty years; they had served together in government and enjoyed each other's company on a personal level.[16] Lenihan's low-key involvement in the Fianna Fáil attempt to pressurise Hillery in January 1982 did not affect their friendship. Hillery held Haughey responsible for the events of 27 January and remained on excellent terms with Lenihan: 'You couldn't be annoyed with the man; I knew it was Haughey. Everyone was afraid of Haughey'.[17] Hillery liked and respected Lenihan, believing that his former colleague's relaxed and affable manner caused him to be underestimated by the media and other politicians, who failed to appreciate Lenihan's intelligence and breadth of knowledge: 'Brian ... was brilliant and very learned and this was not realised by those in the media and public life generally'.[18] Hillery's personal affection for Lenihan did not necessarily translate into political sympathy. The outgoing President thought that John Wilson, the long-serving Monaghan TD and Minister for the Marine, would make an excellent presidential candidate for Fianna Fáil and was surprised when Lenihan decided to run for the office.[19] Moreover, Hillery did not allow his friendship with Lenihan to influence his judgement when the presidential campaign unexpectedly triggered a major political crisis.

The first polls of the campaign in September gave Lenihan a comfortable lead, but Robinson was in second place, while Currie failed to make any impact. In the following month both published opinion polls and private Fianna Fáil research showed Lenihan losing ground and Robinson gradually increasing her support.[20] This was unusual but hardly extraordinary considering the limited appeal of the Fine Gael candidate. Then, only three weeks before the election, the campaign was transformed beyond all recognition. The events of January 1982, apparently safely buried in the past, returned to haunt the main protagonists. It was Brian Lenihan himself who unwittingly played a central part in resurrecting the story, with considerable assistance from a hitherto unknown research student.

The Tánaiste gave an interview in May 1990 to a postgraduate student in UCD, Jim Duffy, who was preparing an MA thesis in political science on the presidency. Lenihan was still recovering from a serious complication arising from his original illness when he gave the interview. This was not, however, widely known until after the presidential election.[21] Lenihan spoke openly about the phone calls to the Áras on the night of 27 January 1982. He confirmed on tape that he himself had made two or three calls to the President, while Haughey and Barrett had also made calls. He told Duffy that 'of course Charlie was gung-ho' and also commented accurately that Hillery 'was annoyed with the whole bloody lot of us'.[22] This was sensational enough, but what followed was even more dramatic. Lenihan told Duffy that he had managed to speak to the President – 'Oh yeah, I mean I got through to him, I remember talking to him and he wanted us to lay off.'[23] As nobody had previously suggested that any of the politicians managed to get through to Hillery, this appeared to be a dramatic new revelation.

In fact, Lenihan had confessed to something that he had not done. Hillery had refused to speak to any Fianna Fáil politician on the night of 27 January and indeed had not spoken to any of them about the phone calls subsequently. He reflected later that Lenihan's comments on the

President's annoyance had to be 'a trick of memory', drawn from a story by Geraldine Kennedy at the time rather than any conversation with Hillery himself.[24] Unfortunately for Lenihan, the rest of his comments to Duffy were broadly accurate and confirmed a version of events that was widely believed in political circles, but consistently denied by Haughey. Moreover, Duffy was a former member of Young Fine Gael, who retained good political connections within the main opposition party.[25] He contributed several articles on the presidency to *The Irish Times* in September, which were based in part on information given by the Tánaiste; in this series Lenihan was named as one of the three politicians who had attempted to speak with Hillery on 27 January, although no indication was given of the existence of the tape.[26] The scene was set for the explosive revelations that would not only rock Lenihan's campaign but shake the government to its foundations.

The controversy ignited in a televised confrontation between Lenihan and Garret FitzGerald on 22 October. Fine Gael strategists decided to raise the issue of the phone calls in an effort to highlight Lenihan's closeness to Haughey; FitzGerald was asked to raise the controversy when he appeared on the panel of RTÉ's *Questions and Answers* programme alongside Lenihan.[27] This tactic proved the only effective move of Fine Gael's disastrous campaign, although it did nothing at all to help their own candidate. When FitzGerald vigorously attacked Lenihan for exerting pressure on the President in 1982, Lenihan responded by categorically denying the whole story, assuring the audience that 'Nothing like that ever happened. I want to assure you that it never happened.'[28] This statement directly contradicted what Lenihan had said on tape to Duffy. Although he did not watch the programme, Hillery himself was astonished by Lenihan's denial: 'Brian with all his experience denied phoning or talking to me. He should have said that there was no offence in trying to call me. But he denied it.'[29] Hillery's reaction underlined his lack of rancour over Lenihan's actions in 1982. Hillery was sympathetic to Lenihan's position and could not understand why the other man did not simply shrug off the accusation by referring to their long-standing friendship: 'Garret threw it at him as an accusation and Lenihan reacted by denying it. He didn't have to. All he had to say was "why not?" I know the man, we're friends.'[30] It is impossible to know what would have happened if Lenihan had simply admitted that he had called his old friend in the Áras rather than confronting FitzGerald. No doubt the Tánaiste would still have faced a certain amount of high-minded criticism, but it certainly would have been a great deal better than the approach he actually adopted.

The stakes escalated dramatically within 48 hours of Lenihan's appearance on *Questions and Answers*. After Duffy contacted *The Irish Times* to reveal the existence of the tape, the paper published a front-page article on Wednesday 24 October, breaking the story that corroborative evidence was available to confirm Lenihan's role in the unsuccessful approach to the President.[31] The story, by Denis Coghlan, was essentially accurate, although it repeated the mistaken claim that Hillery had taken the calls before rejecting the approach.[32] While the Tánaiste himself continued to deny any involvement in phoning Hillery, Fianna Fáil politicians rallied around him, accusing Fine Gael of organising a 'smear campaign' and engaging in 'black propaganda' to discredit Lenihan.[33] But on the following day the axe fell. Duffy, flanked by two journalists from *The Irish Times*, played an extract from the tape to journalists at a packed press conference in the Westbury Hotel. The release of the tape sent shock waves through Fianna Fáil and created a media frenzy around Lenihan's campaign. The candidate's immediate reaction was a spectacular blunder, which further escalated the crisis. Lenihan gave an interview to Seán Duignan on the *Six One News* that evening, in which he declared that 'on mature recollection' he had made no calls to the President and his replies to Duffy were clearly mistaken.[34] The interview had a shattering effect on Lenihan's public credibility and was the principal factor in the rapid collapse in his poll ratings over the following days. The crisis also threatened the stability of the government, as the Progressive Democrats signalled that they were seriously disturbed by the affair and would have to consider their position in any motion of no confidence.[35] Events then took a further extraordinary turn, which threatened to involve Hillery in the election of his successor.

The embattled Tánaiste announced in successive interviews on Thursday 25 October that he would seek a meeting with Hillery to confirm that he had made no phone calls to the President in January 1982.[36] This move threatened to embroil Hillery in the controversy and involve him in a highly charged presidential election. Lenihan telephoned the Áras personally around 5.25 p.m. on Thursday evening, shortly before his fateful interview with Seán Duignan; the Tánaiste asked to see Hillery the following day to confirm his version of events.[37] Hillery was not in the office at the time; Peter Ryan, the assistant secretary to the President, informed him of Lenihan's request later the same evening.[38] Hillery had heard on the radio at 6.30 that Lenihan wished to call on the President. Hillery, however, was determined to stay out of the controversy and had no intention of meeting Lenihan. Moreover, he believed that there was nothing he could do to help the embattled candidate:

> They had the two tapes, Lenihan saying quite the opposite
> in each one, so you couldn't save him. He said he was going
> to see the President; that was typical Lenihan! I heard him
> on the radio. But what could I do, he had said two things
> that totally contradicted each other.[39]

Hillery sympathised with Lenihan's plight on a personal level, but he was well aware that intervening in a presidential election would be both improper and counterproductive. Any attempt to support Lenihan's version of events would constitute a blatant interference in party politics; it would require Hillery to act as a referee between Lenihan and Duffy; and finally, it would do Lenihan little good but would do a great deal of harm to Hillery's own reputation and the hard-won independence of the presidency. As it turned out, it did not prove necessary for Hillery to refuse Lenihan's request. Bertie Ahern, the Minister for Labour, who was Lenihan's campaign manager, acted the following day to persuade Lenihan not to seek a meeting with the President and told journalists that the candidate was no longer pursuing the idea.[40]

Yet this was not the only approach made by Lenihan to Hillery. On

Thursday at 12.45 p.m. Micheál Ó hOdhráin received a phone call from Lenihan's private secretary, Brian Spain, who enquired about the existence of a log of phone calls to the Áras on the night of 27 January 1982. Brian Spain told the President's Secretary that it had occurred to Lenihan that the ADC on duty that night might have logged the phone calls in line with military practice.[41] In fact, Captain Barbour had done just that, and Hillery retained a copy of the ADC's unit journal, which gave a log of all the phone calls received that night, including those from Haughey, Lenihan and Barrett.[42] But Micheál Ó hOdhráin, who was not aware of the log's existence, told Brian Spain that the President's office did not log calls and he knew of no log for the night in question or any other night. The Secretary was by his own account 'taken aback by the call' and immediately reported it in writing to Hillery. Ó hOdhráin was uncertain what Lenihan was trying to achieve: 'Why is the Tánaiste taking such an initiative via Brian Spain? Is he hoping that there exists a log or hoping that such does not or never existed?'[43] The normally diffident Ó hOdhráin was sufficiently alarmed to issue a definite warning to the President: 'I felt that you should know of this strange approach to me, which I understood was on behalf of and at the behest of the Tánaiste. We must keep out of the controversy.'[44] Even this mild warning was entirely unnecessary.

Hillery was consistent in his determination to keep the presidency out of political conflict and he had no wish to be embroiled in the most controversial presidential election of his lifetime. He certainly had no intention of allowing anyone to consult the log in the middle of an election campaign. Hillery moved quietly but effectively to head off any further enquiries about the log. He instructed Ó hOdhráin to contact Frank Murray, assistant secretary in the Department of the Taoiseach, on Friday 26 October; Ó hOdhráin was told to bring Brian Spain's request about the log to Haughey's attention and to ascertain whether he wished to speak to the President about it.[45] This approach was cleverly designed to prevent any further move to embroil Hillery in the campaign. Hillery was well aware of the contents of the log and knew that its records were sufficiently explosive as to make Jim Duffy's tape seem a minor nuisance.

The contents of the log were particularly damaging to Haughey, whose persistent attempts to exert pressure on the President were faithfully chronicled. It is not clear whether Haughey knew of the existence of the log before Ó hOdhráin's call to Murray, but at any rate the Taoiseach's reaction was swift and decisive. Murray phoned back on the same day to tell Ó hOdhráin that Haughey had ordered an end to any enquiries about the log.[46] The Secretary to the President was given the following message for Hillery:

1) that the Tánaiste's office had been instructed that the request is not to be pursued;
2) that I inform the President that the request is not being pursued;
3) the question of a phone call from or request for a visit by the Taoiseach to the President is still with the Taoiseach.

Haughey remembered what had happened only too well. He had good reason to fear for his own hold on power if the existence of the log became a major public issue, and even more so if a documentary record of the phone calls somehow came into the public domain.

Hillery also warned Haughey directly not to involve him in the campaign. The President instructed Peter Ryan to tell the Taoiseach's department that Hillery wished to speak directly with Haughey.[47] The two men spoke on the phone later that day. Haughey asked if Hillery could do anything to help Lenihan, but the President warned that neither Lenihan nor Haughey should attempt to meet him:

Haughey phoned and he said, 'can you do anything, can we do anything?' I said, 'nothing – don't come near me.' But he must have known. I mean it didn't matter who phoned me or who didn't, Lenihan had said contradictory things and they had tapes of the two of them. The fact was that he denied it once and agreed with it the second time

… Haughey was totally stuck to know what to do. There was nothing he could do; nothing I could do.[48]

Haughey made no attempt to pressurise Hillery, probably recognising that any intervention by the President would do Lenihan no good and might well exacerbate the crisis. He had no choice in any event but to accept the President's position, which was not only constitutionally proper but made good political sense. Hillery remained resolutely aloof from the campaign and kept the presidency clear of the political convulsions that ensued.

The crisis unfolded rapidly without any intervention from Hillery. Fine Gael and the Workers Party moved to exploit the government's disarray by putting down a motion of no confidence.[49] It soon became evident that the PDs were not willing to support the government as long as Lenihan remained a member of it. Des O'Malley made clear to Haughey that the price for the Taoiseach's survival was Lenihan's dismissal.[50] Haughey's ruthlessness was never more clearly in evidence. Having failed to persuade Lenihan to resign, he sacked the Tánaiste on Wednesday 31 October, less than an hour before the vote on the confidence motion was taken in the Dáil. The government survived by three votes with the support of the PDs.[51] This denouement appeared to deal the final blow to Lenihan's ill-starred campaign, but the story of the presidential election was not yet over. Lenihan engineered a dramatic comeback in the final week of the campaign. The sacking generated a surge in public sympathy for the beleaguered candidate and Lenihan himself delivered his best performances of the campaign in two televised debates.[52] The final polls showed Lenihan drawing level with Robinson, regaining most of the support he had lost as a result of the tapes affair.[53] But in the end Lenihan's campaign received a direct hit from friendly fire.

On 3 November, the Minister for the Environment, Pádraig Flynn, went on *Saturday View*, RTÉ's current affairs programme on Saturday afternoon, to promote Lenihan's cause. Flynn's intervention had exactly the opposite effect and virtually guaranteed Robinson's election. The Fianna Fáil minister launched into a fervent attack on Robinson; he alleged that 'none of us you know, none of us who knew Mary Robinson very well in previous incarnations ever heard her claiming to be a great wife and mother'.[54] Flynn's comments drew an immediate, furious response in the studio from Michael McDowell, Chairperson of the PDs, who labelled Flynn's intervention 'disgusting' and told him to learn some manners. More significantly, the minister's remarks provoked outrage among women voters, including supporters of Fianna Fáil.[55] Hillery, a shrewd political operator throughout his career, thought that Lenihan would probably have won but for Flynn's intervention: 'He could still have been elected, I think, if Flynn kept his mouth shut. Flynn did for him. Flynn spoke and everyone went for the lady then.'[56] It will never be known whether Hillery's theory was correct. But Flynn's intervention certainly had an important influence on the outcome, costing Lenihan first preference votes that he might otherwise have gained and reducing the momentum of the surge towards the Fianna Fáil candidate in the final days of the campaign.

The electorate voted on 7 November in the most dramatic, contentious and volatile contest in the history of the presidency. Lenihan polled well, securing over 44 per cent of the vote on the first count; but Robinson was not far behind on 39 per cent, while Currie trailed home with 17 per cent.[57] Robinson secured a decisive victory on the second count, capturing the vast majority of Currie's transfers and winning by an eventual margin of 86,000 votes.[58] The success of a female candidate backed by the left-wing parties was an extraordinary outcome to an election that broke almost all the traditional rules of Irish politics. Hillery was abroad during the election count, attending his final official function outside the state, the formal enthronement of Akihito, the new emperor of Japan.[59] When he returned to Ireland shortly after Robinson's election, the Taoiseach was at Dublin Airport to greet him. Hillery wryly recalled another surreal encounter with Haughey:

> They had lost the Presidential election and he had fired
> Lenihan in the middle of it. But he was very positive; when
> I asked him 'how about your position?', he said that the

national executive had been excellent and that all was well. Then he added, 'I made no phone calls!'[60]

Hillery, who was well aware that Haughey had orchestrated the entire episode, kept his counsel and did not respond to this apparently random comment. Hillery believed that Haughey was putting on a brave face after a devastating setback for which he was largely responsible: 'He made an awful mess of it. Losing the presidency: that, for Haughey, was the worst thing he could do.'[61] It was a realistic assessment. The outcome of the presidential election was at least as much Charles Haughey's defeat as Brian Lenihan's.

The result of the election established a series of historic landmarks; the most striking was the election of the first woman to hold the office of President. While Fianna Fáil's failure to win the presidential election attracted considerable attention, not least from Haughey's critics within the party, perhaps more remarkable was the victory achieved by the broad coalition supporting Robinson. The result foreshadowed Labour's dramatic advance in the general election of 1992 and underlined that Fianna Fáil was unlikely to win an overall majority in the foreseeable future. The election was also groundbreaking in its impact on the presidency. Robinson had won a popular mandate to expand the role of the President within the Constitution. While the constitutional powers of the presidency would not change, Robinson's victory signalled that the purely political constraints, which had kept the President as a silent symbol of the state, were about to disappear. The seal of public approval gave the new incumbent powerful leverage with the political establishment, which Hillery had never enjoyed.

Hillery himself was ambivalent about the historic outcome of the election. Despite his distinguished record as a Fianna Fáil minister, he had left party allegiance behind during his term as President and certainly had no emotional attachment to the party under Haughey. Yet Hillery regarded Lenihan as a friend, and privately deplored the Fine Gael attacks on him during the campaign.[62] He knew that Lenihan's part in the events of 27 January 1982 was entirely innocuous and in any event dictated by

Haughey. Hillery sympathised with Lenihan's plight following the revelation of the tape and was shocked at his abrupt fall from office, but he did not allow his personal friendship for Lenihan to dilute his strict neutrality throughout the campaign. Hillery's central concern during the election was to preserve the independence of the presidency and keep the office firmly aloof from party politics. His principled approach during the election of his successor set the seal on the independence of the presidency as an institution.

24.

Retirement

Hillery's retirement from the presidency in December 1990 marked the end of a public career that had spanned four decades. Hillery's feelings about leaving the presidency were unequivocal – he experienced a profound sense of relief. He had been concerned that the campaign for his successor would turn into an inquest on his performance as President, but this never really materialised due to the extraordinary events that shaped the eventual outcome.[1] Hillery never spoke of the presidency in terms that might be seen as disrespectful, even in private to close friends. Instead, he returned after a lengthy break to his taped diary, making a substantial entry for 1991, describing the first year of his retirement. His private reflections on leaving the office bore more than a passing resemblance to those of a man released from prison:

> Once I was out, I did not care. There was a sudden relief. It did not bother me. I was so glad to be out of it. It did not bother me what they said or what they were going to do or how much the new scene was welcomed.[2]

Hillery's feelings were understandable. He had carried the office for fourteen years, with minimal support except from a few devoted staff, while the presidency was largely ignored and neglected by the political establishment. He believed that his work was done and it was time for a new incumbent to make their mark.

Yet returning to private life did not prove as straightforward as Hillery had hoped. He received several requests for interviews immediately after his retirement, mainly from Irish journalists interested in exploring the various controversies in which he had been embroiled, notably the phone calls to the Áras. He was generally reluctant to give interviews, as he had no intention of speaking publicly about the tapes affair, which was then still very much a live issue in contemporary politics. Hillery did not wish to stoke up the controversy and particularly sought to avoid becoming enmeshed once more in disputes that he had found deeply frustrating and upsetting at the time. He had promised RTÉ before standing down as President to co-operate with a documentary on his life, which was to be presented by Siobhan Cleary and produced by Peter Feeney. He had doubts about going ahead with the documentary after his retirement, but was reassured by Cleary that it would focus on his life as a whole and not on particular controversies.[3] He gave several interviews to Cleary in Spanish Point and Maeve also contributed to the programme. When the issue of the telephone calls came up, Hillery remarked that as President he felt he should not have come into controversy and he still maintained that he should not get involved in it now.[4] The documentary proved a balanced and low-key appraisal of his career.

If the RTÉ documentary stirred little public controversy, the same could not be said of an interview that Hillery gave to Joe Carroll, his former press spokesperson in Brussels. Hillery liked and respected Joe Carroll, who had returned to journalism with *The Irish Times*; the two men had known each other for over 20 years. The former President also felt that he owed the journalist an interview due to a misunderstanding eight years earlier. He had told Carroll in 1983 that he was definitely not seeking re-election as President. The journalist printed the story; shortly afterwards Hillery was persuaded to change his mind and announced that he would serve a second term. Hillery, characteristically, felt a sense of guilt about the incident. 'Joe was let down before his colleagues and his boss so I owed him an interview.'[5]

The journalist met Hillery at his house in Sutton; the former President was very relaxed and spoke freely about a wide range of issues. Hillery did not believe that he had said anything very significant, but he had underestimated the news value of his own reflections: 'I was a bit surprised when I saw *The Irish Times* advertising three days of articles by Joe on me and there was quite a response.'[6] The articles, which were published in August 1991, generally provided an informative and sometimes fascinating account of various aspects of his career, including his mission to the UN in 1969 and the negotiations for Irish accession to the EEC. But it was Hillery's comments on his time as President that aroused the greatest interest in the media. He expressed anger at the treatment he had received over the Remembrance Sunday service in 1980 and articulated some of his frustration with the lack of support for the presidency from various governments in the previous decade. Hillery also indicated that the rumours about his marriage in 1979 were not inspired by the KGB, but by unspecified sources closer to home.[7] He did not speak directly about the telephone calls to the Áras, but appeared to give a tantalising hint that he might at a future date: 'I'm holding on to that. A lot of people have asked me. It will surface again … I may say something at a later stage.'[8] This looked like a cryptic warning to his former associates; it was actually a straightforward mistake. He had meant to tell Joe Carroll that he would not talk about 'the night of the phones', but had inadvertently put it in a provocative way. He realised his mistake almost immediately, lamenting his choice of words in his diary: 'Now I don't know why I said it in that form. I meant I am hanging on to that information, but it seemed to be interpreted as a challenge, as if I was going to use it.'[9]

While there were few new revelations in what Hillery said, he had done more than enough to tantalise the national and local media. An editorial in *The Irish Times* declared that Hillery had shown 'a hint of steel' in giving the interview and noted that 'more – perhaps much more – remains to be told.'[10] He received calls from the *Sunday Press*, Clare FM and RTÉ seeking follow-up interviews; he was also invited to appear on Pat Kenny's television show, *Kenny Live*. No newspaper or media outlet wanted to be left behind if the notoriously reticent former President was ready to tell his story and some journalists hoped to coax him into doing so. The intense media interest had exactly the opposite effect. Hillery was horrified at the attention he had unintentionally generated and he refused all further requests for media interviews.[11] He had not attempted to provoke the media, but he had assumed – wrongly – that casual remarks he had made to Joe Carroll would not attract much attention. The media reaction appeared to threaten his hopes of a quiet retirement, far removed from the glare of publicity. He reflected that 'the whole thing has been a great disturbance and it has upset my wife, it has worried me ... and certainly took the peace away from my retirement.'[12] He subsequently adopted a practice that persisted throughout his retirement; he rarely gave public interviews and resolutely declined to speak out on the controversial episodes of his presidency. This approach caused some frustration to journalists, but generally served him well and allowed him to determine the pattern of his life in retirement, which was a luxury often denied him during his public career.

New Horizons

If Hillery had retired in 1983, as he originally intended, he would have returned to medicine, though not in Ireland. He had discussed with Maeve the possibility that they might both go to Africa to work as doctors.[13] He knew that there was considerable scope to make a contribution to medical practice in a developing country and was attracted to it as a fresh challenge. But this prospect was dashed by his reluctant acceptance of a final call to duty. When he finally retired seven years later, he was reconciled to the fact that it was too late to fulfil his cherished dream of returning to medical practice. But retirement did not mean inactivity; he regarded it as a new life after politics.

Hillery took full advantage of the opportunity to pursue old interests and develop new ones. Golf remained an important part of his life. He played regularly in Portmarnock in a four ball including his close friend

Joe O'Keeffe, Michael Mills and Judge Butler. He also devoted more time to his painting. But Hillery's newest pastime was an unusual one for a man of 67: he took up pilot training. He took lessons in a flying school at Celbridge or arranged to meet instructors in Shannon while he was in Clare. He had always wanted to learn how to fly and took to the skies with great enthusiasm. He loved flying, joking that it gave him the chance to get away from people occasionally: 'it's great up there; if you do it once, then once you come down, everything is very congested and everyone is in your way.'[14] He told Joe Carroll that 'It's like being at sea without the waves.'[15] He did not go on to acquire a pilot's licence; his 22 hours of flight training were just short of what was required to be qualified as a pilot, but this did not greatly bother him. It is true that at one time he hoped to fly a plane to Clare and back rather than driving, because 'the roads are terrible for long journeys';[16] but generally he flew for pleasure rather than convenience. Hillery's passion for flying reflected his determination to explore new challenges in his retirement.

Hillery also took up new opportunities in the public arena, contributing especially to several initiatives in higher education. He chaired a committee on the internal structures of UCD, at the invitation of Dr Paddy Masterson, the president of the college.[17] The committee undertook a review of the college's structures in preparation for the establishment of UCD as an independent university, which was accomplished by new legislation in 1997. Hillery's position was not simply an honorary one; he found the role more onerous than he had anticipated, but enjoyed the work and made a substantial contribution to the deliberations of the committee.

The former President developed a more enduring association with a non-profit-making venture, which was designed to promote research links between Ireland and Canada. He was deeply involved in the establishment of the Ireland Canada University Foundation, which set out to facilitate scholarship links between researchers and academic institutions in the two countries. Hillery and Prof John Kelly, the registrar of UCD, were instrumental in bringing the project into being, following a meeting in Newfoundland in 1993 with Craig Dobbin, a wealthy Canadian businessman whose family were originally from Waterford.[18] Dobbin, the CEO of CHC Helicopter Corporation, the largest helicopter company in the world, provided the start-up capital to establish the Foundation and remained a leading supporter of the project for the following decade. Hillery became the joint chairman of the new Foundation in 1994, along with Craig Dobbin, while John Kelly administered the project as its executive director. The Foundation provided funding for short-term scholarships to support visits between Irish and Canadian institutions, by researchers working on projects relating to both countries.[19] The former President was essentially a valued figurehead for the ICUF – he lent his name to the enterprise and took a leading part in its public events, particularly the prize-giving ceremonies for its scholarships. Hillery's involvement in the ICUF was his principal area of public activity during his retirement and his association with the Foundation continued throughout the final decade of his life.

Hillery's new status as an elder statesman also gave him greater scope to express his other political interests, notably his commitment to European integration. He participated in a European conference in June 1991, which explored the new political environment created by the dramatic collapse of the communist regimes in Eastern Europe in 1989.

François Mitterrand, President of France, and Czech President Václav Havel organised the gathering in Prague of former ministers and commissioners, along with younger political activists.[20] The participants, who were drawn from all over Europe, discussed the challenge of enlarging the European Community and creating a unified Europe in the wake of the withdrawal of Soviet power to its own borders. Hillery led an Irish delegation that included former European Commissioner Peter Sutherland and academic Brigid Laffan. Hillery knew most of the European participants in the conference well, including his former colleagues on the Commission, Claude Cheysson and Ralf Dahrendorf, as well as former German President Walter Scheel. Hillery did not overestimate the importance of the event, recognising that it was consultative and that policy decisions were now in the hands of others.[21] But he enjoyed the occasion, revisiting an earlier period of his life with his former colleagues and discussing European issues in which he had a deep interest. The conference also brought some unexpected echoes from the past. He was amused when an Albanian delegate approached him at one of the conference functions and remarked 'You're very famous in my country.'[22] Hillery was convinced that he owed his fame in Albania, such as it was, to his speech at the UN Security Council in 1969 and particularly the positive portrayal that he received in *Pravda*.

The former President also explored the possibility of writing his memoirs. Michael Gill of Gill & Macmillan was interested in publishing a book on Hillery's career. Hillery had maintained a considerable volume of papers that would have facilitated such a project, not to mention his taped recollections of various events. He met Michael Gill to discuss a possible book, but in the end the project did not materialise.[23] Hillery did not go ahead with a book, in part because he had no wish to revisit the public controversies of his presidency, but mainly for less tangible reasons inextricably linked with his character and personality. He had often told officials in the various departments he headed that he was not a writer, though he had no difficulty writing or redrafting speeches about policy; what he meant was that he did not like writing about himself. He was uncomfortable with the idea of writing an autobiography and remained as wary of self-promotion in his retirement as he had been throughout his political career.

This did not mean that he was indifferent to public or scholarly perceptions of his time in office. He took pride in his considerable achievements and was disturbed that public commentary on his career shortly after his retirement appeared dominated solely by the events of his two terms as President.[24] Hillery was concerned that the historical record of his actions be preserved; he took the first step in this direction by giving a substantial collection of his papers to the archives department in UCD. Although the material was not generally available during his lifetime, he himself was readily accessible to researchers. He accepted a wide range of requests for interviews from academics, postgraduate researchers and secondary school students throughout the 1990s. His readiness to facilitate researchers contrasted sharply with his guarded approach towards journalists. Hillery's willingness to help academic researchers undoubtedly reflected his considerate and generous nature, yet it was also influenced by his concern to set the record straight where he felt that his own contribution had been neglected or simply ignored. He increasingly realised that his aversion to publicity had led others to underestimate him. Hillery was deeply concerned that his pivotal role in initiating the transformation of the educational sector in the 1960s had been largely forgotten.[25] He reflected that 'In politics your achievements, even your existence, can be hidden in the media dust created by your successor.'[26] He was keenly aware that Donogh O'Malley's combination of genuine achievement and effective propaganda had essentially blotted out the memory of his predecessors. While he was still a minister, he commented to John McColgan that 'Malley stole my clothes.'[27] Hillery acted quietly but effectively in the 1990s to encourage a reappraisal of the Irish educational revolution; it was significant that he focused his efforts on scholars, rather than on the public. He was not seeking public praise, but to contribute to the first drafts of history, by remedying what he considered an oversimplified and inaccurate perception of the transformation of Irish education. He provided a great deal of assistance to academic researchers who were exploring the origins of the educational reforms in the 1960s. It helped that he had a good case; it was also crucial that his recollections were generally reliable and focused on imparting information rather than propaganda. Hillery's ready availability to researchers and his invaluable perspective as a former minister contributed to a gradual reassessment of the events of the previous generation. This reappraisal occurred primarily within the academic community, as articles by Imelda Bonel-Elliott in *Administration* and Tom Rigney in *Studies* highlighted Hillery's contribution to educational expansion.[28]

Hillery also agreed to participate in the TV documentary *Seven Ages*, a history of the Irish state from its foundation, which was produced by Seán Ó Mórdha, an independent filmmaker, and shown by RTÉ in 2000. *Seven Ages* featured contributions from prominent participants in Ireland's recent political history, including Liam Cosgrave and Charles Haughey, as well as Hillery himself. The former President gave an extensive interview, which illuminated some of his vast – and largely untapped – knowledge of public affairs. He spoke about the origins of the Troubles, identifying the mistakes of the British political establishment as a crucial factor: 'the British in many ways created the IRA.'[29] Hillery also discussed his involvement in the European negotiations and his first term as President. He gave a broad hint of his suspicions about Haughey's involvement in the controversy that engulfed the presidency in October 1979, commenting that he had faced 'structured rumours' about his private life.[30] Hillery's participation in the programme alerted a wider audience to his pivotal role in the politics of the previous generation.

Hillery remained a hugely popular figure in Clare following his retirement, and he maintained strong connections with his native county. He had retained his family home in Spanish Point and kept in contact with his many relatives in Miltown Malbay. He returned frequently to his beloved Spanish Point, where he could sail the bay or enjoy walks along the familiar shoreline. He quietly supported local public services, giving books to the library in Miltown Malbay and providing a substantial collection of artefacts and memorabilia from his career to the Riches of Clare museum.[31] He was keenly interested in the fortunes of the Clare hurling and football teams and was present at Croke Park in September 1995, when the Clare hurlers won their first All-Ireland title since 1914. John Hurley, another native of Miltown Malbay who had served as president of the ASTI, was at the match and vividly remembered Paddy Hillery's emotional reaction when Clare finally ended their long drought:

> One of my abiding memories will be of the day Anthony Daly lifted the McCarthy Cup for us success-starved Clare supporters in 1995. I was fortunate to have a seat near the presentation and I glanced over at Dr Paddy to see the tears streaming down his face.[32]

His devotion to his native county received formal acknowledgement from the local authorities in 2003. His nephew Michael Hillery, who had served as chair of Clare County Council during the 1990s, took the lead in urging that the council should honour the former President in his lifetime. Michael Hillery had no difficulty in persuading his fellow councillors; his only problem came in winning over the intended recipient. 'I had an awful job trying to persuade him. He was afraid that he would be crossing lines that he shouldn't cross.'[33] Michael eventually overcame his uncle's reluctance, pointing out that libraries in Ennis and Shannon carried the names of de Valera and Lemass respectively. Richard Nagle, the Mayor of Clare, proposed that the public library in Miltown Malbay, which had been opened in 1995, should be named after the former President and the council agreed the initiative unanimously. The ceremony dedicating the Dr Patrick J. Hillery Public Library went ahead on 2 January 2003; councillors, officials and former constituents came out to honour the former President. Hillery himself told the crowd that he was 'humbled and somewhat overwhelmed.'[34] Despite his initial doubts, he was delighted by the decision and deeply moved by the honour offered by his county. It reflected the high esteem in which he was held in his native town and was a fitting tribute to Miltown Malbay's most famous son.

Final Days

Paddy Hillery generally enjoyed good health for over a decade after his retirement. But early in the new century he began to suffer serious illness. He developed cancer and had to undergo surgery in October 2001. The surgery was successful and he was able to resume an active life. He would face further health complications over the next six years; age and illness were beginning to take their toll. Many of the physical recreations that he had always valued were no longer possible, and he was no longer able to play golf. His mind remained as acute as ever and his memory of past events in which he had been involved was still impressive, but he was increasingly frail. He knew that he was unwell but did not wish to make a fuss about his illness. He disliked intensely the idea of giving up his independent lifestyle and managed to maintain it until the final months of his life. Strangely enough for a man who had started his career as a much-admired GP, he was wary of doctors. He told his son that 'If you talk to doctors, they'll find something wrong with you.'[35] By January 2008, he was seriously ill and entered the Mater Hospital for treatment; the cancer had recurred. He was able to return home briefly, but it soon became apparent that it would be his final illness. His last days were spent in St Francis' Hospice in Raheny. He died in the early hours of the morning on 12 April 2008, barely three weeks short of his 85th birthday.

The tributes from political leaders were universally warm and generous. His second successor, President Mary McAleese, declared that he had made 'an enormous contribution to this country'; the Taoiseach, Bertie Ahern, said that his 'entire career sums up what is best about politics and public service.'[36] The opposition leaders were equally unstinting in their praise. Labour leader Eamon Gilmore noted that it was a mark of the extraordinary esteem in which Paddy Hillery was held that the tributes from former opponents were as warm as those from political colleagues; this reflected his status as 'one of the most important and influential figures in Irish public life over a period of four decades.'[37] Enda Kenny, the leader of Fine Gael, paid Hillery an even more striking accolade: having lauded the former President as 'an exemplary man, politician and servant of Ireland', Kenny suggested that Fianna Fáil would have been better served with Hillery as its leader in the previous generation.[38]

It was not only politicians who paid tribute. Several hundred people travelled from Clare to pay their respects, including a contingent of students from St Joseph's Secondary School in Spanish Point, the building closest to his home; fittingly enough, it was a school that Hillery had opened in 1959.[39] Appreciation of his public career was not restricted to his native county. Thousands of people lined the streets in the centre of Dublin on 17 April as the funeral cortege passed from the Pro-Cathedral to his final resting place in Sutton.[40]

He received a state funeral, but one marked by a strong input from his family and long-standing friends from Clare. It was a sombre and dignified occasion, which marked a celebration of his personal qualities and political achievements as much as an opportunity to mourn his passing. Dr Fiachra Ó Ceallaigh, auxiliary Bishop of Dublin, who had known Hillery for 57 years and was the son of his former colleague Seán Ó Ceallaigh, was the chief celebrant at the removal on the evening of 16 April, assisted by Bishop Eamonn Walsh.[41] Fr Aidan Lehane, another close friend of the former President, officiated at the Requiem Mass on the following day; Paddy's nephew Fr Des Hillery gave the homily, highlighting the personal qualities of his uncle.[42] Diarmuid Martin, Archbishop of Dublin, provided a memorable accolade, describing the former President as a 'pioneering artisan in building a modern Ireland.'[43] Brian Cowen, the then Tánaiste, gave the graveside oration at the request of the Hillery family. It was a carefully-crafted and elegant address, in which Cowen paid tribute to Hillery both as a man and as a politician. The oration was summed up in the opening line of the English text: 'If greatness is judged by the content of character – we stand at the graveside of a great man today.'[44]

Paddy Hillery was laid to rest in St Fintan's cemetery in Sutton on the afternoon of 17 April. He was buried in accordance with his wishes beside his daughter Vivienne, whose premature passing had been such a shattering blow 21 years before. The funeral did much to underline the high esteem in which he was held across the political spectrum and throughout a wide cross-section of Irish society. He might have viewed the proceedings with a wry smile; as a genuinely modest man, he would have been surprised and not a little embarrassed by the eulogies. Yet it was a suitable farewell for a man who had never sought fame, but had nonetheless served his country well.

25.

Postscript

Hillery was described as 'the quiet man of Irish politics' in an article by Stephen Collins shortly after his death in April 2008.[1] There was undoubtedly much truth in this assessment. Hillery intensely disliked self-promotion and was reluctant to seek publicity for its own sake, but the wider public and media perception of Hillery as a reserved and reticent figure, which flourished particularly around the time of his retirement, was flawed and misleading. This image derived mainly from his time as President, when it had some validity; but even then his public reticence was determined more by the constraints that he faced as head of state than his own preferences. This conventional view took little account of his force of character and toughness, especially in pursuing key policy objectives. As Minister for Education he cajoled and pressured the Catholic bishops to accept comprehensive schools; over a decade later he publicly rebuked the Irish government over its attempt to delay the implementation of the equal pay directive.

He had a relaxed and mild-mannered style, which sometimes veiled his intelligence and shrewd understanding of politics.[2] This low-key style had its advantages, not least when it served to conceal definite and highly controversial political views. His deep hostility to the influence of the Catholic bishops in education never became public, although it was trenchantly expressed in private correspondence and in his own papers. Likewise, his suspicion of Charles Haughey after 1970 was not expressed openly, although it became widely known in political circles. More generally, his natural instinct was to seek conciliation rather than confrontation. Paddy Hillery showed an impressive ability to achieve major policy changes without large-scale conflict.

But Hillery also had a combative side to his character, which usually emerged if his fundamental beliefs or values were challenged. He certainly had no qualms about engaging in public confrontation, as Kevin Boland discovered to his cost. Yet Hillery's occasional public outbursts were usually deliberate; he rarely lost his temper and almost never did so in public. The famous clash with Boland's supporters at the Ard Fheis was undoubtedly a calculated outburst, even if it was not scripted in advance. Similarly, Hillery's vehement attacks on British policy in Northern Ireland were clearly sincere, but equally were designed to reassure Northern nationalists that the Irish government would represent their interests and contain popular outrage in the Republic. There was little sign of reticence in Hillery's resolute opposition to hardline nationalism or his assertive conduct of Anglo-Irish negotiations in the early 1970s.

Hillery was an unconventional politician, as he lacked any great personal ambition. He was a reluctant TD and had no aspiration to be a minister initially. He certainly did not aspire to the highest place in Irish politics:

> There's nothing in the job of Taoiseach that's attractive to
> me. Charlie [Haughey] wanted it; he wanted the power.
> He made use of it, whatever people think of him. But he
> had no inhibition in him. I would have had inhibitions in
> using power.[3]

In view of the excesses of the Haughey era, it might be said that some level of inhibition in using power is no bad thing. But it should also be acknowledged that saints and scholars rarely prosper in politics – Hillery was neither. His toughness and ability to fight his corner were often overlooked. It was no accident that he won six elections in Clare, still less that he remained in government for over thirteen years. His initial unwillingness to serve as a minister soon faded as he became committed to far-reaching policy change in education. He later proposed the establishment of the Department of Labour and accepted appointment as its first minister. He was pleased to be promoted to External Affairs and revelled in the challenges offered by the position, despite the enormous pressure and occasional danger that came with the package. Moreover, he secured the much-desired appointment as Ireland's first Commissioner, a post that he clearly wanted. Hillery was certainly a reluctant President, but not a reluctant politician once he accepted ministerial office in 1959. Indeed, he was reluctant to accept the presidency to a large extent because he recognised that it meant the end of his active political career, not least his aspiration to serve as a member of the first directly elected European Parliament.

Yet it was a passion for achievement, not personal ambition, which drove Hillery throughout his career. He had a compelling desire to succeed at whatever brief he adopted. While he lacked conventional political aspirations, he did not lack political ideals or the ambition to transform them into reality. He was guided by firm political convictions; an unwavering belief in equality of opportunity which remained consistent throughout his career; support for Lemass's strategy of economic development in the 1960s; commitment to a peaceful settlement in Northern Ireland, underpinned by justice for the nationalist community, in the early 1970s; and a conviction that full participation in European integration was indispensable to Ireland.

He was a pragmatic politician; he once told Dennis Kennedy that 'politics is the art of the possible.'[4] But for Hillery, pragmatic methods co-existed with idealistic objectives. A more accurate summary of his own *modus operandi* is that he saw politics as the art of persuasion. He had a shrewd appreciation of what could be achieved in the face of political and economic constraints. As a minister and European Commissioner, he usually prepared the way for major initiatives in a painstaking fashion, through a series of private consultations with policy-makers or interest groups. He sought to win support for his objectives with quiet determination, persistence and considerable political skill. This low-key and conciliatory approach, combined with a clear sense of what he wanted to achieve, often enabled Hillery to change the boundaries of what was politically possible. Certainly the political landscape in education looked very different after his term as minister, to the great benefit of his successors. Similarly he succeeded against impressive odds in converting the vague aspirations for a European social policy into reality.

Paddy Hillery was driven not only by his genuine convictions but also by values that dominated his political life. He had a compelling loyalty to institutions in which he was involved, from the Irish government to the European Commission to the presidency. He gave his allegiance to institutions rather than people. Although he admired Lemass and fought hard to uphold Jack Lynch's leadership, Hillery was not an uncritical follower, and did not elevate loyalty to the leader above all else. His dedication to institutions was based on a profound commitment to basic political values – democracy, social justice and an inclusive nationalism. He was greatly influenced by his own family background; his father had participated in the struggle for an independent state and he grew up in a community marked by recent military conflict. He believed in cherishing the democratic institutions which had emerged from the violence of the 1920s; he was a democratic nationalist long before he entered politics. His family's tradition of service to the local community also shaped his outlook. While he never fulfilled his first ambition to be a country doctor, he was committed to the idea that politics was about public service – initially to his constituents, but later to the nation as a whole. He had a passionate abhorrence of injustice; he did not forget that he was the only member of his class in the national school to go on to Rockwell, because his father was a doctor.[5] Hillery began his career as a fervent supporter of republican ideals, but his distaste for Civil War rhetoric and extreme nationalist posturing provided a revealing indication of things to come.

His nationalism was forward-looking, giving priority to social and economic advances rather than the political battles of the past. Although he was de Valera's loyal running mate, it was Lemass who was his mentor in politics. Michael McInerney, writing in *The Irish Times* in July 1966, described Hillery as a 'Social Republican.'[6] It was an accurate reflection of the mixture of idealistic nationalism and concern for social justice that influenced Hillery in the 1960s.

The most famous public contributions of his career were dictated by his profound commitment to democratic principles and to the institutions in which he served. Hillery played a vital role in preserving Lynch's beleaguered government during and after the arms crisis; his support for Lynch was essential to the Taoiseach's survival. Yet when Hillery faced down the supporters of Blaney and Boland at the Fianna Fáil Ard Fheis in 1971, the conflict was about much more than saving the embattled party leadership. Hillery upheld the right of the majority to determine party policy on the North and ensured the triumph of democratic nationalism in the internal politics of the Republic. It is only necessary to imagine what might have happened if a hardline nationalist administration had been in power in Dublin just after Bloody Sunday to appreciate the importance of Hillery's intervention.

Hillery's only real dispute with the Irish government during his term as a European Commissioner was also driven by principle and institutional loyalty. He stood by the policy of equal pay for equal work, which had been approved unanimously by all the member states and successfully defended the right of the Commission to enforce it against a reluctant Irish government. While Hillery's initiative in this instance might appear to have less dramatic implications than his famous intervention at the Ard Fheis, trade unions and women's organisations had no doubt about the importance of his decision: the Irish state was obliged to implement a long delayed social reform enforcing equality of rights between men and women at work. Hillery placed his commitment to the policy itself and his obligations to the Commission above personal ambition.

It was deeply ironic that Richie Ryan criticised 'the Fianna Fáil-appointed Commissioner' for the decision on equal pay, suggesting that

Hillery had somehow manipulated the Commission in the interests of the Soldiers of Destiny. Hillery had been a loyal member of Fianna Fáil as a TD and minister, but he had a greater loyalty to the institutions of the state itself. His clash with Charles Haughey over the Fianna Fáil leader's attempt to prevent the dissolution of the Dáil in 1982 was driven by Hillery's determination to protect the independence and integrity of the presidency at all costs. But his decision also reflected his private belief that no politician should be allowed to avoid an election for opportunistic reasons; Hillery's action was consistent with his commitment to democratic principles.

Assessing the influence of any political figure is a notoriously subjective occupation; importance often lies in the eye of the beholder. Paddy Hillery's standing in media and political circles fluctuated during the last two decades of his life. Following his death, Hillery was hailed as a great statesman, an architect of modern Ireland and, perhaps above all, as an Irish patriot. This contrasted sharply with the general media reaction on his retirement as President in 1990, or still more in the final years of his second term. Then he was portrayed as a low-key, reticent figure; an invisible President; a decent public servant whose achievements were not very significant and were buried in the distant past.[7] His public standing during the same period is much harder to determine, in the absence of anything beyond anecdotal evidence, which tended to be overwhelmingly favourable. Hillery himself, a naturally modest man, would not have claimed greatness as a public figure. Yet it is possible to reach some general conclusions about his career.

As a reforming Minister for Education, Hillery had a major influence in stimulating the transformation of the educational sector over the following generation. He did not simply prepare the way for others, such as Donogh O'Malley, but initiated far-reaching changes in the state's educational policy. The impact of Hillery's initiatives was still being felt a generation later. His time as Minister for Labour was marked by a mixture of genuine achievement and considerable frustration. There were valuable advances in worker protection legislation and retraining schemes; his attempt to improve the turbulent industrial relations climate had limited success in the short-term and won him few plaudits from the competing forces of capital and labour. Yet managing the confrontation between unions and employers in the late 1960s was a virtually impossible task and many of Hillery's initiatives contributed to the creation of a more stable framework for industrial relations in the long term.

Hillery's term as Foreign Minister made him a major political figure and ensured that he was seen as a potential Taoiseach, even if this was a distinction he would have preferred to do without. He played the pivotal role in the negotiations for Ireland's accession to the European Communities. The achievement of accession on generally favourable terms was no small accomplishment. The referendum that followed, in which Hillery orchestrated the government's campaign, provided the greatest political triumph of his career. His skilful management of the process of accession, from his first visit to Brussels in 1969 to the formal ratification of the terms three years later, was Hillery's most valuable and enduring contribution to the modernisation of Irish society.

There was no comparable triumph in the other main area that took up a great deal of his time and energy – the North. The crisis in Northern Ireland erupted within six weeks of his arrival in Iveagh House, and went from bad to worse in the early 1970s. Hillery's strenuous efforts to persuade British ministers to make timely concessions to nationalist demands largely fell on deaf ears, and he was powerless to prevent a steady escalation of the conflict in Northern Ireland. The divisions within the Irish government also meant that his initiatives at the UN in 1969 were more of an exercise in damage limitation in Dublin than conflict prevention in the North. Yet he was instrumental in preventing a far greater catastrophe, which would have occurred if the Irish state had abandoned democratic nationalism and backed physical force republicanism in Northern Ireland. He did a great deal to uphold Lynch's moderate line within Fianna Fáil; but his most significant contribution was to demonstrate, through intensive diplomatic activity in Britain, America and continental Europe, that constitutional nationalism provided a viable alternative to physical force. He also played a leading part in initiating the first real diplomatic engagement between the two governments concerning Northern Ireland. Anglo-Irish contacts occurred tentatively and sometimes secretly at first, but developed into an open and increasingly constructive dialogue by the summer of 1972.

It was as a member of the European Commission that Hillery enjoyed the greatest scope to express his egalitarian social ideals. Hillery guided the social action programme past the multiple hurdles of the European institutions and secured its adoption within a year of his arrival in Brussels. He drove forward its implementation with remarkable success despite the economic crisis and a declining political will to support social reform among national leaders. The social action programme created a genuine European social policy for the first time, even if it was neither as radical nor as well financed as Hillery had hoped. His achievements here stand the test of time. Women were among the leading beneficiaries of the progressive social policy that he inaugurated. But people with disabilities who benefited from the Social Fund and migrant workers who received aid from the Community for the first time could also testify to the advances delivered by the Commission at Hillery's instigation; so, too, could individuals and families who benefited from the pilot projects to combat poverty. If Hillery's reputation depended solely on his term in the Commission, his status as an outstanding social reformer would be secure.

And then there was the presidency. It was the most prestigious and the least powerful office that he held; it was also the one he was most reluctant to accept. Yet he made a significant contribution to the development of the office especially in his first term. He stabilised the institution following the turbulence that had surrounded the brief terms of his two predecessors. More significantly, Hillery established the independence of the presidency from party politics and politicians; he firmly distanced himself from his former party and faced down the most formidable and ruthless politician of his generation. Hillery often faced criticism in the media, however, as a low profile or inactive head of state. This generally ignored Hillery's considerable workrate and the political realities of the time. There was simply no scope for Hillery to break new ground, due to the political and financial constraints on the presidency that were maintained by successive governments; he lacked both the political mandate and the resources enjoyed by his successors in the 1990s. He was indeed a low-key President, but never an inactive one. Hillery himself was deeply frustrated by the constraints on his freedom of action and at times felt like a prisoner in the Áras. Yet it was an independent and respected office that he passed on to Mary Robinson in 1990.

Following Hillery's death in April 2008, two of his contemporaries, Garret FitzGerald and Gerry Collins, paid tribute to him on RTÉ's *The Week in Politics* programme. The most revealing part of the interview came when they were asked if Hillery would have led the government had he not accepted the presidency. Gerry Collins, a friend and former ministerial colleague of Hillery in Jack Lynch's government, believed that 'Paddy Hillery would undoubtedly have been Taoiseach if he had stayed in the Dáil and not gone to Europe or later accepted nomination as President.'[8] FitzGerald, who led two coalition governments in the 1980s, agreed that Hillery 'probably' would have led a government. It is impossible to know whether they were right. But it is evident that if Hillery had chosen to return to the Dáil in 1977, as many expected him to do, he had several key advantages over the other contenders to succeed Jack Lynch. Hillery had greater ministerial experience than either Haughey or Colley; the Clare man also enjoyed considerable public standing following a highly successful term as a Commissioner. Moreover, Hillery was a unifying figure within the Fianna Fáil organisation; he did not inspire the divisiveness associated with both Haughey and Colley. Perhaps equally important in a party that still prided itself on its republican traditions, Hillery's nationalist credentials were impeccable; no internal opponents could play the green card effectively against the man who had taken Ireland's case to the United Nations and walked the Falls Road as the Troubles erupted. While there are few certainties in politics, the prospects of Hillery taking over the leadership of Fianna Fáil after Lynch were excellent. He also had a better chance of managing a divided party and leading a stable government that could command the confidence of the wider electorate than either of the other contenders. There is little question that Hillery could have been Taoiseach in the 1980s had he wished to be. It is much more doubtful, however, whether he would have been willing to fight for a position that he genuinely did not want. Arguably the most significant obstacle to a Hillery government in the 1980s was the private resistance of Paddy Hillery himself.

Paddy Hillery was not only a formidable politician, but also one of the most creative public figures of his generation. Although he never served as Taoiseach, he was undoubtedly more influential than some of those who did during the second half of the twentieth century. He was also a profoundly decent and honourable man. He acted with scrupulous integrity throughout his career and regarded public service as a noble calling. Hillery made an extraordinary contribution, in a remarkably understated fashion, to the development of the prosperous and peaceful Ireland of the early twenty-first century. Despite his distaste for self-promotion, he left a distinctive imprint on Irish and European political life. His commitment to egalitarian social reform left an enduring legacy, first in the transformation of the Irish educational sector and later on a much wider scale with the evolution of progressive social policies at European level. His other distinctive legacy is less tangible, but no less valuable. Hillery showed that it was possible to succeed in politics while maintaining the highest standards of personal integrity and commitment to public service. Paddy Hillery's career reflected his belief in the power of politics to transform people's lives for the better.

Notes

Chapter 1

1   Samuel Lewis, *A Topographical Dictionary of Ireland*, vol.2 (London, 1837), p.90
2   Private Papers, Hillery Note, *Home*, 1996, p.1
3   Samuel Lewis, *A Topographical Dictionary of Ireland*, vol. 2 (London, 1837)
4   *House of Commons Parliamentary Papers, Accounts and Papers relating to Ireland*, vol.22, 1824, *Abstract of the Answers and Returns under the Population Act of Ireland, 1821*, p.140
5   *House of Commons Parliamentary Papers, Accounts and Papers relating to Ireland*, vol.54, *Census of Ireland for 1861*, Part I, p.22
6   S. MacMathúna, *Kilfarboy: A History of a West Clare Parish* (Lucan, 1974), p.67
7   Ibid., pp.69–70
8   Register of births, no.350, parish records, St Joseph's Church, Miltown Malbay
9   Register of births, no.365; no.392; parish records, St Joseph's Church, Miltown Malbay
10   Ledger for Hillerys' public house, Miltown Malbay, October 1899
11   *Clare Champion*, 'Obituary Notices: Mrs Margaret Hillery', 26 November 1938
12   *Irish Times*, 'Royal College of Surgeons in Ireland', 24 October 1908; *The Irish Times*, 'Royal College of Surgeons in Ireland', 23 July 1910
13   *The Irish Times*, 'Royal College of Surgeons in Ireland', 17 October 1911
14   *Clare Champion*, 'Well-known Clare Doctor's Death', 19 October 1957
15   Interview with David Hillery, 21 August 2008
16   Marriage register, no.166, parish records, St Joseph's Church, Miltown Malbay
17   Interview with David Hillery, 21 August 2008
18   Interview with Paddy Hillery, 3 August 2006
19   *The Irish Times*, 'Dr Hillery: Social Republican', 8 July 1966
20   Private Papers, Hillery Note, *Old IRA*, 1996, p.1; Ernie O'Malley, *Raids and Rallies* (Dublin, 1982), p.67
21   *The Banner*, ed. Thomas Dillon, 'Commandant Martin Devitt Killed in Action', (New York, 1963), XVII

22   Ibid., 'Dr Michael J. Hillery', XVII
23   Hillery Note, *Old IRA*, p.1
24   Ibid.
25   *The Irish Times*, 'Seven police murdered in Co. Clare', 2 October 1920
26   *Clare Champion*, 'Desperate Affair in west Clare', 25 September 1920
27   *Clare Champion*, 'Malicious Injuries in Clare', 2 October 1920; Interview with David Hillery, 21 August 2008
28   *Clare Champion*, 'Desperate Affair in west Clare', 25 September 1920; *Clare Champion*, 'Ennistymon and Lahinch Reprisals Of Last Week', 2 October 1920
29   Paddy Hillery Note, *Old IRA*, p.1
30   Register of births, no.898; no.985; parish records, St Joseph's Church, Miltown Malbay
31   Interview with S. Talty, 21 August 2008
32   Register of births, no.1276, parish records, St Joseph's Church, Miltown Malbay
33   Private Papers, Hillery Note, *Home*, 1996, p.1
34   Interview with Paddy Hillery, 17 May 2006
35   Ibid.
36   Private Papers, Hillery Note, *Gaeilge*, 1996, p.1
37   Ibid.
38   *Clare Champion*, 'Well-known Clare Doctor's Death', 19 October 1957
39   Paddy Hillery Note, *Childhood*, p.1
40   Ibid., pp.1–2
41   Interview with Paddy Hillery, 17 May 2006
42   Pat O'Sullivan, 'Dr Paddy Hillery An Appreciation: Rockwell Remembers a Past Pupil', 15 April 2008
43   Private Papers, Hillery Note, *Rockwell*, 1996, p.1
44   Ibid.
45   *Rockwell College Annual* 1984, p.14
46   *Rockwell College Annual* 1939, pp.136–7
47   *Rockwell College Annual* 1984, p.15
48   Hillery, *Rockwell*, p.1
49   *Rockwell College Annual* 1984, p.15
50   Interview with Paddy Hillery, 17 May 2006

Chapter 2
1   Interview with Paddy Hillery, 17 May 2006.
2   Interview with Dr John Hillery, 19 October 2007
3   Interview with Paddy Hillery, 17 May 2006
4   *The Irish Times*, 'Dr Hillery: Social Republican', 8 July 1966
5   Interview with Paddy Hillery, 17 May 2006
6   Private Papers, Paddy Hillery Note, *Hospital*, 1996, p.1,
7   Interview with Paddy Hillery, 17 May 2006
8   John Corcoran, *Reference*, 22 September 1948,
9   Hillery, *Hospital*, p.1
10   Interview with Paddy Hillery, 17 May 2006
11   Hillery, *Hospital*, p.1
12   Interview with Paddy Hillery, 17 May 2006

13 Interview with Dr John Hillery, 19 October 2007

14 Private Papers, Hillery Note, *Candidate*, p.1

15 Lee, *Ireland 1912–85: Politics and Society* (Cambridge, 1989), p.299

16 Noel Browne, *Against the Tide* (Dublin, 1986), p.110

17 Lee, *Ireland*, p.315

18 Interview with Paddy Hillery, 17 May 2006

19 T.M. Healy, *From Sanatorium to Hospital: A Social and Medical Account of Peamount 1912–97* (Dublin, 2002), xiii

20 Ibid., pp.111–2

21 Ibid.

22 Ibid., pp.109–10

23 Private Papers, Hillery Note, *UNICEF*, 1996, p.1,

24 Ibid.

25 Ibid.

26 Ibid.

27 Interview with Paddy Hillery, 17 May 2006

28 Private Papers, Hillery Note, *Golf*, 1996, p.1

29 Interview with Paddy Casey, 21 August 2008

30 *The Clare People*, 'Dr Hillery the man of sport,' 15 April 2008

31 Interview with Paddy Hillery, 17 May 2006

32 Lee, *Ireland*, pp.315–6

33 *The Irish Times*, 'Dr Hillery: Social Republican', 8 July 1966

Chapter 3

1 Interview with Paddy Hillery, 17 May 2006

2 Ibid.

3 Ibid.

4 Ibid.

5 Ibid.

6 Private Papers, Hillery Note, *Political Life*, p.1

7 Interview with Paddy Hillery, 17 May 2006

8 Ibid.

9 *Clare Champion*, 'Fianna Fáil Team Selected', 12 May 1951

10 UCDA, *The Hillery Papers*, P205, Folder 11, *Election Advertisement 'The Clare Fianna Fáil Candidates Will Not Make False Promises'*

11 Ibid.

12 Private Papers, Hillery Note, Political Life, p.1

13 Ibid.

14 Private Papers, Hillery Note, *Candidate*, p.2

15 *Clare Champion*, 'The Election In Clare: How Parties Fared in '48', 19 May 1951

16 Ibid.

17 *Clare Champion*, 'The Election In Clare', 19 May 1951

18 Hillery Note, *Candidate*, p.2

19 Hillery Note, *Political Life*, p.1

20 UCDA, *The Hillery Papers*, P205, Folder 11, *Election Advertisement 'The Clare Fianna Fáil Candidates Will Not Make False Promises'*

21   Hillery Note, *Political Life*, p.3
22   Hillery Note, *Candidate*, p.2
23   Interview with Paddy Hillery, 17 May 2006
24   Ibid.
25   Hillery Note, *Political Life*, p.1
26   Interview with Paddy Hillery, 17 May 2006
27   Ibid.
28   *Clare Champion*, 'Fianna Fáil's Appeal to Voters: Want Three Clare Seats', 26 May 1951
29   Hillery Note, *Political Life*, p.2
30   Ibid., p.3
31   Interview with Paddy Hillery, 17 May 2006
32   Ibid.
33   Hillery Note, *Political Life*, p.2
34   *Clare Champion*, 'Fianna Fáil's Appeal to Voters: Want Three Clare Seats', 26 May 1951
35   Hillery Note, *Political Life*, p.2
36   Hillery Note, *Candidate*, p.1
37   UCDA, *The Hillery Papers*, P205, Folder 11, *Election Advertisement 'The Clare Fianna Fáil Candidates Will Not Make False Promises'*
38   Hillery Note, *Candidate*, p.2
39   *Clare Champion*, 'Fianna Fáil's Appeal to Voters: Want Three Clare Seats', 26 May 1951
40   Ibid.
41   Ibid.
42   Hillery Note, *Political Life*, p.2
43   Ibid.
44   Interview with Paddy Hillery, 17 May 2006
45   *Clare Champion*, 'The Election In Clare, 2 June 1951
46   Ibid.
47   Ibid.
48   Ibid., Private Papers, Hillery Note, *Candidate*, p.1
49   Interview with Paddy Hillery, 17 May 2006

Chapter 4

1   Private Papers, Hillery Note, *Political Life*, p.3
2   Ibid., p.4
3   Ibid., p.4
4   *Dáil Debates*, vol.126, col.18–75, 13 June 1951
5   Ibid., col.75–80
6   Hillery Note, *Political Life*, p.4
7   Interview with Paddy Hillery, 17 May 2006
8   Private Papers, Hillery Note, *Dev*, p.1
9   Interview with Paddy Hillery, 17 May 2006
10   Private Papers, Hillery Note, *Service*, p.2
11   Ibid.
12   Interview with Paddy Hillery, 17 May 2006
13   Ibid.
14   Ibid.

15   Private Papers, Hillery Note, *Service*, p.1

16   Private Papers, Hillery Note, *Practice*, p.3

17   Ibid., p.2

18   Hillery Note, *Service*, p.1

19   Hillery Note, *Practice*, p.3

20   Interview with Paddy Hillery, 17 May 2006

21   *Who's Who's 1997*, p.915

22   *Clare Champion*, 'Well-known Clare Doctor's Death', 19 October 1957

23   Interview with Michael Hillery, 4 July 2008

24   *Clare Champion*, 'An Taoiseach In Miltown', 1 May 1954

25   *Clare Champion*, 'Speeches from the Election Platforms: Fianna Fáil – "Right In The Past – Right Now"', 15 May 1954

26   *Clare Champion*, 'Speeches from the Election Platforms: Discontented with Everything', 15 May 1954

27   Ibid.

28   *Clare Champion*, 'Retained Their Seats – Record Poll in Clare: Outgoing Deputies Again Re-elected', 22 May 1954

29   Ibid.

30   Interview with Paddy Hillery, 17 May 2006

31   *Politics in the Republic of Ireland*, ed. J. Coakley and M. Gallagher (PSAI Press, Dublin, 1992), p.266

32   *Clare Champion*, 'No Change in Clare Representation: Quietest Election On Record', 9 March 1957

33   Ibid.

34   Interview with Paddy Hillery, 17 May 2006

35   Private Papers, Hillery Note, *Lemass*, p.3

36   Interview with Paddy Hillery, 17 May 2006

37   Ibid.

Chapter 5

1   Interview with Paddy Hillery, 3 August 2006

2   Interview with Dr Maeve Hillery, 29 August 2008

3   Ibid.

4   Ibid.

5   Ibid.

6   Interview with Paddy Hillery, 3 August 2006

7   *The Irish Times*, 'Social and Personal', 8 October 1955

8   *The Irish Times*, 'Obituary: Most Rev. Dr Fogarty', 26 October 1955

9   Register of births, no.1145, parish records, St Joseph's Church, Miltown Malbay

10   Interview with Dr Maeve Hillery, 29 August 2008

11   Interview with Michael Hillery, 22 August 2008

12   Ibid.

13   Interview with Dr John Hillery, 19 October 2007

14   Ibid

15   Ibid.

16   Interview with Paddy Hillery, 3 August 2006

17 Interview with Dr John Hillery, 19 October 2007
18 See Chapter 10, pp. 185–7.
19 Interview with Dr Maeve Hillery.
20 Interview with Dr John Hillery, 19 October 2007
21 Interview with Dr Maeve Hillery, 29 August 2008
22 Interview with Dr John Hillery, 19 October 2007
23 UCDA, *Hillery Papers*, P205, Folder 20, *Marriage notice for John Hillery and Carolyn Curtin*, January 1983
24 Interview with Paddy Hillery, 3 August 2006
25 Interview with Dr John Hillery, 19 October 2007
26 Interview with Paddy Hillery, 3 August 2006
27 Interview with Dr John Hillery, 19 October 2007
28 *The Irish Times*, 'Death of President's daughter', 27 March 1987
29 Interview with Peig O'Malley, 6 May 2008
30 Interview with Dr John Hillery, 19 October 2007

Chapter 6
1 J. Horgan, *Lemass: The Enigmatic Patriot* (Dublin, 1997), pp. 194–5
2 Ibid.
3 Interview with Paddy Hillery, 17 May 2006, Private Papers, Hillery Note, *Lemass*, 1996, p. 2
4 Interview with Paddy Hillery, 17 May 2006
5 Interview with Paddy Hillery, 17 May 2006
6 Ibid.
7 Private Papers, Hillery Note, *Education*, 1996, p. 1
8 Ibid.
9 Private Papers, Hillery Note, *O'Raftery*, p. 1
10 Hillery Note, *Education*, p. 1
11 Interview with James Dukes, 28 April 2003
12 Interview with James Dukes, 4 December 2000
13 Interview with Paddy Hillery, 24 May 2006
14 Interview with Paddy Hillery, 17 May 2006
15 Interview with Paddy Hillery, 25 February 2002
16 Interview with Paddy Hillery, 25 February 2002
17 *Dáil Debates*, vol. 177, col. 200–202, 21 October 1959
18 *Dáil Debates*, vol. 177, col. 470, 28 October 1959
19 Ibid.
20 Ibid., col. 470–1
21 Ibid., Ó Buachalla, *Education Policy*, p. 73
22 Ó Buachalla, *Education Policy*, p. 307
23 Interview with Paddy Hillery, 24 May 2006
24 T. J. McElligott, *Education in Ireland* (Dublin, 1966), p. 50
25 *Dáil Debates*, vol. 189, col. 842, 24 May 1961
26 Circular 22/61, Department of Education, October 1961
27 Ibid.
28 Circular 22/60, Department of Education, June 1960

29   *Dáil Debates*, vol. 195, col. 1377–8, 23 May 1962

30   *Committee of Public Accounts, Appropriation Accounts 1962–63* (Dublin, 1964), pp. 100–106, *Committee of Public Accounts, Appropriation Accounts 1965–66* (Dublin, 1967), p. 117

31   *Dáil Debates*, vol. 191, col. 517–20, 11 July 1961

32   W26/4, M2014/58, *University Scholarships Awarded By County Or County Borough Councils 1958–59,* Department of Education, *Dáil Debates,* vol. 191, col. 521–24, 11 July 1961

33   Interview with Paddy Hillery, 17 May 2006

34   *Dáil Debates,* vol. 191, col. 1683, 25 July 1961

35   Ibid.

36   Ibid., col. 1737–44

37   Ibid., col. 2342–9

38   Ibid., col. 1688–1709

39   *Dáil Debates,* vol. 191, col. 2423–5, 2 August 1961

40   *Dáil Debates,* vol. 206, col. 1083–6, 11 December 1963

41   *Dáil Debates,* vol. 203, col. 384, 29 May 1963

42   Ibid., col. 1684–6

43   *Dáil Debates,* vol. 191, col. 2342, 1 August 1961

44   *Dáil Debates* vol. 182, col. 75, 24 May 1960

45   Circular 11/60, Department of Education, January 1960

46   Ibid.

47   Ibid., O'Connor, *A Troubled Sky*, p. 44

48   W26/2, M2001/5, *Memorandum to the government,* Department of Education, 9 November 1959

49   Ibid., Randles, *Post-Primary Education*, p. 29

50   O'Connor, *A Troubled Sky*, pp. 52–4

51   W26/2, M2001/5, *Memorandum to the government,* Department of Education, 9 November 1959

52   CAB 2/20, G.C.99/28, Cabinet Minutes, 13 November 1959, pp. 3–4, CAB 2/20, G.C. 9/36, Cabinet Minutes, 15 December 1959, pp. 3–4

53   *Dáil Debates*, vol. 182, col. 72–3, 24 May 1960

54   V. Jones, 'Coláiste Moibhí – The Last Preparatory College', *Irish Educational Studies*, vol. 15, 1996, p.109.

55   Circular M19/60, Department of Education, November 1960

56   W26/30, M80/1, *Progress Report for the Quarter ended on 30 June 1960, Department of Education,* 13 July 1960; W26/30, M2001/5, *Memorandum, Additional Gaeltacht Scholarships to be made available,* 15 July 1960

57   Ibid.

58   O'Connor, *A Troubled Sky*, p. 54

59   Ibid.

60   Ibid., pp. 54–5

61   Interview with Paddy Hillery, 25 February 2002

62   Interview with James Dukes, 28 April 2003

63   *Commission on Accommodation Needs,* p. 124

64   NAI D/T S.16803A, *Report of Inter-Departmental Committee on Accommodation for the Faculty of Science, UCD,* 13 November 1959, p. 1

65 Ibid., pp. 11–12, *Reservation by Mr J. Mooney*, pp. 13–14

66 NAI D/T S16803A, C.O.911, *Memorandum for the government, Office of the Minister for Education*, 22 February 1960, pp. 1–10; CAB 2/20, G.C.9/52, Cabinet Minutes, 1 March 1960, pp. 2–3

67 *Dáil Debates*, vol. 180, col. 926–7, 23 March 1960

68 Ibid., col. 945–8

69 Ibid., *Commission on Accommodation Needs*, p. 44

70 *Commission on Accommodation Needs*, pp. 47–8

71 *Dáil Debates*, vol. 180, col. 940–941, 23 March 1960

72 Ibid., col. 940–1

73 O'Connor, *A Troubled Sky*, p. 91

74 DDA AB8/B/XVIII/18, *McQuaid Papers*, McQuaid to Dr P. J. Hillery, 24 March 1960

75 McQuaid to Ó Raifeartaigh, 24 March 1960

76 *Dáil Debates*, vol. 180, col. 955–1172, 23 March 1960

77 *Dáil Debates*, vol. 180, col. 1260–8, col. 1360–85, 31 March 1960

78 Ibid., col. 1507

79 Private Papers, Hillery Note, *Commission*, 1995, p. 1

80 *Dáil Debates*, vol. 180, col. 952–3, 23 March 1960

81 CAB 2/20, G.C.9/90, Cabinet Minutes, 16 August 1960, pp. 3–4

82 Ibid.

83 *Report of the Commission of Inquiry on Higher Education 1960–67, vol. 1: Presentation and Summary of Report* (Dublin, 1967), pp. 1–2

84 Private Papers, Hillery Note, *Commission*, p. 1

85 Ibid.

86 NAI D/T S.16803A, S. MacEntee to Hillery, 26 August 1960; UCDA, *Hillery Papers*, P205, Folder 4, MacEntee to Hillery, 29 August 1960, MacEntee to Hillery (2), 29 August 1960

87 Private Papers, Hillery Note, *MacEntee*, 1998, p. 2

88 Ibid.

89 Ibid

90 CAB 2/20, G.C.9/94, Cabinet Minutes, 13 September 1960, pp. 3–4

91 Private Papers, Hillery Note, *Commission*, p. 1

92 *Clare Champion*, 'Three Outgoing Deputies Retain Clare Seats', 7 October 1961

93 Private Papers, Hillery Note, *Education*, p. 2

Chapter 7

1 *Dáil Debates*, vol. 203, col. 684, 11 June 1963

2 NAI D/FIN 2001/3/546, D500/2/62, OECD *Press Statement*, 5 October 1961

3 Governing Committee for Scientific and Technical Personnel, *STP/GC (61) 13, Policy Conference on Economic Growth and the Role of Investment in Education and Science: Project STP-24*, 22 February 1961, pp. 1–3

4 Private Papers, Hillery Note, *Investment*, 1999, p. 1

5 Interview with Paddy Hillery, 17 May 2006

6 Interview with Paddy Hillery, 17 May 2006

7 S. MacGearailt to M. Breathnach, 15 August 1961

8   NAI D/T S.12891D/1/62, OECD, *STP 62 (1), Pilot Studies on Long-Term Needs for Educational Resources in Economically Developed Countries*, 12 October 1961, p. 1

9   Ibid.

10   O'Connor, *A Troubled Sky*, p. 63

11   S. Ó Buachalla, 'Investment in Education: Context, Content and Impact', *Administration*, vol. 44, no.3 (Autumn 1996), pp. 10–20

12   NAI D/Finance 2001/3/546, D500/2/62, John F. McInerney, Note of meeting, 31 October 1961, p. 1

13   Ibid., O'Connor, *A Troubled Sky*, p. 63

14   O'Connor, *A Troubled Sky*, p. 63

15   Ibid.

16   UCDA, P205, *Hillery Papers*, Folder 4, Hillery Note, undated (1960s)

17   Private Papers, Hillery Note, *Investment,* p. 1; *Dáil Debates*, vol. 210, col. 287, 27 May 1964

18   NAI D/T 97/6/437, S.17913, *Address by Dr P.J. Hillery TD, Minister for Education, on the occasion of his opening the Labour/Management Conference at Shannon Airport*, 22 June 1962, pp. 1–6

19   O'Connor, *A Troubled Sky*, p. 63

20   NAI D/T 97/6/437, S.17913, N.S. Ó Nualláin to C. Ó Dálaigh, Chief Justice, 21 June 1962

21   NAI D/FIN 2001/3/775, D500/8/63, Whitaker to N. S. Ó Nualláin, 20 November 1961, Whitaker to Ó Raifeartaigh, 15 December 1961

22   NAI D/T S.12891D/1/62, *Irish Press,* 'Long-Term Educational Needs will be investigated', 30 July 1962

23   Ibid.

24   NAI D/T 97/6/437, S.17913, *Note of Government meeting,* 26 June 1962

25   Ó Buachalla, 'Investment in Education', *Administration*, vol. 44, no.3 (Autumn 1996), pp. 10–20

26   NAI D/FIN 2001/3/775, Ó Raifeartaigh to Whitaker, 30 April 1962

27   Ó Buachalla, 'Investment in Education', *Administration*, vol. 44, no.3 (Autumn 1996), pp. 10–20

28   *Dáil Debates,* vol. 196, col. 1303–4, 3 July 1962

29   NAI D/T S.12891D/1/62, OECD, *STP 62 (1), Terms of Reference, Pilot Studies on Long-term Needs for Educational Resources in Developed Country*, 12 October 1961, pp. 4–5

30   *Dáil Debates,* vol. 196, col. 1303–04, 3 July 1962

31   *Speech by Dr Hillery to the inaugural meeting of the Steering Committee, October 1962,* Hyland and Milne, *Irish Educational Documents* 2, pp. 30–1

32   Ibid.

33   *Dáil Debates,* vol. 210, col. 287, 27 May 1964

34   *Investment in Education Part 2: Annexes and Appendices to the Report of the Survey Team appointed by the Minister for Education in October, 1962* (Dublin, 1965), pp. 35–6

35   T. A. Ó Cuilleanáin, 'Special Education In Ireland', *Oideas*, no.1 (Autumn 1968), pp. 5–17

36   Ibid.; J. Coolahan, 'Dr P.J. Hillery – Minister for Education: 1959–1965', *Journal of the ASTI Convention*, Easter 1990, pp. 15–19

37   J. Coolahan, 'Dr P.J. Hillery – Minister for Education: 1959–1965', *Journal of the ASTI Convention*, Easter 1990, pp. 15–19

38   Private Papers, Hillery Note, *Education*, p. 1

39   *Investment in Education Part 1*, pp. 228–29 (Dublin, 1965)

40   Ibid., pp. 262–3

41   Ibid., p. 233

42   *Dáil Debates*, vol. 210, col. 333, 14 May 1964

43   W26/30, M80/1, C.O. 704 (3), *Progress Report for Quarter ended 30 September 1964*, Department of Education, 30 October 1964, p. 1

44   Circular 16/64, Department of Education, May 1964

45   Circular 21/63, Department of Education, November 1963

46   W26/30, M80/1, C.O. 704 (3), *Progress Report for Quarter ended 31st March 1964*, Department of Education, 14 April 1964, p. 1

47   *Committee of Public Accounts, Appropriation Accounts 1965–66* (Dublin, 1967), p. 118

48   *Dáil Debates*, vol. 195, col. 1471–93, 23 May 1962

49   Ibid., col. 1493–1514

50   *Dáil Debates*, vol. 195, col. 2185, 6 June 1962

51   Ibid., col. 2185

52   Tuairim, *Irish Education* (Tuairim, London, 1962); Tuairim, *Educating Towards a United Europe* (Tuairim and the European Teachers' Association, Dublin, 1961)

53   The Labour Party, *Challenge and Change in Education*, (The Labour Party, Dublin, 1963), pp. 2–3

54   Ibid., p. 10

55   DDA, AB8/B/XV/b/05, *McQuaid Papers*, Minutes of the Irish Hierarchy, Fergus to McQuaid, 20 February 1963

56   NAI D/T S.12891D/2/62, *Memorandum from the Minister for Education concerning the Small Farms report, 'Post-Primary Education in the Areas Concerned'*, 7 July 1962, p. 1

57   Ibid.

58   Ibid., p. 2

59   Ibid., p. 3

60   T. Ó Cearbhaill to Ministers on the Inter-Departmental Committee on the Problems of Small Western Farms, 9 July 1962

61   E. Childers to Ó Cearbhaill, 11 July 1962, K. Boland to T. Ó Cearbhaill, 13 July 1962, Lynch to Ó Cearbhaill, 14 July 1962

62   Whitaker to Ó Nualláin, 18 July 1962

63   Ibid.

64   T. Leahy to Ó Cearbhaill, 26 July 1962, pp. 1–2

65   Ibid.

66   Ó Cearbhaill to Lemass, 26 July 1962, Randles, *Post-Primary Education*, p. 107

67   NAI D/T S.12891D/2/62, *Outline of Statement of Government Policy on Suggestions in Report of the Inter-Departmental Committee on the Problems of Small Western Farms*, 1 August 1962, p. 8

68   Ibid.

69   Private Papers, Hillery to Imelda Bonel-Elliott, 1995

70   I. Bonel-Elliott, 'The role of the Duggan report (1962) in the reform of the Irish education system', *Administration*, vol. 44, no.3 (Autumn 1996), pp. 42–60

71 Private Papers, Hillery to Imelda Bonel-Elliott, 1995
72 Interview with Paddy Hillery, 25 February 2002
73 Departmental Committee, *Tuarascáil Shealadach ón Choiste a Cuireadh I mbun Scrúdú a Dheánamh ar Oideachas Iarbhunscoile*, December 1962, pp. 5–6
74 Ibid., pp. 10–12
75 NA D/T17405 C/63, *Pilot Scheme related to Small Farm Areas, Proposal for Comprehensive Post-Primary Education*, Department of Education, 9 January 1963
76 Ibid.
77 Interview with Paddy Hillery, 25 February 2002
78 NA D/T 17405 C/63, *Proposal for Comprehensive Post-Primary Education*, 9 January 1963
79 Ibid.
80 Ibid.
81 Ibid.
82 Ibid.
83 Whitaker to Ó Nualláin, 18 July 1962, Interview with Dr Hillery, 25 February 2002
84 NA D/T 17405 C/63, Hillery to Lemass, 9 January 1963
85 Ibid.
86 NA D/T 17405 C/63, Lemass to Hillery, 11 January 1963
87 NA D/T17405 C/63, Lemass to Hillery, 14 January 1963
88 Ibid.
89 NA D/T17405 C/63, *Memorandum from the Department of Education, Proposals relating to comprehensive post-primary education*, January 1963
90 Ibid.
91 Ibid.
92 Interview with Paddy Hillery, 17 May 2006
93 NA D/T17405 C/63, *Statement by Dr P.J. Hillery T.D., Minister for Education, in relation to Post-Primary Education*, 20 May 1963, p. 6
94 Ibid., p. 5
95 Ibid., pp. 7–8
96 Ibid., pp. 8–10
97 Ibid., p. 7
98 Ibid., pp. 9–10
99 Ibid., pp. 8–9
100 Ibid., p. 11
101 Ibid., pp. 12–13
102 Ibid., p. 13
103 Ibid., p. 14
104 *Committee of Public Accounts, Appropriation Accounts 1965–66* (Dublin, 1967), pp. 117–18
105 NAI D/T17405 C/63, *Statement by Dr P.J. Hillery T.D., Minister for Education, in relation to Post-Primary Education*, 20 May 1963, p. 14
106 Coolahan, *Irish Education*, p. 139
107 W26/30, M80/1, *Draft Progress report on secondary education for Second Programme*, Department of Education, February 1965, p. 1
108 Private Papers, Hillery Note, *Education*, p. 1

109 *Irish Press*, 'Dr Hillery Plan is Hailed', 22 May 1963, *Irish Press*, 'New Deal in Education', 22 May 1963

110 *The Irish Times*, Editorial, 21 May 1963

111 *Irish Press*, 'Dr Hillery Plan is Hailed', 22 May 1963

112 Interview with Paddy Hillery, 17 May 2006

113 Interview with Paddy Hillery, 25 February 2002

114 DDA AB8/B/XV/b/05, *McQuaid Papers*, Minutes, General Meeting of the Hierarchy, 1 October 1962, p. 1

115 Fergus to McQuaid, 20 February 1963

116 DDA AB8/B/XV/b/05, *McQuaid Papers*, Hanly to Fergus, 18 February 1963

117 Interview with Paddy Hillery, 25 February 2002

118 DDA AB8/B/XV/b/05, *McQuaid Papers*, Minutes, General Meeting of the Hierarchy, 25 June 1963, p. 3

119 *First Memorandum by the bishops of Elphin and Achonry, The New Post-Primary Schools Scheme*, 28 June 1963

120 Ibid.

121 Interview with Paddy Hillery, 17 May 2006

122 DDA AB8/B/XV/b/05 Fergus to Hillery, 29 October 1963, p. 1

123 Ibid.

124 Ibid., p. 2

125 Hillery to Fergus, November 1963, p. 1

126 DDA AB8/B/XV/b/05, *Memorandum, The Hillery Scheme*, 5 December 1963

127 Ibid.

128 Minutes, Standing Committee of the Hierarchy, 7 January 1964, p. 1

129 NAI D/T S.17592/95, Hillery to Lemass, 4 February 1964, p. 1

130 NAI D/T S.12891E/95, *Speech by Seán Lemass TD, Taoiseach, following address by John Vaizey on 'The Economics of Education'*, St. Patrick's Training College, Drumcondra, 13 February 1964, p. 2

131 Circular M15/64, Department of Education, April 1964

132 NAI D/T S.17592/95, Conway to Lemass, 17 February 1964

133 UCDA, *Hillery Papers*, P205, Folder 3, Hillery Note, May 1964

134 Interview with Paddy Hillery, 17 May 2006

135 ASTI, Minutes, Central Executive Committee, 3 January 1964

136 ASTI, Minutes, Standing Committee, 21 March 1964

137 Private Papers, Hillery Note, *O'Raftery*, p. 1

138 O'Connor, *A Troubled Sky*, pp. 86–87

139 UCDA, *Hillery Papers*, P205, Folder 3, Hillery Note, May 1964

140 DDA, AB8/B/XVIII/18, *McQuaid Papers*, Note by McQuaid, *ASTI*, 28 May 1964

141 Private Papers, Hillery Note, *O'Raftery*, p. 1

142 Ibid.

143 UCDA, *Hillery Papers*, P205, Folder 3, Ó Raifeartaigh to Fr John Hughes, 4 May 1964, Hillery to Fr Tom Counihan, May 1964

144 ASTI, Minutes, Standing Committee, 12 May 1964

145 DDA, AB8/B/XVIII/18, *McQuaid Papers*, Note by McQuaid, *ASTI*, 28 May 1964, Hillery to McQuaid, 6 June 1964

146 CCSS, Minutes, Standing Committee, 3 October 1963

147 UCDA, *Hillery Papers*, P205, Folder 3, Hillery Note, May 1964

148 *Dáil Debates*, vol. 210, col. 336, 2 June 1964

149 UCDA, *Hillery Papers*, P205, Folder 3, Michael O'Connor to Hillery, 18 June 1964

150 ASTI, Minutes, Standing Committee, 12 May 1964

151 DDA, AB8/B/XVIII/18, *McQuaid Papers*, Hillery to McQuaid, 8 June 1964

152 Hillery to McQuaid, 10 June 1964

153 Ibid.

154 ASTI, Minutes, Standing Committee, 15 June 1964

155 UCDA, *Hillery Papers*, P205, Folder 3, Hillery to Conway (draft), May 1964

156 Ibid.

157 UCDA, *Hillery Papers*, P205, Folder 3, Hillery Note, 'attitude of the bishops', undated, 1964

158 D/Education, W26/13, M. 194/4, *Meeting of An Rúnaí with members of the Standing Committee of the Catholic Headmasters' Association in Marlborough Street on 28/1/65 at 2.30pm*, 28 January 1965

159 UCDA, *Hillery Papers*, P205, Folder 3, Draft letter by Hillery to the Catholic bishops, June 1964

160 Interview with Paddy Hillery, 17 May 2006

161 Interview with Paddy Hillery, 17 May 2006

162 Interview with Michael Hillery, 4 July 2008

163 Private Papers, *Fianna Fáil General Election Broadcast, Speaker: Dr Hillery*, 30 March 1965

164 Horgan, *Lemass*, p. 207

165 *Clare Champion*, 'No Change In Clare: Substantial Increase in Fianna Fáil Poll,' 10 April 1965

Chapter 8

1 Interview with Paddy Hillery, 24 May 2006

2 Horgan, *Lemass*, p. 194

3 Ibid., p. 209

4 Private Papers, Hillery Note, *Lemass*, 1996, p. 3

5 Private Papers, Hillery Note, *Transfer*, 1995, p. 1

6 Interview with Paddy Hillery, 24 May 2006

7 Ibid.

8 Hillery, *Transfer*, p. 1

9 *The Second Programme for Economic Expansion, Part I, laid by the government before each House of the Oireachtas, August 1963* (Dublin, 1963)

10 Horgan, *Lemass*, p. 205

11 Ibid., p. 246

12 *Dáil Debates*, vol. 217, col. 1080–3, 13 July 1965

13 Ibid., col. 1095; Horgan, *Lemass*, p. 249

14 *Dáil Debates*, vol. 217, col. 1094, 13 July 1965

15 Ibid., Horgan, *Lemass*, p. 249

16 *Dáil Debates*, vol. 217, col. 1207, 14 July 1965

17 Ibid., col. 1210

18 *Dáil Debates*, vol. 217, col. 1073, 13 July 1965

19 *Dáil Debates*, vol. 217, col. 1218, 14 July 1965

20   Ibid., col. 1207
21   Ibid., col. 1217–18
22   *Dáil Debates*, vol. 217, col. 1091, 13 July 1965
23   *Dáil Debates*, vol. 217, col. 1764–72, 21 July 1965
24   Horgan, *Lemass*, p. 250
25   C. McCarthy, *The Decade of Upheaval: Irish Trade Unions in the 1960s* (Dublin,1973), p. 96
26   Ibid., p. 21
27   *Irish Press*, '2,500 Out – New Strikes threaten', 15 March 1966
28   McCarthy, *Decade of Upheaval*, p. 99
29   NAI, D/T 97/6/216, S.17689A, Lemass to Hillery, 17 June 1965
30   Ibid.
31   NAI, D/T 97/6/216, S.17689A, Hillery to Lemass, 23 July 1965
32   NAI, D/T 97/6/217, S.17689B, *Industrial Relations Legislation, Draft Report of a meeting held in the Cabinet Room*, 5 November 1965
33   *Draft Heads of Bill to amend the Industrial Relations Acts and the Trade Union Acts*
34   N. S. Ó Nualláin to private secretary, Minister for Industry and Commerce, 22 March 1966
35   McCarthy, *Decade of Upheaval*, p. 90
36   *Dáil Debates*, vol. 238, col. 1319, 19 February 1969
37   Private Papers, Hillery Note, *Labour*, 1996, p. 1
38   Interview with Paddy Hillery, 24 May 2006
39   Hillery, *Labour*, p. 1
40   Ibid., Interview with Paddy Hillery
41   Hillery, *Labour*, p. 1
42   NAI D/T 97/6/198, S.17659, Ó Nualláin to all Private Secretaries, Attorney General and Parliamentary Secretary to the Taoiseach, 10 June 1966
43   *Memorandum for the government, Ministers and Secretaries (Amendment) Bill, Office of the Taoiseach*, 8 July 1966
44   *The Irish Times*, 'Cabinet to be Reshuffled? New Ministry for Labour', 8 June 1966

Chapter 9
1   NAI D/T 97/6/218, S.17689C, *Speech by Hillery, Inaugural Meeting of the Advertising-Press Club*, 20 September 1966
2   Interview with Paddy Hillery, 24 May 2006
3   NAI D/T 97/6/198, S.17659, Ó Nualláin to Whitaker, 28 June 1966
4   Interview with Paddy Hillery, 24 May 2006
5   *The Irish Times*, 'Appointed to Department of Labour', 13 July 1966
6   Ibid.
7   *The Irish Times*, 'Hillery Explains Redundancy Plan', 30 December 1967
8   *Dáil Debates,* vol. 230, col. 1937–93, 7 November 1967
9   *The Irish Times*, 'Hillery Explains Redundancy Plan', 30 December 1967
10   Hillery Note, *Labour*, p. 2
11   *The Irish Times*, 'Hillery Explains Redundancy Plan', 30 December 1967
12   NAI D/T 97/6/218, S.17689C, J. O'Brien to Lemass, *Telegram*, 2 June 1966
13   NAI D/T 97/6/218, S.17689C, Lemass to Hillery, 10 May 1996
14   Hillery to Lemass, 11 May 1966

15   Interview with Paddy Hillery, 24 May 2006
16   Horgan, *Lemass*, p. 248
17   Hillery Note, *Lemass*, p. 4
18   Interview with Paddy Hillery, 24 May 2006
19   Hillery, *Lemass*, p. 4
20   Interview with Paddy Hillery, 24 May 2006
21   Horgan, *Lemass*, p. 330
22   Ibid., p. 335
23   Interview with Paddy Hillery, 24 May 2006
24   Ibid.
25   Ibid.
26   Ibid.
27   T.J. Rigney, Interview with Paddy Hillery, 2000
28   *The Irish Times*, 'Government "Among Worst Wage Payers"', 23 November 1967
29   Ibid.
30   *The Irish Times*, 'Desmond Rejects Hillery Claims', 27 November 1967
31   *The Irish Times*, 'Reply to Attack on Unions', 27 November 1967
32   *The Irish Times*, 'Dervish Dance', 27 November 1967
33   *The Irish Times*, 'No Attempt by FF to Split the ITGWU', 28 November 1967
34   Hillery, *Labour*, p. 2
35   UCDA, *Hillery Papers*, P205, Folder 11, MacEntee to Hillery, 29 November 1967
36   *The Irish Times*, 'Dr Hillery: Social Republican', 8 July 1966
37   Interview with Paddy Hillery, 24 May 2006
38   *The Irish Times*, 'No Attempt by FF to Split the ITGWU', 28 November 1967
39   Interview with Paddy Hillery, 24 May 2006
40   *The Irish Times*, 'Conroy Replies to Hillery Speech', 15 December 1967
41   *The Irish Times*, 'Turf Men Go Back Tomorrow: Official Strike later?', 27 November 1967; McCarthy, *Decade of Upheaval*, pp. 138–45
42   Hillery, *Labour*, p. 3
43   McCarthy, *Decade of Upheaval*, pp. 156–7
44   Interview with Paddy Hillery, 24 May 2006
45   McCarthy, *Decade of Upheaval*, pp. 164–6
46   UCDA, *Hillery Papers*, P205, Folder 11, Hillery Note, Meeting with Arthur Rice, March 1969
47   Interview with Paddy Hillery, 24 May 2006
48   UCDA, *Hillery Papers*, P205, Folder 11, Hillery Note, Meeting with Arthur Rice, March 1969
49   Ibid.
50   Ibid., pp. 1–2
51   Horgan, *Lemass*, p. 249
52   *Irish Independent*, 'High Court's E.I. No-Picket Ruling To Be Appealed', 30 March 1969
53   *Irish Independent*, 'Bus Serving E.I. workers burned', 30 March 1968
54   Private Papers, Hillery Note, *General Electric*, 1994, p. 1
55   Ibid.
56   McCarthy, *Decade of Upheaval*, p. 99
57   *The Irish Times*, 'Neutral Committee for ESB Inquiry', 12 April 1968

58   McCarthy, *Decade of Upheaval*, p. 113
59   Ibid.
60   *Irish Independent*, 'Power Crisis Today: Government Acts Against Pickets', 27 March 1968
61   *Irish Independent*, 'ESB Men's Strike Plan Regrettable – ICTU', 26 March 1968; *Irish Independent*, 'Warning To "Pirates" In Power Crisis', 28 March 1968
62   *Irish Independent*, 'Power Crisis Today: Government Acts Against Pickets', 27 March 1968
63   Interview with Paddy Hillery, 24 May 2006
64   Hillery, *Labour*, p. 3
65   *Irish Independent*, 'Twenty-four Strikers Elect to Go to Prison', 29 March 1968
66   Interview with Paddy Hillery, 24 May 2006
67   *Irish Independent*, 'Strikers "Dig In" as Picketers Go to Jail', 29 March 1968
68   McCarthy, *Decade of Upheaval*, p. 115
69   *Irish Independent*, 'Faint Settlement Hopes: Guarded Optimism After Power Crisis Talks', 30 March 1968
70   Hillery, *Labour*, p. 3
71   *Irish Independent*, 'Power Grid Back in Full Operation', 1 April 1968
72   *The Irish Times*, 'Neutral Committee for ESB Inquiry', 12 April 1968
73   McCarthy, *Decade of Upheaval*, p. 125; *Final Report of the Committee on Industrial Relations in the Electricity Supply Board* (Dublin, 1969)
74   McCarthy, *Decade of Upheaval*, p. 119
75   *Dáil Debates*, vol. 240, col. 1126–7, 14 May 1969
76   *Dáil Debates*, vol. 238, col. 1322–5, 6 March 1969
77   Ibid., col. 2357–60
78   Ibid., col. 1328
79   Ibid., col. 1322–3
80   Ibid., col. 1328–30
81   *Dáil Debates*, vol. 239, col. 2274, 24 April 1969
82   McCarthy, *Decade of Upheaval*, p. 31
83   *Dáil Debates*, vol. 238, col. 2361–2, 6 March 1969
84   Ibid.
85   Ibid., col. 1338
86   *Clare Champion*, 'Dr Hillery Regrets Breaching of Clare – But Justifies Size of Breach', 7 December 1967
87   *The Irish Times*, 'Barrett Wins on First Count', 16 March 1968
88   Interview with Michael Hillery, 4 July 2008
89   UCDA, *Hillery Papers*, P205, Folder 11, *Specimen Ballot Paper*, June 1969
90   *Clare Champion*, 'Syl Barrett Tops the Polls for Fianna Fáil,' 21 June 1969
91   Ibid.

Chapter 10
1   Interview with Paddy Hillery, 8 June 2006
2   Interview with Paddy Hillery, 24 May 2006
3   Ibid.
4   Ibid.
5   Ibid., *Dáil Debates*, vol. 241, col. 23–24, 2 July 1969
6   Interview with John McColgan, 20 June 2008

7   Interview with John McColgan, 20 June 2008

8   *Dáil Debates*, vol.251, col.248–9, 28 January 1971

9   Ibid.; *The Irish Times*, 'External Affairs to be Foreign Affairs', 29 January 1971

10 Michael Kennedy, 'Northern Ireland and cross-border co-operation' in Brian Girvin and Gary Murphy, *The Lemass Era* (Dublin, 2005), pp.118–119

11 Lee, *Ireland 1912–1985*, pp. 416–19

12 Ibid., p. 420

13 Justin O'Brien, *The Arms Trial* (Dublin, 2000), p. 35

14 NAI, D/T 2000/6/657, *Note of discussion at the Foreign Office at 12.00pm on Friday 1st August 1969*, pp. 2–3

15 Ibid., p. 8

16 O'Brien, *The Arms Trial*, pp. 38–40

17 UCDA, *Hillery Papers*, P205, Folder 18, *Memorandum for the information of the government: Policy in relation to Northern Ireland*, 28 November 1969

18 NAI, D/T 2000/6/657, Note for Taoiseach, 13 August 1969

19 Nicholas Nolan, *Note of decisions of Government meeting*, 13 August 1969

20 NAI D/T 2000/6/657, *Statement by the Taoiseach, Mr J. Lynch*, 13 August 1969

21 Ibid.

22 Lee, *Ireland 1912–1985*, p. 429; O'Brien, *Arms Trial*, p. 48

23 Private Papers, Hillery, Transcript: Tape 5, *September 1969: N.I*, p. 3

24 Private Papers, Hillery Note, *Arms*, 1999, pp. 3–4,

25 Ibid., p. 3

26 Interview with Paddy Hillery, 24 May 2006; Interview with Paddy Hillery, 8 June 2006

27 Hillery, *Arms*, p. 4

28 NAI, D/T 2000/6/657, *Draft of G.C. 13/12, Cabinet Minutes, Situation in Six Counties*, 14 August 1969; Hugh McCann Note, 13 August 1969

29 NAI, D/T 2000/6/658, *Report of discussion at Foreign and Commonwealth Office, London, concerning Northern Ireland*, 15 August 1969, pp. 1–2

30 Ibid., pp. 2–3

31 Ibid., pp. 18–19

32 NAI D/T 2000/6/658, Draft G.C. 13/14, Cabinet Minutes, 16 August 1969

33 Public Accounts Committee, *Interim and Final Reports* (Dublin, 1972), p. 2

34 Interview with Paddy Hillery, 8 June 2006

35 Public Accounts Committee, *Interim and Final Reports*, p. 49

36 *The Irish Times*, 'Hillery says UN vote on North evaded in 1969', 6 August 1991

37 Ibid.

38 NAI DFA 2000/14/450, *Question of Raising Partition formally by Resolution in International Organisations*, 7 May 1969

39 Private Papers, Hillery Note, *United Nations*, 1999, p. 4

40 NAI D/T 2000/6/657, Memorandum For The Information of the government, *Bringing the Situation in the North of Ireland before the UN*, 16 August 1969, p. 8

41 NAI, DFA 2001/43/848, *Situation in Six Counties before Security Council (August 1969): Programme of Dr Hillery, Minister for External Affairs, in New York*, 16–21 August 1969

42 NAI, D/T 2000/6/659, C. Cremin, *Situation in the Six Counties: Attitude of Members of Security Council*, 25 August 1969, p. 1

43 NAI, D/T 2000/6/658, *Text of letter from the Permanent Representative of Ireland to the UN to the President of the Security Council,* 17 August 1969

44 Note for Taoiseach, *Phone call from Seán Ronan,* 18 August 1969

45 NAI, D/T 2000/6/659, Cremin, *Situation in the Six Counties Before Security Council: Talks with Secretary General,* 28 August 1969, pp. 1–2

46 H.J. O'Dowd, *Note for Taoiseach,* 18 August 1969

47 Private Papers, Hillery, *United Nations,* p. 1

48 UCDA, *Hillery Papers,* P205, Folder 8, *Northern Ireland; Text of a Communiqué and Declaration issued after a meeting at 10 Downing Street,* 19 August 1969, p.3

49 *Irish Press,* 'Sweeping RUC changes: B Specials will go,' 27 September 1969

50 *Northern Ireland: Text of a Communiqué and Declaration issued after a meeting at 10 Downing Street,* 19 August 1969, p.3

51 UCDA, *Hillery Papers,* P205, Folder 8, *Official Records, United Nations Security Council, Twenty-Fourth Year, 1503rd Meeting,* 20 August 1969, p.6

52 UCDA, *Hillery Papers,* P205, Folder 10, *Memorandum, Case for raising the North of Ireland situation in the UN,* p. 2

53 NAI, D/T 2000/6/659, Cremin, *Attitude of Members of Security Council,* 25 August 1969, p. 2

54 Ibid., pp. 6–7

55 NAI D/T 2000/6/658, Note for Taoiseach, 19 August 1969

56 Hillery, *United Nations,* p. 1

57 Ibid.

58 Interview with John McColgan, 20 June 2008

59 NAI DFA 2001/43/848, *Report of Meeting between the Minister for External Affairs, Dr Hillery and the French Foreign Minister, M. Schumann,* 20 September 1969, p. 2

60 NAI, D/T 2000/6/659, Cremin, *Attitude of Members of Security Council,* 25 August 1969, pp. 5–6

61 Ibid., p. 7

62 UCDA, *Hillery Papers,* P205, Folder 10, *Memorandum, North of Ireland situation in the UN,* p. 2

63 *The Irish Times,* 'Crisis of the '70s: UN intervention and the North', 6 August 1991

64 Interview with Paddy Hillery 8 June 2006

65 Philip Ziegler, *Harold Wilson* (London, 1993), p. 175

66 C. Cremin, 'Northern Ireland at the United Nations August/September 1969', 67–73 in *Irish Studies in International Relations,* vol. 1, no.2, 1980

67 NAI, D/T 2000/6/658, McCann, *Note of conversation with Cremin,* 21 August 1969; NAI, D/T 2000/6/659, Cremin, *Attitude of Members of Security Council,* 25 August 1969, p. 8

68 NAI, DFA 2001/43/848, *Situation in Six Counties before Security Council (August 1969): Programme of Dr Hillery, Minister for External Affairs, in New York,* 16–21 August 1969

69 Private Papers, Hillery, *United Nations,* p. 3

70 C. Cremin, 'Northern Ireland at the United Nations August/September 1969', 68 in *Irish Studies in International Relations,* vol. 1, no.2, 1980

71 Ibid.

72 UCDA, *Hillery Papers,* P205, Folder 8, *Official Records, United Nations Security Council, Twenty-Fourth Year, Fifteen Hundred and Third Meeting,* 20 August 1969, pp. 1–2

73 McCann, *Note of conversation with Cremin,* 21 August 1969

74 *Official Records, UN Security Council*, 20 August 1969, p. 2

75 Ibid., p. 3

76 Ibid., p. 5

77 Ibid., p. 5

78 Ibid., p. 5

79 Ibid., p. 5

80 Ibid., pp. 5–6

81 Ibid., pp. 5–6

82 Ibid., p. 7

83 NAI D/T 2000/6/658, McCann, *Note of conversation with Cremin*, 21 August 1969

84 C. Cremin, 'Northern Ireland at the United Nations August/September 1969', 69 in *Irish Studies in International Relations*, vol. 1, no.2, 1980

85 *Ibid.*; D/T 2000/6/659, Cremin, *Attitude of Members of Security Council*, 25 August 1969, p. 8,

86 *The Irish Times*, 'Propaganda Value of Raising North: How UN game was played', 27 August 1969

87 UCDA, *Hillery Papers*, P205, Folder 21, *Note of telephone call from Mr Ronan*, 20 August 1969

88 *The Irish Times*, 'Propaganda Drive Produced Little', 16 October 1969

89 Private Papers, Hillery Note, *New York – Media*, p. 1

90 NAI, D/T 2000/6/660, Eoin Neeson, *Memorandum to An Taoiseach following discussions in New York with Dr Hillery, Ambassador Cremin and Press Attachés*, p. 1, 10 October 1969

91 *The Irish Times*, 'Propaganda Value of Raising North: How UN game was played', 27 August 1969; Interview with Dennis Kennedy, 22 May 2008

92 Hillery to Lynch, 26 August 1969

93 Ibid.

94 Private Papers, Hillery, Transcript 5, *September 1969: N.I.*, p. 3; Kevin Boland, *Up Dev* (Dublin, 1977), p. 12

95 B. Arnold, *Jack Lynch: Hero in Crisis* (Dublin, 2001), pp. 102–3

96 Private Papers, Hillery, *September 1969: N.I.*, p. 1

97 Ibid., p. 4

98 NAI, DFA 2001/43/848, Nolan to John McColgan, 9 September 1969

99 S.417/153/4/III, McCann to all Missions, 5 September 1969

100 NAI, D/T 2000/6/660, Cremin to McCann, *G.A. Note no.1*, 10 September 1969, p. 1

101 Private Papers, Hillery, Transcript 3, *UN: September 1969*, p. 2

102 Ibid., pp. 2–3

103 Ibid., p. 3

104 Ibid., p. 3

105 Ibid., p. 5

106 NAI, D/T 2000/6/661, Cremin, *General Committee: Probable Outcome of Vote on Inscription of Item 102 (Situation in the North)*, 7 October 1969, pp. 6–7

107 Private Papers, Hillery, Transcript 3, *UN: September 1969*, p. 5

108 NAI, D/T 2000/6/661, Cremin, *General Committee: Probable Outcome of Vote*, 7 October 1969, pp. 7–8

109 UCDA, *Hillery Papers*, P205, Folder 8, A/BUR/SR 180, *Transcript of Debate in General Committee*, 17 September 1969, p. 1

110 NAI, DFA 2001/43/848, A/BUR/SR 180, *Meeting of General Committee*, 17 September
     1969, p. 14

111 UCDA, *Hillery Papers*, P205, Folder 8, *Question of inclusion of the item "The Situation in the
     North of Ireland" in the Agenda of the General Assembly of the UN*, 1 October 1969, p. 2

112 Ibid., p. 3

113 Ibid., p. 5

114 Ibid., p. 1

115 *The Irish Times*, 'Hillery's UN Move on North Fails', 19 September 1969; *The Irish Times*,
     'UN protest on North blocked', 19 September 1969

116 NAI, DFA 2001/43/848, Note, *Extracts dealing with Northern Ireland Situation from
     members at 24ᵗʰ Session of UNGA*; Private Papers, Hillery, Transcript 4, *September 1969:
     UN*, pp. 1–7

117 Hillery, Transcript 4, *September 1969: UN*, p. 6

118 NAI D/T 2000/6/660, Hillery to Lynch, 23 September 1969

119 NAI, D/T 2000/6/660, *Speech by the Taoiseach, Mr J. Lynch, at Tralee at a dinner in honour
     of Thomas McEllistrim, former TD*, 20 September 1969, p. 3

120 Ibid., p. 4

121 Ibid., pp. 5–6

122 NAI, D/T 2000/6/659, Cremin, *Situation in the Six Counties Before Security Council: Talks
     with Secretary General*, 28 August 1969, pp. 1–2

123 Cremin, 'Northern Ireland at the United Nations August/September 1969', 68 in *Irish
     Studies in International Relations*, vol. 1, no.2, 1980

124 Private Papers, Hillery, Transcript 3, *September 1969: UN*, p. 3

125 Private Papers, Hillery, Transcript 1, *Attendance at UN as Minister for External Affairs*, p. 1

126 Ibid.

127 Ibid., p. 2

128 NAI, D/T 2000/6/660, A./PV. 1768, *Twenty-fourth Session, General Assembly, Provisional
     Verbatim Record*, 26 September 1969, pp. 22–36

129 Ibid., p. 36

Chapter 11

1   *Dáil Debates*, vol. 246, col. 1628, 14 May 1970

2   UCDA, *Hillery Papers*, P205, Folder 8, *Bulletin of the Department of External Affairs*, no.816,
     p. 5, 30 October 1969

3   *The Irish Times*, 'Blaney Reject, Rift Over Policy: Conflict of views with Lynch over NI
     denied', 12 December 1969

4   *The Irish Times*, 'Force again rejected by Lynch', 10 December 1969

5   UCDA, *Hillery Papers*, P205, Folder 8, Leaflet, *Back Blaney*, January 1970

6   Justin O'Brien, *The Arms Trial* (Dublin, 2000), p. 97

7   Boland, *Up Dev*, p. 21

8   UCDA, *Hillery Papers*, P205, Folder 8, *Presidential Address by the Taoiseach to Fianna Fáil
     Ard Fheis on 17ᵗʰ January 1970*, p. 1

9   Ibid., p. 3

10   Ibid., p. 3

11   305/14/192E, *Memorandum for the Information of the government, Policy in relation to
     Northern Ireland*, 28 November 1969, pp. 1–2

12   Ibid., p. 5

13   Ibid., p. 5

14   Ibid., p. 7

15   Interview with Paddy Hillery, 8 June 2006

16   Correspondence with Seán Donlon, 2008

17   Interview with Paddy Hillery, 8 June 2006

18   UCDA, *Hillery Papers*, P205, Folder 16, Gallagher Note, 12 May 1970,

19   UCDA, *Hillery Papers*, P205, Folder 8, Gallagher Note, 18 May 1970,

20   Correspondence with Seán Donlon, 2008

21   Ibid.

22   Gallagher Note, 8 September 1970

23   Private Papers, Hillery, Transcript 7, *Meeting with Former Ambassador Wright on the night of 12th November, 1969*, November 1969, p. 3

24   Ibid., pp. 1–3

25   UCDA, *Hillery Papers*, P205, Folder 8, *Confidential Report of Discussion about the North of Ireland at the Foreign and Commonwealth Office, London*, 27 April 1970

26   Private Papers, Hillery Note, *Arms*, p. 1

27   UCDA, *Hillery Papers*, P205, Folder 16, Hugh McCann to Hillery, 12 May 1970

28   UCDA, *Hillery Papers*, P205, Folder 11, Hillery Note after Cabinet meeting, *Autumn 1969*

29   Ibid.

30   Interview with Paddy Hillery, 24 May 2006

31   UCDA, *Hillery Papers*, P205, Folder 8, Gallagher Note, 18 May 1970, p. 2

32   Private Papers, Hillery, Transcript 8, *Northern Ireland*, p. 7, May 1970

33   Hillery, Transcript 8, *Northern Ireland*, p. 8, May 1970

34   Ibid., p. 9

35   Private Papers, Hillery Note, *Arms*, p. 3

36   Ibid.

37   Private Papers, Hillery Note, *Arms*, p. 3

38   O'Brien, *The Arms Trial*, pp. 106–7

39   Public Accounts Committee, *Final Report* (Dublin, 1972), pp.61–2

40   O'Brien, *The Arms Trial*, p.118

41   Public Accounts Committee, *Final Report* (Dublin, 1972), p.45

42   Ibid., p.49

43   UCDA, *Hillery Papers*, P205, Folder 8, *Conversation with Mr Gerry Fitt MP*, 13 December 1970

44   Private Papers, Hillery Note, *Arms*, p. 2,

45   O'Brien, *The Arms Trial*, p. 63

46   Interview with Paddy Hillery, 24 May 2006

47   Interview with Paddy Hillery, 24 May 2006

48   O'Brien, *The Arms Trial*, p. 113

49   Ibid., p. 117

50   Ibid., pp. 120–1

51   Stephen Collins, *The Power Game: Fianna Fáil since Lemass* (Dublin, 2001), p. 73

52   Private Papers, Hillery Note, *Arms*, p. 4

53   Interview with Dennis Kennedy, 22 May 2008

54   Hillery, Transcript 8, *Northern Ireland*, May 1970, p. 2

55   Ibid., May 1970, pp. 2–3

56   Ibid., pp. 2–3

57   Hillery, *Arms*, p. 2

58   Michael Mills, *Hurler on the Ditch* (Dublin, 2005), pp. 82–3

59   O'Brien, *The Arms Trial*, p. 124

60   Interview with Paddy Hillery, 24 May 2006

61   *Dáil Debates*, vol. 246, col. 518–19, 5 May 1970

62   *Dáil Debates*, vol. 246, col. 1338, 9 May 1970

63   Private Papers, Hillery, *Arms*, p. 1

64   *The Irish Times*, 6 May 1970

65   Private Papers, Hillery, *Arms*, p. 2

66   Interview with John McColgan, 20 June 2008

67   Ibid.

68   UCDA, *Hillery Papers*, P205, Folder 8, McCann to Hillery, 6 May 1970

69   Ibid.

70   Ibid.

71   Ibid.

72   Private Papers, Hillery, *Arms*, p. 2

73   Ibid.

74   Interview with Paddy Hillery, 24 May 2006

75   UCDA, Fianna Fáil Papers, Minutes of the Parliamentary Party, 6 May 1970

76   Private Papers, Hillery, *Arms*, p.2

77   Ibid.

78   Interview with Paddy Hillery, 24 May 2006

79   Hillery, Transcript 8, *Northern Ireland*, May 1970, p. 5

80   *Dáil Debates,* vol. 246, col. 1624–30, 14 May 1970

81   Ibid., col. 1580–4

82   Ibid., col. 1625

83   Ibid., col. 1625–6

84   Ibid., col. 1626

85   Ibid., col. 1627

86   Ibid., col. 1627

87   Ibid., col. 1628

88   Ibid., col. 1631

89   Ibid., col. 1631

90   Ibid., col. 1763–5

91   UCDA, *Hillery Papers*, P205, Folder 16, Hillery Note, 8 June 1970

92   O'Brien, *The Arms Trial*, p. 147

93   Mills, *Hurler on the* Ditch, pp.82–3; Collins, *Power Game*, pp. 81–3

94   O'Brien, *The Arms Trial*, pp. 187–213

95   Ibid., p. 208, Collins, *Power Game*, p. 84

96   B. Arnold, *Jack Lynch: Hero In Crisis* (Dublin, 2001), p. 152

97   Interview with Paddy Hillery, 24 May 2006

98   Ibid.

99   Collins, *Power Game*, p. 85

100 Interview with Paddy Hillery, 24 May 2006

101 Boland, *Up Dev*, p. 46

102 Hillery, *Arms*, p. 2

103 *The Irish Times*, 'Uproar At Opening of Fianna Fáil Ard Fheis', 22 February 1971

104 UCDA, *Hillery Papers*, P205, Folder 9, Memorandum by Eamonn Gallagher, 20 April 1970

105 Ibid.

106 Ibid.

107 Ibid.

108 UCDA, *Hillery Papers*, P205, Folder 6, *All Irish Traditions: Address by the Taoiseach, Mr John Lynch TD, on Radio Telefís Éireann*, 11 July 1970

109 Ibid.

Chapter 12

1   Collins, *Power Game*, p. 83; T. Ryle Dwyer, *Nice Fellow: A Biography of Jack Lynch* (Dublin, 2001), p. 228

2   Dwyer, *Nice Fellow*, p. 228

3   UCDA, *Hillery Papers*, P205, Folder 16, Hillery Note, 10 June 1970

4   Ibid.

5   UCDA, *Hillery Papers*, P205, Folder 16, Jack Daly to Hillery, 2 June 1970

6   Ibid.

7   UCDA, *Hillery Papers*, P205, Folder 10, *Letter to supporters, Comhairle Dáil Ceanntair an Chláir*, July 1970

8   Ibid.

9   Ibid.

10 Ibid.

11 *The Irish Times*, 'Uproar At Opening of Fianna Fáil Ard Fheis: Blaney Denial on violence', 22 February 1971

12 *The Irish Times*, 'Uproar At Opening of Fianna Fáil Ard Fheis', 22 February 1971

13 Private Papers, Hillery Note, *The Great Ard Fheis*, 1988

14 *Irish Independent*, 'Jack's Their Boy: Bid to disrupt Ard Fheis fails', 22 February 1971

15 Ibid.

16 *The Irish Times*, 'Uproar At Opening of Fianna Fáil Ard Fheis: Scuffles between Lynch and Boland supporters', 22 February 1971

17 Ibid.

18 *Irish Independent*, 'No danger to the leadership of Lynch', 22 February 1971

19 Ibid.

20 Ibid.

21 Interview with Paddy Hillery, 24 May 2006

22 Private Papers, Hillery Note, *The Great Ard Fheis*, 1988

23 *Irish Independent*, 'No danger to the leadership of Lynch', 22 February 1971

24 Ibid.

25 *The Irish Times*, 'Uproar At Opening of Fianna Fáil Ard Fheis', 22 February 1971

26 *Irish Independent*, 'No danger to the leadership of Lynch', 22 February 1971

27 Private Papers, Hillery Note, *The Great Ard Fheis*, 1988

28 *The Irish Times*, 'Uproar At Opening of Fianna Fáil Ard Fheis', 22 February 1971

29 Private Papers, Hillery Note, *The Great Ard Fheis*, 1988
30 RTÉ, *Reeling in the Years* (RTÉ, 1999); *The Irish Times*, 'Uproar At Opening of Fianna Fáil Ard Fheis', 22 February 1971
31 Interview with Paddy Hillery, 24 May 2006
32 *Irish Independent*, 'No danger to the leadership of Lynch', 22 February 1971
33 Ibid.
34 Ibid., Arnold, *Jack Lynch*, p. 162
35 Interview with Paddy Hillery, 24 May 2006
36 *Irish Independent*, 'No danger to the leadership of Lynch', 22 February 1971
37 *Irish Independent*, 'Ard Fheis was rigged, charge by Boland', 22 February 1971
38 Interview with John McColgan, 20 June 2008
39 Interview with Paddy Hillery, 24 May 2006
40 Collins, *Power Game*, p. 90
41 *Irish Independent*, 'No danger to the leadership of Lynch', 22 February 1971; *The Irish Times*, 'Uproar at Opening of Fianna Fáil Ard Fheis', 22 February 1971
42 Interview with Paddy Hillery, 24 May 2006
43 Boland, *Up Dev*, pp. 107–13
44 *The Irish Times*, 'Political Knives May Gleam in Donegal Fight,' 28 June 1972
45 Dick Walsh, *The Party* (Dublin, 1986), p. 129
46 Private Papers, Hillery Note, *The Great Ard Fheis*, 1988
47 UCDA, *Hillery Papers*, P205, Folder 11, Hillery Note, 1969; Private Papers, Hillery Note, *Arms*, p. 2
48 Collins, *Power Game*, p. 98

Chapter 13

1   UCDA, *Hillery Papers*, P205, Folder 16, Gallagher Note, p. 1, 24 June 1970
2   Lee, *Ireland: 1912–85,* p. 434
3   Thomas Hennessey, *The Evolution of the Troubles 1970–72* (Dublin, 2007), pp. 6–7
4   Lee, *Ireland: 1912–85,* p. 433
5   Hennessey, *Evolution of the Troubles*, pp. 9–12
6   Ibid., p. 32
7   Ibid., p. 33
8   UCDA, *Hillery Papers*, P205, Folder 16, Hillery Note, p. 3, June 1970
9   Ibid., p. 4
10 Ibid., pp. 4–5; O'Brien, *Arms Trial*, pp. 154–5
11 Hennessey, *Evolution of the Troubles*, pp. 34–5
12 Ibid., pp. 40–3
13 Hennessey, *Evolution of the Troubles*, pp. 43–5, O'Brien, *Arms Trial*, pp. 158–9
14 UCDA, *Hillery Papers*, P205, Folder 16, Note of activity by Minister and officials of the Department of External Affairs, June–July 1970; *Hansard*, series 5, vol. 803, col. 494, 7 July 1970
15 Private Papers, Hillery Note, *Falls Road*, p. 1
16 UCDA, *Hillery Papers*, P205, Folder 16, Hillery Note, July 1970
17 Hillery, *Falls Road*, p. 1
18 UCDA, *Hillery Papers*, P205, Folder 16, Hillery Note, July 1970
19 Hillery Note, *Falls Road*, p. 1

20 UCDA, *Hillery Papers*, P205, Folder 16, Hillery Note, July 1970

21 Hillery, *Falls Road*, p. 1; Interview with Paddy Hillery, 24 May 2006

22 Hillery, *Falls Road*, p. 1

23 Hennessey, *Evolution of the Troubles*, p. 45

24 UCDA, *Hillery Papers*, P205, Folder 16, Hillery Note, July 1970

25 *The Irish Times*, 'Hillery In Secret Visit to Falls: Diplomatic moves open to prevent holding of Orange parades', 7 July 1970

26 *The Irish Times*, Editorial, 7 July 1970

27 Hennessey, *Evolution of the Troubles*, p. 45

28 *The Irish Times*. 'Hillery In Secret Visit to Falls', 7 July 1970

29 *Hansard*, Series 5, vol. 803, col. 494–6, 7 July 1970

30 UCDA, *Hillery Papers*, P205, Folder 16, McCann Note, 7 July 1970; *The Irish Times*, 'Hillery To Call On Douglas-Home', 8 July 1970

31 UCDA, *Hillery Papers*, P205, Folder 8, *Meeting between Dr P.J. Hillery, Minister for External Affairs and Sir Alec Douglas-Home in London, on Wednesday, 8ᵗʰ July 1970*, p. 3

32 UCDA, *Hillery Papers*, P205, Folder 16, Hillery Note of meeting with Sir Alec Douglas-Home, 8 July 1970, p. 1

33 UCDA, *Hillery Papers*, P205, Folder 8, *Meeting between Dr P. J. Hillery, Minister for External Affairs and Sir Alec Douglas-Home in London, on Wednesday, 8ᵗʰ July 1970*, p. 3

34 Ibid.

35 Ibid., p. 2

36 Ibid., p. 4

37 Ibid., p. 4

38 Ibid., p. 5

39 UCDA, *Hillery Papers*, P205, Folder 16, Hillery Note of meeting with Douglas-Home, 8 July 1970, p. 2

40 Hillery, *Falls Road*, p. 1

41 Ibid., p. 2

42 UCDA, *Hillery Papers*, P205, Folder 8, *Conversation between Dr P.J. Hillery, Minister for External Affairs and Mr Anthony Barber MP, Foreign and Commonwealth Office*, 8 July 1970

43 Ibid.

44 UCDA, *Hillery Papers*, P205, Folder 16, Hillery Note of meeting with Douglas-Home, 8 July 1970, p. 1

45 UCDA, *Hillery Papers*, P205, Folder 18, Gallagher, *Northern Ireland – the present situation*, 17 January 1972, p. 1

46 UCDA, *Hillery Papers*, P205, Folder 11, *Report on Discussion between the Minister and Sir Alec Douglas-Home*, 6 July 1971, p. 3

47 Ibid.

48 UCDA, *Hillery Papers*, P205, Folder 11, *Report on Discussion between the Minister and Sir Alec Douglas-Home*, 6 July 1971, p. 3

49 UCDA, *Hillery Papers*, P205, Folder 8, *Report of Discussion about the North of Ireland at the Foreign and Commonwealth Office*, 27 April 1970

50 Hennessey, *Evolution of the Troubles*, p. 45

51 Ibid.

52 Lee, *Ireland 1912–85*, p. 435

53   UCDA, *Hillery Papers*, P205, Folder 18, McCann Note of meeting with Peck, 22 March 1971

54   Ibid.

55   UCDA, *Hillery Papers*, P205, Folder 21, Gallagher Note, p.1

56   UCDA, *Hillery Papers*, P205, Folder 8, Gallagher Note, *The present political situation in the North*, 19 July 1971, p. 1

57   UCDA, *Hillery Papers*, P205, Folder 19, *Text of a Message from Mr Heath to Mr Lynch*, 8 August 1971

58   Hennessey, *Evolution of the Troubles*, pp. 127–9

59   Ibid.

60   Lee, *Ireland 1912–85*, pp. 437–8

61   Hennessey, *Evolution of the Troubles*, pp. 132–43

62   UCDA, *Hillery Papers*, P205, Folder 19, Statement by Jack Lynch, 9 August 1971

63   UCDA, *Hillery Papers*, P205, Folder 19, Hillery Note, 10–11 August 1971

64   UCDA, *Hillery Papers*, P205, Folder 18, *Report of Meeting at Home Office between the Minister for Foreign Affairs and Mr Maudling, Acting Prime Minister*, 11 August 1971

65   Ibid., p. 2

66   Ibid., p. 7

67   Ibid., p. 3

68   Ibid., p.6

69   Ibid., pp. 5–6

70   Ibid., p. 7

71   Ibid., p. 9

72   Hennessey, *Evolution of the Troubles*, p. 139

73   UCDA, *Hillery Papers,* P205, Folder 18, Note, *Minister's meeting with British Foreign Secretary*, 25 February 1971; Hennessey, *Evolution of the Troubles*, p. 139

74   UCDA, *Hillery Papers*, P205, Folder 19, McCann Note, 23 August 1971, p. 2

75   Ibid.

76   Hennessey, *Evolution of the Troubles*, pp. 178–9

77   *The Irish Times*, 'Lynch-Heath Talks Open Next Monday', 2 September 1971

78   UCDA, *Hillery Papers*, P205, Folder 18, Press Statement, *Text of an Announcement to be made at 16.00 hrs on 1 September*

79   Note for Hillery from DFA, 1 September 1971

80   Hennessey, *Evolution of the Troubles*, pp. 192–7

81   UCDA, *Hillery Papers*, P205, Folder 18, Hillery Note, 1 October 1971

82   TNA, PRO, FCO 33/1596, Activities of Fianna Fáil in the Republic of Ireland, Telegram, Peck to FCO, 15 September 1971, p. 1

83   Ibid.

84   Interview with Paddy Hillery, 25 October 2007

85   Interview with John McColgan, 20 June 2008

86   TNA, PRO, FCO 33/1596, Activities of Fianna Fáil in the Republic of Ireland, Telegram 437, Peck to FCO, 23 September 1971

87   Interview with Paddy Hillery, 8 June 2006

88   Lee, *Ireland 1912–1985*, p. 440, Hennessey, *Evolution of the Troubles*, p. 348

89   Hennessey, *Evolution of the Troubles*, pp. 307–8

90   Ibid., p. 313

91 NA D/T 2003/16/461, Statement issued by the Government Information Bureau on behalf of the Taoiseach, 30 January 1972

92 NA D/T 2003/16/461, Statement issued by the Government Information Bureau, 31 January 1972

93 *The Irish Times*, 'Lynch To Help NI Political Parties: Tour by Hillery to include UN', 1 February 1972

94 Private Papers, Hillery Note, *Murders*, p. 1

95 *The Irish Times*, 'State To Pay For Embassy Burning', 3 February 1972

96 *The Irish Times*, 'Ireland seeking any available help may turn to East – Hillery', 2 February 1972

97 Ibid.

98 *The Irish Times*, 'Lynch To Help NI Political Parties: Tour by Hillery to include UN', 1 February 1972

99 *The Irish Times*, 'Ireland seeking any available help may turn to East – Hillery', 2 February 1972

100 UCDA, *Hillery Papers*, P205, Folder 12, *Hillery Statement at UN press conference*, 2 February 1972, p. 1

101 Ibid.

102 Ibid., p. 2

103 UCDA, *Hillery Papers*, P205, Folder 12, *Summary of Discussion of Dr Patrick Hillery, Minister for Foreign Affairs, with Mr Rogers, Secretary of State*, 3 February 1972, p. 1

104 *Draft Notes On Call of Dr Patrick J. Hillery, Minister for Foreign Affairs on Secretary Rogers*, 3 February 1972, pp. 1–2

105 Ibid., p. 3

106 Ibid., p. 3

107 Ibid., p. 4

108 Interview with Paddy Hillery, 25 October 2007

109 *The Irish Times*, 'US staying neutral on question of North', 4 February 1972

110 Interview with Paddy Hillery, 15 October 2007

111 *The Irish Times*, 'Hillery Did Not Ask For Nothing', 6 March 1972

112 *The Irish Times*, 'Hillery denies that he was rebuffed', 10 February 1972

113 UCDA, *Hillery Papers*, P205, Folder 12, SG/SM/1632, *Extracts from press conference*, 7 February 1972

114 UCDA, *Hillery Papers*, P205, Folder 12, Cremin to McCann, *Secretary-General and good offices on North*, 11 February 1972, p.3

115 *The Irish Times*, 'Hillery sees Rogers on question of North', 4 February 1972

116 Adam Clymer, *Edward M. Kennedy: A biography* (New York, 1999), pp.182–3

117 *The Irish Times*, 'Hillery sees Belgian Minister', 17 February 1972

118 UCDA, *Hillery Papers*, P205, Folder 12, PR(10) 72, Eamonn Kennedy to McCann, 10 February 1972, p. 1

119 Ibid., p. 3

120 Ibid., p. 3

121 *The Irish Times*, 'Government view put to French Ministers', 10 February 1972

122 *The Irish Times*, 'Hillery denies that he was rebuffed', 10 February 1972

123 UCDA, *Hillery Papers*, P205, Folder 12, *Draft Notes on the visit of Dr P.J. Hillery to Rome*, 10/11 February 1972, p. 3

124 PR 3/72, Eoin MacWhite to McCann, *Discussions between the Irish and Dutch Ministers of Foreign Affairs*, 10 February 1972, pp. 1–6

125 PR 3/72, Paul Keating to McCann, *Meeting of Minister with Mr Scheel and Dr Frank at the German Foreign Office*, 18 February 1972, p. 2

126 Ibid., pp. 2–3

127 Ibid., p. 3

128 *The Irish Times*, 'Hillery sees Belgian Minister', 17 February 1972

129 Hennessey, *Evolution of the Troubles*, p. 315

130 Ibid., p. 316

131 Ibid., pp. 333–4

132 Lee, *Ireland 1912–1985*, p. 441

133 *The Irish Times*, 'Whitelaw Tells MPs About Start Of Consultations', 21 July 1972

134 *The Irish Times*, 'Hillery reports on London talks today', 28 April 1972

135 Lee, *Ireland 1912–1985*, p. 442

136 Interview with Paddy Hillery, 24 May 2006

137 UCDA, *Hillery Papers*, P205, Folder 10, *Report of Meeting between the Minister for Foreign Affairs and the Secretary of State for Northern Ireland*, 21 June 1972, p. 1

138 Ibid., pp. 3–4

139 *Notes for meeting with British Minister*, July 1972, p. 2

140 Ibid., p. 3

141 Hennessey, *Evolution of the Troubles*, p. 349

142 Interview with John McColgan, 20 June 2008

143 Interview with John Hillery, 15 May 2008

Chapter 14

1   Private Papers, Hillery Note, *Draft One*, 1997, p. 1, Private Papers

2   Interview with Paddy Hillery, 19 October 2007

3   D. J. Maher, *The Tortuous Path: The Course of Ireland's Entry Into The EEC 1948–73* (Dublin, 1986), p. 229

4   G. Murphy, 'From economic nationalism to European Union', pp. 44–5 in B. Girvin and G. Murphy, *The Lemass Era: Politics and Society in Ireland of Seán Lemass* (Dublin, 2005)

5   *Irish Press*, 'No EEC pact without Ireland', 15 July 1969; Maher, *Tortuous Path*, p. 246

6   Murphy, 'From economic nationalism to European Union', p. 44 in *Lemass Era*

7   Maher, *Tortuous Path*, p. 246

8   Private Papers, Hillery Note, *Brussels*, 1996, p. 1

9   NAI DFA 2000/14/396, *Note on meeting of Minister for External Affairs with President Rey and Signor Martino on 14th July 1969*, p. 1

10   Ibid., pp. 2–3

11   McCann, *Report of meeting between Dr Hillery, Minister for External Affairs and M. Harmel, Belgian Minister for Foreign Affairs on Monday 14th July 1969*, p. 2

12   McCann, *Report of meeting between Dr Hillery, Minister for External Affairs and Dr Joseph Luns, Netherlands Minister for Foreign Affairs on 15th July 1969*, p. 2

13   Interview with Paddy Hillery, 8 June 2006

14   NA DFA 2000/14/396, McCann, *Report of meeting between Hillery and Luns*, p. 3

15   Donal O'Sullivan, *Note of discussion on 16th July 1969 between the Minister for External Affairs and Dr Gerhard Jahn*, p. 3

16   Ibid., p. 6

17   *Digest of Developments in the European Communities and in Trade Groupings during Quarter ended 30/9/69*

18   McCann, *Report of Meeting between Hillery and Schumann*, 25 September 1969

19   Maher, *Tortuous Path*, pp. 248–9

20   NA DFA 2000/14/396, *Note on meeting of Minister for External Affairs with President Rey and Signor Martino on 14th July 1969*, pp. 3–4

21   Maher, *Tortuous Path*, p. 249

22   Ibid., p. 250

23   Ibid., p. 250

24   NA DFA 2001/43/985, *Minister's EEC Discussions: July 1969 to June 1970*

25   Private Papers, Hillery Note, *Brussels*, p. 1

26   Hillery, *Draft One*, p. 4

27   Maher, *Tortuous Path*, p. 254

28   Hillery, *Brussels*, p. 1

29   Maher, *Tortuous Path*, p. 254; Hillery, *Brussels*, p. 1

30   Hillery, *Brussels*, p. 1

31   Maher, *Tortuous Path*, p. 256

32   Interview with Paddy Hillery, 8 June 2006

33   Ibid.

34   Hillery, *Brussels*, p. 1

35   Maher, *Tortuous Path*, p. 257

36   Ibid., pp. 257–8

37   Private Papers, Hillery Note, *Information*, 1995, p. 1

38   Ibid., p. 2

39   *Dáil Debates*, vol. 247, col. 231, 27 May 1970

40   Ibid., col. 233

41   Ibid., col. 236

42   Hillery, *Information*, p. 3

43   Maher, *Tortuous Path*, pp. 263–4

44   Hillery, *Information*, p. 1

45   NA DFA 2001/43/1060, Nolan to McColgan, 19 May 1970

46   NA DFA 2001/43/1060, *Memorandum for the government, Negotiations on Accession to the European Communities*, 14 May 1970

47   Ibid., *Annex, Summary of Recommendations*, p. 4

48   Interview with Paddy Hillery, 8 June 2006

49   Hillery, *Information*, p. 1

50   Private Papers, Hillery, *Europe*, p. 1

51   Hillery, *Information*, p. 1

52   Dennis Kennedy Interview, 22 May 2008

53   Ibid.

54   UCDA, *Hillery Papers*, P205, Folder 16, Harmel to Hillery, 9 June 1970

55   Maher, *Tortuous Path*, pp. 266–7

56   *The Irish Times*, 'EEC Promises Talks Sought by Hillery', 1 July 1970

57   Ibid.

58   Ibid.

59 *The Irish Times*, 'Hillery obtains consultation pledge on EEC entry', 1 July 1970
60 *The Irish Times*, 'Frenchman heads EEC Talks Team', 4 July 1970; *The Irish Times*, 'More Time To Adapt', 20 November 1970
61 Interview with John McColgan, 20 June 2008
62 Maher, *Tortuous Path*, p. 274
63 *The Irish Times*, 'Assurances on EEC sought by Hillery', 21 September 1970
64 Ibid.
65 Maher, *Tortuous Path*, pp. 284–5
66 *The Irish Times*, 'Crisis of the '70s: UN intervention and the North', 6 August 1991
67 *The Irish Times*, 'Hillery asks for talks on EEC integration', 16 December 1970
68 Ibid.
69 Maher, *Tortuous Path*, pp. 290–1
70 *The Irish Times*, 'Hillery asks for talks on EEC integration', 16 December 1970
71 Ibid.
72 UCDA, *Hillery Papers*, P205, Folder 19, Note to Hillery, 2 June 1971, p. 2
73 *The Irish Times*, 'EEC Assurances on Three Main Points: Hillery gets answers on trade, farm finance and dumping', 8 June 1971
74 UCDA, *Hillery Papers*, P205, Folder 19, Hillery Note, *Statement on Ministerial meeting*, 7 June 1971, p. 2
75 *The Irish Times*, 'EEC Assurances on Three Main Points', 8 June 1971
76 Ibid.; Maher, *Tortuous Path*, pp. 290–1
77 UCDA, *Hillery Papers*, P205, Folder 19, Note to Hillery, 2 June 1971, p. 2
78 Hillery, *Statement on Ministerial meeting*, 7 June 1971, p. 2
79 *The Irish Times*, 'EEC Assurances on Three Main Points: Hillery gets answers on trade, farm finance and dumping', 8 June 1971
80 Maher, *Tortuous Path*, p. 316
81 *The Irish Times*, 'EEC Assurances on Three Main Points: Hillery gets answers on trade, farm finance and dumping', 8 June 1971
82 Ibid.
83 UCDA, *Hillery Papers*, P205, Folder 19, Hillery Note, *Ministerial meeting: Note on Dumping*, 7 June 1971
84 *White Paper, The Accession of Ireland to the European Communities, laid by the government before each House of the Oireachas*, January 1972 (Dublin, 1972), p. 91
85 UCDA, *Hillery Papers*, P205, Folder 19, Hillery Note, *Ministerial meeting: Note on Dumping*, 7 June 1971
86 Hillery, *Note on Industrial Incentives*, 7 June 1971
87 *Note for Minister for Foreign Affairs for meeting with M Deniau on 5 July 1971, Export Tax Reliefs*, p. 3
88 *White Paper, Accession of Ireland*, p. 96
89 UCDA, *Hillery Papers*, P205, Folder 19, Hillery, *Note on Industrial Incentives*, 7 June 1971
90 Ibid.
91 *Note for Minister, Export Tax Reliefs*, 5 July 1971
92 Telegram, Seán Kennan to Seán Morrissey, 9 July 1971
93 *Note for Minister, Motor assembly scheme*, July 1971
94 *Transcript, 5th Ministerial Meeting, Resumed Session*, pp. 1–2
95 Ibid.

96 NA DFA 2001/43/1060, *Memorandum for the government, Negotiations on Accession to the European Communities, Annex, Summary of Recommendations*, 14 May 1970, p. 3

97 *The Irish Times*, 'Common Market agrees to Irish Export Aids', 20 October 1971

98 UCDA, *Hillery Papers*, P205, Folder 19, Michael Killeen to Hillery, 26 October 1971

99 *The Irish Times*, 'Common Market agrees to Irish Export Aids', 20 October 1971

100 UCDA, *Hillery Papers*, P205, Folder 19, Hillery Note, *Quotations from Wellenstein*, 19 October 1971, p. 2

101 Ibid.

102 Ibid., p. 1

103 Ibid., p. 3

104 Ibid., p. 3

105 *The Irish Times*, 'EEC agrees to Irish Export Aids: stiffest hurdle cleared as incentives remain', 20 October 1971

106 Ibid.

107 *White Paper, Accession of Ireland*, p. 114

108 Ibid., p. 115

109 *The Irish Times*, 'EEC agrees to Irish Export Aids', 20 October 1971

110 UCDA, P205, Folder 19, *A Note on Discussions in the EEC Negotiations on Export Tax Reliefs*, 2 November 1971

111 Maher, *Tortuous Path*, p. 314

112 Ibid.

113 UCDA, *Hillery Papers*, P205, Folder 19, *Aide-Mémoire of Norwegian position*, 30 June 1971

114 Interview with Paddy Hillery, 8 June 2006

115 *The Irish Times*, 'EEC Assurances on Three Main Points', 8 June 1971

116 *The Irish Times*, 'Crisis of the '70s: UN intervention and the North', 6 August 1991

117 Interview with Paddy Hillery, 8 June 2006

118 UCDA, *Hillery Papers*, P205, Folder 19, *Text of Statement made in the House of Commons by Mr Heath on 24 May 1971*

119 *Main Points of Irish/UK fisheries talks in Brussels*, 30 June 1971, p. 1

120 Ibid.

121 *The Irish Times*, 'Crisis of the '70s: UN intervention and the North', 6 August 1991

122 UCDA, *Hillery Papers*, P205, Folder 19, *Main Points of Irish/UK fisheries talks in Brussels*, 30 June 1971, p. 1

123 *The Irish Times*, 'EEC Talks Stall on Fishing Limits', 10 November 1971

124 Ibid.

125 Ibid.

126 *The Irish Times*, 'EEC Offer Fish Limit Concessions: Marathon talks a pantomime – Rippon', 30 November 1971

127 Ibid.

128 UCDA, *Hillery Papers*, P205, Folder 10, Hillery Note, *The Norwegians and Fish*, 7 January 1972

129 Hillery Note, 21 December 1971

130 *The Irish Times*, 'EEC Fisheries Agreement', 13 December 1971

131 UCDA, *Hillery Papers*, P205, Folder 10, Hillery Note, *Rippon*, 11 December 1971

132 *The Irish Times*, 'EEC Fisheries Agreement', 13 December 1971

133 Interview with Dennis Kennedy, 22 May 2008

134 *The Irish Times*, 'Ireland and EEC Agree on Fisheries: Accession treaty to be signed next month', 13 December 1971

135 Ibid.

136 Ibid.

137 *The Irish Times*, 'EEC Fisheries Agreement', 13 December 1971

138 *The Irish Times*, 'Herring Fishermen Dislike EEC Terms', 14 December 1971; *The Irish Times*, 'EEC fish terms not accepted in Donegal', 16 December 1971

139 UCDA, *Hillery Papers*, P205, Folder 10, Telex from Irish Delegation, *Background Note on the Sugar Production Quota and the Community Offer*, 11 January 1972, p. 2

140 *The Irish Times*, 'Irish Sugar Quota in the EEC', 22 December 1971

141 UCDA, P205, Folder 10, Telex from Irish Delegation, *Sugar Production Quota*, 11 January 1972, p. 2

142 *The Irish Times*, 'Call for bigger sugar quota in EEC', 6 January 1972

143 UCDA, *Hillery Papers*, P205, Folder 10, Hillery Note, 12 January 1972

144 Hillery Note, *Meetings regarding the Sugar Quota*, January 1972, p. 1

145 Ibid., p. 2

146 Ibid., p. 2

147 *The Irish Times*, 'Beet Growers Demand Bigger EEC Quota', 7 January 1972

148 *The Irish Times*, 'Tuam rally for bigger beet quota', 8 January 1972

149 UCDA, *Hillery Papers*, P205, Folder 10, Hillery Note, 12 January 1972

150 Hillery Note, *Sugar Quota*, January 1972, p. 2

151 Hillery Note, 9 January 1972

152 *The Irish Times*, 'Hillery Unable To Accept 150,000-Ton Sugar Quota', 11 January 1972

153 Ibid.

154 UCDA, *Hillery Papers*, P205, Folder 10, Hillery Note, *Sugar*, 11 January 1972

155 Telex from Irish Delegation, *Sugar Production Quota*, 11 January 1972, p. 1

156 Ibid.

157 Interview with Paddy Hillery, 8 June 2006

158 *The Irish Times*, 'EEC Sugar Quota to be Accepted', 12 January 1972; *The Irish Times*, 'EEC Terms on Sugar Quota Accepted', 14 January 1972

159 *The Irish Times*, 'EEC Terms on Sugar Quota Accepted', 14 January 1972

160 Ibid.

161 UCDA, *Hillery Papers*, P205, Folder 10, Hillery Note, 12 January 1972

162 *The Irish Times*, 'What Lynch and Hillery will be signing', 22 January 1972

163 Interview with Dennis Kennedy, 22 May 2008

Chapter 15

1 Helmut Szpott Interview with Paddy Hillery, 29 May 1995

2 Interview with Paddy Hillery, 8 June 2006

3 *Dáil Debates*, vol. 257, col. 1070–1142, 2 December 1971

4 Interview with John McColgan, 20 June 2008

5 *Dáil Debates*, vol. 258, col. 394–484, 25 January 1972

6 Ibid., *Dáil Debates*, vol. 258, col. 623, 26 January 1972

7 *White Paper, Accession of Ireland*, pp. 75–192

8 Ibid., p. 69

9 *Dáil Debates*, vol. 259, col. 2450, 23 March 1972

10 Ibid., col. 2451

11 Ibid., col. 2451

12 Ibid., col. 2453

13 Maher, *Tortuous Path*, p. 348

14 *Dáil Debates*, vol. 259, col. 2437, 23 March 1972

15 Interview with Neville Keery, 16 July 2008; Helmut Szpott, Interview with Paddy Hillery, 29 May 1995

16 Interview with Paddy Hillery, 24 May 2006

17 Interview with Neville Keery, 16 July 2008

18 *The Irish Times*, 'Goods, not people, would be exported', 29 January 1972

19 *The Irish Times*, 'EEC case is defended by Hillery', 7 March 1972

20 *The Irish Times*, 'FF satisfied with canvassing progress', 3 May 1972

21 Interview with Paddy Hillery, 8 June 2006

22 *The Irish Times*, 'Hillery says May 10th Vote is one for Freedom', 29 April 1972

23 UCDA, *Hillery Papers*, P205, Folder 9, *Fianna Fáil: A Referendum Campaign*, 8 June 1972, p. 4

24 *The Irish Times*, 'FF satisfied with canvassing progress', 3 May 1972

25 Interview with Paddy Hillery, 8 June 2006

26 John A. Murphy, *Ireland in the Twentieth Century* (Dublin, 1989), p. 149

27 David Arter, *The Politics of European Integration in the Twentieth Century* (Cambridge University Press, 1993), p. 171

28 *The Irish Times*, 'No EEC vote for internees "treachery"', 29 March 1972

29 Ibid.

30 *The Irish Times*, 'Joining Will Aid Road To Unity – Hillery', 26 April 1972

31 Ibid.

32 *The Irish Times*, 'Ministers see pointers to unity in EEC Membership: Hillery on likely food price rises', 13 March 1972

33 Ibid.

34 *The Irish Times*, 'Hillery Repudiates Corish Assertions', 24 April 1972

35 *The Irish Times*, 'Vote against Europe a denial of Irish Traditions – Hillery', 3 May 1972

36 Ibid.

37 *The Irish Times*, 'Hillery says May 10th Vote is one for Freedom', 29 April 1972

38 Ibid.

39 UCDA, *Hillery Papers*, P205, Folder 18, Hillery Note of meeting with Rogers, 4 October 1971

40 *Sunday Tribune*, 'Garret's brilliance shone as Dev's eyesight faded', 26 January 2003

41 *The Irish Times*, 'Landing rights issue being misused in campaign – Hillery', 9 May 1972

42 Ibid.

43 Ibid.

44 *Clare People*, 'Looking after mná na hEorpa', 15 April 2008

45 Interview with Paddy Hillery, 8 June 2006

46 Interview with Paddy Hillery, 8 June 2006

47 *The Irish Times*, '"Yes" To Europe by 5 to 1', 12 May 1972

48 Interview with Paddy Hillery, 8 June 2006

49 *The Irish Times*, 'Survey has Pro-Marketeers ahead, but only by a Head', 29 April 1972

50 Murphy, *Ireland in the Twentieth Century*, p. 150

51 *The Irish Times*, 'Choice lies ahead for Lynch and Hillery', 13 May 1972

52 Interview with Paddy Hillery, 8 June 2006

53 *The Irish Times*, 'Hillery favoured for EEC post', 10 August 1972

54 Interview with Paddy Hillery, 21 June 2006

55 Ibid.

56 *The Irish Times*, 'Hillery favoured for EEC post', 10 August 1972

57 *The Irish Times*, 'Ó Dálaigh gets EEC court post', 16 August 1972

58 *The Irish Times*, 'Hillery gets the Brussels job: Lenihan for Foreign Affairs?', 27 September 1972

59 *The Irish Times*, 'Hillery chosen as an EEC Commission vice-president', 19 December 1972

60 *The Irish Times*, 'Hillery favoured for EEC post', 10 August 1972

61 *The Irish Times*, 'European Bill passes all stages', 16 November 1972; Maher, *Tortuous Path*, pp. 351–2

62 UCDA, *Hillery Papers*, P205, Folder 11, Secretary General, Council of Ministers, *Telegram to M. Patrick J. Hillery*, 29 December 1972

63 *The Irish Times*, Backbencher, 'Meet the next Taoiseach', 14 October 1972

64 Interview with Paddy Hillery, 21 June 2006

Chapter 16

1 Richard Vaughan, *Twentieth Century Europe: Paths to Unity* (London, 1979), pp. 216–7

2 Ibid., p.140

3 Interview with Edwin FitzGibbon, 2 July 2007

4 Interview with Paddy Hillery, 21 June 2006

5 UCDA, *Hillery Papers*, P205, Folder 14(1), Memorandum, *Social Policy*, February 1973

6 *The Irish Times*, 'Social Progress vital for EEC', 20 October 1972

7 Interview with Paddy Hillery, 21 June 2006

8 *The Irish Times*, 'New EEC commission holds first talks today', 6 January 1973

9 *The Irish Times*, 'EEC Social Affairs Post for Hillery', 8 January 1973

10 Private Papers, Hillery Note, *Langues*, 1995,

11 *The Irish Times*, 'RTÉ man joins Hillery's EEC team', 1 November 1972

12 Private Papers, Hillery Note, *People*, 1996, p. 2

13 UCDA, *Hillery Papers*, P205, Folder 14 (1), Hillery, Transcript, 30 January 1973

14 Private Papers, Hillery Note, *People*, 1996, p. 2

15 Private Information

16 Interview with John Coone, 30 May 2008

17 UCDA, *Hillery Papers*, P205, Folder 14(1), Hillery, Transcript, 8 January 1973

18 Hillery, Transcript, 30 January 1973

19 UCDA, *Hillery Papers*, P205, Folder 14(2), Hillery, Transcript, 9 February 1973, p. 1

20 Ibid.

21 Hillery, Transcript, 17 February 1973, p. 1

22 Ibid., pp. 3–4

23 Ibid., p. 4

24 UCDA, *Hillery Papers*, P205, Folder 14(1), Hillery to Fogarty, 22 February 1973

25 Hillery Note, 16 March 1973

26 Interview with John McColgan, 20 June 2008

27   *The Irish Times*, 'Belgian in Hillery's *cabinet*', 18 January 1973

28   *The Irish Times*, 'Rifflet to be deputy director,' 7 February 1973

29   *The Irish Times*, 'Hillery likely vice-president of European Commission', 11 November 1972

30   UCDA, P205, Folder 14(2), Hillery, Transcript, 13–15 March 1973

31   Interview with Neville Keery, 16 July 2008

32   UCDA, *Hillery Papers*, P205, Folder 12, Hillery, *Notes planning how staff should approach my office in Europe*, December 1972

33   Private Papers, Hillery, *Cabinet*, 1996, p. 1

34   Ibid.

35   Ibid.

36   UCDA, *Hillery Papers*, P205, Folder 14(1), Hillery, Transcript, 17 February 1973

37   UCDA, *Hillery Papers*, P205, Folder 14(2), Hillery, Transcript, 23 March 1973

38   Hillery, Transcript, 19 March 1973

39   Interview with Paddy Hillery, 21 June 2006

40   *The Irish Times*, 'EEC Social Programme Too Limited, Says O'Leary', 29 October 1973; Interview with Edwin FitzGibbon, 2 July 2007

41   Private information.

42   UCDA, *Hillery Papers*, P205, Folder 14(1), Hillery, *Speech to the European Parliament: Report on the Social Situation in the Community*, January 1973, p. 10

43   Ibid.

44   Private Papers, Hillery, *Social Action*, 1995, p. 1; UCDA, *Hillery Papers*, P205, Folder 14(2), Hillery, Note on speech to Parliament, 14 February 1973

45   Hillery, *Social Action*, p. 1

46   Ibid.

47   Ibid., Interview with Edwin FitzGibbon, 2 July 2007

48   UCDA, *Hillery Papers*, P205, Folder 14(1), SEC (73) 597/3, *Projet, Document de travail des services de la Commission sur la programme d'action en matière sociale*, 20 February 1973

49   *The Irish Times*, 'Hillery Outlines Social Programme', 31 March 1973; *The Irish Times*, 'Hillery's social plans agreed by Commission: Minor Changes In Draft', 19 April 1973

50   Hillery, *Social Action*, p. 1

51   Interview with Edwin FitzGibbon, 2 July 2007

52   *The Irish Times*, 'Slight Hold-Up in EEC Social Plan', 10 April 1973; *The Irish Times*, 'What Baulked The Hillery Proposals: Social affairs conflict', 11 April 1973

53   Hillery, *Social Action*, p. 1

54   *The Irish Times*, 'Hillery's social plans agreed by Commission', 19 April 1973; *The Irish Times*, 'EEC Proposals for Work Improvement', 20 April 1973

55   UCDA, *Hillery Papers*, P205, Folder 14(1), Hillery, *Note on Council meeting*, 26 February 1973

56   Interview with Paddy Hillery, 21 June 2006

57   Private Papers, Hillery, *Trade Unions*, 1994, p. 1

58   Ibid., p. 2

59   Ibid., p. 2

60   *The Irish Times*, Tony Brown, 'Patrick Hillery's European legacy', 22 April 2008

61   Interview with Tony Brown, 15 August 2008

62   *The Irish Times*, 'Commission unlikely to pass Hillery's social programme', 27 September 1973; *The Irish Times*, Tony Brown, 'Patrick Hillery's European Legacy', 22 April 2008.

63   Com (73) 1600, *Social action programme (submitted by the Commission to the Council on 25 October 1973)*, p.28, *Bulletin of the European Communities, Supplement 2/74*

64   *The Irish Times*, 'Europe: Hillery's social action programme a blueprint for joint Community effort', 2 October 1973

65   Com (73) 1600, *Social action programme*, October 1973, p. 15, *Bulletin of the European Communities, Supplement 2/74*

66   Ibid., pp. 16–17

67   Ibid., p. 18

68   Ibid., p. 19

69   *The Irish Times*, 'Commission unlikely to pass Hillery's social programme', 27 September 1973

70   Interview with Edwin FitzGibbon, 2 July 2007

71   Private information

72   *The Irish Times*, 'Europe: Hillery's social action programme a blueprint for joint Community effort', 2 October 1973

73   *The Irish Times*, 'Hillery declares himself on side of Workers: Wants equal pay properly implemented', 26 October 1973

74   Ibid.

75   UCDA, *Hillery Papers*, P205, Folder 14 (1), Hillery, Transcript, 16 March 1973, p. 1

76   *The Irish Times*, 'Hillery declares himself on side of Workers', 26 October 1973

77   Ibid.

78   J.P. D. Dunbabin, *The Post-Imperial Age: The Great Powers and the Wider World* (London, 1994), pp. 350–51

79   Interview with Tony Brown, 'Paddy Hillery's European legacy', 15 August 2008

80   *The Irish Times*, 'Social policy is EEC's test, says Hillery', 21 November 1973

81   *The Irish Times*, 'Social plan intact, says Hillery', 11 December 1973

82   *The Irish Times*, 'EEC Social Programme Too Limited says O'Leary', 29 October 1973

83   *The Irish Times*, 'Ministers, not summit to decide social policy: Cost is biggest problem', 12 December 1973

84   *The Irish Times*, 'EEC is to implement Hillery's social plan', 13 December 1973

85   *The Irish Times*, 'Hillery regrets training aid rejected', 15 December 1973

86   Ibid.

87   *The Irish Times*, 'Ministers, not summit to decide social policy: Cost is biggest problem', 12 December 1973

88   Interview with Tony Brown, 15 August 2008

89   Ibid.

90   S.2/74, *Resolution of the Council of 21 January 1974 concerning a social action programme, Official Journal C 013*

Chapter 17

1   Interview with John McColgan, 20 June 2008

2   Private Papers, Hillery, Transcript, 27 May 1974

3   *The Irish Times*, 'Brandt Quits Over Espionage Affair', 7 May 1974

4   Private Papers, Hillery, Transcript, 16 May 1974

5   Private Papers, Hillery, Transcript, 19 September 1974; *The Irish Times*, 'EEC Budget Cuts Could Total £370m', 24 September 1975

6   *The Irish Times*, 'Hillery declares himself on side of Workers', 26 October 1973

7   Interview with John McColgan, 20 June 2008

8   *The Irish Times*, 'Appointed to Hillery's Cabinet,' 16 May 1974

9   Interview with Neville Keery, 16 July 2008

10 *Resolution of the Council of 21 January 1974 concerning a social action programme*, *Official Journal C 013*, S.2/74, p. 10

11 Com (73) 1600, *Social action programme*, Annex II, pp. 21–8, *Bulletin of the European Communities*, Supplement 2/74

12 Ibid., *Annex III*, pp. 29–36

13 74/327/EEC, *Council Decision*, 27 June 1974, *Official Journal* L 185, pp. 20–1; 74/328/EEC, *Council Decision*, 27 June 1974, *Official Journal* L 185, pp. 22–3

14 74/325/EEC, *Council Decision*, 27 June 1974, *Official Journal* L 185, pp. 15–17

15 74/326/EEC, *Council Decision*, 27 June 1974, *Official Journal* L 185, pp. 18–19

16 *The Irish Times*, 'EEC Plans Worker Training Centre', 29 March 1974

17 *Regulation (EEC) No 337/75 of the Council*, 10 February 1975, *Official Journal* L 039, pp. 1–4

18 *Regulation (EEC) No 1365/75 of the Council*, 26 May 1975, *Official Journal* L 139, pp. 1–4; *The Irish Times*, 'Irish-based EEC body meets today', 6 May 1976

19 *The Irish Times*, 'Hillery says new foundation is major step in social research', 7 May 1976

20 *The Irish Times*, 'No cheap cures from Dr Hillery', 26 June 1975

21 Hillery, *Commission*, p. 6

22 *The Irish Times*, 'EEC Ministers defer decision on siting new institution in Dublin', 18 December 1974

23 75/129/EEC, *Council Directive on the approximation of the laws of the Member States relating to collective redundancies*, 17 February 1975, *Official Journal* L 048, pp. 29–30

24 Ibid.

25 *The Irish Times*, 'EEC directive on rights of workers in mergers', 1 June 1974

26 Ibid.

27 Private Papers, Hillery, Transcript, 18 December 1974

28 75/117/EEC, *Council Directive on the approximation of the laws of Member States relating to the application of equal pay for men and women*, 10 February 1975, *Official Journal* L 045, pp. 19–20

29 Ibid.

30 *The Irish Times*, 'Remember yesterday? The day we were to get equal pay?', 1 January 1976

31 Ibid., *The Irish Times*, 'Equal Pay could kill 5,000 jobs, says report', 18 December 1975

32 *The Irish Times*, 'Hillery spells out equal pay directive', 1 March 1975

33 Ibid.; *The Irish Times*, 'Equity at Work', 1 March 1975

34 *The Irish Times*, 'Hillery promises no going back on women's equal pay', 14 June 1975

35 *The Irish Times*, 'Remember yesterday? The day we were to get equal pay?', 1 January 1976

36 Ibid.

37 *The Irish Times*, 'Footwear aid to ease refusal', 12 February 1976

38 *Dáil Debates*, vol. 286, col. 1764, 17 December 1975

39 NAI D/T 2006/133/396, AD 4/17, *Memorandum for the Government, Proposals for legislation to amend the Anti-Discrimination (Pay) Act 1974*, 7 January 1976, pp.6–7

40 AD 4/17, *Memorandum for the Government, Proposals for legislation to amend the Anti-Discrimination (Pay) Act 1974*, 20 January 1976, p.3

41 AD 4/17, *Memorandum for the Government*, 7 January 1976, p.1

42 Daniel O'Sullivan to private secretary, Minister for Labour, 9 January 1976

43 NAI D/T 2006/133/21, *Statement issued on the behalf of the Government*, 21 January 1976

44 Dáil Debates, Vol. 287, Col. 1645, 12 February 1976

45 *The Irish Times*, 'ICTU condemns pay deal', 23 January 1976; *Irish Press*, 'Hillery to sway pay ruling?', 11 February 1976

46 Ibid.

47 Private Papers, Hillery Note, *Equal Pay*, 1994, p. 1

48 Ibid.

49 *The Irish Times*, 'Government will not postpone equal pay if Brussels insists', 6 February 1976

50 European Commission Papers, Hillery to Ortoli, 5 February 1976, p.1

51 NAI D/T2006/133/396, AD 4/17, Memorandum for the Government, Proposals for Legislation to amend the Anti-Discrimination (Pay) Act 1974, 20 January 1976, p. 3

52 Interview with Edwin FitzGibbon, 2 July 2007

53 Interview with Paddy Hillery, 21 June 2006

54 Hillery, *Equal Pay*, p. 1

55 Interview with Edwin FitzGibbon, 4 July 2008

56 European Commission, Hillery to Ortoli, 5 February 1976, p.2

57 NAI D/T 2006/133/396, 'Telephone Call from Ambassador Dillon on Equal Pay', 11 February 1976

58 Ibid., *Irish Press*, 'Equal Pay from EEC: Brussels may foot the Bill', 12 February 1976

59 *The Irish Times*, 'Footwear aid to ease refusal', 12 February 1976

60 Interview with Paddy Hillery, 21 June 2006

61 *Irish Press*, 'Hillery's job on the line', 12 February 1976

62 *The Irish Times*, 'Equal pay law request to EEC to be rejected?', 11 February 1976

63 *Irish Press*, 'Hillery's job on the line', 12 February 1976

64 Interview with Paddy Hillery, 21 June 2006

65 Diarmaid Ferriter, *The Transformation of Ireland 1900–2000* (London, 2004), p.684

66 Interview with Edwin FitzGibbon, 4 July 2008

67 Interview with John McColgan, 20 June 2008

68 Interview with Paddy Hillery, 21 June 2006

69 *The Irish Times*, 'Cabinet accepts EEC "no" on equal pay delay but looks for new aid', 12 February 1976

70 *Irish Press*, 'But where was Richie?' 15 February 1976

71 *The Irish Times*, 'Hillery accused of irresponsible antics', 16 February 1976

72 *Sunday Press*, 'Ryan Attacks Hillery "Antics": Shock Criticism of Commissioner', 15 February 1976

73 Ibid., *Sunday Independent*, 'Ryan Slams Dr Hillery' 15 February 1976

74 *The Irish Times*, 'Embarrassing All Round', 16 February 1976

75 *Irish Press*, 'No Sign of Minister', 15 February 1976

76 Private Papers, Hillery, Transcript, 16 February 1976

77 *The Irish Times*, 'Derogate pay directive or finance it, says Ryan', 17 February 1976

78 *The Irish Times*, 'Ryan to ask EEC to supply equal pay revenue', 16 February 1976

79 Ibid.

80 Minutes of European Commission Com (76) PV 372, Meeting of 17 February 1976, p. 18

81 *Agence Europe*, 'The European Commission Reaffirms Its Position on Equal Pay for Men and Women in Ireland and its Backing for Vice-President Hillery', 18 February 1976

82 *The Irish Times*, 'EEC rebukes Ryan and backs Hillery', 19 February 1976

83 *Irish Press*, 'Hillery's Position', 16 February 1976; *The Irish Times*, 'Embarrassing All Round', 16 February 1976

84 *Irish Press*, 'Hillery's job on the line', 12 February 1976

85 Private Papers, Hillery, Transcript, 4–5 March 1976

86 NAI D/T 2006/133/396, *Note of Government meeting*, 4 March 1976

87 *The Irish Times*, 'EEC to offer £6m on equal pay', 3 March 1976

88 NAI D/T 2006/133/396, *Meeting between EEC Fact finding Team of Officials on Equal Pay and Irish Inter-Departmental Working Group*, pp.1–2

89 European Commission, SEC (76) 871, Report by Directors-General to Commission, *Irlande: Difficultés d'application de l'égalité salariale dans certaines enterprises*, 1 March 1976, pp.5–7

90 Ibid.

91 NAI D/T 2006/133/396, *Questions for decision re Irish alternative proposals on equal pay*, 20 February 1976

92 European Commission, SEC (76) 871, Report by Directors-General To Commission, *Irlande: Difficultés d'application de l'égalité salariale dans certaines enterprises*, 1 March 1976, p.3

93 NAI D/T 2006/133/396, *Memorandum for the Government, Possible Means of obtaining EEC financial assistance towards measures to alleviate impact of equal pay on employment*, 29 March 1976, p.3

94 Private Papers, Hillery, Transcript, 4–5 March 1976, pp. 1–2

95 Ibid., p. 4

96 *The Irish Times*, 'Government to ask EEC again for equal pay aid', 5 March 1976; *Guardian*, 'Dublin plea rejected', 5 March 1976

97 NAI D/T 2006/133/396, *Memorandum for the Government, Possible Means of obtaining EEC financial assistance towards measures to alleviate impact of equal pay on employment*, 29 March 1976, pp.1–4; Note of Government meeting, *Equal Pay: EEC Assistance*, 28 April 1976

98 European Commission Papers, *Memorandum by the Irish Government*, 12 May 1976

99 *The Irish Times*, 'EEC to offer £6m. on equal pay', 3 March 1976

100 *The Irish Times*, 'Hillery Outlines Policy For Working Women', 13 February 1975

101 *The Irish Times*, 'Equal opportunity directive: what happened?' 26 June 1975

102 *The Irish Times*, 'Social affairs Ministers fail to agree', 18 June 1975

103 Ibid.

104 Private Papers, Hillery, Transcript, *Meeting of the Council of Social Affairs with Michael O'Leary in the chair*, 21 July 1975, p. 1

105 Ibid.

106 *The Irish Times*, 'Social affairs Ministers fail to agree', 18 June 1975

107 Interview with Tony Brown, 15 August 2008

108 *The Irish Times*, 'Equal opportunity directive: what happened?', 18 June 1975

109 *The Irish Times*, 'Hillery outlines women's directive', 13 December 1975

110 Private Papers, Hillery, Transcript, 6 October 1975, pp. 1–2

111 *The Irish Times*, 'Hillery outlines women's directive', 13 December 1975

112 *Council Directive 76/207/EEC on the implementation of the principle of equal treatment for men and women as regards access to employment, vocational training and promotion, and working conditions*, 9 February 1976, *Official Journal* L 039, pp. 40–2

113 Ibid.

114 Ibid.

115 *The Irish Times*, 'Hillery to set up women's bureau,' 18 June 1976

116 *The Irish Times*, 'EEC social policy criticised by Cluskey as grossly under-financed', 15 June 1974

117 Ibid.

118 *Council Resolution*, 27 June 1974, *Official Journal* C 080, pp.30–2

119 Ibid.

120 *The Irish Times*, 'Hillery's Social Policy has Concern for the Poor Man', 20 August 1974

121 75/458/EEC, *Council Decision concerning a programme of pilot schemes and studies to combat poverty*, 22 July 1975, *Official Journal* L 199, pp. 34–5

122 *The Irish Times*, 'Social affairs Ministers fail to agree', 18 June 1975

123 Interview with Tony Brown, 15 August 2008

124 Interview with Paddy Hillery, 21 June 2006

125 Ibid.

126 Private Papers, Hillery, Transcript, *Council of Social Affairs*, 21 July 1975, p. 1

127 Ibid.

128 Ibid.

129 Interview with Tony Brown, 15 August 2008

130 75/458/EEC, *Council Decision concerning a programme of pilot schemes and studies to combat poverty*, 22 July 1975, *Official Journal* L 199, pp. 34–5

131 75/459/EEC, *Council Decision on action by the European Social Fund for persons affected by employment difficulties*, 22 July 1975, *Official Journal* L 199, p. 36

132 Hillery, Transcript, *Council of Social Affairs*, 21 July 1975, p. 1

133 *The Irish Times*, 'No cheap cures from Dr Hillery', 26 June 1975

134 *The Irish Times*, 'Ambitious plan to help jobless', 19 November 1974

135 *The Irish Times*, 'Hillery's plan for migrant workers in EEC', 20 March 1975

136 Ibid.

137 European Commission, Com (73) 1600, *Social action programme, Annex II*, pp. 23–4, *Bulletin*, S 2/74

138 Ibid., p. 24

139 *The Irish Times*, 'Charter for migrant workers', 10 June 1975

140 European Commission, Com (73) 1600, *Social action programme, Annex II*, p. 24, *Bulletin*, S 2/74, *The Irish Times*, 'Hillery's plans for migrant workers in EEC', 20 March 1975

141 *The Irish Times*, 'Hillery proposes political rights for migrant workers', 20 December 1974

142 Interview with Edwin FitzGibbon, 2 July 2007

143 *The Irish Times*, 'Hillery proposes political rights for migrant workers', 20 December 1974; *The Irish Times*, 'Hillery's plans for migrant workers in EEC', 20 March 1975

144 Private Papers, Hillery, Transcript, 18 December 1974, p. 2

145 *Council Resolution on an action programme for migrant workers and members of their families*, 9 February 1976, *Official Journal* C 034, pp. 2–3

146 Ibid.

147 Ibid.

148 Private Papers, Hillery, Transcript, 21 July 1976, p. 2

Chapter 18

1   Interview with Paddy Hillery, 21 June 2006

2   Private Papers, Hillery Note, *Presidency*, 1995, p. 1

3   *Irish Independent*, 'Speculation grows on Hillery's plans,' 26 March 1973

4   Ibid.; *The Irish Times*, 'Speculation on future of Hillery in Brussels: Candidate for Presidency?' 26 March 1973

5   *Irish Independent*, 'Hillery will not go for Presidency', 27 March 1973; *The Irish Times*, 'Rumours that Hillery will resign are firmly denied', 27 March 1973

6   Private Papers, Hillery Note, *Cearbhall Ó Dálaigh as Candidate*, November 1974, p. 6

7   Ibid., p. 8

8   Interview with Paddy Hillery, 21 June 2006

9   Horgan, *Lemass*, pp. 201–2

10   Private Papers, Hillery Note, *Presidency*, June 1995, p. 1

11   UCDA, *Hillery Papers*, P205, Folder 20, Hillery to FitzGibbon, November 1974

12   Keery to Hillery, 27 November 1974

13   Private Papers, Hillery Note, *Presidency*, June 1995, p. 1; Interview with Paddy Hillery, 21 June 2006

14   UCDA, P205, Folder 20, Keery to Hillery, 27 November 1974

15   Private Papers, Hillery Note, *Cearbhall Ó Dálaigh as Candidate*, November 1974, p. 10

16   *The Irish Times*, 'FF seeks Donegan's dismissal for remark about President', 19 October 1976

17   Ibid.

18   *The Irish Times*, 'Five Votes decide Donegan should not be asked to resign', 21 October 1976

19   *The Irish Times*, 'Ó Dálaigh will not stand again: Resignation "only way to protect dignity of Presidency"', 23 October 1976

20   UCDA, *Hillery Papers*, P205, Folder 2, Cosgrave to Hillery, 15 October 1976

21   Interview with Paddy Hillery, 21 June 2006

22   Private Papers, Transcript 12, *End of days in Commission*, October 1976, p. 3

23   UCDA, *Hillery Papers*, P205, Folder 2, Hillery to Cosgrave, 28 October 1976

24   Ibid., pp. 1–2

25   *The Irish Times*, 'Hillery non-committal about future after Taoiseach's hint on EEC post', 23 October 1976

26   Private Papers, Transcript 12, *End of days in Commission*, October 1976, p. 2

27   Ibid., *The Irish Times*, 'Hillery non-committal about future after Taoiseach's hint on EEC post', 23 October 1976

28 *The Irish Times*, 'For Hillery, loyalty has had its price as well as its reward', 9 November 1976

29 Private Papers, Transcript 12, *End of days in Commission*, October 1976, p. 2

30 Ibid.

31 Interview with Paddy Hillery, 21 June 2006

32 Private Papers, Transcript 12, *End of days in Commission*, October 1976, p. 2

33 *The Irish Times*, 'Fianna Fáil decides to nominate candidate for the Presidency', 26 October 1976

34 Ibid.

35 Ibid.

36 Private Papers, Transcript 12, *End of days in Commission*, October 1976, p. 6

37 Ibid.

38 *The Irish Times*, 'Hillery, still front runner, awaits FF decision next week', 29 October 1976

39 Ibid., Private Papers, Transcript 12, *End of days in Commission*, October 1976, p. 6

40 Interview with Paddy Hillery, 21 June 2006

41 Private Papers, Transcript 12, *End of days in Commission*, November 1976, pp. 7–8

42 *The Irish Times*, 'For Hillery, loyalty has had its price as well as its reward', 9 November 1976

43 Interview with Paddy Hillery, 21 June 2006

44 Private Papers, Transcript 12, *End of days in Commission*, November 1976, pp. 7–8

45 *The Irish Times*, 'Fianna Fáil names Hillery as presidential candidate', 3 November 1976

46 *The Irish Times*, 'An acceptant Hillery hands in his papers'. 6 November 1976; *The Irish Times*, 'Hillery to become country's sixth President next month'. 10 November 1976

47 Interview with Dennis Kennedy, 22 May 2008

48 Michael Mills, *Hurler On The Ditch* (Dublin, 2005), pp. 94–5; James Downey, *Lenihan: His Life and Loyalties* (Dublin, 1998), p. 102

49 Interview with Paddy Hillery, 21 June 2006; Mills, *Hurler On The Ditch*, p. 94

50 Private Papers, Transcript 12, *End of days in Commission*, November 1976, p. 7

51 *The Irish Times*, 'Hillery to become country's sixth President next month', 10 November 1976

52 *The Irish Times*, 'For Hillery, loyalty has had its price as well as its reward', 9 November 1976

Chapter 19

1 *The Irish Times*, 'Hillery stresses law and liberty in first speech as President', 4 November 1976

2 *The Irish Times*, 'Hillery defends Ó Dálaigh', 8 November 1976

3 Private Papers, Hillery Note, *Presidency*, 1995, p. 3

4 *Constitution of Ireland*, Articles 12–13

5 Hillery, *Presidency*, p. 2

6 Ibid.

7 Interview with Paddy Hillery, 21 June 2006

8 Interview with Peig O'Malley, 6 May 2008

9 NAI D/T 2007/116/61, Minute for Secretary, Department of the Taoiseach, 1 March 1977

10 UCDA *Hillery Papers*, Ó Flathartaigh to Hillery, 15 February 1977, P205, Folder 20

11 Ibid.

12 NAI D/T 2007/116/61, *President: Transport Arrangements*, 23 March 1977

13 NAI D/T 2007/116/61, Minute for Secretary, Department of the Taoiseach, 1 March 1977, p. 1

14 Ibid., p. 2

15 NAI D/T 2007/116/61, *President: Transport Arrangements*, 23 March 1977

16 Interview with Paddy Hillery, 21 June 2006

17 NAI D/T 2007/116/58, *Emoluments, Allowances of the President*, 17 May 1977, p. 2

18 Ibid., p. 3

19 *Note for Secretary, Department of the Taoiseach*, 29 July 1977

20 NAI D/T 2007 116/61, Ibid.; Daniel O'Sullivan, *Note for Taoiseach: Possible Topics*, 24 October 1977, p. 1

21 UCDA Folder 20, P205, Lynch to Hillery, 21 December 1977

22 NAI, D/T 2007/116/58 *Note for Secretary, Department of the Taoiseach*, 29 July 1977

23 O'Sullivan, *Note for Taoiseach*, 5 August 1977; Lynch to O'Sullivan, 11 August 1977

24 NAI D/T 2007/116/61, Lynch to Sullivan, 27 October 1977

25 O'Malley Interview, 6 May 2008

26 Private Papers, Transcript 14, *CJH Elected Taoiseach*, 1979

27 NAI, D/T 2007/116/61 O'Sullivan, *Note for Taoiseach*, 24 October 1977, p. 1

28 Hillery, *Lenihan*, p. 1

29 Hillery, *Presidency*, p. 3

30 *The Irish Times*, 'President's expenses increased to £100,000', 19 April 1991

31 NAI D/T 2007/116/58, *Note for Secretary, Department of the Taoiseach*, 29 July 1977

32 O'Malley Interview, 6 May 2008

33 *The Irish Times*, 'Máirtín Ó Flathartaigh: Private secretary to four Presidents', 19 March 2005

34 Ibid.

35 *The Irish Times*, 'Secretary to President Appointed', 20 May 1978

36 Interview with Paddy Hillery, 3 August 2006

37 Ibid.

38 Ibid.

39 *The Irish Times*, 'Secretary to President Appointed', 20 May 1978

40 NAI D/T 2007/116/315, Peig O'Malley to Daniel O'Sullivan, 10 August 1977, *Address by President Hillery at the official opening of the World Medical Association*, 5 September 1977

41 O'Malley Interview, 6 May 2008

42 Hillery, *Lenihan*, p. 1

43 *The Irish Times*, 'The Presidency and the press: a legacy of outdated attitudes', 5 August 1991

44 Private Papers, Hillery Note, *Rumours*, 1995

45 NAI D/T 2007/116/394, R. Stokes to M. Ó Flathartaigh, 17 December 1976, *Interview by Hillery with Gerd Ludeman, German Press Agency*, pp. 1–3, 21 January 1977

46 Private Papers, *State Visits Abroad by President Hillery*

47 Private Papers, *Other Official Visits Abroad by President Hillery*

48   *The Irish Times*, 'Pope dies after one-month reign', 30 September 1978
49   Hillery, *Presidency*, p. 3

Chapter 20

1   Interview with Paddy Hillery, 18 December 2007
2   *The Irish Times*, 'Emotion and joy filled the day', 1 October 1979
3   *The Irish Times*, 'Half-million in Limerick hear homily on tradition', 2 October 1979
4   Stephen Collins, *The Haughey File* (Dublin, 1992), pp. 24–7
5   Private Papers, Transcript 15, *Rumours*, 2–11 January 1980, pp. 1–2
6   *Irish Press*, 'The President Speaks Out', 4 October 1979, *Irish Independent*, 'Hillery Scotches The Rumours', 4 October 1979, *The Irish Times*, 'President says "I am not resigning" ', 4 October 1979
7   Ibid.
8   Raymond Smith, *Garret: The Enigma* (Dublin, 1985), pp. 125–6
9   Private information
10   Interview with Paddy Hillery, 18 December 2007
11   Ibid.
12   Smith, *Garret*, pp. 125–6
13   *Irish Press*, 'The President Speaks Out', 4 October 1979; Interview with Paddy Hillery, 18 December 2007
14   *The Irish Times*, Editorial 'The Presidency', 4 October 1979, p. 11
15   *The Irish Times*, 'Emotion and joy filled the day', 1 October 1979
16   *The Irish Times*, 'Outpourings of joy and fervour', 1 October 1979
17   *The Irish Times*, 'Emotional farewell as Pontiff leaves from Shannon Airport', 2 October 1979
18   Interview with Paddy Hillery, 18 December 2007; *Irish Press*, 'The President Speaks Out', 4 October 1979
19   *Hibernia*, 'The Week That Shook the Presidency', 11 October 1979, p. 6
20   *The Irish Times*, 'President says "I am not resigning", 4 October 1979
21   Interview with Paddy Hillery, 21 June 2006
22   Ibid.
23   Ibid.; Interview with Paddy Hillery, 18 December 2007
24   *Irish Press*, 'The President Speaks Out', 4 October 1979
25   *The Irish Times*, 'President says "I am not resigning", 4 October 1979
26   Smith, *Garret*, p. 130
27   Private Papers, Hillery Note, 'Editors', undated; Interview with Paddy Hillery, 21 June 2006
28   Interview with Paddy Hillery, 21 June 2006
29   *Hibernia*, 'The Week That Shook the Presidency', 11 October 1979, p. 6
30   UCDA, *Hillery Papers*, P205, Folder 20, *Statement by President Hillery, issued by Áras an Uachtaráin*, 3 October 1979
31   Interview with Paddy Hillery, 18 December 2007
32   *Irish Press*, 'The President Speaks Out', 4 October 1979
33   Ibid.; *Irish Independent*, 'Hillery Scotches The Rumours', 4 October 1979
34   *The Irish Times*, 'President says "I am not resigning", 4 October 1979; *Irish Press*, 'The President Speaks Out', 4 October 1979

35   Ibid.

36   *Irish Press*, 'The President Speaks Out', 4 October 1979

37   *Irish Independent*, 'Hillery Scotches the Rumours', 4 October 1979

38   *The Irish Times*, 'President says "I am not resigning"', 4 October 1979

39   Interview with Paddy Hillery, 18 December 2007

40   *Irish Press*, 'The President Speaks Out', 4 October 1979, *Irish Independent*, 'Hillery Scotches The Rumours', 4 October 1979, *The Irish Times*, 'President says "I am not resigning" ', 4 October 1979

41   *Irish Press*, 'The President Speaks Out', 4 October 1979

42   *Irish Press*, Editorial, 'Dr Hillery's Statement', 4 October 1979

43   *Irish Independent*, Editorial, 'Rumours Scotched', 4 October 1979

44   *The Irish Times*, Editorial, 'The Presidency', 4 October 1979

45   Ibid.

46   *The Irish Times*, 'Lynch supports Hillery's action', 5 October 1979

47   Ibid.

48   *The Irish Times*, 'Lynch supports Hillery's action', 5 October 1979; *Irish Press*, 'Backing for Hillery', 5 October 1979

49   *Hibernia*, 'The Week That Shook the Presidency', 11 October 1979, p. 6

50   Smith, *Garret*, p. 131

51   *Irish Press*, 'Backing for Dr Hillery', 5 October 1979

52   *Hibernia*, 'The Week That Shook the Presidency', 11 October 1979, p. 1

53   Interview with John Cooney, 30 May 2008

54   Ibid.

55   Interview with Paddy Hillery, 21 June 2006

56   Ibid.

57   Collins, *Haughey File*, pp. 30–32.

58   Correspondence with Prof Brian Hillery, September 2008

59   Private Papers, Transcript 13, *Rumours: Áras 1980*, 2-11 January 1980

60   Interview with Paddy Hillery, 18 December 2007

61   Private Papers, Transcript 14, *CJH Elected Taoiseach: Rumours renewed*, December 1979,

62   Private Papers, Transcript 14, *CJH Elected Taoiseach*, December 1979

63   Ibid., p. 2

64   Ibid., p. 1

65   *Report of the Tribunal of Inquiry into Payments to Politicians and Related Matters*, Part 1 (Dublin, 2006), pp.41–2; pp.57–8

66   Interview with Paddy Hillery, 21 June 2006

67   Private Papers, Hillery Note, *Rumours*

68   Interview with Paddy Hillery, 21 June 2006

69   Private Papers, Transcript 14, *CJH Elected Taoiseach*, December 1979

70   Ibid.

71   Private Papers, Transcript 13, *Rumours: Áras 1980*, 16–26 January 1980

72   Private Papers, *State Visits Abroad by President Hillery*

73   *Irish Press*, Editorial 'Dr Hillery's Statement', 4 October 1979

74   *Sunday Independent*, 'How the KGB tried to topple President Hillery' 26 April 1981.

75   Interview with Paddy Hillery, 21 June 2006

76   Ibid.

77   Private Papers, Transcript 15, *Rumours: Áras 1980,* 2–11 January 1980

78   Private Papers, Transcript 14, *CJH Elected Taoiseach,* December 1979

79   UCDA, *Hillery Papers,* P205, Folder 20, Correspondence

80   Interview with Paddy Hillery, 18 December 2007

81   *Hibernia,* 'Hillery To Resign', 4 October 1979

82   *Irish Press,* 'Backing for Dr Hillery', 5 October 1979

83   Private Papers, Transcript 15, *Rumours: Áras 1980,* 2–11 January 1980

Chapter 21

1   UCDA, *Hillery Papers,* P205, Folder 20, Note by Micheál Ó hOdhráin, 11 April 1980

2   Private Papers, Hillery Note, Transcript 18, *C of I Bishop of Armagh,* 1980, p. 1

3   Ibid.

4   *Irish Press,* '"Poppy Day snub" claim', 10 November 1980; *The Irish Times,* 'Hillery refusal seen as snub', 11 November 1980

5   Interview with Paddy Hillery, 11 July 2006; *Irish Press,* 'Legion trouble over Hillery "paraphrase"', 11 November 1980; *The Irish Times,* 'Interview with Dr Paddy Hillery: Remembrance Day, 1980: "I felt I was dropped through the trapdoor"', 3 August 1991

6   Interview with Paddy Hillery, 11 July 2006

7   *The Irish Times,* 'Legion alleges "foreign armies" slight by Hillery', 10 November 1980

8   Ibid., *Irish Press,* '"Poppy Day snub" claim', 10 November 1980

9   *Irish Press,* 'Legion trouble over Hillery "paraphrase"', 11 November 1980

10   *The Irish Times,* 'Legion alleges "foreign armies" slight by Hillery', 10 November 1980; *The Irish Times,* 'Hillery refusal seen as snub', 11 November 1980

11   *The Irish Times,* Editorial, 'The President's "No"', 11 November 1980

12   *Irish Press,* Editorial, 'Regrettable', 11 November 1980

13   Interview with Paddy Hillery, 11 July 2006

14   *Irish Press,* 'Legion trouble over Hillery "paraphrase"', 11 November 1980

15   Ibid.

16   Interview with Paddy Hillery, 11 July 2006

17   Hillery, *Presidency,* p. 3

18   *The Irish Times,* 'Interview with Dr Paddy Hillery: Remembrance Day, 1980: "I felt I was dropped through the trapdoor"', 3 August 1991

19   Interview with Paddy Hillery, 11 July 2006

20   Interview with Peig O'Malley, 6 May 2008

21   Hillery, *Presidency,* p. 2

22   Private Papers, Hillery Note, *Phone Calls,* 1994, p. 1

23   Interview with Paddy Hillery, 21 June 2006

24   Interview with Paddy Hillery, 18 December 2007

25   Collins, *Haughey File,* p. 52

26   Interview with Paddy Hillery, 21 June 2006

27   Smith, *Garret,* pp. 62–4

28   Private Papers, Hillery Note, *Phone Calls,* p. 2

29   Ibid.

30   UCDA, *Hillery Papers,* P205, Folder 7, Capt. Barbour, *Unit Journal,* 27 January 1982

31   Ibid., p. 2

32   Interview with Paddy Hillery, 21 June 2006

33 UCDA, *Hillery Papers*, P205, Folder 7, *Unit Journal*, 27 January 1982, p. 1
34 Ibid., p. 2
35 Ibid., p. 3
36 Ibid., p. 3
37 Ibid., p. 5
38 Interview with Paddy Hillery, 21 June 2006
39 Ibid.
40 UCDA, *Hillery Papers*, P205, Folder 7, *Unit Journal*, 27 January 1982, p. 6
41 Ibid.
42 Interview with Paddy Hillery, 21 June 2006
43 Garret FitzGerald, *All in a Life: an autobiography* (Dublin, 1991), p. 398
44 Ibid., Smith, *Garret*, p. 31
45 Collins, *Haughey File*, pp. 52–3
46 Interview with Paddy Hillery, 11 July 2006
47 Private Papers, Hillery Note, *Phone Calls*, p. 2
48 Interview with Hillery, 3 August 2006
49 Private Papers, Hillery Note, *Phone Calls*, p. 1
50 Collins, *Haughey File*, pp. 180–1
51 Ibid., p. 63
52 Private Papers, Hillery Note, *Phone Calls*, p. 2
53 Interview with Paddy Hillery, 11 July 2006
54 Ibid.
55 Collins, *Haughey File*, p. 62

Chapter 22

1   Interview with Paddy Hillery, 11 July 2006
2   *The Irish Times*, 'Interview with Dr Patrick Hillery', 3 August 1991
3   Interview with Paddy Hillery, 11 July 2006
4   *The Irish Times*, 'Interview with Dr Patrick Hillery', 3 August 1991
5   Private Papers, Hillery Note, *Election 83*, 1995, p. 1
6   UCDA, *Hillery Papers*, P205, Folder 20, Micheál Ó hOdhráin to Hillery, 25 September 1983
7   Private Papers, *Transcript, September 1991*, p. 4
8   Ibid.
9   Interview with John McColgan, 20 June 2008
10 *The Irish Times*, 'A sense of duty led to Presidency', 14 April 2008
11 *The Irish Times*, 'Quiet ceremony for Hillerys', 18 November 1983; *The Irish Times*, 'Hillery inaugurated at simple ceremony', 5 December 1983
12 *Irish Independent*, 'Self-sacrifice the seal of retiring President', 1 December 1990
13 Interview with Peig O'Malley Interview, 6 May 2008
14 *Irish Independent*, 'Youth sets the agenda…for Hillery's city date', 1 December 1990
15 Interview with Paddy Hillery, 11 July 2006
16 *The Irish Times*, 'The Presidency and the press: a legacy of outdated attitudes', 5 August 1991
17 Private Papers, Hillery, *Presidency*, p. 3
18 O'Malley Interview, 6 May 2008

19   Private Papers, Hillery, *Presidency*, p. 3; *The Irish Times*, 'The Presidency and the press: a legacy of outdated attitudes', 5 August 1991
20   *Magill*, 'First Citizen: A portrait of Patrick J. Hillery as President', vol. 6, no.9, pp. 49–55
21   *The Irish Times*, 'The invisible President who maintained stability in silence', 1 December 1990; *Sunday Tribune*, Editorial, 5 July 1987
22   *Irish Independent*, 'Self-sacrifice the seal of retiring President', 1 December 1990
23   Ibid.
24   Private Papers, *Bills Referred to the Supreme Court* by President Hillery
25   *The Irish Times*, 'Supreme Court to test Bill', 14 January 1982; *The Irish Times*, 'Section of Rent Bill declared repugnant to Constitution', 20 February 1982
26   Interview with Paddy Hillery, 3 August 2006
27   Interview with Paddy Hillery, 11 July 2006
28   FitzGerald, *All In A Life*, p. 644
29   Ibid., pp. 644–5
30   Ibid., pp. 644–5
31   Dáil debates, vol. 371, col. 48, 10 March 1987
32   Interview with John Hillery, 19 October 2007
33   Interview with Paddy Hillery, 11 July 2006
34   Private Papers, *State Visits Abroad by President Hillery*
35   Interview with Paddy Hillery, 3 August 2006
36   *Irish Independent*, 'Self-sacrifice the seal of retiring President', 1 December 1990
37   Private Papers, Hillery Note, *Visit I*, 1995, p. 1
38   *The Irish Times*, 'Hillery brings the house down', 17 October 1987
39   *The Irish Times*, 'Irish role in bridging EEC divisions stressed to Hillery', 16 October 1987
40   Ibid.
41   Ibid., Interview with Paddy Hillery, 3 August 2006
42   Interview with Paddy Hillery, 3 August 2006
43   *The Irish Times*, 'Paisley heckles Hillery's speech', 15 October 1987
44   *The Irish Times*, 'Hillery brings the house down', 17 October 1987
45   Interview with Paddy Hillery, 3 August 2006
46   *The Irish Times*, 'Paisley heckles Hillery's speech', 15 October 1987
47   Ibid.
48   Ibid.
49   *The Irish Times*, 'Hillery brings the house down', 17 October 1987
50   Ibid.
51   Ibid.

Chapter 23

1   Emily O'Reilly, *Candidate: The Truth Behind the Presidential Campaign* (Dublin, 1991), pp. 35–6
2   Fergus Finlay, *Mary Robinson: A President with a Purpose* (Dublin, 1990), p. 34
3   O'Reilly, *Candidate*, p. 48
4   Conor Brady, *Up With the Times* (Dublin, 2005), pp. 121–2
5   Private Papers, Hillery Note, *PR Job*, 1995, p. 1
6   Collins, *Haughey File*, p. 177

7   O'Reilly, *Candidate*, p. 83
8   Ibid., p. 69
9   *Irish Press*, 'No Problem for Lenihan', 18 September 1990
10 Ibid.; *Irish Press*, 'No need to reform role of Presidency', 18 September 1990
11 Private Papers, Hillery, *PR Job*, p. 1
12 Ibid.
13 O'Reilly, *Candidate*, p. 76
14 *Irish Press*, 'No Problem for Lenihan', 18 September 1990
15 Private Papers, Hillery, *PR Job*, p. 1
16 Private Papers, Hillery Note, *Lenihan*, 1995, p. 1
17 Interview with Paddy Hillery, 11 July 2006
18 Hillery, *Lenihan*, p. 1
19 Interview with Paddy Hillery, 11 July 2006
20 Collins, *Haughey File*, p. 178
21 Ibid., p. 181; Downey, *Lenihan*, p. 166
22 *The Irish Times*, 'Extract from Interview', 26 October 1990
23 Ibid.
24 Private Papers, Hillery Note, *Election 90*, 1995, p. 1
25 O'Reilly, *Candidate*, pp. 100–1
26 Brady, *Up With the Times*, p. 125
27 Ibid., pp. 112–13; Collins, *Haughey File*, p. 178
28 *The Irish Times*, 'Lenihan denies he tried to prevent dissolution of Dáil', 24 October 1990
29 Private Papers, Hillery Note, *Phone Calls*, p. 1
30 Interview with Paddy Hillery, 11 July 2006
31 *The Irish Times*, 'Lenihan did make call to President he now denies', 24 October 1990
32 Ibid.
33 *The Irish Times*, 'Dukes to table Dáil motion of no confidence in the Tánaiste', 25 October 1990
34 RTÉ, Lenihan interview with Seán Duignan, 25 October 1990; *The The Irish Times*, 'Lenihan says taped replies are mistakes', 26 October 1990
35 *The Irish Times*, 'Lenihan awaits Hillery reply: Government facing no confidence motion', 26 October 1990
36 Ibid.; *The Irish Times*, 'Lenihan insists tape "a casual conversation"', 26 October 1990
37 UCDA, *Hillery Papers*, P205, Folder 7, Note for President, 25 October 1990
38 Private Papers, Hillery Note, *Peter*, 1994, p. 1
39 Interviews with Paddy Hillery, 11 July 2006; 18 December 2007
40 Downey, *Lenihan*, p. 173; O'Reilly, *Candidate*, pp. 133–4
41 UCDA, *Hillery Papers*, P205, Folder 7, Note by Micheál Ó hOdhráin to Hillery, 25 October 1990
42 Capt. Barbour, *Unit Journal*, 27 January 1982
43 Note by Micheál Ó hOdhráin to Hillery, 25 October 1990
44 Ibid.
45 Note by Micheál Ó hOdhráin to Hillery, 26 October 1990
46 Ibid.
47 Private Papers, Hillery Note, *Peter*, p. 1

48 Interview with Paddy Hillery, 11 July 2006
49 *The Irish Times*, 'Government facing no confidence motion', 26 October 1990
50 Collins, *Haughey File*, pp. 183–6; O'Reilly, *Candidate*, p. 135
51 *Irish Press*, 'No Surrender – "Full Steam Ahead" vows axed Brian', 1 November 1990; *The Irish Times*, 'Dismissal strains coalition', 31 October 1990
52 Collins, *Haughey File*, pp. 193–4
53 *Sunday Press*, 'Brian Battles Back in Poll', 4 November 1990
54 O'Reilly, *Candidate*, p. 150; Collins, *Haughey File*, p. 194
55 *Irish Press*, 'Fair Fight claim by Lenihan', 5 November 1990, O'Reilly, *Candidate*, pp. 150–1
56 Interview with Paddy Hillery, 11 July 2006
57 *The Irish Times*, 'Historic Victory for Robinson', 9 November 1990
58 *The Irish Times*, 'Robinson wins by 86,000', 10 November 1990
59 Private Papers, *Official Visits Abroad by President Hillery*
60 Private Papers, Hillery Note, *Phone Calls*, p. 1
61 Interview with Paddy Hillery, 11 July 2006
62 Private Papers, Hillery Note, *Election 90*, p. 1

Chapter 24
1 Private Papers, Hillery, *Transcript, September 1991*, p. 1
2 Ibid.
3 Ibid., p. 2
4 Documentary, *Patrick Hillery: President of Ireland 1976–90* (RTÉ, 1991)
5 Private Papers, Hillery, *Transcript, September 1991*, p. 4
6 Ibid.
7 *The Irish Times*, 'The Presidency and the press: a legacy of outdated attitudes', 5 August 1991
8 *The Irish Times*, 'Remembrance Day, 1980: "I felt I was dropped through the trapdoor"', 3 August 1991
9 Private Papers, Hillery, *Transcript, September 1991*, p. 5
10 *The Irish Times*, 'A Hint of Steel', 7 August 1991
11 Private Papers, Hillery, *Transcript, September 1991*, pp. 5–6
12 Private Papers, Hillery, *Transcript, September 1991*, p. 7
13 Interview with Paddy Hillery, 11 July 2006
14 Ibid.
15 *The Irish Times*, 'Interview with Dr Patrick Hillery', 3 August 1991
16 Interview with Paddy Hillery, 11 July 2006
17 Private Papers, Hillery Note, *Retired*, 1996, p. 1
18 Interview with Prof John Kelly, 16 September 2008
19 Ibid.
20 *The Irish Times*, 'Crisis of the '70s: UN Intervention and the North', 6 August 1991
21 Interview with Paddy Hillery, 11 July 2006
22 *The Irish Times*, 'Crisis of the '70s: UN Intervention and the North', 6 August 1991
23 Hillery, *Transcript, September 1991*, p. 7
24 Interview with Paddy Hillery, 11 July 2006
25 Private Papers, Hillery Note, *Retired*, p. 1

26   Private Papers, Hillery Note, *In Government*, 1996, p. 1

27   Interview with John McColgan, 20 June 2008

28   Imelda Bonel-Elliott, 'The role of the Duggan report (1962) in the reform of the Irish education system', *Administration*, vol. 44, no.3 (Autumn 1996), pp. 42–60; TJ Rigney, 'The Birth of Change in Irish Education with particular reference to Business Studies', *Studies: An Irish Quarterly Review*, vol. 92, no.368 (2003), pp. 329–39

29   *Seven Ages: The story of the Irish State* (Araby Productions and RTÉ, 2000)

30   Ibid.

31   *Clare People*, 'When Miltown honoured a native son', 15 April 2008

32   *The Irish Times*, 'Death of Paddy Hillery', 15 April 2008

33   Interview with Michael Hillery, 30 June 2008

34   *Clare People*, 'When Miltown honoured a native son', 15 April 2008

35   Interview with John Hillery, 15 May 2008

36   *The Irish Times*, 'President says few served country so well', 14 April 2008; *The Irish Times*, 'Taoiseach leads tributes to Dr Hillery', 16 April 2008

37   *The Irish Times*, 'One of the most influential figures in Irish public life', 16 April 2008

38   *The Irish Times*, 'Fine Gael leader notes Hillery's "political nobility"', 16 April 2008

39   *Irish Independent*, 'Community pays respect to county's absolute gent', 17 April 2008

40   *The Irish Times*, 'Rich legacy recalled in tributes as Hillery is laid to rest', 17 April 2008; *The Irish Times*, 'Mourners queue to pay last respects', 16 April 2008

41   *The Irish Times*, 'Hundreds at removal service for former president', 16 April 2008

42   Booklet, 'Paddy Hillery: Iar-Uachtarán na hÉireann: Solemn Requiem Mass', 17 April 2008

43   *Irish Independent*, 'Noble and good man laid to rest', 17 April 2008

44   *The Irish Times*, 'Tánaiste Brian Cowen's oration at the graveside', 17 April 2008

Chapter 25

1   *The Irish Times*, 'Reluctant President did much service for the state,' 14 April 2008

2   *The Irish Times*, 'A sense of duty led to presidency,' 14 April 2008

3   Interview with Paddy Hillery, 24 May 2006

4   Interview with Dennis Kennedy, 22 May 2008

5   Private Papers, Hillery Note, *National School*, 1996, p. 2

6   *The Irish Times*, 'Dr Hillery: Social Republican', 8 July 1966

7   *The Irish Times*, 'The invisible President who maintained stability in silence', 1 December 1990; *Sunday Tribune*, Editorial, 5 July 1987

8   RTÉ, *The Week in Politics*, 13 April 2008

Bibliography

Sᴛᴀᴛᴇ Aʀᴄʜɪᴠᴇs ᴀɴᴅ Rᴇᴄᴏʀᴅs
National Archives of Ireland (NAI)
Department of the An Taoiseach (D/T)
Department of Foreign Affairs (DFA)
Department of Finance (D/FIN)
Minutes of Cabinet Meetings
Minutes of Government Meetings

Department of Education
Circulars for Primary Schools 1957–65, Department of Education
Circulars for Secondary Schools 1957–65, Department of Education
M-Files 1957–65, Department of Education
Progress reports 1957–65, Department of Education

The National Archives, UK (TNA)
Files of the Foreign and Commonwealth Office; telegrams and correspondence

The European Commission
Official Journal of the European Communities
– Decisions of the European Council 1973–76
– Social action programme, October 1973
Correspondence and documents 1973–76

Uɴɪᴠᴇʀsɪᴛʏ Aʀᴄʜɪᴠᴇs ᴀɴᴅ Lɪʙʀᴀʀɪᴇs
Archives Department, UCD (UCDA)
Dr Patrick J. Hillery Papers (P205)
Fianna Fáil Papers, Minutes of the Parliamentary Party (P176)

PRIVATE COLLECTIONS
Private Papers of Dr Patrick J. Hillery, including notes and contemporary transcripts

REPORTS AND OFFICIAL SOURCES
Dáil Debates
Economic Development (Dublin, 1958)
Investment in Education, Report of the Survey Team presented to the Minister for Education in October 1962 (Dublin, 1965)
Report of the Commission on Accommodation Needs of the Constituent Colleges of the National University of Ireland (Dublin, 1959)
Report of the Commission on Higher Education 1960–67, vol. 1 (Dublin, 1967)
Final Report of the Committee on Industrial Relations in the Electricity Supply Board (Dublin, 1969)
Report of Oireachtas Committee on Public Accounts, Appropriation Accounts 1959–70 (Dublin, 1959–72)
Report of the Tribunal of Inquiry into Payments to Politicians and Related Matters, Part I (Dublin, 2006)
Second Programme for Economic Expansion, Part I (Dublin, 1963)
Second Programme for Economic Expansion, Part II (Dublin, 1964)
Thom's Directory of Ireland
Tuarascáil, An Roinn Oideachais, 1957–58 to 1964–65
Who's Who 1997

RELIGIOUS AND DIOCESAN ARCHIVES
Dublin Diocesan Archives (DDA), Archbishop's House, Drumcondra, Dublin 9
— *Papers of Dr John Charles McQuaid, Archbishop of Dublin*: correspondence and papers; Minutes of the Irish Hierarchy, 1957–72
Parish records: Parish office, St Joseph's Church, Miltown Malbay
— Register of Births
— Marriage Register

ARCHIVES OF TEACHING UNIONS AND MANAGERIAL ASSOCIATIONS
ASTI, ASTI House, Winetavern St., Dublin 8
— *Official Programme for Annual Convention*, 1957–65
— Minutes of Standing Committee and Central Executive Committee 1957–65
Central Secretariat of Secondary Schools, Emmet House, Dundrum, Dublin 14
— CCSS, Minutes of Standing Committee and Central Executive Committee

PUBLICATIONS BY POLITICAL PARTIES AND RESEARCH GROUPS
Labour, *Challenge and Change in Education* (Dublin, 1963)
Tuairim, *Educating Towards A United Europe* (Dublin Research Group, Tuairim and European Teachers' Association, 1961)
Tuairim, *Irish Education* (London Research Group, Tuairim, 1962)

NEWSPAPERS AND JOURNALS
Administration
Agence Europe

Belfast Telegraph
Hibernia
Irish Educational Studies
Irish Independent
Irish Press
The Irish Times
Oideas
Studies
Sunday Independent
Sunday Press
The Clare Champion
The Clare People

SECONDARY WORKS

Arnold, Bruce, *Jack Lynch: Hero in Crisis* (Dublin, 2001)

Arter, David, *The Politics of European Integration in the Twentieth Century* (Aldershot, 1993)

Boland, Kevin, *Up Dev* (Dublin, 1977)

Bonel-Elliott, Imelda, 'La politique de l'enseignement du second degré en république d'Irlande 1963–93' (unpublished Ph.D thesis, Sorbonne, 1994)

Bonel-Elliott, Imelda, 'The role of the Duggan report (1962) in the reform of the Irish education system', *Administration*, vol.44, no.3 (Autumn 1996), pp.42-60

Brady, Conor, *Up With the Times* (Dublin, 2005)

Browne, Noel, *Against the Tide* (Dublin, 1986)

Clymer, Adam, *Edward M. Kennedy: A biography* (New York, 1999)

Coakley, John and Gallagher, Michael (eds.), *Politics in the Republic of Ireland* (Dublin, 1992)

Collins, Stephen, *The Haughey File* (Dublin, 1992)

Collins, Stephen, *The Power Game: Fianna Fáil since Lemass* (Dublin, 2000)

Coolahan, John, *Irish Education: its History and Structure* (Dublin, 1981)

Coolahan, John, 'Dr P.J. Hillery – Minister for Education', *Journal for ASTI Convention*, Easter 1990, pp.15–19

Downey, James, *Lenihan: His Life and Loyalties* (Dublin, 1998)

Dunbabin, J.P.D, *The Post-Imperial Age: The Great Powers and the Wider World* (London and New York, 1994)

Ferriter, Diarmuid, The Transformation of Ireland 1900–2000 (London, 2004)

Finlay, Fergus, *Mary Robinson: A President with a Purpose* (Dublin, 1990)

FitzGerald, Garret, *All in a Life: an Autobiography* (Dublin, 1991)

Healy, T. M., *From Sanatorium to Hospital: A Social and Medical Account of Peamount 1912–1997* (Dublin, 2002)

Hennessey, Thomas, *The Evolution of The Troubles 1970–72* (Dublin, 2007)

Horgan, John, *Seán Lemass: The Enigmatic Patriot* (Dublin, 1997)

Hyland, Áine and Milne, Kenneth (eds.), *Irish Educational Documents vol.2* (Dublin, 1992)

Jones, Valerie, 'Coláiste Moibhí – The Last Preparatory College', *Irish Educational Studies*, vol.15 (1996), pp.101–111

Kennedy, Michael, 'Northern Ireland and cross-border co-operation', in Girvin, Brian and Murphy, Gary, *The Lemass Era: Politics and Society in the Ireland of Seán Lemass*, pp.99–121 (Dublin, 2005)

Lee, Joseph, *Ireland 1912–85: Politics and Society* (Cambridge, 1989)

Lewis, Samuel, *A Topographical Dictionary of Ireland, Vol. 2* (London, 1837)

Lyons, F.S.L, *Ireland since the Famine* (London, 1973)

Maher, Denis J., *The Tortuous Path: The Course Of Ireland's Entry Into The EEC 1948–73* (Dublin, 1986)

Mac Mathúna, Seosamh, *Kilfarboy: A History of a West Clare Parish*, (Lucan, 1974)

McCarthy, Charles, *The Decade of Upheaval: Irish Trade Unions in the Nineteen Sixties* (Dublin, 1973)

Mills, Michael, *Hurler on the Ditch: Memoir of a Journalist who Became Ireland's First Ombudsman* (Dublin, 2005)

Murphy, Gary, 'From economic nationalism to European Union', in Girvin, Brian and Murphy, Gary, *The Lemass Era: Politics and Society in the Ireland of Seán Lemass*, pp.28–48 (Dublin, 2005)

Murphy, John, A., *Ireland in the Twentieth Century* (Dublin, 1975)

O'Brien, Justin, *The Arms Trial* (Dublin, 2000)

Ó Buachalla, Séamus, *Education Policy in Twentieth Century Ireland* (Dublin, 1988)

Ó Buachalla, Séamus, 'Investment in education: context, content and impact', *Administration*, vol.44, no.3 (Autumn 1996), pp.10–20

O'Connor, Seán, *A Troubled Sky: Reflections on the Irish Education Scene 1957–68* (Dublin, 1986)

Ó Cuilleanáin, T. A., 'Special Education in Ireland', *Oideas*, no.1 (Autumn 1968), pp.5–17

O'Malley, Ernie, *Raids and Rallies* (Dublin, 1982)

O'Reilly, Emily, *Candidate* (Dublin, 1991)

Randles, Eileen, *Post-primary Education in Ireland 1957–70* (Dublin, 1975)

Rigney, T. J., 'The birth of change in Irish education with particular reference to Business Studies', *Studies: An Irish Quarterly Review*, vol.92, no.368 (Winter 2003), pp.329–339

Ryle Dwyer, T., *Nice Fellow: A Biography of Jack Lynch* (Dublin, 2001)

Smith, Raymond, *Garret: The Enigma* (Dublin, 1985)

Vaughan, Richard, *Twentieth-Century Europe: Paths To Unity* (London, 1979)

Walsh, Dick, *The Party: inside Fianna Fáil* (Dublin, 1986)

Whyte, J. H., Church and state in modern Ireland 1923–1970 (Dublin, 1971)

Ziegler, Philip, *Wilson: The Authorised Life of Lord Wilson of Rievaulx* (London, 1993)

DOCUMENTARY SOURCES (TV/DVD)

Patrick Hillery: President of Ireland 1979–90 (RTÉ, 1991)
Reeling in the Years (RTÉ, 1999)
Seven Ages: The Story of the Irish State (Araby Productions and RTÉ, 2000)

INTERVIEWS AND CORRESPONDENCE
Mr Tony Brown
Mr John Cooney
Mr. Seán Donlon

Mr James Dukes
Mr Edwin FitzGibbon
Dr Garret FitzGerald
Prof Brian Hillery
Dr John Hillery
Dr Maeve Hillery
Dr Patrick J. Hillery
Mr Michael Hillery
Mr John Horgan
Mr Neville Keery
Prof John Kelly
Mr Dennis Kennedy
Mr John McColgan
Ms Peig O'Malley

Index